THE CAMBRIDGE COMPANION TO
CICERO

Cicero was one of classical antiquity's most prolific, varied and self-revealing authors. His letters, speeches, treatises and poetry chart a political career marked by personal struggle and failure and the collapse of the republican system of government to which he was intellectually and emotionally committed. They were read, studied and imitated throughout antiquity and subsequently became seminal texts in political theory and in the reception and study of the Classics. This volume discusses the whole range of Cicero's writings, with particular emphasis on their links with the literary culture of the late Republic, their significance to Cicero's public career and their reception in later periods.

A complete list of books in this series is at the back of the book.

THE CAMBRIDGE
COMPANION TO
CICERO

EDITED BY
CATHERINE STEEL
Professor of Classics, University of Glasgow

CAMBRIDGE
UNIVERSITY PRESS

CAMBRIDGE UNIVERSITY PRESS
Cambridge, New York, Melbourne, Madrid, Cape Town,
Singapore, São Paulo, Delhi, Mexico City

Cambridge University Press
The Edinburgh Building, Cambridge CB2 8RU, UK

Published in the United States of America by Cambridge University Press, New York

www.cambridge.org
Information on this title: www.cambridge.org/9780521729802

© Cambridge University Press 2013

First published 2013

Printed and bound in the United Kingdom by the MPG Books Group

A catalogue record for this publication is available from the British Library

Library of Congress Cataloguing in Publication data
The Cambridge companion to Cicero / edited by Catherine Steel,
Professor of Classics, University of Glasgow.
pages   cm. – (Cambridge companions to literature)
Includes bibliographical references and index.
ISBN 978-0-521-50993-0 (hardback) – ISBN 978-0-521-72980-2 (paperback)
1. Cicero, Marcus Tullius – Criticism and interpretation.   2. Cicero, Marcus
Tullius – Political and social views.   3. Cicero, Marcus Tullius – Appreciation.
I. Steel, C. E. W.
PA6320.C29   2013
875'.01 – dc23   2012035051

ISBN 978-0-521-50993-0 Hardback
ISBN 978-0-521-72980-2 Paperback

To the memory of Sabine MacCormack

CONTENTS

CONTENTS

MAP

CONTRIBUTORS

ANDREW BELL teaches history at the University of Nevada, Las Vegas. He is the author of *Spectacular Power in the Greek and Roman City* (2004).

NICHOLAS P. COLE is Departmental Lecturer in American History at the University of Oxford and a Junior Research Fellow in American History at St Peter's College, Oxford. He read Ancient and Modern History at University College, where he also completed his M.Phil. in Greek and Roman history and his doctorate, which was titled 'The Ancient World in Jefferson's America'. He has been a Visiting Fellow at the International Center for Jefferson Studies at Monticello. He works on the history of political thought, the creation of republican government in early America and on the utility of classical learning in the modern world.

ANTHONY CORBEILL, Professor of Classics at the University of Kansas, is author of *Controlling Laughter: Political Humor in the Late Roman Republic* (1996) and *Nature Embodied: Gesture in Ancient Rome* (2004). He is completing a book on the significance of grammatical gender in Roman society.

EMMA DENCH is Professor of the Classics and of History at Harvard University. Her publications include *Romulus' Asylum: Roman Identities from the Age of Alexander to the Age of Hadrian* (2005). Her current research projects include a thematic study of Roman imperial cultures, and an analysis of the retrospective writing of the Republic in the imperial age.

JOHN DUGAN is Associate Professor of Classics at the University at Buffalo, State University of New York, and co-editor of the interdisciplinary classics journal *Arethusa*. He is the author of *Making a New Man: Ciceronian Self-fashioning in the Rhetorical Works* (2005) and articles on Roman rhetoric and oratory.

LYNN S. FOTHERINGHAM is Lecturer in Classics at the University of Nottingham. Her research deals with rhetorical language and structure, the application of discourse analysis to ancient oratory, and the reception of classical antiquity in contemporary fiction and film. She has published extensively on Cicero's forensic speeches and is currently completing a commentary on *Pro Milone*.

MATTHEW FOX'S work focuses mainly on how the Romans used history as an arena for intellectual and political reflection. Author of *Roman Historical Myths* (1996) and *Cicero's Philosophy of History* (2007), his interest in hermeneutics has led him to publish on a variety of other topics: sexuality in Greece and Rome, the dialogue form and recently the nature of scholarly discourse in the eighteenth century. Since 2007 he has been Professor of Classics at the University of Glasgow.

EMMA GEE lectures in Classics at St Andrews. She was educated at the universities of Sydney and Cambridge and has previously worked in Exeter and in Sydney, where she held the Kevin Lee Lectureship in Ancient Greek. Her main interest is Latin and Greek literature and science, in particular Aratus and his legacy. *Ovid, Aratus, and Augustus* (Cambridge, 2000) is to be followed by a broader study of Aratus, *Aratus and the Astronomical Tradition*. With the help of research grants from the Leverhulme Trust and the Loeb Foundation she is currently working on a book on 'Mapping the Afterlife in Greece and Rome'.

ALAIN M. GOWING is Professor of Classics at the University of Washington in Seattle, where he has been on the faculty since 1988 after receiving his PhD from Bryn Mawr College. His chief interests lie in the area of Roman historiography and literature, especially of the imperial period. His most recent book is *Empire and Memory: The Representation of the Roman Republic in Imperial Culture* (Cambridge, 2005), and he is currently working on a book-length study of the role of Rome and urban space in Sallust, Livy and Tacitus.

JON HALL is Associate Professor in the Department of Classics at the University of Otago, New Zealand. He has published various articles on Cicero's oratory and rhetorical treatises, and a book on the correspondence entitled *Politeness and Politics in Cicero's Letters* (2009).

JILL HARRIES is the Professor of Ancient History at the University of St Andrews. She is the author of various books, including *Cicero and the Jurists* (2006) and *Law and Crime in the Roman World* (Cambridge, 2007).

SABINE MACCORMACK† was the Rev. Theodore Hesburgh Professor of Arts and Letters at the University of Notre Dame. She worked on Roman and late Roman history, the reception of classical traditions, particularly in the Spanish world, and the history of the indigenous peoples of the Andes. Her recent books include *The Shadows of Poetry: Vergil in the Mind of Augustine* (1998) and *On the Wings of Time: Rome, the Incas, Spain and Peru* (2007).

DAVID MARSH studied classics and comparative literature at Yale and Harvard, and is now Professor of Italian at Rutgers, The State University of New Jersey. He is the author of *The Quattrocento Dialogue: Classical Tradition and Humanist Innovation* (1980) and *Lucian and the Latins: Humor and Humanism in the*

Early Renaissance (1998). He has translated Leon Battista Alberti's *Dinner Pieces* (1987), Giambattista Vico's *New Science* (1999) and Paolo Zellini's *Brief History of Infinity* (2004). His editions of humanist Latin texts include Francesco Petrarca's *Invectives* (2003) and the anthology *Renaissance Fables: Aesopic Prose by Leon Battista Alberti, Bartolomeo Scala, Leonardo da Vinci, and Bernardino Baldi* (2004).

RUTH MORELLO is Lecturer in Classics at the University of Manchester. She is the co-editor with Andrew Morrison of *Ancient Letters: Classical and Late Antique Epistolography* (2007) and with Roy Gibson of *Re-imagining Pliny the Younger* (*Arethusa* special edition 36.2 (2003)) and is currently working on a book on encomium in the late Republic and early Empire.

J. G. F. POWELL is Professor of Latin at Royal Holloway, University of London. He has edited Cicero's *Cato Maior De Senectute* (1988), *Laelius de Amicitia* and *Somnium Scipionis* (1990) and *De re Publica and De Legibus* (2006), and was editor or co-editor of the volumes *Author and Audience in Latin Literature* (1992), *Cicero the Philosopher* (1995), *Cicero's Republic* (2001), *Cicero the Advocate* (2004) and *Logos: Rational Argument in Classical Rhetoric* (2007). He is currently working on a new Latin grammar and a study of Latin word order.

MALCOLM SCHOFIELD has spent the last forty years teaching Classics at Cambridge, where he is now Emeritus Professor of Ancient Philosophy, but continuing as a Fellow of St John's College. He has published work in many areas of his subject, but mostly over the last two decades ancient political philosophy. He is co-editor of *The Cambridge History of Greek and Roman Political Thought* (Cambridge, 2000), author of *Plato: Political Philosophy* (2006), and in 2012 delivered in Oxford the Carlyle Lectures on: 'A republican political philosophy: Cicero and Rome'.

CATHERINE STEEL is Professor of Classics at the University of Glasgow. She has written extensively on Roman oratory, Cicero and political life in the Republic, including *Cicero, Rhetoric, and Empire* (2001), *Reading Cicero: Genre and Performance in Late Republican Rome* (2005) and *Roman Oratory* (2006).

ANN VASALY is Associate Professor of Classical Studies at Boston University. Her research focuses on Ciceronian rhetoric and Latin historiography. She is the author of *Representations: Images of the World in Ciceronian Oratory* (1993), as well as a number of articles and book chapters dealing with aspects of Cicero and Livy. She is currently completing a book on Livy's first pentad.

JAMES E. G. ZETZEL is the Charles Anthon Professor of the Latin Language and Literature at Columbia University; he has written extensively about republican and

Augustan literature, textual criticism and the transmission of Latin texts, and the reception of Cicero in antiquity and the nineteenth century. He has also published translations of *De re publica* and *De legibus* (Cambridge, 1999) and *Ten Speeches* (2009). His current project is 'Critics, compilers, and commentators: a guide to Roman textual and grammatical scholarship'.

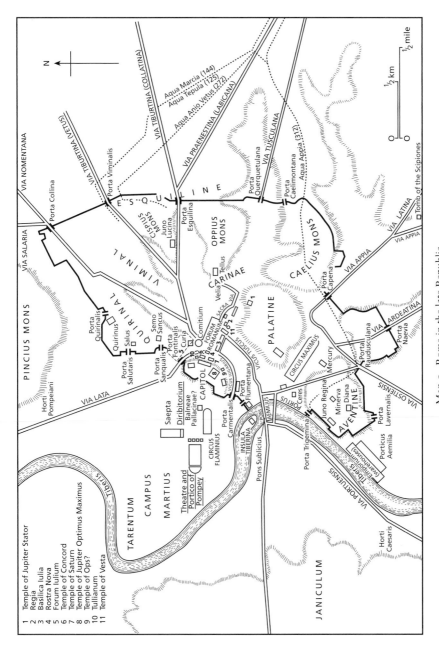

Map 1. Rome in the late Republic

1 Temple of Jupiter Stator
2 Regia
3 Basilica Iulia
4 Rostra Nova
5 Forum Iulium
6 Temple of Concord
7 Temple of Saturn
8 Temple of Jupiter Optimus Maximus
9 Temple of Ops?
10 Tullianum
11 Temple of Vesta

N

½ km

½ mile

VIA NOMENTANA

VIA SALARIA

VIA TIBURTINA (VETUS)

VIA TIBURTINA (COLLATINA)

Aqua Marcia (144)
Aqua Tepula (125)
Aqua Anio Vetus (272)

VIA PRAENESTINA (LABICANA)

VIA TUSCULANA

VIA LATINA

Aqua Appia (312)

Tomb of the Scipiones

Porta Collina

Porta Viminalis

Porta Esquilina

Porta Querquetulana

Porta Caelimontana

Porta Capena

VIA APPIA

VIA APPIA

VIA ARDEATINA

Porta Raudusculana

Porta Naevia

VIA OSTIENSIS

PINCIUS MONS

Horti
Pompeiani

VIA LATA

Porta
Quirinalis

Porta
Salutaris

QUIRINAL

Quirinus

Salus

Semo Sancus

Porta
Fontinalis

Porta
Sanqualis

VIMINAL

CISPIUS MONS

ESQU...

Juno
Lucina

OPPIUS
MONS

Tellus

CARINAE

Velia

SACRA VIA

Comitium

FORUM
ROMANUM

VICUS TUSCUS

CAELIUS MONS

PALATINE

CIRCUS MAXIMUS

Mercury

Juno Regina

Ceres

Diana

Minerva

Porta
Lavernalis

AVENTINE

Porta
Trigemina

PORTUS

Tiberis

Porta
Carmentalis

Porta
Flumentana

CAPITOL

CLIVUS

Curia

AEMILIUS

Pons Sublicius

INSULA
TIBERINA

CIRCUS
FLAMINUS

Balineae
Pallacinae?

Diribitorium

Saepta

Theatre and
Portico of Pompey

CAMPUS
MARTIUS

TARENTUM

Tiberis

JANICULUM

Horti
Caesaris

VIA PORTUENSIS

Porticus
Aemilia
(warehouses)

Emporium

Temple of Jupiter Stator
Basilica Iulia
Forum Iulium
Temple of Jupiter Optimus Maximus
Temple of Vesta

ABBREVIATIONS

Abbreviations of ancient authors and works follow the fourth edition of the *Oxford Classical Dictionary* (Oxford 2012). Other abbreviations used are:

AJPh	*American Journal of Philology*
Anc. Soc.	*Ancient Society*
ANRW	*Aufstieg und Niedergang der römischen Welt*
BICS	*Bulletin of the Institute of Classical Studies*
CAH	*Cambridge Ancient History*
CCSL	*Corpus Christianorum, Series Latina*
CIL	*Corpus Inscriptionum Latinarum*
CJ	*Classical Journal*
ClAnt	*Classical Antiquity*
CPh	*Classical Philology*
CQ	*Classical Quarterly*
CR	*Classical Review*
CW	*Classical World*
G&R	*Greece and Rome*
HRR	*Historicorum Romanorum Reliquiae*
HSCP	*Harvard Studies in Classical Philology*
ILS	*Inscriptiones Latinae Selectae*
JHS	*Journal of Hellenic Studies*
JRS	*Journal of Roman Studies*
MEFRA	*Mélanges de l'Ecole française de Rome: Antiquité*
MEFRM	*Mélanges de l'Ecole française de Rome: Moyen Age*
OCT	*Oxford Classical Text*
P&P	*Past and Present*
PBSR	*Papers of the British School at Rome*
PCPS	*Proceedings of the Cambridge Philological Society*
RÉL	*Revue des Etudes Latines*
RhM	*Rheinisches Museum für Philologie*
SCI	*Scripta Classicala Israelica*
TAPhA	*Transactions of the American Philological Association*
WS	*Wiener Studien*

CATHERINE STEEL

Introduction

Cicero is one of the most prolific authors to survive from classical antiquity; and one of the most varied, whose writings include speeches, letters, poetry and treatises on philosophy, rhetoric, politics and law. He was also part of the ruling elite at Rome during a tumultuous quarter-century, and one of the most self-revealing of ancient figures. He has, as a consequence, multiple characters: a heroic defender of freedom; a political failure, blinded by vanity and oblivious to change; the epitome of oratorical brilliance; the supreme model of Latin; and a human, to whose weaknesses and foibles we have unmediated access.

All these Ciceros, and many others, are discussed in this *Companion*, though its focus throughout is on the textual Cicero. This is the manifestation that has dominated his subsequent reception. Moreover, any attempt to assess his importance as a political figure during his lifetime demands engagement with the complexities of late Republican politics in a manner that is beyond this volume's scope. But some brief biographical notes may provide a helpful introduction to what follows.[1]

M. Tullius Cicero was born on 3 January 106 BC at Arpinum in central Italy, about 60 miles from Rome. This town, despite its distance from Rome, was a community of Roman citizens: it had been in this position since the Roman people had voted in 188 BC to give it this status.[2] As a result, its inhabitants were recorded in the Roman census, and shared rights and duties with Romans across Italy and beyond. We are poorly informed about the use of citizenship, in general, by citizens who did not live in Rome or close to the metropolis; but Cicero's family, which was one of Arpinum's wealthiest, was connected to the political and social elite in

---

[1] Flower 2004 and Rosenstein and Morstein-Marx 2006 offer wide-ranging introductions. There are numerous modern biographies of Cicero: see Fotheringham in this volume (Chapter 19).

[2] Livy 38.36.

Rome.[3] In addition, three days before Cicero was born Gaius Marius, a native of Arpinum and a relative by marriage of the Cicerones, had concluded his first consulship, and was continuing his campaign against Jugurtha as proconsul.[4] Marius was a 'new man': he had no Roman senators among his ancestors, and his achievement in reaching the consulship was exceptional. But an aspiration towards active participation in Roman politics, and entry in the senate, albeit without tenure of the highest magistracies, was certainly realistic for someone from Cicero's background.

Cicero's forebears had not followed this route, and he was, like Marius, a 'new man'. But his father was able to place his two sons into a distinguished circle when he decided to move to Rome, probably in the mid nineties and quite possibly with the specific intention of supporting their education.[5] His acquaintances included M. Antonius, consul in 99 BC, and L. Licinius Crassus (cos. 95 BC).[6] The opportunities to associate with such men were a supplement to formal, structured training in rhetoric, conducted in Greek. Cicero also began his study of law by attending Q. Mucius Scaevola's advice sessions; here he met Atticus.[7] This period was broken by the consequences of the outbreak of the war between Rome and its Italian allies towards the end of 91. Arpinum remained loyal to Rome, as did almost all communities that were Roman or Latin in status, and Cicero served in the armies of Pompeius Strabo and of Sulla. His experiences during this war can only be reconstructed through two anecdotes preserved in works he wrote towards the very end of his life. In the *Twelfth Philippic* he records being present at negotiations between Pompeius Strabo and the Marsic leader Vettius Scato; and in *De divinatione* he records an episode he witnessed when Sulla was

---

[3] Nicolet 1967; Rawson 1985: 5–8; Cébeillac Gervasoni 1998: 205–31; Fantham 2004: 27–9.

[4] Marius' sister was married to Cicero's great-uncle Gratidius; see Evans 1994: 146–52.

[5] Cicero's brother Quintus was a few years younger; he too pursued a political career, though with less dazzling success, reaching the praetorship in 62 BC. He was the recipient of a number of letters from Cicero (particularly in the mid fifties, when he was absent from Rome as a legate), and quarrelled with his brother during the civil war; the two were never fully reconciled (Bailey 1971: 179–85). Quintus Cicero was also killed at the end of 43 during the proscriptions.

[6] Gratidius and Cicero's uncle L. Cicero had served with Antonius (and both died) during the latter's command against the pirates in 102–100 BC; *Brut.* 168; *De or.* 2.2. The link to Crassus may originally have been Crassus' friendship with Cicero's maternal uncle C. Visellius Aculeo (*De or.* 2.2).

[7] *De amicitia* opens with a description of Scaevola attended by a group of his associates (*Amic.* 2). Cicero began to study with Scaevola once he had assumed the *toga uirilis*; unfortunately this event cannot be precisely dated in relation to the outbreak of the Social War.

sacrificing in his camp near Nola.[8] We do not know what position the Tullii Cicerones adopted in the violent struggle between Marius and Sulla during 88; they appear to have avoided harm both then and in 82 when Sulla returned to Italy, which suggests quiescence, but a number of their Roman patrons and Arpinate connections, on both sides, were harmed in various ways.[9] Cicero himself was in Rome throughout the eighties, continuing his studies in rhetoric and engaging with philosophy. He began his legal career in 81 BC, as Rome was adjusting to Sullan despotism; he spoke for a man called Quinctius, who was being sued by his former business partner Naevius. The speech, *Pro Quinctio*, survives; beneath the dense legal argumentation, it offers a fascinating glimpse of Roman business practice and of the disruptions of the eighties.[10] The fact of its survival is also significant; it represents a conscious choice by Cicero to preserve his legal activity and thereby to advertise his skills. The same impulse presumably informed his decision to disseminate, even in unfinished form, his rhetorical handbook *De inventione*.[11]

Cicero's next recorded case was much higher profile: the defence of a man accused of arranging the murder of his father, in one of Sulla's new standing courts. The political significance of the case and of Cicero's involvement in it have been the subject of endless debate.[12] These divergent scholarly analyses can well be seen as demonstrations of Cicero's skill in balancing a powerfully affecting demand for a fresh start in public life with the avoidance of criticism of specific individuals, apart from an otherwise unknown freedman of Sulla.

---

[8] Cic. *Phil.* 12.27; *Div.* 1.72. Cicero is generally assumed to have moved from Strabo's army to Sulla's, but the chronological indicators are not decisive (though *ILLRP* 515 suggests that Cicero was not with Strabo's army when Asculum was captured). He does not even mention military service in the autobiographical notes at *Brut.* 304, which slips seamlessly from Cicero's listening to the *contiones* of 90 (305) to those of 88 (306).

[9] M. Antonius died in 87 in Marius' purge of his enemies after his return to Rome; Scaevola Augur appears to have died of natural causes, but his cousin, the *pontifex maximus* (with whom Cicero studied after the augur's death, *Amic.* 1) was killed in 82 on the orders of the younger Marius. M. Marius Gratidianus, by birth a first cousin of Cicero's father and adopted by Gaius Marius' brother, died after Sulla's capture of Rome, allegedly executed at the grave of Catulus by Catilina (Marshall 1985).

[10] Kinsey 1971; Bannon 2000.

[11] At *Quinct.* 4 Cicero refers to 'other cases' as though he had been involved in them before his speech for Quinctius, but no details survive. *Brut.* 311–14 implies a number of cases prior to Cicero's departure for Athens and Rhodes, though it is not known whether any others predate *Pro Roscio Amerino*.

[12] See Vasaly in this volume (Chapter 8).

At some point during the following year Cicero left Rome for further philosophical and rhetorical study in Athens and then Asia Minor.[13] The details of his trip provide a backdrop to some of his philosophical works from the fifties and forties: *De republica* (set in 129 BC) is presented as the product of Rutilius Rufus' reminiscences, when Cicero met him in Smyrna during his travels, and the fifth book of *De finibus* is a conversation between Cicero, Atticus (by this point resident in Athens), his brother Quintus, his cousin Lucius and M. Pupius Piso (the future consul of 61) in the Academy at Athens in 79 BC.

Cicero returned to Rome in good time to campaign for the quaestorship, to which he was elected in the summer of 76, and allotted to western Sicily. Much later, he offered an amusing glimpse at his chagrin when he returned to Rome, expecting everyone to be talking about his successes, only to find that no-one knew he had been away; and his subsequent resolution to remain firmly in Rome (*Planc.* 62). He resumed his legal activity, but he did not attract prominent clients, and was not notably successful.[14] This may have contributed to the gamble he took in 70, when he prosecuted the former governor of Sicily, Gaius Verres, on *repetundae* charges. Verres' reputation has been so comprehensively blackened by Cicero, and Cicero stresses the scale of his own achievement so emphatically, that it is difficult to assess Verres' standing before the trial and his prospects of reaching the consulship. But Cicero did take a chance with his prosecution; if he failed, he would have to manage the consequences of the subsequent *imimicitia*, and prosecuting itself was socially and ethically dubious. And he exploited his success to the full, with the dissemination of the seven speeches that made up the case, a corpus of oratorical prose writing unparalleled in earlier Latin literature.

After the Verres case and the *Verrines*, and quite possibly as a result, Cicero finally began to defend the political elite, with his first senatorial client in 69. He was elected to the praetorship in the summer of 67 and the following year openly declared himself a supporter of Pompeius in 66 with his first speech at a *contio*, *De imperio Cn. Pompei*. As he began his preparations in the summer of 65 for the consular elections, he had the good fortune of not facing any very strong rivals.[15] Nonetheless, one

---

[13] Cic. *Brut.* 314, which makes health the reason for his departure. Before his departure he had been involved in at least two further defences, those of Titinia and of a woman from Arretium; Marinone 2004: 59.

[14] Scamander and Varenus (both charged under the *lex Cornelia de sicariis et ueneficiis*) were both convicted, but Cicero disseminated his *Pro Vareno* and it was much admired and quoted by Quintilian (Crawford 1994: 7–18); other speeches from this period were in civil cases. See Steel 2005: 24–6.

[15] Cic. *Att.* 1.1.1 offers a list of likely contenders.

might expect that Antonius and Catiline, who emerged as the other serious candidates, would normally have been elected on the basis of the prestige of their families; Catiline's failure to do so – and the gap between the tally of votes for Cicero and Antonius – was because of the inflammatory remarks Catiline made during the campaign, and Cicero's adept exploitation in his own campaigning of his audience's fears about Catiline's intentions and Antonius' reputation.

Cicero's later career appears to be dominated by the choices he made during his consulship: had he not overseen the execution of those of Catiline's followers who were arrested after their failed negotiations with the Allobroges, he would not himself have been exiled with its attendant loss of power and prestige. But, as so often in the late Republic, an apparently simple chain of causation becomes less clear on closer inspection. Clodius was behind Cicero's exile, and in his decision to pursue Cicero combined defence of the rights of citizens with the deep personal hostility that had arisen when Cicero gave evidence against him at his trial in 61.[16] It is impossible to know whether Clodius would have refrained from his *popularis* manoeuvre against Cicero if the two men had not already been enemies for reasons unconnected with Catiline.

Cicero found himself largely irrelevant in political terms after his return from exile; unable to challenge Caesar or Pompeius effectively, he turned to large-scale non-oratorical prose writing, with *De oratore*, *De republica* and possibly *De legibus* between 55 and 51. He was also more intensely busy in the courts than at any time earlier in his career, often at the behest of Pompeius.[17] Whether or not he might have contributed effectively to averting conflict between Pompeius and Caesar, had he not been absent from Rome between the late spring of 51 and the end of 50 as governor of Cilicia, is an intriguing counterfactual.

Cicero's despair and uncertainty following the outbreak of civil war can be traced in the almost daily letters he sent to Atticus during the opening months of 49. In the end, and very reluctantly, he decided that he must actively join Pompeius. His military contribution was of no importance, however; once permitted by Caesar to return to Rome from internal exile at Brundisium he spent his time largely in retirement (a state compounded by the death of his daughter Tullia early in 45).[18] Between 46 and 44 he produced an astonishing set of rhetorical and philosophical texts, fuelled by

---

[16] Tatum 1999: 151–2.

[17] 56 and 54 were exceptionally busy; 55 (the second consulship of Pompeius and Crassus) much less so. For details, see Marinone 2004: 115–38.

[18] For Cicero's relationship with Tullia, see Treggiari 2007.

a commitment to Roman educational practice and a desire to create a Latin philosophical literature.

The final phase of Cicero's career was shaped by the assassination of Caesar in 44. Cicero was not involved in the plot, but was deeply sympathetic to it; intimidated initially by Antonius' assumption of power, he began in the autumn of 44 a sustained attempt to re-assert senatorial authority and to prevent Antonius from taking over Caesar's position through the set of speeches which became known as the *Philippics*. This involved the creation of an enormous coalition of disparate interests, centring upon *imperium*-holders with armies; and the promotion of Caesar's great-nephew C. Octavius as an alternative location for Caesar's residual power. The attempt was a failure; Octavius successfully consolidated his position and joined with Antonius and Lepidus to take control of the state. Once the three men had their position confirmed by the people in November 43, they proceeded to use the Sullan device of proscription to eliminate their enemies, including Cicero, who was killed in December 43.[19]

This volume explores Cicero's writings under three broad headings. The first section relates his work to the intellectual context of Rome in the first century BC. It considers Cicero's contribution to a range of genres and fields, and compares his work to that of other leading intellectuals of the period, particularly Varro and Caesar. In the second section, the focus is on the relationship between Cicero's writing and his political career: here are discussions of his oratory, letters and the relationship between political theory and practice, and a detailed study of the intersection between text and action in the months after Caesar's assassination. The final section addresses the ways in which Cicero's life and writings have been handled subsequent to his death: this is a vast topic, and the approach adopted here is to offer a series of case studies, beginning with Roman treatments in the early empire and concluding with anglophone film and novels in the twentieth and twenty-first centuries.

I am very grateful to Michael Sharp at Cambridge University Press, who first suggested the idea of a *Cambridge Companion to Cicero* and has been a tirelessly supportive editor ever since; to John Henderson, for wise advice at crucial moments; to Clifford Ando, for his assistance with the proofs of Chapter 15; and to all the contributors for their enthusiasm, scholarship and patience. In the very final stages of preparation came the news of Sabine MacCormack's sudden death; it seemed fitting to dedicate the volume to her memory.

---

[19] On the proscriptions which began in 43, see Osgood 2006: 62–81.

PART I

The Greco-Roman intellectual

I

ANTHONY CORBEILL

Cicero and the intellectual milieu of the late Republic

The late Republic marked Rome's zenith of original literary and scholarly creativity. The republican form of government encouraged development of the finest forensic and judicial oratory written in Latin (preserved for us almost exclusively in Cicero); scholars of antiquarianism, with Varro at the forefront, began perfecting linguistic and other tools for reconstructing the history, religion and thought of the seemingly irrecoverable past; a wish to become acquainted with Greek schools of philosophy prevailed among the elite; and developments in history and poetry were preparing the way for great authors of the following generation such as Livy, Virgil, Horace and the elegists. I shall attempt to touch upon some of these areas by focusing on what Cicero viewed as the primary function of intellectual activity, in particular that activity informed by Greek precedents, in the formation of his own political and cultural identity.

Cicero's education

Educating a late Republican Roman meant creating a citizen, but only a citizen of a certain type. State-sponsored schooling was unknown, and the instruction that did become publicly available for a fee beginning in the early first century suffered under the notoriety of both personnel and pedagogy. Teachers supposedly displayed deviance in sexual practice and in political direction, while the actual training occurred in the Latin language, a practice reproved, ironically enough, by the Roman censors in an official edict of 92.[1] Cicero's own education reveals the various manifestations taken by this often uneasy fit of respecting an impressive Greek intellectual heritage while simultaneously embracing native Roman ideals. The elite would normally

---

[1] Teachers' reputations: Kaster 1995: xliv–xlviii (esp. n. 37); edict of 92: Gruen 1990: 179–91 offers an overview, with bibliography. All translations from Greek and Latin are my own.

have undergone the crucial first steps of learning at home, picking up familiarity with Greek language and literature from house-slaves or freedmen in
addition to learning to read and write Latin. Male members of the non-
wealthy classes, by contrast, were probably rarely educated beyond basic
literacy and numeracy, and their familiarity with Greek would have derived
largely from commerce, military service and immigration, yielding a different
sort of vocabulary from that heard in the homes of the wealthy.[2] Outside
the home, elite education can be roughly reconstructed from a variety of
sources, in particular from Cicero's many references to his own. Cicero's
first exposure to philosophy would have been in Greek; his writings refer to
boyhood contacts with the Stoic Diodotus (*Acad.* 2.115) and the Epicurean
Phaedrus (*Fam.* 13.1.2), while he recounts that in 88 he 'devoted himself
entirely' to the teachings of Philo of Larissa, head of the Academy in Athens,
during that philosopher's sojourn in Rome (*Brut.* 306). The one personal
teacher whose name we know with certainty, the Greek poet Archias, is
credited by the mature orator as teaching him in his earliest youth, presumably in literature (*Arch.* 1). Cicero's first instruction in rhetoric was in Greek
as well, beginning when he moved to Rome in the early nineties, and will
have included lessons in dialectic, rhetorical theory and declamation (*De or.*
1.23, 2.2; *Brut.* 310; Plut. *Cic.* 4.6).

Access to the study of Roman topics was more restricted. Cicero asserts
that he and Atticus had memorized as boys the Roman law-code known as
the Twelve Tables, a standard practice since neglected (*Leg.* 2.59). Beyond
this rote learning, no formal education in law is known to have existed.
Rather, a young man learned through personal observation of current practitioners, either in their homes or at the forum; this is also how he would
gain practical training in oratory (*Orat.* 142; *Brut.* 306). An indication of
the type of formal instruction that the young Cicero obtained in this period
can be gleaned from the one prose treatise composed in his youth, the *De
inventione* of the late nineties. During the succeeding decade, when Cicero
was in his late twenties, he studied in the Greek east for two years, a step in
education that by the end of the Republic was to become 'perhaps almost
obligatory for young men of the upper class'.[3] Exposure to this overseas
training was perceived as offering an overt advantage in the courts back
home. In a telling passage from one of his orations, Cicero derides a competing orator for having studied Latin literature in Sicily rather than at
Rome, and Greek literature in Lilybaeum rather than Athens (*Div. Caec.*
39). Once again, a pure Greek training assists in the creation of something
uniquely Roman.

---

[2] Horsfall 2003: 48–63 gives a vivid appraisal of the evidence. [3] Rawson 1985: 10.

Cicero's impressive achievements as an orator and rhetorician occupy other chapters in this volume. Here I shall contextualize Cicero's place in his intellectual milieu by considering principally the origins and development of the mature prose treatises that comprise an equally substantial portion of his corpus. After his consulship in 63, Cicero was to put his hybrid education to work in the service of what he perceived as a broadening of Rome's cultural horizons, by rendering not only in the Latin language but also into a Roman context some of the intellectual achievements of the Greeks that he deemed most relevant to his contemporaries. Of his many programmatic statements in this regard, particularly memorable are the prefatory remarks that Cicero addressed to Marcus Brutus in early 45 as he commenced on an ambitious programme of transmuting the highlights of Greek philosophy into the Latin language: 'I have returned to those studies that are retained in my memory, although circumstances have caused me to neglect them for a long period. And since systematic training for all the arts that pertain to a proper mode of living is bound up in the study of philosophy, I have decided to illustrate this in Latin, not because philosophy cannot be learned from Greek writings and teachers, but because I have always judged that the Romans have in all things either made discoveries on their own with more wisdom than the Greeks or have improved upon what we have learned from them – at least in those areas deemed worth the effort' (*Tusc.* 1.1). Cicero's ultimate view of his project, in other words, entails not Hellenizing Rome but Romanizing Greece, distilling those elements of this heritage that best contribute to a 'proper mode of living' for the rapidly emergent empire. Before examining in more detail how Cicero conceives of his contribution to Rome's intellectual achievements, it will be helpful to put his labours in perspective by discussing briefly three contemporaries whose own career paths diverged from Cicero's in distinct ways, despite their having the same basic educational experience: Atticus the entrepreneur, Varro the scholar and the military leader Julius Caesar.

Atticus

Titus Pomponius Atticus (110–32 BC) was Cicero's fellow student from boyhood, and remained his close friend until Cicero's death.[4] During the conflict between Cinna and Sulla in the eighties he moved to Athens to devote himself to his education. The move allowed him to avoid political inconveniences at home, which was also one of the reasons that seems to have prompted the young Cicero's studies abroad in the next

---

[4] Bailey 1965–70: vol. 1, 3–59 offers the best account of their life-long friendship.

decade.[5] Their sojourns in the east were to prepare these two men for significantly different careers. Cicero describes his time abroad as a quest to hone his already impressive skills in oratory, the ultimate goal being a return to Rome as a rhetorical force to contend with (*Brut.* 315–16). In contrast, Atticus chose to remain in Greece for twenty years, where he proceeded to amass a sizeable fortune through real estate transactions and monetary loans to both individuals and communities.[6] Although he never chose to seek public office for himself, he often used his wealth to support political candidates, even travelling to Rome regularly to vote in the elections, and on many other occasions helping friends and associates when it proved politically expedient (Nep. *Att.* 4.4). Besides the many examples of political savvy that one could cull from the extant letters sent to him by Cicero, Atticus' sensible discretion is best exemplified by his success in surviving the proscriptions of the second triumvirate, despite his close friendship with many of the triumvirate's enemies, including Cicero and Marcus Brutus (Nep. *Att.* 10). The biography composed by his younger contemporary Cornelius Nepos bears out well one modern assessment of Atticus' relationships with the powerful men of his day: his 'only traceable political idea was a hostility in principle to change and change-makers'.[7]

Atticus was a cultured man, much committed to art and literature. Nepos tells us not only that he owned several learned and trained slaves who were capable of performing tasks that required polished literary skills, but that even his footmen (*pedisequii*) could read and write (Nep. *Att.* 13.3). When it came time for Cicero to catalogue one of his own libraries, he enlisted members of Atticus' household staff for assistance (Cic. *Att.* 4.4a.1, 4.8.2). Indeed, Cicero is often asking Atticus for advice in the arrangement and expansion of his personal library, as well as requesting the use of Atticus' own. That collection was clearly extensive, and well used by its owner. Among his limited number of literary compositions, one particularly scholarly work, now lost, came to exert great influence. The *Liber annalis* undertook the difficult task of establishing a chronological order for the holders of Roman magistracies, including along the way notices of wars, the passage of laws and other important historical events (Nep. *Att.* 18.1–2). It marks a significant contrast with Cicero's own writings that Atticus' account seems to have restricted itself to a bare listing of the facts, with no evidence of political partisanship; those genealogies that he assembled of the great

---

[5] Nep. *Att.* 2.2; for Cicero, see Plut. *Cic.* 3.4 (and contrast *Brut.* 314).

[6] Nep. *Att.* 2.2–3, Horsfall 1989: 92–3.

[7] Bailey 1965–70: vol. I 24. Cf. Horsfall 1989: 75 'If Atticus was a "political animal",... he preferred the security of his burrow.'

families of contemporaries, such as the Iunii Bruti and the Cornelii Scipiones, were issued separately from the more comprehensive *Liber annalis*.

A strong adherence to Epicureanism provided Atticus with philosophical justification for not taking a more active part in politics. When one considers that Cicero frequently characterizes the school of Epicurus in his writings as despicable and self-centred, the man's deep love and respect for Atticus becomes especially remarkable. Of the many testimonials that Cicero offers in his correspondence to the special quality of their friendship, one in particular stands out. In 61, two years after holding the consulship, the pinnacle of Republican political achievement, Cicero writes: 'I have always considered that the only difference between you and me is in the way of life that each of us has chosen. A kind of ambition has driven me to pursue political office, whereas a different reason, but one in no way contemptible, has led you to an honourable freedom from such responsibilities. In fact, I consider you superior not only to myself but to everyone when it comes to those truly praiseworthy characteristics – honesty, integrity, care and fidelity' (*Att.* 1.17.5). The rare opportunity that the letters offer in following the relationship between Atticus and Cicero provides a useful reminder that, while Cicero may have been ambitious for his own role in Republican politics (and Roman history), he was well aware that it was not the only respectable way to spend one's life.

Varro

Ancient sources commonly identify Marcus Terentius Varro (116–27 BC) as the most learned man of his day, if not of all Roman antiquity, with well over 600 books attributed to his authorship (e.g. Quint. *Inst.* 10.1.95). What little can be reconstructed of his early life resembles that of Cicero: born outside of Rome in the late second century to a family of probably equestrian origins, as a young man he moved to Rome for his education.[8] Of his teachers, the two whose names have come down to us featured in Cicero's intellectual development as well. Lucius Aelius Stilo, antiquarian and occasional speechwriter, receives mention as a scholar respected by both men in their youth, while the Academic philosopher Antiochus of Ascalon could lay claim to them both as students when Cicero and Varro were young adults.[9] In contrast to Cicero, however, Varro had significant experience in the army, spending probably most of the seventies in various military positions. In the political arena, each man pursued the expected

---

[8] For Varro's early life I follow Cichorius 1922 and Dahlmann 1935.
[9] Stilo: *Brut.* 205–7, Gell. 16.8.2, Kaster 1995: 69–70; Antiochus: August. *De civ. D.* 19.3.

means of advancement, with Varro reaching the praetorship, probably in the late seventies or early sixties, and Cicero the consulship of 63. Each was also a loyal follower of Pompey in the early years of the civil war, with Cicero recording how he was together at Dyrrachium with Varro and Cato the Younger before the battle of Pharsalus (*Div.* 1.68). Yet despite this common biography, both educational and political, and despite the words of praise that Cicero would address to the older scholar as, for example, 'a kindred spirit through the same studies and the length of our friendship' (*Acad.* 1.1), the men seem never to have become close friends.[10]

Although precise reasons for this incompatibility are irrecoverable, a series of letters that Cicero sent Varro during the latter stages of the civil war provides a clear perspective on what Cicero, at least, perceived to be their differences (*Fam.* 9.1–8; none of Varro's responses survives).[11] The correspondence begins with Cicero claiming to emulate Varro, as he turns to books, research and scholarship in consolation for being alienated from his previous role in the Republican form of government. Cicero makes clear his view of how this period of enforced leisure should be spent: he encourages Varro to employ his retirement as Cicero does, in using words and books to govern the republic just as they had both formerly used the senate house and forum (*Fam.* 9.2.5). There is, however, little in the extant works and fragments of Varro's subsequent voluminous output that shows him applying his researches to contemporary problems in the way that Cicero suggests here.[12] Conversely, Varro's antiquarian researches into early human and divine antiquities, the results of which helped shape the patriotic longings for a lost Roman past that drives much of Augustan literature, were alien to Cicero's own way of working.[13] In a later letter, Cicero politely but firmly indicates an awareness of these conflicting notions concerning the ends of scholarly research. As the victorious Julius Caesar approaches Rome in June 46, Cicero compares Varro's literary activity at his Tusculan villa with the civic turmoil going on around them: 'in these stormy times you are nearly the only person safely in port. You reap the greatest fruits of your learning in treating thoughtfully those things that should be enjoyed – in opposition to the hedonistic activities of these contemporaries of ours'

[10] Kumaniecki 1962.

[11] Wiseman 2009 offers a conjectural reconstruction of the ways in which the two men occupied 'opposite sides of an ideological divide' (112).

[12] For popular tendencies in Varro's work, see Wiseman 2009, esp. 115–17, 119–20, 127–9.

[13] A rare exception is Cicero's methods in *De republica*, written in the fifties; see Rawson 1991: 58–79, esp. 65–6. Wallace-Hadrill 2008: 231–9 assesses ways in which antiquarianism, despite its apparent detachment from contemporary concerns, helps subvert the elite system at Rome.

(*Fam.* 9.6.4). The clearly tentative, even sarcastic, tone of Cicero's remarks receives confirmation as he continues in the same letter to ponder whether he could happily lead a life of scholarship detached from concerns for the state, a life that he believes may be inappropriate. Cicero fails to convince himself that such a life is possible, as is apparent from the rhetorical question that concludes these musings: 'So if the state allows it, why should we not pursue those studies that provide, in the opinions of great men, a kind of break from public responsibilities?' (*Fam.* 9.6.5). The protasis here is key – 'if the state allows it' (*concedente re publica*). For Cicero, the state in 46 BC could not afford to excuse learned men from public duties.

The path that Cicero was in fact to take with his scholarly endeavours, and their contrast with Varro's project, is made explicit in the *Academica* of 45. At the beginning of this treatise, dedicated to Varro himself, Cicero depicts a fictional discussion between the two men regarding the merits of rendering the great ideas of Greek philosophy into Latin. 'Varro' objects to the idea, asserting that he refuses to write about things that the unlearned will be unable to understand and the learned unwilling to read (*Acad.* 1.4). As we shall see, such an assertion, if true, would effectively negate much of Cicero's literary activity following the civil war. Accordingly, 'Cicero' responds with a strikingly personal apologia: when in the midst of political turmoil at the helm of the Roman state, he took consolation and guidance in these Greek works; now, in retirement, he finds that making them accessible is equivalent (*consentaneum*) to any political work he has done. 'And if this isn't so, I don't see what else I can do' (*Acad.* 1.11). Varro, it seems, answered Cicero's *Academica* with his only significant venture into Greek philosophy, the *Liber de philosophia* of late 45 (no longer extant). Here, by offering an Epicurean slant to his Academic leanings, he seems to have justified his retreat away from politics and into the world of his studies.[14] Varro, erstwhile Pompeian, was to be elicited for service by Pompey's opponent Julius Caesar as organizer of Rome's first public library (a plan never realized). It is also about this time that Varro dedicates to Caesar his influential compendium on Roman religion, the *Antiquitates rerum divinarum*.[15] After Caesar's death (and Cicero's assassination), Varro continued his private studies – which may have included a treatise providing support for Caesar's deification – as Octavian solidified his hold over the former Republic.[16]

---

[14] Baier 1997: 33–5.   [15] Horsfall 1972: 120–2.
[16] Horsfall 1972: 124–5 (on *De gente populi Romani*).

Julius Caesar

In offering advice to his son Marcus, Cicero recommends a brilliant military career as traditionally the best option for a young man hoping to obtain glory in Rome (*Off.* 2.45; see too *De or.* 1.7). Such was the path adopted by Gaius Julius Caesar (100–44 BC). Prior to this, Caesar followed a course of education similar to that of his older contemporaries, the learned Varro, the entrepreneur Atticus and Cicero. Although details of Caesar's early education are sparse, Marcus Antonius Gnipho, a teacher whose school Cicero frequented even when as old as forty years, is attested as one of his earliest teachers, probably in grammar and rhetoric, perhaps in both Greek and Latin (Suet. *Gram.* 7.2). Afterwards, during travels to the east in his early to mid twenties (delayed by a brief period of captivity among pirates), Caesar pursued more advanced lessons in rhetoric at Rhodes with Apollonius Molon, a teacher with whom Cicero studied in both Rome and Rhodes during the previous decade (Suet. *Iul.* 4.1; *Brut.* 312, 316). By contrast, evidence of any serious studies under Greek philosophers is late and meagre (Rawson 1985: 109–10). Finally, like Cicero, Atticus and Varro, Caesar too dabbled as a young man in composing works of literature; Suetonius mentions a poem entitled 'The praises of Hercules' and a tragedy 'Oedipus' among his juvenilia. The titles alone remain since Augustus mysteriously prevented the dissemination of these works (Suet. *Iul.* 56.7).

Caesar distinguished himself as a talented orator from an early age, so much so that ancient sources are fond of speculating 'what if?'. Quintilian, Cicero's greatest admirer from antiquity, couches the highest praise for Caesar's oratory in a contrary-to-fact condition: 'Had Julius Caesar had much time for the forum, no other Roman could be named as rival to Cicero.'[17] And yet, despite these expressions of apparent regret, Caesar did use his education in grammar and rhetoric in the service of grander ambitions. The elegance of his war commentaries received praise already from his contemporaries (*Brut.* 262), and the propagandistic opportunities that these commentaries provided for Caesar's political promotion and self-preservation have also been apparent since antiquity. Of equal interest are several of Caesar's less celebrated literary endeavours, of which I shall provide one example each from oratory, grammar and political pamphleteering. As early as his praetorship of 62, Caesar exploits in a funeral oration for his aunt Julia the kind of antiquarian researches best associated with Varro.[18] Following a well-established family tradition on his father's side, he traces the line of the

---

[17] Quint. *Inst.* 10.1.114; see, too, e.g., *Brut.* 252, 261; Tac. *Ann.* 13.3.4; Plut. *Caes.* 3.2–3.
[18] On Caesar's use of Varro, see Baier 1997: 65–7.

Iulii back to the goddess Venus, while linking his paternal grandmother's lineage to the early kings of Rome. In this way, Caesar publicly claims his place as a descendant to the divine and human founders of the state (Suet. *Iul.* 6.1). Caesar was to flaunt these associations throughout his lifetime, and his heirs would continue to do so after his death. A less intuitive use of literature to garner a broad base of support has been suggested for the treatise on grammatical analogy that Caesar composed in the fifties (and dedicated to Cicero) while passing over the Alps on his way back to military campaigns in Gaul. In arguing here for a more systematic presentation of the intricacies of Latin grammar, Caesar could be interpreted as attempting to facilitate mastery of the language for non-native speakers, such as future citizens – and therefore likely allies – from the newly conquered Gallic provinces.[19] Finally, after the suicide of the younger Cato in the civil war prompted a series of encomia of his virtues and, by implication, criticisms of Caesar's actions, Caesar wrote two books of declamatory *Anticatones* in response. Their subject matter included hostile invective against Cato's private life. Ideological conflict, it is clear, could display itself both on the battlefield and in the study.[20] Even in the final years of his life, a series of actions planned by Caesar as dictator continue to stress the importance of his education: as a means of attracting the finest minds to the capital, he granted automatic citizenship to all rhetoricians, grammarians and philosophers teaching in Rome (Suet. *Iul.* 42.1); his celebrated reform of the calendar involved consultation with learned astronomers (Plin. *HN.* 18.211, with Rawson 1985: 112–13); other plans, only to be realized after his death, included a codification of Roman law and the establishment of the first public library of Greek and Roman texts (Suet. *Iul.* 44.2).

Caesar well recognized the pragmatic value of education, exploiting his training in antiquarianism, rhetoric and grammar at key moments of his political career, moments when one might think that issues of Latin grammar would be far from his mind. This attitude towards the use of education, just as much as his pursuit of military over oratorical *gloria*, distinguishes Caesar from Cicero, whose main delvings into non-oratorical prose were at explicit times of political 'retirement'.

Physical setting

Cicero's correspondence makes clear that his project of transforming Greek thought into Roman language involved two essential prerequisites: a collection of scholarly texts and a place for uninterrupted work. As already

---

[19] Suet. *Iul.* 56.5, with Sinclair 1994.
[20] Suet. *Iul.* 56.5, with Gelzer 1968: 301–4 and Gildenhard 2007: 39–40.

alluded to above, the Greek-influenced education prevalent during Cicero's youth was made less accessible by the fact that, in contrast with other major Hellenistic centres of learning, Rome lacked a publicly available library.[21] Archival material treating Rome's historical and antiquarian past – such as festival calendars, lists of magistrates, laws and decrees – could be obtained from various governmental collections within the city.[22] For both Greek and Latin literature and history, as well as for the sciences and philosophy, however, the curious had to exploit the resources of friends, or make special visits to established private collections; Cicero, we know, had occasion to consult Lucullus' library at Tusculum and Sulla's at Cumae. These particular collections will have made their way to Rome as a consequence of the systematic military conquest of the east. Several of Cicero's letters to Atticus also refer to the development and care of his own library. This correspondence mentions collections at Ciceronian villas in Tusculum, Antium and Formiae, and a rough notion of their size can be inferred from the fact that he needed to borrow slaves and freedmen to catalogue their holdings.

After the completion of one such major library project at his Antian villa, Cicero writes: 'now that Tyrannio has put my books in their place, it feels as if a mind has been added to my home' (*Att.* 4.8.2). The representation of texts and the building that houses them as analogous to mind and body offers more than a neat conceit. Extra-urban villas provided not simply quiet places for contemplation, but surroundings within which the owner has self-consciously integrated an aura of intellectual accomplishment. And in the late Republic, of course, intellectual refinement entails an intimacy with Hellenic culture. Beginning with the middle of the second century, Greek architectural and artistic motifs come to dominate Roman villa decoration.[23] Several of Cicero's letters discuss various types of artwork that he had acquired for his villas from throughout the Greek world, ranging from painting to exotic furnishing to statuary.[24] Although he occasionally requests that a work illustrate a particular scene from Greek myth and history, he seems hardly concerned about styles or specific artists. Nevertheless, while it is important that we recognize that Cicero is not guided by modern standards in making his aesthetic choices, this nonchalance in fact provides another clear instance of a Roman pragmatizing the Greek abstract, in this case by putting artistic production at the service of a greater goal. As he says explicitly in a revealing letter to his friend Fabius Gallus, filled with complaints about the expense of collecting works of art, his immediate

---

[21] For a survey of public and private libraries, see Casson 2001.
[22] See in particular Rawson 1991: 58–79 (= *JRS* 62 (1972): 33–45).
[23] Zanker 1998: 16–19.   [24] Showerman 1904 catalogues the references.

desire is for statues that will suggest a Greek lecture hall (*gymnasium*), and therefore the most important consideration is obtaining works that conform with this primary intention (*Fam.* 7.23). Decorative and architectural motifs that have been found in surviving villas indicate that Cicero's ideal of creating an appropriate atmosphere for intellectual activity appealed to other wealthy landowners, where decoration establishes a connection with Greek culture that one recent study has termed 'a tourism of the mind'.[25]

At the same time – and this point is important to keep in mind for our concluding section – this hybrid style of villa decor is emphatically *not* Greek. Greek detail exists side by side with Roman motifs – altars for sacrifice to the household Lares, repositories for the ancestral deities, enshrined images of ancestors – so as to forge a new creation: 'for the first time in history a distinct domestic setting had been created for cultural life, to which devotees could withdraw in their leisure time'.[26] An activity towards which Cicero devoted a considerable portion of the final fifteen years of his 'cultural life' occurred in just such a style of villa, as he composed the literary treatises that, in turn, borrow from these physical surroundings as inspiration for their own dramatic settings.

Cicero in retirement

Plutarch represents Cicero's journey to the east in his late twenties as a forced vacation, prompted by fear of reprisal from the dictator Sulla for the young orator's defence of Sextus Roscius.[27] Although the veracity of Plutarch's explanation has been doubted, the young Cicero's activities during this eastern sojourn harmonize well with those that he engaged in during the two later periods when politics again made him absent himself voluntarily from affairs of state: immersed in Greek studies, but with an ever-present awareness of Roman goals. Cicero states in his autobiographical account in *Brutus* that he spent six months at Athens continuing his lessons in philosophy under the Academic Antiochus of Ascalon, and he claims to have travelled throughout the eastern Mediterranean studying rhetoric and declamation in Greek with the greatest teachers then alive. 'After two years', he writes, 'I returned not only better trained but almost a new person.'[28]

Cicero's eighteen months of legal exile from 58 to 57 as a result of his actions after the Catilinarian conspiracy constitute his one period of

[25] O'Sullivan 2006: 134; see too the particular demonstration in O'Sullivan 2007.
[26] Zanker 1998: 18.
[27] Plut. *Cic.* 3.2–5; for an assessment of the claim, see Douglas 1966: 225.
[28] *Brut.* 315–16; Powell 2007: 333–9 offers a clear account of how Cicero's philosophical training contributed to his career as an advocate.

withdrawal from politics during which he did not actively integrate Greek learning with Roman experience. The reasons are not far to seek. His extant literary activity is restricted to personal correspondence, most of which, understandably, seeks to make that exile as short as possible, and in his constant travel during these months he was deprived of the setting and books that, as outlined in the previous section, made such scholarly work possible. Instead, Cicero's two most fertile periods as a composer of prose treatises correspond with those two periods following his exile that offered the most threat to the republican form of government, namely during the first triumvirate of the fifties and during the dictatorship of Julius Caesar. The treatises from both periods are integrally tied with events in his life, personal as well as political. In the preface to the second book of his *De divinatione*, a treatise written around the time of Caesar's assassination in March 44, Cicero looks back on his motivations for producing these tracts: 'as I was contemplating long and hard how I could be of advantage to as many people as possible by not interrupting my service to the state, the greatest benefit that occurred to me was to pass on to my fellow citizens paths toward the highest learning – and I feel that I have done this in several works already ... For in my books I have become the speaker expressing his opinion in the senate and the politician addressing the assembled citizens, in the belief that philosophy had replaced my administration of the state.'[29] This explicit testimony that writing in retirement represented a substitute for political activity shows that modern debates about whether Cicero is an original philosopher or a mechanical copyist of Greek ideas miss an essential point.[30] He intends to make the best of Greek thought available to the young and old in the expectation that it will be of future service to the Roman state (*Div.* 2.4–6).

Before assessing the nature of the contributions that Cicero made to Roman culture as a result of these periods of enforced leisure, we must acknowledge that the haste in which Cicero composed many of these tracts has led not infrequently to inconsistencies and confusion in presentation, in particular for modern readers. Many of these issues are attributable to Cicero's attempt to adapt too closely native Greek ideas to his Roman idiom. For example, the confusing account of prose rhythm in *Orator* has long been recognized as a result of Cicero's misapplying Greek sources to the different principles governing Latin practice (*Orat.* 168–236); a similar explanation underlies the confusing accounts of elision and hiatus in Latin prose.[31] In

---

[29] *Div.* 2.1, 2.7; Cicero repeats similar sentiments over a dozen times in these works (Pease 1920–3: 345).

[30] Douglas 1973 provides a clear discussion of this issue.   [31] Riggsby 1991: 339.

a related fashion, the conflicting views on divination that emerge from a reading of *De divinatione* have been explained as a product of his attempt to interpret traditional religious practice at Rome within a Greek philosophical framework.[32] Other perceived contradictions or ambivalences in Cicero's presentation can be accounted for in similar ways. In transmitting Greek culture as a supplement to Roman, those portions of the Greek inheritance considered intellectually or morally suspect are intentionally simplified or even dismissed: 'Greek learning... could only be rescued, or even understood, by anchoring it once more in a social and moral context – in the service of Roman tradition and Roman values.'[33]

The treatises of the fifties, accordingly, find Cicero putting into Roman context the best Greek writings that treated the two institutions dearest to him: the state (*De republica*; *De legibus*) and public oratory (*De oratore*). The premise of Cicero's *De republica* presents an almost stereotypical expression of Roman pragmatism. Plato's version of an ideal state in his own Republic, Cicero avers, suffered from the fact that the Greek philosopher did not have a contemporary ideal to use as his model. In contrast, at the opening of the second book of Cicero's treatise, the speaker Scipio Africanus the Younger expresses satisfaction that he has the advantage of using as his prototype for the ideal state the historical development of the constitution of Rome itself (*Rep.* 2.3; cf. 2.22). Despite this confident assertion about Roman superiority, Cicero, in reflecting back on the resulting treatise a decade later, remarks that it treated a subject familiar to him not only from Plato but from Aristotle, Theophrastus and all the other Greek-schooled Peripatetics (*Div.* 2.3). Similarly, the companion treatise *De legibus* discusses within a Greek framework laws derived almost exclusively from Roman practice.[34] The potential paradox of a uniquely Roman treatise derived from Greek models could not find clearer expression. Moreover, there survives direct evidence that some, at least, of Cicero's readers also viewed treatises such as the *De republica* as having resonance with contemporary political events. In a letter to his brother Quintus written during the composition of *De republica*, Cicero tells how his friend Sallustius regretted that setting the dialogue in 129 prevents Cicero from making explicit allusions to Roman politics of the fifties. As a result, Cicero states his intention of adding to the treatise a dialogue between himself and Quintus, thereby admitting contemporary concerns.[35]

---

[32] Beard 1986.

[33] Zetzel 2003: 137, an astute analysis of some of the ways that Cicero selectively assesses the value of Greek art, poetry and philosophy.

[34] Dyck 2004a: 12–15; see too his remarks on the Romanization of a Greek setting (21).

[35] *Q fr.* 3.5.1–2; for the interpretation adopted here, see Zetzel 1995: 3–4.

De oratore, published in 55 and viewed by many as Cicero's masterwork, also presents itself as a treatise whose reliance on Greek models allows the author to effect a superior synthesis. One of the major projects of this work is to locate common ground between the two types of training that dominated Cicero's intellectual development throughout his lifetime: that of the philosopher and that of the orator. It would be impossible to deny the immense debt Rome owes to Greece in the field of rhetorical theory, and indeed Cicero acknowledges in the preface to the first book that it was an influx of Greek teachers and texts that inspired Romans to pursue oratory as an art (1.14), and that Greek theorists have left behind a body of writings that cannot be surpassed (1.23). He closes this preface by explaining why, nevertheless, his interlocutors will be Romans of the early first century: since Romans in the intervening period have marked these countrymen for their practical skill in oratory, they must excel over the Greeks in authority (*auctoritas*; 1.23). In the dialogue itself, the interlocutor Scaevola is less politic about making the same point: 'you must cater to Roman youth, who aren't looking for either the everyday blabbing of some Greek without experience or for the sing-song of the lecture-halls, but who are seeking out the wisest and most eloquent of men, a man who is a leader through offering advice and making speeches, and not by means of some teaching but by means of important cases that pertain to our glorious nation' (1.105). Once again, pragmatism prevails over theory.

The general way in which Cicero counters Greek knowledge with Roman experience in his prose treatises should now be clear, as will be some of the ways in which this approach to the relationship between the state and scholarship differed from the concerns of Atticus, Varro and Caesar. I close, therefore, with two examples from Cicero's second period of forced retirement, a period bracketed by Caesar's victory over Pompey in the civil war and his assassination on the Ides of March. In two treatises, *Tusculanae disputationes* and *De officiis*, Cicero's practice of scholarship at the service of the state overlaps with private concerns, in particular regarding his only two children, his daughter Tullia and his son Marcus.

Upon the premature death of Tullia in February 45, Cicero turned away from the composition of the rhetorical and political tracts of the fifties and spent much of the next two years intensely focused on less directly pragmatic works, in particular of ethics and theology. He began with a *Consolatio* to himself that does not survive, a work followed in rapid succession by *Hortensius* (also lost), *Academica*, *De finibus* and *Tusculanae disputationes*. It is probable that consolation for Tullia's death is a driving force in this flurry of literary activity. In March 45, Cicero had received from Servius Sulpicius Rufus a famous letter of consolation for his loss, replete with the conventional elements expected of the genre, such as that death brings welcome release from life's uncertainties and that everything born must die (*Fam.* 4.5). The ultimate import of the letter is to encourage Cicero to return to political activity. In his epistolary reply, Cicero asserts the impossibility of his finding solace in either public or private affairs (*Fam.* 4.6.2–3). We know, however, that at this time Cicero was already busy writing his *Tusculanae disputationes*, marking clearly again that to Cicero the intellectual life is an important aspect of the political life – we will recall that it is the opening paragraphs of this same work that set out most self-consciously his project to render Greek philosophy in Roman terms. As the biographical context for this activity shows, the philosophical also embraces the personal. The first book of the *Tusculanae* deploys well-known Greek sources to prove that death holds nothing to fear – either it provides a welcome end to the pains of life, or the soul lives on in blessed immortality. And yet this life-long sceptic confesses to his young, nameless interlocutor that, like him, he too hopes for immortality: 'I see that you have high hopes of ascending to the heavens. I hope that will happen – for both of us' (*Tusc.* 1.82). Amid the lofty reasoning, the status of Tullia's afterlife is doubtless not far from her father's mind.

In the final year of his life Cicero addressed to his only son, the twenty-one-year-old Marcus, his final major philosophical treatise, *De officiis* – 'On appropriate actions'.[36] A significant portion of the treatise again represents Greek rationalizations, in particular Stoic ethical notions for determining the proper course of action in a given situation, applied to events in Roman history. The Roman element emerges more consistently than it ever had before: in the final, third book especially Cicero claims that he offers arguments to a large extent independent of any Greek predecessor.[37] In the preface to that book he once again alludes to the political circumstances that are forcing his retirement – he is 'fleeing the sight of the wicked' – and he notes that these are the events prompting him to compose a discussion about moral action (*Off.* 3.1–4). Most striking among the historical incidents coming under scrutiny in this book is the assassination of Julius Caesar in the previous spring. This incident provides Cicero with a clear example of how murder, even of a friend, can be justified as morally right (*Off.* 3.19, 82–5). Here, more clearly than anywhere else in his prose treatises, philosophical debate and political realities neatly coexist. The intersection also is reflected in Cicero's public activities during this time. *De officiis* was written as Cicero attempted to return to his role as leading orator and statesman; in particular, he composed the treatise concurrently with his *Second Philippic*

---

[36] On the associations of *officium*, see Dyck 1996: 3–8.
[37] *Off.* 3.34, with discussion of Dyck 1996: 483–96.

against Marcus Antonius. In returning to the political stage that created his career, Cicero uses a speech to justify his own life, one dedicated to service to Rome, in contrast with Marcus Antonius' self-serving quest for individual glory. Here again the justification of murdering tyrants such as Caesar plays a prominent role.

Conclusion

Cicero became notorious in his lifetime for a simple line of verse: *cedant arma togae, concedat laurea laudi* ('let weapons yield to the toga, let the laurel crown [of victory] give way to true praise'). Mocked in antiquity for its vanity, the verse shows an awareness of the two perceived paths to Roman glory – the weapons wielded by the soldier or the deliberation of the politician – and it unambiguously concedes the highest rewards to the politically engaged togate citizen.[38] Inextricably connected to Cicero the politician was Cicero the transmitter of Greek ideas in Roman dress. He never doubted that this two-fold activity constituted a single achievement, and that its rewards were preferable to the commercial successes of the businessman, the hermeticism of the scholar and the personal glory of military conquest.

Further reading

Rawson 1985 is an indispensable distillation of the names and scholarly pursuits of the intellectual elite during the period, and papers collected in Rawson 1991 provide details on particulars; for the nameless plebs, see the invaluable survey of Horsfall 2003. The best single primary source is Cicero's correspondence, particularly with Atticus, accompanied by the valuable commentaries of D. R. Shackleton Bailey. Gildenhard 2007 offers a fine discussion of the political contexts of Cicero's prose treatises, in particular the *Tusculanae disputationes*. Details on the nature of education during the period are assessed in Corbeill 2001. For a basic account of the life of Atticus, see Bailey 1965–70; of Varro, Cichorius 1922 and Dahlmann 1935; of Caesar, Gelzer 1968.

---

[38] Cicero quotes the verse, or part of it, three times (*Pis.* 74, *Off.* 1.77, *Phil.* 2.20); see further Dyck 1996: 208–9 and Gee in this volume (Chapter 5). The adapted phrase *cedant arma humanitati* ('let weapons yield to a sense of humanity') graces the World War II memorial at my home university. I think Cicero would have been pleased to see the potentially confusing *toga* replaced with *humanitas*, a concept he spent so much time developing.

2

JOHN DUGAN

Cicero's rhetorical theory

Rhetoric was the object of profound meditation throughout Cicero's life. The corpus of his rhetorical writings spans nearly the whole of his career, and survives in a remarkable variety of forms, constituting one of Cicero's major contributions to Roman literature and culture. Recent scholarship has deepened our appreciation of Cicero's 'minor' rhetorical treatises:[1] *De optimo genere oratorum* (an introduction to a Latin translation of a pair of Greek masterpiece speeches by Aeschines and Demosthenes); *Topica* (a work written for a lawyer friend of Cicero's, Trebatius Testa, that claims to be a distillation of Aristotle's *Topics*); and *Partitiones oratoriae* (a catechistic account of the basic structure of rhetorical theory written as a dialogue between Cicero and his son). Nevertheless, it is his most developed and elaborate works (*De inventione*, *De oratore*, *Brutus* and *Orator*) that reveal Cicero's use of his rhetorical writings as a sustained and evolving cultural project. Each of these major rhetorical treatises is in its own way a powerful melding of rhetorical theory and literary expression, an inextricable weaving of content and form that itself is one of Cicero's more provocative critical insights (*De or.* 3.19–24).

Fundamental shifts in scholars' approaches to these texts have shaped the recent revival of the study of Cicero's rhetorical theory.[2] The positivistic view of rhetoric as merely a set of abstract guidelines for public speaking has now largely faded.[3] So too scholars no longer limit their investigation of Cicero's

---

[1] See, e.g., Reinhardt 2003 on the *Topica* and Arweiler 2003 on *Partitiones oratoriae*. See also Gildenhard 2007: 1 on the recent trend of re-evaluating Cicero's neglected treatises.

[2] For an attempt to isolate recent trends in the study of Roman rhetoric, see Dugan 2007.

[3] A point made well by Copeland 1991: 4: 'Rhetorical theory has also been a notable victim ... of positivism. It has been viewed as a neutral perceptive system, a descriptive taxonomy of style, or as an academic discipline whose history is constituted by its manifest meanings and whose claims to truth about the nature of language and discourse are accepted on their own terms. But rhetoric as a system, like philosophy, is itself a discursive construct; its language and strategies of self-representation are themselves susceptible of rhetorical explication.'

rhetorica to extracting nuggets of otherwise lost Greek rhetorical wisdom or gleaning from these texts stylistic principles that may underlie his speeches.[4] In each instance this past scholarship had embraced implicit hierarchies – Greek rhetorical thought over Cicero's Roman adaptation of it, and oratorical practice over theory – that set the terms of these investigations. Such trends in Latin literary studies, and their latent assumptions, have been the focus of considerable scrutiny, and the debunking of these presuppositions has cleared the path to the deeper goals of Cicero's rhetorica.[5]

Cicero's rhetorical theorizing performs several interrelated cultural negotiations. It presents Greek rhetorical thought in a form that is both usable by, and acceptable to, his Roman readers. Cicero sought to overcome lingering Roman suspicion of Greek intellectual abstraction by naturalizing rhetorical theory to a Roman cultural context, that is, by talking about rhetoric in such a way that its value and utility would be self-evident. At the heart of Cicero's strategies for Romanizing rhetorical theory is his conviction that oratory is crucial to the health of the Roman state. For Cicero the proper exercise of persuasive speech is not just a matter of individual success, and rhetoric does not simply provide tools for the aspiring orator. Instead, Cicero's rhetorical theory constructs an ideology in which rhetoric is central to the Republic's existence.[6] As a result Cicero does not simply recalibrate the Greek rhetorical tradition to suit Roman use. He is decidedly impatient (or has the interlocutors in his dialogues be) with niggling arguments on specialized questions. Rather, he shapes his society's attitudes towards oratory to present the orator as a figure of profound cultural and political importance. Even in the midst of offering details of technical rhetoric, Cicero directs his readers' attention to the large-scale importance of eloquent speech.

Cicero employed rhetorical theory for such ambitious purposes by leveraging the prestige of being the most celebrated orator of his time. He wrote his mature works of rhetorical theory with the authority (*auctoritas*) of a leading statesman and renowned speaker. Rhetorical theory presented Cicero with an avenue for political influence through intellectual inquiry, especially when more direct routes were closed off to him by the turmoil of the late republic. Cicero's rhetorical theory both presents a view of the global importance of oratory for Rome and defends his own career against attacks from rivals.

---

[4] See May and Wisse 2001: 38–9 on the limitations of source criticism in the study of Cicero's rhetorical works.

[5] On Romanticism's privileging of Greek over Roman culture, see Habinek 1998: 15–33. On Hellenocentric readings of *De oratore*, see Zetzel 2003, esp. 120–3.

[6] Habinek 1995 broke ground on the question of Cicero's dialogues as expressions of ideology. Connolly 2007a is a rich exploration of the political dimensions of Cicero's rhetorical theory.

Cicero uses his own oratorical career to authorize his rhetorical theory, and uses his rhetorical theory to defend his oratorical career. Even within his sweeping arguments about the nature and importance of oratory, Cicero interweaves elements of his own life as an orator and politician, making his rhetorical theory an expression of his identity.[7]

De inventione: textbook interrupted

De inventione provides a crucial reference point for understanding the evolution of Cicero's rhetorical thought. We do not know precisely when Cicero composed this work, though the best estimate is sometime from the mid nineties to the early eighties BC. Therefore it was likely while he was in his teens, years before the speaking career that would bring him fame and power.[8] Nor is it clear why he finished only that section dealing with the discovery of material, *inventio*, leaving out the other canonical divisions of the art: arrangement, expression, memory, and delivery (*Inv. rhet.* 9). The fate of this work has been to be forever labelled 'youthful', yet this designation is less a reflection of a lack of sophistication than it is the result of Cicero's use of *De inventione* as a springboard to launch his later rhetorical theory. Cicero presents *De oratore* as a mature return to the topic of certain juvenilia, notes that had fallen into circulation (without mentioning *De inventione* by name) (*De or.* 1.1). Similarly, Cicero omits *De inventione* from a later list of his books on rhetoric, a canon that includes *De oratore*, *Brutus* and *Orator* (*Div.* 2.4). We can see in this early work more traditional ideas and modes that were part of Cicero's early training in rhetoric from which his later theorizing would depart.[9] Yet *De inventione* also contains seeds of the more global themes that would come to flower in his subsequent rhetorical works.

Cicero emphasizes in *De inventione* that he is composing an *ars*, meaning both 'art' and 'handbook', a term for a rational system that can be taught (where *ars* is a Latin calque for the Greek *techne*).[10] Its specific method of oratorical training is *status* theory, a technique for rhetorical invention credited to the Greek rhetorician Hermagoras.[11] The bulk of *De inventione*'s two

---

[7] An idea explored in Dugan 2005.

[8] On the dating of the *De inventione* see Corbeill 2002: 31–4 and the classic account of Kennedy 1972: 106–10.

[9] See Corbeill 2002.

[10] On rhetoric's status as an *ars* see *Inv. rhet.* 1.7–1.9; reference to competing *artes* (*Inv. rhet.* 1.33; 1.50); on Cicero's text as an *ars* (*Inv. rhet.* 2.4); on Aristotle's collection of early rhetorical *artes* (*Inv. rhet.* 2.6).

[11] On Hermagoras and *status* theory see Kennedy 1963: 303–21; May and Wisse 2001: 32–3; Corbeill 2002: 29–30; Wisse 2002: 356–7.

books gives a detailed account of this highly technical method of argumentation. Yet Cicero prefaces these books with wide-ranging meditations, first, on the significance of oratory and its role within human civilization and then on Cicero's method of adapting Greek rhetorical theory. These expansive theoretical reflections on the nature and function of persuasive speech, and on Cicero's role as a translator of Greek thought for Roman use, anticipate issues that Cicero would develop more fully in his later rhetorical theory. These two parts of the text, the high-flown prefaces and the nitty-gritty of *status* theory, rest somewhat inharmoniously together. Cicero had not yet found a way of integrating the ambitious vision of oratory articulated in prefatory material within *De inventione*'s discussion of the nuts and bolts of rhetorical technique. *De oratore*'s dialogue format, as we shall see, would later give Cicero a framework for harmonizing that work's presentation of rhetorical theory with its over-arching cultural ambitions.

With the passion for classification that is characteristic of ancient rhetorical thought, *status* theory offers Cicero an ever-expanding grid of the classification of notional circumstances paired with the appropriate rhetorical response. In essence, *status* theory (literally, 'postures' or 'stances') presents the orator-in-training with an elaborate menu that categorized various likely oratorical challenges that he might face, and offered suitable responses to those problems. Following Hermagoras, who is thought the inventor of *status* theory, Cicero first distinguishes 'general questions' (*quaestiones*), broad philosophical questions without specific persons involved, and 'special cases' (*causae*), controversies put forward in speech that entail definite individuals.[12] These 'special cases' are further divided into the 'conjectural' (whether or not an act was committed), 'definitional' (how that act should be described in words), 'qualitative' (whether mitigating circumstances should determine the case's outcome), and 'translative' (whether the case should be related to another legal venue) [*Inv. rhet.* 1.10]. The interpretation of legal texts comes under similar schematization, divided into five different sorts of issue that could arise from a disputed law.[13] *De inventione*'s 'positions' branch out in ever more elaborate complexity. In the first book Cicero applies *status* theory to the various parts of an individual speech (exordium to peroration) and, in the second, to the three general classifications of orations (judicial, deliberative and epideictic).

De inventione shows extraordinary confidence in the efficacy of the art of rhetoric, and its rational codifications and systemization, to master the various circumstances that an orator might confront. This is a text in love with its own intricacy. As George Kennedy (1972: 118) notes, for the

---

[12] I borrow the translations of Hubbell 1949.   [13] *Inv. rhet.* 1.17.

readers of this work 'the complexity of the system probably made it seem all the more worth studying'. By offering a map of the linguistic world, *De inventione* presents an image of mastery over that world. *Status* theory serves as a grammar from which its students could generate persuasive language or, in the terms of structural linguistics, a rhetorical *langue* to regulate oratorical *parole*.[14] Such systemization offered its disciples a system of agonistic argumentation that would allow them to overcome their opponents in court. The methodical detail that this text provides, combined with the prestige of Cicero's authorship, made *De inventione* a standard teaching text from antiquity, through the Middle Ages, to the Renaissance.[15]

For its day, *De inventione* was likely an ambitious, even path-breaking attempt to express for a Latin readership important precepts of Greek rhetorical theory.[16] To perform this cultural exchange Cicero, like other Roman rhetoricians, had to develop strategies for appropriating Greek thought without the loss of prestige that would result from subordinating himself to Greek predecessors. Cicero shows symptoms of the anxiety of influence when he offers stern criticism of Hermagoras' theories, though his work serves as the backbone for Cicero's entire treatise.[17] To emphasize his autonomy as a thinker, Cicero offers in the preface to the second book an extended analogy to describe his eclectic handling of Greek sources. His method, he writes, is like that of the fifth-century Greek painter Zeuxis, who chose the five most beautiful women of Croton as his models for his portrait of Helen, selecting their best qualities and combining them in his painting of the legendary beauty. Cicero claims that in composing his art of rhetoric he culled the best ideas from a range of thinkers and combined them like flowers in a bouquet (*Inv. rhet.* 2.4), suggesting that he has control over the entire rhetorical tradition such that he could distil what is best into his own work. Cicero presents himself as focusing his critical gaze over Greek rhetoricians as the artist Zeuxis scanned the beauties of Croton. By implicitly feminizing the Greek rhetorical tradition, Cicero does not allow his readers to imagine that he is dependent upon Greek culture in any subservient fashion. Cicero makes himself the source of the authority in his *ars*, not the various sources he uses. He emphasizes his autonomy in this process – he is not copying Greek rhetorical wisdom, but evaluating and amalgamating material drawn from the treasury of Greek thought. *De oratore* will later develop a more sophisticated method of displacing the authority of the Greek rhetorical

[14] On rhetoric as an intellectual ancestor of structuralism, see Barthes 1986: 6.

[15] See Cox and Ward 2006.

[16] See Steel 2005: 38. On the handbook tradition in Rome, see Gaines 2007.

[17] See Corbeill 2002: 36–46 on the uneasy relationship that *De inventione* and the contemporary treatise *Rhetorica ad Herennium* have with their Greek predecessors.

tradition by making rhetorical theory a performance staged between Roman aristocrats who assert their mastery over Greek thinkers.

In the preface to the first book Cicero presents himself as a committed intellectual in deep, solitary contemplation (*saepe et multum hoc mecum cogitaui*) over the general utility of the art of rhetoric – has it brought humanity more good or evil? *De inventione* is notably lacking a dedicatee, and Cicero as author makes no specific references to his own identity or life circumstances. It is a work that locates its authority apart from the networks of exchange that are characteristic of Roman literary culture. Instead we have an author gazing over the turmoil of his state, and reflecting upon the lessons of human history.[18] In tackling the very legitimacy and efficacy of his enterprise, Cicero shows himself to be a person who has embraced the complexities of public speech, has an understanding of the ethical underpinnings of oratory, and is conversant with philosophy. Cicero's claim that eloquence requires wisdom (*sapientia*) and reason (*ratio*), a *ratio* achieved through study (*studia*), anticipates *De oratore*'s view that the orator should be a figure of broad cultural competence.[19] The harmonious marriage of reason and speech, *ratio* and *oratio*, that *De inventione* presents as essential to the emergence of human civilization will become one of the mainstays of Cicero's view of the global importance of rhetoric in his later works.

While *De inventione* is a handbook whose focus is the art of rhetoric rather than the person of the ideal orator, its description of the role of oratory in humanity's development gives a glimpse of an ancestor of that ideal speaker. Cicero hypothesizes that some great and wise man, in some unspecified time in the past, first civilized humanity (*Inv. rhet.* 1.2). Cicero infers that this foundational figure in the history of human civilization must have had the tool of eloquence – his wisdom must have been articulate in order to succeed in persuading these uncivilized people. Here we see in Cicero's anthropological speculations a prefiguration of the ideal orator, both civilized and civilizing, who will appear in *De oratore*.

De oratore: performing rhetorical theory

In 55 BC Cicero found himself forced to retire from direct political involvement in a Rome dominated by the so-called first triumvirate of Caesar, Pompey and Crassus. His consulate of 63 now a fading memory, and the brutal loss of face of his exile of 58 still stinging, Cicero turned to writing

[18] On the *De inventione*'s lack of a clear audience, see Kennedy 1994: 118 and Wisse 2002: 337–8.
[19] See *Inv. rhet.* 1.1.

his most elaborate and far-reaching work of rhetorical theory, *De oratore*. The over-arching ideological goal of this work is to celebrate the power of oratory to maintain the safety and the stability of Rome. Cicero's ideal orator stands in opposition to the military dynast, and is thus a revival of the role that he created for himself after his suppression of the Catilinarian conspiracy in 63 when he claimed that his oratory was as vital to Rome's salvation as Pompey's military conquests.[20] *De oratore* offered a nostalgic idealization of the orator at a time when speech seemed powerless to influence Roman politics.

De oratore derives its originality from making several profound shifts away from a conventional rhetorical handbook such as *De inventione*. *De oratore* is an anti-textbook – a deconstruction of the generic expectations of a rhetorical handbook. In this dialogue Cicero casts Lucius Licinius Crassus, the person to whom Cicero's father entrusted his sons for their education in Rome, as the primary spokesman, while Marcus Antonius, the other great orator of the day, takes on the role of Crassus' foil. The choice to cast the work with interlocutors from his youth returns to the scene of the composition of *De inventione*, but this return signals change from, not continuity with, that earlier work. Instead of the single voice of a textbook, we have rhetorical theory that emerges from the conversation and interactions of Roman aristocrats. In place of a handbook's standard taxonomies, we have a text that performs rhetorical theory as much as it describes it. The trajectory in *De inventione* towards ever greater particularity, seen in the ramifications of *status* theory, is reversed in *De oratore*, a work which, as it constructs the ideal orator, unites the elements of rhetorical theory rather than divides them.

All of these negotiations rely upon Cicero's bold engagement with Platonic dialogue, and his choice to commandeer the method of rhetoric's great critic from the Greek tradition. Cicero's text invites comparison with Plato's *Phaedrus* early on when the elderly Scaevola proposes to Crassus that they do as Socrates in the *Phaedrus* and sit beneath the shade of a plane tree. Crassus does Plato one better when he suggests that his friends sit not directly on the grass as the barefoot Socrates once did, but on benches with pillows for added comfort. In this gesture of confident cultural appropriation, Cicero's Crassus is not satisfied with mimicking this famous scene in Plato's dialogue. He does not hesitate to improve upon Plato with the unselfconscious aplomb of a Roman aristocrat who knows how to use Greek culture for his own

---

[20] In his poem he wrote on his consulate Cicero attempts to compare his accomplishments favourably with Pompey's with the line *cedant arma togae* ('let arms yield to civilian dress'). Cf. Dugan 2005: 62–4.

purposes.[21] The dialogue ends with a similarly bold allusion to the *Phaedrus*: as Socrates in that dialogue predicts the future oratorical greatness of Isocrates, so Cicero has Crassus predict Hortensius' future glory.[22]

The self-confidence with which Cicero's Crassus treats the *Phaedrus* extends to his brusque dismissal of Plato's *Gorgias*, the philosopher's most sustained critique of rhetoric. Rather than offer a detailed response to Plato's argument, Crassus brushes the *Gorgias* aside with the quip that the chief impression that it left him when he read the dialogue as a student was that Plato was an excellent orator.[23] Reprising his role as an eclectic Zeuxis, Cicero cherry picks ideas from Plato as they suit his purposes in *De oratore*. He finds an ally in Plato's critique of writing in the *Phaedrus*, an attitude that matches *De oratore*'s mistrust of written handbooks, whether the dismally unfunny Greek handbooks on humour (2.217), Antonius' own handbook on rhetoric (1.94 and 1.208), or Cicero's own early attempts at rhetorical theory (1.5). Cicero cunningly melds the aristocratic Roman distrust of committing words to writing (as Thomas Habinek has argued)[24] with Plato's similar suspicion of writing. Cicero's interlocutors keep written oratorical regulations at arm's length. Instead of rules, *De oratore* has Romans speaking of rules, or repeating handbooks' standard treatments, even to the point of parody.[25] This is rhetorical theory in quotation marks, and we as readers are allowed to overhear an expression of rhetorical theory displaced from the standard textbook format.

Cicero's cushioning of Plato can stand as a symbol for strategies for naturalization of rhetoric to a Roman cultural context that *De oratore* performs as a whole. Cicero presents rhetorical theory as a conversation that Roman aristocrats have to relax from the previous day's tense talk about the dire political situation that the interlocutors faced in the dialogue's setting in 91 BC.[26] Rhetorical theory is thus filtered through the etiquette and cultural codes of the Roman elite, persons who have a sceptical view of traditional rhetorical catechisms, dogmas shown by experience in the courts and senate to be insufficient preparation – Roman experience displaces Greek theory.[27]

---

[21] This is the argument of Zetzel's (2003) illuminating treatment of this passage. On the *De oratore*'s relationship with Plato in general see Fantham 2004: 49–77. Cf. Long 1995a.

[22] Compare Phaedrus 279A and *De or.* 3.228–30. On Cicero's relationship with Hortensius, see now Dyck 2008a.

[23] See *De or.* 1.47 and cf. 3.129 (with Dugan 2005: 84).

[24] Habinek 1998: 103–21.

[25] See Crassus' account of standard oratorical regulations in *De or.* 1.134–46 (and cf. 2.41). See May and Wisse 2001: 36 on lists of figures in 3.202–7 as a parody.

[26] See *De or.* 1.26 and cf. Achard 1987: 322.

[27] Hall 1996 demonstrates how the *De oratore* presents rhetorical theory as it arises from Roman aristocratic conversation.

Cicero locates the authority for this account not with the cultural contribution of Greek texts, but with the urbane conversation of Roman aristocrats, persons who have attained prominence according to conventional Roman values (see *De or.* 1.23).

De oratore thus evidences an anxiety over being subjected to external authority, celebrating instead instances of brilliant improvisational oratorical performance.[28] To dispel this anxiety these Roman aristocrats assert their mastery of Greek rhetoric, referring to Greek rhetorical theory as something that they once followed when they were young (*De or.* 1.135). This gesture is a performance of the *auctoritas* of the interlocutors, the quality that Cicero elsewhere calls essential for participants in a literary dialogue.[29] Their attitude towards rhetorical theorizing is essential to the meaning of *De oratore* – the ideal orator is the master of oratorical circumstances, and able to improvise solutions not to be found in handbooks.

Cicero's choice to have his interlocutors refuse to commit to the dictates of rhetorical theory extends to the ironic way that rhetorical theory becomes integrated into performance. The dialogue format of *De oratore* allows the conversation's participants to stage a performance of rhetorical theory.[30] Cicero uses the rhetorical and philosophical technique of arguing a question from two opposing perspectives (*in utramque partem*) to perform a structural role within the work.[31] After Crassus in the first book stakes out positions regarding the need for an orator to be a person of broad and deep familiarity with law and philosophy, Antonius offers detailed refutations of these assertions. Crassus responds by labelling this *in utramque partem* disputation and calling it a favourite practice of philosophers. He questions whether Antonius is offering his sincere beliefs or is demonstrating his talent for this form of argument (*De or.* 1.262–4). Antonius offers a volte-face in Book 2 (2.40) explaining that his positions yesterday were designed to win followers away from Crassus, while today he will present his authentic beliefs. Cicero's interlocutors use rhetorical techniques to discuss rhetoric, and do so with a metaliterary awareness of their status as players within the dialogue.

Presenting rhetorical theory as a literary dialogue also allowed Cicero to make ironic connections between the work's account of the standard

---

[28] See, for example, Cicero's treatment of the Crassus' impromptu wit at *De or.* 2.225. On the ideological significance of Cicero's celebration of spontaneous humour see Krostenko 2001: 218.

[29] See *Amic.* 4; *Sen.* 3; *Q fr.* 3.5.1.

[30] Gunderson 2000: 187–222 is crucial on this question.

[31] On this form of argumentation in Cicero, see Vasaly 1993: 187–90; Hall 1994: 222–3; Long 1995a: 52–8; Narducci 1997a: 32.

elements of rhetoric and the text of the dialogue itself. These resonances highlight *De oratore*'s own rhetorical structures, the rhetoric of Cicero's rhetorical theory. For instance, memory is both an element within rhetorical textbooks and crucial to the dialogue of *De oratore* itself, because Cicero presents his work as the product of memory, both that of one of the participants, C. Aurelius Cotta (who served as Cicero's informant on the dialogue), and Cicero's own recollections of the participants. The art of memory, as Antonius describes it in *De oratore*, arose from the catastrophic death of people caught in a collapsed building. The Greek lyric poet Simonides reconstructs the identities of the deceased by recalling the relative positions of the banqueters at the time the roof fell in. Cicero presents *De oratore* also as an exercise in memory in order to restore his interlocutors, most of whom were destined to die violent deaths soon after the putative date of the dialogue. The memory work that is Cicero's dialogue is thus played out in miniature within *De oratore*'s account of Simonides' invention of artificial memory.[32]

Within *De oratore*'s performance of rhetoric there is a general trend towards reconciliation of apparently opposed elements into a seamless whole. By the time we reach the third and concluding book, philosophy and rhetoric, form and content, innate talent and training (*ingenium* and *ars*), oratory and acting, find their differences fade as Cicero's dialogue works to find kinship at deeper levels. Rhetorical theory within *De oratore* becomes a discourse that resolves these apparent conflicts as it works its way towards its goal of shaping the ideal orator. The dialogue's deconstruction of traditional rhetoric collapses the polarities that form the structure of conventional rhetorical thought. Crassus, after long and deep meditation, offers the insight that words and things cannot be separated, and that the universe itself is one harmonious entity in which all fields of human inquiry share an essential likeness (*De or.* 3.19–24). As opposed to the passion for division and classification that is characteristic of conventional rhetorical theory, Cicero provides a view of eloquence as a single autonomous entity. To express the integrated unity of speech Cicero uses an analogy of the body of a refined and polished Roman aristocrat (*De or.* 3.96). The whole of the third book, in which Cicero combines a discussion of the orator's body in performance with a discussion of oratorical style, enacts this underlying unity for oratory that the work argues for: tropes of the body and tropes of language are treated under the same rubric. The figure of the orator, as an ideal person in whom the various aspects of eloquence are unified, thus

---

[32] On *De oratore* as a memory, a point emphasized in all three of the work's prefaces, see Narducci 1997a: 20. Cicero treats mnemonics in *De or.* 2.350–360. See Dugan 2005: 99–104 for more detailed analysis.

offers Cicero the perfect expression of his view of eloquence as an unbroken whole. The shift from the art of oratory to the person of the orator sets the stage for this integrated view of speech.

Brutus: theories of rhetorical history

After Caesar's victories over the Pompeian forces made him master of Rome Cicero returned to writing rhetorical theory in 46 with *Brutus*. Like *De oratore*, *Brutus* is not conventional rhetorical theory, but here Cicero lays out a history of Roman speech that expresses a theory of how oratory evolves through time. *Brutus* begins with the death of the orator Hortensius, and the lament over this deceased speaker spreads into a more general lament over the ruin of free speech in Caesar's Rome. While *De oratore* presents an optimistic prediction of Hortensius' glory to come, *Brutus* looks back soberly upon Hortensius' career as a squandering of potential. The idealism of *De oratore*'s investigation of the ideal orator meets with the hard facts of history. *Brutus*' diachronic narrative of oratory replaces *De oratore*'s synchronic approach, and urbane conversation yields to a somber wake for Hortensius and the free speech whose demise Hortensius had the good fortune not to live to see.

As in *De oratore*, Cicero frames *Brutus* as a dialogue, but chooses here to cast it between Cicero and his friends Pomponius Atticus and M. Iunius Brutus, not figures from the past. *Brutus* presents itself as recompense for works from each of their pens, Atticus' *Liber annalis* and a letter (really a treatise) from Brutus that has been identified as his *De virtute*.[33] These literary debts form the coordinates for the genre of Cicero's work: *Brutus* is a literary history, dependent upon Atticus' chronological researches, that explores the ethical dimensions of history. The themes of history, oratory, and the moral obligations that history engenders coalesce in *Brutus*' embrace of the Roman aristocratic funeral oration as an organizational motif. *Brutus*' lament over the dead Hortensius grows into an account of his oratorical ancestors within Roman history.[34] Cicero frames his history of Roman oratory within the generic expectations of Roman funeral oration, a series of homages to deceased family members designed to spur the survivors to emulate their glory.[35] Cicero thus again naturalizes oratory within Roman cultural conventions, using here a mode of memorialization that the Roman took as distinctly Roman practice apart from Greek influence. The *laudatio*

---

[33] Hendrickson 1939.
[34] On the *laudatio funebris* motif in the *Brutus*, see Gowing 2000: 58–8 and Steel 2003.
[35] On the aristocratic funeral oration, see Flower 1996: 128–58.

funebris motif also allows Cicero at the conclusion of the dialogue to turn to Brutus, the next in line within the Roman oratorical tradition, and invite him to contemplate his responsibilities within this narrative. How is Brutus to live up to the legacy of a tradition started by that Brutus who both rid Rome of the Tarquins and was Rome's first orator?

The problem of rhetorical theory that *Brutus* faces is how to write a history of the art of oratory. Complicating factors within this history are the absence of direct evidence of early Roman eloquence since no texts of those speeches survived, and the related problem of texts of speeches that fail to live up to the reputation of individuals. *Brutus* engages with the implicit question of the basic status of oratory: is it a transient performance that only becomes a meaningful historical event when represented in a text? Cicero's solution to this problem is to offer a literary history broken up into periods, eras of oratorical history marked both by the general advances in the art of oratory itself and by the technological advances in the writing of speeches. Cicero's history of orators is also a history of writing, of texts of speeches that are ever more potent models of eloquence that extend the influence of individual speakers. The climax of that history, though Cicero puts this compliment in Atticus' mouth, is with Cicero's own speeches, works that have flooded the market and made earlier texts obsolete (*Brut.* 122–6). Following the premise that nothing is simultaneously invented and perfected (*Brut.* 71), this periodic framework constitutes the general shape of the dialogue, and creates a context not only for understanding the evolution of the art over time but also a structure within which one may make legitimate comparisons between different orators.

As with *De oratore*, Plato proves crucial to the structure of *Brutus*. Cicero's choice to present his literary history as a dialogue in the Platonic tradition allows him to make an innovative melding of Aristotelian notions of teleological development – a succession of evolutionary stages directed towards a culmination of that history – and Socratic irony. Near the end of the work Atticus accuses Cicero of acting ironically in his praise of early Roman orators, and faults him for so inclusive a notion of 'orator' that he has included drudges (*Brut.* 292–7). While such irony may suit Socratic dialogue it has no place within a historical enquiry.[36] Cicero's initial response to this accusation of irony is to claim that he has no idea what Atticus could mean. With this ironic response to Atticus' accusation of irony, Cicero further expands the distance between what is said in the dialogue and the intentions of the work as a whole. Such an ironic mode not only allows

---

[36] For a recent, more expansive reading of irony in the *Brutus*, see Fox 2007: 177–208 (esp. 192–203).

Cicero to position himself as the culmination of the Roman rhetorical tradition – the *telos* towards which this narrative is directed – but it also lets Cicero negotiate his way through the political difficulties of writing about oratory, the life's blood of the free republic, under the domination of Caesar. Irony gives Cicero the escape route of plausible denial in the conclusion of the work in which Cicero encourages Brutus to 'reap the benefit of your virtue (*virtus*)' and 'renew – even improve upon – the legacy of the two sides of your family' (*Brut.* 311). This reference could not fail to be taken as an allusion to the Brutus who expelled the Tarquins and the legendary Servilius Ahala (assassin of the would-be tyrant Spurius Maelius). Brutus' later role in Caesar's assassination makes Cicero's call to action appear to have a specificity that his veiled words lacked. Yet it is clear that Cicero concludes the dialogue with a call for Brutus to fulfil his obligations, both political and oratorical, demonstrating the interpenetration of Ciceronian rhetorical theory and politics.

Regardless of Cicero's strategies of ironic dissimulation, *Brutus*, as Cicero's response to the death of oratory after Caesar's victories in the civil war, was inevitably as much a political work as a work of rhetorical theory. Cicero inserts a digression about Caesar (*Brut.* 252–5), and breaks a promise only to speak about dead orators by having Brutus claim that Cicero's opinion of Caesar is already well known. The interlocutors discuss the question of *Latinitas*, or proper Latin diction, as analysed in Caesar's *De analogia*, a treatise of linguistic theory that Caesar wrote in response to the positions that Cicero took in *De oratore*.[37] While Cicero argues that proper Latin arose from the imitation of the speech of others, and offers a *Latinitas* that passed between members of Rome's elite, Caesar instead proposes that Latin could be reduced to a rational system, a method in which words would be formed according to analogy with other similar words. The political implications of the question of linguistic purity have particular force in the context of late republican Rome, where Cicero offers a *Latinitas* that is available only to a political oligarchy, while Caesar's view of Latin as a phenomenon reducible to rational and therefore teachable principles offers a more populist view of language.[38] The politics of this debate reach further into Cicero's positioning of his cultural contributions in relation to Caesar. Cicero takes the opportunity in *Brutus* to quote Caesar's praises of Cicero, comparing his accomplishments in Latin literature favourably with military conquest. We do not have a purely intellectual, disinterested exchange of ideas, but a jockeying for political and cultural positions within the

---

[37] See further Corbeill in this volume (Chapter 1).
[38] This is Sinclair's (1994) brilliant argument. See also Kraus 2005.

fractious world. Rhetorical theory for Cicero is never just 'theoretical', but ideas about language with political meaning.

Orator: the grain of the voice[39]

Cicero wrote *Orator*, his final major rhetorical treatise, in 46 as a letter addressed to Brutus. While ostensibly a return to the question of the ideal orator that Cicero had explored in *De oratore*, *Orator* largely abandons the grand political and cultural ambitions for the orator, and instead focuses upon oratorical style as such. In *Orator* Cicero's rhetorical theorizing takes a distinct turn towards the more technical issues of literary aesthetics. After a quick summary of canonical elements of rhetoric – invention, arrangement, presentation and delivery (*Orat.* 43–60) – Cicero devotes much of the remainder of *Orator* to an investigation of oratorical style, particularly in its most formal capacity: the texture of speech presented by the rhythmical patterns of sound (*Orat.* 149–236). This shift seems a natural consequence of the new political order under Caesar; ambitious claims for oratory would ring hollow after the triumph of the force of Caesar's arms.

The main innovation of *Orator* within Cicero's rhetorical thought is to present the orator, and oratorical style, between opposed poles of abstraction and particularity. On one side, Cicero brings a global philosophical perspective to rhetorical theory. His orator is a Platonic ideal existing in the realm of eternal ideas (*Orat.* 10). The emphatically philosophical cast that Cicero gives to his investigation is both in line with his attempt in *De oratore* to reconcile philosophy and rhetoric and anticipates the final efflorescence of the philosophical works – many of which he will also dedicate to Brutus – that will mark the final years of his life. On the other, Cicero delves into the details of the aural texture of prose – its sound and rhythm – and probes eloquence at the level of the syllable. The radically different perspectives that *Orator* takes in its approach to rhetorical theory, Platonic idealism versus the aural texture of speech, may seem to us incongruous. Yet these perspectives coalesce in *Orator*'s engagement of the critical tradition of sublimity, a strand of ancient literary theory that embraces both the grand effects of literary expression and the details of the artful fitting together of words.[40]

Comparison between *Orator* and the treatise *On Sublimity* attributed to Longinus reveals similar assumptions about the power of language. Cicero both celebrates the ability of speech to overwhelm an audience, uprooting

---

[39] I borrow this phrase from Barthes 1977.

[40] On sublimity as a long-standing tradition within ancient critical thought, see Porter 2001: 72. For a more detailed treatment of the *Orator* and sublimity, see Dugan 2005: 251–332.

old opinions while sowing new ones (*Orat.* 97), and examines the minutiae of prose rhythm. 'Longinus' locates one of the sources of sublimity in the artful arrangement of words (40.1). By tapping into the tradition of the sublime Cicero was able to ally himself with an element of ancient critical thought that suited his immediate needs to answer criticisms from self-styled Atticist orators who appear to have found fault in particular with Cicero's prose rhythms on the grounds that they were somehow effeminate.[41] For Cicero, prose rhythm knits together prose to give a bodily integrity and force that are the antitheses of the slackness and bloatedness imputed to his prose by his Atticist critics; and it also allows the text to have a breath of life like that of a living performance. Cicero thus presents rhythmical prose as crucial to the long-term survival of an oratorical text by replicating the grain of the orator's voice in performance. When Cicero turns to the texts of his own speeches to explore the details of the texture of ornate prose, *Orator* takes on the cast of a career retrospective which offers an implicit defence of Ciceronian aesthetics.

The technical discussion of prose rhythm forces Cicero to deal with the problem of how to talk about such minutiae without suffering diminished *auctoritas*. Cicero appears to try to innoculate himself against accusations of acting like a Greek professor of rhetoric by emphasizing his role as a critic and not a teacher (*Orat.* 112) and by noting that he addresses Brutus not as a pupil but as a peer (*Orat.* 123). Yet, in the elaborate apologetics that precede the section of the *Orator* on prose rhythm (*Orat.* 140–8), we see Cicero struggling with the apparent impropriety of a prominent public figure delving into such a detailed treatment of rhetorical theory. Among other lines of defence, Cicero claims that, now that his oratorical and political career is in ruins, he should be allowed to devote himself to literary study. Cicero then hints at the next turn that his pen would take, the 'more weighty and serious' pursuits that, if finished, will complement his oratorical accomplishments (*Orat.* 148). Here Cicero alludes to the philosophical works that he would compose in such impressive quantity in the final two years of his life. It is as if Cicero decided in this final major work of rhetorical theory to probe into the most formal questions of oratory before devoting himself to the loftier themes of philosophy. The changed political circumstances that ended his oratorical career in the courts and senate made the choice to write philosophy, whose relationship with rhetoric had been Cicero's abiding concern, a natural development from his rhetorical theorizing.

---

[41] Quint. *Inst.* 12.1.22 suggests that the Atticist leaders Calvus and Brutus criticized Cicero's *compositio*. See Dugan 2005: 270–9.

Further reading

Those interested in understanding Cicero's rhetorical theory within a larger Roman historical and intellectual context can begin with Kennedy 1972, a classic still unsurpassed for its breadth of vision and chronological coverage. Habinek 2005 offers a succinct overview of ancient rhetorical theory that distils major themes within contemporary approaches, while Dominik and Hall 2007 and Gunderson 2009 offer excellent collections of more specialized essays by leading scholars. Steel 2005, the best concise treatment of Cicero's literary career in English, situates the *rhetorica* within that larger corpus. Readers with Italian will learn much from Narducci 2005, an introduction to Cicero with excellent bibliographical references.

Within the recent revival of interest in Cicero's rhetorical works the *De oratore* has received by far the most scholarly attention. It has been the topic of a monumental commentary (Leeman et al. 1981–2008) and its third book appeared recently in a Cambridge 'Green and Yellow' edition (Mankin 2011). May and Wisse 2001 gives an excellent translation with introduction and notes. Fantham 2004 is a magisterial treatment of the dialogue. Notable innovative readings of the dialogue include Gunderson 2000 and Connolly 2007a; the former interprets the *De oratore* from the perspective of gender studies and critical theory, the latter from that of political thought.

Readers of the *Brutus* have Douglas 1966, a rich if now dated commentary on the Latin text. For an English translation of the *Brutus* and *Orator* we must resort to Hendrickson and Hubbell's 1962 edition. Gowing 2000 led the revival of critical interest in the *Brutus*, while Fox 2007 offers an engaging treatment of the treatise, and Stroup 2010 situates it within the larger social and literary culture of the late Republic.

Hubbell's 1949 Loeb offers an edition with English translation of the *De inventione*, *De optimo genere oratorum* and *Topica*, the last of which is now served by an excellent modern edition with translation and commentary (Reinhardt 2003). Rackham 1942 translates *Partitiones oratoriae*. While these 'minor' rhetorical works have received less critical attention than the trio of major works from Cicero's maturity, perhaps Gildenhard's (2007) sympathetic re-evaluation of Cicero's formerly neglected philosophical treatise, *Tusculan Disputations*, will inspire fresh readings of these relatively overlooked texts.

3

J. G. F. POWELL

Cicero's style

Introduction

To do justice to Cicero's style in a brief chapter is not easy. One eminent Latinist has called him 'the greatest prose stylist who has ever lived, with the single exception of Plato';[1] another has recently devoted a substantial book to the analysis and exemplification of his style.[2] Several aspects of the topic have received extensive scholarly attention in recent years.[3] The notion of 'style' itself calls for renewed scrutiny. Since the 1970s, Cicero has occasionally been seen as falling short because his cultivation of literary and oratorical style was directed towards practical ends.[4] But elegance of style for its own sake is nowadays less likely to be valued above its practical applications. With the recent growth of interest in the art (or arts) of communication, Cicero can again be studied and enjoyed without apology by academics, students and the general public. At the same time, advances in the study of linguistics are providing new tools for the stylistic analysis of texts. Now is a good time to present the topic afresh.

On the whole, Cicero has probably more often been treated as a stylistic authority and model than as anything else. Besides his explicit and self-conscious role in the fixing of standards for literary Latin, his writing has a number of qualities which, in literary cultures in general, are often valued highly: one may immediately mention (a) observance of linguistic norms and precise choice of words, (b) clarity and articulateness of sentence structure, (c) the richness and abundance of style which the Romans called *copia* or

I am grateful to Dr Kathryn Tempest for reading and commenting on a draft of this chapter. Published translations of passages quoted are acknowledged; others are my own.

[1] Nisbet 1965: 77.   [2] Von Albrecht 2003.   [3] See 'Further Reading' below.
[4] See for example Bailey 1971: ix, 'Not that artistic merits are lacking in his output as a whole; but they subserve some practical purpose, and are not of so high an order as to transcend that purpose.'

41

abundantia.[5] At the same time, each of these three features can be seen in different ways. Adherence to precise norms of language can make the style seem colourless or pedantic. Articulateness of structure can (and in Cicero often does) conceal rhetorical slippages of meaning and tricks of argument. And, most notoriously, the Ciceronian richness and abundance can easily tip over into wordiness and pomposity, features for which Cicero was evidently criticized almost from the beginning.[6]

Cicero's style has often appeared to be easy to imitate, and the activity of imitating him has often been seen as valuable, both as a means of acquiring facility in Latin and as an aesthetic exercise in itself. In the Renaissance, the use of Cicero as a model reached what we might consider exaggerated proportions, though there were always those who insisted that Latin could be effectively written in other ways.[7] Cicero's works have often been plundered for choice Latin words and phrases: Nizolius' *Lexicon Ciceronianum* of 1535 was the first of a long succession of Ciceronian word-lists and phrasebooks. At the beginning of the eighteenth century, a Ciceronian scholar observed: 'Haec ergo & reliqua ejusdem opera, non digniori fine ab aliis leguntur, quam ut verborum inde copiam, tanquam ex repertorio quodam, depromant; quod plurimos induxit, ut nihil in iis praeter verba reperiri censerent.' ('These [the speeches and letters], then, and the rest of [Cicero's] works, are read by others with no worthier aim than to acquire a stock of words from them, as if from a sort of catalogue; and this has led a great many people to think that nothing except words can be found in them.')[8] The writing of 'Ciceronian' prose as an academic exercise has even now not entirely disappeared from our schools and universities.[9] But in order to achieve a better understanding of Cicero's style, one must lay aside his status as an icon of Latin eloquence abstracted from time and place, and take a historical view of the development of the Latin language and Cicero's place within it.

---

[5] These categories are meant merely to provide a convenient way of dividing up the subject matter; they are not primarily meant to reflect ancient classifications of rhetorical 'virtues', though as a matter of fact they do to some extent; cf. Cic. *Orator* 79, referring to Theophrastus; cf. Rowe 1997, Kirchner 2007. More will be said about each of these features in the second half of this chapter.

[6] Hostile criticisms are reported by Quintilian, *Inst.* 12.10.12 '*tumidiorem et Asianum et redundantem et in repetitionibus nimium et in salibus aliquando frigidum et in compositione fractum, exsultantem, ac paene (quod procul absit) viro molliorem...ille tamen qui ieiunus a quibusdam et aridus habetur, non aliter ab ipsis inimicis male audire quam nimiis floribus et ingenii adfluentia potuit*'; similarly Tacitus *Dial.* 18.4.

[7] See the texts collected in DellaNeva 2007.   [8] Toland 1712: 15–16.

[9] For example, the present writer, on going up to Oxford in 1975, was encouraged to read the *De senectute*, not to find out what Cicero had to say about old age, but as a model for Latin compositions.

First, however, one must be clear as to what is meant by 'style'. Apart from the heavily evaluative sense of 'good' or 'correct' style (for which Cicero may or may not be a model, depending on taste), the word has at least two other relevant senses. In the sense in which Buffon presumably meant it in his well-known saying 'le style est l'homme même',[10] it refers to the individuality of an author's manner of writing.[11] The notion of individual style can, and nowadays increasingly does, encompass other areas of behaviour besides the linguistic and literary, extending to the whole of a public figure's self-presentation, and the personality traits to which one's public speeches and writings give expression.[12]

The other relevant sense embraces the variety of ways of writing that may be adopted for different purposes by a single author, even in the course of a single work. Here, especially, the modern study of stylistics (as a branch of linguistics) can help to generate greater clarity, by the use of concepts such as 'register'.[13]

Individuality and comparison

To search for features of Cicero's individual style is to attempt to answer questions like 'What is Ciceronian about this?', 'In what ways is this different from the way another author would have written it?', or even 'Can we be sure that this piece of writing actually is by Cicero?'. So regularly has Cicero been treated as the standard classical prose author par excellence that Latin authors in other periods and genres are more often characterized by the ways in which they differ from a supposed Ciceronian norm, than the other way about. Nevertheless, it is relatively easy to pick out features that distinguish the language of Cicero's time from that of earlier or later authors.[14] One may begin with some straightforward syntactical examples: while in the Latin of

[10] G. L. Leclerc de Buffon 1753. The quotation is often wrongly modernized to 'le style, c'est l'homme'.
[11] This can be seen as equivalent to the set of all constant features of an author's written style, as in the classification adopted by Von Albrecht 2003, who distinguishes consistent features of Cicero's style (125–59) from those which vary between genres (11–77), within individual works (79–95) or according to chronology (97–123).
[12] See 'Further Reading' below.
[13] 'Register' is the technical term for what may otherwise be called 'stylistic level' or 'level of diction': one may talk for example of poetic, prosaic, colloquial, high or low register, or of special registers of the language associated with particular kinds of subject matter and context such as medicine or the law. For an introductory account of register in Latin see Powell 1999, esp. 323; fundamental in this area is Axelson 1945.
[14] On the history of Latin prose style and Cicero's place in it, see Russell 1990: xiii–xxvii; Leeman 1963; Von Albrecht 2003: 125–59; see also more generally (from a linguistic point of view) Rosén 1999; Reinhardt, Lapidge and Adams 2005.

the second century BC indirect questions sometimes have the indicative, Cicero always uses the subjunctive; whereas Cicero's generation is the last to insist on the indicative with *quamquam* 'although' (the subjunctive is found from Cornelius Nepos onwards). Such linguistic differences, trivial though they may seem, can in themselves be significant markers of style.

One of the distinctive features of the Latin prose of the Ciceronian period is its vocabulary. Many items characteristic of the earlier period of Latin have disappeared from ordinary prose, while a large number of innovations in vocabulary (especially abstract nouns) appear in Cicero and Caesar for the first time.[15] There is a tendency for sentence structure in literary Latin to become more complex, though the apparent simplicity of second-century BC Latin may be a deliberately cultivated rhetorical feature rather than (as often perceived) a sign of lack of sophistication.[16] There are equally obvious differences between Republican Latin and the language of later periods, which need not be dealt with here.

However, once we attempt to define Cicero's individuality within his own historical period, we encounter a dearth of comparative material. The accidents of transmission have caused a gross imbalance between the amount of Cicero we can read and what survives of any other Latin literary prose writer of his generation. In the Oxford Classical Texts series, Cicero's works fill sixteen volumes (including three volumes still in preparation). In contrast to this, Caesar and his continuators account for two OCT volumes, and the surviving works of Sallust for one. We do, admittedly, have the four books of the *Rhetorica ad Herennium*, an anonymous handbook on rhetoric most plausibly dated to the eighties BC,[17] when Cicero was a young man; and from Varro's originally vast corpus we have six books excerpted from the philological work *De lingua Latina*, which was dedicated to Cicero, and the three books *De re rustica*.[18] However, Varro's chief contribution in the purely literary sphere – now lost except for scattered fragments – was in the genre of prose satire, a form of writing left untouched by Cicero. Thus the differences of genre make it difficult to compare the major Republican prose authors fairly with one another.

[15] See Rosén 1999: 62–70, noting in particular that while earlier Latin often had a choice of abstract nouns from the same root (e.g. *intemperantia* versus *intemperies*), classical (i.e. late Republican) Latin tended to whittle these down to one. See further below, p. 57.

[16] On 'archaic' prose style, see Courtney 1999; for oratory before Cicero, see Sciarrino 2007, and cf. also my brief remarks in Powell 2011: 390–3.

[17] The arguments for this dating have been restated by Calboli 1993: 12–17. Even partisans of a later dating acknowledge that the examples predate Cicero's maturity (Douglas 1960).

[18] The *De re rustica*, cast in the form of a dialogue, postdates Cicero's dialogues and may be to some extent modelled on them; on Varro's style see Laughton 1960.

Caesar at first sight seems plainer in style than much of Cicero, yet when Cicero writes an official dispatch to the senate from Cilicia, it reads very much like an extract from Caesar's commentaries.[19] Cicero famously praised what one may call the heroic nudity of Caesar's writings;[20] but this is less a reversion to the patterns of ordinary speech than a particular kind of contrived formality.[21] Sallust is agreed to be idiosyncratic even within his genre, and Cicero might have written history differently (*Leg.* 1.5–8), but there is little material for direct comparison. There are passages in Cicero's speeches and philosophical dialogues, especially his excursus on early Roman constitutional history in *De republica* 2, that may be taken as samples of a possible historical narrative style, but we have no passage of Cicero where the narration of events is not subordinated to a wider argument.[22]

No speech of any contemporary Republican orator survives to be compared with Cicero. However, the *Rhetorica ad Herennium*, already mentioned, contains a wealth of examples to illustrate figures of speech and good and bad style. From this it emerges that many of the 'tricks of the trade' were already well established, and not in the least peculiar to Cicero. Take, for instance, this sample of the 'grand' style of oratory, made up by the anonymous author of the *Ad Herennium* (4.12):

Nam quis est uestrum, iudices, qui satis idoneam possit in eum poenam excogitare, qui prodere hostibus patriam cogitarit? Quod maleficium cum hoc scelere comparari? Quod huic maleficio dignum supplicium potest inueniri? In eis qui uiolassent ingenuum, matremfamilias constuprassent, uulnerassent aliquem aut postremo necassent, maxima supplicia maiores consumpserunt: huic truculentissimo ac nefario facinori singularem poenam non reliquerunt. Atque in aliis maleficiis ad singulos aut ad paucos ex alieno peccato iniuria peruenit: huius sceleris qui sunt adfines uno consilio uniuersis ciuibus atrocissimas calamitates machinantur. O feros animos! O crudeles cogitationes! O derelictos homines ab humanitate!

'For who is there among you, gentlemen, who could think of a sufficiently fitting penalty for a person who has thought to betray his country to the enemy? What crime can be compared with this wickedness? For this crime what appropriate punishment can be found? Our ancestors used up their greatest punishments on those who had violated a free-born boy, committed

---

[19] *Fam.* 15.1 and 15.2; on the style of these letters, see Fraenkel 1956.

[20] On Caesar's style and Cicero's judgement of it, see Kraus 2005.

[21] A feature often noticed is the proportion of Caesar's verbs that are placed in final position in their sentence or clause: Linde 1923 called him 'Fanatiker der Endstellung'; cf. Panhuis 1982: 117–18. This is evidently a feature of formal style; Panhuis' view of it as archaic is difficult to reconcile with Caesar's studious avoidance of archaism in other areas such as vocabulary.

[22] Cornell 2001: 56, 'A history by Cicero would have been very different.'

adultery with the mother of a family, had wounded someone or, finally, killed him: but for this most aggressive and nefarious deed they did not leave us a unique penalty. Furthermore, in other crimes the injury arising from another's misdeed affects either individuals or a few; those who are implicated in this crime are plotting the most atrocious calamities for all citizens together at one stroke. O savage minds! O cruel plottings! O humans devoid of humanity!'

Any reader of Cicero will recognize as familiar the exclamations, the rhetorical questions, the anaphora (*Quod?... Quod?*) and parallelisms, the tendency to arrange parallel clauses in triplets with each one longer than the last (technically 'ascending tricolon'), the antithesis (*in aliis maleficiis... huius sceleris*), the emphatic separation of adjectives from nouns (hyperbaton: *satis idoneam... poenam*), the superlatives (*truculentissimo, atrocissimas*), the etymological play on words (*excogitare... cogitarit, derelictos homines ab humanitate*) and the rhythmical sentence-endings (e.g. *cogitarit, comparari, inueniri, machinantur*: for these rhythms see further below, pp. 59–62).

And yet this passage is not quite like Cicero. Take for example the repetition of the word '*maleficium*'.[23] Cicero does something very similar in the *Pro Roscio*, but somehow it seems more pointed and less clumsy:

> Tanti malefici crimen, cui maleficio tam insigne supplicium est constitutum, probare te, Eruci, censes posse talibus uiris, si ne causam quidem malefici protuleris?

> 'Do you think, Erucius, that you can prove to men like this an allegation of such a crime – a crime for which such a spectacular punishment has been devised – if you do not also bring forward a motive for the crime?'

The word order *idoneam possit in eum poenam excogitare, qui...* is difficult to parallel in Cicero;[24] so is the collocation *truculentissimo facinori* (the adjective *truculentus* is more normally used to describe persons). This example, then, shows that Cicero found the grand style ready-made in its outlines; but his own use of it is more careful. As Laurand observed, Cicero speaks the same language as others, but speaks it better.[25]

Written and spoken language: general considerations

Under the surface of the discussion so far lurks the wider question of the relation of Cicero's literary style, or the styles of his contemporaries, to the

---

[23] Repetition of significant or emotionally loaded words is nowadays recognized as an important rhetorical device; for the same phenomenon in Greek prose, see Dover 1997: 131–43.
[24] See Powell 2010.   [25] Laurand 1933: 154.

forms of spoken language that were current in Republican Rome. On this question, only some basic points can be made here.

The two main literary genres in which Cicero wrote – the speech and the dialogue – are both supposed to be representations of oral discourse. Granted, a philosophic dialogue is a fictional composition and may exist only in writing; yet its status as a dialogue lays on the author an obligation to try to reproduce, at least some of the time, the nuances of an actual conversation. A published speech, if it was to carry any plausibility at all, needed to conjure up the authentic phrases and rhythms of the forum or the senate, even if its precise text differed in some respects from what was said on the occasion.[26] A written speech generally[27] purported to represent an oral performance that had already taken place and could be checked against the memories of those who had been present. In the case of just one of Cicero's speeches, the *Post reditum in senatu*, we happen to be told that it was written out in advance and read from a script, because of the importance of the occasion (*Planc.* 74). The style of this speech does not differ greatly from that of other comparable Ciceronian texts, although it is at the more elaborate end of the spectrum.[28] The language or style of a formal speech is obviously different from that of a casual conversation, but the difference is not primarily that between written and oral: it is a difference of register within the oral medium. While the transfer of a speech to writing might make some difference, it must be remembered that it always remained in some sense a script for performance.[29] It is probably, then, more accurate to see the style of Cicero's speeches as an enhanced and polished-up version of ordinary Latin, rather than as something fundamentally distanced from normal speech. Cicero himself, although he prided himself on a forensic style which was *exquisitius et minime uulgare* ('rather careful and not at all hackneyed', *Brut.* 321), took the view that orators should stick to current usage (*De or.* 1.12).

---

[26] On this well-worn scholarly question see e.g. Craig 2002: 515–17; Alexander 2002: 16–25; Powell and Paterson 2004: 52–7.

[27] Not of course always: a speech like the *Second Philippic*, or some of the speeches of Isocrates, might be circulated only in writing; even then, however, a specific occasion tends to be imagined.

[28] Frischer 1996 shows that it has one of the longest average lengths of sentences among the speeches in the Ciceronian corpus; of those in his sample, only *Post reditum ad Quirites* and *In Vatinium* have a higher average. Both of these are exceptional among the speeches: the one relatively short (twenty-five sections) and ceremonial; the other unique of its kind as an interrogation of a witness. For the latter, custom prescribed the form of the indirect question depending on the verb *quaero*, a syntactical feature which is in itself likely to lead to a greater average sentence length.

[29] Cf. Nisbet 1992, analysing in exemplary fashion a passage of the fifth *Verrine*.

It is interesting in this connection to look across at modern research into the differences between spoken and written language, a study that is still comparatively in its infancy. A current textbook of functional linguistics (Halliday 2004: 654–5) remarks that 'written language becomes complex by being lexically dense . . . whereas spoken language becomes complex by being grammatically intricate'. Halliday quotes as a typical example of written English the following sentence:

> In bridging river valleys, the early engineers built many notable masonry viaducts of numerous arches.

He then rewords it 'in a form more typical of the spoken language':

> In the early days when engineers had to make a bridge across a valley and the valley had a river flowing through it, they often built viaducts, which were constructed of masonry and had numerous arches in them; and many of these viaducts became notable.

Obviously, much more analysis of actual texts would be needed to prove this point, and one could not predict with certainty that what was true of modern English would also be true of Republican Latin; yet any practised Latinist will readily recognize that the 'spoken' sentence above is by far the more Ciceronian of the two. The 'written' sentence, with its high lexical density, would be more typical of the historians.

There is one particular feature of Latin prose, uncommon in modern languages, which at first sight looks as though it must be artificial and literary: this is hyperbaton, the separation of noun and modifier. A fairly extreme example is to be found in the following extract from the *First Catilinarian*:

> Magna dis immortalibus habenda est atque huic ipsi Ioui Statori, antiquissimo custodi huius urbis, gratia, quod hanc tam taetram tam horribilem tamque infestam rei publicae pestem totiens iam effugimus. (*Cat.* 1.11)

> 'We owe a great debt of gratitude to the immortal gods and especially to this Jupiter Stator, the god who from the earliest times has stood guard over our city, for enabling us time and again to escape this pestilence, so foul, so revolting, and so deadly to our country.'[30]

The adjective *magna*, 'great', is separated from its noun *gratia*, 'gratitude', by no fewer than thirteen words. But I have argued elsewhere[31] that even this degree of separation may not be unnatural to the language. Hyperbaton (which occurs quite sparingly in Cicero's speeches, but more commonly in

---

[30] Trans. Berry 2006.   [31] Powell 2010.

the letters and philosophical works) may actually be a sign, when it occurs, of oral influence on written style.

Certain linguistic features have been recognized since the time of the ancient rhetoricians as deliberate evocations of the spoken word: these are traditionally classified as aposiopesis (stopping short in the middle of a sentence),[32] anacoluthon (changing grammatical direction in the middle of a sentence),[33] parenthesis (interrupting a sentence with a new observation, then resuming it; after a longer parenthesis one may resume with *sed tamen* 'but anyway')[34] and correction (when one breaks the grammatical flow in order to correct something one has just said; Latin has a special particle for this purpose, *immo* or *immo uero*, corresponding to the corrective use of 'no' in English). There are examples of all of these in Cicero, even in speeches which, according to received opinion, were never actually delivered (e.g. *Verr.* 2.4.5: Cicero, describing some statues removed by Verres, pauses to be reminded of the name of the sculptor); this raises the issue of simulated orality in a written text.[35]

Written and spoken language: Cicero as letter-writer

A good third of Cicero's extant output is comprised by the four collections of letters (*Ad Atticum, Ad familiares, Ad Quintum fratrem, Ad Brutum*). The *Ad familiares* has particular potential for stylistic study as it contains letters to Cicero from various other individuals, with which Cicero's epistolary style can be compared.[36] The letters are at once more and less of a problem from the point of view of their relationship to the spoken language. In one sense, there is no more essentially written medium than the letter;[37] Hutchinson

[32] See Quintilian 9.2.54, quoting a fragment concerning Milo, but not from our extant *Pro Milone*: it has been assigned both to the lacuna at *Mil.* 33 and to the alternative version of the speech taken down in court, to which Quintilian refers elsewhere. But one thing is clear: Quintilian quotes it as an example of a deliberate rhetorical figure, not of failure of nerve on Cicero's part.

[33] On anacoluthon in Cicero, see Mayer 2005: 200–3, suggesting a need for further research.

[34] See, for the letters, Bolkestein 1998.

[35] Fuhrmann 1990. But the issue of non-delivery of the second *Actio in Verrem* is not clear-cut. Although the tradition that it was not delivered at all is ancient (Pliny, *Letters* 1.20.10), this may represent an exaggeration of the real facts; cf. Powell and Paterson 2004: 56. But if the speech was issued only in written form, there is no difficulty in assuming that it represents what Cicero *intended* to say; see Frazel 2004. On the passage see also Nisbet 1965: 56.

[36] See Von Albrecht 2003: 136–7 with references.

[37] For some useful cautionary remarks against identifying informal written style with informal spoken style, in the context of a study of the letters of Caelius, see Pinkster 2010.

has rightly emphasized the literary artistry of Cicero's correspondence.[38] On the other hand, casual correspondence can appear to be virtually a transcription of spoken language. Two complementary conceptions of letter-writing existed in antiquity, one emphasizing the letter's status as a literary artefact ('a kind of present', Demetrius *On Style* 223), the other viewing it as a kind of conversation on paper. In the Ciceronian corpus we can find examples of both kinds. Some are quite formal and rhetorical (consolations, political self-justifications, letters of recommendation) and approach the manner of the public speeches, while others are highly informal and have often been taken to reflect oral features.

Artistry does not necessarily imply artificiality, and it takes a good deal of artistry to achieve a natural-sounding style in letter-writing. Some of Cicero's correspondents do not always achieve it (though others, such as Cicero's protégé Marcus Caelius, often do). For example, the famous consolatory letter of Servius Sulpicius (*Fam.* 4.5), though often praised for its content, is in style rather ponderous.[39] Decimus Brutus, whose style is usually admirably straightforward and businesslike, was doubtless in a panic when he wrote this sentence (*Fam.* 11.20.1; the subject is a man called Segulius Labeo):

> Ipsum Caesarem nihil sane de te questum, nisi dictum quod diceret te dixisse 'laudandum adulescentem, ornandum, tollendum'.

> 'He said Caesar himself (i.e. Octavian) made no complaint about you, except that you had said what he said you said: "the young man is to be praised, honoured, and got out of the way".'

The awkwardness in 'dictum quod diceret te dixisse' is obvious. Cicero's reply (11.21.1) shows his greater confidence in the rhetorical manipulation of language, even in a sticky situation:

> Di isti Segulio male faciant, homini nequissimo omnium qui sunt, qui fuerunt, qui futuri sunt!... Te tamen, mi Brute, sic amo ut debeo, quod istud quidquid esset nugarum me scire uoluisti; signum enim magnum amoris dedisti.

> 'May the gods curse that Segulius, the most wicked of all men who are now, who ever have been, or who ever will be!... But as for you, my friend Brutus, I feel all the affection I owe you, because you wanted me to be informed of that, trivial though it was; for you have given me a great token of your friendship.'

---

[38] Hutchinson 1998.

[39] See Hutchinson 1998: 65–74. Hutchinson makes the comparison between Servius' first paragraph and the opening of Cicero's own consolatory letter to Titius, *Fam.* 5.16, rightly drawing attention to the greater smoothness and tact of Cicero's version; but his order of presentation disguises the fact that Cicero's letter to Titius is in all probability the later of the two, and therefore probably imitates and improves on Servius.

Cicero manages simultaneously to thank Brutus effusively for giving him the information, and to minimize its importance ('trivial though it was'), while he avoids letting Brutus know explicitly whether he really had said what Segulius alleged.

Written Latin does not have as wide a range of graphic conventions to mark oral style as modern English does; even the exclamation mark was unknown to the Romans. There are, indeed, occasional contracted forms like *ain'* (= *aisne?* 'you don't say?', e.g. *Att.* 4.5), comparable with our 'don't' and 'can't'. On the other hand – and this is only partly because of the grammatical inflections – it is easy in written Latin to leave out inessential words, and informal epistolary Latin can display extremes of brevity (as, in other ways, can formal literary or lapidary Latin).[40] Take the following examples, where it has been necessary to add words in the English to clarify the meaning:

> In Equo Troiano scis esse in extremo 'sero sapiunt'. Tu tamen, mi uetule, non sero. (*Fam.* 7.16.1, to Trebatius Testa).

> 'In *The Trojan Horse* you know it says at the end "they are wise too late". But <as for> you, old boy, <it's> not too late.'

> Duas accepi postridie Id., alteram eo die datam, alteram Idibus. Prius ergo superiori. De Bruto, cum scies. (*Att.* 15.17.1)

> 'I got two <letters> on the 14th, one sent that day, the other on the 13th. First, then, the earlier one. About Brutus, <tell me> when you know.'

Regarding this abbreviated style – which might at first sight look like conversation on paper – three points may be made. First, it is probably in general more characteristic of written than of spoken communication, recalling more than anything else the language of today's emails and text messages (which reflect natural spoken language only to a limited extent). Second, its practitioners are sophisticated and literary: it is rarely to be found among the non-literary letters of Egypt or Vindolanda, which are more likely to be stiltedly formal in their syntax. Third, in Cicero's correspondence, it is confined to particular social contexts: either those where the correspondents are intimate (as with Cicero and Atticus) or where the writer is clearly the senior of the pair (as with Cicero and Trebatius). One must therefore be cautious in supposing that it represents a particularly clear window on ordinary spoken Latin.

---

[40] Cf. Kallendorf and Kallendorf 1987.

Style as a means to an end; the 'three styles'

Different 'styles' can be used by the same author on different occasions. This is what the Romans themselves often meant by *stilus* (literally 'pen') or, more often in Cicero himself, *genus dicendi* ('kind of speaking'). Individuals, of course, differ in their ability to achieve such variety, and in the manner in which it is achieved. Within Cicero's works, differences of both style and approach have been noticed not only between the broad genres of speeches, letters and philosophical works, but also between (for example) political and forensic speeches, or between speeches in the senate and those delivered to a popular assembly, or between forensic speeches delivered in public trials and those spoken in private lawsuits.[41] Furthermore, the style and tone can often change between sections of a text. For example, in a lawcourt speech, straightforward narrative, involved legal argument, witty ridicule of the opponents, expansive digressions on wider issues, appeals to sympathy and impassioned denunciation can all occur at different points, and the use of language varies accordingly.

Cicero himself had a good deal of conscious understanding of what he was doing when he adjusted his style to suit the genre of writing or the progress of his argument.[42] But he inherited from the Greek theorists a somewhat over-schematic way of talking about such differences, which has sometimes threatened to dominate modern scholarship on these matters as well: this was the doctrine of the Three Styles. There were supposed to be three distinct types of rhetorical style, plain, middle and grand. Good and bad examples of each of these three varieties are given by the anonymous author of the *Ad Herennium*; the example of the grand style has already been noticed, and while this is closely comparable with Cicero's purple patches, the 'plain' and 'middle' styles are seen differently by different authors. For the author of *Ad Herennium* the plain style in oratory implies a degree of colloquialism which Cicero would not normally approach, except in an intimate letter. The 'middle' style is sometimes defined as lacking the characteristics of the other two, a 'colourless half-way house' in Michael Winterbottom's phrase.[43] The

---

[41] On the differences between senatorial and popular speeches, see Mack 1937; on different styles of forensic oratory, see Laurand 1938, Von Albrecht 2003: 11–27 and 79–85; Powell and Paterson 2004: 9.

[42] See the well-known passages at *Orator* 102 and *Fam.* 9.21, with Von Albrecht 2003: 17–25.

[43] Winterbottom 1989: 127. In *Orator* 91–6, as Winterbottom shows, Cicero characterizes the middle style in terms linked with epideictic (i.e. oratory for ceremonial occasions, for entertainment or for demonstration as in a public lecture), suggesting that Cicero was conscious of introducing epideictic elements into his forensic and political oratory. On epideictic elements in Cicero's speeches see also Von Albrecht 2003: 19–20.

Ad Herennium's example is a piece of political argumentation, while Cicero sees the middle style as suitable for the function of *delectare*, entertainment, as opposed to the giving of information (*docere*, the function of the plain style) or incitement to action or emotion (*movere*, for which the grand style is appropriate).

Part of the reality behind the Ciceronian version of the Three Styles doctrine seems to be this. Variation of style involves distinct sets of variables. One of these is register, and the register of a spoken or written text can often be placed roughly on a scale from 'low' (colloquial) to 'high', though there are different ways of being 'high' (poetic, for example, or formal and official). Another is syntactical elaboration: again a roughly linear scale is possible, from the simplest sentences to the most complex (again there are different ways of being complex, as has already been seen, p. 48). A third is what may be called the 'emotional temperature' of a piece of text, which again can be put on a scale from low to high. Although these factors can vary independently of one another, they are not unrelated: for example, high emotional temperature, especially in formal Latin oratory, generally brings with it relatively high register and a high degree of elaboration in sentence structure, and when all three of these are present, one gets the 'grand style' as one stereotypically imagines it. Cicero, especially in oratory, varies his register (comparatively speaking) less than some other authors, so there are really two variables that count, and practically speaking three common combinations of them: low elaboration + low emotion (plain), high elaboration + low emotion (middle), and high elaboration + high emotion (grand). Thus Cicero's theoretical scheme is more or less true to the broad facts; but it falls short in precision when it comes to details. Some illustration of these different varieties will be found in the second half of this chapter (pp. 66–70).

Stylistic models

Cicero himself writes in *Brutus* and *Orator* about the style of oratory that was in fashion at the beginning of his career. It was called, at least by its critics, 'Asian', and was characterized sometimes by floridity, sometimes by epigrammatic symmetry. From here, it seems, Cicero derived some features of his prose writing, especially his use of rhythm (cf. below, p. 59), although he correctly points out (*Orator* 174–6) that the use of regular rhythms can be traced not only to the Attic orators, especially Isocrates, but also further back to the sophists. By the late fifties BC, a reaction had set in: one of its leading representatives, if not actually its originator, was Licinius Calvus, himself a successful advocate as well as a poet and friend of Catullus. The criticisms levelled against Cicero, and his answers to them, can be traced

partly in Cicero's own *Brutus* and *Orator* and partly in later sources, especially Tacitus' *Dialogus*.[44] Calvus, and maybe some others like him, clearly
thought of his own (evidently highly articulate) style as pure Athenian,
whereas Cicero had allegedly picked up too much from his early travels in
Asia Minor. Cicero's self-defence is based partly on the contention that his
own style had changed – true only to some extent – and partly, perhaps more
plausibly, on the argument that Calvus had too narrow a view of what it
was to be Attic, ignoring the range and power of Demosthenes' style.[45] Such
polemics – friendly, one presumes – between practising orators are interesting in their historical context, but (like the Three Styles doctrine) have been
too prominent in determining the scholarly agenda: the usual view of the
development of Cicero's style throughout his career is based too much on
Cicero's own apologia and not enough on the texts,[46] and Cicero's actual
debt to the Attic orators has tended until recently to be underrated. Here we
happen to have a substantial corpus of texts which were also available to
Cicero and which we know he admired. Recent studies have shown that his
debts in this direction are evident from his earliest speeches, and extended to
argumentative strategies as well as style: he made considerable use not only
of Demosthenes, with whom comparisons have been commonplace since
antiquity,[47] but also of other orators such as Lysias, Aeschines, Isocrates
and Hyperides.[48]

Not only Greek but also Roman models were important, and Cicero
devoted his dialogue *Brutus* to a survey of oratory up to his time. The *Brutus* gives a slanted picture of the history of Roman oratory, partly because
of its heavy concentration on advocacy in the courts, and partly because of
the conspicuous lack of attention paid to certain political figures of whom
Cicero disapproved.[49] Cicero's praise is chiefly reserved for Cato the Elder,
the first Roman to publish a substantial corpus of speeches; for L. Crassus (see esp. *Brut.* 164) and M. Antonius, the two major forensic orators
of the previous generation, whom he had already introduced as the main
characters in his *De oratore*; and for Cotta and Hortensius, the leading
advocates of Cicero's youth, the former of whom had a plain, understated
style of pleading, the latter an elaborate and theatrical delivery. Hortensius
is often assumed to have been a particular influence on Cicero, but this is

---

[44] See Hendrickson 1926.
[45] On the Atticists see esp. Wisse 2002: 364–8, whose discussion well summarizes the
scholarly debate.
[46] For information on linguistic variation throughout Cicero's career, and a review of
scholarship on the subject, see Von Albrecht 2003: 97–123.
[47] See esp. Plutarch *Comparison of Demosthenes and Cicero*, Quintilian *Inst.* 10.1.105–8;
Longinus 12.4.
[48] Weische 1972; Stroh 1982; Wooten 1983; Tempest 2007.   [49] See Steel 2003.

hard to check up on, as his speeches apparently did not transfer well to the written medium, and none has survived. On the whole we know the character of these orators (with the exception of a few fragments of Cato) only through Cicero, and while we may assume that he owed something, perhaps a considerable amount, to earlier Roman oratory, the real extent of his debt remains uncertain. One telling example is a passage of the peroration of the *Pro Murena* (88–9), in which he imagines the consequences of conviction for his client; we happen to know that this echoes a speech by Gaius Gracchus, because Cicero himself quotes from his model in *De oratore* 3.214.

Use of language: vocabulary and register

Before scholars learned to frown on prescriptivism, it was customary to talk of 'correctness' in linguistic matters. As has been remarked, later ages chose Cicero as the norm of correct usage: to call Cicero 'correct' is thus to risk circularity.[50] Historically, the important fact is that Cicero happened to live at a time when the Latin language was going through a process of standardization.[51] Defining correct usage was not yet seen as the privilege of grammarians, since the native speaker was still the arbiter; anyone born at Rome would speak good Latin as a matter of habit (class dialects do not seem to have been a significant issue).[52] Deviations from the urban standard might be stigmatized as countrified or barbarous. Doubts about linguistic usage clearly arose from time to time, and Cicero himself acquired a reputation as an authority on Latinity. (Although opponents such as Catiline drew attention to his rural origin, there is no record that any 'rustic' features were ever detected in his spoken Latin.) When Pompey dedicated his theatre in his third consulship, he wanted to know whether to write *consul tertium* or *consul tertio* on the inscription: Cicero was the obvious person to ask.[53]

But where did Cicero himself get his ideas of correctness? Sometimes he appeals explicitly to current usage, sometimes to literary precedent and sometimes to his 'ears' or, in other words, his intuition as to what sounded

---

[50] An example may be found in *Orator* 160, where he quotes one point of pronunciation where he himself had changed his habits: in his youth, he tells us, he had pronounced *pulcer*, *Cetegus*, *triumpus*, *Cartago*, without aspiration, but adopted the aspiration as a concession to popular usage, 'keeping', as he says, 'his superior knowledge to himself', but refusing to go further and say *sepulchrum* for *sepulcrum*, or *lachrima* for *lacrima*. Modern scholarship has taken its ideas of what is 'correct' from the particular snapshot of Latin usage in 46 BC which happens to be preserved in this text.

[51] Rosén 1999; Clackson and Horrocks 2010, esp. 183–228.

[52] See e.g. Cic. *De or.* 3.39–46 and *Brut.* 258.

[53] He did not know the answer: Gell. 10.1.7; Von Albrecht 2003: 136.

right.[54] Examination of his letters shows that in practice he tends to avoid some linguistic features that his correspondents use (e.g. the colloquial *sane quam* or *valde quam* 'very much'), and this is commonly attributed to his greater fastidiousness.[55] But on the other hand his observations on correct usage in *Orator* are comparatively liberal rather than pedantic, and it should also be kept in mind that the regularity of the language of our texts of Cicero may be partly the result of an artificial smoothing out in the process of manuscript transmission and editing.[56] The purity of language and style aimed at by Cicero and some of his contemporaries was to a large extent a negative quality: a matter of avoiding anything that did not accord with current educated urban usage, whether unassimilated regionalisms or mistaken analogical formations. Cicero was not above fastening on details of linguistic usage to belittle his opponents, as in his criticism of Antony for using the non-standard superlative form *piissimus*,[57] or of his opponent in the Scaurus trial for using a Sardinian word for an overcoat.[58] If this seems odd, we should recall the publicity accorded to Margaret Thatcher's use of a dialectal verb form in the House of Commons.[59]

But Cicero's concern for linguistic detail was not, perhaps, just a source of facile debating points. It should be understood in the context of a general striving towards urbanity and polish and stylistic 'good manners', at least among some members of the Republican aristocracy. Even Caesar, a practical man if ever there was one, evidently occupied himself with what later Italians would call *la questione della lingua* (*Brut.* 253: he wrote *de recta ratione loquendi*, 'on correct speaking'). In *De oratore* and again in *Orator*, Cicero dealt with the question of how a Roman orator and statesman ought to speak and write; the choice of language and style in turn became part of the projection of the speaker's character and hence of its effect on the audience.[60] Linguistic and stylistic models were carefully chosen (for example, Terence was held to write good Latin, Caecilius not) and a careful balance struck between grammatical rule and popular usage. The women of some families were held to speak particularly good Latin and to have brought up their sons to do the same (*De or.* 3.45; *Brut.* 211).

---

[54] See esp. *Orator* 147–62.   [55] Cf. also Von Albrecht 2003: 136–8.
[56] Von Albrecht 2003: 3 remarks that Löfstedt 1928 and 1933 in particular 'defended Cicero against his editors', and (e.g. p. 12) quotes certain apparently irregular forms from existing texts of Cicero. To evaluate these properly, however, one would have to go more fully into the manuscript evidence.
[57] *Phil.* 13.43.   [58] Quint. *Inst.* 1.5.8, cf. *Scaur.* fragment 45h (Isid. *Etym.* 19.23.5).
[59] In Prime Minister's Questions, Tuesday 19 April 1983: 'frit' (= frightened, afraid). A web search on 'Thatcher' and 'frit' reveals many references to the incident.
[60] See Fantham 2004. Cicero's observations on style in this connection are very much in the spirit of Aristotle's *Rhetoric*.

Wider cultural issues were also important. It was evidently a controversial matter for a Roman to advertise in public too much knowledge of Greek language, literature or philosophy.[61] On the other hand, a forensic advantage could clearly be gained from deploying, for example, an allusive familiarity with the Greek-based tragedies and comedies of the Roman theatre. Here Cicero drew on a shared cultural background in order to manipulate the attitudes of the court. It was evidently not too difficult to excite sympathy for his client Caelius by evoking the misjudged Aeschinus in Terence's *Adelphi*; while in the *Pro Roscio comoedo* the great comic actor's adversary is discomfited by having projected onto him the characteristics of the comic villain so often played by Roscius himself.[62] In the *Pro Archia* Cicero famously embarks (after perfunctory apology) on an encomium of poetry in order to bolster Archias' moral claim to citizenship.[63] As so often, what appears initially to be just a stylistic matter – the use of literary quotation and allusion – turns out to serve a definite persuasive purpose.

There was potential in Republican Latin (still the language of Plautus after all) for creativity in the use of language. One area where the late Republic saw a great expansion in the Latin vocabulary was that of abstract nouns, not only in the technical terminology of originally Greek disciplines like rhetoric and philosophy (where we can often see Cicero innovating, or considering whether or not to innovate[64]) but in all areas of the language.[65] In private letters Cicero could introduce nonce words of his own like *sullaturit*, meaning 'wants to be a Sulla' (*Att.* 9.10.6) or *non flocci facteon* (*Att.* 1.16.13), a facetious hybrid with a Greek ending instead of the normal Latin *faciendum*. The phenomena of code-switching into Greek[66] and the use of Greek quotations (the two should be distinguished) are often assumed to have been frequent in letters between intimates: in fact Cicero's correspondence with Atticus may well be a special case, precisely because of Atticus' self-identification with all things Greek. Even within the collection, the purposes for which Greek is used (learned jokes, literary or philosophical allusions, or concealment of the meaning from non-correspondents) vary considerably, and the amount of Greek also varies according to the mood of the moment. There is about

---

[61] See e.g. Oksala 1953; Wallace-Hadrill 1998; on philosophy see also Griffin 1995.
[62] On *Pro Caelio* cf. Geffcken 1973 who risks concentrating on the comic colouring itself at the expense of its persuasive purpose; on *Q Rosc.* see Axer 1980.
[63] See Berry 2004.
[64] Cicero's achievements in rendering Greek terms into Latin were in some cases notable, but it is an exaggeration to credit him with a systematic project of creating a complete Latin philosophical vocabulary: see Powell 1995b.
[65] Rosén 1999: 67 remarks that Caesar's extant writings contain 204 abstracts not previously found in Latin, and there are many more in Cicero.
[66] On code-switching in the letters, see Swain 2002.

half as much Greek in the letters to Quintus as in the Atticus collection,[67] and none in the letters to his wife Terentia, except for one reference to vomit (the Greek medical term being used there for decorum). The use of Greek in letters to other correspondents is sparing, but sometimes striking (e.g. in the series of Homeric quotations in the letter to Caesar, *Fam.* 13.15). Cicero minimizes his use of unassimilated Greek in the philosophical dialogues, probably more for reasons of cultural nationalism than because he thought his readers might not understand it. Partially assimilated Greek borrowings in a Latin context (generally Latinized in spelling and, we may guess, in pronunciation) could have a forceful effect, like *piraticus myoparo* for the pirate ship in the *Verrines* (5.73).

The high literary register of Latin was well established before Cicero's time in Roman epic and tragedy, and beloved of historians as well as poets; but this too appears very sparingly in Cicero's writings. Even in the grandest passages of his speeches, prosaic diction is the norm; the *Ad Herennium* contains an invented object-lesson in the absurdity that resulted if one failed to observe this principle.[68] But an occasional poeticism, again, could be used to good effect. Writing to his family from exile (*Fam.* 14.1.1) Cicero laments the trouble he has caused them, using the high poetic word '*aerumnas*' (recalling the tribulations of tragic heroes and heroines). And in the more exalted passages of his philosophical works, he allows himself some poetic vocabulary, as for example in the *Somnium Scipionis* [Dream of Scipio] which concluded Cicero's great (but now fragmentary) dialogue on the Republic. Even there, it appears only in special contexts: the aged king Masinissa's prayer to the Sun-god, and the admonitions of the departed spirit of Scipio Africanus: voices from a past age, speaking about the most exalted of subject matter.[69] Otherwise, in the dialogues set in the past relative to the time of writing, Cicero inserts occasional touches of old-fashioned diction to accord with the dignity of the characters;[70] and in the *De legibus* he casts his ideal law-code into a version of the highly conservative (but still in Cicero's time current) style of Roman legislation.[71]

Julius Caesar (quoted in Cic. *Brut.* 253) said that the proper choice of words was the source of eloquence, and accorded Cicero high praise in

---

[67] Hutchinson 1998: 14.

[68] *Auct. ad Her.* 4.15. A literal translation may give an impression of the style of this example, which is not only archaic and inflated but ineptly metaphorical: 'For he who has sold his fatherland for treasons, shall not pay sufficient penalty, should he be cast into the Neptunian depths; be therefore avenged on him, who has constructed mountains of war, destroying the plains of peace.'

[69] On the *Somnium*, Powell 1990: 126; in general, Von Albrecht 2003: 30–2; Hine 2005: 229–36, esp. 235.

[70] Bréguet 1964; Powell 1988: 22.   [71] Powell 2005a.

this area. Even within the range of diction characteristic of ordinary prose, there was often a considerable choice of words available: Lucretius' cliché of *patrii sermonis egestas* (the poverty of the native language) should not mislead us into supposing that the Republican Latin vocabulary was really a poor one.[72] Sometimes there is a choice of several near-synonyms with a gradation of meaning; for example, of the various words for 'to fear', *uereor* is weaker than *metuo*, and *metuo* than *pertimesco*; similarly with the words for 'crime', *facinus*, *scelus* and *maleficium*, the last being the strongest. Sometimes there is a fine distinction of meaning: for 'to help', there was a choice of *adiuuare* (implying a common project) or *opitulari* (suggesting that the recipient of help is in trouble); for 'wisdom', one could have *sapientia* (either good sense or philosophical wisdom) or *prudentia* (political foresight or legal learning). In other cases the difference may be mainly one of register (e.g. *pulcher*, beautiful, is higher register than *bellus*; intermediate are *formosus* and *uenustus*). Examples could be multiplied, and sometimes the distinctions are not so clear: one may ask, for example, on what grounds Cicero chose between *puto*, *credo*, *arbitror* and *opinor* for 'I think', or between *adulescens* and *iuuenis* for 'young man'.[73]

Rhythm

The rhythm of Cicero's prose is one of its most pervasive features, and must be understood in broad outline before analysis can proceed further.

All spoken prose has a rhythm of some kind; we are dealing here with observable regularities in rhythm and their stylistic effect, whether or not they are consciously cultivated. Whereas in English we are not usually conscious of the time taken to pronounce individual syllables, in Latin (as also in Greek) almost all syllables could be readily identified as either 'long' or 'short'. Vowel length in classical Latin was phonemic, i.e. made a difference to the meanings of words: *lēuis* 'smooth' was a different word from *lĕuis* 'light [not heavy]'. A short syllable was one containing a short vowel followed by not more than one consonant; other syllables were long, and a long syllable took approximately twice as long to pronounce as a short one. The rhythms produced by the collocation of long and short syllables were evidently noticeable in speech and especially in formal oratory. A strict alternation of long and short syllables led to verse rhythm of one kind (iambic or

---

[72] See Von Albrecht 2003: 136, rebutting the view of Norden 1958: vol. i: 189 on the alleged poverty of the literary Latin vocabulary.

[73] *Adulescens* is largely prosaic or comic (it occurs also in Catullus), while *iuuenis* is common to prose and poetry. Cicero uses both, but seems to prefer *adulescens* in formal and complimentary contexts.

trochaic), while a sequence in which each long syllable is separated from the next by two short syllables produced verse rhythm of another kind (dactylic or anapaestic). Both these types of rhythm could easily produce an undesirable jingle.[74] In the act of avoiding them, Latin tends to fall into a series of 'cretics' (long-short-long), varied by sequences of long syllables and by patterns in which long syllables are separated by three shorts ('paeonic' rhythm, recommended already by Aristotle).

Cicero himself was aware of using these rhythms and cultivated them intentionally, although his observations on the topic in the *Orator* do not do full justice to his own practice. Precise understanding of this did not come until the beginning of the last century, when Zieliński[75] showed that in Cicero's speeches the vast majority of sentence-endings (clausulae) follow one of three basic patterns:

(a) $-\smile- \mid --$ (e.g. *consules possunt*)
(b) $-\smile- \mid -\smile-$ (e.g. *consules audiunt*)
(c) $-\smile- \mid -\smile--$ (e.g. *consules audiebant*).

The length of the final syllable is always immaterial, and any of the non-final long syllables may be replaced by two short syllables; there are also some less common patterns such as $-\smile\smile-$. Further research has shown that rhythmical patterns also very frequently mark subordinate sense-breaks within sentences.[76] Some of Cicero's sentences fall into a virtually perfect succession of cretics and paeons, like the famous opening sentence against Catiline:

Quo usque tānd(em) ăbū | tērĕ, Cătĭ | līnă, pătĭ | ēntĭā | nōstrā?

'How far, I ask you, Catiline, do you mean to stretch our patience?'[77]

If a paeon is substituted for a cretic in the first of the three basic patterns, one gets the rhythm of the notorious sentence-ending *esse videatur* ('it would seem to be'; e.g. *Verr.* 1.37). Tacitus makes one of his speakers in the *Dialogus* (23.1) observe that Cicero ended every other sentence with this cliché: actually it is nothing like as frequent as this would suggest, even if one counts a range of similar phrases (e.g. *posse videamur*, *Leg. Manil.* 68). Other rhythms at sentence-end such as the double trochee (as in example [c] above) could have an equally striking effect: Cicero himself tells us how

---

[74] These basic facts also underlie Greek prose rhythm and are noticed by Aristotle, *Rhet.* 1408b21–1409a21. See in general OCD[3] 1260–2 s.v. 'prose-rhythm, Greek' and 'prose-rhythm, Latin'.

[75] Zieliński 1904.

[76] See esp. Fraenkel 1968; Primmer 1968; Habinek 1985; Nisbet 1990; Berry 1996a: 49–54. Earlier work is conveniently listed in Berry 1996a: 49 n. 247.

[77] Tr. Berry 2006.

such a rhythm could produce spontaneous applause, giving the example of a speech by the tribune Gaius Carbo (*Orator* 214).[78]

There were various linguistic means by which Cicero achieved his rhythmical regularities. One which has received scholarly attention was the choice between the alternatives *atque* and *ac*: the former is often used to achieve a rhythmical sentence-ending such as *atque conspexit*.[79] The flexibility of Latin word order was also brought into play. For example, the 'default' position for the verb in Latin was at the end of the sentence, but the periphrastic passive forms (past participle or gerundive + the auxiliary *esse*) often produced a clumsy rhythm in that position. The rules of Latin grammar, however, provided for the auxiliary *esse* to be placed earlier in the sentence when it was itself stressed or was preceded by an emphatic word.[80] This freedom enabled both rhetorical emphasis and a graceful closing rhythm to be achieved at one stroke, as in a passage like *Verr.* 1.27: *Verri ne noceri possit multis rationibus esse prouisum* ('that by many different means provision had been made to avoid harm to Verres'; emphasis on *multis rationibus*). Or the whole verb could be moved earlier, as in the opening sentence of the *Pro Cluentio*: *omnem accusatoris orationem in duas diuisam esse partes* ('that the accuser's whole speech was divided into two parts'): the word order simultaneously ensures appropriate emphasis on *duas* and a smooth rhythmical ending.[81]

There can be little doubt that Cicero's rhythmical habits were so ingrained that he fell into them unconsciously. They are apparent throughout his published work, even where one might not think they were particularly appropriate. In the *De legibus*, he recites an ideal code of laws in what is supposed to be old-fashioned legal language: but the law code is full of Ciceronian rhythms. In the *De senectute* he introduces Cato the Elder as principal character and clearly makes some attempt to imitate the brusque style of the old censor: but Cicero's Cato still talks in perfect Ciceronian cadences. The rhythms are often apparent, too, in his letters. Only in the letters to Atticus and to his household does he write unrhythmically.[82] So characteristic are these patterns that analysis of rhythm can plausibly be invoked to resolve questions of disputed authenticity.[83] Yet even if it is true that Cicero was the

---

[78] '"*Patris dictum sapiens temeritas fili comprobavit*": *hoc dichoreo tantus clamor contionis excitatus est ut admirabile esset; quaero nonne id numerus effecerit?*' – '"The truth of the father's wise saying was shown by the son's mad behaviour": at this double trochee the public meeting broke into such a clamour that everyone was amazed; I wonder whether it was not the rhythm that achieved that?'

[79] See esp. Nisbet 1990 and Hutchinson 1995.

[80] This principle has been firmly established by Adams 1994.

[81] This sentence was commended by Quintilian 8.6.65 as an example of hyperbaton.

[82] Hutchinson 1998: 10–12.   [83] Berry 1996b.

most consistently rhythmical of all classical Latin writers – and we surely cannot know this in view of the loss of most Republican oratory – the speech of Carbo just mentioned and the sample of the grand style in the *Ad Herennium* (above)[84] are enough to indicate that this stylistic practice was not peculiar to him. 'Ciceronian' rhythms have also been found in a near-contemporary composition in Greek, the memorial inscription of King Antiochus I of Commagene; although this dates from after Cicero's death, it must indicate a shared origin for the style.[85]

Not everybody liked this style; later Latin authors in many cases demonstrate a fairly clear reaction against it. When Brutus (as reported in Tacitus' *Dialogus* 18.5) applied to Cicero's style the picturesque adjective *elumbis* ('with a dislocated hip', *OLD*) it could well be that he meant it with specific reference to the rhythms, which do indeed on occasion recall the progress of a limping horse – *clop*-clip-clip-clip-*clop*-clip-clip-clip. But the rhythmical style served Cicero well, and he never abandoned it.

Periodic style

Much of Cicero's writing is 'periodic', i.e. composed in relatively long sentences constructed of shorter rhythmical units, often with a considerable degree of balance and symmetry. A complete sentence is called a 'period' from Greek *periodos* 'circuit'. Its major divisions are called 'cola' (Greek *kōlon* 'limb', Latin *membrum*) and the smaller divisions 'commata' (Greek *komma* 'cut', Latin *incisum*); our punctuation marks 'colon' and 'comma' derive their names from these terms. The breaks between cola and commata are those where the speaker would naturally pause for breath or for emphasis; they broadly coincide with syntactical divisions but may not do so in detail, since a single syntactical clause may be broken up into a number of co-ordinated cola or commata; a single colon may include more than one short clause. The beginning of a colon may be marked by the occurrence of a normally clause-initial word such as an interrogative, or by the presence of a 'postpositive' near the beginning (e.g. a particle such as *quidem*, *enim* or *autem*, an unemphatic pronoun, or a part of the verb 'to be': all these categories of word tend to gravitate to a position after the first accented word). The end of a colon or comma is likely to be marked by a rhythmical pattern of some kind, and the end of a sentence by one of the characteristic clausula rhythms referred to above. Certain syntactical units, such as

[84] For colometric analysis of that passage, see Habinek 1985: 148–52.
[85] Attention was first drawn to this by Norden 1898; for a sample of the Greek see Nisbet 1965: 51–2.

participial clauses or ablative absolutes, tend to be marked off as independent cola; vocatives are usually followed by a minor sense-break. Lengthy exemplification of these principles is unnecessary, as there are a good number of published examples:[86] here is just one Ciceronian sentence taken at random, not from a speech but from a dialogue (*Brut.* 301). It is not in the least grand or rhetorical – in fact it is very prosaic and ordinary – but it still displays the unmistakable features of the periodic style. Separate cola are placed on separate lines; minor breaks are marked by slashes, and the rhythmical patterns are marked where they occur.[87]

> Hortensius igitur,
> cum ādmŏd(um) ădŭlēscēns / orsus esset īn fŏrō dīcĕrĕ,
> celeriter ad maiores causas ădhĭbērī coēptŭs ēst;
> et quamquam inciderat in Cottae et Sūlpĭc(i) aētātĕm,
> qui annis decēm māiōrēs ērānt,
> excellente tum Crāss(o) ĕt Āntōnĭō, / dein Philīppō, pōst Iūlĭō,
> cum his ipsis dicendi glōrĭā cōmpărābātŭr.

> 'As for Hortensius, then,
> when as a very young man / he started to speak in court,
> he quickly began to be employed in major cases;
> and although he ran into the generation of Cotta and Sulpicius,
> who were ten years older than he was,
> while Crassus and Antonius excelled at that time, / and then Philippus, and
>   afterwards Julius (i.e. Caesar Strabo),
> he was set beside these very men in fame as an orator.'

A sentence can be built up out of smaller syntactical units in two ways: by co-ordination or by subordination. Those who struggle with Cicero's sentences in the course of learning Latin soon learn that it is easier to find one's way through them if one pays attention to the signposts: in the first instance, pairs of co-ordinating conjunctions like *et . . . et* 'both . . . and . . .', *primum . . . deinde* 'first . . . and then . . .', and perhaps most famously, *non solum . . . sed etiam* 'not only . . . but also'. A more subtle device is the forbiddingly named 'contrastive asyndeton', where two phrases are placed in parallel without any expressed conjunction, showing that they contrast with one another. Here is an example from a letter written with great care by Cicero to Pompey in 62 BC (*Fam.* 5.7):

---

[86] See e.g. Fraenkel 1968; Gotoff 1979. On the relationship of rhythm and colon-division see also Habinek 1985.

[87] Even this analysis fails to reflect the complexity of Ciceronian rhythmical composition: clausula rhythms can also run into one another, as shown by Nisbet 1990 and Hutchinson 1995.

Sed hoc scito, tuos ueteres hostes, novos amicos, uehementer litteris perculsos
atque ex magna spe deturbatos iacere.

'But you must know this, that those who were once your enemies and are now
your friends were much surprised by your letter and have had a great blow to
their hopes.'

In the Latin it is just 'your old enemies, new friends': the English paraphrase
is clumsy by comparison.

In Latin as in most other languages, subordinate clauses may either precede or follow their main clauses, depending on the logic. To facilitate the
periodic style, it is often an advantage to put the subordinate clause first: it
creates an expectation, the fulfilment of which in the main clause will then
show that the sentence, or that part of the sentence, has reached its conclusion. To some extent, this was in line with the inherited tendencies of Latin
formal style: for example, preposed relative clauses are a regular feature of
Roman legal language (as in e.g. *qui uolet, petitio esto* 'whoever wishes is
to have the right to prosecute'). The marshalling of clauses was made still
easier by the common device of correlation. Each type of subordinate clause,
in Ciceronian Latin, had its corresponding 'payoff' word to introduce the
main clause: a relative clause was picked up by a demonstrative, a purpose
clause by *ideo* 'for that purpose', a causal clause by *idcirco* 'for that reason',
a concessive clause by *tamen* 'nevertheless'. Here is Cicero at the beginning
of the *Pro lege Manilia* (otherwise known as *De imperio Cn. Pompei*), his
first political speech to the Roman people. The 'quamquam' clause provides
a neat way of getting his flattery of the audience in first:

Quamquam mihi semper frequens conspectus uester multo iucundissimus, hic
autem locus ad agendum amplissimus, ad dicendum ornatissimus est uisus,
Quirites, tamen hoc aditu laudis qui semper optimo cuique maxime patuit, non
mea me uoluntas adhuc, sed uitae meae rationes ab ineunte aetate susceptae
prohibuerunt.

'Although the sight of you, the Roman people, in large numbers has always
been a source of joy to me, and this has always seemed to me the best place
to do business and the most attractive platform to speak from, Citizens –
nevertheless I have so far been kept away from this path to honour, which has
always welcomed the most talented people most of all, not by my own wish,
but by the choices in life that I made at the very beginning of my career.'

Note here also the symmetry and balance of *ad agendum amplissimus, ad
dicendum ornatissimus*: charateristically, the antithesis is used here as a
means of expansion, rather than to point out a contrast. And Cicero's distinction between his 'own wish' and his 'choices in life' – dubious though it

may seem in retrospect – is the beginning of a piece of argumentative sleight-of-hand, designed to show that his absence from popular politics hitherto is a guarantee of his goodwill towards the best interests of the people.[88]

Patterns of argumentation

Cicero's sentence structure can be notably clear and articulate, and this aspect of his style cannot be fully understood without appreciating the sub-structure of real or apparent argumentation on which it rests.[89] A complete survey is not possible here, but if one argumentative tactic can be chosen as typical of the man, it has to be the dilemma and its expansion, the *divisio*; its effect on his style is unmistakable.

Essentially the tactic is to assert that there are only a certain number of possibilities to be considered (two in a dilemma, any number in a 'division'), then take them one by one and pretend to demonstrate that each one entails a conclusion favourable to your case. Suppose you want to argue that I shall be late for work. It is now 8.30; I need to be there at 9.00. '*Either* you will walk,' you say, 'which takes 35 minutes, *or* you will drive – but your car has broken down, *or* you will go by bus – but the next bus is not for half an hour, *or* you will take a taxi – but all the taxis are booked up at this time; so you are bound in any case to be late.'

As Craig has demonstrated, Cicero not only uses real dilemmas, but also has the knack of using an apparent dilemma form in order to increase the air of invincibility that surrounds his arguments.[90] Cicero's apparent clarity is often, let it be clearly admitted, a means of obfuscation, and to present this kind of argument successfully in fact requires considerable stylistic skill. One has to be careful not to let the listener realize that there are other possibilities which you have not considered (e.g. in the example above, I might get a lift from a neighbour); and one has to ensure that the argumentation on each point appears watertight. Too great a complexity in the style might sound a warning that there is some argumentative trickery going on: hence simplicity of presentation may pay dividends. Here is an example from the *Pro Roscio Amerino* (74) – a speech often mistakenly judged, chiefly on the basis of Cicero's own later comments on one famous passage, to be over-luxuriant in style – which exemplifies the effectiveness of reducing such an argument to the bare bones.

---

[88] On this speech see further Steel 2006: 5–7.
[89] See Wisse 2007 for clarity of rational organization as a rhetorical device; Fotheringham 2007 for the devices (unreal conditional clauses, gliding transitions, etc.) used by Cicero in order to run incompatible arguments at the same time.
[90] Craig 1993.

Quomodo occidit? Ipse percussit, an aliis occidendum dedit? Si ipsum arguis, Romae non fuit. Si per alios fecisse dicis, quaero quos: seruosne an liberos? Si liberos, quos homines? Indidemne Ameria, an hosce ex urbe sicarios? Si Ameria, qui sunt ei? Cur non nominantur? Si Roma, unde eos nouerat Roscius, qui Romam multis annis non uenit, neque umquam plus triduo fuit? Ubi eos conuenit? Qui collocutus est? Quomodo persuasit?

'How did he kill him? Did he strike the blow himself, or give others the task of killing him? If you say he did it himself, I reply: he was not at Rome. If you say he did it through others, I ask who: slaves or free men? If free men, what men? Were they from Ameria, like him, or were they some of our own urban assassins? If from Ameria, who are they? Why are they not named? If from Rome, how did Roscius know them? He had not been in Rome for many years, and was never there for more than three days. Where did he meet them? What did he say to them? How did he persuade them to do it?'

Since apparently nobody had alleged that Roscius had hired free men to commit the murder, the argument may appear otiose; but it is a good way to insist that the prosecution has failed to prove its case.

Another example of what may be called the 'dilemma style' is the notorious argument about the bribery of the jury in the defence of A. Cluentius Habitus (*Pro Cluentio* 64):

si constet corruptum illud esse iudicium, aut ab Habito aut ab Oppianico esse corruptum. Si doceo non ab Habito, uinco ab Oppianico; si ostendo ab Oppianico, purgo Habitum.

'Suppose it is agreed that the court was bribed: it must have been bribed either by Habitus or by Oppianicus [his opponent]. If I show that it was not bribed by Habitus, I shall have proved that it was bribed by Oppianicus; if I show that it was bribed by Oppianicus, Habitus is off the hook.'

By his manipulation of symmetrical clauses, Cicero makes it sound simple and obvious. But actually the conclusion does not follow, and Habitus is not off the hook; as has long been recognized, there could have been an attempt to bribe by both sides.[91]

Elaboration: reinforcement, metaphor, emotion

At other times, the argument may be simpler, but the expression of it more elaborate in order to impress it on the listener. Here we have to deal with the qualities of *copia, abundantia, ornatus* – wealth, abundance and ornamentation of style. Two different but related techniques are at work here: first,

[91] Nisbet 1965: 59–60.

reinforcement by repetition (with appropriate variation), and second, the use of striking or unexpected features, such as sound-effects or metaphor, in order to create a memorable impression. Both of these have been features of elaborated speech, especially poetry but also rhetorical prose, since the dawn of human civilization; as far as the Greco-Roman world goes, they were introduced into prose especially by Gorgias and his follower, Isocrates. The orator's trick is to use them without exceeding the bounds of ordinary language, and not to let the self-conscious employment of such devices create an impression of insincerity. The following is a famous passage from the defence of Milo, not a piece of grand public rhetoric, but a confiding explanation to the jury of the moral right to self-defence:

> Est igitur haec, iudices, non scripta sed nata lex; quam non didicimus accepimus legimus, uerum ex Natura ipsa arripuimus hausimus expressimus; ad quam non docti sed facti, non instituti sed imbuti sumus: ut si uita nostra in aliquas insidias, si in uim et in tela aut latronum aut inimicorum incidisset, omnis honesta ratio esset expediendae salutis.

> 'This therefore, members of the jury, is a law that is not written, but born in us; one which we have not learned, received or read, but have seized, imbibed and extracted from Nature herself; one to which we have not been brought up, but created; not taught, but immersed in it: that if our life ever fell into some trap, or came into contact with violence and weapons either of bandits or of our personal enemies, we had the moral right to any possible means of ensuring our safety.'

Cicero could have said just 'This is a law of Nature, not a written law, that if our life ever ran into danger, we had the right to defend ourselves.' But instead, he expands it into three parallel clauses: *est . . . lex*, *quam . . . expressimus*, *ad quam . . . imbuti sumus*, containing within them four parallel instances of 'not A but B' and two triplets of near-synonyms. The memorableness of the passage is enhanced by the ornaments of assonance and rhyme (*instituti . . . imbuti*) and by the striking metaphorical image of the moral law as a nourishing substance provided by Nature (perhaps the more effective for the puzzlement about what it really means: mother's milk, fruit juice or what?).

Cicero is not always thought of as a master of imagery, but he can deploy an effective metaphor for several kinds of purpose; one of these we have just seen. Another is to excite ridicule. In the Caelius trial, it emerges, the prosecution had promised to produce a senator who would testify that Caelius had attacked him physically at the pontifical elections, evidently some time before. Cicero says he will ask the witness why he did not come forward immediately and why he did not prosecute Caelius himself:

> Si mihi ad haec acute arguteque responderit, tum quaeram denique ex quo iste fonte senator emanet; nam si ipse orietur et nascetur ex sese, fortasse ut soleo commouebor; sin autem est riuolus arcessitus et ductus ab ipso capite accusationis uestrae, laetabor, cum tanta gratia tantisque opibus accusatio uestra nitatur, unum senatorem esse solum qui uobis gratificari uellet inuentum.

> 'If he gives me sharp and clever answers to these questions, then I shall ask him, finally, from what source he, that senator of yours, is flowing; for if he rises and springs up from himself, perhaps I shall treat the matter with my usual concern, but on the other hand, if he is just a tributary brought in and drawn off from the fountainhead of your prosecution, I shall be pleased that, while your prosecution relies on such great wealth and influence, only one senator could be found who was willing to oblige you.'

The terminology of rivers and aqueducts (admittedly odd in English) is recalled here no fewer than six times: *fonte, emanet, orietur et nascetur, riuolus, ductus, capite.* The first of the metaphorical words is pointed by a slight adjustment of word order. By placing the pronoun *iste* in the unemphatic second position, Cicero places a slightly greater emphasis on the surrounding phrase *a quo...fonte*; one can imagine the briefest of pauses before *fonte.*

Cicero would regard this type of speaking or writing, elaborated and often figurative, but calm and even in tone, as characteristic of the 'middle' style. But there are times in a speech, especially in the final appeal to the senate to act or to the jury to acquit,[92] where it is necessary to turn up the emotional temperature. Cicero's 'grand' style, used for such occasions, is not necessarily much more elaborate in sentence structure, in rhythm, or in the use of metaphors and other figures, than the style of the passages just considered. The difference is primarily in the degree to which the language is emotionally charged. This can be shown just by the choice of vocabulary: in this style one does not travel but flies, one does not kill but slaughters. Words which in themselves carry a strong emotional overtone will naturally be chosen. 'Fire, sword, etc.' (*de flamma, de ferro*) was Cicero's phrase for this kind of thing, in an ironical but satisfied report to Atticus of a senate meeting (*Att.* 1.14.3, Shackleton Bailey's translation).[93] Blood, religion and the Fatherland also make frequent appearances. In passages of denunciation and invective, highly coloured insults are deployed with a freedom that amazes the modern reader (as it also surprised later Romans).[94]

Emotion can also be indicated by those linguistic devices, morphological or syntactic, that may be classed as 'intensifying': the superlative in -*issimus*,

---

[92] On Cicero's perorations, see Winterbottom 2004.
[93] Shackleton Bailey 1987b.   [94] On invective, see Opelt 1965, Koster 1980, Booth 2007.

the exclamation beginning with a *wh-* pronoun (*qu-* in Latin) or with the grandiose interjection *o* (as in *O tempora, o mores!*)[95], the exaggerated negative or double negative (e.g. 'There is <u>no</u> evil that she has <u>not</u> devised for her son', *Cluent.* 188). Cicero perhaps overuses these features for our taste, but we should beware of our intuitions as non-native speakers.

Among the many rhetorical figures that can be identified in Cicero, that of anaphora, the use of the same word or phrase at the beginning of successive sentences or clauses, deserves particular mention: it is characteristic of rhetorical composition in most times and places, but Cicero combines anaphora with ellipsis (i.e. the use of incomplete clauses) to create a particularly insistent effect (often barely translatable, but in this case Berry has succeeded in reproducing the anaphora in English):

> Nihilne te nocturnum praesidium Palati, nihil urbis uigiliae, nihil timor populi, nihil concursus omnium bonorum, nihil hic munitissimus habendi senatus locus, nihil horum ora uultusque mouerunt? (*Cat.* 1.1)

> 'Have the nightly guards on the Palatine, have the patrols in the streets, have the fears of the people, have the gatherings of all loyal citizens, have these strongly defended premises in which this meeting is being held, have the faces and expressions of the senators here had no effect on you at all?'[96]

Although the grand style in Cicero is typically periodic, moving in long, well-planned, balanced sentences, a striking effect within a grand passage can be achieved by means of occasional brevity. In this example, the effect is increased by the alliteration as the clauses get shorter:

> Quae cum ita sint, Catilina, perge quo coepisti: egredere aliquando ex urbe: patent portae: proficiscere. (*Cat.* 1.10)

> In view of this, Catiline, finish what you have started: leave the city at long last. The gates are open: go.[97]

It is unnecessary to illustrate the qualities of *copia* and *ornatus* further by quotation: those new to the topic may get an idea of them simply from reading, for example, the excursus on the punishment for parricide in the *Pro Roscio Amerino* (for Cicero's own later comments on this see *Orator* 107), the prayer to the gods at the end of the second *Actio* against Verres, the appeal to mercy at the end of the defence of (for example) Murena or

---

[95] Neither English 'O' (poetic vocative) nor 'oh' (colloquial expression of surprise, disappointment, etc.) will do for the Latin *o*. For *O tempora, o mores!* we have to say something like 'Look at the times we live in! Look at the standards we observe!' or, if in a very exalted mood, 'Alas for our times, alas for our morals!'.
[96] Tr. Berry 2006.   [97] Tr. Berry 2006.

Milo ('we know your little teardrops', said his opponent Laterensis in the trial of Plancius), the praise of poetry in the *Pro Archia*, the noble gesture of defiance to Antony at the end of the *Second Philippic* or – to add an example from the philosophical works – the apostrophe to 'Philosophy, the light of life' in the prologue to the last book of the *Tusculan Disputations*.[98] Without meaning to diminish the impressiveness of these passages, part of the aim of this chapter has been to show that there is much more to Cicero than rhetorical ornamentation, and that if we pay attention to him only when he is in *fortissimo* mode, we shall miss the greater part of his artistry.

Epilogue: fashion, form and function

For Quintilian, writing barely a hundred years after Cicero's death, 'Cicero' was '*non hominis nomen, sed eloquentiae*':[99] 'not the name of a person but the name of Eloquence itself'. He was thinking not just of style, but of Cicero's all-round skill as an advocate and politician. But around the same time, Tacitus in the *Dialogus* could make a contemporary advocate, Marcus Aper, criticize Cicero (especially the early Cicero) for being primitive, unsophisticated and utilitarian. 'He is slow in the beginnings of his speeches, long-winded in his narrations, leisurely in his digressions; he takes a long time to get up any interest, and he rarely gets heated; few of his sentences end aptly or with any kind of brilliance; there are no good quotes, nothing to take away with you; and as in a primitive building, the construction is strong and durable enough, but not sufficiently polished and splendid.'[100] From the point of view of many public speakers in Tacitus' time (including perhaps Tacitus himself), the supreme virtues were rapidity, brilliance and quotability; Cicero had lived before the age of the soundbite.[101] These differences of opinion, barely a century after Cicero's own lifetime, go to show just to what extent judgement of style is a matter of subjective taste, preference or fashion.

---

[98] On the last-mentioned passage, see Hommel 1968.

[99] *Inst.* 10.1.112.

[100] Tac. *Dial.* 22.3; cf. Quint. *Inst.* 12.10.12–13. On Aper's criticism of Cicero see Goldberg 1999; Dominik 2007: 331.

[101] Even so, his work is not devoid of *sententiae*, which are perhaps the more effective for their rarity: note e.g. *Mil.* 11 *silent leges inter arma* ('the laws are silent among weapons'); *Sest.* 98 *cum dignitate otium* ('peace with honour'); *Clu.* 146 *legum idcirco omnes servi sumus ut liberi esse possimus* ('the reason we are all servants of the laws is in order to be free'); *Div.* 2.58 *nihil tam absurde dici potest, quod non dicatur ab aliquo philosophorum* ('there is no opinion too absurd for some philosopher to state it'); *Leg.* 3.2 *magistratum legem esse loquentem, legem autem mutum magistratum* ('a magistrate is a speaking law, a law is a silent magistrate'); *Rep.* 6.30 OCT = 6.26 Ziegler = *Somn.* 18 *mens cuiusque is est quisque* ('you are your mind').

Yet it would be a bad mistake to dismiss the style of Cicero or any other great writer as merely a matter of preference with no significance beyond the superficialities of language. In general terms, it is often very difficult and not even always desirable to disentangle the purely stylistic question of *how* something is said from the questions of *what* is said and *why* the author chose to say exactly that and not something else. The problem of form versus function was addressed by Dover at the beginning of his book on Greek prose style.[102] Dover suggests that one can isolate distinctions of 'linguistic style' which make no difference, or as nearly as possible no difference, to the meaning and function of the text, 'as I may choose ... a red-handled screwdriver in preference to one which has identical length, weight and blade but a green handle'.[103] But Cicero was too much of a rhetorician to see things this way. If he had used such a metaphor, one may reasonably suppose that he would have compared style not to the colour of the handle, but to the precise shape and finish of the blade. For him, aesthetics could not be separated from function, even in theory, since the aesthetic effect of an oration on its audience, or of a letter on its recipient, was necessarily part of its practical effect in gaining their attention, goodwill, understanding or sympathy. The ability to put the right words in the right places, with the right stylistic 'finish', was precisely where the really accomplished orator could gain an edge over his opponents. Without this ability, he would not, it may be, have been able to get Roscius or Cluentius acquitted, to eject Catiline from the senate, to explain Greek philosophy to his fellow-Romans or (since the oratorical ideal extended also to tact in private life) to maintain his friendship with Atticus for so many years. We may also add, as Juvenal did (*Satire* 10.114–26), that it was partly Cicero's stylistic genius that caused him to end with his severed head and hands displayed on the Rostra.

Further reading

The fullest recent study of Cicero's style is Von Albrecht 2003, which is indispensable for the serious student of Cicero in Latin, especially as regards detailed chronological and generic variations; it contains a useful bibliography of earlier work on the subject (247–71). Other significant studies include Hutchinson 1998 on the letters and Usher 2008 on the speeches. May 2002 contains several chapters relevant to style and includes a useful critical survey of work in the period 1975–2000 by Craig (Craig 2002), esp. 524–31. Fantham 2004 on *De oratore* includes chapters on stylistic theory. Fraenkel 1968, Johnson 1971, Gotoff 1979 and 1993, and Cerutti 1996 focus on the

---

[102] Dover 1997.   [103] *Ibid.* 13.

practical analysis of texts. Scholarship on Cicero's philosophical works has generally been less concerned with stylistic questions, but two related areas that have received attention are Cicero's dialogue technique (see e.g. Becker 1938, Süss 1952, Ruch 1958, Zoll 1962, Görler 1988, Powell 2005b: 233 and 2007a: 340) and his translations from Greek and creation of technical terms (e.g. Poncelet 1957, Jones 1959, Lambardi 1982, Puelma 1980, Powell 1995b and 2007b). For the details of Ciceronian language and style, older works such as Lebreton 1901 and Laurand 1938 still merit consultation, and some commentaries on Ciceronian texts are particularly valuable on linguistic and stylistic points, ranging from Madvig 1876 on *De finibus*, via Landgraf 1914 on *Pro Roscio*, to Berry 1996a on *Pro Sulla*.

On the history of ancient prose writing in general, the fundamental work of Norden 1898 is still worth reading; after going through five German editions (1898, 1909, 1915, 1923, 1958) it has been republished in Italian translation, with addenda by Calboli (Calboli 1986). Compare also Dover 1997 on the evolution of Greek prose style; and for an anthology of Latin prose with brief introduction on the evolution of classical Latin style, see Russell 1990. Leeman 1963 provides a valuable survey of the stylistic theory and practice of Roman prose writers, containing much of relevance to Cicero. Works more generally on rhetoric often touch on stylistic matters (see Dominik and Hall 2007 and their bibliography). For recent interest in Ciceronian style as an aspect of a broader project of self-projection, see e.g. Hariman 1989, Narducci 1997a, Krostenko 2001, Dugan 2005, Steel 2005. On the inseparability of Cicero's style from the process of rhetorical persuasion, see esp. Classen 1982 and 1985.

4

MALCOLM SCHOFIELD

Writing philosophy

Scholars of Plato and Aristotle would give their proverbial back teeth to have in the record anything remotely resembling the remarkable passage that opens Book 2 of Cicero's *De divinatione*. Here Cicero presents a retrospective catalogue of his philosophical oeuvre as it stands at the time of writing: soon after the assassination of Julius Caesar in March 44 BC. The catalogue is to a degree selective, but it has the added bonus of explicit or implicit indications of order of composition for a fair proportion of the items mentioned. In many cases these can be confirmed by the evidence of Cicero's correspondence, something else Platonists and Aristotelians must envy keenly. Especially in his letters to Atticus, we find frequent references to his philosophical writing: what work he is engaged on at the moment, how he is getting on with it, which persons in Roman political and intellectual circles would be suitable interlocutors in a particular dialogue (and why he has made the choices he has made in the past), what books he is in urgent need of, future writing plans, impact of some of the dialogues he has already published – and so on.[1]

All this information can be further supplemented by one more kind of evidence lacking for Plato or Aristotle: the Ciceronian preface. It was Cicero's frequent if not invariable practice to launch his philosophical dialogues with an authorial introduction, where often enough (Book 2 of *On Divination* is only one among several examples) he takes opportunity to comment on many aspects of his own writing of philosophy, including accounts of what he has attempted in previous works, and sometimes discussion of how that has been received.

This chapter of the *Companion* will effectively consist in commentary on the *On Divination* catalogue. That way we shall get a sense of why and when Cicero wrote most of the philosophy he wrote, and indeed how he conceived

---

[1] See n. 3 below (referring to Griffin 1997). A particularly stimulating discussion of the role of philosophy itself in Cicero's letters is Griffin 1995.

of the very idea of philosophy. For these issues the very first sentences of the preface provide an immediate manifesto (*Div*. 2.1):

> I ransacked my brain and pondered a great deal and for a long time how I could be as helpful to as many people as possible, and not interrupt at any point the service I perform for the commonwealth. No more important project occurred to me than the idea of transmitting to my fellow citizens the ways of the best of the arts. And I think that through numerous books I have now achieved that aim.

'Not interrupt...the service I perform' – or, more literally, his active attempts to deliberate the best interests of the commonwealth – is the key phrase here. It is Cicero's way of reminding his reader that the scope for playing any significant role on the political stage had become extremely restricted for a senior politician who like him had taken Pompey's side in the civil war. And this is how he tries to insist that the writing of philosophy is nonetheless a means – as the next sentence says, the most important he can conceive – of still doing something that will benefit the country at large. Retirement from politics does not mean retirement from public-spirited activity. Philosophy is not or need not be merely a way of whiling away the hours and days of enforced leisure, but service to the commonwealth pursued in another mode. This stance of Cicero's is of course provocative, undermining both the Greek dichotomy between the active and the contemplative life, and the Roman polarity of *otium* (leisure) and *negotium* (public or private business). It also doubtless carries the subtext that while others are effectively negating the very idea of the commonwealth, Cicero's labours will help keep it alive.

The same manifesto is articulated in a number of the prefaces to the philosophical dialogues of the previous year (45 BC), as for example in Book 1 of *On Ends* and at the very outset of the *Tusculan Disputations*, where to Brutus, dedicatee of this as of several among the dialogues of this period, Cicero tactfully indicates that it was chiefly because of encouragement from that quarter that he has resumed the study of philosophy (*Tusc.* 1.1). Not that public duty is quite the main note he strikes in one of the earliest prefaces to survive from the sequence: the dialogue he writes between the polymath Varro and himself in the final edition of the first of his *Academic Books*. Here he claims to be seeking in philosophy healing for his grief (over the death of his daughter Julia in February 45: he mentions the *Consolation* he wrote in this connection later in the catalogue in *On Divination*), and 'a most honourable means of making leisure delightful' (*Acad.* 1.11). He goes on to give some options as to why writing philosophy can be considered in this light: either it is what is suitable for a person of his age, or it is particularly in tune with the distinction of his achievements, or again as an instrument for educating citizens it has no superior. Even if none of these justifications were valid, he would be left having to face the fact that he cannot see what else he can do. There follows a compliment to Brutus for the model he himself has set as writer of philosophy in Latin. These are the urbane accents of dignified regret and resignation, not the ring of the public mission statement Cicero is anxious to make dominant as his writing programme develops in later works.

What *was* the principal public service he thought the programme could deliver? The compliment to Brutus foreshadows the theme to which Cicero returns again and again in his *apologiae* for his philosophical compositions. 'I thought it mattered a lot for the glory and honour of the state', he says in the preface to *On the Nature of the Gods*, 'to give ideas of such importance and so greatly respected a place in Latin literature' (*Nat. D.* 1.7). It is not just a question of instructing his fellow citizens in the subject, but of illuminating philosophy *Latinis litteris* (*Tusc.* 1.1) – which means at once in the Roman script (not Greek characters), in the Latin language and with a Latin philosophical vocabulary he himself will largely forge, and in writings which constitute a rich and sophisticated body of literature that can challenge comparison with Greek philosophical literature.

The most extended treatment of this theme is given in the preface to *On Ends* (*Fin.* 1.1–10), where Cicero defends the decision to write philosophy in Latin against a variety of actual or imagined objections from those who think the subject should or indeed can be studied only in Greek (see *Acad.* 1.4–8), if indeed it should be studied – or studied seriously – at all. Here and elsewhere he waxes eloquent against the idea that Latin does not have the linguistic resources for philosophical vocabulary commanded by Greek (quite the contrary, he argues: *Fin.* 1.10, *Nat. D.* 1.8); and he attacks other insufficiently equipped attempts to produce Latin philosophical writings (*Tusc.* 1.6, 2.7). For Cicero the perfect philosopher is also the perfect orator (the thesis he argued at length in *On the Orator* back in 55 BC). Writing philosophy properly is something that demands supreme rhetorical gifts and skills. And those gifts and skills are what above all he claims he himself has been able to bring to the presentation of philosophy in Latin: mastery of their own language in this most challenging of intellectual projects is the great benefit he has rendered his countrymen by precept and example (*Off.* 1.1–3).

The catalogue of philosophical works

Cicero begins the catalogue of the 'numerous books' to which his opening remarks in the second book of *On Divination* refer as follows (*Div.* 2.1):

> In my book entitled *Hortensius* I encouraged readers as best I could to take up
> the study of philosophy; and in my four *Academic Books* I displayed the brand
> of philosophizing I thought least arrogant and most consistent and elegant.

Hortensius and the work which eventually became the *Academic Books*
were in all probability conceived originally as a trilogy of philosophical
dialogues, *Hortensius*, *Catulus* and *Lucullus*, named after leading figures in
Roman public life from Cicero's early days as an advocate and politician,
and set apparently a year or so after his consulship in 63 BC in their country
villas, with the conversations between them (and Cicero himself) imagined
as following each other on successive days. *Hortensius*, celebrated for its
impact on the young Augustine (*Conf.* 3.4.7), was a protreptic in which
Cicero evidently rebutted arguments attacking philosophy put in the mouth
of the elderly orator Hortensius, as well as singing its praises as the path
to virtue. Only quotations in later authors survive. In a famous letter of
June 45 (*Att.* 13.19.3–5) Cicero explains his subsequent decision to write
Hortensius, Catulus and Lucullus out of the script of *Catulus* and *Lucullus*,
and to make Varro and himself do all the talking where 'the Academic
question' is concerned – and comments that he has also turned the two books
into four. The arguments they contained 'were more technical than anybody
could ever suppose they [viz. Catulus, Lucullus and Hortensius] dreamed
of'; and indeed great tracts of *Lucullus* are of remarkable philosophical
sophistication – which to be sure is present in abundance although less
consistently elsewhere in Cicero's dialogues (of course, the material is much
of it translation or paraphrase or intelligent summary of what he found in
his Greek sources; sometimes we could wish that there had been more logical
precision in the summarizing). So though, as with *On the Orator* and *On
the Commonwealth* a decade or so before, Cicero was drawn to insinuating
the importance of philosophy to the Roman reader by presenting it as the
subject of learned discussion between the members of the Roman nobility
(*homines nobilissimi*),[2] the final version made no such pretences where this
particular subject was concerned.

What remains of the treatment of 'the Academic question' is only the first
half of the first book of the final edition.[3] But fortunately, despite Cicero's
intentions, the *Lucullus* survives intact. One way of putting the issue at stake
is as a dispute about the true identity of the Academy. Is it the Academy

---

[2] On the importance of this dimension of Cicero's philosophical dialogues, see Steel 2005.
[3] Brittain 2006 is the best guide to the *Academic Books* and the scholarship devoted to
them. A particularly important collection of articles is Inwood and Mansfeld 1997, which
includes a study of the tangled tale of the composition of the different versions – making
exemplary use of the evidence of Cicero's letters of the period – by Miriam Griffin.

of the Hellenistic sceptics Arcesilaus and Carneades, who argued – in a Socratic spirit – against the claims made by Epicureans and Stoics alike that we have absolutely reliable means of access to the truth about things (in other words a 'criterion of truth')? Or is it the Academy of Cicero's older contemporary Antiochus of Ascalon? Antiochus portrayed the sceptic stance, particularly as developed by his and Cicero's teacher Philo of Larissa, as aberrant within the tradition of Plato and his heirs (counting among these both Aristotle and the Stoics). He branded its proponents the 'new' (i.e. new-fangled) Academy, in contrast to his own revival of what he portrayed as the doctrine of the true 'old' Academy – although he himself embraced some of the Stoic Zeno's 'reforms' of the school's teaching, accepting in particular the doctrine of cognitive presentations, i.e. the thesis that things generally present themselves to us in a way that guarantees the absolute reliability of the presentation.[4]

In *Lucullus* it is Lucullus who puts the argument for the Antiochean position and against the sceptical counter-arguments, with Cicero himself responding and upholding the superior rationality of the sceptical stance. He begins with a few words about himself. He is not taking the sceptic line 'out of ostentation or from a desire for contention', nor does he claim wisdom for himself. His motivation is a burning desire for discovering the truth – and 'I think what I say', as he would swear to heaven if this were a public debate (*Luc.* 64–6). Is this Cicero the author speaking, or is it no more than *captatio benevolentiae* on the part of his character 'Cicero'? In prefaces to later writings in the sequence of philosophical dialogues, Cicero the author repeatedly represents his *Academic Books* as designed to articulate his own position.

Thus in *Tusculan Disputations* he states that while *Hortensius* replied to critics of philosophy in general, the *Academic Books* explain the things that are to be said in favour of the Academy in particular (*Tusc.* 2.4). In *On the Nature of the Gods* he refers to the work as his response to those who are surprised that this is the school he is following (*Nat. D.* 1.11). Here in *On Divination* he talks of displaying it there as the least arrogant mode of philosophizing (evidently because it makes no claim to absolutely reliable access to truth), and as superior in both consistency and elegance. Consistency is for Cicero a key requirement we expect a philosophical position or stance to satisfy (e.g. *Fin.* 5.83–6). But equally he demands of philosophy the stylishness appropriate to properly fluent treatment of the subject matter (e.g. *Off.* 1.1–2), something whose absence he

---

[4] For Philo see Brittain 2001, for Antiochus Barnes 1989 and now the essays collected in Sedley 2012.

frequently deplored in Stoicism, but which he often trumpets as a hallmark of the Academic tradition (e.g. *De or.* 3.65–8, *Parad.* 1–5).

Cicero's catalogue next mentions *On Ends* (*Div.* 2.2):

> Since the foundations of philosophy are set at the limits of good and evil, I gave a thorough treatment of the subject in a work of five books, so that readers could appreciate what different philosophers say, and what can be said against each of them.

Philosophy for Cicero, as for Socrates and one way or another for every philosopher who functioned within the Socratic tradition, is fundamentally an ethical project: reasoned guidance for living – philosophy of life. The foundations of philosophy so conceived will therefore require a proper understanding of what the supreme good and correspondingly the greatest evil consist in: the limits (*fines*), as Cicero puts it (*Fin.* 3.26). If the Epicureans are right, and pleasure is ultimately the sole good, and pain the sole evil, then hedonism will be the philosophy to go for; whereas if virtue is the only good, moral wickedness the only evil, a sound philosophy of life will be found in Stoicism.[5]

Accordingly Books 1 and 2 constitute a dialogue between Torquatus and Cicero set in 50 BC debating the merits of Epicurean ethics, and Books 3 and 4 one between the younger Cato and Cicero set in 52 BC dealing with what is represented as the more challenging subject of Stoic ethics (*Fin.* 3.2–5), the settings on both occasions country villas belonging respectively to Cicero himself and to Cato. Book 5 is rather different: a richly evocative trip Cicero takes down memory lane, imagining a conversation back in Athens in 79 BC following a stroll through the walks of the deserted Academy, in the company of his brother, a young cousin, his great friend Atticus and their mutual friend Marcus Piso. They have all been to a lecture by Antiochus; and the bulk of Book 5 is taken up with an exposition by Piso (represented as an adherent) of Antiochus' version of Aristotelian ethics, which is then fairly briefly challenged from a Stoic perspective by Cicero, to whom Piso responds at similar length.

Much could be said about the role of Book 5 – not easy to divine – within the overall economy of *On Ends*. One thing it clearly does and is meant to do is remind us of the way time in Athens or in the company of Greek philosophers was for Cicero and some of his Roman contemporaries part of their intellectual and cultural formation in their younger days – so that in later life the ideas and vocabulary of Greek philosophy and the differences between the philosophical schools would become an often playful lingua

---

[5] For orientation on *On Ends*, see Annas and Woolf 2001.

franca, available also however for more serious debating of ethical issues. Particularly important for Cicero himself was Philo of Larissa, last head of the Academy before Sulla laid siege to Athens in 86 BC, with whom he studied in Rome (*Brut.* 306), and from whom he learned his Academic scepticism (*Nat. D.* 1.6, 17), and conceivably also his conceptualization of philosophy as a guide for living, with protreptic its natural and necessary prelude (see Stob. *Ecl.* 2.39.20–41.25).[6]

In his catalogue's account of the work as a whole, what Cicero stresses is its ambition to be comprehensive ('a thorough treatment of the subject'). He makes the consequential assumption that the reader will therefore need to be presented with systematic expositions of opposing viewpoints ('what different philosophers say, and what can be said against them'). Both the ambition and the assumption deserve some comment. The idea that the search for truth in any area of philosophy requires a comprehensive approach, in ethics (for example) identifying and examining all the serious candidates for the *summum bonum* which had been or might be proposed, was associated particularly with the name of Carneades, the greatest philosopher of the second century BC, and head of the Academy for three decades. Cicero in fact reproduces in the fifth book of *On Ends* (*Fin.* 5.16–23) a version of Carneades' classification of the principal options that he found in Antiochus.

One might then wonder how it is that he can think he has fulfilled his brief by limiting himself to Epicureanism, Stoicism and Aristotelianism. Isn't he really considering only the ethical systems most favoured in the social and intellectual circles he moved in? Without denying that there is probably some truth in that suggestion, it is worth recalling that his contemporary Varro, though in his *On Philosophy* he had elaborated the Carneadean classification into a truly baroque scheme with no less than 288 different possible candidates for *summum bonum*, nonetheless ended up reducing the options to just three: we seek the primary objects of natural desire (e.g. pleasure or tranquillity) for the sake of virtue; virtue for the sake of them; or both for their own sake (Varro's own preferred solution) (August. *De civ. D.* 19.2.3). Cicero might similarly have wanted to say that at the end of the day pleasure and virtue (whether alone or with such things as health and wealth) are the two candidates really needing extended discussion (cf. *Fin.* 3.1–2) – which is precisely what treatment of the three schools he considers delivers.

That the appropriate form of discussion is in general systematic exposition of opposing viewpoints is something on which Cicero frequently comments.

---

[6] This suggestion is argued in Schofield 2002.

In the *Tusculan Disputations*, for example, he associates it with both Aristotelian and Academic practice (*Tusc.* 2.9):

> The custom of the Peripatetics and the Academy – of arguing on opposite sides about all subjects – always commended itself to me, not only for the reason that approximation to truth on each subject could not be discovered in any other way, but also because it afforded maximal practice in speaking. Aristotle was the first to follow this custom, then those who followed him.

Here in a nutshell is the rationale for Cicero's adoption and indeed very likely invention – in *On Ends* as in many others of his philosophical writings of 45 and 44 BC – of what we might call the Academic dialogue-treatise. For a philosophical position to be presented properly, it must be developed with rhetorical as well as logical skill. But it needs to be balanced with counter-argument. Challenging a position in dialogue is the only way to discover what it is that approximates to the truth (approximation, not Stoic certainty, is the best the Academics think can be hoped for).[7]

The method and the objective were clearly inspired by Carneades' notorious delivery in Rome of speeches for and against the natural basis of justice on successive days, when on a delegation as an Athenian envoy in 155 BC (e.g. Lactant. *Div. inst.* 5.14.3–5 [= Cic. *Rep.* 3.9]). Nowhere are they stated more clearly than on the final page of Book 2 of *On Divination* itself (*Div.* 2.150):

> But since it is characteristic of the Academy not to introduce any judgement of its own, but to approve what seems most like the truth; to compare cases and to express what can be said against each view; and (without bringing in play any of its own authority) to leave the judgement of the audience free and all their own – we shall hold to this practice, which was inherited from Socrates.

That does not mean that Cicero in the arguments he represents himself as putting in *On Ends* does not take a position. 'Are you forgetting', he says at one point (*Fin.* 5.76), 'that it is quite open to me to approve the claims you have made? After all, who can fail to approve (*probare*) what appears to him persuasive (*probabilia*)?' But such approval is not a matter of Stoic certainty. The opening of Book 3 is particularly indicative. In addressing Brutus in the preface, Cicero makes it plain that he regards the case he has just put against Epicureanism in Book 2 (where as in Books 4 and 5 he himself assumes the role of critic) as conclusive. No candidate for supreme good will command approval (*probetur*) if virtue is missing – nothing could surpass virtue (*Fin.* 3.1–2). Nonetheless it is for us the readers to decide whether we give that approval ourselves.

---

[7] On the Academic dialogue-treatise, see further Schofield 2008.

On the next of the writings from the *annus mirabilis* of 45 BC the catalogue has this to say (*Div.* 2.2):

> My five subsequent books of *Tusculan disputations* explained the key prerequisites of a happy life. The first is about making light of death, the second is on putting up with pain, the third deals with the alleviation of distress, and the fourth with other mental disturbances. The fifth covers the subject which sheds more light than any other on the whole of philosophy. It teaches that virtue is sufficient on its own for a happy life.

This account of the *Tusculan Disputations* indubitably constitutes the climax of the whole opening section of the catalogue. Uniquely the topic of each of the five dialogues that make up the work is separately, albeit succinctly, listed. And Book 5 is singled out as addressing the key issue in the whole of philosophy, confirmation of the way Cicero conceived philosophy as at its heart an ethical enterprise. Nor is the book described as merely developing a particular point of view about it. Cicero claims that it teaches the truth – or as he would presumably prefer to put it, 'what seems most like the truth' (cf. e.g. *Tusc.* 4.7).

The *Tusculan Disputations* in fact represent a bold and radical departure from Cicero's entire approach hitherto to the writing of philosophical dialogues, ever since he first started composing them – in the shape of *On the Orator*, *On the Commonwealth* and *On Laws* – in the fifties BC.[8] Gone are the elaborate settings in time and place, gone are the exchanges of urbanities between discussants given the identity of high status Roman dignitaries, most of them afforded opportunities to put their own viewpoints at length. Instead we find Cicero after a visit from Brutus at his villa in Tusculum in the company of unnamed friends, some at least adolescents (*Tusc.* 2.28), giving lectures (*scholae*) 'in the Greek manner' (*Tusc.* 1.7), unmediated by cultured introductory banter or thicker physical description. The Greek paradigm in question is another variant of the Socratic method (*Tusc.* 1.8), in *On Ends* said to have been revived by the Academic sceptic Arcesilaus (*Fin.* 2.2).

One of the company volunteers a commonplace ethical viewpoint: e.g. death is something evil, pain is the greatest of evils, virtue cannot suffice for living happily. Then after some 'Socratic' quizzing of the speaker, Cicero himself eventually settles into a sustained defence of the opposite and less intuitively attractive thesis, designed to 'marry wisdom with eloquence' (*Tusc.* 1.7). In *On Fate*, the one other partially surviving dialogue which he was to write in this manner (his role in it is one he undertakes 'as

---

[8] On this dimension of *Tusculan Disputations* – and many others – see Gildenhard 2007.

a Roman, as venturing nervously upon this genre of argument'), it is suggested that the genre is appropriate when interlocutors wish only to listen, not to develop at length a position or theory of their own (*Fat.* 4). What Cicero doesn't admit is that this particular kind of *schola* gave him much more freedom than in a work such as *On Ends* to use whatever material he wished as he wished. No other work of his in any genre contains so many citations of the old Latin poets, or so many of his own translations in both prose and verse from named Greek authors, as do the *Tusculan Disputations*.

When Cicero says of Book 5 that it 'teaches' the doctrine that virtue on its own is sufficient for a happy life, are we to suppose that this is his own ethical position? 'Nothing can surpass virtue' – but quite what more he thought one could safely say is a much-debated issue, and indeed it seems likely that he found it difficult to settle into any one particular stance. He represents the difficulty as one characteristically felt by an Academic sceptic (*Luc.* 134):

> Zeno thinks the happy life is found in virtue alone. What does Antiochus say? 'Yes', he says, 'the happy life, but not the happi*est*' . . . I am torn. Sometimes the one view seems more persuasive to me, sometimes the other. Yet unless one or other of them is right, I think that virtue lies utterly prostrate.

In *On Ends* Cicero indicated in the preface that as well as setting out 'what is said by each of the systems of philosophy', he would indicate 'what I give my approval to' (*Fin.* 1.12). He undertakes the critique of Stoic ethics in Book 4 of that work from an Antiochean standpoint. In Book 5 of *Tusculan Disputations* he makes his interlocutor refer back to Book 4 of *On Ends*, and accuse him of inconsistency with the Stoic line he is now taking. He does not deny it. His last pronouncement on the subject in the last of his philosophical writings – Book 3 of *On Duties* – is this (*Off.* 3.33: he is again referring to the Stoic and Aristotelian theories): 'Now one view, now the other seems to me more deserving of acceptance (*probabilius*).' Along the way, however, some of the subtlest and certainly some of the most complex philosophical analysis Cicero ever wrote is devoted to debating the relative consistency of Stoic and Aristotelian ethics (see especially *Fin.* 5.77–95, *Tusc.* 5.21–34). He was impressed by the logic of the Stoics, who held that, provided what is morally admirable is the only good, virtue is all we need to have a life of happiness, but at the same time found irritating their insistence that (for example) there is nothing really bad about pain. The Aristotelians, by contrast, are liable to the objection he says he put to Antiochus: if as most of us agree there are afflictions of the body and blows of fortune that do count as truly bad things, is it consistent (as Antiochus maintains) to think anyone subject to them can be happy – because he must be without some good, and nobody who suffers from a deficiency in what is good can be happy?[9]

The next entry in the catalogue – and the last to be examined in this chapter – reads as follows (*Div.* 2.3):

> After publishing this material I finished three books *On the Nature of the Gods*, which covers every issue relating to that topic. To ensure that the issue was brought fully and more than amply to conclusion, I started to write these books *On Divination*. And if I add to them one *On Fate*, as I have it in mind to do, I shall have done full justice to this entire issue.

Hellenistic philosophers regarded the epistemological questions with which the *Academic Books* engage as falling under logic, among the three main divisions of philosophy – logic, physics, ethics – that they recognized, and to which Cicero often refers in his writings. It is natural to wonder whether at any point he conceived a plan to write a systematic sequence of works covering the whole of philosophy and its traditional three parts. By the time he wrote the words just quoted, he had published two sets of dialogues on ethics. He had also completed one substantial work on theology, which is much preoccupied with questions to do with the nature of the physical world, and with the views of the Epicureans and Stoics on many of the fundamentals of physics. This trajectory does map fairly well on to the standard tripartition, as he could hardly have been unaware.

Cicero's claim that he will have done full justice to the whole theological issue when he completes the trilogy he has in mind sounds as though he may be meaning to imply that he will thereby have covered the whole of philosophy in the sequence of writings beginning with the *Academic Books* (and prefaced by *Hortensius*), an encyclopaedic ambition he does occasionally profess (e.g. *Nat. D.* 1.9, cf. *Div.* 2.4). On the other hand, there is more to physics than theology and its physical and cosmological underpinnings. And the preface to *On the Nature of the Gods* provides a strong clue as to what especially tempted him to write on theology. It is an issue, he says, on which there are a great number of different views, and one which prompts a lot of debate – with Carneades in particular having held forth provocatively and at length on the subject (*Nat. D.* 1.1–5): in short, the ideal topic for the systematically opposed arguments of an Academic dialogue.

---

[9] Annas 1993 is an excellent guide to this issue as to many other topics in Hellenistic ethics.

Some parts of *On the Nature of the Gods* are written with more relish than others. Cicero clearly enjoyed deploying all his rhetorical resources of mocking wit in the critiques of Epicurean theology (in the second half of Book 1) and Stoic theology (in Book 3, where however virtually the whole of the onslaught on the Stoic case for the providential government of the universe is missing in the manuscripts, thanks perhaps to the Christian piety of a scribe). But he invests no less of himself in the extended and elaborate presentation of the Stoic theory of providence, particularly in an eloquent passage where – 'putting argumentative subtlety aside' – readers are invited to gaze at the beauty of the universe. Cicero takes the opportunity to quote liberally from his own youthful verse translation of the astronomical poem of Aratus, a sure sign that his heart was in his work (*Nat. D.* 2.98–115).

Divination in particular seems to have been a subject of huge intellectual interest in late Republican Rome, where its practices were fundamental to the way the state functioned. Among philosophers Cicero's older contemporary Posidonius had written a work in five books about it. This was another subject on which Carneades had had much to say, and once again it provided wonderful material for a vigorous Academic dialogue, this time saturated with stories illustrating what the Romans took to be their historical experience of divinatory successes, to which is counterpoised more of Cicero's satirical rhetoric.[10] Even more remarkable is the substantial surviving fragment of *On Fate*: technical, dense, intense, full of subtle dialectical twists and turns, very much focused on Epicurus, Chrysippus and Carneades, and devoted to the abstruse metaphysical topic of what Milton was to call 'providence, foreknowledge, will, and fate, fix'd fate, free will, foreknowledge absolute'. It conveys the interplay of ingenious minds arguing and putting fresh and unexpected lines of thought to each other better than any of Cicero's other philosophical writings, even though it is formally presented as the continuous discourse of a *schola*.[11]

After its account of the theological dialogues, the catalogue becomes more retrospective, taking in the writings of the fifties (no mention however of the unpublished and probably unfinished *On Laws*),[12] as well as more recent productions such as his lost *Praise of Cato*, and the still extant *Brutus* and *Orator* (both dealing with rhetoric). However, despite Cicero's gradual resumption of political activity after *On Divination* (the assassination of Julius Caesar is commented on a little later in Book 2: *Div.* 2.23), more philosophical writings were still to come. *On Fate* is the only such work explicitly

---

[10] See further Schofield 1986.   [11] A useful edition with translation is Sharples 1991.
[12] Discussed by Zetzel in Chapter 11 of this volume.

projected in the catalogue. But those that followed certainly included *On Friendship* and the lost *On Glory*.[13]

Above all there was to be a final work, *On Duties*, composed in the autumn of 44 BC.[14] Exceptionally *On Duties* has the form not of a dialogue but of an address to Cicero's son Marcus: advice on ethical matters, written from a Stoic standpoint (Panaetius is the source avowedly drawn upon) but, as the author makes clear particularly in the preface to Book 2, because this is what in exercising the freedom of judgment of an Academic sceptic he finds most deserving of acceptance for the purpose. Of the three books the first is billed as dealing with what is honourable or morally admirable, the second with the sphere of the advantageous and the third with conflicts or supposed conflicts between the two (Panaetius' scheme).

A better summary of their actual substance would be to say that Book 1 presents a treatment of the principal moral attributes of a good man: justice, or more broadly the virtue associated with fulfilling our social obligations; 'lofty spirit' (*magnitudo animi*) – the attitude of mind traditionally associated with courage, enabling us to rise above ordinary human limitations of whatever kind; and the consistency, fittingness and courtesy which Cicero calls *decorum*, and is taken to flow from the traditional virtue of moderation or restraint. The shorter Book 2 identifies support from one's fellow men as the greatest advantage one can acquire, and dwells in this context especially on ambition and liberality, and on how unless regulated by the virtues – justice especially – they will prove disastrous. Book 3 (where Cicero says he had no Panaetian model to follow) is an extended exercise in practical ethics, working through a whole range of ethical dilemmas: along with Seneca's *On Acts of Beneficence* much our richest source for this kind of moral philosophizing to survive from classical antiquity. Considerations of justice, interpreted as the principle of never harming another for the sake of one's own advantage, are made the rule (*formula*, a term borrowed from Roman civil law) that needs applying whenever problems of this kind present themselves.

What this account of *On Duties* so far leaves out is its Roman dimension. The political realities at Rome in the uncertain period following Caesar's assassination (which is justified as tyrannicide at several junctures) are the backcloth against which Cicero writes; and the fabric of Roman society and of its legal institutions is frequently visible when not the actual focus. What Cicero is imagining in making young Marcus his addressee is someone on

---

[13] There are interesting comments on this work and the importance of its theme in *On Duties* in Long 1995b.

[14] See the translation with introduction and notes in Griffin and Atkins 1991.

the verge of a career in public life, and much of the material illustrating problems to be thought through, behaviour to be encouraged or deplored, and qualities of character to be emulated is chosen accordingly. It is no accident that the first individual example of all is Marcus Crassus, as a paradigm of the morally equivocal desire to amass wealth, which leads into discussion of the desire for power and glory that usually makes persons such as Julius Caesar (his first mention) oblivious of the constraints of justice (*Off.* 1.25–6). Book 3, by contrast, ends with a protracted treatment of the moral heroism of Regulus in an earlier age, who by keeping an oath sworn to the Carthaginians guaranteed a cruel death at their hands in preference to breaking it to save his own skin (*Off.* 3.99–115).

Back in the *Tusculan Disputations* Cicero had written a passage of high-flown rhetoric, extravagant even by his own standards, apostrophizing philosophy as the guide to living, with the power to instil virtue and expel vices (*Tusc.* 5.5). With *On Duties* Cicero's single-handed endeavour to supply Romans and Latin with a philosophy for living really did bear fruit. It was to prove the most influential of all Cicero's writings over the centuries. Both for its Latinity and for its moral teaching it was a widely disseminated text, with nearly 700 manuscript copies extant, mostly dating from the high Middle Ages, and still taken seriously by thinkers such as Montesquieu, Voltaire and Kant in the eighteenth century, when as Hume put it 'the fame of Cicero flourishes'.[15]

Further reading

A useful comprehensive survey of all Cicero's philosophical writings, extant and fragmentary, is MacKendrick 1989. There has been a revival of interest in Cicero as a philosophical writer since MacKendrick's book was conceived and published. The scholarship this has generated is reflected in editions of some of the major works as translated into English, which make an excellent introduction to Cicero's thought. Three outstanding examples are Brittain 2006 (which includes *Lucullus* and the surviving fragments of the *Academic Books*); Annas and Woolf 2001; Griffin and Atkins 1991.

Sharples 1991 is a useful Latin and English parallel edition. A book offering a comprehensive exploration of the way Cicero used his philosophical and other writings to operate within the public sphere is Steel 2005; see also Long 1995b. Schofield 2008 is a general treatment of Cicero's

---

[15] This legacy is helpfully surveyed in Dyck 1996, a commentary rich in information if less incisive philosophically.

use of the philosophical dialogue form. Powell 1995a is an excellent collection of essays on particular topics. Gildenhard 2007 is an important monograph.

Introductory guides to Hellenistic philosophy are supplied in brief compass by Sharples 1997 and more amply by Long 1986.

5

EMMA GEE

Cicero's poetry

> As he advanced in age and tackled this art at a more complex level, he
> was thought to be not only the Romans' best orator but also their best
> poet. His reputation for oratory, however, remains safe to the present
> day, although there has been not a little innovation in prose style, but
> it so happens that his poetry, many talented poets having come after
> him, has fallen completely into disrepute and dishonour.[1]

Why should Cicero's poetry have fallen into disrepute and dishonour?
Plutarch seems to suggest that he was eclipsed by those who came after;
surely this is not the whole story. Cicero's poetic output, even as preserved,
represents a good proportion of what remains of Roman epic in the generation before Virgil.[2] We have substantial fragments of two of the poems,
namely the *Aratea,* or translation of Aratus, composed perhaps as early as
the eighties BC, and *De consulatu suo,* an epic on his consulship, composed
in 60 BC. An extended fragment (seventy-eight lines) from the beginning of
Book 2 of the *Cons.* is the longest quotation of Latin poetry in existence: a
self-quotation.[3] Of uncertain date is Cicero's epic on his fellow-townsman
Gaius Marius, of which thirteen lines were again quoted by their author
in a later work.[4] Cicero also composed many short passages of translation
from Greek for his Latin philosophical dialogues, presumably as a means of
replicating Plato's practice of literary quotation.[5]

What has survived is only a portion of Cicero's poetic oeuvre. Apart
from the *Aratea,* Cicero's early works – *Pontius Glaucus, Nilus, Uxorius,
Alcyones, Limon, Thalia Maesta* – survive only in trace form, as titles or brief
quotations.[6] The *De temporibus suis,* an epic about Cicero's exile, probably

---

[1] Plut. *Cic.* 2.4–5, tr. Moles 1988. On this passage of Plutarch, and other ancient
comments on Cicero's poetry, see Moles 1988: 149.

[2] For a general chronology of the poems alongside Cicero's other works, see Steel 2005:
163–5.

[3] Cicero quotes the fragment at *Div.* 1.17; see Courtney 2003: 162.

[4] *Div.* 1.106. Commentary and brief discussion of date appears in Courtney 2003: 174–8.
There is a more extended discussion in Steel 2005: 30.

[5] See Goldberg 1995: 135–57.

[6] On the early poems, see Soubiran 1972: 5–27; Courtney 2003: 149, 152–6.

composed during the years 56–54 BC, is lost to us.[7] Nor do we have Cicero's epic, apparently begun in 54, on Caesar's expedition to Britain.[8]

It is sometimes said that there is a progression in Cicero's verse career from Alexandrian or 'neoteric'-type works to epic writing;[9] but while this is a frequent scholarly narrative, we should also note Cicero's continuing interest in his *Aratea*, the possible addition to it of the *Prognostica* ('Weather-signs') in *c*. 60 BC, and its extended quotation in the *De natura deorum*, composed in 44.[10] In fact, Cicero's poetry forms a coherent and relatively uniform body of work, both in style and in intention. The attribution of sobriquets such as 'Ennian' or 'neoteric' to various aspects of Cicero's work can be as much a result of scholarly preconceptions as of stylistic development.[11] As far as uniformity of intention goes, the purpose of the poetic corpus could be described, as Catherine Steel does, as 'the relentless subordination of the text to his public personae and aspirations for political success'.[12]

Although Cicero's poetry may represent in itself an essential unity, it is important not altogether to elide the differences between Cicero's poetic output and the other types of texts he produced. Nor must we forget, conversely, that the poetry is embedded in various later prose contexts: the *Aratea* in *De natura deorum*, the *Cons.* and the *Marius* in *De divinatione*, and so on.[13] Any serious student of Cicero's poetry must take account of these issues.

It is customary to apologize for Cicero's poetry, citing negative copy from antiquity; even the most sympathetic critics are guilty, at least, of omission.[14] I do not propose to follow this route, but to evaluate his poetic

---

[7] Courtney 2003: 173–4. See also Harrison 1990.

[8] *Q fr.* 3.7.6. The project of Caesarian epic was not unique: Furius Bibaculus and Varro Atacinus may have written similar poems (see Wiseman 1969: 41; Courtney 2003: 199–200; Goldberg 1995: 135). It has been thought that Cicero's agenda in the *Marius* may also have been to celebrate Caesar: see Benario 1957.

[9] For instance, Courtney 2003: 200: 'Cicero himself graduates from his *Alcyones* and *Pontius Glaucus* . . . to epics.' See Neudling 1955: 169–71; Steel 2005: 15–16 and 28–32.

[10] Gee 2001.

[11] Kubiak 1994: 63–5. In particular, Kubiak illustrated (64) how features such as compound adjectives are described as either innovative or archaizing according to the context in which they appear. See also Goldberg 1995: 145 n. 10: 'Cicero's poetry displays from first to last a striking unity of style.'

[12] Steel 2005: 21.

[13] The *Aratea* is unique among Cicero's poems in also having an independent tradition. Ewbank 1933: 98–9 helpfully quotes the fragments together with their prose contexts: more than half of the fragments of the *Prognostica*, for example (five out of nine), are from Cicero's *Div.*

[14] On the negative criticism, see Ewbank 1933: 10–13 and 123–4; Soubiran 1972: 69–72; Steel 2005: 28. Note, however, that the volume of independent criticism may be less

impact by other means, positive rather than negative. Cicero casts a long shadow on the works of more lauded poetic contemporaries and successors, and this is the clearest index of the value of his poetry. I shall therefore examine instances where it can be sufficiently demonstrated on the existing evidence that Cicero has influenced (a) Lucretius, and (b) Virgil. During this discussion we should be aware that Cicero's influence on both of these was probably more thoroughgoing than we are able to perceive. I shall then try to illuminate an issue of a more general nature, namely Cicero's place in the literary environment of the late Republic, by taking a Catullan snapshot.

Lucretius and Cicero

I cannot here replace the seminal study of Merrill (1921) on Lucretius and Cicero's verse, although such a study is due. For the purpose of this volume I aim to show in a practical way, through study of some key examples, first how Ciceronian influence on Lucretius makes itself felt on the level of echo and allusion, and then the possible consequences for underlying philosophical debate.

Paradoxically, since Lucretius opposed Cicero philosophically, it is in the *De rerum natura*, perhaps, that Cicero's poetry finds its most striking setting. Lucretius engaged primarily with the *Aratea*, although it is probable that the *Cons.* was also 'out' by the time Lucretius was writing.[15] Lucretius had his reasons for concentrating on the *Aratea*, as will become clear: the *Aratea* was, for him, a powerful weapon. Looking at Buescu's definitive list of *loci similes* in his edition of the *Aratea*, there is hardly a passage of that work which cannot be matched by some Lucretian parallel.[16] These parallels are of various kinds, ranging from formulaic correspondences and simple collocations to more thoroughgoing allusions. Some correspondences may be explained by common Ennian ancestry; in others, Lucretius is clearly responding to Cicero.[17]

---

than it looks: for example, Quintilian's criticism of Cicero's *Cons.* at Quint. *Inst.* 11.1.24 is apparently dependent on [Sall.] *In Ciceronem* 4.7. It is also notable that the negative reception of Cicero's poetry in antiquity is based solely on the *Cons.* (Courtney 2003: 150). For omission, see for example Goldberg 1995: 150 n.16: 'I do not mean to slight the merits of Cicero's *Aratea*, merely to ignore them.'

[15] 'Lucretius himself read the *Aratea* with care and was greatly influenced by its versification and language' (Courtney 2003: 150).

[16] Buescu 1941: 331–59.

[17] I have elsewhere identified a passage in which I think that Lucretius may be replying directly to the *Aratea*, with his use of the striking collocation *fortis equi vis* at *De rerum natura* 3.8, which conflates *Aratea* 54, *fortis equi*, with *Aratea* 57, *equi vis*: see Gee 2008: 486–9.

It is undoubtedly the case that Lucretius has the *Aratea* in mind from the outset of his *De rerum natura*. Consider the statuesque pose of Venus and Mars, frozen in embrace at the beginning of the *De rerum natura* (1.35–6):

> atque ita suspiciens *tereti ceruice* reposta
> pascit amore.

'And so looking up, with his smooth neck angled back, [Mars] feeds on her love.'

In *Aratea* fragment 9.5–6, Cicero strikingly describes the relative position of the Bears and Draco in the sky:

> obstipum caput a *tereti ceruice* reflexum
> obtutum in cauda Maioris figere dicas.[18]

'You might say that [Draco's] head, turned on its rounded neck, fixes its gaze on the tail of the Great [Bear].'

In the Lucretian passage, we see the gods in a state of love-fuelled Olympian ataraxia; in Cicero, we perceive the stars in schematized relation to one another. Is this just a near-borrowing by Lucretius of a convenient line-end collocation from Cicero? Or is there more at stake in such an echo? With the model in mind, one is led to look at Mars and Venus as though they are emblazoned on the heavens, hieratically gesturing figures looking down upon mankind. Unlike Ciceronian (and Aratean) constellations, which act as guiding images of divine Providence,[19] they do not take an active part in human affairs, but have become in Lucretius' universe static figures, as it were, in eternal artistic repose. The theological debate concerning the role of the gods in the Epicurean and the Stoic worlds may be adumbrated in the echo.

The process of dialogue between Cicero and Lucretius was two-way. Later, in the *Somnium Scipionis* (the closing part of his *Republic*, composed 54–51 BC), Cicero, having recently read the *De rerum natura*, was to restore divinity to the sky, through the influences of the stars – among them Venus and Mars, cast as planets now – on mankind.[20] We know from a key piece of evidence that Cicero engaged with Lucretius' work at the same time as he was writing his *Republic*: a letter he wrote to his brother in 54

---

[18] All quotations of Cicero are taken from Ewbank 1933.

[19] All of Aratus' constellations are set up by Zeus: 'For it was Zeus himself who fixed the signs in the sky, making them into distinct constellations, and organised stars for the year to give the most clearly defined signs of the seasonal round, so that everything may grow without fail' (*Phaenomena* 10–13, tr. Kidd 1997). Lucretius' gods have no such role.

[20] Cicero, *Rep.* 6.17 (= *Somnium Scipionis* 4:9 in Powell's 1990 edition).

BC (*Q fr.* 2.10), in which, scraping the barrel, he insists, for news from Rome, he says *Lucreti poemata ut scribis ita sunt, multis luminibus ingenii, multae tamen artis*, 'The poetry of Lucretius is as you write, containing many shafts of brilliance, but at the same time very artful.'[21]

It is a lot to pin a whole process of dialogue on individual collocations, as I have done above, so let us consider a larger vignette, with a view primarily to establishing to what extent Lucretius can be seen to-rely on Cicero's *Aratea*. The most immediate way to do this is to take a passage from the *Aratea* and mine it for Lucretian 'hits'. For instance, *Aratea* 223–34, on the planets, made a big impact on the poet of the *De rerum natura*. In these lines there are as many as eight noteworthy parallels, even discounting common formulae, or 'Ennianisms' such as *caeli sub tegmine* (*Aratea* 233, Lucretius 1.992, 2.663, 5.1016).[22] We shall consider several significant points of contact. First, the Ciceronian passage:

> haec sunt quae uisens nocturno tempore signa
> aeternumque uolens mundi pernoscere motum,
> legitimo cernes caelum lustrantia cursu.   225
> nam quae bis sex signorum labier orbem
> quinque solent stellae simili ratione notari
> non possunt: quia quae faciunt uestigia cursu,
> non eodem semper spatio protrita feruntur.
> sic malunt errare uagae per nubila caeli,   230
> atque suos uario motu metirier orbes.
> hae faciunt magnos longinqui temporis annos,
> cum redeunt ad idem caeli sub tegmine signum:
> quarum ego nunc nequeo tortos euoluere cursus[.]

'Seeing these constellations at night and wishing to discern the never-ending motion of the heaven, you will realize that they wend their way through the sky on a course determined by law. But those five bodies which move in the circle of the zodiac can't be understood in like fashion, because the tracks they make in their course are not carried on a worn path always in the same place. Thus they prefer to wander footloose through the clouds of heaven and to measure out their circuits with varying motion. They create the "great years" of long duration when they return to the same zodiacal sign under the canopy of heaven. Of these I am not now able to set forth the twisting courses[.]'

---

[21] On the letter, see Shackleton Bailey 1980 n. 14, with the commentary; Sedley 1998: 1–2. On the meaning and significance of *poemata*, see Shackleton Bailey 1980.

[22] Buescu 1941: 338, ad *Aratea* 47.

The first Lucretian parallel we might note is *De rerum natura* 4.443–5. Points of contact are italicized:

> raraque per caelum cum uenti nubila portant
> *tempore nocturno*, tum splendida *signa uidentur*
> *labier* aduersum nimbos atque ire superne
> longe aliam in partem ac *uera ratione* feruntur.

'When the winds carry the scattered clouds through the sky at night-time, then the shining constellations seem to glide in opposite direction to the clouds and move on high on a course far removed from actuality.'

Here Lucretius is describing, not just the ostensibly wandering motions of the planets, but the apparent wandering of all the constellations under certain conditions. But in doing so, he draws on Cicero's description of the planets, beginning with the collocation *nocturno tempore*. He also picks up *Aratea* 223, *quae uisens nocturno tempore signa*, in *De rerum natura* 4.444.[23] Lucretius can be seen to be reacting to Cicero, both by imitation and by opposition. Lucretius' *uera ratione* may 'correct' Cicero's *simili ratione* in *Aratea* 227. In the *Aratea*, Cicero describes the planets, wrongly thought to be 'wandering' in their courses (note the *figura etymologica* of *errare* in *Aratea* 230).[24] For Cicero, the movement of the planets cannot be described *simili ratione* to that of the 'fixed' stars. Lucretius, on the other hand, condemns the false perception that the stars *all* wander with the clouds at night: this *perception* is what strays *uera ratione*, not the heavenly bodies themselves. Lucretius can thus be interpreted as saying that, just as the planets' 'wandering' is false in Cicero, so Lucretius will nullify false perceptions about *all* the stars.

Lucretius also interposes the Epicurean understanding of nature between himself and his model: for Lucretius it makes no difference whether the planets wander, or all the heavenly bodies do: as we learn later in the *De rerum natura* (see below), Epicurean astronomy presupposes no divine, rational system for *any* stars. One could see Lucretius as using Ciceronian material in a counterblast against the Stoic notion of divine governance, the very notion which informed Cicero's *Aratea*.

Note further Lucretius' astronomical programme at *De rerum natura* 5.78–80:

> ne forte haec inter *caelum* terramque reamur
> libera sponte sua *cursus lustrare* perennis
> morigera ad fruges augendas atque animantis[.]

---

[23] See also *De rerum natura* 5.766, *perlabier orbem*.
[24] Compare *Cons.* 2.8, *quae uerbo et falsis Graiorum et uocibus errant*.

'...lest perchance we might assume that they [the sun and moon] wend their eternal courses between heaven and earth freely and of their own accord, obligingly bent on increasing the crops and livestock[.]'

Lucretius' agenda at this point is to demolish any notion of 'intelligent design' in the universe. Here again, Cicero's passage on the planets is implied. *De rerum natura* 5.78–9 picks up *Aratea* 225, *legitimo cernes **caelum lustrantia cursu*** (there of the fixed stars). Lucretius, in setting out the programme of *De rerum natura* 5, is implicitly arguing against the worldview of the *Aratea*, in which (following Aratus' broadly Stoic programme) the fixed stars obey readily discernible laws. For Lucretius, the proposition that they somehow 'choose' to follow such laws, and in doing so bring benefit to mankind *sponte sua*, is ludicrous.

Thirdly, at *Aratea* 232–4, Cicero refers to the 'great year' (*magnos longinqui temporis annos*), the period of time it takes for all the heavenly bodies, including the planets, to return to the same place relative to one another.[25] Lucretius may echo Cicero's *magnos...annos* a couple of times in the *De rerum natura*, first, at 1.1028–9:

> qualibus [primordiis rerum] haec rerum consistit summa creata,
> et multos enim *magnos* seruata per *annos*

'Formed from primary bodies such as these, the whole created universe subsists and endures over great periods of time[.]'

In Lucretius, Cicero's phrasing is transferred from a description of the regular clockwork motion of the heavenly bodies, to refer to the constancy of *atoms*: in pragmatic Lucretian rationalism, it is the atomic nature of the world, rather than Cicero's celestial clock, which is the measure of constancy.

Later, Lucretius does apply the formulation to the heavenly bodies, at *De rerum natura* 5.643–4:

> et ratione pari lunam stellasque putandumst,
> quae *uoluunt magnos* in magnis orbibus *annos*

'and the moon and stars, which spend long periods of time in their great orbits, can be understood in the same way[.]'

At this point, Lucretius is advancing various rationalistic theories as to the movements of the heavenly bodies. Ostensibly copying Cicero's, his planets also complete a 'great year', but, in opposition to the intelligent design theory of Stoicism, Lucretius advances the happily random explanation that

---

[25] The concept is perhaps first found in Plato, *Timaeus* 39d. See Powell 1990: 163.

they may be blown about by winds. Cicero does not expound the theories of planetary motion in this passage of the *Aratea*, but leaves their motion in the realm of the mysterious: Lucretius is careful to respond with unremitting rationalist elucidation. Costa, commenting on the Lucretian passage, remarks, 'The Great Year, with its mystic and astrological implications, seems alien and irrelevant to L[ucretius]'s thinking'.[26] This is the *point*: Lucretius is debunking the 'mysticism' inherent in his model, while at the same time drawing attention to that model by verbal echo.

To sum up, then, Ciceronian material forms a significant part of the hinterland to the *De rerum natura*. The relationship between 'model' and 'copy' is largely one of antagonism: in Cicero, the layout of the heavens is evidence of divine providence;[27] Lucretius' task, on the other hand, is to prove *quo quaeque modo fiant opera sine diuum* (*De rerum natura* 1.158), how everything comes into being without divine agency. Small wonder that Lucretius chose to engage to a significant degree with the *Aratea*, particularly in *De rerum natura* 5, his exposition of astronomy: in so doing he was arguing against the Stoic position, using language taken from a presumably well-known contemporary exponent of that tradition to make his point. He was able to play this game because of the significant place of the *Aratea* in his literary milieu: he and his audience read the *Aratea* and traded blows.

Virgil and Cicero

Next, we can invoke a more sympathetic, but no less engaged, reader of Cicero's poetry, namely Virgil. Let's begin with a famous passage. Most of us are familiar with the beginning of Anchises' cosmological explanation of the destiny of souls, *Aeneid* 6.724–34:

> Principio caelum ac terras camposque liquentis
> lucentemque globum lunae Titaniaque astra   725
> spiritus intus alit, totamque infusa per artus
> mens agitat molem et magno se corpore miscet.
> inde hominum pecudumque genus uitaeque uolantum
> et quae marmoreo fert monstra sub aequore pontus.
> igneus est ollis uigor et caelestis origo   730
> seminibus, quantum non noxia corpora tardant
> terrenique hebetant artus moribundaque membra.

---

[26] Costa 1984: 90.
[27] Compare *Cons.* 2.10 (also of the planets): *omnia cernes **diuina mente** notata*.

hinc metuunt cupiuntque, dolent gaudentque, neque auras
dispiciunt clausae tenebris et carcere caeco.

'First of all, Spirit sustains from within the heaven and the earth and the watery plains, the luminous globe of the moon and the Titan star [the sun], and Mind animates the whole mass and mixes itself with the great body, distributed through all its limbs. From this source comes the race of men, of beasts and of birds, and those strange beings which the sea bears under its marbled levels. The power of these seeds is fiery, their origin heavenly, so far as harmful bodies do not impede them, or earthly limbs and mortal consituents blunt their force. From here they feel fear and longing, they grieve and rejoice, and they do not see the outside air, enclosed as they are in shadows and prison darkness.'

Anchises' opening words at *Aeneid* 6.724–7 employ the standard divisions of the upper world, namely earth, sea and sky. Within these divisions the heaven is given the greatest colour: the sun and moon together take up the whole of line 725, and are more vividly described than the world-divisions in the previous line. Our eyes are forced upwards at this point in the narrative, rather than down into the epic underworld. The upward-tending gaze is both literal and metaphorical: the higher contemplation of philosophy. There is a concatenation of philosophical ideas in this passage: *spiritus* or *mens* as the animating force of the universe (724–7); the fiery nature of the particles of soul situated within living things (728–31); the idea that the soul is hindered by the body (731–2), and that the latter is a pernicious emotive force, a prison in fact, for the soul (733–4). Despite the initial Lucretian *principio* and ongoing echoes of the *De rerum natura*, these ideas are not Epicurean in origin, but Platonic and Stoic.[28]

Should we be surprised to find Cicero's poetry among Virgil's models for this passage? There is a parallel for Virgil's philosophical cosmology in Cicero, *De consulatu suo* 2.1–10:

Principio aetherio flammatus Iuppiter igni
uertitur et totum conlustrat lumine mundum
menteque diuina caelum terrasque petessit,
quae penitus sensus hominum uitasque retentat
aetheris aeterni saepta atque inclusa cauernis.
et, si stellarum motus cursusque uagantes
nosse uelis, quae sint signorum in sede locatae,

---

[28] Best on the various philosophical currents in *Aeneid* 6 is still Norden 1916. Also very useful is Austin 1977; specific studies include Feeney 1986, Habinek 1989 and Braund 1997.

> quae uerbo et falsis Graiorum uocibus errant,
> re uera certo lapsu spatioque feruntur,
> omnia iam cernes diuina mente notata.

'First of all Jupiter, set alight, whirls in the heavenly fire and illuminates all the world with his light; with his divine mind he strikes through heaven and earth. The divine mind, bounded and enclosed in the caverns of eternal ether, sustains from deep within the sentience and life of humans. And if you want to understand the movements and the wandering courses of those heavenly bodies which are located in the seat of the constellations, which by their name as well as in the false discourse of the Greeks are said to "wander", but in fact traverse a fixed course and track, you will now understand it all, marked out as it is by the divine mind.'

Here again we have *principio* (Ciceronian, as well as Lucretian! – which came first?).[29] In Cicero, the Stoic Jupiter, like Virgil's *spiritus* (*Aen.* 6.726), permeates the world *diuina mente* (compare Virgil's *mens* in *Aen.* 6.727). Cicero's is a more intimate connection than Virgil's between the divine *spiritus* and the human soul, and makes more immediate sense. While Virgil's connection is loose – living things come *inde*, 728, 'from' (or 'after', thinking in cosmogonic terms?) the spirit, Cicero's syntax makes it clear that it is the *diuina mens* which holds fast (*retentat*) human sentience and existence (*sensus hominum uitasque*), even though the proper home of that *mens* is the heavens (*aetheris aeterni saepta et inclusa cauernis*, *Cons.* 2.5). Cicero thus plays on the Stoic idea of the balance and interrelatedness of macrocosm and microcosm which is only implied in Virgil.

Likewise, the point of the celestial imagery is immediate in Cicero. Just as Jupiter permeates the world *mente divina* (*Cons.* 2.3), so the heavenly bodies are laid out *diuina mente* (*Cons.* 2.10); the parallel is elegant, the repetition pointed. All in all, the Virgilian passage makes more sense when read with the Cicero in mind: the predominance of celestial imagery, otherwise dissonant in the underworld setting, is explained, as is the connection between the *spiritus* which runs through the universe, and the human soul. Even apart from its obvious verbal and thematic similarity with these lines of *Aeneid* 6, the protrepic rationale behind the cosmology in Cicero's poem is the same as that in Anchises' speech: in the *De consulatu suo*, as in *Aeneid* 6, 'scientific' cosmology is the prelude to Roman history.

---

[29] 'The speech of Anchises in *Aen.* 6.724ff begins, like here, with the didactic *principio* familiar from Lucretius, and so much of Cicero's phraseology recurs here that Vergil must be considered to have had this passage in mind' (Courtney 2003: 163).

Both passages are to be understood in the context of the peculiarly Cicero-nian tradition of philosophy, which sought to yoke Rome and the cosmos. We remember that Cicero himself quoted our fragment from *De consulatu suo* at *De divinatione* 1.17. The concepts Urania is led to espouse in the poem of 60 BC are those which found a home in Cicero's philosophy in the forties BC. As in the case of the *Aratea*, which I have written about elsewhere, Cicero's own poetry provides *exempla* of the 'here's one I made earlier' vari-ety, which can be tailored to various contexts in the philosophy of twenty years on.[30] Moreover, these ideas span Cicero's philosophical works, going beyond the immediate context of *De divinatione*. Take, for example, the notion of *spiritus* we have just seen, and compare it with *De natura deorum* 2.19, *haec ita fieri omnibus inter se concinentibus mundi partibus profecto non posset, nisi ea uno diuino et continuato spiritu continerentur* ('in fact, these things couldn't happen in this way as a result of the harmony of all the parts of the world unless they were held together by one divine and thoroughgoing spirit').

What is more natural than that Virgil, seeking to integrate Roman phi-losophy into his imperial myth, should draw on Ciceronian ideas, and, in particular, on these ideas in their *poetic* form?[31] Cicero's poetry, there-fore, was influential in the conception as well as the construction of Virgil's Roman myth.

This is not the only instance of the influence of Cicero's poetry on Virgil, and it is not only the *Cons.* that Virgil read. In fact, *Aeneid* 6 is framed by allusion to Cicero. We have already seen how Virgil alludes to Cicero near the end of the book, in the speech of Anchises. Now let us look at Virgil's description of the flight of Daedalus near the beginning of the book, at *Aen.* 6.14–16:

> Daedalus, ut fama est, fugiens Minoia regna
> praepetibus pennis ausus se credere caelo
> insuetum per iter gelidas enauit ad Arctos
> . . .

'Daedalus, as rumour has it, fleeing the kingdom of Crete and daring to trust himself to the heaven on swift wings, journeyed to the frosty Bears – by an unprecedented passage.'

---

[30] Gee 2001.

[31] See further Wiseman 1994: 57 on the hypothetical borrowing by Virgil from the *Cons.* of an episode involving Catiline in Tartarus (*Aen.* 8.666–70).

It has been demonstrated that *praepetibus pennis* in line 15 alludes almost beyond doubt to Cicero's *Marius*.[32] The Ciceronian passage is as follows (*Marius* fragment 2.9–13):

> Hanc ubi praepetibus pinnis lapsuque uolantem
> conspexit Marius, diuini numinis augur,
> faustaque signa suae laudis reditusque notauit,
> partibus intonuit caeli pater ipse sinistris.
> sic aquilae clarum firmauit Iuppiter omen.

'When Marius, augur of divine power, saw [the eagle] soaring on swift wings in flight, and interpreted it as a favourable sign of his fame and his return, the Father himself thundered in the left part of the heaven. Thus Jupiter confirmed the clear omen of the eagle.'

Here Marius takes the auspices on his own behalf, imitating, in so doing, what must have been a famous part of Ennius' *Annales* in which Romulus took the auspices for the founding of Rome.[33] *Praepes*, which occurs in Ennius, is a term of augury.[34] The collocation *praepetibus pennis* does not, however, so far as we know, occur in Ennius, only in Cicero; Virgil echoes Cicero's collocation, at the same time, however, changing its significance to indicate the very fallibility of those 'swift wings' of omen. This is appropriate, because the fallibility of knowledge, particularly prophecy, is a key theme of the *Aeneid*, darkening (perhaps) the ostensible optimism of the Ciceronian vision.

Virgil can also play off the *Marius* against its epic models.[35] The scene of a snake and eagle fighting, which precedes the lines from the *Marius* just quoted, also finds its echo in Virgil. The Ciceronian passage begins (*Marius* 2.1–3):

---

[32] Wigodsky 1972: 112–13. Another intriguing instance of the *nachleben* of Cicero's expression is in the poetry of the Scottish humanist George Buchanan, who borrows it, almost certainly through the Virgilian passage, in his neo-Latin didactic poem *De sphaera* 5.20, there used in an address to astronomers: *praepetibusque uehet per postera saecula pennis*, '[Glory] will carry you through centuries to come on rapid wings.' Whether or not the humanist was aware of its ultimate origin in Cicero's *Aratea*, the Virgilian 'tag', through its own poetic ancestry, takes him back to an astronomical context particularly appropriate for his own astronomical didactic undertaking in the *De sphaera*. On the Buchanan passage, see further Gee 2009.

[33] Ennius, *Ann.* 1.86–9, Skutsch 1985 (*praepes / avis, . . . praepetibus sese pulchrisque locis dant*). Cicero quotes this passage in the *Div.* straight after the *Marius* excerpt.

[34] Originally meaning (as here) a bird or place of good omen, coming to mean simply 'swift': see Ewbank 1933: 128; Austin 1977: 39–40; Skutsch 1985: 233–4.

[35] Ewbank 1933: 124–9; Goldberg 1995: 143–4. The Ciceronian passage is based on *Iliad* 12.200–29 (see Ewbank 1933: 125–7).

> hic Iovis altisoni subito pinnata satelles
> arboris e trunco, serpentis saucia morsu,
> subrigit ipsa feris transfigens unguibus anguem[.]

'Here suddenly the winged attendant of high-thundering Jupiter rises up from the trunk of a tree, wounded by a serpent's bite, itself piercing the snake with its ferocious talons[.]'

Virgil adapts the scene to a simile in *Aeneid* 11.751–6:

> utque uolans alte raptum cum fulua draconem
> fert aquila implicuitque pedes atque unguibus haesit,
> saucius at serpens sinuosa uolumina uersat
> arrectisque horret squamis et sibilat ore
> arduus insurgens, illa haud minus urget obunco
> luctantem rostro, simul aethera uerberat alis[.]

'just as when a golden eagle, flying high, carries the snake it has seized and restrains it with its feet and grips it with its talons, but the wounded snake winds its twisty coils and bristles with erect scales and hisses through its mouth, drawing itself up to its full height, but the eagle, beating the air with its wings, presses upon it no less with its beak as it struggles[.]'

The relationship is clear: Virgil has *unguibus* at the same point in the hexameter as in *Marius* 2.3; he retains the Ciceronian sibilance and the expression of *serpentis saucia* in *saucius at serpens*. But otherwise, Virgil reworks the image, not in Cicero's ornate style, but apparently in the simpler style of the Homeric original, and uses it in simile rather than in narrative. The points of *variatio* would surely not have been lost on Virgil's first readers.[36]

This is only one point of contact between the *Aeneid* and Cicero's *Marius*: it could be demonstrated that Virgil may have in mind passages of the *Marius* which *we* happen to know in at least three passages of the *Aeneid*.[37] If we had any of the *Marius* apart from the bit that survived by being quoted by its author, we should probably find its influence on Virgil more significant. Why would Virgil not have been vitally interested in an earlier epic on Roman history? Perhaps we might see him as choosing to react to the Ciceronian poem by turning its myth/history connection inside out: whereas Cicero, in the *Marius* and elsewhere, used mythic paradigms to

---

[36] Goldberg 1995: 143 refers to 'Cicero's traditionally elaborate diction' (cf. Ewbank 1933: 128).

[37] Virgil may also have this passage from the *Marius* in mind at *Aen.* 12.247–56. See also *Aen.* 2.691–3 and *Aen.* 9.630, with *Marius* lines 12–13 (Courtney 2003: 176).

illustrate history, in Virgil history becomes ancillary to the myth of Roman foundation.[38]

What we have seen thus far flies in the face of the impression of the value of Cicero's poetry we gain from almost all critics. Lucretius may be debunking some of the ideas behind the *Aratea*: but, poetically, his debt to Cicero is great. Virgil apparently draws on at least two of Cicero's poems, and his myth-historical vision of Rome is informed by frameworks, be they philosophical or historical, already explored by Cicero.

Catullus and Cicero

Cicero's poetry is tightly implicated in the literary activities of the late Republic and early empire. We have considered direct allusion. But when we get to testimony about Cicero's place in the Republican socio-literary milieu, the picture becomes a bit more complex. Take for example the testimony provided by Cicero's poetic contemporary Catullus. Catullus and Cicero knew each other, and Catullus even wrote a short poem addressed to Cicero:

> Disertissime Romuli nepotum,
> quot sunt quotque fuere, Marce Tulli,
> quotque post aliis erunt in annis,
> gratias tibi maximas Catullus
> agit pessimus omnium poeta,
> tanto pessimus omnium poeta,
> quanto tu optimus omnium patronus.[39]

'Marcus Tullius, most eloquent of the descendants of Romulus, as many as there are, and have been, and as many as there will be in future years: Catullus, the worst poet of all, gives you greatest thanks – the worst poet of all, by the same amount that you are the best advocate of all.'

Catullus 49 has been dated to 56 BC; its occasion may have been Cicero's delivery of his famous speech in defence of Caelius.[40] At face value, this is a poem in praise of Cicero, but many editors of Catullus read it ironically.[41]

---

[38] This is not by any means the limit of Virgilian allusion to Cicero. There are also documented parallels between Cicero's *Aratea* and Virgil's *Georgics*. Thomas 1988 ad *Geo.* 1.244–6 notes in particular Virgil's interlacing of Cicero with Aratus and Homer. In another case of multiple reference, *Geo.* 1.374–8, Virgil 'has referred to Aratus, to Cicero, through Cicero to Aristophanes [*Frogs*], and by omission to Varro [of Atax]' (Thomas 1988: 132).

[39] Catullus 49. Text taken from Goold 1989.   [40] Quinn 1970: 233–5.

[41] In addition to Goold, discussed in the text above, Quinn 1970: 233–5, Godwin 1999: 168 and Svavarsson 1999 take the poem ironically. Krostenko 2001: 272, n. 92 argues that the poem is indecipherable for us, but he nonetheless aligns its opening *disertissime*

George Goold, for instance, describes the poem as 'a saucy expression of thanks to Cicero for having paid some compliment to Catullus as a poet. The grandiose apostrophe, the formal style of the vocative, and the exaggerated portraits of the poet and the orator show that . . . Catullus is writing tongue in cheek. And there is a sting in the tail of the poem, where *optimus omnium patronus* can mean not only "the best of all advocates", but also "the best advocate of all", i.e. the greatest unprincipled advocate.'[42] Catullus' phrasing reminds me, at least, of Cicero's jab at Clodia in the *Pro Caelio* itself: *neque enim muliebres umquam inimicitias mihi gerendas putaui, praesertim cum ea quam omnes semper amicam omnium potius quam cuiusquam inimicam putauerunt* ('Nor do I think its worthwhile my bearing a grudge against women, least of all against her whom everyone always thought of as being everybody's "friend" rather than anyone's enemy' *Cael.* 32). With Cicero's own formulation in the *Pro Caelio* in mind, one is tempted, perhaps, to read Catullus 49 as though Catullus is accusing Cicero of prostituting his rhetorical wares.

In the case against Cicero, Catullus comes out looking like a better witness for the defence or the prosecution, depending on the degree of irony one is prepared to inject into 49. But what does this mean for our purposes? The main drawback in this evidence is that, whatever degree of irony we consider appropriate, it is not obvious that it is Cicero's *poetry* Catullus is talking about. It might be assumed that it is Cicero's forensic work at stake here: *di(s)sertus* is perhaps best taken as 'eloquent' in the sense of giving speeches, and *patronus* as a '(defence) advocate'.[43] One thing may help us to establish whether Cicero's poetry is implicated in Catullus 49, namely the relationship of 49 with another poem in the Catullan corpus. The topos of the *pessimus poeta*, found in 49, also appears in 36. The setting of the latter is Lesbia's promise to dedicate 'the choicest writings of the worst poet to the slow-footed god' (*electissima pessimi poetae / scripta tardipedi deo daturam*, 36.6–7). According to the most common reading of the poem, that poet is Catullus himself; Catullus, however, turns mock-dedication into a literary-critical manifesto, by substituting the *Annales* of one Volusius for his own poetry.[44] In 36 we have an ironic displacement of the *pessimus poeta*, from Catullus to Volusius. What if we similarly read an ironic displacement of

with the genre of 'ironic or cloying compliments' (286, n. 126). Fordyce 1961: 214, on the other hand, is not disposed to accept its irony.

[42] Goold 1989: 245.

[43] Only one critic (Green 2005: 227) chooses to read poetic significance into Catullus' criticism of Cicero in poem 49: 'Catullus is saying, in effect, I may be a bad poet, but at least I am a poet; you're a distinguished lawyer, but a poet you're not.'

[44] See, for example, Morgan 1980: 59. The seminal literary-critical reading of poem 36 is Buchheit 1959.

the topos in poem 49? In other words, what if we are meant to think that it is not *Catullus* who is the *pessimus poeta* in 49 – just as he was not in 36. Then who is? Cicero, the dedicatee of 49, presents himself as the obvious and immediate candidate.

In 36, the term *pessimus poeta* implies poetry of a type that Catullus thinks risible, designated by the generic title *Annales*. Presumably such poetry is ponderous, since we might take it that *tardipedi* puns on *pes* meaning metrical 'foot' as well as the lameness of Vulcan. It is most logical to take this kind of poetry as annalistic compositions of the Ennian kind, antithetical to the neoteric aesthetic. So in 36, the best example of the 'worst poet' is someone who writes this type of poetry, rather than Catullus himself. If in 49 Catullus is looking for a proxy as the 'worst poet', he could not do better than Cicero himself, who, by 56, had already written one, possibly two, epics, the *Cons.* and the *Temp.* Cicero's regard for Ennius over the neoterics is self-confessed, as at *De opt. gen. orat.* 1.2, *itaque licet dicere et Ennium summum epicum poetam.* We might read Catullus 49 as saying, in fact, that the worst poet is not Catullus, but *Cicero*, in proportionate degree to his success in oratory (i.e. by a *very long* way). This nicely catches the ambiguity in the repetition of *pessimus poeta* in Catullus 49, which I have also tried to bring out in my translation (does it refer to Catullus, or to Cicero, the second time around?). Such a reading is, of course, hypothetical (like most interpretations of Catullus 49): for our purposes it has the advantage of showing how Catullus' poem could be interpreted in relation to Cicero's poetry. What more natural for a poet intimately concerned, as we see elsewhere in the Catullan corpus, with the poetic landscape of his day? If you accept this hypothesis, then the consequences are, first, to give support to the 'ironic' reading of Catullus 49, and, second, that Catullus represents the first beginnings of the criticism of Cicero's poetry. Cicero may have attempted to hit back by peppering his works with disparaging remarks about the neoterics;[45] his extensive self-quotation of his poetry in later works may also have been part of an attempted rehabilitation by Cicero of his poetic reputation. Yet it was the negative view of his poetry that prevailed.

So, to return to the question with which we began, why was this? Multiple factors were probably at work, salient among which might have been (a) Cicero's propensity for self-praise, over-the-top even by Roman standards, different though these were from ours; and (b) Cicero's political fate, bound up with what we now see as the end of the Republic.

On the first point, we have ample evidence that Cicero regularly badgered his associates to write panegyrics for him; in fact, it seems that, between

---

[45] *Tusc.* 3.45; *Att.* 7.2.1; *Orat.* 161: see Neudling 1955: 169.

c. 60 and *c.* 49, and in the years 56–54 in particular, post-exile, Cicero was in a great welter of self-commemorative fervour. Even as early as 62, Cicero had hoped that Archias might finish his verse account of Cicero's consulship.[46] Cicero's own composition of the *Cons.* in 60 might have been in response to Archias' failure to do so. Cicero was nonetheless unsatisfied, apparently, with self-commemoration only. In the same year (60), Cicero also approached Posidonius with a view to having him compose a Ciceronian panegyric. In *Att.* 2.1.1–2 (60 BC), Cicero laments that Posidonius had been scared off (*plane deterritum*) by Cicero's memoir, which presumably was to provide him with the raw material for an epic. But Cicero wants his memoir distributed anyway – albeit in the provinces – so his deeds may be properly understood.[47]

By 55 his pleas for commemoration, in any form, verse or prose, seem to have reached fever pitch. *Fam.* 5.12, which Shackleton Bailey dates to April 55, appeals to the historian Lucceius in the strongest terms (5.12.1): *ardeo cupiditate incredibili, neque, ut ego arbitror, reprehendenda, nomen ut nostrum scriptis illustretur et celebretur tuis* ('I am alight with an unbelievable desire, nor one I deem reprehensible, that my name should be glorified and promulgated in your writings'). Cicero at this point compares himself in his desire for remembrance to various historical figures, not least Alexander (5.2.2, 7): hardly modest! Taking his cue from Cicero, Lucceius must disregard the decorum of history and exaggerate (5.12.3). He is to write a history of the Catilinarian conspiracy (5.12.4). If Lucceius does not do this, Cicero will be obliged to do it himself: *cogar fortasse facere, quod nonnulli saepe reprehenderunt – scribam ipse de me* ('Perhaps I shall be forced to do what not a few have criticized me for: I shall write about myself', 5.12.8).

Here we have it: the admission by their author that Cicero's autobiographical writings bugged his contemporaries. We might imagine that key instances of this kind of writing were poetic: the *Cons.* and the *Temp.*, possibly also the *Marius*, if one considers it a work informed by Marius' and Cicero's shared Arpinate descent and *novus homo* status. A powerful answer to the question of the fate of Cicero's poetry is that it tracked its author's political fate and to some extent shared his annihilation in 43, from which it has not recovered to this day. The waters have become muddied, and political imprudence conflated by critics with stylistic infelicity.

The seeds were sown in Cicero's own lifetime. Piso, consul of 58 BC and supporter of Caesar, apparently kept Catullus company as one of the earliest critics of Cicero's poetry, if we are to give credence to Cicero's own

---

[46] *Pro Archia* 28–30, on which see Steel 2005: 53–4.
[47] On this letter, and on Cicero's early readership in general, see Murphy 1998.

tongue-in-cheek dramatization at *In Pisonem* 72. Cicero appears to be reply-ing to an *obiter dictum* of Piso, who had attributed Cicero's exile, not to his unsanctioned execution of the Catilinarian conspirators, but to his verses:

> qui modo cum res gestas consulatus mei conlaudasset, quae quidem conlauda-tio hominis turpissimi mihi ipsi erat paene turpis, 'non illa tibi', inquit, 'inuidia nocuit sed uersus tui.' nimis magna poena te consule constituta est siue malo poetae siue libero. 'scripsisti enim: "cedant arma togae".' quid tum? 'haec res tibi fluctus illos excitauit.' at hoc nusquam opinor scriptum fuisse in illo elo-gio quod te consule in sepulcro rei publicae incisum est: 'VELITIS IVBEATIS UT QUOD M. CICERO VERSVM FECERIT', sed 'QUOD VINDICARIT.'

'Indeed, when he had praised the achievements of my consulship, which praise, coming as it did from the most disgraceful of men, was almost distasteful to me, he said "It was not this hatred that did you harm, but your poetry." The punishment ordained in your consulship was too great a punishment for a poet, whether that poet was a bad poet, or too outspoken. "But you wrote – 'Arms must yield to the toga'." So what? "This was what stirred up the backlash against you." But I don't think that funerary inscription, inscribed on the tomb of the republic while you [Piso] were consul, read as follows: "You hereby decree that because Marcus Cicero has written poetry . . . " but "because he punished the guilty".'

Piso's reference to Cicero's poetry is harsh perhaps, and Cicero counters it with a fictional rewrite of the bill of exile posted by Clodius,[48] but there may be some truth in the allegation that it contributed to its author's downfall. Piso's criticism had apparently rested on an infamous line of the *Cons.*, *cedant arma togae, concedat laurea laudi* ('let arms yield to oratory, laurel to fame'). But it is not so much because this is bad poetry, but because it could have been taken as 'too outspoken', that is, as Cicero's placing of his own forensic achievements over and above the military achievements of Pompey. Regardless of the quality of the verse, such political hubris may well have contributed, at least, to Cicero's exile.

Maybe this was a cue to the linking by some of Cicero's eventual fate with his poetry. Bitingly ironic, as befits the satirist, but perceptive nonetheless, Juvenal goes so far as to link Cicero's poetry directly with his assassination, beginning with a quotation of the most ludicrous line from Cicero's *Cons.* (*Satires* 10.122–6):

> 'O fortunatam natam me consule Romam!'
> Antoni gladios potuit contemnere, si sic
> omnia dixisset. ridenda poemata malo

---

[48] On the interpretation of *Pis.* 72, see Nisbet 1961.

quam te, conspicuae diuina Philippica famae,
uolueris a prima quae proxima.

'"O fortunate Rome, born in my consulship!" He could have scorned the sword of Antony, if he had said everything in such a way. But I prefer the poems, risible as they are, than to unroll you, divine Philippics of eternal fame, from beginning to end.' In other words, although it was the *Philippics* which got Cicero assassinated, nonetheless the poems failed to save him.

At the beginning of the empire, Cicero, his life and death, lapsed into political irrelevance; his poetry would hardly have been feted as one of the grand monuments of a time of political excess, knockdown blows and eventual civil war. Nonetheless, the paradox is that it was read, among others by Virgil, the poet who best came to represent the new regime. Cicero was still involved in poetic dialogue even after his lifetime, through Virgil and beyond. It is on this level that Cicero's poetry is best understood, and on which it has its most enduring afterlife, fulfilling, although not perhaps exactly in the way Cicero would have envisaged, his wish in *Pro Archia* 30: *ego uero omnia, quae gerebam, iam tum in gerendo spargere me ac disseminare arbitrabar in orbis terrae memoriam sempiternam* ('I judged that in performing all the deeds I performed, I scattered myself and sowed the seed of eternal memory about the globe'). Even if his self-panegyrics generated ridicule, and his death was arguably one of the most wasteful of the late Republic, Cicero did indeed scatter his poetic seed, which bequeathed its genetic material to Latin poetry.

Further reading

Steel 2005 is best on the subtleties of interpreting Cicero's poems in his wider oeuvre. A recent addition to Cicero bibliography is May 2002; this concentrates on the rhetorical works at the expense of the poetry. Ewbank 1933 remains the only English edition of Cicero's poetry. The best edition of the poetry is Soubiran 1972; of the *Aratea* alone, Buescu 1941. The best commentary on the poems, including this fragment of the *Cons.*, is Courtney 2003: 149–78; but Courtney omits the *Aratea*.

6

The law in Cicero's writings

Cicero's analysis of law in the senses of legal right (*ius*) and positive law (*lex*) shaped the content of his speeches and was integral to his concept of the Roman citizen community (*civitas*) and its political expression, the *res publica*. As the pupil in the late nineties and eighties of two distinguished jurists, Q. Mucius Scaevola the Augur (consul 117) and his namesake the Pontifex (consul 95),[1] Cicero was fully acquainted with the *ius ciuile*, the law as it applied to Roman citizens, although he often expressed impatience with juristic concern for technicalities.[2] He reflected on law in the context of advocacy, in both theory and practice, exploiting ideas of law appropriate to his arguments in his speeches and instructing others in his theoretical works on how legal arguments should be deployed by the public speaker. His ideas on the philosophy of law were explored both in his writings on rhetoric and philosophy and in his published speeches.[3] While the expression of his thinking was affected by the genres in which he operated, the core content of his thought was consistent. Two legal or quasi-legal concepts in particular were central to his philosophy: natural law as the expression of mankind's innate attachment to justice, and partnership (*societas*) as the contractual basis of a citizen community.

The advocate, jurists and the *ius ciuile*

In his first work on rhetoric, *De inventione*, which signalled his determination to make his mark as an orator,[4] Cicero offered advice to advocates on how to discuss the law. After a discussion of natural law and how custom,

---

[1] On the Augur, Cic. *Amic.* 1; *Brut.* 212; on the Pontifex, *Rosc. Am.* 33; *Verr.* 2.3.209; 4.133; *Nat. D.* 3.80; Asc. 67C; *Sest.* 30; *Att.* 6.1.15; *Fam.* 6.2.4; *Off.* 3.62; 3.70. Harries 2006: 17–26.

[2] E.g. *Mur.* 23–8; *Leg.* 1.14; *Fin.* 1.12.

[3] *Nat. D.* 1.6 *quod et orationes declarant refertae philosophorum sententiis.*

[4] Steel 2001: 165–6.

or agreed legal principles, could come to be expressed in statute, Cicero explained that the ideas contained in customary law could be found in the Praetor's Edict, the annual declaration by the Roman praetor on how he would administer the laws (*Inv. rhet.* 2.66); aspects of law were also now established by custom, of which the most important were legal agreements (*pactum*), fairness (*par*) and judicial decision (*iudicatum*). The first two in particular were validated by their context in social expectations. Thus the agreement has priority in law because 'it is thought' to be 'just' or in accordance with *ius*. Equity was 'what is fair to all', although what was 'fair' in practice could be disputed. On *iudicata*, arguments based on 'decisions' by individuals empowered to make them, their use in court, usually through arguments based on analogy, reflected Roman respect for *auctoritas*. However, the clever advocate confronted by inconvenient precedents could cite competing cases or seek to undermine the precedent as irrelevant.[5]

'Fairness' could depend on perspective. When defending Cluentius in 66, Cicero reminded the jury that the citizen body was framed by law, invoked as the 'foundation of our liberty, the fountain-head of equity'. The law was the 'bond' of honour (*dignitas*), which linked citizens together and was the 'mind, soul and source of wisdom for the *civitas*' (*Clu.* 146). All who were part of the process were 'servants of the laws, that we might be free'. Cicero also offered a characteristically Roman insistence on law as procedure, the means by which remedies for wrongs were sought and achieved: the law, he said, guaranteed the authority of its own procedures and those who operated and participated in them.[6] The existence of the courts was integral to the operation of a free state, and the failure of the courts, as Cicero would argue in the fifties, signalled the failure of the entire *res publica*.

Three years earlier in his defence of Caecina, he had connected the law explicitly with the safeguarding of property rights (*Caecin.* 75):

> Therefore you should hold fast with equal care to the public heritage of law, which you have received from our ancestors, no less than that of your private means; not only because they are protected by the *ius civile* but also because an inheritance is lost only to the detriment of an individual, but law cannot be forfeited without great harm to the citizen community.

The impact of the message would have been enhanced by the context; the trial concerned the praetor's interdict on armed violence (*de ui armata*) and the *recuperatores*, sitting as a board of judges, would have sympathized with Cicero's insistence[7] that violence was the opposite of law, that the intention

---

[5] cf. *Clu.* 139; *De or.* 2.292–4.   [6] *Clu.* 147. On legal process, see Greenidge 1894/1971.
[7] *Caecin.* 5; on the interdict, Frier 1985: 171–83.

of law was always just and wise and that therefore a principle applied in one case could reasonably be extended to other analogous situations.[8]

Thus the task of the advocate in discussing law was to respect the concept of 'Law', while undermining interpretations unfavourable to his client. A much-used device was analysis in terms of 'letter' and 'spirit'. The advocate whose case was supported by the text of a law or other written legal document would obviously focus on the 'letter', but would also be careful to establish that the law was directly applicable to the case in question and that the 'letter' of the law accorded with the intention of the lawmaker. His opponent would seek to prove the opposite. A variant on this theme was provided by the *causa Curiana* referred to by Cicero on several occasions:[9] a trial before the Centumviri in the nineties on a contested will, which featured the jurist Q. Mucius Scaevola Pontifex against L. Licinius Crassus, his colleague as consul in 95 and principal speaker in Cicero's *De oratore*.[10] The testator, one Coponius, expected a son to be born to him and made him his heir in his will, making Manius Curius the reversionary heir. No child was born, Coponius died and Manius' title as reversionary heir was challenged on the grounds advanced by Scaevola, that his status as heir depended on the existence of the son, who had either failed to be born or had died prematurely. Crassus argued that Coponius had wished Manius Curius to inherit if no son came of age, regardless of the reasons. Although often seen as a clash between advocates of the 'letter' (Scaevola) and the 'spirit' or intention (Crassus) of Coponius' will, in fact both advocates advanced an interpretation of written text and intention, as inferred from the text, and both used authorities, precedents and forms of wills in support of their case. Crassus prevailed because he was more attuned to audience reaction than Scaevola, not because his understanding of 'the law' was superior.

The *causa Curiana* also offered an example of a jurist whose rhetorical skills fell short, although Cicero acknowledged that Scaevola was 'the best orator among jurisprudents and the best jurisprudent among orators' (*De or.* 1.180). Cicero's attitude towards jurisprudents, such as Scaevola, Servius Sulpicius Rufus (consul, 51) and C. Aquillius Gallus, his fellow praetor in 66, was respectful but wary. In 63, in his defence of the consul-elect Murena on a charge of electoral corruption, Cicero took Servius to task for the

---

[8] *Caecin.* 34 (intention of interdict *de ui armata*); 51–2 (legal chaos if arguments from intention not admitted); 19.54 (arguments from analogy extending application of a legal ruling); 80 (*aequitas* and intention matter more than wording). See also Harries 2002: 65–8.

[9] *De or.* 1.180; 2.142; *Brut.* 144–9; 194–8; *Top.* 44.

[10] For modern refinements of the letter/spirit distinction in this case, see Wieacker 1967; Zimmermann 1996: 628–32.

alleged triviality of lawyers' arguments, asserting that lawyers created work for themselves by inventing obscure legal formulas and clever dodges to frustrate the clear intention of the laws (*Mur.* 25–7). In the early chapters of *De legibus*,[11] Cicero explicitly sidelined the jurists as irrelevant to his project of expounding the laws of the best possible state. Their horizons, he asserted, were limited to the practical application of the law to the interests of their clients, and, through their preoccupation with 'regulations for party-walls and gutters', they were oblivious of the big picture of the law as a whole. They would probably not have approved of his project, set out in his lost work *De iure civili in artem redigendo*, the systematization (and simplification) of the *ius ciuile* into a teachable form.[12]

In other contexts, Cicero's attitude to the jurists was more positive. For practical purposes such as estate management jurists were routinely invoked as experts in their chosen specialism;[13] for example Q. Cascellius[14] was the recognized authority on praedial servitudes (rights of way).[15] Jurists were given honourable places among the discussants described in his treatises of the fifties, Scaevola the Augur in *De oratore* 1, and Manius Manilius in *De republica*. Both act in character, the former insisting on the importance of juristic law (minus eloquence) for the state, the latter displaying a typically juristic interest in the finer points of ancient history. More subtly, Cicero chose topics for legal discussion on which his interlocutors were already experts; Servius may have been surreptitiously flattered in this manner in *Pro Murena*[16] and Trebatius is known to have had interests in questions of rainwater damage used by Cicero for illustrative purposes in *Topica*.[17] Despite their relative lack of a public profile, the authority of jurists was also invoked in speeches. In his defence of Caecina Cicero insisted on the importance of jurists as interpreters of law; their role mattered, because the law mattered (*Caecin.* 68–9). If the law could not be invoked to protect the innocent from unlawful violence, then the innocent law-abiding Roman had no protection (*Caecin.* 34). In the same speech, however, he took issue with arguments based on the difference of one letter between '*deicio*' and '*reicio*'; whatever the merits of such an approach, the intention of the legislator should prevail (*Caecin.* 68).

---

[11] *Leg.* 1.14. Cf. *Fin.* 1.12, where Cicero admits that he enjoys reading legal treatises but is sceptical as to the value of disputes on the ownership of a hired slave's children.

[12] Gell. *NA* 1.22.7; cf. Cic. *De or.* 2. 137–42.   [13] *De or.* 1.66–7.

[14] Quaestor *c.* 73, Bauman 1985: 119, n. 322.

[15] *Q fr.* 3.1.3. A servitude is a right over property, including land, belonging to another; praedial servitudes are attached to land or buildings for the benefit of the owner, giving, for example, rights of access over adjacent property.

[16] Michel 1975.   [17] *Top.* 9.39 with Dig. 39.3.1.1; 3–5.

Disputes on matters juristic underpinned the happy relationship of Cicero with the young jurist and follower of Caesar, C. Trebatius Testa; on one occasion, Cicero reported to Trebatius that he returned home late at night after a lively legal discussion[18] and promptly resorted to his copy of the eighteen-book treatise *De iure ciuili* of Scaevola the Pontifex to clinch his argument. Trebatius was the dedicatee of Cicero's most legally orientated treatise on rhetoric, the *Topica*, written in the summer of 44.[19] While it covered familiar ground, it also used examples derived from legal discourse to support a thesis that jurists used methods of argument similar to those employed by orators, and indeed would be required to do so, if their meaning was to be made clear (*Top.* 65–6). In this theoretical context, he offered a specimen *definitio* of the *ius ciuile* as 'a system of proportional fairness (*aequitas*) set up for those with a shared citizenship to claim what is rightfully theirs'.[20] Later he offers a list of the components of the *ius ciuile* as an example of enumeration.[21] The '*membra*' – statutes, senatorial resolutions, judicial decisions, opinions of the jurisprudents, edicts of magistrates, custom and equity – are not connected to each other; they all contributed to the *ius ciuile*, but how the *ius ciuile* was meant to be read as a sum of its constituent parts is not made clear.

Moreover, Cicero knew that the elite jurists shared the intellectual preoccupations of their class. Etymology was a recognized form of discourse: Trebatius is reminded of the derivation of *assiduus*, tax-payer, from *aere dando*, 'paying money', first advanced by L. Aelius Stilo Praeconinus (*Top.* 10). He would have been familiar with the disagreement between Q. Mucius Scaevola Pontifex and Servius on the meaning of *postliminium* (*Top.* 36–7). The authority of Scaevola is invoked elsewhere in connection with the creation of a definition, a process, which consisted of accumulating attributes to the point when they can apply only to the thing defined (*Top.* 29). Cicero would also have known of Scaevola's formulation in his *De iure ciuili* of concepts in terms of *genus* and *species*; on guardianship, Cicero's other friend, Servius, had reduced Scaevola's five *genera* to three.[22] C. Aquillius Gallus, too, though not named at this point, is behind Cicero's definition of fraud as 'doing one thing while pretending to do another'.[23] Yet it had to be conceded that the correspondence between the orator and the jurist was not absolute (*Top.* 41); jurists would not employ the device of similarity using fictitious examples, as an orator might, as jurists were not supposed

---

[18] *Fam.* 7.22.   [19] Reinhardt 2003; Harries 2006: 126–32.
[20] *Top.* 9, cf. also *De or.* 1.188.
[21] *Top.* 28. On defining the *ius ciuile* in rhetorical terms, see Harries 2002.
[22] Dig. 26.1.1.   [23] *Top.* 7.32; cf. *Top.* 11.51 and *Off.* 3.14.60–1.

to make things up (although this did not apply to imaginary cases, devised to illustrate a legal point).

Oratory and philosophy combine in the *De oratore*, which contains Cicero's fullest exploration of the place of the *ius ciuile* in the education, culture and practice of the advocate.[24] The much-respected Q. Mucius Scaevola the Augur is made to argue from history (as jurists often did) that eloquence is not required for wise governance of the state (*De or.* 1.35–44). The clever speaker, Scaevola argues, might also mislead, and the founders of Rome – Romulus, Numa, Servius Tullius and L. Brutus – were men who did a good job, not men who talked well. They and others like them created the ancient statutes, custom, religious law and the *ius ciuile*. To illustrate the dangers to the state of eloquence without judgement, he offers a contrast between the wise father, Tiberius Sempronius Gracchus the elder, who guided public policy without eloquence, and his two eloquent sons, Tiberius and Gaius, who destroyed it.

It was agreed by the other speakers (although Antonius appears more sceptical) that the advocate did require a working knowledge of the *ius ciuile*, although it was more effective if also grounded in history, which could supply precedents.[25] The consequences of ignorance were illustrated by Crassus' citation of a series of real cases, where advocates had let down their clients by arguing the opposite of what they should have done.[26] But eloquence on the advocate's part was also necessary, if the law was to be effectively communicated and debated. Some famous jurists, such as Publius Mucius Scaevola (consul 133) and his son, the Pontifex, had also been distinguished orators (*De or.* 1.170–2). A series of real cases is cited[27] on such matters as wills and a controversial house sale, to illustrate the requirement that an advocate be able to advance a legal argument in support of his case, which would convince a jury. Without such communication skills, arguments based on specialist jurisprudence would be of no avail. But without knowledge of law, even as an 'attendant and servant' (*De or.* 1.75) of oratory, the orator too would fail in his task.

Public and natural law

For Cicero, law was embedded in history. Early man, wrote the aspiring orator in *De inventione*, relied on physical strength and knew nothing of right reason (*ratio*) in connection either with right worship of the gods or the duty (*officium*) of men to each other. Their ignorance of this and of *ius*

---

[24] Fantham 2004: 26–48; 102–30.   [25] *De or.* 1.18; Harries 2004: 155–8.
[26] *De or.* 1.166–9; for hack lawyers in the forum, *De or.* 1.173; 2.101; Harries 2004: 154.
[27] *De or.* 1.175–8.

aequabile, law based on fairness, was put right by the guidance of a wise and eloquent man who taught the primitives to keep faith (*fides*) and observe justice (*Inv. rhet.* 1.1–3). Although good men were to be sidelined later by crooked advocates, Roman statesmen such as Scipio and Laelius (and the Gracchi) understood that wisdom and eloquence together were needed to preserve the state.

Roman *ius publicum*, public law, is an elusive concept, because it too was rooted in the long history of the evolving Roman *res publica*. Cicero wrote no treatise on *ius publicum* but he had dealings with aspects of it. 'Public law' related to how the public institutions of the *res publica* operated and were regulated (although much of this must have depended on custom rather than formal rules). Chief among the residents in the community were the gods and the *ius publicum*, which included the *ius sacrum*, related to their place in the *ciuitas* and how that was to work and be acknowledged. How rituals were conducted was the responsibility of the college of *pontifices*, two heads of which, Publius and Quintus Mucius Scaevola, were also pioneers in the formulation of the *ius ciuile*. As the life of the household also revolved around religion and right cultic observance, much family law was also part of the *ius publicum*, including adoption (*adrogatio*), which entailed the end of a *familia* by descent, guardianship, wills and funerals.

De domo sua shows public law in action. In this speech (September 57) Cicero argued before the Pontifices that his house should be restored to him and that Clodius' dedication of a shrine to *Libertas* on part of the site should be nullified. The remit of the *pontifices* was limited to a recommendation to the senate on the disputed point of law, which was based on two precedents. Although the senate had the final right to decide, the college consisted of a representative selection of senators, and the senate would be expected to follow their lead. The bulk of the speech consisted of an attack on the validity of Clodius' adrogation in the first place (and thus on his right to be a tribune at all), and on his behaviour during his tribunate, not least his unlawful exiling of Cicero himself. The aim of this was to establish a general prejudice in the complainant's favour, which would then influence the *pontifices'* decision on the specific precedents at issue. The precedents appear narrow: first the *pontifices* refused in 154 to give the consul permission to dedicate a shrine to Concord (*Dom.* 130); second, a dedication already made by a Vestal Virgin, Licinia, in 122 was ruled unlawful because it was made 'without a (formal) order from the *populus*' (*Dom.* 136). Yet they were the only issue addressed by the College: provided that the dedicator (Clodius) was not given authority to do so by name (*nominatim*), or ordered to do so, by the *populus* or plebs, their legal opinion was that Cicero could receive back that part of the site.[28] Despite Cicero's best efforts, they offered no opinion on the questions of fact.[29]

The religious law of the ideal state was the subject of a separate 'codification' in *De legibus* 2; it bore a remarkable resemblance to Roman religious institutions. Its distinctive character and importance were underlined by the priority given it over the secular public law, which followed in Book 3, and it provided a context for Cicero to reflect on the evolution of the *ius ciuile* away from its roots in pontifical law. In particular, Cicero questioned the approach of the pontifical jurists to the transformation of pontifical to civil law in the case of family *sacra* (*Leg.* 2.48–53) and liability for the conduct of funerals.[30] In his view, regulations introduced by the Scaevolae, which affected the hierarchy of heirs named in a will and responsible for funeral rites, were counter-productive and broke the link between family and funerals. He was also concerned that the pontifical jurists gave sanction to legal dodges, ignoring the possibility that the ideas for getting round the law may have originated elsewhere. For Cicero's discussion of *sacra* did not take into account the effect on public religious law of other developments, such as the growing popularity of privately made wills or gifts to take effect on the death of the giver (*donatio mortis causae*). This was the more important because regulations on other matters, such as mourning and the avoidance of ostentation, were present in the Twelve Tables, and some derived from Solon; they were also, in Cicero's opinion, in accordance with the law of nature (*Leg.* 2.58–62).

A historical foundation for law at Rome of a different kind is offered in *De republica*. 'Scipio's' thesis is that the early history of Rome down to the publication of the Twelve Tables in *c.* 450 was the story of how the *populus* acquired freedom, but not to excess, resulting in the evolution of the ideal balanced or mixed constitution, of which Rome was the finest example (*Rep.* 2.1–63). Although senate and people had reached the desired equilibrium and harmony by the mid fifth century, they suspended their constitution and appointed a Board of Ten lawgivers, from whose decisions there was no appeal.[31] The Board drew up the original ten Tables, which were admirable but were then replaced by one (or two) successor-boards. These degenerated into lawlessness, and were overthrown. Cicero thus creates a dramatic tension between the ideal of law, as represented by Rome's first law-code, still much revered in his own day, and the flawed characters and tyrannical behaviour of the legislators. Despite the excellence of the mixed

---

[28] *Att.* 4.2.3.   [29] Harries 2006: 156–62; for a different approach, see Stroh 2004.

[30] Dyck 2004a: 381–3; Harries 2006: 149–52.

[31] Although this right did exist in relation to other magistrates, *Rep.* 2.53–4.

constitution, even at its best, it was vulnerable to subversion by the imperfections of bad citizens, a lesson that Cicero would apply also to events in his own time.

Present in Rome's constitutional history, as Cicero saw it, was a dichotomy between a legal ideal, understood and aspired to but not always attained, and the imperfections of laws and states in history. Cicero's rationalization of this derived from his understanding of natural law. This was first expressed in *De inventione* (2.65):

> Its beginnings appear to derive from nature; certain elements on grounds of their usefulness, which are either obvious to us or obscure, seem to have evolved into custom. Later, certain matters, tested by custom or beneficial for other reasons, were confirmed by statutes (*legibus*). And the law of nature is what is ingrained in us, not by opinion but a sort of inbred conviction (*innata uis*), such as worship of the gods (*religio*), duty to gods and men (*pietas*), gratitude (*gratia*), revenge (*uindicatio*), respect (*obseruantia*) and truth (*ueritas*).

Natural law, therefore, was based on a set of moral values, which are assumed to be universal. Its evolution into 'customary law' was sanctioned by the acceptance of custom over time, requiring no sanction by statute (*Inv. rhet.* 2.67). These legal principles could prevail without being written down but were nonetheless incorporated, not only into statute but also into the Praetor's Edict, the Roman praetor's annual statement of how he would administer the law. Cicero did not add that the Edict was also shaped by the advice of the jurists, who, through their writing on the civil law, could also count as interpreters of custom. This textbook version of law in history, designed for use in speeches, would re-emerge in modified form in *Pro Sestio*, supporting the argument that law and violence are opposites, the former being required for a state to be viable (90–2).

A more sophisticated explanation of natural law is offered in *De legibus* (1.15), which is explicitly offered as a companion piece to *De republica*, echoing Plato. Cicero and Atticus agree that legal knowledge (*iuris disciplina*) is not to be derived from the Praetor's Edict or the Twelve Tables but from philosophy and a true understanding of the nature of Justice (*Leg.* 1.18–19):

> Law (*lex*) is the highest reason, rooted in nature, which commands the things that should be done and forbids the opposite. That same reason, when it is established and fully integrated into man's intellect, is law. And so they (the most learned) think that law is that kind of wisdom, the nature of which is to order right actions and forbid wrongdoing.

After commenting that the Greeks thought that the word for law in Greek derived from giving every man his due, while the Romans' *lex* derived from *legere*, to choose, Cicero reiterated his thesis that legal right (*ius*) originated in the law of nature, which he now equated with the intellect and reasoning power of the wise man. Despite this, however, Cicero remained mindful of his audience: it would also be necessary to label as 'law' what the *populus* decreed in written form.

However, the 'law' of the *populus* was not invariably compatible with the law of nature or justice; nature could be corrupted by bad custom.[32] It was therefore possible for laws passed by states and communities to be unjust (*Leg.* 1.42):

> Now, this is the most foolish idea, that one should believe that everything is just, which is established by the conventions and laws of peoples. Is that so, if the laws were those of tyrants? If the infamous Thirty at Athens had wished to impose laws on the Athenians, or if all the Athenians had welcomed the laws passed by the tyrants, would those laws be held to be just on those grounds? No more, I think, should those laws, which that *interrex* of ours (L. Valerius Flaccus) passed that the dictator could kill any citizen he wished without fear of the consequences, even without a trial. For legal right (*ius*) is one, by which associations of men are bound together, and one law (*lex*) has established it.

The question Cicero avoids, but to which he would return in later writings, is whether or not the citizen was obliged to obey laws contrary to the justice embedded in nature. Yet the answer is implied in the lengthy discussion on virtue, which follows: virtue alone, which is based on nature, law and justice, and exercised in the service of the community, should be the guide of right actions. A philosopher who followed the dictates of the universal norms based on nature could well find himself violating the positive laws, even the conventions, of a corrupted state.

Cicero's version of natural law thus permitted the orator to claim justification from 'universal' norms for undermining the formal laws and institutions of the *res publica*. In general, he avoided open conflict with statutes, lawfully passed. In 63, Cicero argued that the followers of Catiline were not citizens but *hostes*, enemies, who had forfeited the right of a citizen to a fair trial (*Cat.* 1.28); this – and the senate's debate and vote on the matter – justified the summary executions of Lentulus and his colleagues in December 63. When arguing against his exile and its consequences, brought about by the tribune Clodius in 58, Cicero maintained that Clodius' law against 'those who had executed Roman citizens without trial' had been improperly passed

---

[32] *mala consuetudine*, *Leg.* 1.12.33.

by a packed assembly and by a tribune whose 'adoption' as a plebeian by someone younger than himself was also open to legal challenge. It had also violated Cicero's own rights as a citizen (who had not been proclaimed a *hostis*) to a fair trial. The returned exile went further, arguing in *Pro Sestio* that, when lawful process was suspended and the *res publica* could no longer function as a viable state, violence in its defence was justifiable. The debate between two sets of gangsters was thus elevated to a competition for legitimacy; the party that could successfully lay claim to representing the *res publica* would also have 'natural law' on its side.

Cicero's exploitation of this argument in the service of what others labelled as a faction[33] reached its culmination in his *Philippics* against Antonius in 44–3. Like Catiline, Antonius was labelled by the orator as a *hostis*, and Cicero made repeated, but unsuccessful, attempts to formalize that status through senatorial resolution. Like Clodius, Antonius allegedly passed laws that were not laws at all because of procedural irregularities.[34] Their content was flawed, because they permitted government by violence[35] and they did not represent the true will of the *populus*. Cicero's consistent line, that Antonius was isolated from the Roman community, allowed him to argue also that those who were opposed to Antonius – the tyrannicides (whose unlawful action was also justified), and later Octavian – were acting in accordance with natural law, even when what they did contradicted positive law or lacked senatorial sanction. Thus Decimus Brutus was urged to pre-empt the decision of the senate to legitimize his position in Cisalpine Gaul, as the senate was 'not yet free' (*Fam.* 11.7); Marcus Brutus' disputed occupation of Macedonia, earlier allocated by law to Antonius, was justified because Antonius had attacked the *res publica* (*Phil.* 10.12); and Brutus was not required to wait for the senate before attacking Dolabella, who had disposed of Trebonius in Asia and was now formally a *hostis* (*Phil.* 11.27). The legal right of both M. Brutus and Cassius to grab what provinces and armies they could in the East, regardless of statutory provincial allocations, was confirmed by an explicit reference to the divinely sanctioned power of natural law (*Phil.* 11.28):

> Juppiter himself has ordained that all, which contributes to the safety of the *res publica*, should be held to be lawful and right. For Law (*lex*) is nothing else but a right form of reasoning (*ratio*) drawn from the gods, which commands what is honourable and forbids the opposite.

For this strategy to work, Cicero's assertion that his *res publica* was the true one had to be beyond challenge. In a period of factional struggle, this

---

[33] Antonius, in his letter, cited at Cic. *Phil.* 13.42.
[34] *Phil.* 1.6; 5.7–8.   [35] *Phil.* 1.22; 26.

was impossible, and Cicero's argument that law-breaking was lawful, if in accord with the 'higher' natural law, has obvious dangers: who decides when law-breaking is lawful? However, the implications of his rhetoric of legitimacy for the appearance of constitutional rule were not lost on the future Augustus.

Partnership and community

Both human and legal relationships were based on right behaviour, in particular trust, *fides*, a quality so important that it was also connected with the gods. In late Republican jurisprudence and legal process, the legal implications of *fides* were analysed and applied to real cases heard before judges, who had special discretion when dealing with legal actions *bonae fidei*. Because they had initially trusted each other, parties to many such cases would not have expected to arrive in court, and indeed, may not always have been aware that they were incurring legal obligations. So, for example, lawsuits on mandate, the process by which one individual instructs another to carry out some transaction, and trusts him to do so honestly, may not have been initially anticipated by either of the parties, who could well have neglected such formalities as formally agreeing to the mandate, or checking first before changing the conditions.[36] Yet, as Cicero insisted in his defence of Roscius of Ameria in 80, abusing a mandate for personal gain, or merely carrying it out in a negligent way, was utterly disgraceful, and in fact equivalent to theft. Indeed, one who failed to perform a task entrusted to him also damaged the community as a whole, by undermining its safeguards based on social values.[37]

Social expectations also shaped legal actions on partnership (*pro socio*), which, like those on mandate, concerned good faith (*bona fides*). In Roman law a partnership, *societas*, was an agreement between two or more parties entered into by deliberate action on a voluntary basis for the benefit and profit of all concerned. The consenting parties made agreed contributions and their share of the profits (and losses) were agreed accordingly; the contribution could be assessed in terms of services rendered, as well as material assets.[38] The assets of the partnership were owned by the partnership and would probably be redistributed on the death of one of the

---

[36] Dig. 17.1.22.10, the mandatary must accept the commission; *Fam.* 7.23.1, the mandatary must not exceed his mandate without authorization.

[37] *Rosc. Am.* 38.111–39.113; cf. *Fam.* 7.23.1; *Nat. D.* 3.30.74; *Top.* 10.42; 17.66; Watson 1965: 147–56.

[38] *Q Rosc.* 10.28; Dig. 17.2.5.1.

parties.[39] There was also a fuller form of partnership, which incorporated all the assets of the parties.[40] For a partnership to function properly, all the partners were required to act in good faith (*bona fide*) towards each other. This legal contract, therefore, depended for its effectiveness on adherence to moral standards, which were reflected in the legal formula, 'as ought to be good conduct between good men'.[41]

Two of Cicero's early civil cases concerned the consequences of the breakdown of partnerships between friends or family members, who might have been expected to work well together. Because individuals do not necessarily expect to end up in court, such cases could have a long history, stretching back over several years and perhaps entailing other court appearances. P. Quinctius, the uninspiring hero of the *Pro Quinctio*, delivered before C. Aquillius Gallus in 81, was the unlucky inheritor of his brother's partnership debts[42] but, as a result of a series of praetorian interventions,[43] the dispute with his relative by marriage, Sex. Naevius, was now about possession by praetorian order, not the partnership; the present judge, C. Aquillius Gallus, had already been involved in previous hearings. Quinctius' brother-in-law, Sextus Roscius the actor, was also, after some fifteen years, still seeking his rightful share of compensation due after the killing of a slave held in common with his partner, C. Fannius Chaerea.[44]

In *Pro Quinctio*, Cicero's portrayal of Quinctius' opponent, Naevius, as a false partner, though not relevant to the point at issue, depicts what was required morally of a person in a legal partnership; the focus of the argument is the ethics of *societas*. By contrast, the failings of Roscius' opponent are set in the context of other legal failings in trusts or guardianship,[45] a line of argument not followed in the Quinctius speech. The original partnership between Naevius and Quinctius' brother, Gaius, was freely entered into, but Gaius was mistaken in the character of his partner, who was not morally equipped to understand the 'legal duties of partnership'.[46] Naevius is represented as fraudulent and deceitful, offering to lend Publius money to tide him over but then changing his mind at the last minute, insisting that issues relating to the partnership (which had already been under review for more than a year) be settled first (*Quinct.* 19). Even Naevius' agreement to

---

[39] Dig. 17.2.59; in classical law (but perhaps not earlier) it was not possible for the *heres* to take over, even with the agreement of the surviving partners.

[40] *societas omnium bonorum*, Dig. 17.2.1.1.

[41] Formula cited *Top.* 17.66; cf. *Rosc. Am.* 40.116, *in rebus minoribus socium fallere turpissimum est*. On *societas* under the Republic, Watson 1965: 125–46.

[42] Dig. 17.2.63.8, the *heres* was liable for the debts of the deceased.

[43] E.g. *Quinct.* 30, 32.   [44] *Q Rosc.* 33.   [45] *Q Rosc.* 16.

[46] *iura societatis*, *Quinct.* 12.

an attempt at settling the matter by arbitration is represented as insincere, when he appoints a crony as his legal representative, rather than someone who might act as a neutral arbitrator.[47] Although technically peripheral to the main issue, Cicero's technique was to undermine the credibility of Naevius by reference to his past misconduct. In the process, he bridges the divide between the 'legal' and the 'moral', knowing as he did so that the *iudex*, Gallus, was an expert on the legal applications of 'good' and 'bad' faith.[48]

The implications of the definition of community offered by 'Scipio Aemilianus' in the *De republica* over twenty-five years later can be fully understood only if the legal character of *societas* as a contract based on consensus is taken into account (1.39).

> 'So', said (Scipio) Africanus, 'the *res publica* is the property (*res*) of the people (*populus*). But the people is not a universal gathering of men brought together in any old way, but a gathering of a large number (*multitudo*) bound together in partnership (*sociatus*) by legal consent (*iuris consensus*) and for the shared benefit of all (*utilitatis communione*).'

Every element required for the legal partnership contract is present. The people are designated the owners of the *res publica*, which is their shared asset, and the people themselves are partners with each other, having deliberately agreed to the contract, with the aim of benefiting or profiting from it. Moreover, whatever the form of government chosen (monarchy, aristocracy or 'popular government'), for any system to be even viable, the bond created by the partnership agreement must hold firm.[49] The terminology of contractual law is not here used for linguistic effect; it is integral to the argument.[50]

Societas was not to be applied only to the behaviour of communities in the abstract, but also to the dealings of members of communities with each other. It thus bridged the gap not only between the moral and the legal but also between the public and the private; what private individuals did had a direct impact on the community. *De officiis*, Cicero's last philosophical work, returned to the application of *societas* to human relations in the context of what was expected of the virtuous citizen. Q. Mucius Scaevola Pontifex's development of *fides* in its legal application is fused with the Roman requirement of *fides* in dealings with the gods, friends and enemies, marital relationships and friendship. Good government required good faith

---

[47] *Quinct.* 21. The conduct of Quinctius' representative Alfenus is in fact far from neutral.

[48] See also *Quinct.* 26, *si veritate amicitia, fide societas, pietate propinquitas colitur*; also 48; 55.

[49] *Rep.* 1.44 *si teneat illud vinculum, quod primum homines inter se rei publicae societate devinxit.*

[50] Cf. also *Leg.* 1.35 on mankind as bound together *societate iuris*; in general, Asmis 2004.

in the keeping of oaths by judges and office-holders[51] and loss of reputation was incurred by those who breached *fides* through false swearing, treachery, cheating of any kind or acting with bad intent.[52] One exemplar of the man who dealt honourably, against his own self-interest, was Scaevola himself, who, when offered the chance to buy a farm on the cheap, insisted on paying the true value.[53]

Cicero's ideas on legal partnership as the foundation of a successful community should be taken in conjunction with his theory of natural law, if the implications of the latter are to be fairly assessed. Cicero did not believe that 'natural law' should be invoked lightly against the laws of the state; it was not up to the individual alone and unaided to ascertain what *his* justice was, and then act upon it. The situation in which resort could legitimately be made to the justice innate in natural law was created when the 'legal consent', on which community was based, had been withdrawn or made void. Such was the situation created by the dictatorship of Caesar – hence the argument that his murder was justified, even though homicide was contrary to positive law. Despite the potential for abuse inherent in his doctrine of natural law, the contribution of Cicero's legal writings was to demonstrate how the legal procedures and social values of the *ius ciuile* were essential both to the effective functioning of the orator as statesman and advocate, and to the identity and survival of the Roman community of citizens.

Further reading

Niall Rudd's translation of *The Republic and The Laws* (1998), has an excellent translation of two key texts with introduction to the main lines of argument; also see introduction and translation of *On Duties* by Griffin and Atkins 1991. On Cicero and law, see Harries 2006. On lawyers and legal culture in general, see Buaman 1985 and Frier 1985. Powell and Paterson 2004 has useful chapters on Cicero's use of law as an advocate.

---

[51] *Off.* 3.104; 111 on sanctity of oaths in context of the story of Regulus.
[52] *Off.* 1.13–14; cf. Livy 28.42; Caes. *B Civ.* 2.14.1.
[53] *Off.* 3.62. On Scaevola's perhaps unworldly attitudes to business, see Plin. *HN* 18.32; Columella, *Rust.* 1.4.6; Dyck 1996: 572.

7

EMMA DENCH

Cicero and Roman identity

Remembering Cicero's Roman identity

Of all the posthumous ancient evaluations of Cicero's life, death and cultural legacy, the Elder Seneca's presentation of multiple perspectives on 'Cicero considers whether he should beg Antony for mercy' (*Suas.* 6) best illustrates the complexity that made the figure of Cicero so good to think with as a Roman exemplar in the early imperial period. This *Suasoria* turns on the ethics of negotiating with a tyrant in order to save one's life, and the different responses represented within it focus on the value of Cicero's life and the meaning of his death. These perspectives on Cicero, presented in a quintessentially early imperial educational format, illustrate and debate major socio-specific ways of thinking about what it meant to be Roman, in terms of the ethical continuity suggested by the concept of *mos maiorum*, in terms of culture and descent (surprisingly important in a socially mobile society with a comparatively permeable citizenship) and in political terms of identification with the *res publica*, all increasingly vexed concepts during a period of profound social, political, demographic and cultural change.[1]

Cicero was a more equivocal figure than others whose life and death might inspire early imperial reflections on how to behave when faced with tyranny. There was intense interest also in Brutus, Cassius and Cato the Younger as characters in a drama at one remove from, but with powerful resonance for, the political situations and personalities of the present regime. All three could be cast as martyrs for Roman liberty, a highly contentious term in the early imperial period.[2] However, the possibility of characterizing Cicero as a binding-link to the present as much as an epitome of the vanished past encouraged intense engagement with his status as a figure who

---

[1] Richlin 1997; David 1980; Nicolet 1991; Moatti 1997; Habinek 1998; Linke and Stemmler 2000; Pina Polo 2004; Dench 2005; Bell and Hansen 2008; Wallace-Hadrill 1997 and 2008; and see Gowing in this volume (Chapter 14).
[2] Wirszubski 1950; Macmullen 1966; Gowing 2005: 5.

represented Roman values that were alternatively compromised or continued after Actium. The identification of Cicero as quintessentially Roman in his dedication to the state and resistance to tyranny was also to form a powerful strand in European Republican thought of the early modern period.[3]

In Tacitus' dramatic recreation of Cremutius Cordus' trial under Tiberius, however, it is Cassius whom the historian allegedly called the 'last of the Romans': Cassius' death at Philippi is equated with the death of Rome itself (*Ann.* 4. 32–4). The episode of the trial, Cremutius Cordus' defence and subsequent suicide, and the futile book burning that follows is highly charged within the *Annals* as a whole, and alerts us to the complex role played by the Republican past in the *Annals* as a repository of Roman values with which the present can strive to compete.[4] While earlier Roman texts had raised issues of the decline of, threats to and change in the *res publica*, Tacitus is the first ancient author whom we can see periodizing the Republic as a distinctive, past era, an idea that is standard in the second- and third-century Roman historians writing in Greek on whom we substantially rely for the detail and colour of our Republican narratives.[5] The idea of the Republic as decisively past is introduced at the beginning of the *Annals* in a notorious rhetorical question that closes off the relentless, unstoppable and inevitable advent of monarchy at Rome: 'Who was there left who had seen the Republic?' (1.3.5).

The various meanings attributed to Cicero's death within more favourable later accounts were less decisive than 'Cremutius Cordus'' depiction of Cassius as the 'last of the Romans', but certainly played on his identification with the Roman state or with Roman cultural life. Several authors considered the relationship between Cicero's life and that of the *res publica*, the Roman state that Cicero in his *Letters* had himself lamented as lost, or in desperate straits, as early as 59 BC, threatened by the domination of individuals, although potentially 'recoverable' even in the autumn of 44 BC.[6] In Varius Geminus' version, Cicero was made to beg for his life not for his own sake but for the survival of the *res publica*, a twist on the motif of Cicero as saviour of the state that originates in his own portrayals of his consulship of 63 BC (Sen. *Suas.* 6, 13).

These allusions to the endangered nature or death of the *res publica* suggest what an emotive and contested term this was in the last decades of the Republic and in the early imperial period. This is a world away

---

[3] Fox 2007: 19; 73. See further, Chapter 17 below.
[4] Moles 1998; cf. Ginsburg 1981 and 1993.
[5] Sion-Jenkis 2000: 23; 51; 55–63; Gowing 2005: 1–27.
[6] *Q fr.* 1, 2, 15; *Att.* 2, 25, 2; *Att.* 15, 13, 4; 15, 13a, 3.

from the finality suggested by Tacitus' rhetorical question. Ironically, in the last century of 'the Republic', dominant individuals increasingly identified themselves as saviours of the *res publica*, equating the safety of their own persons with that of the state. The rhetoric of Cicero, Sulla, Julius Caesar and Augustus shares much common ground, as does the double-edged reception of these figures, each perceived in some measure as both saviour and tyrant.[7]

Velleius Paterculus' *Roman History*, written during the reign of Tiberius, insisted that the Augustan principate marked not change but the revival of the 'traditional and antique form of the *res publica*', shifting subtly but decisively the rhetoric of Augustus' own principate (2.89.3).[8] Velleius' Cicero strengthens the link between past and present, encouraged by the complex political allegiances in the last years of his life, not least by his sponsorship of the future emperor Augustus against Antony. Both his actions and his personal history are tied inextricably to the beginnings of the principate, a motif that is developed in later biographical treatments. Thus for Velleius, the emperor Augustus was born in the year of Cicero's consulship, while Suetonius goes one further and makes him born on the very day the Catilinarian conspiracy was uncovered in the senate (Vell. Pat. 1.36; Suet. *Aug.* 94).[9] According to tradition, in Plutarch's *Cicero*, Cicero identifies the then unknown future emperor as a man pointed out by Zeus/Jupiter as the future ruler of Rome (ch. 45).[10] Cicero was, Velleius says, elevated by the state to such a position of esteem that he could by his recommendation confer *principatus* ('princeps-ships') on pretty much anyone he wished (2.128.3). This concept picks up on a repetition of the term princeps and its cognates with reference to individuals from Republican history, including the notoriously austere middle Republican general Ti. Coruncanius, and Marius (2.128.1; 2.128.3).

In evocations of Cicero's death, allusions to his dismemberment, the removal of his head and hands, occur frequently, highlighting insistence in the early imperial period on Cicero as primarily an orator rather than a 'politician', but also suggesting injury to the metaphorical body of Rome.[11] For Velleius, Antony's murder and mutilation of Cicero effectively sever the *uox publica*, the collective voice of the Roman people, while his memory will co-exist with 'the continuation of the body of the universe which he almost alone of the Romans saw in his mind, embraced with his intellect, illuminated with his eloquence' (2.66.3–5). In Cornelius Severus' poetic version of the death of Cicero, 'the eloquence of the Latin tongue was made silent with

---

[7] E.g. App. *B Civ.* 1, 57; cf. 1, 77; Caes. *B Civ.* 1, 1–12; August. *RG* 1 cf. 34.
[8] Cf. Millar 1973 and 2000; Judge 1974.   [9] Cf. Schmitzer 2000: 184–9.
[10] Cf. Pierini 2003.   [11] Butler 2002; Narducci 2003b; Pierini 2003.

grief', and 'the glorious head of his fatherland' was lamented (Sen. *Suas.* 6.26; cf. 6.27). A fascinating spurious tradition on Cicero's murder holds that he was killed by Popillius, a man he had once successfully defended for parricide. The story turns on the ironic detail of Cicero, a man once hailed as *pater patriae*, 'Father of the Fatherland', killed by the accused father-killer whose name he had cleared.[12]

In these different ways, Cicero's life, his personal history and even his body were inextricably linked to the history and fortunes of Rome itself. Later traditions also explored the question of how 'Roman' Cicero really was, and the different suggestions reveal broader preoccupations with questions of Roman identity. Evaluating 'Roman' behaviour could be a question of ethics, as it frequently was in the exemplary tradition.[13] Thus, in Latro's apparently hostile version, Cicero's death was fundamentally unRoman, since it would be shameful for any Roman to beg for his life, let alone Cicero (Sen. *Suas.* 6.8). Cicero's descent could also feature in the consideration of how Roman he was, so that his self-identification as a 'new man', someone not 'ennobled' by illustrious senatorial ancestors, was picked up in reception traditions. In Sallust's *Catiline*, 'Catiline' is made to contrast his own patrician status and his extensive services to the Roman people with Cicero's status as an *inquilinus ciuis*, a 'resident alien' of the city of Rome, by implication a most unlikely saviour of it (Sall. *Cat.* 31.7; cf. [Sall.] *In M. Tullium Ciceronem oratio* 4). Cicero's 'newness' is emphasized in Velleius Paterculus' *Roman History*, providing one of several honourable precedents for Tiberius' elevation of his equestrian prefect Sejanus (2.127–8). 'New men' are a major theme of Velleius' work as a whole, one that unites his personal history with the history of Rome: his own senatorial promotion in the principate mirrors that of Sejanus, a culmination of a long-standing tendency to unite the pasts of Rome and Italy.[14]

Interestingly, Cicero's 'newness' is absent from the second- to third-century Greek narratives of the late Republic and even from Plutarch's biography. It does not figure in the long invective that Cassius Dio attributes to 'Calenus' (46.1–28), set in 43 BC and focusing rather on the 'class' issue that is a more universal feature of classical rhetoric. It is Cicero's father's supposed status as a fuller that is at the centre of the diatribe, rather than any question of how 'Roman' he is. Plutarch's biography is wholly silent on Cicero's Arpinate origins, despite its focus on Cicero the man: only Tusculum features as Cicero's place of retirement and private land (*Cic.* 40.3;

---

[12] Sen. *Controv.* 7, 2, 8; Wright 2001: 437 n. 5.
[13] Pina Polo 2004; Linke and Stemmler 2000; Bell and Hansen 2008.
[14] Gabba 1973; Dench 2005: 119–20.

cf. 47). The significant silence of Plutarch and Dio suggests that interest in figures of Italian 'new men' with origins outside the city of Rome is limited to the context of the last decades of the Republic and the early principate, the aftermath of the enfranchisement of peninsular Italy following the Social War of 91–81 BC, the period when the entry of the Italian elites into the Roman senate was such a keen issue. Fine distinctions between Romans and Italian locals made little sense to later Greek writers for whom Rome and Italy seemed essentially to be as one.[15]

On the other hand, Plutarch is interested in invective against Cicero that styles him *Graikos* as well as *scholastikos* (5.2). Plutarch's transliteration of a specifically Latin term for 'Greek' underlines the distance between his own narrative and the world of the Roman invective, remote in time as well as space. Plutarch is in general very interested in the increasingly convergent worlds of 'Rome' and 'Greece', an interest illustrated by his very choice of writing individual 'Greek' and 'Roman' lives in parallel.[16] It is Plutarch too who cites Apollonius' assessment that *paideia* ('education'), and *logos* ('speech'), the only fine things left to the Greeks after the Roman conquest, are now also in the possession of the Romans through the person of Cicero (4.5). This is a personalized twist of the adage of the Greek cultural conquest of Rome that follows the Roman military conquest of Greece, first attested in the later Republic and made famous for us in Horace's *Graecia capta ferum uictorem cepit* ('captured Greece made captive her wild conqueror') (Hor. *Epod.* 2.1.156–7).[17]

The making of Roman Italy

The figure of Cicero suggested to later authors multiple different personae and ways to think about his connection with Rome past and present. These different takes had some basis in interpretations of Cicero's own writings, and it is to these that I turn now, exploring his writing of Roman Italy before examining his constructions of himself. At the beginning of the second book of *De legibus*, Cicero, representing himself in dialogue with his brother Quintus and with Atticus, formulated an ideal relationship between individuals like Quintus and himself, or Cato the Censor before them, and their two *patriae*, Rome and the municipal town of their origins, Tusculum or Arpinum. Both the 'natural' and 'adopted' fatherlands should engender

[15] Mouritsen 1998: 9, 87–91; Dench 2005: 128–9.
[16] Jones 1971; Swain 1990 and 1996; cf. Preston 2001.
[17] Cf. Porcius Licinus fragment 1 (Courtney 2003); Cic. *Brut.* 254–5; Whitmarsh 2001: 9–12.

love and loyalty, but a hierarchy of allegiance is desirable. Thus the adopted fatherland of Rome demands total dedication, including self-sacrifice if need be (*Leg.* 2.4–5). Cicero's formulation represents one resolution of the complex political, social and cultural issues presented by the mass incorporation of the peoples of peninsular Italy into the Roman citizenship in the decades following the Social War of 91–89 BC, a radical development in the Mediterranean world, wholly unprecedented in scale. This mass enfranchisement stretched the traditional understanding of a civic community within the Greco-Roman world beyond recognition, and made Rome's political and civil institutions accessible to large numbers of Italian elites of proudly diverse cultural and linguistic backgrounds.[18] The terms of continued local self-government and the relationship with the Roman state were worked through in part via legal documents traditionally referred to as municipal 'charters'.[19]

Both the duality and the hierarchy of Cicero's formulation in *De legibus* are striking. Across the corpus of Cicero's writings, there are only hints of any local political scene, in the gentle gibes at others' attachment to their local *patria*. Marcus Marius, who stays at home in Pompeii, missing Pompey's games in 55 BC, is said to be able to enjoy the 'Oscan farces' in his local senate, while Cicero's grandfather vigorously opposes a ballot law at Arpinum that was proposed by M. Gratidius, a paltry 'storm in a wine-ladle', in contrast with the grand 'storm in the Aegean' wreaked by M. Gratidius' son, Marius Gratidianus (*Fam.* 7.1.3; *Leg.* 3.36). Any sense of local distinctiveness is rare, such as the occasion when he tries to pass off the allegation that his client raped an actress in his hometown Atina as a wholly excusable local festival version of a *droit de seigneur* (*Planc.* 12, 30–1).[20] In other contexts, Cicero invokes the regionally specific, moral-geographical categories, the association of lush peoples with lush lands or morally upright peoples with rough landscapes that recalls much older explanations of human difference in Greek thought. One such example is the speech before the people in 63 BC, where Cicero represents himself as a *popularis* consul who has the interests of the Roman people more genuinely at heart than P. Servilius Rullus, the tribune of the people who has proposed the law to allot land to the Roman poor, including a colony to Capua (*Leg. agr.* 2). Cicero portrays the landscape of Capua and the broader territory of Campania in the traditional ancient mode of 'environmental determinism',

---

[18] Wallace-Hadrill 2008: 73–143.
[19] Frederiksen 1965; Crawford 1998; Dench 2005: 173–93; Bispham 2007.
[20] Dench 2005: 186–7.

of a lush landscape that engenders decadent and tyrannical behaviour (*Leg. agr.* 2.95–7).[21]

Elsewhere, Cicero frequently represents Italian locations as essentially an extended rustic hinterland of the city of Rome, a trope that can be traced back at least to the second century BC.[22] Thus he constructs an idealized role for Italian townsmen as a supporting cast, bastions of the moral high ground, an image to which he returns frequently throughout his life, as natural supporters of himself and of various clients, as horrified witnesses of disreputable behaviour on the part of Roman magistrates, and as opponents of tyranny. These moral worthies play an important role in his constructions of various political interest groups that cut across and subvert contemporary political rhetoric. In *Pro Sestio*, Cicero counters his opponents' popularist slogan of an exclusive *natio optimatium*, 'breed of optimates', by recasting 'optimate' as a broad and inclusive term that represents the 'best' moral concerns rather than anti-popularist concerns more narrowly focused on senatorial interests. He claims that the *optimi*, the 'best', include '[Italian] townsmen, Roman country-folk, traders and also freedmen', a list that proceeds in declining order of possible appeal to images of moral worthiness (96–8).[23]

While Cicero occasionally makes appeal to the specific moral worthiness of townsmen from particular regions of Italy, a subtle clue to the importance of regionalism that we see played out in other evidence from this period, Italy and Italians are elsewhere notable rather for their vast and amorphous moral presence. Thus Cicero's *tota Italia*, 'the whole of Italy', a highly emotive slogan that will ultimately be appropriated by Augustus, is invoked as a witness to the trial of Verres in 70 BC, all in town for the elections, games and census (*Verr.* 1.54). Decades later, in the *Philippics*, Antony's procession through Italy is represented in full tyrant colours, a non-stop low-life party, while Antony indulges his appetites rather than receiving local dignitaries, and his brother is responsible for executing some of the 'best' citizens of Parma, and abusing their wives and children (*Phil.* 2.105–6; 14.8–10). The horror of this behaviour is highlighted by the backdrop of shocked Italian worthies, occasioning the pronouncement that *tota Italia* wants *libertas*, freedom from tyranny that is championed by the 'new man' Octavian. This invocation of 'new man' ideology illustrates beautifully the fluidity of its application in rhetorical contexts (*Phil.* 3.15–17; 3.32; 10.19; 13.39).

---

[21] Capua's likely effect on the colonists is also mentioned briefly in Cicero's speech before the senate (*Leg. agr.* 1, 18); for Cicero's engagement with geographical and ethnographical tropes see e.g. Vasaly 1993: 218–22; Ando 2002: 131–4; Dench 2007.

[22] Dench 1995: 85–94; Dench 2005: 172–3.   [23] See Kaster 2006; cf. Dench 2005: 182–3.

Cicero's writings dominate our evidence for first-century BC Roman Italy. Although there are hints of a different story that would put greater emphasis on local allegiance and regionalism, a keenly Romanocentric perspective on political and social life dominates. It is true that the transfigured Roman state was centripetal: political office, political institutions and the rituals of state were all based in the city of Rome, and remained so even through the considerable disruptions of the civil war of 69 AD. This insistence on Roman centrality required much energy that is visible in the peculiar emphasis on 'writing Rome' in the late Republic and early imperial period.[24]

At the level of the local town, dramatic alterations to the fabric of the community suggest the impact of political incorporation, such as monuments to Roman patrons, profound urban development, and aqueducts and baths representing the amenities of a Roman 'good life', even in more remote parts of Italy. There is a complex relationship between these developments and the increasing entry of local elites to the Roman senate at precisely this period.[25] However, there is also considerable evidence to suggest that regional specificity continued to be promoted after incorporation. This specificity is by no means antithetical to political integration. Roman institutions could enhance or recreate a sense of 'tribal' community and identity, as in the persistence of 'ethnic' units in the Roman army in the first century BC, and the combinations of peoples within the Roman voting tribes. There is intense interest in myths of origins at the end of the Republic and early imperial period, exactly at the moment when local cultures and languages were becoming less visible.[26] Individual members of the Roman senate promoted themselves by appeal to their Italian towns of origin, particularly on coinage, distinguishing themselves in the competitive environment of late Republican politics.[27] Some members of the Roman elite almost certainly enjoyed very different lifestyles when they went 'home' to their *origines*: we should not minimize the realities of cultural difference that continued well into the principate in areas such as north Etruria.[28] The dynamics of the local *patria* continued to be vital despite success in Roman politics, as suggested by the monument of the people of Superaequum honouring their patron, the Augustan proconsul Q. Varius Geminus, as 'first of all the Paelignians' to become a Roman senator (*CIL* 9,3305 = *ILS* 932).

---

[24] Giardina 1997; for the phenomenon of 'writing Rome', see Edwards 1996.
[25] Torelli 1991; Patterson 1991; Dench 1995: 140–53.
[26] Bradley 2000: 239–45; Dench 2005: 176; 200–4.
[27] Farney 2007.   [28] Terrenato 1998.

Cicero's multiple identities

This complex background of relationships between Roman and local identities highlights the particularity of Cicero's various constructions of his own personae and the spaces they inhabit. Cicero's 'foreignness', as we have begun to see, was the subject of invective, and 'newness' is certainly one of his modes of self-representation. The rhetorical figure of a 'new man', reliant on his own merits rather than on those of the ancestors paraded by the Roman 'nobility', may not actually have been invented by Cicero, but was certainly exploited extensively by him. The 'new man's' claims to be the rightful heir of the 'nobility' through his deeds and morally upright behaviour represent a brilliant strategy that both reflects and negotiates major changes in the composition of the Roman elite. To a considerable degree, assuming the figure of the 'new man' naturalizes the 'foreignness' of the individual with a place of origin outside the city of Rome. 'Newness' is a far from stable rhetorical category. The glide between 'newness' and 'nobility', to be experienced by the 'new man's' descendants, and even by himself, when he is 'ennobled' by high office, mirrors the glide between 'Roman' and 'foreign' that is exploited by Cicero in *Pro Sulla* (22–5) and that will become an increasingly potent idea in the course of the early principate as Roman citizenship is progressively extended beyond Italy.[29]

While Cicero certainly does play the role, or roles, of the 'new man', it is not clear that we should understand this 'new man' *persona* to be Cicero's 'real' identity, the key to reading the corpus as a whole. The intimate, 'confessional' tone of the *Commentariolum petitionis*, supposedly written by Quintus, with its advice to repeat as an almost daily mantra when going down to the forum, 'I am new, I seek the consulship, this is Rome', might encourage us to believe that this was a constant voice in Cicero's head (1; cf. 54). There have long been arguments about the authenticity of the text, but at the very least we might suspect that the intimate tone is highly self-conscious in a piece of electoral propaganda, within which Cicero's 'new man' *persona* is a manifesto.[30] If this were so, it would, to some extent, anticipate the fictions and adoption of personae in later 'confessional' texts, closer to Seneca's *Letters* than to Marcus Aurelius' *Meditations*.[31] In the first book of *De officiis*, an equally 'confessional' work that is framed as philosophical advice on statesmanship to Cicero's son Marcus, the subject of 'newness' is

[29] Earl 1961: 28–40; Wiseman 1971; Brunt 1982b; Flower 1996: 61–70; Dugan 2005.
[30] For the interesting recent argument that the tract was a later, tongue-in-cheek account of getting on in Roman politics, with Marcus Cicero as a negative exemplum, as well as useful references to the long debate about authenticity, see Alexander 2009.
[31] Nardo 1970; Brunt 1974; Edwards 1997.

barely raised. Marcus has his father's example to follow, so that he might be imagined to be more like the named men who either continued their fathers' particular talents or added their own than the unnamed successful men who set high goals for themselves 'despite being sprung from obscure forefathers' (*Off.* 1.116).

The lack of emphasis on 'newness' in *De officiis* can be partly explained by the transience of this attribute, but we should also take care to note the contexts within which Cicero does emphasize his own newness. This tends to happen within some of his most elaborately crafted attacks and defences, such as the *Actio secunda* of the *Verrines*. This section of the speech, which was never delivered, contains towards the end one of the fullest expositions of 'new man ideology', a reversal of assumptions about the inherited virtues of the *nobiles*. Cicero sets himself up as peculiarly suitable to take on the corruption that has destroyed the reputation of Rome, exemplified by the outrageous deeds of Verres, with the alleged complicity of his friends, including P. Scipio Nasica and Q. Hortensius, the famous orator who was defending Verres, and by the behaviour of the all-senatorial juries that had been reinstated by Sulla (a measure that would soon be partially reversed with the instatement of mixed senatorial and equestrian juries). One irony here is that Verres is arguably 'new' himself, involving Cicero in some fancy footwork in order to make his lack of awareness of the past and his pretentiousness the real problem.[32]

Cicero's emphasis here on his own 'newness' is deeply political and 'popularist' in a very Roman way, fitting for one who promises to be the champion of the Roman people in his aedileship the following year (2.1.36). The equestrian juries instituted by C. Gracchus for extortion trials had shown the 'power of the Roman people' to check senatorial behaviour (2.1.38). This tendency to collapse the equestrian order into the category of the 'Roman people' is typical of Roman 'democratic' thought in the second and early first centuries BC.[33] Cicero's insistence that the trial go forward in the presence of a large crowd 'from the whole of Italy' suggests his early political exploitation of the new electorate, and particularly the vastly expanded pool of wealthy Italians who could be mobilized to attend the voting assemblies (2.1.54). Any doubts we might still have about the extent to which Cicero is playing a role should be set aside when we witness him pretending unfamiliarity with the names of artists, such a 'textbook'

[32] Steel 2001: 35–6; 44–5.
[33] See e.g. Sherwin-White 1982 for the application of Greek democratic ideas in Gaius Gracchus' *repetundae* law, and Polybius' emphasis on the involvement of the Roman *demos* in contracts (6.17).

version of 'new man ideology' that it reminds us powerfully of Sallust's Marius.[34]

If the rhetoric of 'newness' can emphasize 'revolutionary' and popularist aspects, elsewhere the conservatism suggested by the idea that 'new men' are the rightful heirs of noble exempla and the values of *nobilitas* itself is more apparent. Thus Cicero offers a lesson in manners to the blue-blooded Appius Claudius Pulcher after the latter claims to have been snubbed in Cilicia in 51 BC. When Cicero pointedly 'teaches' Appius the true meaning of *eugeneia*, 'good birth', the nonchalant use of the Greek term and allusion to Stoic philosophy asserts a shared, privileged educational background (*Fam.* 3.7.5). At other times, Cicero's assimilation of himself to the old nobility is so complete that any indication of 'newness' disappears altogether. While Cicero in some contexts took care to line himself up with notable 'new men' of a more venerable past, such as Manius Curius Dentatus, Cato the Censor and Marius, the virtual communities that he created by the exempla he chose and the individuals he selected to play roles in his dialogues included members of the oldest and noblest Roman families. In *De oratore*, Cicero's linguistic ideal of a 'pure' Latinity is associated with old, upper-class families of Rome, best preserved, interestingly, in the female members of these families: there is a marked contrast here with Julius Caesar's apparently more 'democratic' notion that a target Latinity could be acquired by *ratio* ('reason') (*De or.* 3.45).[35] While setting himself up as arbiter of Latinity, Cicero interestingly condemned what one might have imagined to be a variation on his own self-portrayal as a 'popular' statesman: the vice of L. Cotta who, by affecting a 'rustic' accent, sought to endear himself to the Roman people (*De or.* 3.42).

Both insistence on 'newness' and assimilation to the old nobility are strikingly Romanocentric strategies. In order to explore how far Cicero's other modes of self-construction suggest a more variegated vision of Roman Italy, I shall briefly examine the various locations in which he places himself. Cicero's appeal to topography is an effective and self-conscious aspect of both his courtroom rhetoric and his philosophical treatises, and is also important in his self-representation.[36] Cicero imagines an intimate relationship between himself and the city of Rome, expressed especially through his retelling of his role in saving the city when he put down the Catilinarian conspiracy. It is closely tied to the image of a primarily civil 'politician' that he forges for himself in contrast with the military achievements, much

---

[34] Cic. *Verr.* 2.4.4; cf. 2.4.5; 2.4.134; Sall. *Iug.* 85; for 'new man' ideology, see the classic account of Wiseman 1971: 107–16.
[35] Cf. *Brut.* 211, 252, 132; Dugan 2005: 177–89; Dench 2005: 298–301.
[36] See, especially, Vasaly 1993.

promoted geographical range and imperial ambitions of other contemporary individuals and predecessors, such as Marius, Pompey and Caesar.[37] However, he also regularly goes 'on location'.

Cicero occasionally uses Arpinum as a rustic foil for the Roman centre, 'rugged Arpinum', his Ithacan homeland peopled by country bumpkins (*Att.* 2.11; 15; 16). In *De legibus*, set in Arpinum, the associations are more developed, although his formula of two *patriae* ultimately subordinates his homeland to Rome, as we have seen. In this highly crafted treatise, Arpinum is a down-to-earth, homegrown counterpart to Atticus' Athenian adoptive home or to his country house in Epirus, and the specificity of place seems to be connected with the dialogue's meditations on fiction, truth and memory. The reference at the beginning of the dialogue to the 'Arpinate oak' that figured in Cicero's lost, and perhaps quite recent poem *Marius* remind us that Arpinate origins connect him also with C. Marius, one of his new man 'ancestors' as well as, in reality, a kinsman by marriage (*Leg.* 1.1–4; 2.1–6).[38] Reading across the corpus we can see the importance of Tusculum as a third homeland of sorts, alongside Arpinum and Rome. Tusculum is at one remove, more obviously a chosen, constructed 'not-Rome', the *origo* of other notable Romans, but not of himself, and one of multiple resonances. His villa at Tusculum (a Latin town about fifteen miles to the south-east of Rome) is a frequent point of reference in letters and philosophical writings alike. It can be used to express withdrawal, the *otium* that suggests in Latin the opposite of business, *negotium*, and the pursuits that belong in such a sphere, such as philosophy and art collection. It can be the perfect space to 'go Greek', the language and culture of philosophy, art and leisure in the Roman imagination.[39] On the other hand, Tusculum is solidly 'Roman' in a very Ciceronian elision of the local Italian and Roman, as the birthplace of Cato the Censor, in subtle ways invoked as another virtual ancestor of Cicero.[40]

The 'Greekness' and the 'Romanness' of Tusculum come together in the conceit of Cato the Elder as protagonist of *De senectute* arguing 'somewhat more eruditely than he does in his books', because he has been hard at work on Greek literature in later life (*Sen.* 3). It is typical of Cicero's engagement in the connection and disconnection between business and leisure, philosophy and history, and Greekness and Romanness that he should bring together these very different kinds of values in association with Tusculum.[41] To

---

[37] Steel 2005: 32–3; 45; 63.
[38] Recent discussions of the dynamics of place in *De legibus* include Dyck 2004a; Dolganov 2008; Krebs 2009; for Cicero's representation of Marius, see Carney 1960.
[39] Cf. Wallace-Hadrill 1998.   [40] E.g. *Div.* 2.8; *Tusc.* 2.9; *Rep.* 1.1.1; *Sen.* 55.
[41] Fox 2007: 29–32.

some extent, Cicero's chosen, alternative space in which to locate himself anticipates a later, high imperial phenomenon in Italy, a kind of small-scale 'globalization' in which attachment to particular origins was increasingly challenged by mobility and lessened cultural differences.[42] The very different, still very culturally and ethnically diverse, world of Italy in which Cicero lived highlights the particularity of his constructions of person and place.

Cicero's Roman past

Cicero wrote no prose historical narrative, but was demonstrably interested in the idea and ideals of history, its relationship to truth and fiction, and its educational purposes.[43] Cicero evokes and reconstructs the past frequently, in different registers across the range of his writings, including the use of exempla in forensic contexts, the recurrent theme of his own political life and vicissitudes, and historical dialogues. Two issues are of particular relevance within a discussion of Roman identity: questions about the ownership of the past, particularly in terms of social and ethnic exclusiveness, and the use of the past as a location in which essential Roman traits, values, problems and institutions may be explored.

Issues of cultural identity, of authority over the past and of the role of individuals as protagonists within the past are already apparent in early Roman historiography. Rome's arrival as a major power within the Hellenistic world provided impetus for the kinds of history and epic poetry that located her as a member of an international community with a shared canon of Greek literature. Nevertheless, Roman writers insisted in different ways on Roman particularity, not least through specifically Roman morals and virtues that may characterize Rome in contrast to other peoples or the Roman past as distinct from its more degenerate present. The Elder Cato's *Origines* is distinctive in a number of ways, including its composition in Latin, surely an indication of the desire to particularize further. Cato apparently tended to omit the names of Roman magistrates in most of the work, perhaps suggesting some 'democratization' to counter the traditional tendency to commemorate the deeds of notable families (*HRR* F88). His inclusion of origin myths and local lore for Italian communities in the body of the work, sandwiched between Roman origins and the historical narrative, suggests some interconnection between Roman and Italian pasts,

---

[42] Purcell 1983; Purcell 2000.

[43] E.g. *De or.* 2.62; *Fam.* 5.12.3; *Leg.* 1.1–14; the beginning of *Brutus* flirts extensively with the notion of chronological narrative as a means of thinking about the subject of oratory: e.g. 14; 19; 62.

another strikingly original feature. Ultimately, the social and geographical breadth of Cato's *Origines* must be reconciled with the work's insistence on its author as prime protagonist within the making of contemporary history.[44] Literary self-commemoration, preserving and correcting memories of actions, is a marked Roman trait from the second century BC, and its authors include both members of renowned families and those from obscure backgrounds.[45]

Increased pressure on the traditional shapes of Roman society and culture, and the whole vexed question of what it meant to be Roman with a vastly expanded citizenship, find reflections in late Republican and early imperial constructions of the past. These are all issues that find particular resonance in the works of Cicero, and his crafting of his own *persona*, as we have begun to see, and they also resonate in the works of his contemporaries and near contemporaries. The writings of Varro suggest substantial interest in the geographical interconnectedness (for good or for ill) of Rome and Italy, and in the plural roots of the Latin language, which consist of numerous languages of Italy and even beyond. In Sallust's *Jugurtha*, the permeability of the Roman empire is explored through traditional tropes of moral corruption attendant on empire. Both 'new men' and foreigners learn undesirable ways from the old nobility, partially anticipating the interconnection between imperial expansion and moral corruption of Rome's subjects that is a theme of the works of Tacitus.[46] Focus on the remote past is particularly keen in the late Republic and early imperial period, and this can include both reflections on the beginnings of Rome, an essentially mythical space in which to explore traits of the present-day society, including ethnic and cultural complexity, civil war and tyranny, and myths of origins of Italian peoples. The first book of Livy's history and Virgil's *Aeneid* both attest this intense, and sometimes creative, interest.[47]

In contrast, the Roman past that Cicero recreates over the course of his dialogues is tightly focused on the city of Rome and on individual Roman statesmen. Set between 150 BC (*De senectute*) and the present day (e.g. *De legibus*), with recurrent, intergenerational casts of characters, the relationship with the present is emphasized by stories of how the dialogue was remembered and transmitted to Cicero (e.g. *De republica* 1.13), by a preface set in the present day relating the problems of the present to those of the past (e.g. *De republica* 1.1–13) or, more obliquely, by reminiscences of present-day problems in the world depicted by the historical speakers.[48] Cicero is clearly writing a certain kind of Roman historical continuity through the

---

[44] Badian 1966; Walter 2004; Beck 2007.   [45] Fox 2007: 260; Riggsby 2007.
[46] Dench 2005: 80–91.   [47] Miles 1995; Horsfall 2000.   [48] Cf. Fantham 2004: 306–7.

dialogue form, and building an eclectic virtual ancestry for the circle that he creates around himself as well as hinting at the role of the dialogues in the education of future generations. Cicero's historical settings are never entirely removed from contemporary political and social problems: Ciceronian respite is to be found in moments of pause rather than in any extended golden age. Both *De republica* and *De oratore* anticipate the violent deaths of some of their major statesman protagonists as they are caught up in a string of events known to us as 'the fall of the Roman Republic'. These deaths undermine any real confidence in the success or efficacy of individuals, including perhaps Cicero himself. Insofar as Cicero writes a historical continuity across the dialogues, it is a continuity of effort, intellectual engagement and struggle.[49]

In Cicero's version of Plato's *Republic* his characters put forward the Roman constitution as the ideal state, a jarring juxtaposition of the historical and the philosophical ideal. When pushed to choose between 'simple' constitutional forms rather than selecting the complexity of the 'mixed constitution', 'Scipio' expresses his preference for monarchy (*Rep.* 1.35; 54–5). This choice is by no means incidental: the virtues of kings during Rome's regal period anticipate the *rector* in Books 5 and 6, the idealized statesman who acts in the best interests of the *res publica*.[50] The early Rome of *De republica* is most unlike the microcosms of Roman society and its strengths and weaknesses that we see in other accounts of Rome's beginnings, and looks far more like a Never Never land. The primitivism and barbarism that are important for the 'developmental' scheme of other accounts are almost totally denied, and the role of individuals is the real point, rather than political theory, environmental considerations or any of the other more 'structural' features that one might anticipate (1.58; 2.4; 2.12; 2.17–21). The odd, unreal and disconnected nature of the benign monarchy of *De republica* might do something to lessen the shock of 'Scipio''s preference for monarchy in a world in which *regnum* was perceived to be a real threat.[51] The early Rome of *De republica* pushes to extremes several recurrent features of Cicero's constructions of Roman identity: the tight focus on the city of Rome itself, a Rome that engages with and transfigures Greek cultural contributions, and the best traditions of Rome continued by the dedication of statesmen to the *res publica*.

---

[49] Steel 2005: 136–40.
[50] For the political theory of the *De republica*, and particularly for Cicero's relationship with 'democracy', see the excellent account by Zetzel in this volume (Chapter 11).
[51] Zetzel 1995; Fox 2007: 80–110.

Conclusion

The later retrospectives on Cicero's life, death and relationship with the *res publica* with which we began suggest different resolutions of the paradoxes of his person. These are suggested either by the variant interpretations of individual authors or by formulae that bridge gaps and inconsistencies, such as Velleius Paterculus' characterization of Cicero in relation to Catiline as 'a man of the noblest newness' (*uir nouitatis nobilissimae*) (*Cat.* 2.34.3). The 'real' identity of Cicero remains, and should remain, elusive to us, although the parts that he played himself and those that he wrote for others reveal highly significant (and ultimately influential) choices about the relative positions of Rome and local *patriae*, especially if we try hard to tune in to other conversations, both those hinted at within Ciceronian texts and those suggested by other evidence.

Further reading

Cicero's self-fashioning, the socio-specifics of Roman memory and the institutional, political and cultural 'making of Roman Italy' have all been the subjects of stimulating discussion in recent years. Close readings of Cicero's self-fashioning, in his own writings, particularly as a 'new man' (excellent examples of which include Fantham 2004, Dugan 2005 and Steel 2005), as well as explorations of the afterlife of Cicero in literature of the imperial age (e.g. Wright 2001, Butler 2002, Narducci 2003a), should ideally be considered alongside broader discussions of the construction of memory and identity in the late Republic and early empire.

Cicero's tendency to populate the past with idealized individual Roman statesmen, as well as his own role in imperial memories of the Republic, encourages us to consider the broad importance of family and collective memory in Roman culture, and particularly the socio-specific emphases on *exempla* and *mos maiorum*. Stimulating contributions include Linke and Stemmler 2000, Pina Polo 2004, Gowing 2005 and Bell and Hansen 2008. Finally, Cicero's writings shape and are shaped by the enormous political, cultural and social changes of the first century BC: the after effects of the enfranchisement of Italians following the Social War and Rome's growing confidence as an imperial centre. Recent treatments, with different emphases, include: Giardina 1997, Dench 2005, Bispham 2007 and Wallace-Hadrill 2008.

PART II

The Roman politician

8

ANN VASALY

The political impact of Cicero's speeches

The subject of this chapter immediately raises a few definitional problems. First, what do we mean by 'Cicero's speeches'? The gap in time between their delivery and publication, as well as the difference in the composition and responses of a reading versus a listening audience, suggests that the same analysis would not necessarily apply to the political goals and effect of both the original and published orations. In this brief chapter I shall restrict myself to discussing the political impact of the speeches as delivered. The exact relationship of the extant texts to the original oral performances cannot be determined, but if it is reasonable to assume that one of Cicero's chief aims in publishing the works was to furnish models of his response to specific oratorical challenges, then we can presume a close similarity between what Cicero said at trial and what he later published, since the intent of both was to make the 'best case' – not only in a rhetorical, but also in a moral, legal and political sense.[1] This conclusion is not undermined by the recent work of Narducci, Habinek, Dugan, Steel and others, who propose wide-ranging social/cultural/political aims and impact for Cicero's written texts (including certain speeches), since these studies simply make clear that Cicero's purpose in publishing his speeches was not *limited* to the didactic (in a formally rhetorical sense).[2] It is still reasonable to assume, therefore, that Cicero's desire to 'monumentalize' various rhetorical events not long after they took place would have been realized only in texts that reflected reasonably accurately the arguments he made, in the way he made them.[3]

---

[1] For Cicero's desire to furnish oratorical models to the young, see Stroh 1975: 31–54. For an overview of the question, see Powell and Paterson 2004: 52–7. Lintott 2008: 15–32, like Humbert 1925, sees a number of the published speeches as a mélange of what was delivered at various points in a trial or trials. *Contra* see Vasaly 2009: 110–12, 111 n. 33.

[2] Narducci 1997a; Habinek 1998; Dugan 2005; Steel 2005 and 2006: 25–43.

[3] See, e.g., *Orat.* 131–2 for speeches illustrating how Cicero manipulated the emotions of his audience; and Narducci 1997a: 157–73 for evidence of Cicero's desire to reproduce for a reader the effect of the speeches as delivered.

An enquiry into the political impact of the speeches also raises the necessarily related topic of the nature of political power in late Republican Rome.
The question of how Cicero used his speeches to consolidate and expand
his political influence is one of extraordinary complexity, since it concerns
the relative weight of many sources of power: constitutional and extra-
constitutional, military and non-military, economic, social and religious.
An approach that dominated scholarly work in the first half of the twentieth century, and that found its most powerful expression in Ronald Syme's
Roman Revolution, tended to devalue oratory as a source of political power,
as it was based on the assumption that behind the theoretical sovereignty of
the *populus Romanus* lay an oligarchy composed of a narrow group of individuals whose influence stemmed from (1) networks of alliances within and
between elite *gentes*, supported by large numbers of compliant clients among
subordinate classes and subject peoples; and/or (2) military power, acquired
by individuals through both regular and irregular commands, and which, in
turn, provided further sources of wealth, clients and military strength.[4] In
more recent times, however, successful challenges to this approach, famously
termed the 'frozen waste theory of Roman politics' by John North, have
become common.[5] The prosopographical research that underlay the work
of Syme and others – and which used evidence of kinship and intermarriage,
mapped against the identity of those supporting or opposing this or that law
or prosecution, as a means of distinguishing consistent and persistent *factiones* – now seems to lead to a different conclusion: namely, that political
combinations in this period, if recoverable at all, often were neither consistent nor persistent, since individuals of both elite and subordinate classes
responded to a wide range of factors in responding to any particular issue.[6]
Although this does not necessarily require a positive re-evaluation of the
political impact of Cicero's speeches, the notion that the nature of political
alliances and the distribution of political power were much more complex
than previously acknowledged does raise the possibility that Ciceronian oratory might have tapped into various sources of power in ways not previously
acknowledged.

---

[4] This view of the sources of political power sharply minimized the role of Cicero's oratory
in his advancement. Syme, for instance, wrote that 'ambition and vanity blinded [Cicero]
to the true causes of his own elevation'. Syme 1939: 11.
[5] North 1990: 7.
[6] See esp. discussions of *amicitia*, *clientela* and *factiones* in Brunt 1988: 351–81, 382–442,
442–502; with overview of Alexander 2007: 102–3.

The speeches as sources of *gratia*

An ancient work that illuminates for us at least some general aspects of how the *quid pro quo* between advocacy and political support functioned in Cicero's early speeches is the treatise in letter-form attributed to Q. Cicero, the *Commentariolum petitionis*.[7] The author, advising Cicero as candidate in the run-up to the election for the consulship of 63, asserts at the outset that Cicero's success was owed entirely to his oratory: 'Whatever you are, you are because of this' (2: *quicquid es ex hoc es*). He then goes on to provide an extremely hard-headed, if not cynical, view of the role that oratory played in the creation and expansion of Cicero's influence among the individuals and groups on which his election would depend. To be constantly seen surrounded by an attendant crowd of those he had successfully defended is said to bring him *summa dignitas* (38); such individuals, in turn, could give the orator access to an extensive group of enthusiastic supporters, who were friends, clients, fellow townsmen and fellow tribesmen of those he had defended. Cicero might count, for instance, on the energetic support of many of the *publicani* and other members of the equestrian order who had frequently received his legal help, as well as on the enthusiasm of the masses and of popular leaders who had been won over by his praise of Pompey and by his willingness to take on the cases of the *populares* C. Manilius (*tr. pl.* 66) and C. Cornelius (*tr. pl.* 67).[8] Towards the end of the work, the author even advises Cicero to pretend to accept cases he had no intention of arguing, in order to avoid angering potential supporters.

Similar indications of the political utility of advocacy appear in Cicero's own works. In his judicial speech of 63 for L. Murena, for instance, Cicero patiently explains to Sulpicius Rufus, the eminent jurisconsult defeated by Murena in the consular elections of that year, that only excellence in either military affairs or oratory could create the kind of public presence that would lead to election to the consulship. In regard to the latter, he states that it was not surprising that even *noui homines* had achieved the consulship through oratorical ability, since it created *plurimas gratias, firmissimas amicitias, maxima studia* (24, 'the greatest influence, the strongest friendships, and

---

[7] See general introduction to the work by Laser 2001: 3–52. The date and authorship of the treatise remain unclear. Lintott 2008: 130–3 does not rule out the possibility that it was in fact written *c.* 64 by Quintus and meant for 'discreet circulation' (131).

[8] *Comment. pet.* 50–1. On the speech for Cornelius (*tr. pl.* 67), see Crawford 1994: 33–41; Laser 2001: 179; Lintott 2008: 112–25. It is unclear whether Cicero merely agreed publicly to defend Manilius (*tr. pl.* 66) or actually did so at the latter's aborted trial in 65. See Ramsey 1980; Crawford 1994: 67–148; Laser 2001: 174–5.

the highest enthusiasm'); or, as he says later, oratory involved *magna res, magna dignitas, summa autem gratia* (29, 'great affairs, great reputation, and, moreover, the most extensive influence'). Cicero also highlights the political rewards of successful oratory in the *Brutus*, whose extended roll call of successful orator-politicians constitutes a testament to such rewards. Included is a certain Q. Arrius, elected praetor for 73. Cicero compares Arrius to another orator who, although lacking talent, possessed a certain 'verbal fluency' (242: *uerborum copiam*) that produced an enthusiastic following among the public. Cicero continues (242–3):

> He [Arrius] ought to be an example to all how much potency there is in this city in serving the needs of many and being of use to many either in their campaigns for office or legal peril. For by doing these things, although born of the lowliest rank, he achieved offices and money and influence; and without learning, without inborn talent, he even achieved a place among the ranks of advocates.[9]

Even those most sceptical of the importance of Cicero's oratory in his advancement would acknowledge the role it played in the accumulation of the political capital vital to his attainment of the various steps in the *cursus honorum* prior to his election as consul for 63. By means of his speeches, especially the judicial speeches, he obligated many of those on whose behalf he acted to support his electoral ambitions. Building on family connections that procured him early training from and access to such eminent statesmen as L. Licinius Crassus and the Mucii Scaevolae, he enlarged his circle of associations through assiduous cultivation and legal support of individuals from various classes, especially the *equites* – including younger members of noble families, municipal elites and those involved in commercial ventures, the *publicani*.[10] *Pro Roscio Amerino* provides a good example of how this worked. The defence was risky, as it necessitated an attack on a freedman of Cornelius Sulla, who at that time wielded a dangerous degree of power within the state. Taking on this, his first criminal defence, however, ultimately proved prudential, since he thereby strengthened his connections to

---

[9] *is omnibus exemplo debet esse quantum in hac urbe polleat multorum oboedire tempori multorumque uel honori uel periculo seruire. his enim rebus infimo loco natus et honores et pecuniam et gratiam consecutus etiam in patronorum, sine doctrina, sine ingenio, aliquem numerum peruenerat.* Cf. Cicero's discussion of the success of M. Crassus (triumvir), who lacked both natural talent and an impressive delivery, and in whose case *gratia* is both a consequence and a tool of advocacy: *quod adhibebat ad obtinendas causas curam etiam et gratiam in principibus patronis aliquot annos fuit* (He was for some years among the chief advocates because he brought diligence and even influence to bear in winning legal cases) (*Brut.* 233). On the more tangible rewards of prosecution, such as money and/or offices, see Alexander 1985.

[10] On Cicero's forensic success and the *equites*, see Berry 2003.

the powerful young *nobiles* who had asked him to take on the case, while the resounding success of his performance resulted in greatly increasing the requests for his advocacy, leading in turn to the multiplication of such ties.[11]

Also potentially risky was his prosecution of Verres in 70, since the gratitude to be expected from the Sicilians and others who wished Verres punished might have been offset by the ill-will created among Verres' powerful defenders, including leading members of the senate such as Verres' advocate (and consul-elect) Q. Hortensius, Q. Lutatius Catulus and certain of the Metelli.[12] Furthermore, while it was expected that high-profile prosecutions would be launched by ambitious young politicians at the beginnings of their careers, Cicero was already thirty-six years old at the time of the trial and aedile-elect, leaving him open to charges of using the resources of the state for his own aggrandizement, while destroying the life and career of a fellow citizen. His rhetorical transformation of the prosecution into a defence – of just provincial government, of an honest court system, ultimately of the *res publica* itself – was successful, however, in maximizing the positive impact of the case, and he emerged as the leading judicial orator in Rome and, somewhat ironically, the recipient of requests for his services from prominent ex-provincial governors like M. Fonteius, who was accused of the same sort of actions in Gaul as Verres had been in Sicily, and whom he successfully defended, probably in 69.

The latter part of his career shows the functioning of *gratia* in somewhat different ways. In a letter to Atticus in 59, for instance, Cicero mentions the widespread good will (*studia*) he believed he was accumulating from his constant advocacy, asserting that this had made him confident that he would not need to fear a coming clash with Clodius (*Att.* 2.22.3). After his return from exile many of Cicero's judicial orations more clearly reflect his need to repay obligations rather than to create new ones. Men like Sestius and Milo, for instance, who loyally supported him during the Catilinarian crisis and throughout his exile, received his enthusiastic, if not always successful, advocacy when they were attacked in these years. Assuming such *officia* was not simply an ethical obligation but was vital to Cicero's ability to maintain some degree of political power, since those who were seen as incapable of rewarding their friends or punishing their enemies naturally suffered a marked diminution of influence. Calculating the 'cost-benefit ratio' in certain requests for legal representation entertained by Cicero in the fifties, however,

---

[11] Cicero states that the status of those who asked him to take on the case, and his
    obligations to them, were such that a refusal would have been impossible (*Rosc. Am.* 1).
    For their identity, see Gruen 1968: 266.
[12] For a summary of the many theories concerning the identity of Verres' supporters and
    opponents, see Vasaly 2009: 103.

is anything but straightforward for us (nor was it for Cicero). The case of A. Gabinius is illustrative. Few individuals were more publicly denounced by Cicero as an enemy than Gabinius. As consul with L. Calpurnius Piso in 58 he had refused to intervene on Cicero's behalf when threatened by Clodius, and upon Cicero's return from exile Cicero had attacked him virulently in a number of speeches. Even remaining neutral when Gabinius was on trial in 54, therefore, would have highlighted (and thus contributed to) Cicero's lack of political influence, given this well-aired hostility. The orator, however, was under obligation to all three of the so-called 'triumvirs' for his continued immunity from the attacks of Clodius and his many other enemies, and when Pompey pressed Cicero to defend Gabinius (much as Caesar had done in the case of Vatinius a few years earlier), Cicero ultimately agreed, despite the fact that he had earlier said that doing so would bring him 'everlasting shame' (*Q fr.* 3.4.3: *infamiam sempiternam*). His submission to such demands thus smacked more of a response to intimidation, rather than to a traditional request for repayment of a political obligation.[13]

The speeches and the Roman crowd: contional oratory

Interpreting Cicero's oratory in this way – i.e., viewed externally, as a bargaining chip in a political game, more or less valuable as circumstances varied – cannot stand alone as an accurate description of the role that the speeches played in Cicero's political career. As mentioned above, many challenges have arisen to the idea that power in the late Republic was what happened behind the scenes rather than in public, and some of the most significant focus on the role that the Roman voter played in the political process. Not only have many become sceptical of the idea that large blocks of voters could be effectively controlled by a small number of noble *patroni*, but Fergus Millar has argued that 'our whole conception of the Roman Republic has been distorted by theories that have allowed us not to see [the] open-air meetings (*contiones*) of the *populus Romanus* as central to Roman politics'. Millar's intention, therefore, has been 'to place the *populus Romanus* – or the crowd that represented it – at the center of our picture of the Roman system'.[14]

---

[13] Cicero masks his shame for acceding to such demands in his letter to P. Lentulus (*Fam.* 1.9) by citing his personal relationship to Pompey and Caesar, the prudence of bowing to superior power and the *inconstantia* of many of the so-called *optimates*. For discussion of ancient evidence, see Fantham 1975. Cf. Crawford 1984 *ad loc.* for the unpublished *Pro Messio, Pro Druso, Pro Caninio Gallo, Pro Gabinio*, and Crawford 1994: 271–80 for discussion of *Pro Vatinio*, all delivered at the urging of the 'triumvirs'.

[14] Millar 1998: 1. On scholarly overstatement of the importance of clientage in elections, see Brunt 1988: 382–442 ('*Clientela*').

How this popular element functioned and what weight it carried in the political arena continues to generate fierce debate among historians, and Cicero's contional speeches constitute key pieces of evidence. In Millar's view, the restoration in 70 of full tribunician powers, especially that of proposing legislation, represented a turning point, after which the Roman forum for some twenty years became the chief venue for discussion of key issues affecting 'the constitution of the republic and the government of the empire' (84). While acknowledging the increasing use of violence during this period and the 'need to control the Forum physically' (84), Millar nevertheless argues that contional oratory involved genuine debate by opposing politicians on fundamental political issues, followed by the final test of the relative success of these competing appeals through the votes of the people in the *comitia tributa*. His analysis of *Pro lege Manilia* of 66, for instance, highlights Cicero's argument that the assignment to Pompey of command in the war against Mithradates was demanded by the practical needs of empire, which took precedence over the tradition of shared command, an argument that was opposed by Hortensius, Catulus and others, who warned of the dangers to the state if such great power were concentrated in the hands of a single individual.

This somewhat idealized view of the political impact of Cicero's contional speeches has been questioned by, among others, Robert Morstein-Marx, who – covering much the same territory as Millar – steers a thoughtful middle course between those, on the one hand, who see these public debates as largely irrelevant to decisions about legislative initiatives since the outcomes were ultimately determined by a combination of factional coalitions, violence, intimidation and bribery; and those, on the other, who find in them the workings of a genuinely democratic constitution, in which key questions affecting the state were resolved by appeal to the judgement of those members of the *populus Romanus* who took part in the *contiones* and voted on any particular issue.[15] Morstein-Marx does not doubt the enormous power that the masses exercised in late Republican politics, but believes that this power was not an avenue for constraining the elite to respond to their needs. Rather, popular power became another means by which competing members of the elite sought to bludgeon their opponents. In his view, *contiones* were often carefully orchestrated events used by one side or another to demonstrate, and thereby expand, consensus, and to put pressure on opponents (even when the latter were given a nominal opportunity

[15] Morstein-Marx 2004; cf. an even stronger challenge to Millar in Hölkeskamp 2010. See also Tan 2008 on the use of the *contio* by *populares* more frequently than by their opponents. For a good introduction to the subject of popular power, see Yakobson 2006. On the *contio* generally, see Pina Polo 1996.

to make their case) to accede to the 'popular will'. Given the volatility and heterogeneity of contional audiences, however, as well as the varying rhetorical and organizational abilities of *contio*-holders, their success as instruments of 'opinion-and-will-formation' (158) was never a given, especially in the early run-up to legislation.

Viewed in this way, the putative aims and possible impact of the contional speeches cannot be clearly discerned merely through study of their content, but must be carefully read against the particular circumstances surrounding the holding of the *contio*. Thus Cicero's delivery of *Pro lege Manilia* on behalf of a cause that had already developed almost unstoppable momentum enlarged the orator's political status by putting him at the centre of a successful demonstration of mass support for the assignment to Pompey of the command against Mithradates, rather than because it showed his ability in open debate to convince still-undecided voters of the wisdom of a particular course of action. *De lege agraria* 2, on the other hand, in which Cicero as consul countered the proposal of a tribune of the people to distribute land to the poor by 'proving' that behind the bill was a plot to remove the people from Rome to undesirable lands, undermine Pompey's status and assign quasi-regal powers to the proposal's chief sponsors and supporters, did reflect a stage during the law's progress towards passage in which genuine debate was possible. The speech therefore highlighted and extended Cicero's influence by showing his effective use of *popularis* rhetoric to defeat a *popularis* proposal before the very people who would have profited by its passage.

Considering the effect of Cicero's speeches upon the Roman public leads to another aspect of this interaction. The 'master of special speech' – as Thomas Habinek describes the Roman orator-politician – was constantly an object of display and evaluation: when he received *salutatores* in the morning; when he emerged from his house and descended to the forum, accompanied by a crowd of supporters; when he greeted and engaged in conversation with various individuals of all classes in the course of the day.[16] Whom he spoke to and how, what he wore, how he wore it, the appearance of his face and body, his gestures, the pitch and rhythm of his voice, all carried cultural, and therefore political, meaning. Public address was therefore not the only opportunity for image formation and self-representation, but it was surely the most critical, for here the orator exposed himself to the highest

---

[16] For the phrase, see Habinek 2005: ch. 1 *passim. Comment. pet.* 17 advises the orator to pay close attention even to the impression he makes on his slaves, since 'almost all the gossip that creates public reputation springs from sources within the household'. Cf. Connolly 2007a on the role of the Roman public in judging the worth of the public figure through his performances before them.

expectations regarding his appearance and performance in front of the largest number of judges. He risked not only failure to persuade his audience on the particular subjects on which he spoke, but overall diminishment of his *dignitas*, a key form of political capital. Conversely, a performance that was approved and admired (even, in some cases, if it were not ultimately successful in swaying the votes of jury, senate or assembly) increased that capital. The many scholarly forays in recent years into such issues, which depend especially on the texts of Cicero to explore cultural norms of appearance and behaviour in the late Republic, illustrate Cicero's ability to undermine the *dignitas* and *auctoritas* of his opponents – and increase his own – by placing them outside these norms. In the *Second Catilinarian* (17–23), for instance, he castigates not only the aims of the conspirators, but also the effeteness of their dress and hairstyles; in a number of speeches following his exile he ridicules L. Calpurnius Piso for his long 'philosophical' beard and dour manner, which belied his true character, while at the same time criticizing Piso's fellow consul of 58, Gabinius, as a fop and a dancer; and throughout much of his career he refers with devastating effect to the physical deformities of the popular politician, P. Vatinius.[17] Within the defensive passages in the speeches we also find evidence of ways in which Cicero's own public performances might have been targeted, especially in the latter part of his career: e.g., for excessive humour, theatricality, appeal to the emotions, aestheticism and effeminacy, much of which material can be subsumed under aspects of oratory associated with 'Asianism'.[18]

The speeches and the Roman crowd: judicial oratory

While it can thus be argued that every Ciceronian speech was 'political' in this larger sense, how do we assess the impact of the explicit political commentary in some of the judicial speeches? Current scholarly orthodoxy tends either to limit absolutely the political aims of such speeches to the *gratia* and *dignitas* associated with an admirable performance and a positive outcome or, at least, rigorously to subordinate political content to these aims.[19] In

---

[17] For a survey and interpretation of such characterizations, and the related issues of invective and wit/humour, see Corbeill 1996: esp. 14–56; and Corbeill 2002. Cf. Dyck 2001; Craig 2004; Arena 2007.

[18] For Cicero's literary attempts to adapt his style and action to the narrow limits of normative elite behaviour, or to widen those limits, see esp. Dugan 2005. On aestheticism, see Krostenko 2001: 154–201. Concerning issues of gender, sexuality and rhetoric, see Richlin 1992 and 1997; Gleason 1995; Gunderson 2000; Langlands 2006: 281–318; Connolly 2007b. On social norms more generally, see Edwards 1993.

[19] The discussion that follows is in part reproduced from Vasaly 2009 (there with specific application to the First Action of the *Verrines*).

what is termed the 'persuasive process' approach in rhetoric, we are asked to read a Ciceronian forensic speech as the reflection of the progressive manipulation of an audience in which each part in sequence attempted to move its hearers towards a desired practical end, namely judicial victory. Political comment is thus interpreted, first and foremost, as a means of achieving this goal.[20] And, indeed, sophisticated analysis has shown that even passages in the judicial speeches that at one time were interpreted as clearly digressive – *Pro Sestio* provides perhaps the best examples – in fact can be shown to serve the practical needs of advocacy.[21]

The idea that the political content of a judicial speech should be read in this way has also found support in an often-quoted passage from *Pro Cluentio* of 66, in which Cicero responds to the fact that his opponent had read a passage from an earlier speech (probably *Verr.* 1.38–40), suggesting that Cicero believed that an earlier trial had been corrupt, whereas in his defence of Cluentius eight years later he argues that the verdict in the same trial had been correct. Cicero states that the opinions voiced in the earlier speech responded to 'my circumstances rather than my considered judgement' (139: *potius temporis mei quam iudicii et auctoritatis*). He continues (139):

> But a person would be greatly in error if he were to think that our formally attested judgements are contained in the speeches we have given in the law courts. For all of these belong to particular circumstances and occasions, not to the men or advocates themselves.[22]

Cicero then recalls that the great orator L. Licinius Crassus had been embarrassed when an opponent read out contradictory passages concerning the authority of the senate contained in two of the latter's deliberative speeches. While Crassus was able to deflect this attack with wit, Cicero speculates that he was nevertheless annoyed to have been criticized 'in respect to those

---

[20] A second, related issue is whether jurors were assumed to base their decisions (and the advocate, his chief arguments) on an assessment of the legal guilt or innocence of the accused, rather than on extraneous matters, such as, e.g., the advocate's (or prosecutor's or defendant's) *auctoritas*, or their own interests as a political/social class, or their pity for or anger at the accused. If Riggsby 1999 and others are correct that this, indeed, was the expected criterion of judgement, then Cicero's extant forensic speeches – which regularly encourage jurors to base their decisions on other issues and often give only *pro forma* attention to legal proof – show that this expectation was regularly flouted in the published (i.e., paradigmatic) works of the acknowledged master of forensic oratory. For discussion of juror expectations, see Powell and Paterson 2004: 1–43.

[21] Cf., e.g., Classen 1985 for the contribution of political material to Cicero's legal strategy in several judicial speeches. On *Pro Sestio*, see esp. Craig 2001; Kaster 2006.

[22] *Sed errat uehementer, si quis in orationibus nostris, quas in iudiciis habuimus auctoritates nostras consignatas se habere arbitratur. Omnes enim illae causarum ac temporum sunt, non hominum ipsorum aut patronorum.*

speeches he had given about political matters [i.e., deliberative orations], in which, perhaps, consistency ought more to be demanded'.[23]

Even this passage, however, seemingly a straightforward caveat against taking political comment in a judicial speech 'politically', hints at a more complex way of reading this material. In the reference to Crassus, Cicero notes that he took pains to clarify to his audience the differing circumstances surrounding his two speeches so as to explain how each responded to a different 'reality and motivation' (*Clu.* 141: *exposuit utriusque rationem temporis ut oratio ex re et ex causa habita uideretur*). Although Cicero's diction here is vague, the passage suggests that Crassus was not seeking simply to argue that his inconsistency was unimportant, but rather that it arose from reading his words out of context, and that once that context was restored the inconsistency disappeared. Cicero's diction in the statement quoted from *Pro Cluentio* (139) is also noteworthy. The words he uses to refer to an orator's 'real' opinions, as opposed to those he might espouse in a judicial speech, *auctoritates consignatas* (cf. 139: *iudici et auctoritatis*), are decidedly legalistic; they refer not to what the orator simply believed but what he had formally attested to. Cicero seems to be saying, then, that political opinions voiced in a judicial speech do not have the status of senatorial *sententiae*, much less of testimony taken under oath. As an advocate in a judicial case, the orator was free to alter earlier judgements made in the same milieu without having his ethical status impugned.

We should note, here, that at no point in *Pro Cluentio* does Cicero admit that his earlier statement about Oppianicus' trial had been a lie; rather, he claims that he had believed 'rumour' (139) and 'popular opinion' (142) about the matter, which he later determined to have been in error. This is unsurprising, since if an advocate were to admit that any statement in a past oration was false and made simply to win his case, he would lead his audience to assume that the same might be true of what he was saying to them in the present. In *Pro Roscio Amerino*, for instance, Cicero states in the exordium (1–5) that one of the reasons that he had been asked to defend Roscius was that the case demanded that Roscius' advocate speak about the political situation, which he would be able to do more easily than more eminent men because, as a young and relatively unknown orator, his comments would be less likely to be misinterpreted and, in any case, would be less widely circulated. Towards the end of the speech Cicero states that not all of his remarks were made as part of his advocacy for Roscius, but rather respond to his own feelings and beliefs (129); and in the peroration

---

[23] *Clu.* 141, *in eis orationibus . . . quas de re publica habuisset, in quibus forsitan magis requiratur constantia.*

he makes an eloquent plea for the return of *humanitas* to a state that had
become inured to the habits of cruelty brought on by the civil war (153–4).

Now, whether or not we wish to argue that Cicero wanted his audience
to remember these remarks beyond the time of the trial and use them as a
guide to his political stance, it seems clear that at the time he delivered them
he wanted his audience to believe that he was speaking truthfully about his
own political beliefs. Allowing them to question the sincerity of his remarks
De republica could not help but simultaneously undermine the *ethos* he
had crafted throughout the speech – one crucial to his defence of Roscius.
Whatever we make of the broader impact of such passages, Cicero would
have realized that, to the same degree that they were persuasive (and he could
not but hope that they would be persuasive), these remarks would have been
received seriously by the audience as a form of political self-representation.
This insight, in turn, should help us to see the passages in *Pro Cluentio* for
what they are: part of Cicero's efforts to prevent what he had said in an
earlier trial from harming his defence of Cluentius in 66. The very fact that
he took such pains to prevent the audience of *Pro Cluentio* from taking his
earlier remarks as representing his authentic political beliefs indicates that
this was exactly what Roman orators must have expected their audiences to
do.[24] Cicero's assertion here that political comment within a judicial speech
should not be connected to the orator as a public figure ought not, therefore,
to be taken as a general guide to interpreting this material.

Simply demonstrating that political material in a judicial speech advanced
the goals of practical advocacy is not sufficient to show that this was the primary reason that Cicero included it within a speech or that broader political
goals might not have been as important as its usefulness in persuading a jury
to find in the advocate's favour. After all, Cicero enjoyed virtually unlimited
licence in what he chose to say in a prosecution or defence speech. Unlike his
modern counterpart, a Roman advocate was not prevented from introducing topics that were 'irrelevant and immaterial', from personally vouching
for the truth of his assertions or from encouraging 'jury nullification'.[25]

[24] Cf. Powell and Paterson 2004: 19–29; Burnand 2004. The latter sees the remarks in *Pro
Cluentio* as part of an (unresolved) tension between disinterested professionalism and
personal patronship in the Roman advocate's role. Note, however, the disdain often
connected by Cicero precisely to advocacy that could be pictured as 'professional'.

[25] The following is quoted by Goodwin 2001: 58 n. 7: 'A lawyer shall not...in trial,
allude to any matter that the lawyer does not reasonably believe is relevant or that will
not be supported by admissible evidence, assert personal knowledge of facts in issue
except when testifying as a witness, or state a personal opinion as to the justness of a
cause, the credibility of a witness, the culpability of a civil litigant or the guilt or
innocence of an accused' (American Bar Association 3.4[e]). The issue of 'vouching' has
been discussed by Frier 1997.

His motivation for including political comment within a particular judicial speech might, on the one hand, represent a short-term strategic move intended to make a fleeting impact on a jury and then fade from public memory; or it might represent an attempt by the orator to use aspects of the speech as crucial to a consistent, long-term programme of 'political self-fashioning'. No matter where Cicero's aims fell on this spectrum in any particular speech, we would expect that he would have been able to find ways to make political comment also serve the interests of practical advocacy. In fact, this would not be particularly challenging since (1) much 'political' material readily falls into the categories of *inventio* laid out in late Republican rhetorical handbooks which advise the orator e.g., to create a positive *ethos* for himself as a *ciuis bonus*, or to argue the qualitative status of an act by claiming that his client's action served the *res publica*, or to 'generalize the case' by showing how an issue that might otherwise seem of importance only to his client was of crucial importance to the state; (2) a Roman jury was sensitive to the political status of an advocate, so any attempt to draw on and enlarge a speaker's *auctoritas* and *dignitas* served both short-term practical goals and long-term political goals; and (3) the general understanding that in the *iudicia publica* the larger interests of the state were at stake made it easier for either a prosecutor or a defence attorney to introduce political topics into the proceedings.[26]

Although space does not permit a detailed investigation of the range of recent explorations of the possible political aims and impact of various judicial speeches, in general such work tends to move analysis of the construction of Ciceronian *ethos* beyond the pragmatic goal of persuasion of a particular jury in a particular case.[27] At key moments in his career Cicero seized the public platform furnished by a high-profile trial to craft (or recraft) his public image in memorable ways: thus in the defining moment of his early career, the prosecution of Verres, he injected himself into the contemporary debate on jury composition and treatment of provincials, cleverly defining himself as both critic and defender of senatorial power; during the Catilinarian

---

[26] On the *iudicia publica*, see Riggsby 1999: 157: 'The public courts are those where the community protects itself, its property, and its rights.' Since, on the one hand, scholars wishing to demonstrate how political comment supported Cicero's attempts to win his legal cases frequently acknowledge that such comment enhanced Cicero's overall political position; and, on the other, those describing the importance of such material to the orator's political self-representation often readily concede the part played by the same material in persuading the jury, we may have arrived at a distinction without a difference.

[27] For analyses of how political content functioned at the same time within and outside the court in Ciceronian forensic speeches, see, e.g., Axer 1989; Rose 1995; Narducci 1997a: 3–18; Leff 1998; Steel 2001; Dugan 2005: 55–66; Stem 2006; Vasaly 2009.

crisis he turned his defence of Murena into a revelation of and referendum on his own political-philosophical principles; in the year following his consulship, he countered the attacks of the tribune Nepos and others by using his judicial speech on behalf of P. Sulla to defend both his execution of the conspirators and his subsequent use of his *auctoritas* to convict others accused of complicity in the plot; and confronting his greatly diminished role in politics in the fifties, he exploited both deliberative and judicial speeches to recast his exile as a heroic self-sacrifice for the good of all, while building on the disjunctive political rhetoric employed during his consulship to cast his opponents (like the Catilinarians before them) as enemies of the *res publica* and of all loyal citizens, while casting himself and his allies as the Republic's true defenders.[28] It should be noted that such approaches implicitly reject the idea that Cicero's judicial orations are morally and ethically neutral instruments of legal argumentation. Rather, they force us to reconnect the speeches to the world outside the confines of the court and to make Cicero – for good or ill – responsible for the political impact of the strategies he chose to employ.

Cicero's ideal orator

How did Cicero himself describe the goals that should be attached to oratory? The conception of the ideal orator contained both in the speeches and in the theoretical works is intensely 'political' insofar as it rejects the idea of facility in speaking as narrowly circumscribed by the exigencies of any particular event, but rather views it as a means by which the best statesman achieved an ethically virtuous end: i.e., the preservation of the state in its best form. Indeed, this is the only thing that distinguishes the ideal orator from the popular demagogue, since both are willing to use oratory to rouse the emotions of the masses.[29] In *De oratore* 1.102, for instance,

---

[28] On creation of *ethos* generally, see May 1988. For the *Verrines*, see Vasaly 2009; for *Pro Murena*, see, e.g., Leff 1998; Steel 2001, who reads the speech as part of an enactment of Cicero's value to the state at a moment of crisis that goes beyond what is needed simply to support his client (172), although in general she claims only the 'weaker senses' (15) of political content in the forensic speeches; Stem 2006. For aims of, and appeal to, *auctoritas* in the *Pro Sulla*, see Berry 1996a: esp. 26–33, 293–4; Goodwin 2001. For Cicero's recasting of exile, see Claassen 1992: 31–40; Robinson 1994; Narducci 1997b; Dyck 2004b. For rhetorical 'creation' of the *res publica*, see discussion in Dugan 2009: 180–3.

[29] For *De oratore*, see May and Wisse 2001. See Narducci 1997a: 93–5 on Crassus' recognition in *De or.* 3.55 of the dangers of the orator's mastery of *simulatio* and the requirement, therefore, that his broad education make him a *uir bonus* (since, as Crassus says, giving such powers to a person without integrity and wisdom (*probitate summaque prudentia*) would be like 'giving arms to madmen').

L. Crassus – after noting the ability of the ideal orator to expose and punish criminals and protect the innocent – summarizes his powers in the following way:

> [he is] one who can arouse an apathetic and erring people to what is fitting, or lead them away from error, or inflame them against wicked men or allay their anger against good men; who, finally, through his oratory, is able to excite or calm any emotion in men's minds as circumstances and occasion may require.[30]

Cicero's ideal use of oratory in politics, then, is never 'democratic', in the sense that he does not conceive of its optimal function as presenting the best possible arguments on any issue to the people, who then are meant to weigh each side dispassionately and make an informed decision. Rather, oratory is a tool to manipulate an audience, most effectively by playing on their emotions. The point is not necessarily for them to understand or reason, but to respond, by thinking and acting in a way that the orator alone has determined to be most advantageous to the state. Revealing in this regard is Cicero's frequent metaphor of the ideal orator as the pilot or helmsman who guides the ship of state.[31] While the masses are to be counted among the souls on board who depend on the wisdom and experience of the helmsman (as in, e.g., *Dom.* 137: *demerso populo Romano*), at the same time they are implicitly envisioned as the storm itself, who, when whipped up by the demagogues, create the greatest danger to the survival of the ship.[32] It is the highest office of the statesman-orator, therefore, to control this element for the good of all.

At few points in Cicero's career do we see him embodying this ideal. Certainly not in the latter fifties, when, starting with his 'palinode' supporting the extension of Caesar's power in Gaul, he bowed to the prevailing winds and put his oratorical skills at the service of Pompey, Crassus and Caesar.

---

[30] *idemque languentem labentemque populum aut ad decus excitare aut ab errore deducere aut inflammare in improbos aut incitatum in bonos mitigare; qui denique, quemcumque in animis hominum motum res et causa postulet, eum dicendo uel excitare possit uel sedare.* Cf. *De or.* 1.30.

[31] For discussion of the metaphor, see May 1980. Cf. Quint. *Inst.* 2.17.26–9 for defence of an orator's use of deception and appeals to the emotion to achieve laudable ends (following his comparison of the orator to the ship's pilot in 2.17.24).

[32] Cf. Piso and Gabinius as *duo turbines rei publicae* (*Sest.* 25); the *tempestates* of *seditiones* and *discordia* (*Sest.* 46); Cicero's withdrawal into exile as avoiding *fluctus* and *tempestas* of sedition roused by his opponents (*Sest.* 73); the *multitudo* who arouse *fluctus* in the state (*Sest.* 99); Cicero like a ship's pilot who has braved the *tempestates* and *praedones* (i.e., of the conspiracy) (*Mur.* 4); electorate as sea strait with *motus, agitationes, commutationes fluctuum* (*Mur.* 35); electorate compared to *tempestates* (*Mur.* 36).

With the exception of the period after Caesar's assassination (covered elsewhere in this volume), it is only in the orations of his consulship that we see Cicero's astonishingly successful use of a variety of oratorical genres – contional, senatorial, judicial – to achieve his overriding political goals: preservation of the republic as a system of government and of the power and privileges of the senate within that system (on both of which his own *auctoritas* and *dignitas* rested).[33] In the *De lege agraria* speeches, Cicero acted in defence of what might be termed 'conservative interests' – not only in opposing a land distribution bill, but in successfully opposing a bill on public policy that originated with a *popularis* tribune of the people, rather than in the senate. In the defence of C. Rabirius against the legal attack launched by Julius Caesar and others shortly thereafter, Cicero argued the legality of Rabirius' ostensibly unconstitutional action when, some thirty-seven years previously, the latter had murdered the radical tribune Saturninus under the auspices of the *senatus consultum ultimum*, 'the ultimate decree' – a tellingly prescient defence of the very powers Cicero himself would exercise in executing the Catilinarian conspirators a few months later. In this speech Cicero experimented – as he had in the *De lege agraria* speeches – with a number of rhetorical themes that would loom large during the Catilinarian crisis, most notably: the characterization of his opponents as false friends of the people and himself as a true *popularis* (the reverse template of his frequent strategy before his consulship of using rhetoric that was ostensibly sympathetic to conservative interests in support of popular positions);[34] and the characterization of the political composition of the state as consisting of a minority who aimed to undermine it and a united majority of loyal men

---

[33] Cicero's political vision in the latter part of his career (often summarized both personally and politically in the phrase *cum dignitate otium*) receives its most extensive articulation in *Pro Sestio* (esp. 96–143) and the closely related *De republica*. For comment and bibliography on the former, see Kaster 2006. Although Kaster takes careful note of the many correspondences between the speech and the *De republica*, he generally rejects the idea of the speech as 'a serious exercise in political thought' (35). Of the voluminous scholarship on *De republica*, see, e.g., Powell and North 2001; Zetzel 1995. On Ciceronian oratory in the period after Caesar's assassination, see Hall in this volume (Chapter 13).

[34] A model for the tactic was perhaps furnished by the speeches of L. Licinius Crassus and M. Antonius, who had delivered both *popularis* and anti-*popularis* orations. Note, e.g., Crassus' speech on the *lex Servilia Caepionis*, which Cicero called his *magistra* in oratory (*Brut.* 164) and which Fantham 2004 believes contained a 'conservative message in a populist style' (33); or Antonius' defence of the *popularis* ex-tribune Norbanus (c. 95), containing a justification of certain popular uprisings (*De or.* 2.199). Although Antonius did not commit his speeches to writing, Cicero's *Brutus* and *De oratore* indicate knowledge of the most famous of them.

of all classes who wished to preserve it, later termed a *concordia ordinum* and *consensus omnium*.[35]

The most dramatic of the extant orations of 63 were surely the four deliberative speeches known as the *Catilinarians*.[36] The first of these, delivered in the senate, is couched as a spontaneous and emotional reaction to Catiline's unexpected appearance in that body on 7 or 8 November, but actually makes a strikingly subtle response to a variety of political challenges, including, on the one hand, that of convincing Catiline that his (Cicero's) control of the city was so firm that the conspirator's only choice was to join Manlius and declare himself in open rebellion against the state, and, on the other, that of convincing the senate that Catiline represented so great a danger that the strongest legal and moral support of the heroic consul – on whom their safety depended – was crucial. Here we see Cicero confidently facing down Catiline's threats, putting backbone into senatorial resistance and fear into his opponents, and inducing Catiline to leave the city for Manlius' camp without recourse to a senatorial vote for arrest or exile which he might well have lost. The *Third Catilinarian*, delivered at a *contio* before the people, was equally successful: first it helped to bring about a mass revulsion from the conspiracy – whose popular support had rested to a great extent on Catiline's promised cancellation of debts – through Cicero's revelation that the conspirators' plans had called for mass murder and arson; and secondly, the oration effectively presented the arrest of the conspirators as an expression of the gods' intervention on Rome's behalf, with Cicero playing the part of divinely ordained instrument of the Republic's preservation. In the *Fourth Catilinarian* Cicero found ways of assuring the senate of his support for execution of the conspirators and of his confidence in the political resources to defend that verdict, while preserving the superficial neutrality expected of a magistrate putting a question to the senate for debate.[37]

Two further speeches from this year, only the first of which is extant, also deserve mention. In *Pro Murena*, referred to above, Cicero was able to preserve Murena's consulship, while capitalizing on and enhancing his own *auctoritas* as a leader possessed of the temperament, pragmatism and

---

[35] Lintott considers but ultimately rejects the notion that the similarity of themes might argue for the later alteration of the speech (which, with a number of his other consular orations, was published in 60). See Lintott 2008: 120–5 for the complicated (and unclear) circumstances surrounding the speech and its date.

[36] For recent approaches and bibliography, see Cape 2002; for (relatively) recent work on all Cicero's speeches, see the extensive bibliography in Craig 2002: 533–90.

[37] See Cape 1995.

patriotic vision to lead the state through the present crisis. Almost nothing remains of *De Othone*, an impromptu *contio* speech of 63 in which Cicero chastened the masses for voicing their displeasure at a theatrical performance to the special seating privileges recently given to the *equites*, but here we find Cicero at the pinnacle of his powers, demonstrating his mastery of the orator's most difficult challenge: 'the rhetoric of reprimand' before a mass audience.[38]

Cicero's consulship is usually viewed not only as the period in which his oratory was most effective in achieving his political and ideological ends, but also as one which sowed the seeds of his political destruction, since his success in building a broad consensus supporting his actions and those of the senate nurtured the delusion that his status as *dux togatus* could continue after his consulship ended and the threat of Catiline's rebellion was crushed. Doubtless his execution of the conspirators in Rome gave his enemies a platform from which to attack him (in much the same way that the irregularities of Caesar's consulship of 59 gave his enemies a way to threaten him); and doubtless he completely misread the political situation shortly before his exile, as demonstrated by letters such as *Att.* 2.1.3. One might ask, however, what a more dispassionate and clear-sighted Cicero might have done in the period after his consulship to achieve his political goals and maintain his political influence in the face of the power wielded by the 'triumvirs', on the one hand, and Clodius' popular gangs, on the other. As he himself realized, oratory was helpless against those commanding such resources.[39] We may debate whether the rhetorical strategies Cicero employed to further his goals ultimately benefited the system he fought to maintain; we may also debate whether Cicero's political aims for himself and the state were attainable and desirable. Less debatable is the notion that, what oratory could achieve in attaining these goals, Cicero's oratory achieved.

Further reading

For a general introduction to the role of rhetoric in Roman politics, see David 2006. Current scholarly approaches to the issue are reviewed in Alexander 2007 and Dugan 2009. For a valuable survey and discussion (with extensive

---

[38] For the phrase, see Hölkeskamp 2000: 222. On *De Othone*, see Plut. *Cic.* 13.2–4; Crawford 1994: 213–18. Of the fourteen speeches of his consulship, Cicero chose, in 60, to publish twelve, almost all deliberative. In addition to those listed above, the following are mentioned in *Att.* 2.1.3 (neither extant): *De proscriptorum filiis, Cum provinciam in contione deposui*. On reasons for publication, see Steel 2005: 49–53.

[39] Cf. *Fam.* 9.1.21: *nam neque pugnandum arbitrarer contra tantas opes.*

bibliography) of conceptions of ancient politics, see Hammer 2009. See also Hölkeskamp 2000, who in his review of Millar 1998 describes the many factors that a 'thick description' of Roman political culture should include. Assessing the effect of Cicero's speeches – whether deliberative or forensic – on his own political status and on the political milieu at the time they were delivered depends on an understanding of the history of the late Republic, always the subject of intense scholarly debate. See, e.g., Brunt 1988; Crook, Lintott and Rawson 1994. For trends in interpreting late Republican history, see Beard and Crawford 1999; Jehne 2006; Hölkeskamp 2010. Still valuable in contextualizing Cicero's literary output within its historical milieu are Mitchell 1979 and Mitchell 1991. Recently, see Tempest 2011.

An understanding of the political milieu is only a first step towards understanding the interaction between orator and audience at any specific oratorical event. An excellent introduction to scholarly approaches to analysing the political impact of speechmaking before the mass audiences of the *contio* is Morstein-Marx 2004: 1–33. Yet if, as I have argued, the *content*, not just the fact or outcome, of the many forensic speeches that attracted extensive audiences could also constitute an essential mode of political communication, further study of the persuasive strategies of Cicero's judicial speeches and the multiple audiences to which they were addressed is called for. Of special interest are discussions of Cicero's rhetorical use of historical *exempla* casting persons and actions in the past as guides to current political debates and to representation of individual political actors: Walter 2004: 51–70; Bücher 2006; Blom 2010; similarly Gildenhard 2010, which explores the creative (re)definition in various speeches of certain terms and ideas pertinent to Cicero's political representation of himself, his allies and his enemies.

9

CATHERINE STEEL

Cicero, oratory and public life

Oratory was, according to Cicero on certain occasions, a minority pursuit. In the opening chapters of *De oratore*, he emphasizes how the demands of oratory always restrict its successful pursuit to a small number of men. Its rewards are great, and yet: 'who would not rightly be amazed that, over the whole range of time, situation and states such a small number of orators can be found?'.[1] In *Brutus*, however, he explores the opposite possibility, with the character Cicero using a very inclusive definition of 'orator': activity, combined with the state of being dead, is presented as being sufficient for inclusion.[2] Cicero, indeed, regularly draws attention to this approach, and it is challenged towards the end of the dialogue by the character Atticus, who complains that Cicero is including in his catalogue men who, in Atticus' view, do not deserve to be considered orators since they were not very good speakers.[3] Atticus' alternative, and very selective history of Roman oratory implies that the term 'orator' makes a claim about quality: it does not, or should not, simply describe the fact of activity. He appears, therefore, to be operating with an exclusive idea of oratory reminiscent of *De oratore*'s claims.

The difference between the two dialogues can be understood in the context of the differing ends of each work. *De oratore* is concerned to set up oratory as a force that can preserve and guide the *res publica*: a challenging prescription of what an orator is supports the seriousness of this claim. *Brutus*, however, written during Caesar's dictatorship, emphasizes the contrast between the vibrant political atmosphere of the free *res publica* with

---

[1] Cic. *De or.* 1.16, *quis non iure miretur ex omni memoria aetatum, temporum, ciuitatum tam exiguum oratorum numerum inueniri?*

[2] Cicero does not literally follow this prescription. Steel 2003 discusses some high-profile absences, Marius and Sulla above all; Cicero is also clearly using some unstated minimum of activity to count, since speaking in public was much more widespread than even the *Brutus*' inclusiveness suggests: see below.

[3] Cic. *Brut.* 292–7.

the constraints of autocracy. A densely populated environment of public speech, now lost, contributes to the work's atmosphere of loss and mourning. But both works acknowledge the possibility of establishing a definition of 'orator' that does not simply involve the act of public speaking.

We can see how selective even *Brutus* is in its list of orators if we compare the activity it documents with what we may reasonably suspect was the level of activity gauged by a minimal definition of public speech. If we define this as speaking in the senate (with more than a token formula of assent) or to the Roman people, then it is difficult to see how consuls, praetors, aediles and tribunes of the people can have entirely avoided the task.[4] That is more than twenty men a year; if we reduce it to twelve, to allow for successive office holding, we are still faced with well over 1,500 speakers between the end of the second war against Carthage and the end of the Republic. *Brutus* includes 221.[5] The standard modern edition of the fragments of the Republic orators lists 176.[6] For every orator who commended themselves to Cicero's attention, or who has left a direct trace in the surviving ancient evidence, we can reasonably conclude that at least another seven men spoke in public at Rome.

This conclusion is hardly surprising: Rome's political culture was public and oral, as has been increasingly emphasized over the last three decades.[7] The decisions made by assemblies of citizens were not determined in advance by members of the elite exercising their influence through bonds of friendship and patronage, but reflected instead the majority opinion of the groups of citizens by which that assembly was structured. This opinion was potentially influenced by the speeches delivered in the public meetings that characteristically preceded legislative assemblies.[8] In addition, oratory had the potential to contribute to individual political success.[9] The *Commentariolum petitionis* makes the point emphatically: 'You will compensate for your "new man" status most of all through the glory won by speaking.'[10]

---

[4] Lintott 1999a: 9–15 provides a useful account of the annual cycle of Roman political life, which demonstrates the frequency with which oral communication took place. These figures may well underestimate the range of those contributing to senatorial debate: see Ryan 1998.

[5] Sumner 1973. [6] Malcovati 1976.

[7] Major discussions include Millar 1984 and Millar 1986; Jehne 1995; Mouritsen 2001; Flaig 2003; Morstein-Marx 2004; Hölkeskamp 2010.

[8] The relationship between oratory and electoral assemblies is less obvious; Tatum (2013) argues that the separation of elections from public speech may have been a response by the elite to the perceived distorting effect of speech on the choice of magistrates and public officials.

[9] See further Vasaly's chapter in this volume (Chapter 8).

[10] Q. Cicero, *Comment. pet.* 2, *nominis nouitatem dicendi gloria maxime subleuabis* and see Dench and Vasaly in this volume (Chapters 7 and 8). Q. Cicero's authorship has

Forensic oratory made the biggest contribution towards this end, though political oratory was not entirely irrelevant, since it offered the opportunity to affirm links through public demonstrations of support. When Cicero supported the *lex Manilia* in 66, for example, his speech was hardly necessary for the measure's success; it served rather to demonstrate, both to Pompeius and to the Roman people, Cicero's alignment with Pompeius. Oratory would seem, therefore, to be a skill highly relevant to the politically active.

We are left, then, with an interesting tension in Cicero's presentation of oratory. On the one hand, it is presented as a skill of immense importance to the practice of politics (and one, therefore, which we might think would logically attract a large number of users); on the other, it was one whose exercise was limited to a relatively small number of men with the talent and application to master its difficulties. The tension can be resolved through the unifying force of Cicero's ambition: he wished to enhance his own achievements in the written record he left behind by emphasizing the decisive role he played in political life by virtue of his skill as a speaker, and at the same time demonstrate that his skill was unique or, at the very least, rare. A sceptic can indeed argue that the apparent importance of public speech at the end of the Republic is a Ciceronian mirage, which in turn distorted the transmission of the Republic through the early empire and beyond. That argument is too large to pursue here. We can note, however, the importance of forensic oratory as a category in defining different kinds of oratorical activity and presence. Unlike public speech more generally, which was an unavoidable aspect of public life, forensic speech represented a choice, and required commitment and training.[11] Nor was it coterminous with political activity. Only some senators were forensic orators; only some forensic orators were politically active.

Cicero was not only active as a forensic orator for most of his career, the gaps being explained by his absences from Rome or by political changes affecting the operation of the courts; he also created a very substantial textual record of his forensic activity. Nonetheless, the corpus of his speeches, despite its size, represents a heavily edited version of his oratorical activity, both forensic and deliberative. Some of that editing is the result of subsequent losses in transmission; but a very great deal was imposed by Cicero

been challenged by Alexander 2009. His arguments would support the hypothesis that Cicero's example and output substantially inflated the importance of oratory at this period, with significant consequences for the subsequent historical record.

[11] On advocacy and advocates in Republican Rome, see David 1992; Crook 1995; Burnand 2000.

himself, through the decision he made, every time he spoke in public, on whether or not to publish a written version of what he had said.[12]

The standing courts at Rome had developed to take over from the Roman people the task of trying those whose alleged offences were of consequence to the state as a whole.[13] Consequently, forensic oratory in the jury courts (unlike that in civil cases) ought always to have had the potential to touch on matter relevant to the *res publica*; and as early as *Pro Sexto Roscio Amerino* Cicero exploited this link to demonstrate his position as somone who speaks for and about the state.[14] But in practice the potential wider significance of jury trials varied considerably, not least because not all jury trials dealt with defendants whose actions were of immediately obvious and wide-ranging public significance. Whereas offences under the laws on *res repetundae* and *maiestas* were difficult (though not impossible) for non-*imperium* holders to commit, and the definition of *uis* was closely tied to the interests of the state, electoral bribery could be alleged for any office, and murder was not confined to the political classes.[15] My purpose in this chapter is to examine Cicero's tactics in two such cases, the defences of Archias and of Plancius, where despite the relative obscurity of the defendants, Cicero chose to disseminate a written version of his speech.

Pro Archia deals with an allegedly fraudulent claim to the possession of Roman citizenship. The *lex Papia* of 65 expelled from Rome non-Romans who lived outside Italy. It was, presumably, very frequently ignored but it provided the means to challenge individuals' claims to be Roman citizens. Citizenship had, of course, been a matter of urgent political debate in Cicero's youth; and to a certain extent had remained on the agenda in the post-Sullan period because of Sulla's attempts to disenfranchise some Italian communities because of their resistance to him.[16] The passage of the *lex Papia* suggests that the matter retained its sensitivity, even as the reality of pan-Italian Roman citizenship became embedded in political and

---

[12] Crawford 1984 and 1994 reveal the scale of both kinds of losses.

[13] Riggsby 1999: 151–71.

[14] On the speech *Pro Roscio Amerino*, see Dyck 2010; on universalizing tendencies in Cicero's works more generally, Gildenhard 2010. Cicero stopped disseminating written versions of his speeches in civil cases by the time he held the praetorship: it is reasonable to assume that the difficulty of introducing convincing *amplificatio* into such cases was a factor in this decision.

[15] See in general Robinson 1995; on the definition of *uis*, Nippel 1995; Lintott 1999b; Kaster 2006. Robinson 2007: 187 points out the sketchiness of our information about the punishment of 'ordinary criminals', i.e. those of citizen status lower down the social scale than the relatively wealthy men who were Cicero's clients.

[16] Cicero himself had defended the claim to citizenship of an inhabitant of Arretium, a town from which Sulla had removed its (recently acquired) right to Roman citizenship (*Caecin.* 96–7).

social affairs. Despite this, the aims of those who prosecuted Archias in 62 remain something of a puzzle.[17] The defendant was a Greek-speaking Syrian, originally from Antioch, who had moved to Rome as a young man some forty years earlier and made a living as a poet under the patronage of a number of elite Romans. He had allegedly become a Roman citizen in the immediate aftermath of the Social War under the *lex Plautia Papiria*, a law which apparently allowed those who were citizens of allied states to become Roman citizens on the basis of domicile in Italy and a personal declaration to the urban praetor.[18] Archias was eligible to benefit from the *lex Plautia Papiria* because he had earlier become a citizen of Heraclea.

Cicero himself hoped that his achievements as consul would be recorded by Archias, and his own relationship with Archias is an important factor in his defence. But what Cicero offers the jury is not a simple exchange, whereby he trades his personal standing for Archias' acquittal. Instead, he translates his links with Archias into a nexus which embraces the entire *res publica*: the quality that attracts Cicero personally to Archias and his literary outputs is the same that makes literary activity important to all citizens. The movement of this short speech's argument is from contrast to harmony: the audience starts with surprise at Cicero's tactics and ends with universal conviction.

Thus the speech begins with a long sentence – at sixty-four words, a notorious stumbling block to the student in a work which is otherwise pedagogically attractive – which makes Archias, or rather, the citizen denominated Aulus Licinius, the creditor for those aspects of Cicero's rhetorical skill which derive from the pursuit of literary studies (if that is a reasonable translation of the phrase *optimae artes*). Cicero's claim balances grandiose syntax with modest content: Archias has not made him the orator that he is today, but is merely responsible for whatever part of his oratory comes from literature. That claim provides the basis for the heart of the speech. Once Cicero has provided a brief account of the facts of Archias' citizenship, he resumes the discussion of literature (12–30) with an explanation of why he values literary studies. He does so because they make him a better orator: first by providing relaxation from forensic activity (12) and then through the encouragement to ambition which literature provides through its store of *exempla* (13–14). His personal experience is the starting-point for a survey of Roman history that focuses on the literary studies of great Romans and their relationships with poets (15–28). At the end of that section, Cicero returns

---

[17] Taylor 1952; Luisi 1996; Berry 2004. Some connection between Archias' links to Lucullus and the fact of the prosecution is likely, but it seems implausible that Pompeius himself was seriously interested in the outcome.

[18] Cic. *Arch.* 6–7; Bispham 2007: 172–3.

to his own experience, mentioning Archias' planned poem on his consulship and relating his actions then to his hope of memorialization ('Indeed, as I was doing everything that I did, I was conscious that I was scattering and sowing myself into the world's everlasting record').[19] But the end of the speech moves, via a reminder of Archias' links with Licinius Lucullus and Metellus Pius, back from individual to collective: poets in general have always been considered holy, and Cicero's argument should appeal to all. Cicero's talent, achievements and personal relationship with the defendant are part of his strategy, but they are embedded in a much wider argument that involves the Roman *res publica* and, ultimately, the whole of humanity.[20]

Cicero's tactics here can be compared with another case under the *lex Papia* in which he was involved, the prosecution in 56 BC of L. Cornelius Balbus. Balbus, originally from Gades, was distinctive because of his *political* (rather than cultural) importance; initially the protégé of Pompeius during the latter's Spanish commands of the seventies, he subsequently became Caesar's *praefectus fabrum*. Whereas the motives for Archias' prosecution are obscure, the much higher-profile Balbus emerges as a victim of his association with Pompeius and with Caesar, and was defended by Pompeius and Crassus as well as by Cicero. Balbus' prosecutor – whose name does not feature in Cicero's speech – was from Gades; but this man was presumably a front for those who wished to test out the solidity of the renewed alliance between Pompeius, Crassus and Caesar and the level of its popular support. Cicero's line of argument in *Pro Balbo*, as in *Pro Archia*, emphasizes the significance of citizenship as a reward for those who serve Rome faithfully. But, whereas Cicero combines in his defence of Archias this broad argument with his own links to the defendant, his approach in *Pro Balbo* is to underplay his personal stake in the outcome. In a strategy that may reflect Cicero's unease at the forensic activity he engaged in during the mid fifties at Pompeius' request, the case for Balbus' acquittal lies in the relationships between him, Pompeius and Caesar, and the *res publica* alone: Cicero has detached his own interests from the case.

Archias became a citizen because he fitted the criteria of the *lex Plautia Papiria*: other men will have done likewise, though he is the only attested beneficiary. Balbus, by contrast, received his citizenship as a personal favour from Pompeius during the war against Sertorius, possibly on the recommendation of a Cornelius Lentulus; these Pompeian grants were confirmed *en bloc* by a *lex Gellia Cornelia* of 72 BC, the wording of which, as Cicero

---

[19] Cic. *Arch.* 30, *ego uero omnia, quae gerebam, iam tum in gerendo spargere me ac disseminare arbitrabar in orbis terrae memoriam sempiternam.*

[20] See further Steel 2001: 82–98; Dugan 2005: 31–58; Panoussi 2009; Nesholm 2010.

records it, demonstrates that it concerned individual grants.[21] Balbus is Pompeius' creation; and the prosecutor did not dispute Pompeius' grant of citizenship. The legal point of the case concerned the capacity of Balbus to change his citizenship, and the prosecutor claimed that he could not because Gades did not permit it.[22] Cicero addresses the substantive legal arguments, but these give way in the structure of the speech as a whole to other considerations. The first major section is a eulogy of Balbus which emphasizes his links to Pompeius and Pompeius' own achievements (4–10), and in the handling of citizenship the legal issue of dual citizenship within the framework of the treaty between Rome and Gades is subordinated to emotional appeals to citizenship and the need of the Roman state to have the capacity to reward service through the bestowal of citizenship. Citizenship is presented as an aspect of imperial power.[23]

Balbus was unpopular in Rome, for his wealth and influence; Cicero acknowledges this unpopularity, in some detail, in his speech (56–7). Whatever the effectiveness of this tactic in terms of jury response, it also underscores Cicero's detachment from the case. This is not a situation in which Cicero is appealing on behalf of a close friend, with whom he is emotionally involved: Balbus is, simply, a client, whose case Cicero presents as effectively as he can. This aspect of the speech can be linked to its *exordium*, where Cicero draws the jurors' attention to the qualities of the two advocates, Pompeius and Crassus, whom they have already heard. The speech starts with a question arising from a statement: 'If the reputation of advocates carries any weight in judicial proceedings, the case of L. Cornelius has been defended by men of the highest standing; if experience does, by the most skilled; if talent, by the most eloquent; if enthusiasm, by his closest friends and those linked to L. Cornelius by the exchange of services and by the greatest intimacy. What, then, is my contribution?'.[24] The answer is limited amounts of *auctoritas*, *usus* and *ingenium*; we note the absence of *studium*. The effect is to separate Cicero from the other members of the defence team, and this may even be emphasized in the brief section much later where

---

[21] Cic. *Balb.* 19, *ut ciues Romani sint ii, quos Cn. Pompeius de consilii sententia singillatim ciuitate donauerit.*

[22] Brunt 1982a; Sanchez 2007.

[23] Steel 2001: 98–112. How far the case may have reflected discussion about the exclusivity of Roman citizenship is difficult to establish. Cicero combined an emphatic statement of the impossibility of dual citizenship (28) with acknowledgement of the breach of this principle by his peers (30); by 41 BC a framework for dual citizenship existed (*FIRA* 1.55).

[24] Cic. *Balb.* 1, *si auctoritates patronorum in iudiciis ualent, ab amplissimis uiris L. Corneli causa defensa est, si usus, a peritissimis, si ingenia, ab eloquentissimis, si studia, ab amicissimis et cum beneficiis cum L. Cornelio, tum maxima familiaritate coniunctis. quae sunt igitur meae partes?*

Cicero acknowledges his personal debt to Balbus (58). The obligation turns out to arise from Balbus' behaviour at the time of Cicero's exile. Not only did Balbus 'not delight in my downfall'; he 'supported all my people by every kind of dutiful action, by his tears, his deeds and his sympathy during my absence'.[25] In contrast with the heightened language with which Cicero often treats his exile and the reactions of others to it, including Plancius (discussed below), this is a modest claim for Balbus' involvement. And Balbus managed to do this whilst remaining *in intima familiaritate*, on the closest of terms, with a 'very powerful man'. This allusion to an unnamed (and absent) Caesar in the context of Cicero's exile, when put together with the visible presence of Pompeius and Crassus in court, encourages a listener to think about Cicero's exile, and the role that Caesar and Pompeius played in bringing it about.

The defence of Balbus involved Cicero in a self-consciously detached pose. His relationship with the defendant is not presented in his speech as close or affectionate. The jurors are instructed to pity Balbus, but to do so because he risks falling foul of an issue of public law, *ius publicum*, through an action of Pompeius (64). The focus in the closing words of the speech is on Pompeius and Caesar: should their friendship be the source of benefits or of disaster? Cicero uses his speech to unveil what he presents as the real motive behind the prosecution: Balbus is a victim of his association with Pompeius and Caesar. This enables him to suggest to the jurors that their verdict should be on Pompeius and Caesar, rather than on Balbus, or indeed on Cicero himself.

It is unusual for Cicero, particularly after his consulship, to present the level of his own involvement in a case at such a minimal level. The speech *Pro Plancio*, which also dates from the mid fifties, presents the more familiar tactic of relating the trial's outcome closely to Cicero's own well-being. This speech was a defence against a charge of electoral bribery: Plancius, Cicero's client, was prosecuted by M. Juventius Laterensis, an unsuccessful candidate for the position of aedile that Plancius had secured. Plancius himself is so obscure a figure that we do not even know whether he was acquitted or not; his next impact on the record is letters which Cicero wrote to him in 46 (*Fam.* 4.14, 4.15).[26] Laterensis is a slightly better-attested figure; despite

---

[25] Cic. *Balb.* 58, *non modo non exsultauit in ruinis nostris . . . sed omni officio, lacrimis, opera, consolatione omnes me absente meos subleuauit.*

[26] These put Plancius on Corcyra; exile (which could have followed conviction, or support for Pompeius during the civil war) is a likely though not certain explanation. Cicero's letters involve familiar tropes of self-exculpation, combined with bitter references to domestic troubles; they tell us little about Plancius' views or activities, beyond attesting to an ongoing friendly relationship with Cicero. Plancius' slaves appear as couriers for Cicero's correspondence in *Fam.* 6.20.1; 16.9.2

his setback in these elections, he reached the praetorship in 51 and, having passed through the civil war unrecorded, committed suicide in 43 after Lepidus, whose legate he was, joined forces with Antonius. Unlike Cicero's other surviving *ambitus* defence, of the consul-elect Murena in 63, this trial did not involve major figures.

One of the issues which, according to Cicero, faced him in his defence of Plancius was his obligations to both sides, arising from their support for him during his exile. We are entirely dependent on this speech for evidence of that support: Plancius was quaestor in Macedonia in 58, and consequently in a position to help Cicero during his exile (26, 98–101); Laterensis offered support in Rome (2). Laterensis, moreover, apparently claimed that Cicero had fabricated the closeness that he claimed with Plancius (4; 72: 'It was rather harsh for you to claim that I was lying in what I said about Plancius and making it up because of the exigencies of circumstance').[27] But Cicero puts these personal relationships at the heart of the speech. He begins (1) by drawing a direct connection between his exile, Plancius' support then, and the support that Plancius is now receiving from others because he earlier helped Cicero. Cicero then claims that the prosecution of Plancius was being promoted by his, Cicero's, enemies; a bold move insofar as he then insists on the close relationship which exists between the actual prosecutor, Laterensis, and himself: 'and I am more surprised, gentlemen of the jury, that M. Laterensis, a man who is most supportive of my standing and my safety, has marked out this defendant, of all people, for himself, than afraid that you may think he has good reason to have done so'.[28] The contrast suggests that Laterensis himself is utterly confused about his motives and actions. The nexus between Laterensis, Plancius and Cicero dominates the opening of the speech, with Cicero presenting his dilemma as the balancing of two sets of obligations: 'Either I must damage the reputation of a very dear friend, if I follow the example of the prosecution, or I must abandon the safety of one who has done me great service.'[29] Perhaps not coincidentally, Plancius is never described as Cicero's friend: friendship remains Laterensis' attribute.[30] And the links between Cicero and Plancius, and Cicero and

---

[27] Cic. *Planc.* 72, *illud fuit asperius, me, quae de Plancio dicerem, mentiri, et temporis causa fingere.*

[28] Cic. *Planc.* 2, *saepiusque, iudices, mihi uenit in mentem admirandum esse M. Laterensem, hominem studiosissimum et dignitatis et salutis meae, reum sibi hunc potissimum delegisse, quam metuendum, ne uobis id ille magna ratione fecisse uideatur.*

[29] Cic. *Planc.* 6, *ita aut amicissimi hominis existimatio offendenda est, si illam accusationis conditionem sequar, aut optime de me meriti salus deserenda.*

[30] The discussion of gratitude (80–2) links it to friendship in general terms, and Cicero makes a general statement about his friendship being more a source of pleasure than of

Laterensis, should have prevented this trial from taking place: Laterensis has forgotten that he gave Cicero permission to support Plancius (73).

This presentation of a three-cornered relationship between prosecutor, defendant and defence advocate is reflected in Cicero's handling of the charge of electoral bribery. Laterensis' argument was, it seems, that the difference between his status and Plancius' and their respective qualities meant that it was impossible for Plancius to have been elected without bribery. Cicero responds by setting up a model of elections for more junior positions, such as the aedileship, in which personal qualities are subordinated to unpredictable popular decision-making, with the result that defeat does not necessarily involve a judgement of quality.[31] Not only does this line of argument help Cicero in providing an explanation for Plancius' success: it also enables him to maintain a friendly stance towards Laterensis. Nonetheless, at the end of the speech Cicero deploys the tactic which Laterensis had been trying to prevent by claiming that the relationship between Cicero and Plancius was not close. The final section is a description of Plancius' conduct towards Cicero during his exile and Cicero concludes by linking Plancius' fate directly to his own, through the tears which he and, he claims, the court president and the jurors are shedding: his closing words are, 'Your tears, and yours, gentlemen of the jury, prevent me from saying more – not just my own: and they give me a sudden hope, in the midst of great fear, that you will show the same qualities in saving this man as you showed towards me, since these tears remind me of those which you have often poured out in great quantity on my behalf.'[32] By the end, then, Laterensis has been replaced as the third element in the emotional equation by Gaius Flavus and the jury, and Plancius' safety is presented as the inevitable concomitant to Cicero's own position and authority.

The cases of Archias and Plancius have a significance, according to Cicero, which ties the fate of the defendants to wider concerns of the *res publica*, and consequently of the jurors. But whereas Archias' prosecution raises questions about the ways in which Roman achievements are recorded for posterity and the value of that record as a stimulus for contemporary excellence, Plancius matters to the *res publica* because he is a proxy for Cicero: attacked by Cicero's enemies, he will be saved by Cicero's popularity. In Cicero's forensic

protection, in a context which implies that Plancius is one of those affected; but he never explicitly uses *amicus*, or cognate, of Plancius.

[31] Steel 2011.

[32] Cic. *Planc.* 104, *plura ne dicam, tuae me etiam lacrimae impediunt uestraeque, iudices, non solum meae: quibus ego magno in metu meo subito inducor in spem, uos eosdem in hoc conseruando futuros qui fueritis in me, quoniam istis uestris lacrimis de illis recordor, quas pro me saepe et multum profudistis.*

world, the interests of the *res publica* and those of its leading men (including Cicero) are interchangeable: Cicero's position guarantees the concern of his listeners, and at the same time enables him, in speaking, to make the fate of other men equally serious.

Cicero was able to use his rhetorical skill and resources to amplify the defences of Archias and Plancius into cases of urgent importance for his jury. It is, of course, impossible to prove that the possibility of such amplification was a factor in Cicero's decision to publish these speeches: we do not know enough about the cases in which Cicero chose not to disseminate a written version to assert confidently that they were all beyond Cicero's capacity to rescue from triviality.[33] But it is apparent that the record of his career that Cicero was writing through his speeches was one which demonstrated the importance of his oratory to the *res publica*, even if that record omitted some supporting material. By examining the defences of Archias and Plancius, we can see in practice how Cicero articulated this importance, whatever the identity of his defendant.[34]

Further reading

Whereas Crawford 1994 offers an edition of the fragments of Ciceronian oratory from speeches which he disseminated, but have failed to survive in the direct tradition, Crawford 1984 embarks on the rather different task of identifying and cataloguing the speeches which Cicero delivered but did not choose to record in written form. The result is in parts inevitably speculative but offers an essential tool to understanding Cicero's tactics in forcing writing to serve his purposes. The introduction to Powell and Paterson 2004 provides an excellent discussion of the factors surrounding the publication of Cicero's speeches and of the vexed relationship betweeen spoken and written texts; on writing and Cicero's public persona, see Dugan 2005 and Steel 2005.

[33] The verdict was a major factor: only in two cases (the defences of Varenus and Milo) is Cicero known to have disseminated a version of a speech from a trial at which his client was known to have been convicted, and both these cases were exceptional. The shift from civil to criminal cases in the written record of his career is noted above, n. 14.
[34] Archias – along with Quinctius – exemplifies the obscure defendant for Maternus in Tacitus' *Dialogus* (37.6).

10

ANDREW BELL

Cicero, tradition and performance

In his dialogue *Brutus*, Cicero talks about a young, rising statesman, C. Scribonius Curio, who was the son of an accomplished orator. The young Curio also possessed great natural gifts of eloquence. But he chose not to follow the example of Cicero. Instead he established an allegiance with Julius Caesar, in part to secure funds that could pay off debts incurred in providing lavish, spectacular entertainments. Consequently, Cicero asserts, he chose power and wealth rather than the true distinction that comes from the judgement and the enthusiastic support of his fellow citizens (*Brut.* 280–1). Cicero was writing the dialogue *Brutus* (and also the *Orator*) in 46, at a time when Caesar and his legions were fighting other Roman commanders and legions in North Africa. Caesar's soldiers were loyal to their charismatic commander rather than to the *res publica* itself – that is to say to the traditional, republican state in which the people (*populus*) were sovereign. Even if Caesar's final victory was not yet certain, it was clear that the *res publica* would not exist in the condition that Cicero desired. Throughout his life, Cicero naturally was committed to the advancement of his own career towards the heights of prominence in the state. But equally this commitment entailed investment of his energies and his hopes in a conception of the *res publica* as peaceful, ordered and fundamentally inseparable from the assumption that there would be competition for rewards of honours and glory, bestowed by contemporaries and bequeathed to posterity. Principally the competition to make manifest one's qualifications for enduring significance in the life and the history of the *res publica* was to be conducted by the power of oratory.

Accordingly Cicero's determination, both self-serving and high-minded, to monumentalize this power is the most salient feature of the legacy he has left for the history of the late Roman Republic. Greeks had long recognized the power (*vis*) of public speech and pioneered its development through teaching in the fifth century (*Brut.* 30). But it was *vis* in the form of the power of violence, and especially that of military force, that was a chronic phenomenon or threat during Cicero's own lifetime.[1] When Cicero was an adolescent, for instance, the Italian countryside provided battlegrounds for clashes between Romans and sometime Italian allies determined to win either liberty and autonomy or at least the dignity of full, enfranchised inclusion in the *res publica*. In the eighties there was struggle between adherents of Marius and of Sulla. In the seventies there was insurrection in the countryside and later a massive uprising of slaves. In Cicero's own consulship in 63 there was a battle between Roman soldiers and poorly armed countrymen. And, of course, Cicero eventually lost his own life in the turbulent aftermath to the battles between followers of Caesar and followers of Pompey. In Cicero's legacy there are surviving speeches and also his treatises on the theory and practice of oratory at Rome. The speeches inevitably tackle political circumstances determined or affected by armed force. His treatises make relatively little mention of what were surely great dislocations to any confidence in the ideal of a *res publica* steered by men of eloquence who were able to sway the minds and emotions of fellow Romans in the venues of oratorical competition: the senate, the *contiones* – the public meetings held when humbler citizens were addressed by the more important political personages prior to voting in the assemblies – and in legal trials, held in public and where the audience would frequently comprise a throng much larger than just the jurors alone. Cicero has left to posterity a teleological history of Roman oratory that culminates in the glory of his own (possibly, when all was said and done, vainglorious) career. It is nevertheless a splendid legacy, not least because we can understand just how masterfully Cicero deployed the power of eloquence to rise to great prominence in the *res publica*. In peaceful times, eloquence could readily enjoy primacy (e.g. *Orat.* 141). In this chapter we shall seek to understand how this power operated.

Cicero's legacy appears all the more impressive because of the absence of surviving speeches from other orators, whether predecessors and exemplars or contemporaries and competitors. As he explains in the *Brutus*, speeches were available to Cicero for careful study and emulation in his formative years, although some of these could only be found with difficulty towards the end of his life (*Brut.* 129). Cicero even learned the peroration of a speech of C. Sempronius Gracchus by heart (127), although throughout his life he was adamantly hostile to the populism and policies of Gracchus and his older brother Tiberius. Nothing much, however, could be found that preceded the time of Cato the Elder, with the exception of some laudatory speeches

---

[1] The most accessible introductions to the career of Cicero are Stockton 1971 and Habicht 1990.

preserved within families (62), whereas Cicero had read more than 150 of Cato's speeches (65). Other speeches that were extant in Cicero's day might, in his judgement, be mediocre or not those that once had been the most famous ones of particular, noted speakers. Many had disappeared among a throng of more recent texts – including, of course, Cicero's own productions (117 and 122). Others simply could not be bothered to write. They did not want to add toil at home to that exerted in the courts before the jurors (91).[2]

This assertion raises the important but vexing question of the relationship between a written – and, in the case of Cicero, surviving – speech and its delivery as an actual performance before an audience. The heart of the matter is that it is simply impossible to talk with any confidence about this relationship. Cicero delivered more than 160 speeches. Out of these, 58 have survived to the present, of which all but the first of his speeches in prosecuting Verres and the one in defence of Milo were actually delivered. But it is clear that most speeches that were circulated as texts were written in that form after delivery and not before; it appears too that it was possible to read some sort of a record or transcript of the proceedings at a *contio* (*Har. resp.* 51). Speeches attributed to an orator might in fact have been written by somebody else (*Brut.* 205–6). In any event, Cicero observes that others do not work hard to construct their speeches, although nothing contributes as much to good speaking as writing. (We might note in passing that some of the more wearisome instrumentality involved in writing could have been eased by employment of skilled slaves – e.g. *Brut.* 87–8.) Furthermore, they do not crave to leave posterity with a memorial of their ability. They are content with the glory they have from their speaking and think it will be greater if their writings are not subjected to the judgement of critics. Others are aware that they speak better than they write, which happens in the case of those of great natural ability but insufficient formal training. Galba for instance not only had a force of intellect but was fired up when speaking so as to be passionate, earnest and vehement. But afterwards the storm had subsided when he took up his pen and his speech drooped (*Brut.* 91–3). Clearly there is, according to Cicero, an intimate relationship between writing and speaking. Indeed he insists that good orators cannot earn applause and admiration (*clamores* and *admirationes*) unless they have written extensively. Just as when the crew of a boat stops rowing and yet the vessel still keeps moving, so an orator can continue to speak extemporaneously in a style similar to that he was using when his words were

---

[2] For an excellent discussion of Cicero's training as an orator, see Fantham 2004: 78–101. A valuable overview of Roman oratory is provided by Kennedy 1972.

based upon what had already been written (*De or.* 1.152–3). An orator did not speak with his eyes glued to a script or notes – although Pompey could be critiqued along those lines (*Sest.* 129) – but needed to employ the important capability of memory. If an orator, while writing, forgot what he had just written, it was hardly surprising that often he suffered complete loss of memory when speaking extemporaneously (*Brut.* 219 and *Orat.* 129).

There were other important preliminaries of training before an effective oratorical performance could be staged. Obviously one should know what one was talking about, including presumably the contents of a bill in a *contio* or in the senate. The finer points of law were obviously crucial in forensic speeches but so too was a knowledge of history (*Orat.* 120). Given the really rather impressive dedication of Cicero to writing about philosophy, there is no surprise in finding him stressing its importance for the orator, allowing him to give a full exposition of matters likely to come up in speeches (e.g. *Orat.* 118): reverence, death, loyalty, patriotism, discrimination between good and bad things, virtues and vices, duty, grief, pleasure, disturbances and mistakes of mind, and also natural law. In general, Cicero stresses the necessity for a speaker to have a broad education, especially in philosophy, history and law. Wisdom and eloquence must go together: these are key themes in the *De inventione* and the first book of the *De oratore*. Clearly Cicero was extremely well trained in rhetorical theory, as has been shown earlier in this volume. But he could claim that eloquence was not a product of rhetorical theory but rather theory developed from eloquence.

In Cicero's assessment of the rise of Roman eloquence in the *Brutus*, the glory of Greek oratory was not matched by Latin until the careers of M. Antonius and L. Licinius Crassus, who died in 87 and 91 respectively (138). Both chose to write little. Had they done so, they would have left to posterity both memory and instruction in their writings (163). Both men prepared very carefully and well for their public appearances but they also had excellent delivery (*actio*) when it came to actually performing (141 and 158). *Actio* (or in Greek *hypocrisis*), as Demosthenes, the most accomplished Athenian orator, had stressed, is paramount (142; cf. *Orat.* 56). Cicero divides Antonius' excellence in performance into gesture and voice. His use of gesture chimed with not just his words but also his thoughts, in the movement of his hands, shoulders, chest, the stamp of a foot, and posture, whether standing still or pacing. His voice was somewhat husky but he turned this to his advantage (141). Crassus displayed no great movement of his body, no modulation of his voice, no pacing to and fro, no frequent stamping of his foot. In the *Orator* (59–60), Cicero further expounds upon such particularities, adding such details as the desirability of an erect posture, and of avoidance of effeminate bending of the neck, twiddling of the fingers or marking the rhythm of speaking with the finger joints; the orator should also carefully control his eyes. Successful oratory naturally depended upon physicality and visibility.[3]

Such finer points regarding performance readily suggest that there were basic similarities between the performing skills of an orator and those of a stage-actor. Q. Hortensius was the orator who in Cicero's judgement was the greatest until Cicero himself attained primacy as a public speaker – Cicero notes in particular that Hortensius ceded to Cicero the responsibility of delivering the peroration when both were appearing for the defence (*Brut.* 190). Hortensius was remembered as having noted that the leading actors of the late Republic, namely Aesopus and Roscius, actually watched him perform (Val. Max. 8.10.1). Roscius, in turn, wrote a work comparing the art of the orator with that of the actor (Macrob. *Sat.* 3.14.12). Cicero himself observes that it was as if the forum at Rome was a theatre for Hortensius' talents (*Brut.* 6); and that Hortensius spoke better than his written speeches might suggest (*Orat.* 132). The parallels between the stage and a *contio* were especially conspicuous (e.g. *Amic.* 97). Cicero himself defended Roscius in a speech in 76 (the *Q Rosc.*) packed with theatrical allusions. At both performances the crowds were large and they always stood at *contiones* and often at the theatre (for not until 55 was there a permanent theatre constructed of stone at Rome). Furthermore, a great deal of noisy applause and shouting, as we shall see, was to be expected – and often to be welcomed: both actors and politicians wanted *clamores* and *admirationes*. But the similarities were also disquieting, for several related reasons. In the first place, only important individuals spoke as orators. This was especially so at *contiones*: Cicero did not make his debut in such a venue until 66, when he was not only sure of his abilities but as a praetor possessed substantial political authority (*De imp. Cn. Pomp.* 39). Actors did not enjoy high social prestige even if they became wealthy, and their manners and their language backstage could be crude (e.g. *Auct. ad Her.* 4.14); both Roscius and Aesopus were freedmen – slaves given their freedom. Above all they were, in a way like slaves or for that matter gladiators, mere instruments of another's will, expressed through a script that they performed but had not written. They were inherently *levis*, trivial – as was their skill (*De or.* 1.18) Their speeches could not possibly be construed as expressions of their sincere thoughts.

---

[3] Very useful accounts of oratorical gestures are to be found in Aldrete 1999 and Corbeill 2004.

Yet an audience's reaction to the performances of both the actor and the orator was obviously the most important gauge of their skills and overall effectiveness. An orator should instruct, please and stir his audience (*Brut.* 185). Orators, however, might have been judged less indulgently than actors (*De or.* 1.124–5). Cicero points out that the orator should have a full and keenly attentive audience – so much so in fact that a passer-by would recognize that a Roscius was upon the stage (*Brut.* 290). Romans of every social class and order of formal status attended the theatre and Roscius was always careful to ensure that he earned the goodwill of both the ordinary people (*vulgus*) and the leading individuals (*principes*) of Rome (Plin. *HN.* 7.128). When it suited the needs of the case he was pleading, Cicero could claim to jurors that the *vulgus* had no deliberation, intelligence, judgement or attention (*Planc.* 9). But Cicero comes much closer to a truthful admission when he avers that, while he would prefer his discussion of the grounds for appraising an orator to be approved by the likes of his friends Atticus or Brutus, he wants his eloquence to be approved by the people (*populus*); he insists too that oratory approved by the *multitudo* must inevitably be approved by the experts as well (*Brut.* 184). Furthermore, while a *contio* might consist of the most ignorant sorts of people, it nevertheless might still be able to discriminate between someone whom Cicero deemed to be a *popularis* trimmer and someone else who was resolute, sincere and serious (*Amic.* 95).

Certainly those that comprised a *contio* lived in a world in which oral expression could be evaluated in a manner that was far more sophisticated than in our modern world, drowning as it is in text. Cicero could write at great length – and frankly sometimes repetitiously – about oratory, but he hailed the ears of an audience as supremely important. To be sure, he cavils, sometimes the *vulgus* cannot tell that a speaker is really not that good: the ears of the people can be compared to a wind instrument: if it does not accept what is blown into it, then there is nothing that can be done (*Brut.* 192–3). These tend to include those whose politics he abhorred, namely those whom he deems to be 'radicals' (*seditiosi*) – populists who were active after the Gracchi brothers, including L. Appuleius Saturninus, C. Servilius Glaucia and Sextus Titius (*Brut.* 224–5). Nonetheless, he has seen *contiones* cry out when words have had a nice cadence (*Orat.* 168). Likewise entire theatres have cried out if a single syllable in verse is too short or too long (*Orat.* 173). Cicero himself was standing in a *contio* when C. Carbo (the younger) finished a sentence with the unexpected metrical pattern of a ditrochee: it was wonderful what *clamor* was aroused (*Orat.* 214). Such aesthetic appreciation was not based upon training or knowledge; rather nature has put into our ears the power of judging long and short sounds and also high and low pitch in words (*Orat.* 173). Cicero's own speeches were indeed theory in action. He modulated, he explains, his style to the needs of a particular performance: there was detailed legal exposition of the meaning of words in the speech for Caecina, calm praise for Pompey in his speech supporting the Manilian law and blazing amplification of his themes in the speech in defence of Rabirius, when Cicero thought the majesty of the *res publica* was at stake; every style can be found in the *Verrines* (*Orat.* 102–3).

Clearly the big shouting came in *contiones*. It is hard not to be intrigued by an anecdote that reports that once upon a time a crowd at a *contio* shouted so loudly that a crow fell stunned from the sky (Cass. Dio 36.30.3). Even the toughest of Romans might be apprehensive. C. Marius, whose military victories at the end of the second century caused many to view him as the saviour of Rome and who boasted of the scars upon his chest, was thought to have feared the roar of such assemblies (Plut. *Mar.* 28). In such a political environment, shouting could be seen as integral to the very liberty of the *res publica* (Val. Max. 6.2.6). And whenever there was great *clamor*, it could be read as consensus for a political position (e.g. Cicero's hopefulness regarding a *contio* discussing Cassius, an assassin of Caesar, in March 43: *Fam.* 12.7.1), regardless of whether there was a subsequent vote in the assembly. Popular expressions of feeling at the assemblies and at the theatre were also carefully noted (*Sest.* 106). Accordingly some sought to sway sentiment. The populist tribune Clodius was particularly effective at arranging for orchestrated chanting (e.g. *Q fr.* 2.3.2). The *contio* lay at the heart of all that the *res publica* was.

Indeed the determination to sway popular sentiment and the necessity of influencing the outcome of voting in the assembly testify to the importance of a popular sovereignty in the later Republic.[4] As tribune of the plebs C. Gracchus changed his stance when speaking at a *contio*: he turned away from facing the senate-house and directly addressed his audience (Plut. *C. Gracch.* 5; but Cicero (*Amic.* 96) attributes the change to C. Licinius Crassus). Ever after that move, which was as ideological as it was merely physical, the dynamic between orators and their audiences in large part defined the nature of politics in the *res publica*. Increasingly historians have stressed the crucial role of the popular assembly in enacting laws. There was indeed a democratic element in the workings of the constitutional system of the

---

[4] Millar 1998 draws extensively on the evidence of Cicero's speeches in order to argue that the late Republic was more democratic than has traditionally been thought. Much of the groundwork for such a view was established in essays that are to be found in Brunt 1988. The broader social and political dimensions of the Republic are splendidly covered in Nicolet 1980.

res publica. Appreciation of this should, however, be balanced by the consideration that only an elite took political initiatives. Unlike a democratic assembly in classical Athens, those in the audience at a *contio* could not take their turns in stepping up to speak. Eloquence was a potential possession for very few. Nevertheless Cicero's oratory will remain at the heart of scholarly debate as it is important evidence for consideration of political dynamics in the late Republic. Yet such textual evidence needs to be accompanied by apprehension of all the other types of performance that shaped politics in this period, such as religious ritual or spectacular entertainment. When one looks beyond the *contio* and the voting-pens, the courts or the senate, it is clear that an elite had a ritualized authority that complicates and diminishes the strength of any claim that there was a democratic nature to the *res publica.*

There were then other reasons for Cicero's persuasiveness.[5] A consul was able to bring authoritative and charismatic appurtenances to his *actio*.[6] Thus as consul Cicero had an official entourage of lictors carrying the *fasces* that symbolized his official power in the state. As consul he also took a central part in the religious rituals that maintained Rome's good relations with the gods. In the previous century the Greek historian Polybius had seen for himself, and been impressed by, Roman rituals. Funerals of notable individuals articulated their significance (Polybius, *Histories*, 6.53.1–10). Religious rites had a theatrical quality, and they served to keep the humbler citizens in check (6.56.8–11). There was a great gulf that separated political actors such as Cicero from their audiences and rituals confirmed that sociopolitical divide. Indeed they surely helped to make it seem wholly normal and natural. When we try – as we must – to visualize an orator addressing a crowd in the forum, we need also to be aware of the implications of the full aesthetic and emotional context of the ritualized performance. Indeed, Cicero's speeches consistently and effectively paint for the mind's-eyes of his audience vignettes of such things as places and distinctive individuals' appearances.[7]

Other spectacular performances certainly had increasing, popular appeal. The historian Tacitus, looking back with nostalgia from imperial times upon the Republic, considered it a time when citizens had persuaded themselves that only with eloquence could anybody reach or maintain a position of conspicuousness or prominence in Rome (Tac. *Dial.* 37.6). But already in the

---

[5] See further Bell 2004: 199–239.

[6] A stimulating introduction to thinking about rituals and ritualization in general remains Bell 1992.

[7] Vasaly 1993 provides a fascinating analysis of how Cicero drew great persuasive power from representations of places and spaces familiar to his audience.

time of Cicero, eyes were being drawn increasingly to – and *clamores* aroused by – other spectacles: theatre offered not just skilled actors but also massively elaborate staging and more and more violence in gladiatorial contests and killings of exotic wild animals.[8] Curio had not been foolish in neglecting the pursuit of greater eloquence for the sake of competing for other forms of power. But once the *res publica* became in fact a monarchy, spectacle became the monopoly of the dynasty. There was no longer competition in either the forum or the theatre.

Still, given Cicero's insistence upon the approval of the *multitudo*, success in *contiones* should be taken to constitute validation of his prowess as an eloquent orator – and also as a central and glorious figure in the *res publica* itself. His speech had been carefully prepared and written beforehand and his memory had been applied. And then he performed. Perhaps his greatest successes came with his speeches *De lege agraria* 2 and *In Catilinam* 2. In the former he opposed passage of agrarian reform legislation and in the latter he turned sentiment against a radical, aristocratic renegade of potentially popular appeal. Both performances were in the year when he was consul; and upon each occasion Cicero posed as a champion of popular interests. In large measure he was insincere – but at least there was something of sincerity in his insincerity in so far as it was as necessary for him to appear to defer to popular sensibilities as it was for him to speak to them in the first place. He had attained the highest office in the *res publica* in large measure through his talents as an orator, which meant saying what was necessary.

Sadly, Cicero died somewhat ingloriously, beheaded on the orders of M. Antonius, the grandson of the orator whom Cicero so admired.[9] Although his political influence had waned after his consulship, vehement hostility to Antonius late in his life notwithstanding, his ambition has prevailed. While at times he might claim not to crave *honores* or *gloria* (writing to his brother in late October 54 (*Q fr.* 3.6.2)), Plutarch was surely right to identify in Cicero a powerful ambition to be held in the highest repute, even going so far as to ask the oracle of Apollo at Delphi how he could attain this goal (*Cic.* 1 and 5). It would be very interesting to know just what he wrote in his treatise *De gloria* (Gell. 15.6.1), which unfortunately is not extant. Those words that have survived, however, are a legacy that both testifies uniquely to an extraordinary talent in understanding and practising oratory and also allows analysis of the fundamental dynamics of political power in the last years of the *res publica*.

---

[8] Fagan 2011 provides an invaluable discussion of Roman spectacles of violence.
[9] See further Butler 2002.

Further reading

A valuable overall introduction to Roman oratory is Kennedy 1972. For a more detailed focus upon Cicero, an excellent starting-point is Vasaly 1993, which provides a fascinating analysis of how Cicero drew great persuasive power from representations of places and spaces familiar to his audience. A very useful account of oratorical gestures is to be found in Aldrete 1999. A stimulating introduction to thinking about rituals and ritualization in general remains Bell 1992.

Helpful accounts of Cicero's political career are to be found in Stockton 1971 and Habicht 1990. With particular regard to political dynamics, Millar 1998 draws extensively on the evidence of Cicero's speeches in order to argue that the late Republic was more democratic than has traditionally been thought. Much of the groundwork for such a view was established in essays that are to be found in Brunt 1988. The broader social and political dimensions of the Republic are splendidly covered by Nicolet 1980.

11

JAMES E. G. ZETZEL

Political philosophy

At the end of July 54 BC, Cicero wrote to his brother Quintus and his good friend Atticus (*Q fr.* 2.15.4, *Att.* 4.15.8) describing in virtually identical words the tribunician elections about to take place. Every candidate had given a deposit to Cato; if Cato decided they had behaved corruptly, then they would forfeit half a million sesterces. And if this plan works, Cicero says, 'Cato on his own will have had more effect than all the laws and all the judges.' The contrast Cicero draws between the authority of a single man of character and courage and the governmental structure (laws and judges) supposed to be in control is striking. It is perhaps no accident that these letters were written only a few months after Cicero wrote (again, to both Quintus and Atticus: *Q fr.* 2.13.1, *Att.* 4.14.1, 4.16.2) to describe the beginnings of his work on the dialogue *De republica* (*On the Commonwealth*). It is also no accident that the principal concern of the dialogue is the same as that of the letters about Cato: what is the relationship between the individual statesman or citizen and the structure of government? What kind of political organization can combine the routine and predictability of a traditional society with the need for a charismatic figure to take decisive action in a crisis?[1] And what is the relationship between virtue on the individual level and virtue on the societal level: do good men make a good society, or does a good society create good men?

None of these questions, certainly not the last, was novel in 54 BC: the relationship between individual morality and civic success is a fundamental question in Aristotle's *Politics*, and while Cicero knew that work only indirectly, he certainly knew the work of Aristotle's followers Theophrastus

---

[1] This chapter will not make frequent reference to modern political theory, but Max Weber's categories (Weber 1978 vol. II: 212–54) of 'traditional' and 'charismatic' authority are the most useful way to describe the conflicting power structures analysed by Cicero. For comments on an earlier draft, I am grateful to Gareth Williams.

and Dicaearchus.[2] In the late fifties, however, such questions had a peculiar urgency: the rise of the dynasts Caesar, Pompey and Crassus; the power wielded by demagogues and street-politicians like Clodius and Milo; the ability of a Cato to have a greater effect than all the organs of government – the personal politics of the decade before the civil war gave a terrifying reality to theoretical questions that had been discussed for generations. 'It's a long time since we lost the commonwealth', Cicero wrote in despair later in 54 (*Att.* 4.18.2); he said so again in the preface to the fifth book of *On the Commonwealth*.[3]

During the early fifties BCE, Cicero spent a brief but traumatic period in exile (58–57); during the latter half of the decade he experienced a kind of internal exile from public life after being warned by Caesar and Pompey not to interfere with their control. From 55 to 51, Cicero appeared in court and in the senate, but under serious constraints; one of the effects of his circumstances was that he undertook an ambitious programme of writing. Two great works were completed, another left unfinished. The first, *De oratore* (*On the Orator*), concerned oratory and the role of the orator; the second, *De republica*, concerned political theory and civic life; the unfinished third, *De legibus* (*On Laws*), was meant to propose an ideal law-code for Rome consistent with the natural law described in the first book. All three were dialogues, modelled on Plato: *Gorgias* and *Phaedrus* in the first case, *Republic* in the second, *Laws* in the third. *De legibus* is set more or less in the present, with Cicero himself, his brother and his close friend Atticus as protagonists, while the others involve elaborate recreations of precise historical contexts highly significant for their arguments, and highly evocative of an earlier, better day. *De oratore* claims to record the last conversation of Lucius Crassus in September 91, before his sudden death and the outbreak of the Social War. In *De republica*, the dramatic setting in 129 BCE is a crucial element in the argument of the dialogue. Four years earlier, in 133, Tiberius Gracchus as tribune had carried legislation for agrarian reform and when he sought re-election had been murdered by a senatorial mob. In 129, his brother-in-law and cousin Scipio Aemilianus led senatorial opposition to the law, but he died suddenly and mysteriously (Cicero thought it was murder, although it probably was not) in the middle of disputes about the effect of the agrarian law on Rome's Italian and Latin allies. The conversation of *On the Commonwealth* takes place just before Scipio's untimely death early in 129. The

---

[2] For more detailed discussion of Cicero's sources, cf. Zetzel 1995: 13–29. For fuller discussion of content, characters and structure, see the introductions to Zetzel 1995 and 1999.

[3] This was neither the first nor the last time he said so, over a long period; for examples and further bibliography, see Dyck 1996 on *Off.* 2.29.

nine participants include Scipio – a man Cicero revered for his combination of political and military skill with high cultural attainments and interests – and his two closest friends Gaius Laelius and Lucius Furius Philus, together with representatives of an older and a younger generation (respectively the great jurist Manius Manilius and Laelius' two sons-in-law Scaevola and Fannius). The conversation begins from the recent astronomical portent of a double sun (parhelion) and moves rapidly to the corresponding divisions in Roman society. From there, Scipio leads his friends through a detailed examination of government and civic life, ultimately returning to a cosmic context in the prophetic *Dream of Scipio* which concluded the work.

The scope, the style and the careful attention to setting and context in all three dialogues display the goals and the magnitude of Cicero's project: on the one hand, to create a philosophical literature in Latin comparable to Plato's major dialogues; on the other, to explore the moral and intellectual underpinnings of Roman public life at a time when they were all in question. Each dialogue addresses an area of social and cultural theory – rhetoric, politics, law – of critical importance to the success of civil society; at the same time, however, each one focuses less on the grand structure of theory than it does on the ways in which individual citizens inform and are informed by these practices. Even the title of *On the Orator* makes this clear: it is the orator, not rhetorical theory, that is central. The focus of *On Laws*, although it was never finished, seems to have been on the shared reason that unites gods and men as fellow-citizens ruled by the same law, the law that is simultaneously our own and that of the cosmos as a whole.[4] The focus on the citizen is even more apparent in *On the Commonwealth*: the preface and the conclusion (*The Dream of Scipio*) emphasize the responsibilities and rewards for individuals of engagement in public life, and the historical narrative of Roman development in Book 2 stresses the importance of individuals in effecting change and maintaining order.

In *De oratore*, when illustrating the difference between proper definitions and the mere accumulation of examples, after defining 'general' Cicero moves on to 'statesman':

> But if we were asking who it is, who brought his experience and knowledge and energy to the guidance of the commonwealth, I would give a definition like this: the man who understood and made use of those things by which the interests of the commonwealth were developed and advanced, is the one who should be considered the guide and author of public wisdom. And I would name as instances Publius Lentulus the leader of the senate and the elder

---

4 On some of the peculiarities of *On Laws*, see Harries 2006: 51–6.

Tiberius Gracchus and Quintus Metellus and Publius Africanus and Gaius Laelius and countless others both from our state and from others. (1.211)

The first term for this sort of statesman, *rector*, is one that reappears in *On the Commonwealth*: not a ruler (*rex*) but a guide (*rector*). The latter dialogue in many ways is a sequel to the former: the Ciceronian orator is a figure of immense political importance and integrity, the man who can direct public policy through the power of language.[5] But rhetorical theory itself, both in *On the Orator* and in Cicero's early treatise on rhetoric *De inventione*, raises an important question: how can one ensure that moral integrity and rhetorical power are found in the same person?[6] How can we be certain that the good speaker is also a good man? Although the argument of *On the Commonwealth* incorporates much else, that is unquestionably Cicero's central concern. In particular: if good institutions make good men, and vice versa, then how can we (as writers, as readers, as citizens) understand or create the framework in which those good institutions and good men can work? Cicero at times speaks of outstanding figures as leaders and guides, but in fact leadership for Cicero is secondary to political participation itself, and the whole dialogue is structured as a protreptic to politics.[7] One may, in moments of crisis, require a leader; but if the citizens are not also both loyal and moral, then who will follow? Cicero's fundamental political allegiance was to property, stability and senatorial control, but as will become clear, he also believed in some sense in popular sovereignty and governmental accountability.[8] Cicero believed in inherited Roman customs and traditional institutions; and yet he also believed in the ethical grounding of political life emphasized by Plato and Aristotle.

Not much more than one-third of *On the Commonwealth* survives, and for the purposes of reconstructing the philosophical argument it is the wrong third. Although the dialogue was widely read and admired in antiquity, it largely disappeared from sight after the fifth century CE apart from the short and mystical *Dream of Scipio* that served as its conclusion. Otherwise, only quotations and paraphrases were known from late antiquity until 1819, when the prefect of the Vatican library discovered under a copy of Augustine's commentary on the Psalms a palimpsest, an erased and rewritten text of part of *On the Commonwealth*.[9] Most of the first two books of the

---

[5] On rhetoric as a theory of political life, see Connolly 2007a.

[6] See above all Skinner 1996: 66–110; Connolly 2007a: 118–29 is inadequate.

[7] On *De republica* as protreptic, see Zetzel 1998.

[8] On the uneasy balance between popular sovereignty and the rights of property in Cicero, see particularly Wood 1988: 123–42. Wood is wrong, however, to minimize the ethical element of Cicero's politics.

[9] On the recovery of *De republica* in its nineteenth-century context, see Zetzel 2011.

dialogue, on the theory of constitutions and on the history of the Roman constitution, were recovered, but very little of the remainder: the coherent portion of the palimpsest breaks off with the restoration of constitutional government after the fall of the Decemvirate in 449 BCE, a few pages survive from Books 3–5 and nothing at all from Book 6.

Even though reconstruction is necessarily speculative, the overall structure of the argument is clear. After two books on the theory of constitutions, the central pair (Books 3–4) concerned the social institutions of government and civil society and the final pair (5–6) were about the statesman – the training and actions of the individual leader. Within each pair, the first book (equipped with a separate preface in Cicero's voice) concentrated on theory, while the second was more concerned with particulars: Book 2 on the development of the Roman constitution, Book 4 on institutions such as education and the censorship, Book 6 on the actions of particular statesmen in crises, in which a reference to the behaviour of Scipio Nasica in the suppression of Tiberius Gracchus led to the concluding *Dream of Scipio* about the afterlife of great citizens.[10]

As even this brief description implies, however, and as Laelius' comments (2.21–2) about Scipio's account of the reign of Romulus make explicit, Cicero's theoretical project in *On the Commonwealth* is two-fold. On the one hand, he is trying to construct a description of the logic of political society, the basic assumptions and institutional structure of government; on the other hand, he is proposing an analysis of the government of Rome in particular, showing how it conforms to the theoretical framework being developed. These two approaches dominate respectively the odd-numbered and even-numbered books, but the separation is by no means absolute: empirical and theoretical clearly blend, and the overall structure of the dialogue is meant to draw together ever more closely the actual behaviour of citizens and the eschatological structure of the cosmos itself.

Although Cicero had Greek models in mind in his account of political theory, he clearly had his own ideas as well. Thus, the constitutional theory presented by Scipio in Book 1 is very familiar in its outlines: the identification of the three primary forms of government (monarchy, aristocracy, democracy; rule by the one, the few and the many) goes back at least to Herodotus (3.82–4) and by Cicero's time it had been refined and elaborated to an intricate theory of constitutional development and change, best attested for us in Book 6 of Polybius' *Histories*.[11] Each of the three basic

---

[10] On the structure of the dialogue, see Ferrary 1995: 48–51.

[11] An intelligent summary of the theory, its history and modern analysis is in Wood 1988: 159–68. For Cicero's modifications of Polybius, see particularly Ferrary 1984. Asmis 2005 adds little.

constitutions has its evil twin: monarchy paired with tyranny, aristocracy with oligarchy, democracy with mob rule. Unless checked, constitutional change moved from one of these to the next in inexorable order, starting from the primordial chaos that produces a single, powerful leader and degenerating at the end back into chaos from mob rule. At that point, according to Polybius, the cycle of constitutions (*anakuklosis*) begins again. But the means of resisting, if not stopping, the cycle exists in the so-called mixed constitution, a form of government blended from the three primary forms. Because each of them resists the others, the progress of decay is slowed, if not ever stopped entirely.

Cicero accepts the basic form of this theory – the six types, the *anakuklosis* and the superiority of a mixed constitution to any of the simple forms – but his description of how such things actually work resolutely eschews rigidity either of constitutional development or of the way in which it is described. Scipio describes the virtues of democracy and aristocracy from the point of view of their advocates, who also give succinct and vivid explanations of the drawbacks of the other forms. The arguments of these two groups are practical and prudential; but when Scipio gives an account of monarchy it is in his own voice and uses arguments from analogy with the soul and the cosmos, and while he remains firmly in favour of the mixed constitution as the best, he views monarchy as the best of the simple forms. What is more, he does not believe in the fixed order of the cycle of constitutions set out by Polybius, but argues that any form of government can change to any of the others (1.45, 65, 68).

Cicero's differences from Peripatetic theory are indicative of his general approach, above all his emphasis, even when discussing structures of government, on the role of individuals. Monarchy is the best simple form not merely because an executive of some kind is the one essential element in all government, and not merely – although it is important – because Rome began as a monarchy, but because Cicero constantly chooses to emphasize the role of individuals in government. His first mention of the variability of constitutional change is also the first mention of the role of the wise and provident statesman (1.45): 'There are remarkable revolutions and almost cycles of changes and alterations in commonwealths; to recognize them is the part of a wise man, and to anticipate them when they are about to occur, holding a course and keeping it under his control while governing, is the part of a truly great citizen and nearly divine man.' This abstract description of the statesman becomes concrete in the account of Roman constitutional development in Book 2. There, in describing the role of Lucius Junius Brutus in expelling the Tarquins, Scipio draws the moral that 'he was the first in this state to show that in preserving the liberty of citizens no-one is a private person' (2.46); so too, the antitype of the tyrant is described (2.51) as 'almost a tutor and manager of the commonwealth . . . he is the one who can protect the state by his wisdom and efforts'. The fullest description of this figure – the guardian, the helmsman, the man of foresight – at the end of Book 2 is unfortunately very fragmentary, but is of critical importance: he is compared (2.67) to the mahout, the single man who can control a huge elephant; he is also a musician, the one who creates and maintains the harmony of the state (2.69).

The nature, role and institutional position within Cicero's ideal government of this single leader have always been problematic.[12] It is one thing to advocate a constitutional structure with a strong executive; it is another to emphasize the role of the individual citizen in recognizing and even supervising constitutional change. At the same time, however, this odd position is consonant with another difference between Cicero's account of the mixed constitution and that of Polybius (and, indeed, that of the American constitution): Cicero believes not in a system of checks and balances, in which the vices to which the simple forms are prone are repressed by the presence of the other forms, but in a system that harnesses the virtues of each of the simple forms so that they complement one another. At most times, from Cicero's point of view, the collective wisdom of the aristocracy will guide the state, but at other times, quite clearly, the authority of a charismatic leader is essential. But what place is there for the virtue of the third form, the *libertas* that characterizes democracy?

Cicero was, to be sure, no democrat, and nor is his protagonist Scipio. In praising the constitution of Servius Tullius, he emphasizes the importance of its weighted voting system: 'He made certain (something that must always be secure in a commonwealth) that the greatest number did not have the greatest power' (2.39). But despite Cicero's strong support of property and senatorial rule, he is not quite as un-democratic as one might expect, either in *On the Commonwealth* or in other contexts. Thus, in the speech supporting the Manilian Law of 66 BCE, he makes a claim that the *auctoritas* of the people is at least as important as that of the senate; indeed, the fundamental argument of *every* speech before the people is an endorsement of their sovereignty.[13] At times, notably in the fragmentary speech in defence of the tribune Cornelius

---

[12] The so-called *princeps* has unfortunately been the most discussed element of Cicero's political theory – in part because it was distorted (particularly by Pöschl 1936) into an unsavoury amalgam of Platonism and Nazism. The essentials were seen by Heinze 1960: 141–59 (originally published 1924); restated and slightly amplified by Powell 1994. Asmis 2005 wrongly believes that this was some kind of permanent office; it was not. The most useful recent discussion is in Ferrary 1995: 51–66.

[13] *De imp. Cn. Pompei* 63–4. On the political rhetoric of public oratory (*contio*), see Morstein-Marx 2004: 119–59.

on a charge of treason in 65, he seems to go even further: there, he argues (following the famous speech of the orator Antonius in defence of his former quaestor Norbanus) that popular resistance of the kind that led in 494 BCE to the secession of the plebs and the creation of the tribunate is justified (fr. 48–9 Crawford). Cicero does not, indeed, go so far as Machiavelli or Jefferson in arguing the need for regular revolutionary upheaval,[14] but he does firmly believe that the establishment of the tribunate was both necessary and justified and that the legitimacy of government ultimately rests on the consent of the people.

Cicero's belief in the necessity of the tribunate is clear both from *On the Commonwealth* and from the comparable discussion in *On Laws*.[15] In *On the Commonwealth*, in discussing the origins of the tribunate (2.57), Scipio says that it was natural, after the fall of the monarchy, for the people to assert themselves. The fuller discussion of the tribunate in *On Laws* is more explicit. Here, Cicero's brother Quintus, speaking as an unrepentant Sullan (3.17), calls the tribunate 'a great evil' reducing the power of the optimates; Cicero disagrees, arguing in favour of moderation and 'wise blending' before the text breaks off. In the subsequent discussion (3.19–26), Cicero allows that some tribunes – like some holders of other offices – are difficult and problematic, but that the office itself is necessary, and that in the absence of absolute monarchy, the people needed 'real, not nominal, freedom' (3.25). Cicero's description of his ideal ballot law is more revealing, and matches the views Scipio expresses about the weighted voting in the Servian constitution. In *On Laws* he advocates giving plebeians the vote – but requires that they show their ballots to the optimates. 'The liberty should consist in this, that the people are given the power of honorably pleasing the respectable citizens... [M]y law gives the appearance of liberty while keeping the authority of the respectable and eliminating an occasion for dispute' (3.39). In a certain sense, then, Cicero seems genuinely to believe in recognizing the authority of the people – but it is much more important that the people believe they are respected than that they actually, under normal circumstances, control daily governmental affairs. The law gives them authority and respect; it does not give them control of government.

---

[14] Machiavelli 1994: 189–93; Jefferson to William Smith, 13 November 1787: 'God forbid we should ever be 20 years without such a rebellion. The people cannot be all, and always, well informed. The part which is wrong will be discontented in proportion to the importance of the facts they misconceive. If they remain quiet under such misconceptions it is a lethargy, the forerunner of death to the public liberty... The tree of liberty must be refreshed from time to time with the blood of patriots and tyrants. It is it's natural manure' (Jefferson 1955: 356).

[15] For Cicero's views on the tribunate and popular sovereignty, see particularly Girardet 1977. Many scholars exaggerate Cicero's conservatism in this regard.

The most important difference between Cicero and Quintus concerning the tribunate is not that one accepts it and the other does not, but that Cicero thinks not just that it is tolerable, but that it is right and necessary as a confirmation of the legitimacy of even aristocratic government.[16]

If we accept the possibility that Cicero has a genuine belief in at least limited popular sovereignty – the right to representation by the tribunes, a (restricted) right to vote and (more or less) equal access to law – then the definition of the *res publica* from which Scipio begins his account of constitutions deserves careful scrutiny. According to Scipio's account of political origins (1.39), human beings are naturally gregarious and in the first instance that is why they form societies: 'The first cause of its [sc. a people's] assembly is not so much weakness as a kind of natural herding together of men: this species is not isolated or prone to wandering alone.' The dismissal of weakness as a cause is a deliberate rejection of the kind of rudimentary contract theory proposed by Glaucon in Plato, *Republic* 2 – that society (and hence justice) is a compromise between being able to harm others and the fear of being harmed by them; an agreement to do neither is the basis of society. Cicero's approach in this respect is more Aristotelian: he believes that the urge to form societies is natural, even if he never follows the Aristotelian pattern of viewing the *polis* as logically prior to the individual or the family. Indeed, Scipio, in Cicero's account, explicitly rejects (1.38) the idea of tracing the origins of society to the family. But beyond natural gregariousness, Cicero adds two important criteria for the creation of a legitimate society.[17] One derives from his use of the language of property to define the relationship of people to commonwealth (*res publica/res populi*).[18] Given the strong meaning of ownership in Roman law, a definition of the commonwealth as *owned* by the people implies the necessity for popular consent: one may lose possession of property unintentionally, but one can not lose ownership without choosing to do so. Second, the notion of political organization as a form of popular ownership depends on the definition of the *populus* to whom it belongs. Cicero defines this *populus* by two criteria. One, *iuris consensus*, is ambiguous, but must at a minimum mean agreement on law: again, it defines the people as created by, and existing through, their consent to a legal system.[19] The other, *utilitatis communio* (community of

---

[16] See also Wood 1988: 170–1.

[17] On the interpretation of Cicero's definition, I largely follow Schofield 1995. The discussion of Harries 2006 on law, *societas* and the *populus* is also extremely valuable.

[18] On the importance of property in Cicero's political definition, see also Wood 1988: 125–6.

[19] For its second, stronger meaning ('agreement with the [universal] law') in Book 3, see below (pp. 192–3). On the significance of the change, see Zetzel 1996.

interest) again implies agreement, in this case in defining the best interests of the community.

What is important about this combination of features is that, although there is a close connection between the notions of consent and contract, the consensual *populus* of Cicero's *Commonwealth*, unlike the participant in the Hobbesian covenant, does not give up freedom to the selected government, it merely entrusts (in a Lockean sense) the administration of its wishes to a government. And, as Cicero goes on to say, any form of deliberative control is acceptable, but it 'must always be connected to the original cause which engendered the state' (1.41).[20] Thus, although Cicero obviously cares a great deal – both in the account of government he assigns to Scipio and in his own public statements – about senatorial control and the centrality of property and aristocracy, the story he tells about political origins is firmly based on popular sovereignty. He may believe that the wisdom of aristocracy is necessary and that direct popular rule is terrible; but he consistently believes that, ultimately, the success of government depends on the satisfaction and acquiescence, if not the participation, of the legitimate community of all citizens.

If Cicero were simply saying that the rule of law creates a legitimate community it would be tautological; but the argument is more complicated than that. To say that for all individuals in a community the sense that the community is governed by the rule of law legitimates the political system is not trivial: my belief that I am governed by a law that I accept (or indeed ratify) not only legitimates the political system, it creates a sense of loyalty and identification. Without the creation of a belief in a legally constituted community (in *On Laws*, the belief that one's vote matters, even if it doesn't), Cicero believes, there can be no enduring community. But on the one hand, if one accepts, at least theoretically, the right of popular resistance and ultimate popular sovereignty; and on the other hand, if one is committed to a conservative and traditional form of government and society, what is to ensure a continuing sense of political obligation? What makes the people accept the law? Cicero's definition risks condoning a very utilitarian (or Epicurean) definition of law and justice as contingent and based on circumstance; but it also clearly risks serious social instability. It is precisely these problems that the dialogue begins to address immediately after Scipio finishes his account of Roman constitutional development – and it is not

---

[20] The original cause at 1.39 (sociability and weakness) is modified in a more Aristotelian direction ('shared association in a happy and honorable way of life') at 4.3a. On the importance of fiduciary responsibility, see Wood 1988: 132–42.

coincidental that these are precisely the issues confronting Scipio and his friends in 129 BCE.[21]

Although the end of Scipio's narrative (with the restoration of constitutional government after the expulsion of the Decemvirate in 449) is also the point where the palimpsest begins to be very discontinuous, some aspects of the discussion are clear. In the first place, after Tubero criticizes Scipio's account as panegyric rather than analysis of constitutional theory, Scipio emphasizes the importance of the man of foresight (*prudens*) in managing and controlling constitutional change, something that has already been repeatedly mentioned in the narrative. But now the qualities of this statesman are described more fully: he is first compared to a mahout, the elephant-handler who can control the direction of a huge animal, and then Scipio emphasizes his ability, like a musician, to maintain harmony in the state: 'What musicians call harmony with regard to song is concord in the state, the tightest and the best bond of safety in every republic; and that concord can never exist without justice' (2.69a).

The fragment on harmony, concord and justice is of critical importance, both in the structure of the dialogue and in the argument itself.[22] In terms of the argument, it returns to the definition of the *res publica* at 1.39 and the problem of popular allegiance and political obligation. Structurally, it leads to the analogy of state and cosmos that animates the *Dream of Scipio* at the end of the work; it also implies (what is demonstrated by Laelius in the debate on justice that follows in Book 3) that just as harmony has an objective existence and truth, so too does concord and therefore justice. We are left, then, with the double problem of determining the substantive content of justice and of learning how and why people accept it.

The debate on justice was the centrepiece of the dialogue and, directly or indirectly, influenced political theorists at least down to Grotius.[23] It was based on the pair of speeches delivered by the Academic Carneades in 155 BC in Rome, in which on the first day he spoke of the necessity of justice for human society and on the next day of the necessity of injustice. Carneades was reversing the order of arguments in Plato, *Republic* 2–4; in reproducing the debate, Cicero reversed the arguments again. Philus, given

---

[21] On the sources of law and obligation, see also Ferrary 1995, to which I am much indebted although I disagree with his understanding of Ciceronian natural law and hence reach somewhat different conclusions.

[22] On the harmony fragment, see the discussions of Wood 1988: 162–8, Ferrary 1995: 64–6, Asmis 2005: 404–6.

[23] For discussion and reconstruction of the debate, see Zetzel 1996 with fuller bibliography. Powell's arrangement of the fragments (Powell 2006) is unhelpful; my own version (which I follow here) in Zetzel 1999.

the job of attacking justice, speaks first; Laelius, defending it, is given the last word. In the course of his (very fragmentary) speech, Laelius not only refutes Epicurean notions of the relativity and contingency of justice, but also establishes that morality (including justice) is based in nature and that there is such a thing as natural law. The famous paragraph (3.33) defining natural law – preserved by Lactantius, who says that it might well have been written by a Christian – describes it as eternal, universal, unchangeable and unbreakable. More important, observing the natural law defines one as a human being. The Stoic argument, elaborated in much more detail in Book 1 of *On Laws*, is that the natural law is identical to right reason; that reason is shared by all humans (and gods as well); and therefore that the proper use of reason both leads one to recognize the natural law and to obey it. Not everyone, of course, does make proper use of reason: it is the inspired statesmen who are most in harmony with the justice and reason of the universe, and who therefore (in the *Dream*) most rapidly receive an eternal reward for their lawfulness.

The abstract Stoic argument about natural law and right reason seems a very long way from the practical workings of government and the creation of a sense of civic obligation. And, in fact, not enough of the second half of *On the Commonwealth* survives to allow any certainty about how Cicero makes the connection. But what Cicero says in Book 4 about the social institutions that animate Roman morality and government repeatedly (4.4, 4.6d, 4.6f = 4.2a, 4, 8 Powell) link them to the concept of *uerecundia*, the sense of shame, which in turn is defined by Scipio (5.6) in terms that identify it as Stoic *aidôs*: 'The leader of commonwealths strengthens this sense of shame by his opinions, and he brings it to perfection by institutions and education, so that shame does as much as fear to keep citizens from crime.'[24] In other words, Cicero argued that the traditional institutions of Rome were consonant with the natural law – representations of reason as applied by enlightened statesmen to the government of their country.

If that is the case, then it is not hard to imagine how Cicero dealt with the basic issues of obligation and popular sovereignty. If Roman custom is a manifestation of reason/natural law, and if all people who use their reason properly have access to that natural law, then those people will naturally recognize the validity and enduring merit of Roman traditional institutions. At the same time, the institutions of Roman government – being attuned to the natural law – will normally produce citizens who are

---

[24] This is part of a leaf of the palimpsest that Powell wrongly assigns to the preface of Book 3 (3.3) rather than (as Ziegler 1958) to a speech of Scipio in Book 5 (5.6). For reconstruction of the argument, see Zetzel 2001.

indeed capable of reasoning properly, or at least of accepting the validity of their betters' reason. In the conversation that follows his speech on justice, Laelius brings back the phrase used by Scipio in 1.39 to define the *populus*, namely *iuris consensus*, agreement on law. But when Laelius repeats it, it is in connection not with positive law or law by consensus, but in connection with the natural law itself. The agreement on law that is the contractual basis of social order becomes an agreement with natural law, something that all reasonable people will accept. And by accepting natural law through reason, the people are indeed sovereign – although no more so than any other truly rational person.[25]

There are two problems with this reasoning. One is that it can be understood to produce a very feeble version of Rousseauian or Kantian autonomy – we are all rational and therefore we are all somehow sovereign, we all will what reason (and the law) demand – that resolves nothing about political order or constitutional structure; the other is that reason itself is not infallible, as is made very clear in the account of the origins of the tribunate discussed above: 'The nature of commonwealths often overcomes reason' (2.57). But the weakness of reason itself explains the need for authority and for traditional institutions. The Roman social and political system was not the result of one person's wisdom or one generation (2.1); it involves trial and error as well as the cumulative wisdom of the *maiores*. Nor, indeed, do all people want to spend their time in contemplation of reason, natural law and their own political and ethical beliefs and actions. That is the role of the statesman: as Scipio says of him at the end of Book 2 (2.69a), his responsibility is 'that he never cease educating and observing himself, that he summon others to imitate him, that through the brilliance of his mind and life he offer himself as a mirror to his fellow citizens'.[26] As with the ballot law of *On Laws* Book 3, according to which the citizen shows his ballot to some respectable citizen, so with the relationship between ruled and rulers in political society: the people are sovereign, but are expected, collectively and individually, to recognize the brilliance of their leaders and to accept that leadership.

But what of the leaders themselves? In Cicero's own preface to Book 3, he speaks of outstanding citizens – like Scipio, Laelius and Philus, who go beyond the philosophers who attain theoretical understanding of

---

[25] This is, fairly evidently, a version of the Stoic cosmopolis, in its weaker form (as in *On Laws* 1): not (as, for instance, in Philo or Marcus Aurelius) a city composed only of the wise, but a city of all rational beings. See above all Schofield 1991. For another account of the role of natural law in the definition of citizenship in the last years of Cicero's life, see also Harries 2006: 204–29.

[26] For the mirror argument, see Ferrary 1995.

the ethical life to combine with it an understanding of the Roman past: 'In order to achieve the highest glory of great men, they added to the traditional knowledge of their own ancestors the imported philosophical knowledge of the Socratic school. The person who has had the will and capacity to acquire both . . . is the one who I think has done everything deserving of praise' (3.5–6a). By looking both ways, to the traditional institutions of Rome and to the cosmic order of reason which animates them, they provide a model and an instrument for the preservation of a just society. That is the role of Scipio in providing guidance in the crisis of 129 – guidance that he did not live to offer – and, as transmitted through Cicero himself, for the crisis of the fifties.

One last feature of the political theory of *On the Commonwealth* needs to be noticed. Unlike Athens or Plato's Kallipolis and Magnesia, Roman government had to take account not just of the city, but of the world. The end of Laelius' speech on justice makes it clear that a moral government could not treat its citizens well only at the expense of its subjects and allies: the eternity of government requires just treatment of all its subjects (3.41).[27] So too in Scipio's dream, reference to the Latins and the allies is crucial: 'the senate, all upstanding citizens, the allies, and the Latins will look to you; you will be the one person on whom the safety of the state rests' (6.12). Equally striking is Cicero's account of the extent of wise leadership (3.7): 'And if we take the praiseworthy states which exist and have existed (since the foundation of a state capable of lasting for a long time takes greater judgment than anything in the world), and if we count one person to each state, then how great a multitude will we find of excellent men! If in Italy we consider Latium, or the Sabine and Volscian nations, or Samnium, Etruria, and Magna Graecia, and add to them the Assyrians, Persians, Carthaginians.' Good institutions are not limited to Rome, governments consonant with the principles of morality and law are not limited to Rome (or to metropolitan Greece, which is conspicuously not mentioned in this list); the natural law is represented anywhere morality and tradition coincide in the persons of enlightened citizens and statesmen.[28] What follows from this is that no government, particularly not an imperial government like that of Rome, can limit its sense of justice to a single city, but must respect on the one side its place in the cosmic order and on the other its relationship to everyone under its control. Cicero, we know from as early as the *Verrine*

---

[27] Cf. Zetzel 1996.

[28] It is this universality of natural law that makes it impossible to follow Girardet 1983 and Ferrary 1995 in identifying the ideal Roman law-code of *On Laws* 2–3 as being the same thing as, rather than a reflection of, the natural law. This identification leads them to adopt a much weaker (non-Stoic) interpretation of natural law itself.

Orations down to his governorship of Cilicia in 51 and later, was acutely aware of the inequity of much of Rome's treatment of its allies and subjects. In *On the Commonwealth*, he extends the ethical responsibility of government far beyond what Aristotle acknowledges; for the first time, he offers a justification and a critique of empire. 'We are not born for ourselves alone, but for our country' is one of Cicero's favourite tags from Plato (*Epistles* 9.358a). Cicero goes beyond Plato: we have a responsibility not just for our own country, but for the world.

Further reading

Cicero's political theory has been discussed very little in English until fairly recently and there is still no satisfactory full-length treatment of *De republica*, although Atkins 2000 provides a serviceable brief account. Wood 1988 has much of value but is marred, sometimes seriously, by frequent errors in Latin, overemphasis on economic structures of power and too little attention to the ethical element in Cicero's politics. Connolly 2007a is a fascinating study of rhetoric and politics in Cicero, but is much more concerned with constructing normative theory than with explaining Cicero. Harries 2006 focuses on Cicero's views of law, but in the process says much about his ideas about government. Gildenhard 2010 offers a useful account of what Cicero says about society and law in his speeches, but very little about his political theory. Much is still written about the mixed constitution, but very little of interest has been said on the subject in many years. So too with the issue of leadership and the *rector*: most of what is said (to the extent that it is right) simply restates Heinze 1960 with minor modifications.

There are, however, some admirable studies of particular issues. Above all, anyone interested in *De republica* should start by reading the work of Malcolm Schofield and Jean-Louis Ferrary; for titles, see the bibliography. But to place Cicero in his context in the history of political theory, the best starting-point is the work of J. G. A. Pocock and Quentin Skinner on early modern republican theory.

12

RUTH MORELLO

Writer and addressee in Cicero's letters

Omnes autem Ciceronis epistulas legendas censeo, mea sententia uel
magis quam omnes eius orationes: epistulis Ciceronis nihil est
perfectius.
(Fronto *Ed. ad Ant. Imp.* 2.5 = 3.8 van den Hout 1988)

Elite Romans in the late Republic lived in an epistolary culture, one into which the extant Ciceronian collections give us invaluable, but still only partial, insight. The collections contain over 900 of Cicero's surviving letters, including 435 letters *Ad familiares*, 426 more *Ad Atticum*, plus 53 (combined) *Ad Quintum fratrem* and *Ad Brutum*. They preserve pieces about personal or professional dilemmas, gossip, parental worries, gubernatorial successes, architectural renovations, literary projects and political speculation.[1] Indeed, such profusion and variety, even within the bounds of single letters, came to characterize the Ciceronian collection for later readers, as did the weight and solemnity of much of Cicero's political material.[2] The surviving letters are the products of his maturity, and many of them cluster around the most traumatic times of his life; for example, the transmission includes only eleven letters from the years before 61 BC, but distinctive parts of the collections belong to two periods of enforced absence from Rome (exile in 58–57 and proconsular service in Cilicia in 51–50), while there is also a particularly rich vein of letters on the political cataclysms and private griefs of his final years; roughly a quarter of the *Ad familiares* dates, indeed, from 46 BC,[3] while there is a further flurry in the immediate aftermath of Caesar's assassination.

---

[1] On the extant letters as a tiny fraction (potentially only 1 per cent) of Cicero's total epistolary output, see Hall 2009: 16; Achard 1991: 139; on 'missing letters' and the editorial selectivity of the transmitted collections, see White 2010: 31–61, especially 34–41. Other sets of books to (e.g.) Pompey, Caesar, Octavian and Cicero's son, which were certainly known even in late antiquity, are now lost. For Cicero's own plans for publication of a selection of his own letters, see *Att.* 16.5, *Fam.* 16.17; cf. Nep. *Att.* 16.2–4. On fragments of lost Ciceronian letters, see Weyssenhoff 1966. On the extant remains of pre-Ciceronian Latin letters, see Cugusi 1983: 151–7.

[2] See, e.g. Sen. *Ep.* 118. For a Ciceronian letter as a mélange of topics, see *Att.* 6.1.17.

[3] Leach 1999: 139.

Chronological arrangement, however, is not the dominant principle in the transmitted Ciceronian letter books. The unknown ancient editors of the collections tended to group letters first of all by addressee, and only thereafter, as a secondary organizational principle, to arrange the letters in chronological sequences. In consequence, the books of letters *Ad Atticum* need relatively little rearrangement to restore chronological sequence, while even the sixteen books *Ad familiares* (containing letters to over seventy individuals, as well as about ninety specimens of their replies) arrange letters by correspondent in more or less chronologically coherent subgroups. For example, all but one of the letters in *Fam.* 1 are addressed to Lentulus Spinther, most of them written in 56–54, during Lentulus' proconsulship in Cilicia, while Book 3 is devoted to the letters to Appius Pulcher in 52–50. The gathering of letters according to addressee applies even when the dominant selection principle in a book is more obviously a thematic or formal one, as it is, for example, in Book 13 of the *Fam.*, in which several of the book's seventy-nine recommendation letters are arranged in small groups according to addressee. Moreover, meaningful patterns may be detected in the groupings of addressees: *Fam.* 2, for example, which contains letters to Curio and to Caelius, as well as one letter to Cicero's unsatisfactory quaestor, Coelius, is delightfully characterized by Leach as 'the book of the reformed scapegraces'.[4] *Fam.* 14 contains letters to Cicero's wife and children, and *Fam.* 16 those to his freedman Tiro, while sixteen letters from Caelius fill *Fam.* 8 (the only book to contain no letters at all from Cicero's pen).

The primary focus of this chapter is upon the letter-writer's handling of individual addressees and particularly upon Cicero's sophisticated techniques for involving his addressee in the topic or event which forms the central material of a letter.[5] It looks first at 'conversational' elements of letters, before examining, as case studies, four individual letters (*Fam.* 9.21 to Papirius Paetus, *Fam.* 2.4 to Curio, *Att.* 1.14 and *Fam.* 7.1 to Marius) in which Cicero successfully constructs a close link between his addressee and the central topic of the letter itself. Finally, it considers the effects achieved by the ancient editors of the *Fam.* collection in gathering and arranging a famously more problematic letter exchange, namely that between Cicero and Cato at the end of Cicero's governorship of Cilicia (*Fam.* 15.3–6).

---

4 Leach 2006: 256.
5 For a study of Cicero's readiness to adapt (e.g.) oratorical material in order to find the right approach to an addressee, see Bernard 2007.

Epistolary 'talk'

Letters are an interactive genre – one half of a dialogue, according to Artemon's famous characterization.[6] It is, indeed, a cliché of epistolary theory that letters are a substitute for conversation.[7] They anticipate an answer,[8] and by retaining the flavour of conversational exchange, they maintain an apparent realism and seek to minimize the sense of geographical separation between writer and addressee.[9]

A distinctively 'realistic' feature of the letters in the Ciceronian collections is the remarkable amount of spoken material which is woven into them; not only are they 'conversations' between writer and addressee, but they also allow the addressee to 'hear' what is being said by third parties in his absence. Caelius, for example, relays the gossip while Cicero is away in Cilicia – including a rumour of Cicero's own death.[10] Indeed, *Fam.* 8.1, Caelius' manifesto for his role as Cicero's trusted political correspondent, promises two 'epistolary' products, both stuffed with 'talk' of all kinds: an encyclopaedic *uolumen* (an information pack, as it were), compiled regularly by an assistant, which will report everything from senatorial edicts to rumours and popular gossip, and – as separate items – Caelius' own, shorter letters, intended to cover any material too important for the 'hack' to report properly.

Cicero's reply, preserved as *Fam.* 2.8, begins with humorous criticism of the excessive detail in the 'information pack': if he were in Rome, he says, no-one would dare to waste his time with such stuff. In this respect, one might say, these reports are the antithesis of proper letters, which should mimic the experience of being in the thick of things in Rome and reduce the recipient's sense of separation from the writer and from home. So Cicero

---

[6] Reported and refined by Demetrius, *De elocutione* 223–4.

[7] See most recently White 2010: 18–29. Cf. Thraede 1970: 27–47; Williams 1991: 170. On conversational style in letters, see (e.g.) Seneca *Ep.* 75.1.

[8] Some letters, indeed, present themselves as little more than a request for a reply (see e.g. *Att.* 14.12.3 *scribo tamen, non ut delectem is litteris sed ut eliciam tuas*, 'still I go on writing, not to give you pleasure with my letters but to evoke yours').

[9] An emphasis upon the situation or location in which the writer composes, or from which he sends, his letter, is one of the many features of ancient letter-writing which are suggestive of the dialogue; just as Cicero's philosophical dialogues often begin by setting the scene for the conversation in a garden, or at one of the protagonists' villas, so too do many epistolary 'conversations' highlight the motif of separation by noting the place of composition (*Att.* 1.10.1 provides a humorously competitive example: *cum essem in Tusculano (erit hoc tibi pro illo tuo 'cum essem in Ceramico'*, 'I was at my place in Tusculum – that will do in return for your "I was in Ceramicus"').

[10] *Fam.* 8.1.4. 'Talk' is epistolary currency, and Caelius expects in return for his trouble a full account of Cicero's conversation with Pompey (*Fam.* 8.1.3). On the dissemination of political rumour, see Laurence 1994; Hall 2009: 25.

wants to see reports only from Caelius himself, but he also further defines Caelius' own epistolary role (*Fam.* 2.8.1):

Ne illa quidem curo mihi scribas, quae maximis in rebus rei publicae geruntur cotidie, nisi quid ad me ipsum pertinebit; scribent alii, multi nuntiabunt, perferet multa etiam ipse rumor. Qua re ego nec praeterita nec praesentia abs te, sed ut ab homine longe in posterum prospiciente futura exspecto, ut, ex tuis litteris cum formam rei publicae uiderim, quale aedificium futurum sit scire possum.

(I do not even particularly want you to tell me day-to-day political developments in matters of major consequence, unless I am affected personally. Others will be writing, I shall have plenty of oral informants, even common report will transmit a good deal. So I do not expect things past or present from *your* pen. What I want from so far-sighted a fellow as yourself is the future. From your letters, having seen, as it were, an architect's drawing of the political situation, I shall hope to know what kind of building is to come.)

This request compliments this addressee as the expert political commentator who can (like Atticus) intelligently *interpret* events which others can only report.[11] Conversations, anecdotes and rumours are natural epistolary material, but Caelius is distinguished by his ability to move beyond them.

The rich variety of human talk underpins epistolary realism more successfully in *Att.* 2.15:

Vt scribis ita uideo non minus incerta in re publica quam in epistula tua, sed tamen ista ipsa me uarietas sermonum opinionumque delectat. Romae enim uideor esse cum tuas litteras lego et, ut fit in tantis rebus, modo hoc modo illud audire.

(Evidently it is as you say, things are as uncertain in the political field as in your letter; but it is just this diversity of talk and comment that I find so entertaining. When I read a letter of yours I feel I am in Rome, hearing one thing one minute, another the next, as one does when big events are toward.)

In realistic fashion (*ut fit in tantis rebus*), Atticus' letter had reflected the rich variety of human talk to be heard in the city of Rome, and subsumed the lone voice of the writer himself into the voices of an urban population, transporting Cicero's imagination back home by means of clever epistolary staging of multiple conversations.

The conversational quality inherent in many types of letter has obvious stylistic consequences – in theory, if not always in practice. Ovid advises a deceptively natural style for letters of seduction (*Ars am.* 1.457–68): they

---

[11] *Att.* 5.14.3.

should be composed in *credibilis sermo* and in everyday language, to mask, in Hardie's words, 'the care and artifice required to create the illusion of unmediated presence and the effect of being natural'.[12] The expectation of relative simplicity in epistolary language itself became an epistolary topos, and excessively lofty vocabulary was felt to endanger the realism of letters and to unmask a writer's wish to target readers other than the addressee himself. In *Fam.* 16.17, for example, Cicero pokes fun at Tiro for a rather highfalutin declaration that he is 'faithfully studying' his health (*ualetudini fideliter inseruiendo*). Tiro's self-conscious style, Cicero suggests, betrays a secret ambition to see *his* letters, too, collected and published (*uideo quid agas; tuas quoque epistulas uis referri in uolumina*).[13]

This is not to say that we should expect no complexity or stylistic sophistication in letters, or even that such qualities required disguise.[14] Indeed, in a famous letter to Papirius Paetus (*Fam.* 9.21) the topos of epistolary simplicity itself provides the framework for a complex set of jokes. Cicero contrasts two 'Ciceronian' styles: his Jove-like grandeur in his oratory (*fulmina* which Paetus had recently attempted to emulate), and the 'plebeian' epistolary simplicity he ascribes to *Fam.* 9.21 itself:[15]

> Ain tandem? Insanire tibi uideris, quod imitere uerborum meorum, ut scribis, 'fulmina'? Tum insanires, si consequi non posses... Verum tamen quid tibi ego uideor in epistulis? nonne plebeio sermone agere tecum? nec enim semper eodem modo; quid enim simile habet epistula aut iudicio aut contioni? quin ipsa iudicia non solemus omnia tractare uno modo: priuatas causas, et eas

---

[12] Hardie 2002: 108.

[13] Cf. *Fam.* 7.5.3 where Cicero, mindful of Caesar's mocking response to his earlier failure to find the *mot juste*, relies upon 'plain Latin' in his recommendation on behalf of Trebatius.

[14] On Cicero's use of a virtuoso's rhythmic prose for his letters, for example, see Hutchinson (1998): 9–12; cf. Hutchinson 1995. Cicero's correspondents rarely produce rhythmic letters; as Hutchinson suggests, even to elite contemporaries Cicero's letters 'would have seemed highly distinctive and distinctively polished' (Hutchinson 1998: 12).

[15] On this letter, see Hutchinson 1998: 5–6; 191–8. This addressee is also the recipient of another letter about vocabulary (*Fam.* 9.22), this time on the criteria for using obscene words. 'Getting the right tone' for an addressee might be a matter of perceived manner – so, for example, Cicero complains to Atticus that Brutus' letters tend to be rather arrogant and insufficiently mindful of addressee (*sed plane parum cogitat quid scribat aut ad quem*, Att. 6.3.7). However, Cicero painstakingly selects metaphors and jokes which will have special relevance to the addressee; for example, he famously builds *Fam.* 6.6, an encouraging letter to the exiled Caecina, around a metaphor of augury, an especially apt image from Cicero the augur to the addressee whose father wrote a well-known treatise *De Etrusca disciplina*. In a different vein, Caelius makes a cheekily apt joke instructing Cicero the proconsul to 'give himself an order' (*impera tibi hoc*) and sort out some panthers for the games (*Fam.* 8.9.3). On Cicero's equally humorous response, see Hutchinson 1998: 178.

tenues, agimus subtilius, capitis aut famae scilicet ornatius; epistulas uero quotidianis verbis texere solemus.

(Really? You think you are out of your mind to be imitating my 'verbal thunderbolts'? You would be if you could not make a success of it...But tell me now, how do you find me as a letter-writer? Don't I deal with you in colloquial style? The fact is that one's style has to vary. A letter is one thing, a court of law or a public meeting quite another. Even for the courts we don't have just one style. In pleading civil cases, unimportant ones, we put on no frills, whereas cases involving status or reputation naturally get something more elaborate. As for letters, we weave them out of the language of everyday.)

The match between style and status really matters in oratory, but Cicero disingenuously characterizes all letters as woven from humble yarn.[16] This letter, however, builds a sophisticated joke about literary style and social class, constructing parallel contrasts of grandeur with simplicity, both in speech and in family breeding. Cicero reassures Paetus as to the sanity (*insanire tibi uideris*) of his attempt to be (grandly) Ciceronian, but uses self-consciously 'plebeian' language to question the mental state which led this addressee into erroneous claims about his own family's social status ('Be that as it may, my dear Paetus, what possessed you – *qui tibi uenit in mentem* – to say that all the Papirii without exception were plebeians?'). Cicero corrects the mistake, and exhorts his addressee to 'return to the fathers' (*ad patres censeo reuertare*); this play upon a senatorial technical term (properly used of the reversion of auspices to the patrician senate in the absence of patrician magistrates) humorously redirects his friend's attention away from the more disreputable plebeian branches of his clan towards its noble pedigree. Thus, in return for Paetus' flattering imitation of his oratorical grandeur, Cicero reminds him (in language pointedly labelled 'plebeian' but crowned by a distinctly patrician metaphor) that Papirii are true grandees. The letter tells us much about how to deal elegantly with a friend's mistake, but as an instance of epistolary simplicity it is a deliberately piquant failure.

Another classic piece of Ciceronian theorizing about letters functions similarly as a rhetorical device to highlight a letter's main topic (*Fam* 2.4.1):

Epistularum genera multa esse non ignoras sed unum illud certissimum, cuius causa inuenta res ipsa est, ut certiores faceremus absentis si quid esset quod eos scire aut nostra aut ipsorum interesset. Huius generis litteras a me profecto non exspectas...Reliqua sunt epistularum genera duo, quae me magno opere delectant, unum familiare et iocosum, alterum seuerum et graue. Utro me minus deceat uti non intellego.

---

[16] The characteristic unhelpfulness of Cicero's epistolary theorizing is noted by Hutchinson 1998: 7.

(That there are many different categories of letters you are aware. But the most authentic, the purpose in fact for which letter-writing was invented, is to inform the absent of what it is desirable for them to know, whether in our interest or their own. Letters of this kind I suppose you do not expect from me...That leaves two categories which give me great pleasure; one familiar and jocular, the other serious and grave. Which would be the less fitting for me to use I don't know.)

In a brisk priamel, three epistolary options of topic or style are mooted and dismissed (as inappropriate to the political circumstances), before Cicero briefly exhorts Curio to fulfil the promise of his talents and to strive to win fame as a committed citizen of the *res publica*. This exhortation, however, is understated, so that it appears not as the climactic (and preferred) epistolary mode, but merely – *faute de mieux* – as a closural device characteristic of letters (perhaps to *this* addressee above all):[17]

> Quam ob rem, quoniam mihi nullum scribendi argumentum relictum est, utar ea clausula qua soleo teque ad studium summae laudis cohortabor.
>
> (Well then, having no topic left, I shall resort to my usual conclusion and urge you to strive for glory.)

Exhortation can be an uncomfortable project; Cicero's careful discussion of epistolary modes mitigates potential offence by depicting Curio as a fellow patriot with as sensitive an understanding of the interaction of style and politics as Cicero himself – the right sort of addressee.[18]

The addressee as expert audience

In *Fam.* 9.21, as we have seen, Cicero contrasts his oratorical output with his epistolary one on stylistic grounds, taking the addressee as inspiration for topic and style. Ciceronian oratorical style is the subject also of *Att.* 1.14, which reports to Atticus on the situation in Rome in 61 BC after the breaking of the Bona Dea scandal. In this letter, Cicero locates himself at the heart of the action first at a *contio* in the circus Flaminius and then again at a meeting of the senate:

---

[17] In *Fam.* 2.1.2 (the first letter to Curio in the collection) Cicero similarly dismisses the topic of letters and turns to exhortation of his addressee: *sed de litteris hactenus...breue est quod me tibi praecipere meus incredibilis in te amor cogit.*

[18] On this letter, cf. Hall 2009: 16, 66–71; Leach 2006: 251, 256. Cf also *Fam.* 6.10b, and *Fam.* 4.13 (in which Cicero once again rejects other epistolary modes in favour of exhortation).

Prima contio Pompei qualis fuisset, scripsi ad te antea, non iucunda miseris, inanis improbis, beatis non grata, bonis non grauis; itaque frigebat. Tum Pisonis consulis impulsu leuissimus tribunus pl. Fufius in contionem producit Pompeium. Res agebatur in circo Flaminio . . . Quaesiuit ex eo, placeretne ei iudices a praetore legi, quo consilio idem praetor uteretur . . . Tum Pompeius μάλ' ἀριστοκρατικῶς locutus est senatusque auctoritatem sibi omnibus in rebus maximam uideri semperque uisam esse respondit et id multis uerbis. Postea Messalla consul in senatu de Pompeio quaesiuit, quid de religione et de pro-mulgata rogatione sentiret. Locutus ita est in senatu, ut omnia illius ordinis consulta γενικῶς laudaret, mihique, ut adsedit, dixit se putare satis ab se etiam 'de istis rebus' esse responsum.

(I have already given you a description of Pompey's first public speech – of no comfort to the poor or interest to the rascals; on the other hand the rich were not pleased and the honest men were not edified. So – a frost. Then an irrespon-sible tribune, Fufius, egged on by Consul Piso, called Pompey out to address the Assembly . . . Fufius asked him whether he thought it right for a jury to be selected by a Praetor to serve under the same Praetor's presidency . . . Pompey then replied, very much *en bon aristocrate*, that in all matters he held and had always held the senate's authority in the highest respect – at considerable length too. Subsequently Consul Messalla asked Pompey in the senate for his views about the sacrilege and the promulgated bill. He then addressed the senate, commending in general terms all decrees of that body, and remarked to me as he sat down beside me that he hoped he had now replied sufficiently to questioning on these matters.)

Cicero reports the question put to Pompey in the two separate public dis-cussions (*quaesiuit . . . quaesiuit*), each instigated, directly or indirectly, by one of the consuls; each response is marked out with a Greek adverb – a touch of grandiose irony, perhaps, given the otherwise poor impression left in the reader's mind by the repetition of *quaesiuit* and by Pompey's verbose but unspecific replies. Only then does Cicero reveal his own precise where-abouts – just at Pompey's elbow, a position that allows him to hear not only Pompey's 'public' speech, but also his *sotto voce* expression of (ill-founded) satisfaction with his own performance (*mihique, ut adsedit, dixit se putare satis ab se etiam 'de istis rebus' esse responsum*).

Crassus' speech which follows trumps Pompey's both in its compliments to Cicero on his successful consulship and in the 'Ciceronian' tone and language in which it is couched.

Crassus posteaquam uidit illum excepisse laudem ex eo, quod suspicaren-tur homines ei consulatum meum placere, surrexit ornatissimeque de meo consulatu locutus est, cum ita diceret, 'se, quod esset senator, quod ciuis, quod liber, quod uiueret, mihi acceptum referre; quotiens coniugem, quotiens domum, quotiens patriam uideret, totiens se beneficium meum uidere.' Quid multa? totum hunc locum, quem ego uarie meis orationibus, quarum tu Aristarchus es, soleo pingere, de flamma, de ferro (nosti illas ληκύθους) ualde grauiter pertexuit. Proximus Pompeio sedebam. Intellexi hominem moueri, utrum Crassum inire eam gratiam, quam ipse praetermisisset, an esse tantas res nostras, quae tam libenti senatu laudarentur, ab eo praesertim, qui mihi laudem illam eo minus deberet, quod meis omnibus litteris in Pompeiana laude perstrictus esset.

(When Crassus saw that Pompey had netted some credit from the general impression that he approved of my Consulship, he got to his feet and held forth on the subject in most encomiastic terms, going so far as to say that it was to me he owed his status as a Senator and a citizen, his freedom and his very life. Whenever he saw his wife or his house or the city of his birth he saw a gift of mine. In short, he worked up the whole theme which I am in the habit of embroidering in my speeches one way and another, all about fire, sword, etc. (you are their Aristarchus and know my colour-box), really most impressively. I was sitting next to Pompey and I could see he was put out, whether at Crassus gaining the credit which might have been his to realize that my achievements are of sufficient consequence to make the Senate so willing to hear them praised – praised too by a man who had all the less reason to offer me such incense in that everything I have written glorifies Pompey at his expense.)

This section is once again rounded off by a report of Pompey's reaction (perceived by Cicero in the seat right next to him), but it is also enriched by a peculiarly epistolary phenomenon: just as the writer appeared on stage, as it were, after Pompey's speech, now, after that of Crassus, the addressee is given a role in this scene. Atticus is presented as a privileged audience, with specific expertise: as a scholarly connoisseur of *genuine* Ciceronian style (*quarum tu* Aristarchus *es*), capable (by implication) of distinguishing between the master's original works and spurious imitations, Atticus can appreciate Crassus' 'Ciceronianism' better than any other addressee.

Both Pompey and Crassus, of course, are to be outclassed by the real thing, as the master orator turns to the memory of his own performance. The letter opened with a reminder of Pompey's flop in his first *contio*, which was not significantly improved upon in second and third outings (when he produced only pompous declarations of respect for the senate), and then 'reviewed' Crassus' fine quasi-Ciceronian performance; the climax comes, however, in the riotous virtuosity of Cicero's display before the senate and Pompey, in which he pronounces both more widely and in greater detail than Pompey had, speaking not only upon the role of the senate, but upon a familiar range of related national issues and class interests.

> Ego autem ipse, di boni! quo modo ἐνεπερπερευσάμην nouo auditori Pompeio! Si umquam mihi περίοδοι, si καμπαι, si ἐνθυμήματα, si κατασκευαί suppeditauerunt, illo tempore. Quid multa? clamores. Etenim haec erat ὑπόθεσις, de grauitate ordinis, de equestri concordia, de consensione Italiae, de intermortuis reliquiis coniurationis, de uilitate, de otio. Nosti iam in hac materia sonitus nostros. Tanti fuerunt, ut ego eo breuior sim, quod eos usque istinc exauditos putem.

> (As for myself – ye gods, how I spread my tail in front of my new audience, Pompey! If ever periods and *clausulae* and enthymemes and *raisonnements* came to my call, they did on that occasion. In a word, I brought the house down. And why not, on such a theme – the dignity of our order, concord between Senate and Knights, unison of Italy, remnants of the conspiracy in their death-throes, reduced price of grain, internal peace? You should know by now how I can boom away on such topics. I think you must have caught the reverberations in Epirus, and for that reason I won't dwell on the subject.)

This time the Greek comes not in single adverbs but as a colourful verb and a torrent of nouns, to underline Cicero's mastery of both style and content (so unlike Pompey's lofty vagueness). Autopsy, connoisseurship and authentication are prominent themes of this section of the letter, and all depend upon Atticus' persona and point of view as expert reader and audience. Once again this section's closural device is another reference to Atticus' expertise in Ciceronianism (*nosti . . . nosti*), as the letter transports him into a front-row seat, and even imagines him as virtually able to hear the whole show himself by the end – a humorous twist on conventional epistolary efforts to minimize geographical distance whereby this letter almost tries to make itself redundant. By skilfully building this addressee into the letter in this way, Cicero can summon him into this scene of competitive oratory as special witness and guarantor of Ciceronian quality. From *frigebat* to *clamores*, then, in four carefully controlled narrative steps, with Atticus implicitly called upon first to validate Crassus' good 'reproduction' copy, and then to put a hallmark upon the genuine Ciceronian oratory which is the climax of the whole sequence.

Epistolary realism

The letters discussed so far all demonstrate close engagement with the addressee, and their emphasis on speech of all kinds is part of the 'realism' of the Ciceronian letter which has led many readers to see it as the record of his innermost thoughts, and to compare Cicero favourably with his epistolary successors.[19] There are, of course, exceptions, and some letters have failed to convince as 'realistic' or 'natural'. Stockton, for example, describes *Fam.* 7.1 (his letter 14), Cicero's letter to Marius congratulating him on his absence from Pompey's games, as a 'literary exercise' rather than a 'real letter' (by this he means a letter written primarily to 'convey information and points of view on matters of current importance and immediate relevance to writer and recipient').[20]

However, both Cicero and Marius would surely have scratched their heads at the suggestion that this piece was not a 'real' letter. It is certainly carefully – even self-consciously – written, and its dominant theme (the futility of public games in comparison with a day of bookish *otium* in a seaside retreat) becomes a familiar topos.[21] Nevertheless, the letter sustains its epistolary colour and function throughout: it reports a recent social event, expresses concern for the addressee's health and looks forward to a day when the correspondents will meet again. Above all, Cicero tries to see through his addressee's eyes at every stage of the letter. In a version of a classic epistolary feature, for example, he skilfully contrasts their respective environments in order to highlight Marius' viewpoint (both physical and metaphorical) and to demonstrate his prudent deliberation in managing his intellectual (and visual) life. Even Marius' living quarters, indeed, attest his conscious efforts to design the scenic backdrop that will most please him as a spectator in the mornings. His *cubiculum* does not just happen to look out over the bay; rather, he has deliberately had it remodelled for that purpose (*in illo cubiculo tuo, ex quo tibi Stabianum perforasti et patefecisti sinum*). His afternoon pastimes are similarly tailored to his personal tastes (*reliquas uero partes diei tu consumebas iis delectationibus, quas tibi ipse ad arbitrium tuum compararas*). In contrast, his theatre-going friends in Rome have had to endure entertainments staged by an uncongenial impresario, events which Cicero describes in terms of his addressee's imagined aversion to virtually every detail.[22] Finally, Cicero reveals that even the letter itself is the product

---

[19] E.g. Stockton 1971: 304, 'the true Cicero is the writer of the letters'. The more private the letter, the more 'real' the sentiments: see, e.g., Stockton 1971: 180 on *Att.* 2.19: 'we cannot doubt the truth of Cicero's reporting; he is writing a private letter to Atticus, not making a speech'.

[20] Stockton 1968: 28. Cf. Shackleton Bailey 1977: 324: 'a literary exercise . . . reminiscent of the younger Pliny'.

[21] See, e.g., Plin. *Ep.* 4.22, 9.6. Seneca *Ep.* 7.

[22] *Nosti enim reliquos ludos; non dubito quin animo aequissimo carueris; delectationem tibi nullam attulissent; si tu . . . operam dedisti Protogeni tuo . . . non enim te puto Graecos aut Oscos ludos desiderasse; quid ego te athletas putem desiderare; saepe uidisti.*

of Marius' genius for planning his own pleasures and anticipating his own requirements, since he had virtually 'commissioned' it as a compensation for missing the games:

> Haec ad te pluribus uerbis scripsi quam soleo, non oti abundantia sed amoris erga te, quod me quadam epistula subinuitaras, si memoria tenes, ut ad te aliquid eius modi scriberem, quo minus te praetermisisse ludos paeniteret.

> (I have written at unusual length, out of an abundance, not of spare time, but of affection for you, because in one of your letters you threw out a hint, if you remember, that I might write something to prevent you feeling sorry to have missed the show.)

Just like *Att.* 1.14, then, *Fam.* 7.1 constructs what the addressee would have thought of the events he missed, and reports the games in a tone precisely calibrated to his persona, giving him a role as a kind of spectator. These two letters differ in style and tone, but the intense and recurring focus upon the addressee's persona gives them both their epistolary quality and their artistic complexity alike.

Epistolary persuasion

Thus far we have looked only at letters that seem to reflect good relationships between writer and addressee. Moreover, we have looked at individual letters in isolation, without considering the interpretative consequences of reading letters in the sequences in which they are preserved in the transmitted collections. One might usefully contrast one of the most famous examples of an uncomfortable letter exchange, namely Cicero's correspondence of 51–50 BC with Cato, in which he lobbies Cato to support a supplication for him after the military action at Pindenissum. The central pair of letters, *Fam.* 15.5–6, is often seen as an extreme case of disparity in epistolary style and approach between correspondents; as Steel has observed, readers 'are left with a strong impression, albeit one that is difficult to articulate, that Cicero is by far the more competent manipulator of the epistolary medium'. One important factor in this seeming disparity is the greater effort Cicero appears to make in constructing a favourable epistolary persona for his addressee as well as for himself.

Cicero constructs a more formal persona for Cato than those we have seen him crafting for the addressees discussed so far; this comes into high relief if we return both letters to their context in Book 15, taking the unknown editor's cue to read in sequence the handful of letters which leads up to this pair in that book.[23] The Cato series proper begins (out of chronological order) at *Fam.* 15.3, in which Cicero reports Antiochus' intelligence about Parthian incursions. He explains that he has as yet sent no formal public letter to the senate (*putaui pro nostra necessitudine me hoc ad te scribere oportere. publice propter duas causas nihil scripsi, Fam.* 15.3.1–2), since he awaits further intelligence and assumes that Bibulus, the proconsular governor of Syria, will cover the matter in his own official dispatches. However, a sequential reader of the book will already have read the public dispatches Cicero did eventually send to the magistrates and senate in Rome, namely *Fam.* 15.1 on Antiochus' intelligence and the need for significant Roman military investment, and *Fam.* 15.2, sent a few days later, on Cicero's obedience to the senate's mandate to protect king Ariobarzanes. The proximity of 'public' to 'private' letters here encourages us to notice similarities in content and style between *Fam.* 15.3 and the opening sections of the (chronologically later) *Fam.* 15.1.[24] Such an overlap is not in itself necessarily remarkable in letters written to different addressees about the same event, but here it also seems symptomatic of a conscious rhetorical decision on Cicero's part to write to Cato as if to the senate and to model his letter on the more formal genre of the official dispatch.

Fam. 15.1 and 15.2 are both considerably shorter than the next letter in the Cato sequence. *Fam.* 15.4, addressed to Cato himself, contains a more extended version of the account Cicero has (from the sequential reader's point of view) already given to the senate of his activities between late July and late October of 51.[25] The letter retains elements of the official dispatch but ties its narrative specifically to Cato's views and interests. It now 'reveals' to the sequential reader, for example, that senatorial protection of Ariobarzanes as a special ally (highlighted in *Fam.* 15.2) was Cato's own particular project (*Ariobarzanem, cuius salutem a senatu te auctore commendatam habebam, Fam.* 15.4.6). Above all, Cicero lists his own prestige as a 'standing item' on Cato's senatorial agenda (*Fam.* 15.4.11):

> Tu es enim is qui me tuis sententiis saepissime ornasti, qui oratione, qui praedicatione, qui summis laudibus in senatu, in contionibus ad caelum extulisti.

> (I am writing to one whose motions in the House have again and again done me honour, and who both there and at public meetings has praised me to the skies in language of unstinted panegyric.)

---

[23] On the value of reading books of Ciceronian epistles whole, and seeking to interpret the letters in the transmitted sequences, see Beard 2002.

[24] One might contrast *Fam.* 15.13.3 (to the consul L. Paulus), in which Cicero merely refers the addressee to earlier dispatches for details of the grounds on which Cicero wishes to be considered for a supplication.

[25] Contrast the accounts written to Atticus (*Att.* 5.20) and Caelius (*Fam.* 2.10)

It is conventional in any persuasive genre, of course, to invoke past favours as precedent for new ones, and to dwell upon the writer's admiration for the addressee. Cicero caps Cato's past support of him, warm though it was, with a reminder of his own lavish and (more) varied panegyric of the addressee in every area of his public, intellectual and literary work (*Fam.* 15.4.12):

> A me autem haec sunt profecta . . . ut praestantissimas tuas uirtutes non tacitus admirarer . . . sed in omnibus orationibus, sententiis dicendis, causis agendis, omnibus scriptis Graecis, Latinis, omni denique uarietate litterarum mearum te non modo iis quos uidissemus sed iis de quibus audissemus omnibus ante-ferrem.

> (On my side there has been forthcoming this much . . . , that I have not confined myself to tacit admiration of your extraordinary qualities . . . , but have publicly exalted you beyond any man we have seen or of whom history tells us. This I have done in all my speeches, whether addressing the senate or pleading in court, in all my writings, Greek or Latin, in fact throughout the entire range of my literary output.)

This is an appeal for reciprocity in expansiveness and enthusiasm on Cato's part – an appeal doomed to failure, one might think, but nevertheless one that will make Cato's brief response all the more startling when it arrives.

Subsequent paragraphs match Cicero's gubernatorial style still more closely to Cato's agenda, and, in a carefully calibrated appeal to his Stoic addressee, play a variation upon the emphasis in *Fam.* 15.3.2 upon *mansuetudo* and *continentia* (*Fam.* 15.4.14):

> Equidem etiam illud mihi animum aduertisse uideor (scis enim quam attente te audire soleam), te non tam res gestas quam mores instituta atque uitam imperatorum spectare solere in habendis aut non habendis honoribus. Quod si in mea causa considerabis, reperies me exercitu imbecillo contra metum maximi belli firmissimum praesidium habuisse aequitatem et continentiam.

> (Furthermore, I think I have observed (you know how attentively I listen to you) that in conceding or withholding such distinctions it is your practice to pay greater regard to a commander's conduct, his principles and way of life, than to his operations in the field. If you apply such considerations in my case, you will find that with a weak army I made fair and clean administration my bulwark against the threat of a major war.)

In this letter, Cicero has already presented his 'report' on his own achievements, and has done so at greater length and in greater detail than he thought appropriate in his letters to the senate. The placement of this letter *after* the more official reports highlights the differences in its treatment of the single (difficult) addressee, and throws into high relief the passages in which Cicero links his own principles of virtuous behaviour when serving as commander in the field directly to an awareness of Cato's views on such matters and to the influence he exerts.

Finally, Cicero makes his famous appeal to shared interests and common endeavours in pragmatic philosophical living (*Fam.* 15.4.16):

> Haec igitur, quae mihi tecum communis est, societas studiorum atque artium nostrarum, quibus a pueritia dediti ac deuincti soli prope modum nos philosophiam ueram illam et antiquam, quae quibusdam oti esse ac desidiae uidetur, in forum atque in rem p. atque in ipsam aciem paene deduximus, tecum agit de mea laude; cui negari a Catone fas esse non puto.

> (Think then of the pursuits and acquirements we have in common and to which we have been devoted heart and soul since we were boys. We two almost alone have brought the old authentic philosophy, which some regard as an amusement of leisure and idleness, down into the market-place, into public life, one might almost say into the battlefield. This companionship of ours pleads with you on behalf of my renown. I do not think Cato can in conscience say no.)

Thus far, then, we have seen Cicero marrying the structures and language of panegyric with classic epistolary motifs of shared values and proven mutual admiration.[26] As Ebbeler notes in her study of 'epistolary codes' in the letter corpora of late antiquity, 'letter exchanges are textualised social performances, carried out in accordance with a scripted set of conventions and coded rhetoric. Correspondents constructed "faces" for themselves and each other.' In *Fam.* 15.4, Cicero constructs an 'epistolary code' which figures Cato as synecdochically representative of the senate as a whole, makes him first recipient (before even the senate) of official news from a proconsul in the field, and highlights the distinctively 'Catonian' mandate for Cicero's campaign.[27] Thus Cicero turns to flattering use the persona he depicts in more critical terms in *Att.* 2.1.8 where he makes his famous joke that Cato speaks as if he were in Plato's Republic rather than Romulus' cesspit, and then again more positively in *Att.* 6.1.13 where he measures contemporary governors (including himself) against what he calls Cato's 'blueprint' ('*politeuma*').[28]

It is all the more startling that Cato's reply to this letter (*Fam.* 15.5) does so little, despite its formally complimentary language, to reflect Cicero's best self and his chief interests back to him, and I suggest that it is this practice – one of the most important features of Ciceronian letter-writing

---

[26] Griffin 1989: 34–5.   [27] Ebbeler 2007: 322.
[28] On Cato's 'blueprint', see Steel 2001: 204–5.

at its best – which determines the apparent difference in epistolary skill between the two men. As a rebuff *Fam.* 15.5 works well enough, but there seems little else to be gained from the letter as it stands.[29] Each section of Cato's response seems oddly truncated. For Cicero's impassioned exposition of long-standing association and mutual admiration, Cato returns a brisk *nostra amicitia*; he begins and ends not with their friendship, but with the *res publica*. The insistent repetition of abstract nouns seems almost to parody Cicero's earnest declaration of his own virtues as a governor (*uirtutem, innocentiam, diligentiam*; *innocentia consilioque tuo*; *summa tua ratione et continentia*; *mansuetudine et innocentia*; *seueritatem diligentiamque*). At the same time, in the terse response to a governor's exposition of a pressing issue, a reader almost catches an anachronistic flavour of the imperial rescript.

The self-conscious epistolary reflections of the second paragraph which follow then seem almost comical:

> Atque haec ego idcirco ad te contra consuetudinem meam pluribus scripsi ut, quod maxime uolo, existimes me laborare ut tibi persuadeam me et uoluisse de tua maiestate quod amplissimum sim arbitratus et quod tu maluisti factum esse gaudere.

> (I have written to you at some length on this subject (contrary to my normal habit) so that you may realize, as I most earnestly hope you will, my anxiety to convince you of two things: firstly, as touching your prestige, I desired what I conceived to be most complimentary to yourself; secondly, I am very glad that what you preferred has come to pass.)

Cato not only eschews close engagement with his addressee, but the sole reference to his own letter *as a letter* seems inappropriate to its text: that this letter, barely twenty-three lines long in the Oxford Classical Text and a markedly self-conscious representation of Catonian severity and brevity, should be excused for its unusual fullness suggests – particularly when read in the light of the whole sequence of letters here – an implicit criticism of Cicero's unusually lengthy appeal for support in *Fam.* 15.4. Letters which reflect and foster a good relationship between writer and addressee might be expected to engage with previous letters in the shared correspondence in greater detail than Cato allows himself in this instance; as Shackleton Bailey notes, both letters (that of Cicero as well as Cato's reply) betray discomfort;[30] however, it is Cicero who seems more successfully to have

---

[29] For a more positive view, see Griffin 1989: 35.

[30] On the 'humbug' of Cato's second paragraph (and speculation that 'it was obviously not an easy letter to write'), and the 'well-grounded nervousness' of *Fam.* 15.4, see Shackleton Bailey 1977: 446; 449. Cf. Stockton 1969: 169 on *Fam.* 15.5: 'a rather laboured piece of writing totally lacking in any hint of sincerity'. One might (perhaps

injected the sense of friendly reciprocity that underpins the best epistolary relationships, even while simultaneously setting out his narrative (in quasi-Caesarian style) as a version of the official dispatch.[31]

One should acknowledge that the *initial* reaction of Cicero (as the first reader of Cato's brief, almost impersonal letter) is not hostile, and in this sequence's final letter (*Fam.* 15.5) his warm thanks for the *iucunda laus* of *Fam.* 15.4 are echoed in his report to Atticus on Cato's *iucundissimas litteras* (*Att.* 7.1.7). A change of heart came later, however, when Cato supported honours for his son-in-law, Bibulus, on the basis of a dispatch from Bibulus which Cicero regarded as fraudulently boastful;[32] Cicero might have been influenced also by the letters from Caesar that are mentioned already in *Att.* 7.1.7, in which Caesar ignored Cato's laudatory speech and focused solely on his failure to support the supplication.[33] By the time Cicero writes *Att.* 7.2.7, the damage is complete and Cicero sees the disjunction between his request and Cato's response (once again brooding upon the effects of Caesar's letters too) (*Att.* 7.2.7):

> Hortensius quid egerit aueo scire, Cato quid agat, qui quidem in me turpiter fuit maleuolus: dedit integritatis iustitiae clementiae fidei mihi testimonium, quod non quaerebam; quod postulabam negauit. Itaque Caesar iis litteris quibus mihi gratulatur et omnia pollicetur quo modo exsultat Catonis in me ingratissimi iniuria!

> (I am longing to know what Hortensius has done and what Cato is doing. To me he has been disgracefully spiteful. He gave me an unsolicited testimonial for uprightness, justice, clemency and honourable dealing, while what I asked for he refused. Accordingly Caesar, in a letter of congratulation in which he offers me full support, is fairly cock-a-hoop at Cato's 'most ungrateful' ill-usage.)

Cato's response to Cicero's request failed to 'answer' point by point to the terms of the request itself – and, as we have seen, this is reflected also in the partial mismatch in the language and in the expansiveness of their respective letters.

Meanwhile, Cicero's final letter in the Cato sequence, *Fam.* 15.6, seems all the richer and more urbane by contrast with Cato's brief, almost impersonal,

---

unfairly) contrast Caelius' breezy (and more informative letter) on the headaches Cicero's supplication has given everyone (*Fam.* 8.11).

[31] See Hutchinson 1998: 98 on the Caesarian qualities of the narrative in *Fam.* 15.4. Cf. Hall 2009: 103; 232 n.50.

[32] *Att.* 7.2.6. On a similar change of attitude in Cicero (this time towards letters from Caesar), see Hall 2009: 79.

[33] Contrast *Fam.* 8.11.2, from Caelius.

letter, and in the light of his own change of heart shortly afterwards.[34] He focuses initially on the positive reports he has received of Cato's speech of praise, which he says he values more than laurels or triumphal chariot (*Fam.* 15.6.2). Nevertheless, insisting upon retaining his hope that he may yet obtain the honours he has asked Cato to help him achieve, he refers Cato to his earlier letter on the subject (*causam meae uoluntatis, non enim dicam 'cupiditatis,' exposui tibi superioribus litteris, Fam.* 15.6.2) and also 'recycles' Cato's own language from *Fam.* 15.5:

> Quod si ita erit, tantum ex te peto, quod amicissime scribis, ut, cum tuo iudicio quod amplissimum esse arbitraris mihi tribueris, si id quod maluero acciderit, gaudeas.
>
> (If it so turns out, all I ask of you is that (to use your own very kind expressions), having accorded to me what in your judgement is most complimentary to myself, you should be glad if what I prefer comes about.)

Cato had declared his support for Cicero *pro meo iudicio*, and expressed joy in a successful request for a supplication if Cicero really preferred his hard-won success to be ascribed to the benevolence of the gods (*Fam.* 15.5.2). Cicero now requires him to be as good as his word, and to live up to the image constructed for him as Cicero's epistolary addressee (*Fam.* 15.5.2):

> Sic enim fecisse te et sensisse et scripsisse uideo, resque ipsa declarat tibi illum honorem nostrum supplicationis iucundum fuisse, quod scribendo adfuisti; haec enim senatus consulta non ignoro ab amicissimis eius cuius de honore agitur, scribere solere.
>
> (Your actions, your views as expressed in the Senate, your letter, and the very fact that you were present at the drafting of the decree are clear evidence to me that the grant of the Supplication in my honour was agreeable to you. For I am well aware that such decrees are usually drafted by the closest friends of the persons honoured.)

In the earlier letters, Cicero constructed Cato as the public man, so eminent as to be almost synecdochically representative of the whole senate, whose statesmanlike 'blueprint' has been Cicero's handbook of conduct in his province; he now holds up to his addressee a protreptic image of Cato as Cicero's benevolent supporter whose *sententiae* and letters suggest – despite that awkward 'nay' vote – that his pleasure in the prospect of Cicero's honours (*honorem... iucundum, Fam.* 15.6.2) matched Cicero's delight in Cato's good opinion (*iucunda laus, Fam.* 15.6.1).

---

[34] On Cicero's exaggeratedly lengthy reponse to a more openly offensive short letter from Metellus Celer (*Fam.* 5.1 and 5.2), see Hall 2009: 153–60.

Despite the ultimate failure of this particular letter exchange, then, Cicero seems a 'more competent manipulator of the epistolary form' at least partly because he can design, and then creatively manipulate or adjust, a highly distinctive 'epistolary code', building a persona for his addressee which can fruitfully mesh with the topic and the dominant motifs of his letter. He retains and enhances such epistolary features as are useful to him, in some instances playing upon the relationship between letters and conversation, while in others (such as this correspondence with Cato) enriching a 'private' letter with the flavour of a formal gubernatorial dispatch. Above all, it is Cicero's irresistible focus on the epistolary addressee, and his dexterity in responding appropriately to a friend's temperament and interests and tailoring his text to suit them, which make his letters so peculiarly effective.

Further reading

The extensive learned literature on Cicero's letters can be daunting, but good starting places include (most recently) Hall's study (2009) of the conventions of elite letter-writing in the late Republic and how epistolary conventions shaped the relationships between powerful correspondents, and White's guide to Cicero's letters (2010). Hutchinson 1998 is also essential on the literary aspects of the letters. Important shorter pieces of scholarship which have been influential include Beard's excellent paper (2002) on why the inherited order of Cicero's letters in the extant collections matters, and Griffin's two papers (1995 and 1997) on philosophical aspects of the letters.

The indispensable aids for any reader of the letters are Shackleton Bailey's volumes of text, commentary and translation. Shorter volumes of commentary on selections of the letters include Stockton 1969, Shackleton Bailey's own selection, published in the 'green and yellow' series of Cambridge University Press (1980), Willcock 1995 and Treggiari 1972.

On letters more generally, readers will want to consult Trapp's edition of selected Greek and Roman letters (2003), as well as the collected papers in Morello and Morrison 2007.

13

JON HALL

Saviour of the Republic and Father of the Fatherland: Cicero and political crisis

During his long career as senator and statesman, Cicero found himself confronted on several occasions with moments of grave political crisis, moments that threatened both his political survival and personal safety. His reactions to these crises offer significant insights not just into his character and political acumen; they demonstrate too the importance in aristocratic life of assertive self-promotion. Over the course of his career, Cicero worked hard to construct a distinctive political image and to manipulate the ways in which he was perceived by his peers and the wider public. At times we may be able to discern a distinct gap between this image and the realities on which it was based; but in a political environment where opponents were ruthless in their denigration of a rival's character and policies, the ambitious aristocrat needed to be assertive and creative in the promotion of his achievements.

Cicero and Catiline

The controversy that followed Cicero's handling of the Catilinarian conspiracy illustrates the point well. The consul quickly found himself under sustained attack. Soon after his execution of the conspirators on 5 December 63, two of the new tribunes for 62, L. Bestia and Q. Metellus Nepos, prevented Cicero from delivering the customary speech to a public assembly on the final day of his consulship (*Fam.* 5.2.7; *Pis.* 6; Plut. *Cic.* 23.1–2; Cass. Dio 37.38). Then on 3 January Nepos stirred up hostility against him at a *contio*, presumably criticizing Cicero's infringement of the Roman citizen's basic right to a trial in front of the people, which the executed conspirators had not been granted (*Fam.* 5.2.6; cf. Cass. Dio 37.42.2). Bestia seems to have followed a similar course (Sall. *Cat.* 43). Indeed, these attacks assumed a sharper focus in the ensuing months and years. Cicero was portrayed as an arrogant autocrat (*tyrannus* or *rex*: *Att.* 1.16.10; *Sull.* 22; *Dom.* 94; *Vat.* 23, 29), whose actions against the conspirators were savage and blood-thirsty (*crudelis*: *Sull.* 8; *Dom.* 94; cf. *Pis.* 14). His consulship was thus a despotism (*regnum*: *Sull.* 21; cf. Plut. *Cic.* 23.2–3), and the armed support of equestrians that he deployed during the debate on the punishment of the conspirators led him to be branded the 'enemy of the Capitoline' (*Dom.* 7: *hostem Capitolinum*). These attacks acquired their most dramatic manifestation during Cicero's exile in 58–57 BC, when Clodius Pulcher destroyed his house and dedicated on the spot a shrine to Freedom (*Libertas*). For a few months it looked as if Cicero would be remembered not as the consul who saved the state, but as the tyrant who callously oppressed the Roman people.[1]

These persistent and damaging criticisms called for vigorous countermeasures, and we can trace with some precision Cicero's cultivation of promotional slogans to aid his cause. The first – his claim to the title *parens patriae* or 'father of the fatherland' – seems in fact to have been initiated by allies in the senate who immediately rallied to his support. Cicero tells us that Q. Catulus, after the arrest of the conspirators on 3 December, 'addressed me (*me . . . nominavit*) in a packed meeting of the senate as father of the fatherland (*parentem patriae*)' (*Pis.* 6). The choice of verb here is important. Cicero does not claim that this title was officially conferred upon him. He notes merely that a leading member of the senate spoke of his achievement in glowing terms.[2] Cato the Younger seems to have supported him in similar fashion. Plutarch (*Cic.* 23.2–3) records that, at the start of 62, as Metellus Nepos launched his attacks, Cato at a political rally persuaded the crowd to hail Cicero as father of the fatherland (πατέρα πατρίδος). Again, the acclamation probably had no official status; but the anecdote provides a plausible picture of the politicking of the time. In the face of concerted criticisms, Cicero's allies came to his aid by promoting his actions in a positive and celebratory way.[3]

Cicero's second bold claim – that his actions as consul had saved the Republic – seems to have had its origins in his wrangling with the tribunes on his final day of office. Although denied a proper speech, evidently Cicero was able to contrive an oath that asserted the great significance of his achievements (*Pis.* 6): 'I swore that the republic and this very city had been saved (*esse salvam*) through my efforts alone.' The assertive hyperbole is understandable in this specific context of public confrontation. But Cicero evidently discerned broader self-promotional potential in the claim, and in the years that followed he cultivated it with considerable energy.

[1] On Clodius' destruction of Cicero's house, see Allen 1944; Tatum 1999: 156–8.
[2] Cf. Kaster 2006: 353–4.
[3] On Cato's support, see further *Fam.* 15.4.11; App. *B Civ.* 2.7. L. Gellius Poplicola also supported Cicero's actions, asserting in the senate that the consul deserved a civic crown (*ciuica corona*, *Pis.* 6; cf. Gell. *NA* 5.6.15).

The *Catilinarian Orations* in particular, which probably received their final editorial touches in 60 BC (*Att.* 2.1.3), incorporate frequent references to the theme, as Cicero strives to endow his actions with a heightened grandeur and significance.[4]

Cicero further attempted to bestow a unique quality upon his consulship by characterizing himself as *dux togatus* ('military commander in civilian dress'). The phrase appears, for example, in an address to the Roman people following the arrest of the conspirators (*Cat.* 3.23): *erepti sine caede, sine sanguine, sine exercitu, sine dimicatione; togati me uno togato duce et imperatore uicistis.* ('You, [citizens of Rome], have been rescued without slaughter, without bloodshed, without recourse to an army, without fighting. You have won your victory in civilian dress, with me as your civilian general and commander.') It is important to appreciate the paradoxical element of the image. Roman magistrates who were about to depart the city at the head of an army (as *dux*) would ceremoniously exchange their toga for military dress in a very public and highly formal ritual.[5] The image of a toga-clad general, then, is a striking and unusual conceit (as unusual as the image today of a soldier fighting in a jacket and tie). Cicero thus contrives to cast his actions as consul in a distinctive and memorable light. He stresses that he has dealt with Catiline's coup without the trauma of armed violence (*sine caede* etc.); and yet he also claims for himself some of the glamour and prestige of the military commander (*dux et imperator*).[6] This conceit was facilitated by the fact that the senate had just awarded him a *supplicatio*, an honour usually associated with military success (*Cat.* 3.15 *mihi primum post hanc urbem conditam togato contigit*). He is therefore able to give his achievements a novel twist: he is a civilian magistrate (*togatus*) whose deeds rival those of Rome's great generals.[7]

Manufacturing slogans, then, was an established part of the political game, deployed by Cicero and his opponents alike. But while both sides made extensive use of oratory and invective in their attempts to shape public opinion, Cicero took matters considerably further.[8] In addition to preparing

[4] See *Cat.* 2.14 (*conservandae rei publicae*) and similar phrases at 3.2, 3.15, 3.25, 4.18, 4.20, 4.23. On the publication of these speeches, and whether a (potentially different) text had been circulated before 60 BC, see Settle 1962: 127–46; Cape 1995: 257–9; Dyck 2008b: 10–12. The argument of McDermott 1972 relies more on supposition and inference than on positive evidence.

[5] See Marshall 1984.

[6] See also *Cat.* 2.28; *Har. resp.* 49; *Pis.* 6; *Off.* 1.77. Cf. Nicolet 1960; May 1988: 56–7; Kurczyk 2006: 178.

[7] For strained elements in Cicero's claim regarding his *supplicatio*, see Dyck 2008b: 187 on *Cat.* 3.15.5–7.

[8] These efforts seem to have acquired particular urgency from July 61 (or thereabouts), as Cicero became aware that the controversy regarding his actions as consul was not going

a volume of his consular speeches, he composed in 60 BC an account in Greek of his suppression of the conspiracy, as too did Atticus, who had played a minor but noteworthy role in the events of 5 December 63 (*Att.* 1.19.10; *Att.* 2.1.2 and 7). These volumes were to serve as a foundation from which Greek writers could compose a more extensive, celebratory opus. Indeed, Cicero notes that he had already tried (unsuccessfully) to enlist the talents of Posidonius the philosopher in such a pursuit, and he claims that other Greek writers had expressed an interest in the project (*Att.* 2.1.2; *Arch.* 28). He intended to finish a Latin summary of his achievements as well (*Att.* 1.19.10).

No less remarkable was his decision to compose a Latin poem on his consulship, a work that was evidently completed by March 60 BC.[9] Although its precise contents are debated, it is clear enough that the poem attempted to develop at least two of the promotional slogans that we have already identified. Its best-known (and most notorious) verse, *o fortunatam natam me consule Romam*! ('O happy Rome, given new birth during my consulship!'), seems to promote the notion of Cicero as *parens patriae*: the consul has brought about the rebirth of the city through his generative powers as parent.[10] And the verse *cedant arma togae, concedat laurea laudi* ('Let weapons yield to civilian toga, let the general's laurel give way to social repute') attempts a variation on the *dux togatus* motif.[11] In this case, the toga-clad politician is to take precedence over the military man, and civic recognition (*laus*) is to be preferred to military honours. The statement presents an ambitious, perhaps naive challenge to the accepted hierarchy of values in ancient Rome; nevertheless, it succeeds in portraying Cicero as a man of non-violence – a smart move given the prevailing accusations of *crudelitas*.[12]

In disseminating these promotional materials, Cicero was to a degree simply following established practice. Other Roman politicians had likewise

---

to fade quietly away. See *Att.* 1.16.7; also 1.18.4–8 (January 60); 1.19.5–8 (March 60); Rundell 1979: esp. 304–6; Tatum 1999: 79–80.

[9] See *Att.* 1.19.10. It appears to have consisted of three books in hexameter (*Att.* 2.3.4) with elements of traditional epic machinery. See Ewbank 1933: 75–7; 109–24; Harrison 1990; Kurczyk 2006: 76–103; in this volume, Gee (Chapter 5).

[10] For the metaphor, cf. *Flac.* 102: *diem uere natalem huius urbis*. See further Allen 1956: 139–43; Goldberg 1995: 151; also Horace's apparently serious echo at *Epist.* 2.1.256.

[11] This is the text given by Cicero himself at *Pis.* 74. Quint. *Inst.* 11.1.24 quotes a slightly different version (*laurea linguae*), probably a parody then in common currency. See Allen 1956: 132–3.

[12] Cf. May 1988: 56–7. Elsewhere Cicero addresses this charge more directly by laying claim to the qualities of *lenitas*; see *Cat.* 2.14, 3.29, 4.1 and 4.11, as well as *Sull.* 1 (probably delivered mid 62 BC).

composed self-serving memoirs and been celebrated in poems.[13] But Cicero's rush to compose such works himself smacked both of desperation and conceit, and it is no surprise to find his enemies ridiculing these efforts.[14] Nevertheless, this self-promotion seems to have succeeded in establishing what today's marketing consultants would refer to as Cicero's 'brand' – as we can see from the redeployment of these slogans by his supporters during his exile. Pompey, for example, whose initial reaction to Cicero's achievements as consul was distinctly frosty, delivered a speech to the senate in 57 BC, in which he proclaimed Cicero to be the saviour of the state (*Sest.* 129: *mihi uni testimonium patriae conservatae dedit*).[15] A senatorial decree acknowledging his achievements was then passed in essentially the same terms (*rem publicam meis consiliis conservatam*), and several leading figures repeated these claims at a political rally on the following day (*Red. sen.* 26). Public demonstrations of support for Cicero were also engineered at the dramatic performances taking place when the senate finally voted for his recall from exile. The tragic actor Aesopus (we are told), while performing Accius' *Eurysaces*, introduced a phrase (*o pater!*) from a play by Ennius in order (apparently) to evoke Cicero's *pater patriae* slogan.[16]

The slogans and general 'spin' surrounding the Catilinarian conspiracy naturally make it difficult to assess how well Cicero actually handled the crisis that confronted him. Where does reality end and embellishment begin? Perhaps the most useful perspective is provided by a letter to Atticus written some eighteen years later (*Att.* 12.21). From this we learn that Marcus Brutus has in fact recently praised Cicero's handling of the situation. In particular, Brutus compliments his decision to put Cato's motion to the vote, at the conclusion of the senatorial debate on the fate of the arrested conspirators (*Att.* 12.21.1: *quod rettulerim*). The compliment is significant, in that it provides an independent assessment of events, written at some remove from the self-interested posturing of the time. (This fact does not of course remove the possibility of Brutus' own biases and misunderstandings.) Perhaps most importantly, Brutus' comment reminds us that matters that

[13] On memoirs, see *Brut.* 132, Plut. *Sull.* 37.1 and Tac. *Agr.* 1. Fragments in Peter 1967: 185–204. Cf. *Arch.* 24 on Theophanes' prose writings celebrating Pompey. On poems, see *Tusc.* 1.3, *Arch.* 19–21 and Gell. *NA* 4.7.3. Useful discussion in Gruen 1990: 108–23 and Goldberg 1995: 111–34.

[14] See e.g. *Pis.* 72–5; *Phil.* 2.20; *Off.* 1.77; Quint. *Inst.* 11.1.24; Sall. [*Cic.*] *Inv.* 5.

[15] See Kaster 2006: 363 and 401; cf. *Red. pop.* 16; *Red. sen.* 29; *Dom.* 30.

[16] See *Sest.* 121, with Kaster 2006: 352–3; cf. Ribbeck 1871: 25 (fragment 81). On aristocratic exploitation of such plays for political ends, see Wright 1931: 5–9; Kaster 2009: 314–17.

day could have turned out quite differently. According to some accounts of the debate, Caesar's speech against the execution of the conspirators (Sall. *Cat.* 51) had raised considerable misgivings among the assembled senators (Sall. *Cat.* 50.4; Suet. *Iul.* 14; Plut. *Cat. Min.* 22–3). A different consul, then, may have been tempted to prevaricate or adopt a less controversial, more moderate stance. Indeed, the proposal of Tiberius Nero to adjourn the debate and reconvene the next day (Sall. *Cat.* 50.4; App. *B Civ.* 2.5) offered a convenient means of delaying any fateful decision. Instead, Cicero chose to put to the vote Cato's decisively phrased motion with the intention of resolving the matter by nightfall.[17]

As he did so, Cicero would have been well aware of the precariousness of his position. Certainly, a senatorial decree approving the executions gave that course of action a degree of moral and political cover, and in fact on occasions Cicero tries to spread the responsibility for the decision across the senate as a whole (*Pis.* 14; Quint. *Inst.* 9.3.45). From a strictly legal perspective, however, the liability was all his.[18] Indeed, the trial earlier in the year of C. Rabirius Postumus would have made all too obvious the possible ramifications of the executions.[19] Thus, pushing the matter to a vote was not a course to be taken lightly, and, in Brutus' eyes, Cicero deserved some credit for refusing to take an easier, less decisive path – although his opponents would no doubt characterize such a course as typical of his tyrannical arrogance.

Cicero also seems to have shown a creditable degree of diligence and initiative in uncovering the full extent of the conspiracy. In particular, his covert operation to catch the conspirators plotting with the ambassadors of the Allobroges (*Cat.* 3.4–13; Sall. *Cat.* 41, 44–7; Cass. Dio 37.34) was astute and carried out with disciplined efficiency (it could easily have been bungled). Cicero's own self-promotion at the time made an effort to emphasize these aspects of his actions as well, and it may well be true that without such irrefutable evidence of Catiline's plans, the senate's reaction to the escalating crisis would not have been as energetic as it (eventually) was.[20] In these respects, then, the consul had shown himself to be capable and resolute at a time of real danger to the city.[21] As we have seen, however, as the criticisms

---

[17] See *Cat.* 4.6; Cass. Dio 37.35.3–4 claims that plans were being made to rescue the conspirators.

[18] See Greenidge 1901: 400–1; Hardy 1924: 86–9; Drummond 1995: 108–13; Lintott 1999a: 86–93; cf. Cass. Dio 38.14.4–6.

[19] See Cass. Dio 37.26–7; Tyrrell 1973; Lintott 2008: 120–4.

[20] See e.g. *Cat.* 2.26; 3.3; 3.27; 4.14; *Sull.* 3; 14; *Flac.* 5. Cf. also the praise of Cicero's *vigilia curaque* at Vell. Pat. 2.34.3.

[21] For modern discussions of the threat posed by Catiline's conspiracy and its true extent, see Further Reading below.

of his actions intensified, he was soon obliged to represent them in rather more grandiose and hyperbolic terms.

Cicero and civil war

The need for such posturing diminished considerably, however, following his return from exile, as Cicero slowly managed to broker unhappy compromises with the dominant political players of the day. Indeed, with the unexpected murder of Publius Clodius at the start of 52 BC, he may well have thought himself permanently relieved of the need to engage in this kind of aggressive self-promotion. But a new crisis soon emerged, when, towards the end of 50 BC, it became clear that the confrontation between Caesar and Pompey would end in armed conflict.

Cicero's previous experience with the two men seems to have led him to adopt a mainly cautious and circumspect approach as he weighed his political options. His initial reluctance to join Pompey's side, for example, evidently derived in part from a concern that the generals might quickly resolve their differences, and thus leave him open to criticism for having turned so readily against Caesar (*Att.* 7.26.2; 10.8.5). For similar reasons, he also took care to manoeuvre his way out of the military responsibilities at Capua that Pompey was trying to place upon him (*Att.* 7.17.3; 8.11D.5; 8.12.2; *Fam.* 16.12.5).[22]

In pursuing this course of neutrality, Cicero was strongly influenced by the counsel of Atticus, a skilled exponent of political quietism (see e.g. *Att.* 7.23.2; 8.2.2; 8.9a.1; 9.6.5). As the orator recognized, however, even neutrality was not without its risks (*Att.* 8.3.6; 9.15.2). Moreover, as a senator he was encumbered with greater obligations and responsibilities than Atticus, and his correspondence during these months highlights the nexus of conflicting expectations that confronted a man in his position. He broods anxiously over his ethical duty as a citizen of standing and influence (*Att.* 7.21.2; 7.26.2; 9.4.2; 10.8.4); the safety of his family (*Att.* 7.12.6; 7.13.3; 7.17.4); the approval of his political peers (*Att.* 7.12.3; 8.16.1; 9.1.3); and, not least, his personal obligations as an *amicus* of Pompey and Caesar (*Att.* 9.2a.2; 9.6.4; 9.7.3).[23]

To this extent, we can perhaps sympathize with Cicero's emotional distress at the crisis and the intractable dilemmas that it posed. Indeed, his criticisms of the two generals in the course of these ruminations are often trenchant and insightful, and his observations regarding the past and future intentions of the opposing camps offer valuable material for modern historians of the

---

[22] See further Bailey 1965–70: vol. IV, 438–40.   [23] See further Brunt 1986.

period.[24] Overall, however, his attempts to pursue a course of prudent, self-interested caution would be more convincing, if his views on his own intended actions did not veer so wildly from day to day. At times, his ability to analyse a situation from every conceivable angle appears to have produced, not calm and measured resolve, but anxious vacillation.[25]

Throughout this period, however, Cicero also tried to claim for himself a rather more noble and active political role as peace-maker. How committed he was to this cause – and how seriously Caesar and Pompey engaged with it – is difficult to judge. In two letters from the end of January 49, Cicero states that he has been working hard for some kind of peaceful solution to the worsening conflict (*Att.* 7.14.3; *Fam.* 16.12.2). In part, this involved corresponding with Caesar on the subject (*Fam.* 16.12.5) and receiving encouraging words from him in return (*Att.* 7.21.3). Moreover, during February he appears to have been working on a peace proposal that depended in some way on the consuls – a plan that was derailed when the consuls themselves fled Italy with Pompey (*Att.* 8.11.7; 8.12.4–6; 9.7.3; 9.9.2).

But while these negotiations may have been undertaken with the best of intentions, it is clear that Caesar and Cicero both had plenty to gain from such a pose, whatever the outcome. In general terms, both were able to present themselves as patriots concerned for the welfare of the state and keen to avoid bloodshed; and more specifically, the role of peace-maker afforded Cicero some honourable cover while he sat on the political fence.[26] Such a situation also suited Caesar. So long as Cicero remained as peace-maker in Italy, he was conspicuously not allied with Pompey. Caesar was thus more than happy to encourage Cicero's diplomatic efforts, and seems even to have enlisted the aid of his colleagues, Balbus and Matius, in his attempts to keep the orator on this path (see *Att.* 8.9a.2; 9.11.2; also 9.18).[27]

In the end, though, Cicero departed from Italy and ended up in Pompey's camp. He does not, however, seem to have been particularly welcome there or to have contributed energetically to the cause (Plut. *Cic.* 38.2–6). Indeed, his actions during the crisis seem to have succeeded only in alienating him from both parties. Despite the attempts to present himself as peace-maker, he achieved little that might have helped to sustain any image of him as saviour of the republic or *dux togatus*. Moreover, when Caesar was formally

---

[24] On Caesar, see e.g. *Att.* 7.7.6–7; 7.9.4; 7.11.1; on Pompey, *Att.* 7.11.3; 8.3.2; 8.8.1; 8.11.2; 9.5.2.

[25] See, for example, the fluctuations between *Att.* 8.12.5 and 8.14.2; 9.19.2 and 10.1a; 10.8 and 10.9.2.

[26] See, for example, his letter to Pompey written at the end of February, where Cicero stresses his efforts to act as a constructive negotiator (*Att.* 8.11D.6–8).

[27] See Bailey 1965–70: vol. IV, 461–9 for discussion of other more ambitious plans that Cicero may have entertained briefly.

voted the title of *parens patriae* by the senate (probably in 45 BC), Cicero's earlier claims must have seemed well and truly eclipsed.[28] It is something of a surprise, then, to find these slogans given new life in the aftermath of Caesar's assassination, as Cicero engaged in a bitter struggle with Antony that would end in the orator's murder.

Cicero and Antony

Cicero's initial response to this new political crisis was in fact (once again) one of prudent withdrawal. After an apparently significant role in helping to broker an amnesty between the assassins and the Caesarians (*Phil.* 1.1; Plut. *Cic.* 42.2 and *Brut.* 19.1), he soon retreated to his country residences and played little direct part in affairs at Rome. By now over sixty years old, he commanded a degree of respect as one of the elder consular figures in the senate; but without any constitutional post with *imperium*, his influence was limited. Moreover he had little affinity with the consul Antony, and within a few months he had decided to leave Italy, at least until the end of the year and its anticipated change of magistrates. It was only chance weather conditions that thwarted these plans and set Cicero on a course of active political confrontation.[29] Even as he returned to Rome, however, his precise plan of action was far from clear.[30] The prominent role that he ended up taking during the ensuing crisis is perhaps best viewed as the result of a sequence of *ad hoc* decisions made in response to a rapidly changing and unpredictable political landscape.

With this return to the political stage came the need to resuscitate and reinvigorate his earlier self-laudatory slogans. When Antony on 19 September, for example, delivered in the senate a vitriolic denunciation of the orator's whole career, including many criticisms of his consulship (see *Phil.* 2.3–42), Cicero immediately reverted to his own promotional rhetoric from this period.[31] Thus we find references to the *parens patriae* motif (*Phil.* 2.12), to his role as saviour of the state (*Phil.* 2.2; 2.17; 2.60) and to his image as *dux togatus* (*Phil.* 2.13). This sloganeering, however, took a further intriguing twist in the following months.

In the *Sixth Philippic* (delivered on 4 January 43), Cicero claims that, at a *contio* on 20 December, the crowd declared that his opposition to

---

[28] See Stevenson 2008: 104–13 for details.

[29] For details, see Mitchell 1991: 289–301; Ramsey 2001.

[30] See *Att.* 16.7.7 (19 August 44): *nec ego nunc, ut Brutus censebat, istuc ad rem publicam capessendam uenio.*

[31] Cicero was not present when Antony delivered the speech (*Phil.* 5.19–20).

Antony had now saved the state a second time (*Phil.* 6.2: *iterum a me con-servatam esse rem publicam*). The claim is open to suspicion, since Cicero's published speech from 20 December (the *Fourth Philippic*) makes no mention of such an acclamation.[32] Nevertheless, there are hints elsewhere that the notion of Cicero's second coming as saviour of the state was already gaining a wider currency. In a letter to Atticus dated 5 November 44, for example, Cicero reports that the young Octavian had tried to flatter him by inviting him to save the republic a second time (*Att.* 16.11.6: *iterum rem publicam servarem*). And some months later, Cassius Parmensis sent a letter to Cicero (*Fam.* 12.13.1, dated 13 June 43) extolling the fact that the orator's *toga* had surpassed the weapons of everyone else, and that he had once more rescued the republic (*nunc quoque... rem publicam ex manibus hostium eripuit ac reddidit*). If Cassius and Octavian contrived these compliments independently, we have fascinating evidence for the effectiveness of Cicero's earlier promotional campaign and its continuing legacy. (The *Catilinarian Orations* and *In Pisonem* had been in circulation for over a decade by now and were evidently studied in schools.)[33] But it is no less likely that Octavian and Cassius were influenced by a line of propaganda that Cicero's supporters were actively encouraging in this conflict with Antony.

Cicero's more general tactic during this period is to identify himself closely with the welfare of the *res publica*. For the most part, he does this indirectly rather than via explicit slogans. By associating the safety of the commonwealth with the policies of himself and his allies, Cicero deftly assumes the guise of its protector, whose sole aim is to defend the established freedoms of republican government.[34] This image is given yet sharper relief by its juxtaposion with depictions of Antony as a monstrous oppressor of Rome's citizenry.[35] This tendentious slant characterizes the *Philippics* in other ways too. We may note, for example, the partisan gloss given to the actions of commanders such as Decimus Brutus and Octavian. Their potentially revolutionary use of military force is described euphemistically by Cicero as undertaken through 'private initiative' (*priuato consilio*) – a deliberately bland phrase that conceals a host of uncomfortable truths (*Phil.* 3.5; 3.14; 10.23). Likewise, when M. Brutus and C. Cassius engage in significant military operations without senatorial approval, they are not damned as dangerous

---

[32] Cf. Manuwald 2007b: 750–1.

[33] See *Att.* 2.1.3; 4.2.2; *Q fr.* 3.1.11; cf. Stroh 1975: 52–3.

[34] See e.g. *Phil.* 1.38; 2.1; 2.50; 3.35; 6.2; 8.8; 12.30; 13.47; 14.20. For the association of his allies with the *res publica*, see *Phil.* 3.5, 4.2, 5.46 (Octavian), 10.12 and 23 (M. Brutus), 11.35 (C. Cassius), 5.24 and 7.11 (D. Brutus), 9.16 (Servius Sulpicius Rufus).

[35] See e.g. *Phil.* 2.70; 10.12; 13.32; cf. May 1996; Lévy 1998.

renegades, but lauded as men able to formulate policy unilaterally on behalf of the senate (*Phil.* 11.27). Cicero's rhetoric bends the truth to suit his desired political agenda.

But Cicero's response to the crisis was not limited to public political rhetoric. No less significant were his diplomatic attempts to stitch together a coalition of both the willing and the ambivalent in the service of the 'republican' cause. His extant correspondence preserves letters to (and from) various military commanders whose aims and ambitions he hoped to align with his own: men such as Munatius Plancus, Asinius Pollio and Q. Cornificius, as well as major players such as Lepidus, Octavian, Decimus Brutus and Marcus Brutus.[36] Cicero was matched in this energetic diplomacy, however, by Antony's own extensive efforts to broker deals and alliances (see further below), and his public rhetoric too cleverly disseminated its own half-truths and distortions. Those opposing his cause (he asserted) were not noble defenders of the Republic, but a self-interested political clique (*Phil.* 5.32 and 13.47, *contentio / certamen partium*); worse than this, they were *Pompeiani* (*Phil.* 13.28: *Pompeianum senatum*; 13.38: *Pompeianorum causa*).[37] Cicero himself was branded a war-monger, when in January 43 he vigorously challenged all attempts to resolve through diplomatic channels the military stand-off between Antony and Decimus Brutus at Mutina (*Phil.* 7.3: *bellicum me cecinisse dicunt*). Indeed, Antony cleverly styled himself as a man of peace and compromise. He was said to be ready to give up his claim to Cisalpine Gaul in exchange for control of *Gallia Transalpina*, and even to relinquish his army entirely, if the other generals would agree to do the same.[38] Cicero, by contrast, was striving to have Antony declared an enemy of the state (*hostis*) and to thwart all attempts at peaceful negotiation.[39]

Once again, then, our view of Cicero's political acumen at a time of crisis is obscured by both his own rhetoric and that of his opponents. So when we find the historian Aufidius Bassus asserting (Sen. *Suas.* 6.23) that Cicero's most significant flaw (*uitium*) was that he thought Rome's safety could be achieved only through Antony's destruction, we are faced with a quandary: is this an astute historical judgement or merely a re-packaging of Antony's depiction of Cicero as a reckless, relentless war-monger? In the end, our view on the matter must depend on how we judge Antony's

---

[36] See e.g. Willcock 1995; Hall 2009: 178–90.

[37] See Welch 2002: 9–11; Matijevic 2006: 261.

[38] For Antony as a man of peace, see *Phil.* 7.3 (*suscipiunt pacis patrocinium*); also 5.3; 8.11. On his negotiations, *Phil.* 5.5; 7.2–3; 8.25–28; 12.13.

[39] See e.g. *Phil.* 5.33: *cum hoc, patres conscripti, bello, <bello> inquam, decertandum est.* Cf. 5.3–5; 6.2–6; 6.15; 8.1–9. On Antony as *hostis*, see *Phil.* 3.14; 4.8; 5.25; 7.10–18; 8.4; 13.32; 14.6.

wider political aims. He could in fact claim with some plausibility that his actions in the wake of Caesar's assassination had been characterized by negotiation and compromise rather than violence. In addition to his diplomacy in the days immediately after the murder (praised by Cicero at *Phil.* 1.31–2), he had conceded official positions to the leading assassins, Brutus and Cassius (*Att.* 15.9.1; 15.10; 15.11.2–3; 15.12.1). Indeed, rather than behaving autocratically, he had engaged in negotiations with many prominent politicians of the day, including Plancus (*Fam.* 10.6; *Phil.* 13.44), Hirtius (*Phil.* 13.22), Dolabella (*Phil.* 13.42), Lepidus (*Fam.* 10.27; *Phil.* 13.43) and Octavian (*Phil.* 13.22). Perhaps most conspicuously of all, he had stepped aside from his post as consul at the allotted time, thus ostensibly re-establishing the time-honoured republican principle of the rotation of public office. From this perspective, the war that Cicero was advocating could be regarded as unnecessary and misguided. Antony had steered the state successfully through a time of crisis and was now handing over the reins of power. Far from saving Rome, Cicero's *Philippics* arguably drove the city onto a course of chaos and destruction that could otherwise have been avoided.[40]

We should pause, however, before we accept an image of Antony as entirely selfless and benign. While his policy of compromise was executed with a degree of finesse, it was one over which he perhaps had little choice. The highly volatile situation following Caesar's assassination virtually forced this diplomatic approach upon him. The dictator's violent end sent a clear message that autocratic inclinations would not be tolerated. Antony's prudent politicking, then, does not preclude a degree of ambition in the man. Moreover, Octavian's growing influence among the Caesarian veterans seems to have forced his hand in the latter months of his consulship. Antony's efforts in particular to acquire the province of Cisalpine Gaul for a period of five years suggest a determination to entrench his position for the future.[41] Having gained command of these legions on Italy's doorstep, he would be well poised to exert a louring influence on affairs in the capital (see *Phil.* 7.3; 10.9; 13.37; also 3.27; 5.21). Indeed, his new policy, adopted towards the start of 43, of seeking to avenge Caesar's death must have heightened further the element of intimidation and menace.[42]

---

[40] For this general line of argument, see the (possibly fictional) remarks put into the mouth of L. Piso at App. *B Civ.* 3.54–60. Cf. Syme 1939: 106; 170; Chamoux 1986: 120–1; Matijevic 2006: 256; 374.

[41] See Manuwald 2007a: 12–15 on Antony's assignment of provinces in 44 and the chronological difficulties; cf. Matijevic 2006: 220–37. On the senatorial decree of 20 December 44 supporting D. Brutus, see *Phil.* 4.7–9; 5.36.

[42] See Welch 2002: 9.

Certainly Cicero presents Antony's intentions in starkly exaggerated and alarmist terms; but this does not in itself mean that these concerns were bogus or misplaced.

But if there is still room for debate today regarding the extent of Antony's ambitions and the wisdom of Cicero's policy of aggression, a rather more settled view of their political legacies seems to have developed within a couple of decades or so of their deaths. The school declamations described by Seneca the Elder tend in particular to portray Antony as a violent and menacing opponent of free speech. *Suasoria 7*, for example, which requires students to imagine Cicero pondering whether to burn his writings in order to save his life, encourages reflection on issues such as freedom of oratorical expression, and on the conflict between political principle and personal safety.[43] Most students (we are told) – although not all – chose to depict Cicero as showing a brave defiance in the face of Antony's intimidation (Sen. *Suas.* 6.12).[44] By this time, however, the latter's reputation had suffered yet further at the hands of Octavian's victorious propaganda.[45]

These declamations may tempt us perhaps to endow the *Philippics* themselves with a similarly lofty significance. Certainly, from a historical perspective, they constitute something of an oratorical watershed: the last extant examples of the frank, often rancorous style of debate that typified the Republican senate. Indeed, for many young students of oratory brought up during the more constrained political conditions of the principate, the direct, confrontational manner of these speeches must have held considerable allure.[46] From a practical perspective, however, their success as instruments of political persuasion was often limited. Cicero's attempt in the *Fifth Philippic*, for example, to have a state of emergency (*tumultus*) declared at the start of January 43 was unsuccessful, as were his attempts to discredit and derail the first peace embassy to Antony (*Phil.* 5.31; 6.2–3). His proposal in the *Eleventh Philippic* to have Cassius appointed governor in Syria did not prevail over the opposition of the consul Pansa (*Phil.* 11.29–31; *Fam.* 12.7; *Brut.* 2.4.2); and even his arguments against the second peace embassy to Antony in the *Twelfth Philippic* may not have triumphed as decisively as is sometimes claimed. The speeches thus document a determined, but highly

---

[43] See also Sen. *Suas.* 6, in which Cicero deliberates whether to beg Antony's pardon (cf. Quint. *Inst.* 3.8.47). Sen. *Controv.* 7.2 seems designed to have students explore rather different issues; see Roller 1997: 112.

[44] See Fairweather 1981: 104–31; Richlin 1999: esp. 203–6; Gowing 2005: 45–8. On the speakers who argued Antony's side, see Roller 1997: 116–17; Wilson 2008.

[45] See Charlesworth 1933; Scott 1933; Syme 1939: 459–75.

[46] See e.g. Tac. *Dial.* 37.7; 40–1; Gowing 2005: 110–12. Cf. Winterbottom 1982: 240–5 and Kaster 1998 on the elevation of Cicero to the status of oratorical exemplar.

contentious and not always successful struggle, against opponents who were able at times to nullify or outmanoeuvre his rhetorical gambits.[47]

Moreover, despite the generally positive view of Cicero revealed in the declamations, it is also clear that many students were encouraged to engage more critically with his political legacy. They attacked his character and policies in the style of late Republican invective and in letters written in the guise of contemporary rivals and colleagues.[48] To develop a patina of authenticity, it was natural for such writers to incorporate phrases and ideas culled from their reading both of Cicero's works and of those of his critics. Thus we find resurfacing in various forms and across various genres the same distorting slogans that were deployed during the late Republic. To take two examples from more established writers: in Sallust's monograph, Catiline is depicted lamenting the possibility of Cicero 'saving' the city (Sall. *Cat.* 31.7: *cum eam servaret M. Tullius*). The notion of Cicero as saviour of the state seems a little odd this early in the narrative (Catiline has not yet left Rome and the other conspirators are still to be arrested). Thus, Sallust's phrasing here probably derives from his broader view of the conspiracy and his retrojection upon it of elements from Cicero's later propaganda campaign.

Livy's presentation of the orator's final words, by contrast, appears a little more sly and knowing (Sen. *Suas.* 6.17): '*moriar*' *inquit* '*in patria saepe servata!*' ('I shall die,' he said, 'in this fatherland I have so often saved!') The exclamatory form here suggests a degree of self-importance in the orator – a trope regarding Cicero's character that was well established by the fifties BC. Likewise, the inclusion of *saepe* seems to allude – perhaps wryly – to Cicero's recycling of the 'saviour-of-the-republic' slogan at various points in his career.[49] Moreover, Livy's more directly damning remarks in his death-notice for the orator (Sen. *Suas.* 6.22) may reflect the tradition that condemned Cicero for cruelty.[50]

In death, then, as in life, Cicero's political legacy continued to be a matter of dispute. What is remarkable is the extent to which the labels 'saviour of the republic', 'father of the fatherland' and *dux togatus* continued to be associated with him throughout the centuries that followed. We can discern their

[47] On the *Fifth* and *Sixth Philippics*, see Steel 2008; on the *Twelfth Philippic*, see Hall 2008.

[48] See Syme 1964: 314–51; Bailey 2002: 339–41. On the (probably) spurious letters preserved as *Brut.* 1.16 and 1.17, see Bailey 1980: 10–14; for a different view, Moles 1997. On mock-Ciceronian speeches composed by teachers and students, see Sen. *Controv.* 3, pref. 15; Quint. *Inst.* 10.5.20; Clift 1945: 91 and 95.

[49] On his return from exile, Cicero had tried on several occasions to claim that his departure abroad too had saved the Republic (see *Dom.* 76; 99; *Sest.* 49).

[50] See in general Pomeroy 1991: 146–68; also Roller 1997: 123; Wright 2001: 448–9.

traces in an array of later writers, including Velleius Paterculus (2.66: *conservator rei publicae*), Cremutius Cordus (Sen. *Suas.* 6.19: *multorum capita servaverat*), Pliny the Elder (who claims that Cicero was the first civilian to win a triumph, *HN* 7.117), Cornelius Severus (Sen. *Suas.* 6.26), Lucan 7.63–4 (*sub iure togaque*), Juvenal (*Sat.* 8.240–3: *toga... gladio* and *Sat.* 8.244: *Roma patrem patriae Ciceronem libera dixit*), Plutarch (*Cic.* 22.3:) and Appian (*B Civ.* 2.7). These vestiges are a testament both to Cicero's prodigious energy for self-promotion, and the place that his writings assumed in the literary canon of later generations. As we have seen, these slogans are fundamentally misleading; but, in a political environment characterized by aggressive personal attack and distorting rhetoric, that was precisely their point.

Further reading

On Cicero's public presentation of his personal and political achievements, see Allen 1954; Graff 1963; May 1988; Steel 2005; Kurczyk 2006. For a concise account of the Catilinarian conspiracy and associated orations, see most recently Dyck 2008b: 1–20; for fuller treatments, Hardy 1924; Gelzer 1969: 80–104; Rawson 1975: 69–87; Mitchell 1979: 205–42. The ancient sources are usefully gathered together (with German translations) in Drexler 1976. For historical analyses of Catiline's coup and its significance (from various perspectives), see Yavetz 1963; Waters 1970; Seager 1973; Phillips 1976; Wiseman 1994b. On the debate regarding the fate of the conspirators, see Ungern-Sternberg 1970; Cape 1995; Drummond 1995.

For convenient introductions to the political events following Caesar's assassination, see Syme 1939: 97–111; 162–75; Frisch 1946; Mitchell 1991: 289–301; Rawson 1994. Matijevic 2006 provides a useful revisionist interpretation of Antony's policies, with copious references to modern authors. The recent commentaries on the *Philippics* by Ramsey 2003 and Manuwald 2007a and 2007b supply expert discussions of individual points. For attitudes to Cicero in later authors, see Broughton 1936, Millar 1964: 46–55, Winterbottom 1982, Stone 1999 and Gowing in this volume (Chapter 14).

PART III

Receptions of Cicero

14

ALAIN M. GOWING

Tully's boat: responses to Cicero in the imperial period

Quintilian, on whom Cicero exerted a deeper and more readily discernible influence than on any other imperial author, conjures in the preface to the twelfth and final book of the *Institutio oratoria* a memorable image: Cicero sailing in a boat, alone, far from the safety of port. I shall have more to say about this curious tableau and its context presently, but for the moment it will suffice simply to note that Cicero is omnipresent in Quintilian in ways large and small, the *sine quo non* of his masterwork, the standard by which he defines the arts and practitioners of oratory and eloquence. By contrast, Cicero appears comparatively seldom in the work of Seneca the Younger. Despite some obvious parallels in their literary interests – both write dialogues, letters, poetry, philosophy – and even their lives (both experienced exile, both 'retired' from public life in the face of a tyrant), Seneca cannot be said to have openly promoted Cicero as a *model* for much. Of the forty or so direct references to Cicero spread across all of Seneca's extensive extant oeuvre, few adduce Cicero as a positive *exemplum*; most are simply no more than colourless passing references, suggesting a reluctance to give Cicero too prominent a place in his writings. Yet there are occasions when Cicero, apparently seldom far from his mind, lurks below the surface of what Seneca writes. Such is the case with *Epistula* 51, a moralizing account of a trip to Baiae that alludes to Cicero while seeming deliberately to overlook or exclude him.

While my brief for this paper is early imperial responses to Cicero (the chronological range extending from the Augustan period through the reign of Trajan), I should like to focus attention on these two texts because they represent what I see as the two most significant responses from the early imperial period: one that readily acknowledges and holds up Cicero as a model, another that seems to marginalize him. Yet both make one point crystal clear: Cicero could never simply be ignored. Before I turn to these two texts, however, an overview of the principal responses to Cicero in the 100 years or so after his death in 43 BC will provide some necessary context.

A century of (relative) silence

The subject of responses to Cicero, it should be stressed, has not lacked study and investigation.[1] Given the profound importance of Cicero as an orator, writer, stylist and thinker, his influence on subsequent writers must have been considerable. Nonetheless, his *direct* appearances in the extant literature produced subsequent to his death down to the Tiberian period are few if well known.

He has a role in Sallust's *Bellum Catilinae*, of course, published soon after the orator's death in 43 BC, but a role not quite in proportion to Cicero's own account of his part in suppressing the conspiracy. Whether Sallust was 'fair' to Cicero, whether he cast him in a positive or negative light, has been the subject of much enquiry.[2] The lack of scholarly agreement in itself should tell us something. The fact is that Sallust does not go out of his way to praise Cicero (contrast the Tiberian historian, Velleius Paterculus, at 2.66, discussed below); his most laudatory remark is aimed not at Cicero *per se*, but at the *First Catilinarian* (*orationem . . . luculentam atque utilem rei publicae*, Sall. *Cat.* 31.6). As so often, it is Cicero's eloquence that receives approval, less so Cicero himself. He virtually disappears from the latter part of the narrative. Sallust deems it imperative *not* to 'pass over in silence' (*silentio praeterire non fuit consilium*, 53.6) the lives of Caesar and Cato, who are therefore accorded special treatment (54), but not that of Cicero. Sallust himself hints at the hostility Cicero endured during his lifetime (23.5–6, 48.7–9), a hostility that dogged him even (and perhaps especially) after his death. The existence of the Pseudo-Sallustian invectives, comprising an exceptionally bitter attack on 'Cicero' by 'Sallust' and an equally bitter response, suggests that at least some of Sallust's ancient readers perceived an antipathy worth exploiting in the rhetorical schools. Why Sallust should harbour such antipathy can only be surmised, but he was after all a Caesarian partisan, and thus on the opposite side of the political fence from Cicero. Those political lines were even more distinctly drawn (and harder to cross) after Caesar's assassination and Cicero's own murder (discussed below), when Sallust was writing. Even Sallust's style has been deemed to be a studied and conscious rejection of Cicero, despite the fact that he often mines Cicero's own language to good effect.[3] As a historical source, however, Cicero seems to have held little weight for Sallust. He cannot write Cicero

[1] See Further Reading.   [2] See McGushin 1977: 154–5, Syme 1964: 105–11.
[3] Thus Syme 1964: 111, maintains that Sallust 'transmutes personal hostility into emulation in the field of letters, wilfully creating a style and manner that defies and denies everything that is "Ciceronian"'. Sallust's best-known allusion to Cicero is Catiline's *quo usque tandem* of *Cat.* 20.9, echoing Cic. *Cat.* 1.1 (often interpreted as a spiteful gesture

out of history, but he can diminish his part in it, and in this Sallust was not alone.

A corrective to Sallust's perspective may well have been supplied by the now lost biography of Cicero published in the mid to late thirties, within a few years of the appearance of the *Bellum Catilinae*, by his friend Cornelius Nepos. This was certainly eulogistic in tone, and perhaps an important source for subsequent historians.[4] Strikingly, however, between Sallust's *Bellum Catilinae* and Velleius Paterculus – the entire Augustan period – scarcely a single extant writer mentions Cicero by name. This is a telling fact, although not the sole criterion by which we should gauge Cicero's influence. That manifests itself in far more subtle ways that are admittedly a greater challenge to detect and confirm. The *De officiis*, for instance, is often cited as a source for some of the sentiments found in Ovid's *Amores* and Horace's *Odes*.[5] No doubt, in short, that Cicero was read, and perhaps even heeded, but hardly ever referenced or acknowledged directly. Why should that be? I am hesitant to deduce, with Weil, that the Augustan silence about Cicero signals a reluctance to identify with the great defender of the Republic – a virtual 'ban' on Cicero.[6] On the other hand, it is also difficult to reconcile this silence with Syme's view that Cicero's 'whole conception of the Roman State triumphed after his death'.[7] Virgil's own silence may support a more nuanced view.

In the *Aeneid* Virgil has two particularly good opportunities to refer to and even name Cicero. One is on the scene on the shield of Aeneas in Book 8, where we see depicted Catiline tortured in the underworld, followed hard on by Cato 'giving laws' (*dantem iura Catonem*) (8.668–70). No mention is made of Cicero's part in the Catilinarian conspiracy (contrast Lucan a couple of generations later at 7.62–6, discussed below). Virgil has done what the historian Sallust could not or would not do, write Cicero out of Catiline's story. He has, in fact, written Cicero out of Roman history altogether, for nor does Cicero find a place in Virgil's underworld in Book 6 and the survey of Roman history. One could argue that in the scene on the shield he doesn't *need* to name Cicero, but why Cato and not Cicero?

The answer to this, and to the post-mortem silence about Cicero generally, is that Catiline and Cato both serve a useful purpose that Cicero at this point

towards Cicero), but traces of the orator's language are apparent elsewhere as well, e.g., Cic. *Cat.* 1.14 ≈ Sall. *Cat.* 15.1–3; Cic. *Mur.* 51 ≈ Sall. *Cat.* 31.6–32.1.
[4] See Peter 1967: 2.xxxx–xxxi, liii–lv, fragments on p. 34.
[5] See Gibson 2003: 22 n. 57 and passim; Dyck 1996: 40–1.
[6] Weil 1962: 46; his chapter on Cicero's reputation in the early imperial period is entitled 'Der Bann gegen der Redner'.
[7] Syme 1939: 318.

does not, as *exempla*, a status denied Cicero, and not merely in the *Aeneid*. Catiline personifies the forces of subversion in the state and punishment that awaits those who deploy them; Cato, 'the ideals of just and virtuous republican statesmanship'.[8] Cicero does not. The omission therefore seems quite deliberate,[9] and offers a clue as to why Cicero occupies a relatively small place in very early imperial literature.

One Augustan writer who does name Cicero as a source – or rather as a source of inspiration – is the architect Vitruvius, but this too is suggestive. In the preface to Book 9 of the *De architectura* (coincidentally, in the midst of a passage quite fascinating for what it tells us about the Roman view of memory), he imagines 'discussing' with Cicero the *ars rhetorica*. Through his writing, Vitruvius argues, Cicero becomes virtually 'present' (*praesens*) or alive (9.*praef.*17). This sort of imaginative move is not so unusual, but it is curious not only that he cites Cicero as a source (of inspiration) but that he focuses on his rhetorical works. The relevance of such works to a book about architecture might not seem obvious, but as Wallace-Hadrill astutely remarks, Vitruvius discerned in Cicero's *rhetorica* a model for '[marrying] Greek *ratio* with Roman *consuetudo*'.[10] Here, then, Cicero's method matters as much as, if not more than, the substance of his work.

If these few sources may be trusted, the vague lines of a pattern begin to emerge. Cicero's authority as an orator and writer, and in particular as an authority on rhetoric, seems assured (though up to this point it is impossible to be very precise about the extent of his influence), but as a historical figure he possesses little clout. This is not to deny him importance in the course of events in the waning years of the Republic, but he had not earned through his actions a place in the Roman moral and ethical universe that manifested itself in the ever-evolving *exemplum* tradition. This general pattern is confirmed by one of the most important sources for early imperial responses to Cicero on the part of historians, *Suasoria* 6 of the Elder Seneca, a product of the thirties AD and the Tiberian period, when the silence surrounding Cicero seems to be broken.

The first half of this rhetorical declamatory exercise is given over to the question of whether or not Cicero should beg Mark Antony for his life; the context prompts Seneca to quote or paraphrase accounts of Cicero's death by various historians and other writers in the second half (*Suas.* 6.14–26). It would be interesting to know just how much space these historians accorded the *other* events of Cicero's life, but we simply cannot know.

---

[8] Gransden 1976: 173.
[9] Highet 1972: 141–5, 284–5, discusses these passages and Virgil's evident 'hostility' to Cicero.
[10] Wallace-Hadrill 2008: 145–6.

Perhaps, however, the view of Bruttedius Niger was a common one, that the period from the time of his consulship in 63 BC down to his conflict with Antony in 44–43 BC was a 'nadir of servitude' (*miserrimi temporis seruitutem*, *Suas.* 6.21) and not worth much attention; some, like Asinius Pollio, were manifestly hostile to the memory of Cicero (*Suas.* 6.24).[11] The *Suasoria*, however, zeroes in on the death, a particularly brutal event: Cicero, tracked down at his villa at Caieta in November of 43 BC, was beheaded and his hands cut off – these were brought to Rome and stuck on a pole in the Roman forum for public viewing.[12] Some of these narratives are largely sympathetic (Livy, Aufidius Bassus, Cremutius Cordus, Bruttedius Niger – with the exception of Livy, all essentially Tiberian authors), but their final assessments of Cicero, also quoted or paraphrased by Seneca, are guarded. Almost all remark the enmity Cicero stirred up in the course of his lifetime, and describe a man whose faults too often cast his virtues into the shadows. None disputes (and most praise) Cicero's eloquence, but none offers up Cicero's life and career as something worthy of emulation. Not even the Tiberian historian Velleius Paterculus, whose *History* is the fullest and in some respects most laudatory source for the life of Cicero prior to Plutarch, *quite* does this.

Velleius' abbreviated account of Roman history in two books appeared a few years prior to the publication in the late thirties AD of Seneca's *Controversiae* and *Suasoriae*. This historian does in fact give Cicero his due, terming him not only the *princeps* of *eloquentia* (1.17.3; cf. Sen. *Contr.* 7.4.6) but a man distinguished as much for his life as he was for unparalleled intellectual achievements (2.34.3).[13] His death, however, elicits extraordinary outrage from Velleius – and the longest passage about Cicero in the entire work (2.66.1–5).[14] In it he laments the passing of the *conseruator rei publicae*, the 'saviour of the Republic', and the *uox publica*, the 'voice of the people', embodied in Cicero. Velleius' remark that Cicero's renown has been increased, if not actually ensured, by Antony's vile actions underscores the notion that one's reputation, and perhaps Cicero's in particular, rests as much on deeds (and not necessarily one's *own* deeds) as it does on words. Thus in Velleius' view Cicero's death is far more important for its symbolic value than its historical details (note that he does not actually narrate the

---

[11] Winterbottom 1982: 241–2; Syme 1939: 318.

[12] Apart from *Suasoria* 6, the chief sources are Cassius Dio 47.8 and App. *B Civ.* 4.19–20. For the scholarship on the treatment of Cicero's death, see references in n. 15.

[13] Valerius Maximus, Velleius' coeval, similarly admires Cicero as the *summa vis Romanae eloquentiae* (2.2.3) and the *caput Romanae eloquentiae* (5.3.4). Valerius is more generous to Cicero than most (see, e.g., 4.2.4 on Cicero's *praecipua humanitas*, 8.5.5).

[14] For discussion, see Woodman 1977: 144–5, Gowing 2005: 44–8. Despite Velleius' remarks about the success of Cicero's life, he does not make him much of a player.

murder itself). This fits with the historian's desire to locate in the most significant players from the Republic exemplary qualities that anticipate those displayed, and inevitably surpassed, by Tiberius (Gowing 2007).

In sum, the fixation on the death of Cicero – as opposed to the details of his life and career – is not simply an accident of the sources, nor is the confusion generated by those sources.[15] Here, too, we run up against the pull of the *exempla* tradition, and the wish to salvage from Cicero's final hours an *exemplum* on the order of Cato, Brutus or Cassius – or to discredit him. The difficulty is that while Cicero may hardly be said to have died a cowardly death, the manner and circumstances of his demise did not match those of the men who became known as the martyrs for the Republic (cf., e.g., Sen. *Suas.* 6.2).[16] Velleius, as I have argued elsewhere (Gowing 2007), circumvents this problem by perpetuating the myth that the Republic persists, if not unchanged then certainly resuscitated by Tiberius. On that view, Cicero could hardly be considered a threat nor does he need to be made a 'martyr' because the survival of the Republic was not in doubt; his death was the fault of one particularly villainous individual, Mark Antony, not of a 'Roman Revolution' aimed at transforming the Republic.

These, in brief, are the chief sources for responses to Cicero in the 100 years or so after his death. A couple of facts are clear: opinion about Cicero, especially about his life and achievements, is to this point sharply divided; starting with the Tiberian period, at least to judge from the extant sources, Cicero begins to appear more explicitly in the literary record, especially among the historians. The question of Cicero's exemplary value appears especially to come to the fore. And thus as Rome completed the transition from Republic to principate – a gradual process that reaches a watershed moment in the Neronian period when few would deny that the old Roman Republic had indeed been replaced or 'changed' (Seneca refers to the *mutatio rei publicae*, *Ep.* 71.12) – this question seems to acquire fresh significance: what, if anything, is the relevance of Cicero in the new society and the new political order? Is there a sense, that is, in which he could finally find a

---

[15] The substantial disagreements between the sources show that the facts of Cicero's death (and indeed of his life) could be manipulated in the interests of a dramatic and skewed narrative. See esp. on this point Wright 2001; the confused traditions surrounding Cicero's death are well discussed as well by Homeyer 1964 and Roller 1997. Valerius Maximus also sympathetically references Cicero's death 1.4.6 and 5.3.4. His death continued to intrigue subsequent writers: e.g., Sen. *Dial.* 9.16.1; Martial 3.66, 5.69 (on which see Pierini 2003: 44–47); Tac. *Dial.* 17.3, 24.3.

[16] Kaster 1998: 254, analysing the perspective on Cicero in these Senecan texts, puts it thus: 'what is "going on" is that Cicero is being heroized: he is becoming a culture hero, an icon more important as an abstract representation than the historical reality of the man and the sensible reality of his words'. For Cicero's exclusion from the cast of Republican 'martyrs', see Wirszubski 1950: 128–9.

niche as an *exemplum*? To this point Cicero's political views hardly seem to have held much weight; his reputation as a great orator and the master of eloquence seems secure; as a player on the historical stage, however, his impact is seen to be minimal. If we consider that the oratorical arts were for Cicero the foundation of political power, as they were for anyone living under the Republic, what could be his role in the imperial period, when public oratory and the free exchange of ideas no longer mattered in quite the same way?

Seneca in the *umbra Ciceronis*

Seneca the Younger, who was well aware of Cicero's influence (he coined the phrase 'the shadow of Cicero', *Q Nat.* 2.56.1), has seemed to many a logical source to seek an answer to this question. While this is not the place for full discussion of the oft-examined relationship between Seneca and Cicero, especially with respect to their shared interest in philosophy,[17] Grimal's conclusion, that Seneca never formed a universal opinion of Cicero that was either wholly positive or wholly negative, is certainly correct.[18] Rather, as Grimal and others have shown, Seneca's view of Cicero is complex and nuanced, and doubtless changed over time. Yet despite the many similarities between the two men – similarities so striking that Grimal can observe 'une parenté spirituelle' (Grimal 1984: 656) between them – Seneca does not see a kindred spirit in his Republican predecessor.

But he does understand his debt to him. It is conceivable that Seneca was fully aware of and even promoted the temptation to compare him with his Republican predecessor, not to highlight similarities but rather to emphasize contrasts – to put it more bluntly, to suggest ways in which Seneca succeeded where Cicero failed. Thus, for instance, Grimal plausibly suggests that among the sort of excessively ambitious and foolish men attacked at the conclusion of the *De brevitate vitae*, men who live their lives 'fruitlessly, with no pleasure, no mental improvement' (*sine fructu, sine uoluptate, sine ullo profectu animi, Dial.* 10.20.5), is none other than Cicero himself.[19] And indeed, earlier in this work Seneca launched one of his most scathing attacks on Cicero, essentially accusing him of not being a 'wise man' (*sapiens*, 10.5.3). In a general sense, of course, Seneca was, like Cicero, very much

---

[17] See Further Reading. The full scope of Seneca's indebtedness to – and disagreements with – Cicero on philosophical matters may be easily appreciated through Inwood 2005.

[18] Grimal 1984: 666.

[19] Grimal 1984: 660–5. See further on Seneca's fundamental dislike of Cicero, Kennedy 2002: 485; Leeman 1963: vol. I, 271–9.

concerned with personal conduct, if less explicitly personal conduct in a *political* sphere. In this respect Cicero had fallen short.

This sort of vague allusiveness noted by Grimal – where Seneca will engage and perhaps even contrast himself with Cicero without directly adducing him – may be more prevalent than we have yet realized. There can be no doubt that Seneca read very deeply in Cicero, especially but not exclusively his philosophical works, and thus Cicero may seldom be far from Seneca's mind, an often unspoken standard against which he measures himself and others. *Epistula* 51 offers an example.[20]

The letter's subject – life at the Campanian resort town of Baiae and Seneca's rejection of that life – invites a comparison between Seneca and Cicero on several levels. This is the gist of the letter: Seneca has gone on holiday to Baiae, that notorious seaside resort outside of Naples famous for its decadence, but as he informs Lucilius, who took his holiday in Sicily, he left the day after he arrived, in fear of the effects such an extended stay in this decadent place might have. It is difficult to read this letter without being put in mind of Cicero's famous description of Clodia's escapades with Caelius at Baiae in the *Pro Caelio*; Seneca's vivid description of the region's decadence (*Ep.* 51.3–4) so closely echoes what we read in Cicero's *Pro Caelio* (*Cael.* 27, 35, 38) that commentators on both texts invariably cross-reference the relevant passages.[21] Seneca may well have in mind a related speech, the *In Clodium et Curionem*, a (to us) less well-known and now lost speech composed in 61 BC.[22] In *Epistula* 97, dated to AD 63, Seneca quotes at length from a letter by Cicero (*Att.* 1.16) that describes this speech and Clodius' response, so he obviously knew it (so did Quintilian, *Inst.* 5.10.92, 8.3.81, 9.2.96). (It is worth emphasizing, by the way, that Seneca's reference to the letter to Atticus is the first such reference to this particular corpus we have, leading scholars to conclude that the *Epistulae ad Atticum* were only published in the Neronian period.[23] If true, this attests to a renewed interest in Cicero himself; the corpus would clearly have been responsible for providing a fresh perspective on Cicero, an opportunity of which Seneca evidently takes full advantage.) From this and other fragments

[20] So, too, does Henderson 2004: 166–9, discover traces of Seneca's subtle engagement with Cicero in *Ep.* 86. This sort of Cicero-hunting in Seneca is a familiar task for those interested in Seneca's philosophy (a good example of this is Inwood's 2005: 271–301 exegesis of *Ep.* 120, where Seneca clearly debates Cicero without naming him) and thus neglects the non-philosophical components of Cicero's corpus with which Seneca was familiar. For the familiarity of imperial readers with Cicero's work, McGill 2005 makes for useful and interesting reading.

[21] E.g., Summers 1968: 217, Austin 1960 on 35.10. Cf. Hönscheid 2004: 17.

[22] For the fragments of the speech, with commentary, see Crawford 1994: 226–63.

[23] See Bailey 1965: 59–76, with Steel 2005: 44–6.

of the speech we know that accusations of living the high life at Baiae figured prominently in that exchange (in this instance, the charges are laid against Cicero himself) as they did later in the *Pro Caelio* of 56 BC.[24] I shall return to this point presently.

One device common to both the *Pro Caelio* and *Epistula* 51 is the use of *exempla*. Memorably, in the *Pro Caelio*, Cicero brings out the dead Appius Claudius Caecus, the stern censor of 312 and ancestor of Clodia, so that we might hear what he would say about her questionable behaviour (*Cael.* 33–4). In *Epistula* 51, Seneca similarly summons dead characters from the Republican past to reinforce his condemnation of Baiae. The *Epistulae* feature *exempla* less often than other Senecan texts – in this respect, then, the letter is a bit of an anomaly; and here, as often, he deploys standard *exempla* in ways other than what one would expect.[25] Seneca's first *exemplum* is Hannibal, adduced as an example of someone who had been corrupted by Baiae. Seneca fudges a little, for it is nearby Capua that is typically identified as the culprit (it was here that Hannibal's men were allegedly corrupted by the pleasures of Campania during a prolonged stay in the year 216 BC, for which see Livy 23.18; cf. 23.44–5). Cicero himself adduces this tale, as an illustration that even great men may be corrupted by bad places (*Agr.* 1.20, 2.95). As Cicero puts it, 'that luxury which, through pleasure, conquered Hannibal, so far unconquered by arms' (*ea luxuries quae ipsum Hannibalem armis etiam tum inuictum uoluptate uicit*); Seneca gestures to precisely this passage, 'a single winter stay undid Hannibal, and Campanian tenderness slackened a man unsubdued by snow and Alps; he conquered through arms and was conquered by vices' (*una Hannibalem hiberna solverunt et indomitum illum niuibus atque Alpibus uirum eneruauerunt fomenta Campaniae: armis uicit, uitiis uictus est*) (*Ep.* 51.5). While this line certainly owes something to Livy as well, the historian focuses attention on Hannibal's men, not, in contrast to both Seneca and Cicero, on Hannibal himself.[26]

But Seneca applies a significant corrective to Cicero's use of Hannibal: it is not places that corrupt, Seneca argues, but people and their bad habits. The wise man (*sapiens*) will steel himself against all corrupting influences (*voluptas*), indeed against all external forces; his goal must be *libertas* – a loaded Republican word – but Seneca's *libertas* means having the ability to withstand the whims of *fortuna*, to rise above circumstances (51.8–9). In Seneca's view of him, Cicero never managed to do that (e.g., *Dial.* 10.5.1–3, the passage which, as we have seen, leads Seneca to infer Cicero was not a

---

[24] See esp. Crawford 1994, fragment 1.96–105 = Cic. *Att.* 1.16.10.

[25] On this point see Mayer 1991.

[26] Hönscheid 2004: 35–7 draws attention to the similarities between Seneca and Livy, but not between Seneca and Cicero. Cf. Summers 1968 on 51.5.

sapiens). This section of the letter, however, actually comes quite close to the moralizing lecture Cicero delivers in the *Pro Caelio* (46–7), where he advises that 'all pleasures' (*omnes uoluptates*) must be abandoned by those who wish to achieve success;[27] and here Cicero, like Seneca, argues that Baiae is not the culprit, but rather the depraved and seductive Clodia who lured Caelius to Baiae.

As proof of his argument about strong moral character he adduces an interesting collection of Republican *exempla* (51.11–12): Scipio Africanus (here because he had defeated Hannibal), Marius, Pompey the Great and Julius Caesar. They all have something in common with Hannibal: they are all generals, as all of Seneca's readers would be aware. Yet here Seneca uses them as examples of people who were able to resist temptation. In contrast to Hannibal, they resisted the lures of Baiae, despite having actually lived nearby. The villas built by Marius, Pompey and Caesar were in fact constructed on the hilltops surrounding Baiae: this was more 'military', and permitted a sweeping view of what lay below. They were, as Seneca says, more like military camps than villas (51.11). Of course no criticism of luxury can be complete without Cato, so he deftly brings him on (much as Cicero brings on Appius Claudius Caecus in the *Pro Caelio*), asking us to imagine Cato at Baiae – or rather, to imagine that Cato would never be caught dead at Baiae, gazing at prostitutes on yachts and at gaily decorated dinghies, listening to a chorus of drunks (51.12).[28]

Missing from this cast of exemplary characters is Cicero, yet it could be argued that he certainly belongs among them. Apart from connecting Seneca's condemnation of Baiae with Cicero's well-known pronouncements, knowledgeable readers would similarly be aware that Cicero himself owned a villa (or villas) in this vicinity.[29] Cicero had evidently purchased the first of these shortly before 61 BC, prior to the delivery of the *In Clodium et Curionem*. We learn of this via Cicero's retelling of the altercation in the letter to Atticus, the letter cited by Seneca in *Epistula 97*, as well as from

[27] Some important distinctions between Cicero and Seneca may be glimpsed here. Cicero is interested in the *praemia* of eloquence (*Cael.* 46), because that leads to a successful political career; Seneca is interested in the *praemium* afforded by a moral life, namely, *libertas* (*Ep.* 51.9). Cicero, that is, constantly thinks in political terms; Seneca, in personal terms, even when using a term as loaded and fraught with political connotations as *libertas*.

[28] A further reason for this condemnation of Baiae, it should be mentioned, may be to underscore Seneca's growing disapproval of Nero and his well-known Baian escapades, not least of which was the murder of his mother (cf. Suet. *Ner.* 27).

[29] For Cicero's Campanian villas (as well as for the various villas mentioned in *Epistula* 51) see D'Arms 1970: 44–56, 198–200 and passim. On this particular villa, probably his *Pompeianum*, see Bailey 1965 on *Att.* 1.16.10 (p. 320).

a fragment of the speech.[30] Accusing him of visiting the region, Clodius had cited Cicero's purchase of a villa at Baiae as evidence of weak moral character. 'What business does a man from Arpinum have with the hot springs?' (*quid . . . homini Arpinati cum aquis calidis?*, *Att.* 1.16.10), he said. Cicero's response to this was, 'Tell that to your patron, who coveted the springs of a man from Arpinum' (*narra . . . patrono tuo, qui Arpinatis aquas concupiuit*). As he explains to Atticus, this was a veiled allusion to Curio, who had recently purchased the villa owned by the famous Marius (like Cicero, from Arpinum) at Baiae. This is the same villa referenced by Seneca at *Epistula* 51.11.

Villas figure prominently in Seneca's *Epistulae*. As Henderson has shown, Seneca closely links morals and villas: 'Seneca's *localized* expatiation [provides] models of moralization' wherein 'imagery plumbs the depths to implant lessons in morality topicalized through mimesis'.[31] What does it mean, therefore, to exclude Cicero and his villa near Baiae from this letter, in which the villas and their equally famous owners are deployed in the service of Seneca's moralizing? Why does the Baian villa-owning, ethical Cicero not warrant a place among these men? In leaving him out Seneca denies him the moral authority Marius, Caesar, Pompey and most significantly Cato enjoy. In short, Cicero does not make the grade as an *exemplum*, at least not in this context.[32] Seneca does, however, align *himself* with these famous characters who had the moral character to resist the temptations of Baiae. If, for the reasons I have suggested, readers could not help but think of Cicero when they read this letter, it would be equally apparent that Seneca supplants and surpasses Cicero as the moral paragon. The letter showcases a tendency in Seneca generally: to value Cicero at best as essentially a literary or oratorical figure, at worst as a man whose flawed and perhaps even hypocritical life undermined any claim to ethical authority. Thus while Cicero does not earn *explicit* mention here, as do Cato, Caesar and the others, his presence is implicit through reference to well-known speeches. He remains an important, useful, even reliable point of reference. But Seneca, and others too for that matter, could not, or would not, separate Cicero's life from his work; the authority of the latter to some degree was determined by how he had conducted his life.

Quintilian will openly dispute this point of view, but it is worth noting before we take leave of Seneca Cicero's place in the epic of his nephew,

---

[30] Crawford 1994, fragment 19.   [31] Henderson 2004: 4.

[32] Winterbottom 1982: 241–4 explores the various ways in which Cicero served as an *exemplum* in the imperial period, but it is important to note the almost complete absence of consensus about what he exemplified. Quintilian, I would argue, manages to change that.

Lucan. Cicero's role in the *Pharsalia*, a poem contemporary with Seneca's *Epistulae*, is small – he appears only once – but notable because it is utterly unhistorical and fictitious: Lucan places him at the battlefield at Pharsalus, where, speaking for the other senators and the soldiers, he angrily upbraids Pompey for his hesitation and timidity (7.45–85).[33] This is not the Cicero we are accustomed to, yet Lucan suggests that his anger at Pompey is of a piece with his suppression of Catiline, an event he mentions specifically (7.63–4); at the heart of that event, and of his outburst against Pompey, is Cicero's overriding desire to preserve the Republic. If Virgil writes Cicero out of history, Lucan writes him back in, albeit with a dramatic twist of fact. The fiction, however, allows Lucan to create a scene in which the man most closely identified as the voice, if not the soul, of the Republic is made to confront the man whose defeat at the hands of Caesar ensured the Republic's demise. Ahl may well be correct to infer that the scene does not put Cicero in an entirely positive light (he certainly does not achieve the status of an *exemplum* in Lucan), but rather illustrates that the 'strength of senatorial *libertas*', instantiated in Cicero, 'becomes its critical weakness in time of war'.[34] Seen in this way, Lucan's Cicero appears slightly misguided, even (and perhaps deliberately) out of place, though there is no mistaking the positive nature of the poet's characterization of Cicero as 'the greatest practitioner of Roman eloquence', *Romani maximus auctor / Tullius eloquii* (7.62–3). Even Seneca would agree with this, though it will be left to Quintilian to reconcile the facts of Cicero's life with his authorial and oratorical legacy.

Quintilian: setting sail with Cicero

By the time we reach the latter part of the first century and essentially the reign of Trajan, writers are less troubled by the details of Cicero's personal and political life, and more inclined to recognize that his accomplishments as an orator warranted serious study and emulation. This may well be the consequence of several factors, among them the increased stability afforded by a maturing principate and the simple fact that after 150 years or so the particulars of Cicero's life seemed less important than the lasting legacy of his literary and oratorical accomplishments. Whatever the reason, this is the period when we can speak of an emerging 'Ciceronianism' as the basis of one's education in oratory and, in Brink's term, of a 'general civic culture'.[35] The text that best illustrates the neo-Ciceronianism of the

---

[33] See discussion by Ahl 1976: 160–3.   [34] Ahl 1976: 163.
[35] Brink 1989: 486 with n. 53.

period, and indeed the text largely responsible for it, is Quintilian's *Institutio oratoria*.

Composed in the latter part of the reign of Domitian, in the nineties AD, Quintilian's masterwork is essentially a handbook on the education and training of an orator. The work is unabashedly inspired by the example of Cicero, who had of course written several treatises on roughly the same subject and who is liberally cited (and praised) throughout.[36] Where Seneca rejects the Ciceronian ideals (or at least questions Cicero's claim to moral authority), Quintilian avidly embraces and promotes them. Indeed, his own well-documented antipathy towards Seneca may in part be a reaction to the perceived anti-Ciceronian perspective of the Neronian author.[37] The *Institutio* is a work designed to rethink the relevance of those ideals, born under the Roman Republic, for the Roman principate. At the hands of Quintilian, this Ciceronianism is largely devoid of any overt political meaning,[38] especially in contrast to, say, 'Republicanism', another term used to describe a spirit of resistance to the principate. But Ciceronianism is not synonymous with Republicanism. Rather, Quintilian's Ciceronianism aims at the cultivation of the *vir bonus dicendi peritus*, the 'good man skilled at speaking' (*Inst.* 12.1.1) – not because 'speaking' is any longer the key to wielding political power but because the training required for such skill in consequence produces a 'good man'. Character is what matters here, not power. As Connolly neatly summarizes it, '[Quintilian] transposes Ciceronian public performative ethics into a domestic key, and redefines the enlargement of thought by Ciceronian rhetoric as the project of becoming a *vir bonus*, a "good man"'.[39]

It is striking, however, that there is virtually no biographical information about Cicero in Quintilian – very little attempt, that is, to justify the authority of Cicero through reference to his own life. Until, that is, one reaches the opening chapters of the twelfth and final book of the *Institutio* (*Inst.* 12.1.14–20). Here, as Quintilian defends the connection between being 'good' and an orator, Quintilian directly confronts the question of Cicero's character. Admitting that many fault Cicero on exactly this point, Quintilian confirms what we have already surmised, that there existed a persistent hostility towards Cicero, a hostility born of the fact that his life was seen by many to have been less than perfect and thus not worthy of emulation. This clearly still matters to Quintilian, who must at last address the issue directly: if Cicero were not a 'good man', then how could he have been a 'good' (and imitable) orator? But he *was* a good man: Quintilian

---

[36] See in general Kennedy 2002: 486–7, and Further Reading.
[37] So Dominik 1997: 51; see also Leeman 1963: vol. I, 278–82. [38] Brink 1989: 475.
[39] Connolly 2007a: 256. Connolly's is an important reconsideration of the political dimension of Quintilian and Ciceronianism.

offers as evidence the highlights of Cicero's career (including his celebrated death, *finem vitae clarum*, 12.1.15) in order to argue that in everything he acted as 'the best citizen' (*optimus civis*, 12.1.16) and a 'perfect orator' (*perfectus orator*, 12.1.19). This may not entirely convince, but he does soften it a bit by conceding that Cicero may not have been wholly 'perfect' in his oratory, and thus not wholly 'perfect' as a man. Still, he *came* closer than anyone ever *has* – the tense of his *accessit* is important – thus leaving open the possibility that Cicero may be surpassed (12.1.20).

That Quintilian should, however, hold up Cicero as the standard towards which all well-educated Romans should strive, and against which they should measure themselves, marks a significant transformation in the imperial responses to Cicero. Quintilian does have to confront the weight of prior opinion, as he does here, but if Tacitus and the Younger Pliny are any indication, Quintilian had converts to his point of view.

Something should briefly be said about these two important authors. Both the Younger Pliny, Quintilian's pupil, and Tacitus, whose debt to (and possible disagreements with) Quintilian has been noted,[40] evince renewed respect for Cicero. In Tacitus' case, this is most apparent in his *Dialogus*: in terms of style and subject matter, the text itself constitutes a nod to Cicero; Tacitus draws on some specific Ciceronian texts, in particular the *Brutus*; and a good deal of the conversation revolves around Cicero and his influence (or lack of it).[41] The *Dialogus*, then, is the affirmative answer to a broad question, 'does Cicero still have any value?' Pliny the Younger, on the other hand, offers in the *Panegyricus* the best example of imperial oratory we possess, and a speech that owes a great deal to Cicero.[42]

In short, by the time we reach this period, there emerges something of a consensus about why Cicero matters: because as an orator and authority on rhetoric he had no equal. Quintilian makes a cogent case for why oratory, and the education and training it demands, still matters; Cicero was the logical cornerstone on which to build that argument. In this context, however, Cicero's *political* relevance had no bearing (he certainly was not held up as a martyr and poster boy for the Republic), though Quintilian nonetheless believed that the facts of Cicero's life, which he felt compelled to defend, validated his views on oratory and citizenship. What Quintilian in essence achieved was to create a niche for Cicero in the *exempla* tradition that he could comfortably fulfil – and in fact a niche that in some respects he could

---

[40] See most importantly Brink 1989; cf. Austin 1965: xxvi–xxvii, Barnes 1986: 229–30, 234–6, Goldberg 2009: 76–9.

[41] See Brink 1989: 489 and passim, Gowing 2005: 109–20, Goldberg 2009: 80–1, Stroup 2010: 272–3.

[42] See now esp. Manuwald 2011.

uniquely fill. In Quintilian's moral universe, real or imagined, Cicero had a pre-eminent place.

But has Quintilian in fact stripped Cicero of all political significance? Perhaps not entirely, and this brings me to the passage to which I referred at the outset, wherein Quintilian imagines Cicero in a boat:

(2) Quare nunc quoque, licet maior quam umquam moles premat, tamen prospicienti finem mihi constitutum est uel deficere potius quam desperare. Fefellit autem quod initium a paruis ceperamus: mox uelut aura sollicitante provecti longius, dum tamen nota illa et plerisque artium scriptoribus tractata praecipimus nec adhuc a litore procul uidebamur et multos circa uelut isdem se uentis credere ausos habebamus: (3) iam cum eloquendi rationem nouissime repertam paucissimisque temptatam ingressi sumus, rarus qui tam procul a portu recessisset reperiebatur; postquam uero nobis ille quem instituebamus orator, a dicendi magistris dimissus, aut suo iam impetu fertur aut maiora sibi auxilia ex ipsis sapientiae penetralibus petit, quam in altum simus ablati sentire coepimus. (4) Nunc 'caelum undique et undique pontus'. Vnum modo in illa inmensa vastitate cernere uidemur M. Tullium, qui tamen ipse, quamuis tanta atque ita instructa naue hoc mare ingressus, contrahit uela inhibetque remos et de ipso demum genere dicendi quo sit usurus perfectus orator satis habet dicere. At nostra temeritas etiam mores ei conabitur dare et adsignabit officia. Ita nec antecedentem consequi possumus et longius eundum est ut res feret. Probabilis tamen cupiditas honestorum, et uelut tutioris audentiae est temptare quibus paratior uenia est. (Quint. *Inst.* 12. *praef.* 2–4)

(2) Therefore now, too, although a weight heavier than ever presses upon me, I have nonetheless determined, as I look toward the end, that I may simply lack the strength to finish rather than despair of finishing. Moreover, I was fooled by the fact that I started the work with smallish matters. But soon, although I had been carried rather far out by a stiff breeze, as long as I was teaching skills well known and discussed by many authorities, I did not seem to be far from shore. There were also many around me who dared to trust in the very same breezes. (3) But *now*, as I embark on an account of eloquence that has only recently been discovered and tested by very few, rare is the person found to have left port so far behind. Indeed, after that man, who has been trained by us to be an orator and has been discharged by his instructors in oratory, is either carried along on his own steam or seeks greater help for himself from the inner recesses of philosophy, we begin to understand how deep are the waters into which we have been drawn. (4) Now, 'on all sides, the sky, on all sides, the sea'. In that vast emptiness I seem to see only one man: Marcus Tullius [Cicero]. Yet he himself, although he set sail on this sea in a large and fully fitted-out boat, furls his sails and ships his oars. About that very kind of oratory through the practice of which an orator becomes perfect, he has enough to say. But I in my rashness will try to equip the orator with morals

and to counsel him as to his duties. In this case I cannot sail past someone who has gone on before me, yet I must go farther, however the subject will take me. And then, too, the desire for what is honourable warrants praise, and it is the mark of, as it were, cautious boldness to attempt those things for which pardon is readily given.

It is worth attempting an explanation for why Quintilian should choose *this* image at precisely *this* moment in his text, when he turns his attention to the training in ethics required to elevate the orator from one who is merely well trained to one who is a *vir bonus dicendi peritus*, 'the *good* man skilled at speaking' – to 'perfect' that man. The image of the orator as sailor is not unprecedented in Quintilian (e.g., 10.7.23), though this is the only occasion on which Cicero is so described. It is, moreover, a poignant image, of a man so skilled that he is virtually without equal, a navigator who has dared venture farther out to sea than anyone else. Given the plausible argument that in this book Quintilian looks directly to Plato to help him define what he means by the 'good man',[43] it is possible that in this preface, as he pictures Cicero in his boat, he similarly makes reference to Plato's famous parable of the philosopher-king as navigator (*Resp.* 6.488a–489c). I am not suggesting that Quintilian offers Cicero up as the ideal philosopher-king, but rather that he embodies some of the virtues Plato demands of a master navigator and wise ruler. Socrates' description of the training required of the ideal *navigator* who by virtue of his training also acquires the wisdom to serve as *captain* (*Resp.* 6.488d–e) looks rather like Quintilian's own approach to the training of the orator who acquires by virtue of *his* training – and the supplementary training Quintilian will sketch out in Book 12 – the wisdom to become a *vir bonus dicendi peritus*. It may be no coincidence that Pliny seems to invoke this very image, of the wise ruler and skilled navigator, in connection with the emperor Trajan (*Pan.* 81.4).

There is more at stake here in the *Institutio*, in short, than merely the ability to speak well. The *Institutio*, after all, has as its aim the production of an educated ruling class – from whose ranks the emperor will ultimately come. Indeed, Quintilian had been chosen as the tutor to potential future emperors (*Inst.4.praef.*2–3). Seen in this light, Cicero, in his capacity as a model for Quintilian and others, clearly enjoys some political relevance. Isolating and highlighting Cicero here, alone in his boat, as the one man capable of navigating this particular 'sea', sets him apart from ordinary mortals – while imagining (and this is important) that it is possible, even necessary, to sail further than Tully's boat, and thereby surpass the man himself. This is a far cry from the ambivalence and outright hostility towards Cicero apparent in

---

[43] Brinton 1983. For Quintilian's explicit admiration of Plato, see *Inst.* 10.1.81, 12.22.24.

some writers, and even well beyond the occasional admiring notices we have remarked upon in others. Quintilian rescues Cicero from the aporia evident in earlier generations, according him a status that the orator will enjoy in the Middle Ages and the Renaissance, when he becomes, as Quintilian hoped he might, the foundation of a good education.[44]

This underscores a fundamental difference between the two responses I have articulated here. Quintilian's Cicero is not one who would have been embraced, or perhaps even been recognized, by an earlier generation (cf. Aper's rejection of Cicero in Tac. *Dial.* 22). Rather, Quintilian returns to us a Cicero reconfigured for the future, and a Cicero that proved to be quite durable. Seneca's response, in hindsight, seems firmly rooted in the political and even literary culture of the early imperial period. It is doubtless of some significance that not only did Quintilian take Seneca to task for his views on Cicero, but that those views essentially died with Seneca. Not quite able to disentangle himself from the divided tradition over Cicero, and from a memory that still seemed quite fresh and serviceable, Seneca sees Cicero more as a rival, literary and otherwise, than a pedagogical paradigm. For Seneca, Cicero's questionable moral authority still matters, and thus he excludes him from the canon of acceptable *exempla*, as did Sallust, Virgil and others. This seems to me to have been a central problem for those attempting to figure out what to do with Cicero, but a problem that disappears with time. The details of his life aside, to those living under Claudius and Nero the political views of Cicero must have seemed irretrievably outdated. It is all the more remarkable, then, that Quintilian, whose career after all began under an emperor not much better than Nero, retrieves Cicero from the dustbin of irrelevance and refashions him as an imperial *exemplum* par excellence.

Still, Quintilian perhaps would not have discerned the irony of his remark in Book 1 that the name 'Cicero' denotes not so much a 'man' (*homo*) as it does 'eloquence' (*eloquentia*) (1.1.112). This sits rather awkwardly with his defence of Cicero the man in Book 12. In the end, however, Quintilian is right, as Kaster puts it, to have 'reduced [Cicero] to his *ingenium*'.[45] As early as Sallust, and then again in the Tiberian historians featured in *Suasoria* 6 of the Elder Seneca, the historical facts – or rather the 'truth' – of Cicero's life seem to matter little. Thus, as we have seen, with impunity can Lucan place Cicero, *Romani maximus auctor / Tullius eloquii*, at Pharsalus and equip him with a stirring exhortation, something that simply never happened (*Phars.* 7.62–86). Rather, as early as Velleius Cicero is seen not so much as a static

---

[44] For this see Connolly 2007a: 262–73, with references to the considerable body of work about the influence of Cicero in these periods.

[45] Kaster 1998: 262.

historical character as a symbol, the *uox publica*. (It will be up to the imperial Greek historians to rethink the historical relevance of Cicero.) Cicero rapidly became a character larger – and more important – than his life. Yet not even Velleius could have imagined just how accurate his verdict on Cicero would prove to be: *vivit vivetque per omnem saeculorum memoriam*, 'He lives and he *will* live in memory for all eternity' (2.66.5). Cicero's prodigious intellect and achievements are of course largely responsible for this, but his durability owes much to the immediate, widespread and long-lasting impact his work and his life have had on the many generations of writers, politicians and philosophers who have carried, and continue to carry, his memory forward.

Further reading

Surveys and discussions of the imperial and later afterlife of Cicero are plentiful. In English, Kennedy 2002 is the most recent, accessible and thorough (his survey ranges from antiquity through the nineteenth century). Winterbottom 1982, far more restricted in scope, is an important and thought-provoking essay on the subject that offers more by way of analysis than Kennedy; so too Richter 1968, in German. Pierini 2003 (in Italian) focuses a good deal of attention on accounts of Cicero's death, but nonetheless usefully discusses some of the less-studied references to Cicero in imperial literature. I have not seen Gambet 1963. For those who read German, however, the book-length studies of Cicero's *Nachleben* by Zieliński 1912 and Weil 1962, while dated, remain essential, especially for the post-classical reception of Cicero. The debt of specific authors to Cicero has often received special treatment, and much may be learned from these. This is especially true of Seneca, for whom see Gambet 1970, Grimal 1984, Griffin 1988 and Setaioli 2003; and of Quintilian, whose debt to Cicero is discussed by virtually every scholar who works on him but is perhaps best appreciated through Cousin's massive study in French in 1967.

15

SABINE MACCORMACK†

Cicero in late antiquity

Cicero, whose name evoked, as Quintilian had it, not just the person, but eloquence itself, was remembered, for sure, in the schools of grammarians and rhetors. Here the young studied and sought to emulate his polish and charm, his marvellous confidence as a speaker, his ability to lead his listeners to the desired result and, in a word, his 'divine eloquence'. Even beginners, Quintilian was convinced, could enjoy this 'great author'.[1] It was not merely a question of the written word, for in the city of Rome, in the mid second century, the figure of the 'head and wellspring of Roman eloquence' still seemed to hover around the rostra as an exhortation to orators of that time, even if their work was left in the shadow by the great master.[2] The very stones of Rome spoke of Cicero's linguistic finesse and his personality. An anecdote to this effect was recorded by Aulus Gellius, involving the temple of Victory at the top of the cavea of the Theatre of Pompey that had been dedicated during Pompey's third consulship. Men of learning had disagreed about the correct phrasing of the inscription to be carved on this building. Should it read that Pompey had been consul *tertio* or *tertium*? Each phrasing had its supporters, with Varro favouring the latter. When Cicero was consulted, however, he recommended that the abbreviation *tert.* be used, so as to avoid giving offence to those whose wording had been rejected.[3]

---

[1] Quint. *Inst.* 10.1.112, Cicero as eloquence personified; 10.1.113 his polish; 5.13.52 his confidence; 2.16.7 his divine eloquence; 2.5.20; 9.4.16, 'great author'. In general Zieliński 1912/1929; Plasberg 1962, with Lintott 2008. For the educational worlds where Cicero was read and studied, see Marrou 1965; Bloomer 2011; Haarhoff 1958; Riché 1962.

[2] Fronto is cited from Haines 1919 (chronological arrangement of the letters), with Naber 1867 (arrangement as in the palimpsest, for which cf. below n. 293) in brackets. Haines 1919: vol. I, 4 (Naber 1867: 63) *fons caput atque romanae facundiae*; Haines 1919: vol. II, 64 (Naber 1867: 145) the rostra; Haines 1919: vol. II, 100 (Naber 1867: 183–4) Cicero unsurpassable.

[3] Although, when, years later, the inscription was restored, another solution was found – to wit, writing the third consulship 'by three small incised lines', i.e. in Roman numerals,

But it was not merely Cicero's oratory, mastery and sophistication of language and his diction that was remembered and touched his readers.[4] The young Marcus Aurelius was 'deeply moved' by one of Cicero's letters, and quoted, by way of bantering with his teacher Fronto, who liked drawing attention to Cicero's diction, a piece of philosophical advice from the *Tusculan Disputations*.[5] Years later, during the Parthian war waged by Marcus Aurelius' adoptive brother Lucius Verus, Fronto sent to his former student a copy of the speech that Cicero addressed to the Roman people on behalf of Pompey in 66 BC. 'It seems to me', he explained, 'that no-one has ever been praised in a popular assembly more eloquently in either the Greek or the Latin language than has Pompey in this speech. I think, therefore, that Pompey was named "the Great" not so much for his own merits as for Cicero's praises.' 'You will find there', Fronto added, 'many carefully weighed chapters relevant to your present deliberations, touching the choice of generals, the interests of allies, the safeguarding of provinces, the discipline of soldiers, and the qualifications of commanders in the field and elsewhere.'[6]

Others were interested in Cicero the philosopher, among them the real or imagined scholars and men of letters whose conversations make up Aulus Gellius' *Attic Nights*. In one such conversation, Cicero's *De amicitia* was criticized by an unnamed *rhetoricus artifex*, a master of both Greek and Latin, who found fault with Cicero's manner of formulating the argument that friendship should be cherished for the sake of virtue and honour even if no practical advantage could be derived from it.[7] Cicero's argument was circular, this critic asserted, only to find his interlocutors rejoining that he had misapprehended the cultural and social environment in which the dialogue *De amicitia* unfolded. Accordingly this, like so many other criticisms of Cicero's choice of terminology and content, was disallowed in the learned circles of Rome – indeed, cultivated converse, whether spoken or written, required appreciation of his elegance, of his choice of words and figures

Gell. *NA* 10.1; cf. Richardson 1992, s.v. Theatrum Pompeii. One may also think of the Hadrianic inscription on the Pantheon, *ILS* 129, which (repeating the original inscription?) adopts Varro's solution, M. AGRIPPA L.F.COS. TERTIUM FECIT.

[4] Haines 1919: vol. I, 4; 6 (Naber 1867: 63) discussing Cicero's choice of words; Haines 1919: vol. I, 110 (Naber 1867:.25) he will himself end a speech with *aliqua... Tulliana conclusio*; Haines 1919: vol. I, 68, 70 (Naber 1867: 44) on Cicero's *modus*; Haines 1919: vol. II, 98; 100 (Naber 1867: 183–4) comparing a speech of his own to one by Cicero and acknowledging that Cicero is better.

[5] Marcus Aurelius moved by one of Cicero's letters, Haines 1919: vol. I, 100 (Naber 1867: 52); *Tusc.*, Richlin 2006, Letter 37: 129 with n. 7.

[6] Fronto to Marcus Aurelius, AD 162 (ed. and tr. Haines 1919, with some changes), vol. II, 20–30, section 10 at 30 (Naber 1867: 217–22 at 221–2).

[7] Gell. *NA* 17.5.

of speech, of the sheer accessibility and lucidity of his arguments, not to mention his wit, precisely what had also pleased Quintilian.[8]

Among historians, by contrast, Cicero found few if any friends: they judged both his personal and his political life with some severity. In particular, Dio Cassius, who was familiar with a substantial corpus of anti-Ciceronian literature of Cicero's own and later times, repeatedly described him as a traitor. Adding to this corpus, he portrayed Cicero in exile as bereft of all fortitude and a victim of despair, and attributed to Q. Fufius Calenus, a partisan of Antony, an entire speech discrediting Cicero's politics.[9] Such interest in Cicero's political and personal life, in his friendships and enmities, made sense as long as the complexity and detail of the history of the late Republic continued to appeal to readers – which was no longer the case once historical epitomes replaced more detailed narratives, especially that of Livy.[10] But Cicero the writer, as distinct from Cicero the person, was far from forgotten. Indeed, it was once Cicero's personal characteristics, his wit and gift for repartee, his passionate devotion to the *res publica*, his periodic fragilities and propensity for vain glory, whether real or amplified by critics and admirers, were beginning to fade into the past, that his intellectual presence became more distinct.[11] Perhaps this shift describes one at least of the beginnings of late antiquity.

Not that Cicero's literary and rhetorical achievement and his personal and political life were entirely forgotten. Even so, a different wind blows in the account of the development of Roman law in the *Enchiridium* by the jurist Sextus Pomponius, a late contemporary of Aulus Gellius. The *Enchiridium* contains an account of the development of Roman law and was incorporated into Justinian's *Digest*. Discussing the succession of eminent jurists of the later Republic, Pomponius mentioned Lucius Crassus, of whom 'Cicero says that he was the most eloquent of the jurisconsults.'[12] Lucius Crassus was the owner of the Tusculan villa where Cicero located his dialogue *De oratore*, with Crassus himself as the principal interlocutor. Another

---

[8] Criticism of Cicero disallowed, Gell. *NA* 17.1; Cicero's wit, 12.12. On the Ciceronian commentator Statilius Maximus, a contemporary of Gellius and Fronto, see Zetzel 1973; Martin 1984. For the period as a whole, Sallmann 1997 (257–8 on Cicero's speeches).

[9] Millar 1961: 11–22; Millar 1964: 46–55; Lintott 1997; Richter 1968. Plutarch's biography of Cicero contains much material that appears to have been collected by Cicero's critics.

[10] Steinmetz 1982: 145–6.

[11] The exception here is Macrobius, who included a long section on Cicero's jokes in his *Saturnalia*: see below, n. 195.

[12] Pomponius in *Digest* I.1.2.40, perhaps echoing Cic. *Brut.* 145. Cf. his comment in *Digest* I.2.2.40 on Coelius Antipater, perhaps linked to Cicero *Brut.* 102 and *De oratore* 2.54.

of the eminent jurists whom Pomponius listed was Servius Sulpicius who underwent something of a conversion to the civil law, since earlier in his career, according to Pomponius, he had held 'the first place in pleading cases, or to be sure the first place after Marcus Tullius', but when reprimanded for his ignorance of the law decided to devote himself to its singleminded study and wrote a number of books, some of which were still circulating in the later second century.[13] Readers of Cicero's *Pro Murena* will remember Servius Sulpicius in precisely this context, as the austere jurist who held the practices of legitimate electioneering in contempt and hence failed to be elected consul for the year 62 BC.[14] Finally, Pomponius recalled Cicero's speech, *oratio satis pulcherrima*, in defence of the Pompeian Q. Ligarius, delivered in the forum in the presence of Julius Caesar who was much moved by it despite himself. But the reason for Pomponius' recollection of this speech was that the charge against Ligarius had been brought by the jurist Q. Tubero who was 'considered most learned in public and private law and left behind several books in both fields'.[15]

Pomponius thus remembered Cicero the great advocate and orator, but, like other jurists of his own and an earlier time, he also incorporated some at least of Cicero's reflections on natural law into his own work.[16] A generation later Ulpian in his *Institutes* and elsewhere thought in some detail about Cicero's *De legibus*, the first book of which comprises an extended discussion on natural law and *ius gentium*. Indeed, this first book acquired new relevance in the late second and early third centuries, during the years preceding and following the *Constitutio Antoniana* that bestowed Roman citizenship on all freeborn residents of the empire, thereby foregrounding issues as to how Roman civil law related to the legal traditions of the Roman provinces, or – more broadly – to the *ius gentium* and natural law.[17] While Cicero was inclined to leave the interpretation of details of the civil law to jurisconsults, he had an exalted idea of the law as such because – he thought – it lay at the root of the formation of society, 'of what unites human beings and what natural fellowship exists among them'. Hence, following 'the methods of philosophers', knowledge of law was to be drawn 'not from the praetor's edict as many people now think, nor from the Twelve Tables as our ancestors thought, but from the very heart of philosophy'. This

---

[13] Pompon. *Dig.* I.1.2.42 and 43.

[14] Cf. Pompon. *Dig.* 1.2.43 on the statue erected in honour of Servius Sulpicius after his death, information that Pomponius could have drawn from Cic. *Phil.* 9.6.

[15] Walser 1959; although pardoned, Ligarius was among Caesar's assassins, which endowed Cicero's speech, for those who knew this, with additional poignancy. Pompon. *Dig.* I.2.2.46; *Dig.* I.2.2.45 also mentioned the jurist Trebatius, but without referring to Cicero's *Topica* which is addressed to Trebatius.

[16] Kaser 1993: 162–4.   [17] Ando 2008: 59–92.

conception of law as a philosophy was taken up by Ulpian when in his *Institutes* he defined law as 'the art of goodness and fairness' of which jurists were the priests, *sacerdotes*, 'professing true philosophy, not a semblance of it'.[18]

Ulpian wrote from within the Roman law tradition, as one of its upholders, and as such looked to Cicero. Possibly the statement by the jurist Gaius, that 'what natural reason has established among all human beings...is called law of nations',[19] also has a Ciceronian origin, as when Cicero wrote in *De legibus* that law is an expression of 'the highest reason', and not merely of the customs and traditions of this or that polity; similarly in *De republica*, 'true law is right reason in harmony with nature, spread through all people'; and finally in *Tusculan Disputations*, 'the unanimity of all nations should be described as the law of nature'.[20]

Whether or not the Christian apologist Tertullian is identical with the jurist of the same name, Tertullian the apologist, a man of formidable rhetorical and literary skill,[21] approached these questions in an entirely different light, as a critic, rather than an exponent of Roman legal traditions. Christians were persecuted, but why? What response could be made to statements such as, 'Gaius Seius is a good man, except that he is a Christian?'[22] Although Tertullian rarely quoted earlier authors, whether Greek or Latin, and for the most part disdained even mentioning their names, his critique of Roman law as applied to Christians evokes Cicero's contrast in *De legibus* between true law, 'reason derived from the nature of things' and 'pernicious and unjust commands' that ought to be and periodically were repealed.[23] Tertullian in his turn defined law in Ciceronian terms as existing by virtue of reason[24] and, listing bad laws that had been rescinded, asked: 'Shall we wonder that a human being can be wrong in issuing a law, or can recover

---

[18] Cic. *Leg.* 1.36 with Dyck 2004a: 164–5; Cic. *Leg.* 1.17 with *Dig.* I.1.1 from Ulpian Book 1 *Institutionum*.

[19] Gaius *Instit.* 1.1 (ed. Zulueta 1922; also in *Dig.* I.1.9). Cf. Kaser 1993: 17, 39. But see Thomas 1991: 203–4.

[20] Cic. *Rep.* 3.27; *Leg.* 1.18, 2.8; *Tusc.* 1.30.

[21] Fragments of the jurist Tertullian in Lenel 1889: vol. II: 342–3; Kunkel 1967: 236–40 thought identity of jurist and apologist to be possible but not provable. Barnes 1971: 22–9 thought it impossible and judged Tertullian's legal expertise to be minimal; Steiner 1989: 20–32 modifies this view. On Tertullian's culture, see Barnes 1971: 187–232; on Tertullian and Cicero, Steiner 1989: 50–2; 95–7; 177; 229; note especially, Fredouille 1972: 235–49; 343; 382–424 passim; Tertullian's 'rhetorical habit of thought' analysed, Sider 1971.

[22] Tert. *Apol.* 3.1; cf. 4.4 a pagan addressing a Christian: *non licet esse uos*. On the date and two distinct recensions of *Apol.*, Sordi et al. 2008: 11–20; 67–81.

[23] Cic. *Leg.* 2.10; 2.11; 2.14.

[24] Tert. *De corona* 4.5 cited by Fredouille 1972: 242 and 235–49.

his senses when repealing it?'[25] The direction of his argument, however, differed from Cicero's. For Cicero's Roman past contained examples to be followed and others to be eschewed, whereas Tertullian claimed that these same examples deserved attention because they fitted into a scheme of history that was altogether different from the Roman one because it had been prophesied in Scripture.[26] Not that Rome did not matter: but the exhortations by Cicero in *Tusculan Disputations*, and by others elsewhere, that pain and death should be patiently endured, were suspended because 'the blood of Christian martyrs is a seed'.[27]

However, not everyone was planning to build Christian community on martyrdom. For other Christians, what mattered about Cicero was not so much his thinking about law, or – as in the *Tusculan Disputations* – his thinking about pain and death, but the discontinuities and discrepancies in Roman notions of the gods that he had written about in *De natura deorum*. For generations of Christian writers, the vantage points there portrayed, that is the philosophical theodicies of two of the interlocutors, the Epicurean Velleius and the Stoic Balbus, as critiqued by the adherent of the Academy and *pontifex* Gaius Cotta, provided arguments both to attack Roman and in general pagan religion, and simultaneously to affirm the truth of Christian monotheism. In the dialogue *Octavius*, the very form of which was inspired by Cicero, Tertullian's near contemporary Minucius Felix thus adapted and incorporated statements by Cicero's Balbus about the order and harmony of the cosmos as proofs of the existence of god into his defence of Christianity, while statements by Velleius and Cotta were recycled to demonstrate that the religion of ancient Rome and pagan religion in general were erroneous.[28]

Possibly, this reuse of the argumentation of *De natura deorum* was not unique, for in the early fourth century the African apologist Arnobius told an anecdote which, even if he invented it, highlights the potential utility for Christians of Cicero's dialogue. People were saying, Arnobius claimed, that the Roman senate ought to order copies of *De natura deorum* to be destroyed, because this book by 'Tullius, the most eloquent of the Romans' who had 'so fearlessly, fittingly, steadfastly and freely' unveiled the many fictions about the gods, 'confirmed the Christian religion and crushed the

---

[25] Tert. *Apol.* 4.6 *miramini hominem aut errare potuisse in lege condenda, aut resipuisse in reprobanda?*

[26] Tert. *Apol.* 20.

[27] Tert. *Apol.* 50.15. Cf. Klein 1968: 42–5 passim: Tertullian saw the Christians as the true Romans, cf. Augustine, below n. 138.

[28] Latin text in Halm 1867; translation in Clarke 1974 with excellent detailed commentary. Clarke 1970: 503–4 considers the possibility that Minucius Felix was responding to Fronto's speech against the Christians, pointing out that what joined the two was their admiration for Cicero's style; see also Opelt 1966.

authority of the ancients'.[29] Arnobius himself, accordingly, made use of the text to highlight the contradictions of polytheism.[30] For example, having dissected the Stoic understanding of the cosmos as a whole and of the different celestial bodies as animate beings – for if the whole cosmos had an animate physical identity, how could its parts have such an identity too?[31] – Arnobius took from Cotta's critique of Stoic theodicy the query about multiple gods bearing the same names, among them Jupiter, Sol, Mercury and Minerva.[32] But where Cicero's Cotta raised the query by way of seeking clarification of Stoic teaching, Arnobius addressing his pagan contemporaries raised it to prove that the entire fabric of ancient religion and philosophy lacked cogency. In short, he turned Cicero's dialogue into an armoury of arguments against the religious system within which Cicero, for all his scepticism, lived. In the process, a new Cicero came into existence. No Roman Christian then or subsequently neglected complimenting Cicero on his eloquence, but not infrequently the compliment turned into a tool to attack Roman errors. As Arnobius' student Lactantius had it: 'I would like Cicero to rise for a while from the nether world, so that this most eloquent man might be taught by a lesser and far from eloquent man . . . where the discipline of virtue, since it does exist, is to be sought.'[33] Simultaneously, the range of discussion broadened, for Lactantius' engagement with Cicero reached far beyond *De natura deorum* into his other philosophical and his political writings, in particular *De republica*.[34] According to Jerome, the eloquence of Lactantius matched that of Cicero. And indeed, the connection between the two was a matter not just of style but of

---

[29] Arn. *Adv. nat.* 3.6–7. For the date of *Adv. nat.*, written between AD 302 and 305, Simmons 1995: 47–93; in general, Herzog 1993.

[30] Le Bonniec 1984: 89–101.

[31] Arn. *Adv. nat.* 3.35; cf. Cic. *Nat. D.* 2.21–43; 66–71. But here, Arnobius' description of the cosmos differs from Cicero's and he may have had in mind another source: e.g. Arn. 3.35 *uniuersam istam molem mundi, cuius omnes amplexibus ambimur, tegimur ac sustinemur, animans esse unum sapiens rationale consultum probabili adseueratione definiunt* ('they declare, with convincing argument, that the whole mass of the world, in whose folds we are encompassed, covered and supported, is a single living, wise, rational and planned entity', with Cic. *Nat. D.* 2.21 (Balbus speaking): *ratione igitur mundus utitur. similiter effici potest sapientem mundum, similiter beatum, similiter aeternum* ('The world therefore employs reason. In a similar way it can be shown that the world is wise, good and everlasting'); 2.36 *necesse est intellegentem esse mundum et quidem etiam sapientem* ('The world must possess understanding and indeed even wisdom'). Regarding the parts of the universe, Cic. *Nat. D.* 2.30; 39 (divinity of the stars); 49–55 (sun, moon, planets, fixed stars); 66–71 (personified elements).

[32] Arn. *Adv. nat.* 4.14–16 with Cic. *Nat. D.* 3.53–60: Le Bonniec 1984: 89–101.

[33] Lactant. *Div. inst.* 3.13.13; similarly *Div. inst.* 1.15.16; 3.13.10.

[34] Cicero was the classical author whom Lactantius cited most frequently, see the index of citations in the edition by Brandt and Laubmann 1890–7: vol. II, 245–51; Ogilvie 1978: 58–72.

content, for Ciceronian allusions, quotations and ideas pervade most of what he wrote.[35]

The text of *De republica* had also figured in the learned conversations of Aulus Gellius whose *Attic Nights* Lactantius knew, but none of the interlocutors took an interest in the dialogue's arguments; Minucius Felix and Tertullian may also have read it, but again without pausing to consider its arguments.[36] For Lactantius, however, *De republica* provided the infrastructure for a far-ranging critique of Roman governance, and he quoted it often. Embedded in the dialogue's principal theme, the chronological development of the Roman constitution, is a pair of speeches in which Cicero replicated the arguments for and against justice as the necessary guideline in individual and collective action that had been presented before the Roman senate by the philosopher Carneades in 156 BC. Defending justice in the first speech, Carneades in the second described justice as 'the height of foolishness', because, so he claimed, to act justly contravenes individual and collective self-interest.[37] But in *De republica*, Cicero reversed the order of the two speeches, thereby giving greater weight to the second one which he placed in the mouth of Laelius: 'True law is right reason in harmony with nature, spread through all people, steadfast and everlasting. It summons to duty by its orders and deters from crime by its prohibitions... All nations will be bound by this one eternal and unchangeable law.'[38] The thought was echoed by the jurists.[39] Lactantius in turn used the first speech which Cicero had attributed to L. Furius Philus, in order to formulate his attack on pagan Rome and the Tetrarchic empire. The second speech by contrast yielded material for his exegesis of a just and as he envisioned it Christian empire.

---

[35] Jer. *Ep.* 58.10 (addressed to Paulinus of Nola), evaluating Christian writers: *Lactantius, quasi quidam fluvius eloquentiae Tullianae, utinam tam nostra adfirmare potuisset, quam facile aliena destruxit* ('if only Lactantius – a river of Tullian eloquence – had been able to support our position as easily as he destroyed others'). Possibly Jerome's hesitancy was occasioned by Lactantius' theology, cf. *Div. inst.* 2.8.3–4, about the creation: God *produxit similem sui spiritum, qui esset virtutibus patris dei praeditus... deinde fecit alterum, in quo indoles divinae stirpis non permansit* ('brought forth a spirit resembling Himself, because it was endowed with the virtues of God the Father... then he made a second, in which the stamp of its divine origin did not remain'. Or possibly given Lactantius' Ciceronianism, this was what led Jerome to consider him as lacking in originality: see Perrin 1988: 108–14.

[36] Gell. *NA* 1.22.8; 7.16.11; 12.2.6–7; 16.10.10; Min. Fel. *Oct.* 12.7 with Cic. *Rep.* 1.30; Tert. *Apol.* 25.14–15 with Cic. *Rep.* 3.20.

[37] Fuchs 1964: 3–5; Cic. *Rep.* 3.21 (Ziegler 1958; Powell does not include the passage in his text but cites it in the apparatus (Powell 2006: 96)) *aut nullam esse iustitiam, aut si sit aliqua, summam esse stultitiam.*

[38] Cic. *Rep.* 3.33 (Ziegler 1958 = Powell 2006: 3.27 p.107 f.), tr. Zetzel 1999 with adjustments.

[39] See above, notes 19–20; Ulpian in *Dig.* I.1.1.1.

Circumstances had changed since a generation earlier Arnobius had written his *Contra gentes*, for by the time Lactantius completed the *Divinae institutiones*, persecution of Christians was a thing of the past, which helped to inspire his confident tone in the concluding book and lent momentum to his argument that prophets, poets and philosophers – Cicero among them – were in some agreement about the one God.[40] Even before the edict of toleration, it was possible for Lactantius to point to the ever-growing number of Christians, and to query the legitimacy of persecution.[41] Indeed, it was persecution that led Lactantius to transform Furius' speech against the feasibility of justice as a guide for policy into a programmatic statement of the pagan Roman empire, where, quoting Cicero's L. Furius Philus, a 'good man is harassed, dragged away, his hands are cut off and his eyes gouged out'. The wicked man by contrast is 'praised, cultivated and cherished by all'.[42] In *De republica* these views were advanced in order to be refuted in the second speech, but Lactantius reproduced them by way of describing what he saw as the concrete reality of his time,[43] simultaneously accepting the charge that justice was 'the height of foolishness'. For, as Paul had said, 'just as the wisdom of men is the height of foolishness before God, and foolishness the height of wisdom, so whoever will have been notable and exalted on earth is small and abject before God'.[44] And why were the Christians hated? Because, as Cicero had said long ago, quoting Terence: 'Truth begets hatred.'[45]

Having thus shown 'from their own authors' that no-one could be just 'unless he appeared to be foolish', Lactantius relocated Cicero's political ideals for Rome into the Christian Rome that he anticipated would emerge under Constantine. In *De natura deorum* and elsewhere, Lactantius thought, Cicero had conceded the inadequacies not merely of Roman religious observance but also of philosophical theology and philosophical concepts of happiness, that it was easier, in his words, 'to say what is not, than what is'.[46]

---

[40] Lactant. *Div. inst.* 1.3–5; on its dating Digeser 1994; Digeser 2000 on the implications of dating of both versions before and in the year 313. For the presence of Cicero in Lactantius, *De opificio dei*, see Perrin 1974: 40–2.

[41] Lactant. *Div. inst.* 5.13.1–2.

[42] Lactant. *Div. inst.* 5.12 = Cic. *Rep.* 3.27 (Ziegler 1958 = 3.13 Powell 2006).

[43] A vantage point he pursued at length in *De mortibus persecutorum*, cf. Digeser 2000: 54–6.

[44] Lactant. *Div. inst.* 5.15.8 with *I Cor.* 3.19: *sicut enim sapientia hominum summa stultitia est aput deum, stultitia, ut docui, summa sapientia est, sic deo humilis et abiectus est qui fuerit conspicuus et sublimis in terra.*

[45] Ter. *An.* 1.1.41 quoted in Cic. *Amic.* 89. Lactantius repeats the same line of Terence in *Div. inst.* 5.9.6 and 5.21.1. It was a famous line in its own right, quoted also by Jerome *Comment. in Epist. ad Gal.* ch. 4, 15–16 (*Patrologia Latina* 26, col. 409).

[46] Lactant. *Div. inst.* 1.17.4, cf. Cic. *Nat. D.* 1.60 (Cotta speaking).

Lactantius in turn, while frequently referencing Cicero for errors and negativities, drew on him equally for his positive content by way of supplying revisions and improvements. The extent of Cicero's presence in Lactantius' mind emerges all the more clearly in tacit, indirect allusions. For example, when launching on his discourse about natural law and law as 'right reason' in *De legibus*, Cicero with a touch of humour had questioned his interlocutors whether they wanted him 'to write pamphlets on the law about rain water running off roof tops and shared walls', or 'formulas for contracts or civil judgements', phrases that Lactantius echoed at the beginning of the *Divine Institutes*. His programme, he declared, had nothing to do with the civil law or with 'rain water running off roof tops and keeping it away'; rather, it was 'about hope, life, salvation, immortality and God'.[47] Later on, now citing Cicero explicitly, Lactantius converted Laelius' refutation of L. Furius Philus into an incipiently Christian statement. 'True law is right reason', Laelius had said, explaining that God 'is the author, expounder and mover of this law', which led Lactantius to ask: 'who is there who, knowing the mysteries of God, is able to declare the law of God as powerfully as did a man far removed from the knowledge of truth?'. Had Cicero also expounded the content of this law, Lactantius concluded, he would have performed the task not of a philosopher, but of a prophet.[48] The task of the *Divine Institutes* therefore was to provide this as yet missing information, where Cicero emerged as an authority not only on justice and law, but also on ethics, ethical conduct – or virtue – being the precondition to true worship.

Here, Lactantius foregrounded *De officiis* and *Tusculan Disputations*, and once more Cicero emerged as something of a forerunner to Christianity whose errors and omissions Lactantius undertook to rectify. According to Lactantius' streamlined version of Cicero's ideas about virtue in *De officiis* and elsewhere, Cicero said that virtue is 'to know what is good and evil, what is morally wrong and right, what is useful and what is less so'.[49] Lactantius first corrected the statement: 'knowledge cannot be virtue because it does not reside within us but comes to us from without', whereas 'virtue belongs to each one individually'; and next he completed it: 'knowledge is to know God and virtue is to worship him: wisdom resides in the first, justice in the second'.[50] On this basis, Lactantius adduced Cicero's statement about virtue as expressed for example in service to one's country, 'what we

---

[47] Cic. *Leg.* 1.14 with Lactant. *Div. inst.* 1.1.12.
[48] Lactant. *Div. inst.* 6.8.7–9; Cicero as potential prophet, *Div. inst.* 6.8.10–12; Heck 1978.
[49] Lactant. *Div. inst.* 6.5.5 with reminiscence (perhaps) of Cic. *Off.* 3.7; 3.81.
[50] Lactant. *Div. inst.* 6.5.6 (with 6.6.1): cf. Cic. *Nat. D.* 3.86; *Div. inst.* 6.5.19.

normally call upright', only to point out that, even according to Cicero, the performance of this obligation conflicted with the higher one obtaining 'within the common fellowship of humankind, and when this is removed, kindness, generosity, goodness and justice perish utterly'.[51] Confronting Cicero's evaluation of obligations to smaller, defined communities in relation to obligations owed to all humanity, even to those who have harmed us, Lactantius quoted Cicero's own words to Caesar in *Pro Ligario*: 'you who are accustomed to forget nothing except your wrongs'.[52] That Ligarius, whom Caesar pardoned, was later among Caesar's assassins could only confirm Lactantius' point that – despite the emerging Christian empire that he welcomed – mankind's ultimate goal is attained in the resurrection of the dead.[53]

Christian apologists found in Cicero's dialogues a voice that they used so as to explain their religion while at the same time claiming to support the established order of things by way of offering a better way of maintaining it. In their different ways, Tertullian, Minucius Felix, Arnobius and Lactantius all interpreted Ciceronian ideas in ways that were not entirely incompatible with what Cicero had written. Even so, the theological framework by means of which they incorporated Cicero's writing into their own did clash with what the 'excellent orator and philosopher'[54] had written about Rome and with his love for Rome. Although Christian children and young people, notwithstanding periodic misgivings, attended the same Roman schools as everyone else,[55] Christian writers responded to Cicero in their own way with intense interest in his dialogues, especially *De republica*, *De natura deorum*, the *Tusculan Disputations* and his rhetorical works. Their pagan contemporaries by contrast were more interested in Cicero's diction, and this not so much in the dialogues but in the speeches, given that the primary purpose of education was to prepare the young for public service and for public speaking in the law courts and

---

[51] Lactant. *Div. inst.* 6.6.21–7, citing Cic. *Off.* 3.28; 3.69; 3.16. That the *officium* owed to one's *patria* conflicts with one's officium to humanity at large does not harmonize well with Cicero's statement in *Rep.* 1.12 with 6.13 describing service to one's country as the highest achievement. The point was taken up by Macrobius, see below, notes 178–82.

[52] Lactantius discusses passages from Cicero's *De officiis* in *Div. inst.* 6.11 on defined communities as objects of beneficence, but beneficence should be extended to all, even the poor; similarly, *Div. inst.* 6.12; 6.17; 6.18.35 quoting Cic. *Lig.* 35.

[53] But Lactantius may not have known that Ligarius was among the conspirators against Caesar, given increasing ignorance of the historical circumstances of Cicero's life and career (see above, n. 15); Hildebrandt 1894: 43–63. On the resurrection, Lactant. *Div. inst.* 7.23, adducing Cicero.

[54] Lactant. *Div. inst.* 1.15.16 *Cicero qui non tantum perfectus orator sed etiam philosophus fuit.*

[55] Marrou 1965: chapters 7–9.

elsewhere.[56] How Cicero's speeches were studied can be learned not only from the early imperial commentaries by Asconius that were still circulating,[57] but also from several late Roman ones containing summaries of the speeches along with notes on historical context and on Cicero's rhetorical method and legal arguments and their desired effects.[58] Another approach to Cicero's speeches was taken by – among others – the rhetor Romanus Aquila who in response to a request by one of his students wrote the treatise *De figuris* about figures of thought and speech.[59] 'By this means, the orator exalts small and expands on narrow topics, adding vivacity and brilliance along with energy and weight to his words and thoughts: for moving the soul of the listener or judge there is no better tool.'[60] In order to demonstrate this fact, Romanus Aquila enumerated the names of the different figures in Greek and Latin and, drawing on a Ciceronian repertoire more ample than the one that survived the post-Roman destruction and disappearance of classical manuscripts, illustrated each of them with a phrase or sentence from Cicero's speeches. Cicero's prominence among the authors studied in Roman schools is brought home by a fourth-century bronze statuette from a Roman villa in the province of Gallia Narbonensis. It is of a teacher dressed in a pallium and holding an open book. The inscription on the pedestal of the statuette carries the opening words of Cicero's *First Catilinarian Oration*.[61] The speech appears also to have been known to the historical epitomator Eutropius, who included Cicero's defeat of the Catilinarian conspiracy and his death in the proscription of 43 BC in his summary of Roman history.[62] A somewhat more detailed account of Cicero's life appears in the anonymous *Liber de uiris illustribus*.[63]

Among Cicero's rhetorical writings, as distinct from his speeches, it was not so much the dialogues of his maturity and later years that he valued himself, namely *Orator, De oratore* and the history of Roman rhetoric entitled *Brutus* after its dedicatee, that attracted the attention of the late Roman rhetors who were teaching the young, but *De inventione*, his very first book, with which later in life he was not entirely satisfied. Remembering

---

[56] Millar 1977: 98–9.   [57] Clark 1907.
[58] Hildebrandt 1894 discusses the different strands of commentary that were combined in the *Scholia Bobiensia*; Stangl 1912; Herzog 1993: 159–62 suggests that the *Scholia Bobiensia* are the Cicero commentary by Volcacius mentioned by Jerome, *Contra Rufinum* 1.16 (*Patrologia Latina* 23, col. 428C).
[59] Elice 2007; Halm 1863: 22–37; Elice 2007: xl–lii discusses date. Rutilius Rufus, *Schemata lexeos*, Iulius Rufinianus, *De figuris sententiarum et elocutionis*, the anonymous *Carmen de figuris* and the anonymous *Schemata dianoeas quae at rhetores pertinent* (all in Halm 1863) all use examples from Cicero.
[60] Elice 2007: 7 (Halm 1863: 22–3).   [61] Passelac 1972.
[62] Eutropius 6.15; 7.2.   [63] *Vir. ill.* 81.

the two books of *De inventione* in the dedication of *De oratore* to his brother Quintus, Cicero wrote: 'as you have often said to me, because those preliminary and unpolished essays that slipped out of my notebooks when I was still a boy or rather a young man are hardly worthy of my present time of life and the experience I gained in the many important cases I have argued, you now wish me to publish something more polished and complete on these same topics'.[64] What made *De inventione* attractive to readers, however, was precisely its relatively straightforward, didactic content that Cicero had assembled from earlier philosophical and rhetorical authorities after these had been coordinated into compendia for teaching the art of speaking. 'All these,' Cicero wrote, 'and those earlier works I have myself consulted as best I was able, and have added some material from my own knowledge.'[65] This process of collecting and selecting, summarizing and amplifying in light of the diverse interests and priorities of teachers in Roman schools continued over the generations and made of Cicero's text just one component within an ever-growing number of instructional treatises and commentaries of varying length and complexity. In the mid fourth century, the African rhetor Marius Victorinus, who was teaching in Rome, wrote an extended rhetorical and philosophical commentary on *De inventione*,[66] and this was later followed by another more concise commentary by Grillius, who also wrote for students of rhetoric.[67]

In short, familiarity with some at least of Cicero's life and writings was part and parcel of the late antique literary and cultural literacy that was taught in Roman schools. The orations brought together in late antiquity in the collection of *XII Panegyrici Latini,* which – other than the first one, by the younger Pliny – were composed by rhetors from Gaul, reveal what this could mean in practice. An orator's awe in the imperial presence and his sense of inadequacy at having to describe the imperial *res gestae* are regularly voiced in Ciceronian terms,[68] and further reminiscences and allusions to and quotations from Cicero adorn most of these speeches. One of the panegyrists, the rhetor Eumenius, an early contemporary of Lactantius, addressed an oration to an imperial official in the late third century requesting support for rebuilding the schools of Autun. Like other panegyrists, he used the opportunity to recommend his students to the attention

---

[64] Cic. *De or.* 1.5.   [65] Cic. *Inv. rhet.* 2.8.

[66] Marius Victorinus, *Explanationum in Rhetoricam M. Tullii Ciceronis* (Halm 1863: 153–304). Hadot 1971: 73–101.

[67] Jakobi 2002 (partial earlier edition in Halm 1863: 596–606); Jakobi 2005.

[68] Galletier 1949–55 and Nixon and Rodgers 1994 present the *Panegyrici Latini* (excluding that by Pliny) in chronological order; Mynors 1964 in the same order as the MSS, which is used here. Klotz 1911 collects Ciceronian and other literary allusions and quotations in the *Panegyrici*; Herzog 1993: 185–98.

of his distinguished listener and adorned his speech with numerous Ciceronian allusions and quotations. Particularly fitting in this context were the
rhetorical and argumentative precedents that could be derived from Cicero's
encomium of literature in the speech for the poet Archias.[69] A speech more
generally germane to the purposes of the panegyrists, which they cited with
some regularity, was *Pro Marcello*, which could be deployed in the praises
of emperors once the political ambiguities amidst which Cicero was constrained to formulate his complex message had been forgotten.[70] Other
speeches the panegyrists alluded to – but more for their diction than any
specific parts of their content – were *Pro Ligario*, *Pro Sestio*, *Pro Roscio
Amerino* and the *Catilinarians*.

Among all these orations the one that Cicero addressed to the Roman
people on behalf of Pompey, already earmarked by Fronto for the attention
of Marcus Aurelius, occupied a special place: the panegyrists cited it more
than any other, and not only for its diction.[71] The qualities of Pompey that
Cicero highlighted were Knowledge of military affairs, Virtue, Authority and
Felicity.[72] In late antiquity, *felicitas* was an imperial quality frequently adver-
tised on the coinage; the theme was taken up by the panegyrist of AD 291
who praised the *felicitas* of the Emperor Maximian and demonstrated familiarity with the oration for Pompey and several more from among Cicero's
speeches.[73] In 389, the panegyrist Pacatus ascribed *felicitas* along with *virtus*
to the Emperor Theodosius.[74] That *felicitas* was not simply a slogan, or a
synonym for *fortuna* or luck, and that its Ciceronian contours were recognizable at the time is made clear by the historian Ammianus Marcellinus in his
character portrayal of the Emperor Constantius II. Ammianus appreciated
Constantius' dignity and imperial poise, but found fault with his relentless
prosecution of civil war. As Cicero had said in a letter censuring Julius
Caesar which Ammianus quoted: 'Felicity is, quite simply, success in noble
actions. Or to define it differently: felicity is fortune when it furthers worthy designs, without which a person cannot be happy. Lawless and impious
plans such as those of Caesar therefore allowed no scope for felicity.'[75] The
felicity that Cicero denied to Caesar but ascribed to Pompey also caught
the attention of the illustrator of the *Notitia dignitatum*. The *Notitia* of

---

[69] *Pan. Lat.* 9.5.3–4; on references to Cic. *Arch.* in this speech see Nixon and Rodgers
1994: 149–50, correcting Klotz 1911: 540–2. On Eumenius, Nellen 1981: 19–20,
148–50, who sees the successful careers of 'gebildete Aufsteiger' like Eumenius and his
students, unqualified as he considers them to have been for effective administrative
work, as one of the causes of imperial decline in the West. Note the prosopography of
the 'Aufsteiger', 19–97. See also Pichon 1906: 36–150, cited by Rees 2002: 196.

[70] Dyer 1990.   [71] On Fronto, above n. 6.   [72] Cic. *De imp. Cn. Pomp.* 28.

[73] On *felicitas*, see *Pan.Lat.* 9.19.2 with Klotz 1911: 532–4.   [74] *Pan. Lat.* 2.6.1.

[75] Amm. Marc. 21.16.13 (the letter to Nepos here mentioned is not found elsewhere).

the Eastern empire concludes with a pair of full-page images without any accompanying text. The first image of the pair shows a set of *codicilli*, diplomas to be bestowed on imperial officials, in a rectangular frame surmounted by a shallow triangle with the bust of a personified *Divina Providentia*, an imperial quality,[76] at its apex. At the four corners of the frame, in clear juxtaposition with Cicero's speech for Pompey, appear the personifications of *Virtus, Scientia Rei Militaris, Auctoritas* and *Felicitas*. The second image, with the same overall design, shows at the apex the bust of *Divina Electio*, that is, the divine election of the emperor,[77] or, perhaps, the emperor's divinely guided choice of governmental officials. In the four corners of the rectangular frame enclosing an identical set of *codicilli* appear busts of the four seasons, representing the order of nature within which imperial administration unfolds. In short, imperial administration is depicted as enduring throughout the ever-recurring cycle of the seasons under the guidance of divine election and thanks to the military virtues as defined by Cicero, under the guidance of divine providence.[78]

Ammianus, although fond of citing Cicero for purposes of adornment,[79] did so primarily in order to add authority to his statements. Quoting Cicero amounted to tacit juxtaposition of a better Roman past with the failings of his own time, especially when it came to the judicial abuses that make so dark a thread in his narrative.[80] The message is especially clear where Ammianus commented on the careers and doings of powerful residents of the city of Rome. The wealthy and supremely well-connected C. Anicius Petronius Probus, for example, would have done well to take to heart the questions Cicero addressed to Antony in the *Second Philippic*: 'What is the difference between someone who encourages an action and one who approves it? Or between one who wishes that something were done and one who rejoices that it has been done?'[81]

---

[76] Ando 2000: 34.   [77] MacCormack 1981: 247–56.

[78] Burger 1981: 134–41 with figures 44–5, who thinks that the busts in the apex of the two images are of the emperor. The MS she discusses is Munich, Staatsbibliothek Clm. 10291, fols. 178r–222r. Cf. Neira Faleiro 2005: 307, where the bust under Divina Electio is clearly female, and 309, that under Divina Providentia is male. Both are with halo, whereas in the Munich codex Divina Electio (who also appears to be female) is not. Similarly, the line drawings in Seeck 1962: 101–2. If the personages depicted in these busts were indeed emperors (and imperial consorts?), one would expect them to wear diadems, but they do not. The issue merits further attention.

[79] Amm. Marc. 14.2.2; 15.12.4; 16.1.5; 22.15.24; 26.9.11; 27.4.8; 31.14.8.

[80] Amm. Marc. 15.3.3; 19.12.18; 26.10.12–13; 28.1.40; 30.4.7–10. On Ammianus' understanding of Cicero and the late Republic, in particular Cicero's view of divination, see Matthews 1989: 128–9; 428–31.

[81] Amm. Marc. 27.11.4 quoting Cic. *Phil.* 2.29; see also Amm. Marc. 28.4.26 quoting Cic. *Amic.* 79.

Ammianus took Cicero seriously – the attitude, perhaps, of a man who learned Latin as a second language. At any rate, others who were also familiar with Cicero took a less carefully deliberated approach.[82] Ammianus' contemporary Symmachus alluded to or echoed Cicero periodically, and he is also mentioned in the imperial biographies of the *Historia Augusta*. *Inter alia* we learn there that Severus Alexander kept a portrait of Cicero in his *lararium*, read his *De officiis* and *De republica* and accepted his life and career as something of an example for himself.[83] Cicero also supplied material for some invented personages in the *Historia Augusta*, and altogether helped to endow the compilation with an air of authenticity that is not warranted by its overall content.[84]

The *Historia Augusta* was known to Jerome who, in the life of the desert father Hilarion, adapted a phrase from the speech *Pro Archia* that he found in the biography of the emperor Probus.[85] Not that Jerome did not produce a very large number of Ciceronian quotations, allusions and reminiscences of his own. As the student in Rome of the grammarian Aelius Donatus whom he remembered with admiration as *praeceptor meus*, Jerome had received the best of schoolings, and throughout his life quoted, along with Cicero, all the other Latin authors of the curriculum in almost everything he wrote.[86] But Cicero occupied a very special place in his mind. Having renounced family and kin and adopted an ascetic lifestyle, he found that he could not give up his library 'which I had assembled in Rome with the utmost care and labour'. So it was that while he was on his way to Jerusalem in 374, 'fasting in order then to read Cicero', he fell ill and suddenly found himself in a blaze of terrifying light before the tribunal of the heavenly judge, where he identified himself as a Christian. But the judge rejected this self-description: 'you are a Ciceronian, not a Christian. Where your treasure

---

[82] Cameron 2011: 384, 'I myself would turn the traditional hypothesis (sc. that pagans were especially devoted to the authors of classical antiquity) on its head and argue that knowledge of the classics was taken far more seriously by people of modest origins, well aware that literary culture was their avenue to positions of profit and power. Two examples we can document are Augustine and Aurelius Victor, both Africans.' Cf. above n. 69.

[83] SHA *Alex. Sev.* 8.5 f.; 30.1 (see SHA *Clod.* 2.5 for an indirect mention of *De republica*); SHA *Alex. Sev.* 30.2; 42.4; 62.3. SHA *Hadr.* 25.6–7 asserts: *apud ipsas Baias periit die VI iduum Iuliarum. inuisusque omnibus sepultus est in uilla Ciceroniana Puteolis* ('he died at Baiae itself on July 10th, and, hated by all, he was buried at Cicero's villa at Puteoli') – a remarkable statement, since Hadrian had been buried very visibly in his own Mausoleum. But we may perhaps take it that the villa was still known as formerly Cicero's property at the time of writing (i.e. in the later fourth century).

[84] For the Ciceronian personages, see Syme 1968: 168–9. Cameron 2011: 743–82 dates the *Historia Augusta* to the years 375/380, i.e. written before Ammianus, and describes it as not a work of pagan propaganda (on Cicero, note 761–70).

[85] Cameron 2011: 764–70.   [86] Pease 1919; Hagendahl 1958: 91–328; 331–46.

is there your heart is also.'[87] Endeavouring, at least for some years, to avoid reading the Latin classics, Jerome learnt Hebrew but felt profoundly deprived: 'what I accomplished from my tireless study of that language I leave to the judgement of others. What I lost in my own language, I do know.'[88] That said, Jerome did not relate to Cicero in the same way as had Arnobius, Minucius Felix and Lactantius, who engaged with Cicero's arguments with some passion, whether in agreement, or, more usually, in disagreement. Jerome, by contrast, quoted Cicero's words in pursuit of his own topics and generally independently of the original larger contexts in which those words were to be found.[89]

What mattered to Jerome was the beauty of classical Latin, *Latini eloquii uenustas*, this being one reason why he introduced so many samples of it into his own writing, while simultaneously pillorying the stylistic failings of his opponents. But this was not the whole story, for, as he wrote to Magnus, orator of the city of Rome, Christianity was not a self-contained system. Not only had earlier Christian writers quoted 'secular letters', *saeculares litterae*, but the author of the Acts of the Apostles and Paul did too. As for the Old Testament, 'Hosea took as wife the daughter of Debelaim, that is "of delights", and from the prostitute was born his son Iezrahel, who is called "seed of God"' – which Jerome interpreted as additional authority for resorting to both the content and the formal beauty of 'secular letters' by way of explaining and adorning Christian teaching.[90]

However, regarding Cicero, more than this general principle was at issue because Jerome regarded him as something of a model in his own work as a translator. Jerome's first translation was the *Chronicle* of Eusebius, which he modified and continued to the year AD 378, adding much new information, not all of it correct, concerning Roman history and his own

---

[87] Jer. *Ep.* 22.30 to Eustochium, with Matthew 6.21. This 'dream' has generated much interest. Kelly 1975: 41–4; Feichtinger 1991: 54–77; Feichtinger 1997: 41–61; Rebenich 2002: 7–10 and literature there cited.

[88] Jer. *Comment. in Epist. ad Galatas* III, preface. Kamesar 1993: 48–9 on Jerome's Hebrew studies as compensation for giving up enjoyment of the literary beauty of the Latin classics: 'Having been schooled in the great Latin tradition, he was capable of appreciating the aesthetic merits of works in a language not his own.'

[89] Hagendahl 1958: 337: 'Apart from his sincere admiration for their literary qualities and his ambition to enrich his own works in matter and form by all kinds of imitations and borrowings, he shows a remarkable lack of interest in or esteem for pagan philosophers and their ideas. Jerome was a Christian from the very beginning, he never had to fight his way, like Augustine, through philosophy to Christian faith.' But this assessment requires some modification: Adkin 1997.

[90] Jer. *Ep.* 70.1–2; he continues with a commentary on Christian writers and their engagement with secular letters. The date of the letter, AD 397, corresponds to Jerome's renewed engagement with secular letters after his 'dream', see Hagendahl 1958: 325–6; Kelly 1975: 213.

times. This information included the dates of Cicero's birth and death, of his consulship and the Catilinarian conspiracy, with a wrong date for his exile – and, not to forget, the dedication of a statue to Marius Victorinus, the commentator on Cicero's *De inventione*, in the Forum of Trajan.[91] At a time when Christian writers were already accustomed to differentiate their own, i.e. 'our', authors from those who were not Christians, Jerome in the preface to the *Chronicle* referred to Cicero as 'noster Tullius', designating him, no doubt, as a Latin rather than a Greek author, but also making room for a broader identification between Cicero and himself. Cicero's translations highlighted the difficulty of translating, for in them the 'golden flow of his eloquence is so often arrested by those obscure, confusing impediments which lead readers unaware that the words are translations to disbelieve they are by Cicero'. And thus, Jerome added, 'If I translate literally, it sounds incongruous; if out of necessity I change something in the word order or the discourse, I will appear to have wandered from the duty of translator.'[92]

Even while working on the *Chronicle*, Jerome was thinking ahead about translating Scripture, and before long embarked on this *pius labor sed periculosa praesumptio*.[93] Here also, Cicero accompanied him. Defending his translation from Hebrew of the Pentateuch against critics who claimed that the Septuagint had been inspired by the Holy Spirit and left no room for a new translation from Hebrew, he once more adduced Cicero the translator. The Septuagint was a translation pure and simple, not a prophetically inspired text. 'It is one thing to be a prophet, another to be a translator. In the former, the Spirit foretells the future; in the latter learning and fulness of expression translate what is understood – unless we believe that Tullius translated the *Oeconomicus* of Xenophon, the *Protagoras* of Plato and *De Corona* of Demosthenes under the inspiration of the spirit of rhetoric.'[94]

---

[91] Most of these data were incorporated into the chronicle of Prosper Tiro. Generations later, the Venerable Bede entered Jerome's words about Cicero's birth into his own chronicle – and thus, Jerome's much-consulted *Chronicle* helped to pass Cicero's name to post-Roman Europe. *Hieronymi Chronicon* (Helm 1956) ad ann. 106 BC, *Cicero Arpini nascitur matre Helvia, patre equestris ordinis ex regio Vulscorum genere*; *Prosperi Tironis Epitoma Chronicon* (Mommsen 1892), *Huius regni anno VIII Cicero oritur matre Hevia patre equestris ordinis ex regio Vulscorum genere*; *Bedae Chronica* (Mommsen 1898), *Cicero Arpini nascitur matre Helvia, patre equestris ordinis ex regio Vulscorum genere*; the use of the verb 'nascitur' rather than Prosper's 'oritur' suggests Bede was here reading Jerome. Marius Victorinus' statue, Jerome, *ad ann.* AD 354.

[92] *Chronik des Hieronymus* (Helm 1956: 1–2).

[93] 'A pious task, yet perilous presumption': Jer. *Biblia sacra iuxta vulgatam versionem* (Gryson et al. 1994), preface to the Gospels, addressed to Pope Damasus.

[94] Jer. *Vulgata*, preface to the Pentateuch pp. 3–4. Cf. Jerome's comments on Cicero's translations in the Preface to the *Chronicle* of Eusebius (Helm 1956: 1–2). Cic. *Opt. Gen.* was designed as the preface to his projected translation of Aeschines and Demosthenes, see Giomini 1995.

Translation thus had nothing to do with inspiration or prophecy, because to translate, one had to understand what had been said by someone else.[95] Next came the difficulties of an author's diction. The elegant, urbane diction of the prophet Isaiah presented problems all of its own, and once more, Cicero came to Jerome's mind. In the preface to his translation of Isaiah he explained the distinct layout of the text on the page that he wished to be followed here. Isaiah's phrases and clauses, *cola et commata*, were to be separated by line breaks to convey his meaning more adequately, but this did not mean that Isaiah had written in verse. Rather, 'as happens in Demosthenes and Cicero, who write in phrases and clauses, that is in prose not in verse', so did the prophets. And hence 'we, considering the interest of readers, distinguish this new translation with a new method of presenting the text'.[96]

This comparison between Isaiah on the one hand and Demosthenes and Cicero on the other implies a larger issue that Jerome also addressed in a letter to his friend Pammachius about translating Scripture and other texts. Scripture, 'where even the order of the words contains a mystery', had to be translated literally, word by word, but elsewhere Jerome followed the example of Cicero's translations from Greek: 'I here omit mentioning', he wrote, 'what additions, omissions and changes Cicero made, replacing the idiom of Greek with that of Latin', and then went on to quote Cicero himself: 'I did not translate as an interpreter but as an orator, keeping the same ideas and their expressions and, as it were, figures, in words adjusted to our usage. I did not think it needful to translate word by word, but preserved the general character and force of the words.'[97] The matter had already arisen in Jerome's preface to the *Chronicle*. Even so, as Jerome himself implied in describing his handling of the 'phrases and clauses' of Isaiah, translating Scripture word by word was not always possible, not only because the 'general character and force' of Hebrew and Greek differed

---

[95] Jer. *Vulgata*, Preface to Job, *hoc unum scio non potuisse me interpretari nisi quod ante intellexeram*. In the same preface, Jerome comments on issues relating to the translation of the verse and prose parts of the book of Job, an issue also noted by Augustine who refers to this passage, *De Doctrina Christiana* 4.20.41.

[96] Jer. *Vulgata*, preface to Isaiah. See also Jer. *Hebraicae quaestiones in libro Geneseos*, preface (Patrologia Latina 23, col. 983): *sed et Tullius, qui in arce eloquentiae romanae stetit, rex oratorum et latinae linguae inlustrator, repetundarum accusatur a Graecis* ('But even Tullius, who stood on the citadel of Roman eloquence, the king of orators and the illuminator of the Latin language, was accused of *repetundae* by the Greeks'). Similarly, Jerome expects to be accused of plagiarisms from Jewish learning. The preface is a masterpiece of bitingly learned and amusing self-defence. On *cola* and *commata*, cf. Donatus, *Ars Maior* 1.6 in Holtz 1981: 612, cf. 62–3.

[97] Jer. *Ep.* 57.5 quoting Cic. *opt. gen.* 13–14.

from Latin vocabulary, but because the syntax of these languages differed too.[98]

Among all the Christian and pagan writers of his own, earlier and subsequent times, Jerome was the most deeply devoted to the habits of erudite, scholarly reading, of exegesis and of translating that could be learned in Roman schools.[99] A Christian from birth, he appears to have had no pagan friends. Yet his labours as a translator and his love of textuality and Latinity, where Cicero proved to be so ineradicable,[100] approximated him more closely than other Christian writers to those traditions of scholarship that in origin at least were pagan, and it was this same love that set him at odds with numerous Christian contemporaries,[101] among them Ambrose and Augustine, whose reading and reception of Cicero differed greatly from his.

Jerome's love for the classics is patent. He could not forget Cicero even in the introductions to his translations of Scripture – and the issue was not some classical nostalgia, but the living awareness that Cicero, 'the king of orators and light of the Latin language', was there to stay.[102] Ambrose, for whom Jerome came to feel a vigorous dislike,[103] had also grown up with Cicero but responded differently. He had been bishop of Milan for less than three years when in 378 his brother Satyrus died and he was called upon to address the people of Milan in a consolatory oration during the funeral, followed seven days later by another oration that was delivered next to the tomb. As might be expected, he began the first oration with a scriptural quotation, but the very next sentence contained a reminiscence

[98] Brown 1992: 104–8, on Jer. *Ep.* 57 and the preface to the *Chronicle*. On the chronology of Jerome's scriptural translations, Kelly 1975: 158–63. Bartelink 1980: 1–7 on the circumstances and content of this letter; see here section 5.2 with Bartelink's commentary, which points out (44–7) that even by his own account elsewhere Jerome did not consistently translate Scripture *verbum e verbo*. See further, Lardet 1993: numbers 79b; 174a; 177; 207; 349a; 410.

[99] Holtz 1981: 37–46; Gilliam 1953; on Jerome as book collector and textual critic (primarily of Scripture), see Brown 1992: 21–54.

[100] Note Jerome's frustrations with the prophet Daniel: *Vulgata*, Preface to Daniel (1341).

[101] For Jerome's many quarrels and controversies with contemporaries, friends and former friends, in particular Rufinus, see Kelly 1975.

[102] Jer., *Hebraicae quaestiones in libro Geneseos*, preface; Jerome here sees Cicero's experiences as an antecedent to his own.

[103] See Jerome's attack on Ambrose's treatise *De Spiritu Sancto libri tres* (much of them taken from Didymus' treatise on the Holy Spirit) in Jer. *Liber Didymi Alexandrini de Spiritu Sancto, praefatio*; accusing Ambrose of plagiarism he writes: *malui alieni operis interpres exsistere, quam – ut quidam faciunt – informis cornicula, alienis me coloribus adornare* ('I preferred to be the interpreter of another's work rather than – as others do – adorn myself with stolen colours, like an ugly crow'). On this passage, and on Jerome's estimation of Ambrose's *De officiis*, see Testard 1988: 227–54.

of Cicero's *Tusculan Disputations*, small for sure, but recognizable.[104] For all that Ambrose spoke to his people as their bishop,[105] both orations are steeped in Ciceronian sentiment. In the *Tusculan Disputations*, Cicero had observed that evils when anticipated are easier to bear – but Satyrus had died unexpectedly and Ambrose's grief was all the greater.[106] Elsewhere, Ambrose echoed Cicero's sentiments on the cares of life, the frailty of the body and on man's unsteady heart and feeble spirit,[107] from all of which death is a release. Satyrus died in troubled times. The Roman legions had recently suffered a crushing defeat at Adrianople and Italy stood in fear of the enemy.[108] Here in the footsteps of Cicero it was possible to seek another kind of consolation: Satyrus would not see 'the end of the world, the burial of his kinsfolk, the death of citizens'. Indeed, he had been blessed in 'so timely a death' – a thought reminiscent of Cicero's repeated reflections near the end of his life on the sorrows from which he himself and others would have been saved had they died earlier.[109] And in any case, death was part of the course of nature, and new life would spring from the seeds that rested in the ground, a passage where Ambrose spoke of the resurrection and also echoed words from Cicero's *Cato Maior*.[110] Perhaps most striking of all is another allusion to the *Cato Maior* where the elder Cato summed up his ideas about the afterlife: 'If I am mistaken on this point, believing that the souls of human beings are immortal, I am willingly mistaken, and do not want this error that delights me in this life to be wrested from me.' When Ambrose pondered, near the end of the second oration on Satyrus, how the resurrection from the dead might take place, he reformulated Cicero's thought like this: 'If I am mistaken on this point, seeing that after death I prefer to be in the company of angels...I am willingly mistaken and will never in this life allow myself to be cheated of this opinion.'[111]

Even so, these and other Ciceronian echoes are no more than a partial infrastructure to the primary themes pursued by Ambrose, who was in any case much more interested in Greek than Latin philosophical writings.[112] This is the case even in *De officiis*, a treatise he designed as a response

---

[104] Ambr. *De excessu fratris*, 1.1 with Cic. *Tusc.* 3.30.
[105] For the circumstances, see McLynn 1994: 68–78.
[106] Ambr. *De excessu fratris* 1.35 with Cic. *Tusc.* 3.29.
[107] Ambr. *De excessu fratris* 2.29 with Cic. *Rep.* 3.1.1, cf. Heck 1966: 105.
[108] McLynn 1994: 68–78.
[109] Ambr. *De excessu fratris* 1.33; 2.14. 2.18; 2.22; Cic. *Tusc.* 1.83–6; *De or.* 3.12. The 'death of citizens' etc., Ambr. *De excessu fratris* 1.30. Favez 1937: 63–6, on timely death in Cicero, Ambrose and elsewhere as a topos of consolatory discourse.
[110] Ambr. *De excessu fratris* 2.61 with Cic. *Sen.* 53.
[111] For this surprising statement (that he is willingly mistaken about eternal life, a doctrine stated in all the Creeds), see Ambr. *De excessu fratris* 2.134 and Cic. *Sen.* 84.
[112] Pépin 1962; Zelzer 1977 discusses Ambrose's Greek and Latin sources.

to and reformulation of Cicero's *De officiis* and for the guidance – so he claims – of his clergy: 'just as Cicero wrote to instruct his son, so I write to guide you who are my sons. For I love you, whom I brought forth in the gospel no less than if you were my sons born in marriage: nature is no stronger in loving than grace.'[113] As a former provincial governor, Ambrose felt ill-equipped to teach things Christian and began by searching for a scriptural antecedent of the very notion of an *officium*. He found it in the gospel pericope involving the time of service, *officium*, that Zacharias the father of John the Baptist served in the temple.[114] The argument pursued by Ambrose in his *De officiis* follows that of Cicero: in three books he proceeds from obligations the fulfilment of which is honourable, to those which may be complied with for the sake of advantage or self-interest, to criteria whereby to resolve conflicts between the two. But the content that Ambrose placed into this form was designed to supersede Cicero's guidelines. For example, Ambrose accepted from Cicero the schema of the cardinal virtues, as he also did in *De excessu fratris* and elsewhere.[115] In describing the virtues, Cicero had followed not only a philosophical but also a cultural and political programme: his aim was to show that Roman was equal to and indeed at times superior to Greek virtue.[116] In this way, he peopled the annals of philosophy with Roman exemplars to stand alongside and at times to supplant the Greek ones.[117] Ambrose in his turn did the same, replacing Cicero's Romans with scriptural personages, and redefining the virtues in light of the theological virtue of faith.[118] In so far therefore as Cicero's *De officiis* was a narrative of Roman history and of eminent Romans both ancient and contemporary, Ambrose made of his *De officiis* a narrative of scriptural history, of patriarchs, prophets and kings, and also of Christian heroes such as the Roman martyrs Agnes and Laurentius.[119]

---

[113] Ambr. *Off.* 1.24; see also Davidson 2001.

[114] Luke 1.23, discussed in Ambr. *Off.* 1.25. The passage suggests that Ambrose compiled *De officiis* from sermons or talks and wrote linking passages to create a continuous text, see Testard 1989; Davidson 2001: vol. I, 36–44 argues for composition as a book.

[115] Ambr. *De excessu fratris* 1.42; 44; 51; 57 on *prudentia, fortitudo, simplicitas* (or *temperantia*) and *iustitia* respectively; cf. *Off.* 1.115; 126; 129; 210. See also Colish 2005.

[116] E.g. Cic. *Amic.* 15, on pairs of friends.

[117] E.g. the lamentations about death and pain uttered by figures from Greek tragedy in *Tusc.* Books 1 and 2. As a counter-example, Cicero mentions his countryman Marius, *Tusc.* 2.35; 53; cf. 55 (*Twelve Tables*).

[118] Ambr. *Off.* 1.110 (*fides* and *iustitia* of Abraham); 142 *fundamentum ergo iustitiae est fides*; 148 *liberalitas* and *fides*; 178 *fortitudo* with *fides*; 196 *fortitudo* and *fides* of Joshua; 253 *sapientia* and *fides* of Solomon; 2.20 *fides* of the patriarchs, David and Job; 99 of Moses; 154 of Josiah; 3.83 of Judith.

[119] On Agnes, Amb. *Off.* 1.204; on Laurentius, 1.205–7 (with reminiscence of Cic. *Amic.* 24); 2.140–1.

Finally, Ambrose claimed chronological priority for Scripture. The wise men of Greece had learned from Abraham, David, Solomon, Job and Daniel, not the other way round,[120] and this – so Ambrose implied – also affected the interpretation of Cicero the imitator of Plato, for Plato in his time had learned about justice and injustice not from other Greeks but from the Book of Job.[121]

Ambrose appears to have worked on *De officiis* during just the period when Augustine, then rhetor of Milan, was struggling towards his conversion and heard Ambrose preach sermons in which perhaps he picked up themes derived from the *Tusculan Disputations* and *De natura deorum*.[122] For Ambrose as a well-connected Roman,[123] reading Cicero could be taken for granted. For Augustine whose education began in a small African town, access to Cicero was not quite so natural, but the consequences were all the more far-reaching. Cicero accompanied him, it is no exaggeration to say, from youth to old age, beginning with his reading of the *Hortensius* at nineteen: as he recalled in the *Confessions*, the book redirected his life.[124] During the months of preparation for baptism that Augustine spent at his patron's country estate of Cassiciacum, the *Hortensius* was prescribed reading for the students who accompanied him there, and many years later, when seeking to understand and write about the Trinity, it was still present in his mind and he quoted it at some length.[125]

---

[120] E.g. Ambr. *Off.* 1.31; 2.6 on David; 1.44 on Job; 118 on Abraham, David, Solomon; 2.48 on Daniel; also 1.92; 94. Further, on Solomon, Ambr. *De excessu fratris* 2.30 with Cic. *Tusc.* 1.114 on Trophonius and Agamedes.

[121] Ambr. *Off.* 1.43–4. Ambrose here mentions the argument against justice in Cic. *Rep.* demonstrating that he had read the book. On Ambrose's thesis of the chronological priority of Scripture, Davidson 2001: vol. I, 21–2.

[122] Davidson 2001: vol. I, 3–5 suggests he composed the *De officiis* 'some time in the late 380's'. Augustine knew of the work (but did he read it?) and mentioned it in his *Ep.* 82.21, addressed to Jerome. In light of Jerome's sentiments about Ambrose, the reference cannot have been helpful in this particular letter, which Augustine wrote in an endeavour to improve his relations with Jerome. For the possible impact on Augustine of Ciceronian themes in Ambrose's preaching, Testard 1958a: 119–28.

[123] McLynn 1994: 31–5; 68–71; 264–75.

[124] August. *Conf.* 3.4.7; cf. August. *De Beata Vita* 4. Testard 1958a, a work of enduring importance, describes Augustine's evolution in relation to Cicero. See also Testard 1958b and Hagendahl 1968. Testard organizes the testimonia in accord with the work of Augustine where quotations of Cicero occur, whereas Hagendahl organizes them by works of Cicero; Testard 1986; Lancel 2003; on the course of Augustine's education, career as a teacher and critique of the Roman educational 'system', Voessing 2003.

[125] August. *De Trinitate* 14.9.12 on the place of the virtues in the next life; 14.19.26 on death and the pursuit of wisdom; see also 13.4.7 citing the words of the *Hortensius*, *beati certe omnes esse uolumus*. The same passage is quoted in August. *C. acad.* 1.5 (words put into the mouth of Trygetius); *Hortensius* prescribed reading, *ibid.* 1.4. Among late references to the *Hortensius* are those in *De civ. D.* 22.22 (Hagendahl

Augustine's Ciceronian repertoire was extensive, but his interest in Cicero changed in the course of his long life. At Cassiciacum, finally convinced of the Christian truth and preoccupied with the education of his students, he was troubled by the Academic scepticism of 'our Cicero',[126] and by the very idea that certainty might be unattainable.[127] In the dialogue *Contra Academicos* he thus wrote: 'I ask your very own legal advice, Marcus Tullius: we are considering the conduct and lives of the young, over whose education and training all those writings of yours have kept watch.' How would the young thrive without moral guidance? Besides, how was it that with such a philosophy, Cicero had been able to 'govern the commonwealth'? Beyond asking rhetorical questions, refutation of the Academic position was the essential preliminary to remapping the world of philosophy in light of Augustine's newly found Christian convictions.[128]

Yet, although Augustine was distancing himself from Cicero, his ideas proved vital. In the resulting process of adoption and adaptation, Augustine transformed and remade Cicero's thoughts and precepts into Christian ones, as when in *Contra Academicos* he narrowed Cicero's definition of the wisdom that was to be sought as 'the knowledge of things human and divine' into 'the knowledge of things human and divine, but only of those that pertain to the blessed life'.[129] But we can perhaps take it to be a further Ciceronian twist that for Augustine as earlier for Cicero 'things human and divine' meant not so much natural as moral philosophy and its practical,

1968, testimonium 200) and in *Contra Iulianum* (Hagendahl 1968, testimonia 188; 191). See also Doignon 1993.

[126] August. *C. acad.* 1.7 *placuit enim Ciceroni nostro, beatum esse qui ueritatem inuestigat, etiamsi ad eius innentionem non ualeat peruenire* ('Cicero thought that he who sought the truth was happy, even if he did not manage to find it').

[127] August. *C. acad.* 2.11. Further details of Augustine's engagement with Cic. *Acad.* in this dialogue are found in the *notes complémentaires* in Jolivet 1948. See also August. *Conf.* 5.19 with O'Donnell 1992.

[128] August. *C. acad.* 3.35; 44–5; here, with a touch of humour, Augustine anticipated that his friend Alypius would take up Cicero's arguments and defeat his own arguments against the Academics – a thought that he rejected as too light-hearted when he came to write the *Retractationes*, see *Retract.* 1.1.13. Note also August. *C. acad.* 3.43 suggesting that the Academics had propagated their scepticism in public, in order to protect their actual, Platonic philosophy that they did not wish to expose to controversy.

[129] August. *C. acad.* 1.23 Trygetius says to Licentius, tell me: *si sapientiam rerum humanarum diuinarumque scientiam dicamus, sed earum quae ad beatam uitam pertineant*, with Cic. *Fin.* 2.37 (vs. Epicurus): *aequam igitur pronuntiabit sententiam ratio, adhibita primum diuinarum humanarumque rerum scientia, quae potest appellari rite sapientia, deinde adiunctis uirtutibus, quas ratio rerum omnium dominas, tu uoluptatum satellites et ministras esse uoluisti.* Augustine did not mention Cicero here, but the Ciceronian tone of the phrase was very recognizable, see e.g. *Tusc.* 4.57; *Tusc.* 5.7; *Off.* 1.153; *Off.* 2.5.

lived applications.[130] Cicero's views on human relations, the virtues, passions and emotions, thus resonated even among the members of Augustine's monastic community[131] and in the text of Augustine's monastic rule.[132]

Even so, in such Christian formulations Cicero's ideas, however vital, were reshaped. This was the case throughout Augustine's writings, and especially in his grand renewed encounter with Cicero and the Roman past in general in the *City of God*.[133] The aim of the book was, *inter alia*, to reeducate Romans as Christians in their personal and public life and thus to rewrite Roman ethics, history and political theory. Here Cicero – along with Sallust, Virgil and Livy among others – provided points of departure, as he also did in Augustine's correspondence with Roman dignitaries and public officials. Exhorting 'you, the excellent progeny of Rome, the descendants of Regulus and Scaevola, of Scipio and Fabricius', to become Christians, Augustine included in the *City of God* a critique that was simultaneously an appreciation of Cicero's *De republica*.[134] Having read the *Divine Institutes* of his African predecessor Lactantius, Augustine nonetheless did not approach *De republica* with any expectation that the Christian Roman empire constituted a perfectable society for the success of which Cicero's work could provide guidance.[135] For, until the *civitas dei*, held together by love, not institutions,[136] came into its own at the end of time, it was a stranger

---

[130] MacCormack 1998: 126–7.

[131] August. *De Diversis Quaestionibus Octoginta Tribus* question 31, quoting Cic. *Inv. rhet.* 2.159–67, with August. *Retract.* 1.26.32. See Testard 1958a: 320–2; Hagendahl 1968: testimonia 336–9.

[132] Cic. *Amic.* 71: Laelius advises his interlocutors *ut igitur ei qui sunt in amicitiae coniunctionisque necessitudine superiores, exaequare se cum inferioribus debent, sic inferiores non dolere se a suis aut ingenio aut fortuna aut dignitate superari* ('and so just as in the bond of friendship and relationship the superior ought to equal himself to the weaker, so the weaker ought not to be upset that they are overtaken by their circle in talent or luck or status') – even if the latter may still not be content; cf. August. *Praeceptum* 1.3–7 (in Lawless 1987: 80–2). Here Augustine urges the brothers that in accord with the precedent of the early church in Acts 4.35 where distribution was made to each according to his need, those who had been affluent in the world should share with all, while those who had been poor should accommodate the distinct needs of their formerly wealthy brethren. That Augustine had read *De amicitia* is clear from C. *acad.* 3.13 and from his *Epistula* 258, to Marcianus, quoting *Amic.* 20.

[133] That Augustine reread the pagan classics in order to write *De civitate dei* is the view of O'Donnell 1980; see also Scheele 1978: 66–7.

[134] *De civ. D.* 2.29. On correspondence with public officials, see Atkins and Dodaro 2001; on Augustine's reception of Cicero, primarily in the *City of God*, Dodaro 2004: 6–26.

[135] August. *De civ. D.* 18.23, discussing the Sibyls to whom Lactantius devoted considerable attention. For Lactantius' Christian empire, above at notes 46–53.

[136] The *res publica* held together not by institutions, least of all juridical ones, August. *De civ. D.* 2.21, but by love, *De civ. D.* 19.21–4. This idea was developed throughout the work, see especially *De civ. D.* 14.28. See also *De civ. D.* 18.54 (end of this chapter); Markus 1970: 64–9; 97–100.

'journeying in this world' whose citizens for now remained hidden within the terrestial city.[137] This was not to set aside the obligation to correct its ills and errors and to work for its peace and continuance – where Augustine, in a passage reminiscent of Cicero's juxtapositions of the potentially conflicting calls of morality and expediency in *De officiis*, insisted that the wise person will desist from taking refuge in philosophical solitude: for 'human society which he considers it a crime to abandon constrains him to perform this duty, *officium*'.[138]

The *City of God* opens with an extended critique of pre-Christian Rome, where Cotta's critique of Stoic theology in *De natura deorum* proved as useful as it had been a century earlier to Arnobius and Lactantius, but now in the larger context of the role of religion in the Roman state.[139] For Augustine sought to demonstrate from Roman writers that the pagan gods, so far from furthering Rome's glory and power, had corrupted individuals and the social fabric from within, *inter alia* by pandering to the licentious pleasures of the stage. The Romans themselves, so Augustine recalled from Cicero's *De republica*, had misgivings about the theatre and unlike the Greeks did not allow poets to lampoon public figures. But this did not prevent them from staging plays representing the sexual and other escapades of the gods, thereby compromising public morality, not to mention the dignity of the gods.[140] Augustine thus approved of Cicero's censure of Homer's gods: 'Homer invented these things and attributed human feelings to gods; I wish he had attributed divine feelings to us.'[141] Here and elsewhere, Augustine used Cicero's theological dialogues[142] not in the light of the purpose for which they had been written, i.e. in pursuit of describing Roman religious

---

[137] *De civ. D.* 15.20.

[138] Cic. *Off.* 3.17; August. *De civ. D.* 19.6; Fuchs 1965 (first published 1926): 11 refers the thought to Varro.

[139] In Cic. *Nat. D.* 3.39–62, Cotta ridicules the multitude of deities that must result from Balbus' cosmic theology (2.45–72). Augustine returned to this argument, while also drawing on Varro and Virgil, see e.g. *De civ. D.* 4.30; with Varro as his primary source, *De civ. D.* 6.9; 7.2–28 on the fragmentation of divine functions. Further, O'Daly 1999.

[140] August. *De civ. D.* 2.8–16 passim, with Hagendahl 1968: testimonia 260–3, 303; cf. Testard 1958b: 37–8.

[141] Cic. *Tusc* 1.25 in *De civ. D.* 4.26 (already in August. *Conf.* 1.25). In *De civ. D.*, Augustine added after the critique of Homer the story of how the gods most cruelly punished Titus Latinius for failing to pass on their message to the Roman senate, from Cic. *Div.* 1.55 to conclude (here as elsewhere) that the gods were 'malignant demons'.

[142] See especially August. *Ep.* 118, of AD 410 or 411, to Dioscorus, discussing Stoic, Epicurean and Platonist theodicies on the basis of *Nat. D.*, especially its early sections. See also *De civ. D.* 4.30 (pagan internal contradictions about the gods) with Cic. *Nat. D.* 2.70–72; Cic. *Div.* 2.24; 36–38; August. *De civ. D.* 5.9 (divine foreknowledge and human free will) with Cic. *Nat. D.* 3.95 and further passages from *De fato* and *De divinatione*.

practice within frameworks provided by the different Greek philosophical schools of Cicero's day,[143] but for the purpose of undermining Roman religious practice by separating Cicero's statements from their discursive context and inserting them into a new Christian discursive context in which Scripture, 'which by the decree of supreme providence has subjected to itself every kind of human genius, outstripping all by its divine authority', constituted the ultimate court of appeal. It was on the basis of Scripture that Augustine arrived at his conception of *civitas dei*: 'Glorious things are spoken of you, city of God.'[144] Consequently, Augustine was able to elicit from Cicero conceptual tensions – other than the ones that Cicero himself introduced for reasons of his own – that appeared to be present in his texts, but only in light of this new contextualization.[145]

Distinct purposes converged in this process. In discussing Cicero's ideas in *De republica* about justice at Rome that had also interested Lactantius, Augustine produced in the first instance a refutation. In the persona of the younger Scipio Africanus, Cicero had illustrated the harmony and concord of the different parts of Roman society by comparing it to the musical harmony of different voices – but all this was being destroyed by internal conflict because justice, 'without which the *res publica* cannot be governed', had been set aside. Cicero himself had concluded that 'our time, having received the *res publica* like a noble picture, but fading with age, not only failed to restore it in the colours that it possessed, but did not even care merely to preserve its form and basic features'. Hence, according to Augustine, Rome had not even before the birth of Christ conformed to Scipio's definition of a *res publica* or 'weal of the people', *res populi*. A people, Scipio had said, is 'not any gathering of a multitude, but a gathering brought together by consent about law and community of interest'.[146] However much, Augustine concluded, this state of affairs might have obtained in Rome's ancient days, true justice did not exist even then, but is only found in 'that *res publica* whose founder and ruler is Christ'.[147]

---

[143] Cf. Beard 1986; Schofield 1986.

[144] August. *De civ. D.* 11.1 with Psalm 87.3 cf. the opening words of *De civ. D.* in the preface, *Gloriosissimam civitatem dei*.

[145] Recontextualization is part and parcel of reading and interpretation, but among the Christian writers of late antiquity, Augustine stands out for the extent and depth both of his recontextualizations and of his internalization of Cicero's arguments.

[146] Cic. *Rep.* 1.39.

[147] August. *De civ. D.* preface, *aduersus eos qui conditori eius deos suos praeferunt*; 2.21, citing Cic. *Rep.* 2.42 (musical harmony and social concord); *Rep.* 5.1; 1.39. *Conditor rectorque Christus*, *De civ. D.* 2.21. Regarding music as an image of a harmonious polity, see *De civ. D.* 17.14, on the music of King David.

Having completed his extended argument against Roman religion and statecraft, and also against the deficiencies of ancient philosophy in terms of discovering the worship of the true god, and having explained the parallel histories of the two cities, Augustine in Book 19 resumed his response to Scipio's definition of the *res populi*: 'where there is no true justice, there cannot be a gathering of human beings and therefore, according to that definition of Scipio or Cicero, no people. And if no people, then no *res populi*, but some multitude unworthy of the name of people.' In addition – here Augustine added and adapted a definition of justice from Cicero, 'justice is that virtue which distributes to each his own'[148] – 'what kind of human justice is it that takes a human being away from the true god and subjects him to unclean demons?' Next, reviewing the argument between Philus and Laelius as to whether government was possible without committing injustice, and mentioning Laelius' claim that imperial power rightly holds sway over subjects just as god rules human beings, the soul rules the body and reason rules the passions, Augustine refocused this claim by adding that 'this analogy demonstrates that subordination is beneficial for some people, and subordination to god is beneficial for all'. But once more, since the Roman gods were 'impure demons', justice did not prevail in ancient Rome.[149]

However, this was not the end of the story because Augustine proceeded to offer an alternative definition of people, *populus*: 'a people is a gathering of a multitude of rational beings united in a common agreement about the objects of their love'. 'According to this definition of ours, the Roman people is a people, and its estate undoubtedly is a *res publica*.' History related the many wars and discords that marked its progression through time and that Augustine had outlined earlier, but none of this compromised the validity of his definition even if the objects of a people's love varied in quality. This new definition in turn, while it recognized Rome as a *res publica*, did the same for all other polities,[150] depriving Rome of the unique position in history that Cicero – and not only he – at times strove to attribute to it. Further, because God did not rule in any of those polities, even if the two cities, the terrestrial

---

[148] Cic. *Nat. D.* 3.38: Cotta asks, by way of problematizing Balbus' theodicy: *iustitia quae suum cuique distribuit, quid pertinet ad deos? hominum enim societas et communitas, ut uos dicitis, iustitiam procreauit.* Cic. *Inv. rhet.* 2.160 *iustitia est habitus animi communi utilitate conservata suam cuique tribuens dignitatem*; cf. August. *De Libero Arbitrio* 1.13.27: *iustitiam quid dicamus esse, nisi uirtutem qua sua cuique tribuuntur?*

[149] August. *De civ. D.* 19.21; see also Testard 1958b: 64–6. The point is reiterated in *De civ. D.* 19.23 (at end). Augustine here implies a criticism of Roman imperialism such as was not present in Lactantius. See also *De civ. D.* 4.4 on Alexander the Great and the pirate, derived from Cic. *Rep.* 3.24. Cf. Heck 1974: 181.

[150] August. *De civ. D.* 19.24.

city and the city of God on its journey in the world, were 'intermingled', *permixtae*, these polities did not possess true justice.[151]

A new concept of polity thus emerged from Augustine's conversation with Cicero, and along with it a new concept of being human, a new psychology. He was deeply familiar with the *Tusculan Disputations*, where Cicero analysed the emotions and passions, exploring from an Academic and Peripatetic point of view the propositions that 'distress (*aegritudo*) affects the wise man', and that 'the wise man cannot escape every disturbance of the soul' (*omni animi perturbatione*).[152] Augustine agreed with these propositions: 'as one of the learned men of this world has expressed it, entire freedom from pain (of soul) "cannot be attained without the great cost of savagery of mind and stolidity of body"'.[153] As a result, he rejected the Stoic argument that freedom from *perturbatio* and *aegritudo* or sadness, *tristitia*, was attainable and should be attained.[154] In any case, sadness could be useful, where Augustine cited from the *Tusculan Disputations* the example of Alcibiades who wept because Socrates called him foolish, for in such sadness 'a person grieves that he is what he should not be', this being a necessary preliminary of reform.[155] But Augustine's reasons for agreeing with Cicero were his own and entailed a larger disagreement with him. For Augustine engaged in his discussion about emotion and distress of soul in order to contradict the argument that the body was the cause of human sin, or, as Cicero had said, that the soul lived in the body 'as in a stranger's house' from which it would be freed at death – this being one aspect of Augustine's larger argument about the resurrection of the body on the last day.[156] Demonstrating by reference to Cicero among others that emotions and passions arose not in the body but in the soul provided the infrastructure for his explanation of the resurrection which also gave access to Augustine's interpretation of

---

[151] August. *De civ. D.* 19.26; Dodaro 2004.

[152] Cic. *Tusc.* 3.7 and 4.8 with Graver 2002, introduction, and Long 1995a. In *De civ. D.* 8.17 Augustine quoted *Tusc.* 4.11 about the passions in the course of his argument about demons as mediators as envisioned by Apuleius in *De deo Socratis*. Here, the argument about the passions as lived out by demons in their capacity of mediating between human beings and the high gods feeds into the larger argument – against Porphyry – about Christ the true mediator. As for Cicero, the meaning of his texts changed by virtue of being read in circumstances that he did not and could not have envisioned.

[153] August. *De civ. D.* 14.9 quoting Cic. *Tusc.* 3.12.

[154] August. *De civ. D.* 9.4 (e.g. in *Tusc.* 4.11). There follows the story from Gell. *NA* 19.1 about the Stoic philosopher who grew pale with fear in a storm at sea. For *aegritudo*, see *De civ. D.* 14.7. See with this passage, Cic. *Tusc.* 3. 22–3, esp. *aegris enim corporibus simillima animi est aegritudo*, a statement Cicero goes on to qualify.

[155] August. *De civ. D.* 14.8 (at end) with *Tusc.* 3.77.

[156] Cic. *Tusc.* 1.51; for Augustine on body and soul, see e.g. *De civ. D.* 14.3. The resurrection of the body is the subject of *De civ. D.* Book 21.

Scripture and Christian ethics for those not familiar with either. Emotions could indeed be positive. The apostle Paul had been afraid for the sake of the Christian congregation at Corinth. More important, Christ had wept at the tomb of Lazarus, and his soul was grieved, *tristis*, at the approach of his passion: 'he accepted these emotions in his human soul by the grace of his sure design when he so willed, just as he became man in the manner he willed'.[157] Augustine's understanding of the will as the defining component of positive and salutary and also of negative and sinful emotions had been anticipated by Cicero who described emotions as a matter of our forming an opinion and thus as outcomes of what is willed.[158] But the purpose to which Augustine directed his reading of Cicero was designed not so much to modify Stoic severity as Cicero had done, but to demonstrate that freedom from emotion and even from distress was unthinkable in this present life.[159]

In the final dénouement of his long conversation with Cicero in the *City of God*, Augustine did not mention the name of the 'founder of Roman eloquence'.[160] Similarly, in Book 4 of *De doctrina Christiana* which he finished at the same time as the last books of the *City of God*, Cicero is present but not named. The primary subject of *De doctrina Christiana* is the exegesis of Scripture, which Augustine here envisioned – as any teacher of rhetoric would have done – as the two-fold task of discovering what had to be understood, and then putting it across. For discovery, *inventio*, discussed in the first three books, he worked mainly from Scripture and Christian authors, but for communicating what had been discovered, *modus proferendi*, he repeatedly referred to Cicero while maintaining that 'our authors', among whom the apostle Paul was his favourite example, possessed all the virtues of eloquence and of the ornaments of speech of which secular authors could boast.[161] In effect it was Christian, especially scriptural, writers who best exemplified Cicero's dictum that 'wisdom without eloquence is of small use to states, whereas eloquence without wisdom is frequently most detrimental and never useful'.[162]

---

[157] August. *De civ. D.* 14.9.   [158] August. *De civ. D.* 14.6; Cic. *Tusc.* 4.11–12; 82.

[159] Augustine also adduced the *Tusculan Disputations* in his discussion of the role of the theatre in Roman public life, *De civ. D.* 4.26 with *Tusc.* 4.26 (cf. *Conf.* 1.25); and of the theory of Apuleius about demons as false mediators between human beings and the immortal gods, *De civ. D.* 8.17 with *Tusc.* 4.11.

[160] August. *De Doctrina Christiana* 4.17.34 *Romani auctor eloquii*.

[161] August. *De Doctrina Christiana* 1.1.1 on *modus inveniendi* and *modus proferendi*, reiterated in 4.1.1 along with explaining the structure of the work. On Paul, August. *De Doctrina Christiana* 4.4.11. Eskridge 1912 assembled and discussed Augustine's quotations from Cicero in *De Doctrina Christiana*.

[162] Cic. *Inv. rhet.* 1.1, quoted by August. *De Doctrina Christiana* 4.5.7; a similar point at 4.28.61.

Wisdom was attained by studying and understanding Scripture, where formal training in rhetoric was superfluous. Indeed, trying to observe precepts of rhetoric while speaking was a hindrance because it compromised spontaneity.[163] Within this framework, however, Augustine did reiterate the advice of 'an eloquent man' that one should speak 'so as to teach, to delight, and to sway'. And then he added: 'teaching is a necessity, giving delight is agreeable and to sway is victory'.[164] In implementing this advice, the Christian orator like his Roman predecessor was first to instruct his listeners, then to engage their emotions and finally to move them to action. Here Augustine recalled how in the course of an address he had reduced the people of Mauretanian Caesarea to tears and lamentation with the purpose of persuading them to discontinue their traditional ritual battle in which every year many lost their lives: 'when I saw the tears, I knew that this monstrous custom, handed down from their fathers, grandfathers and remote ancestors . . . had been overcome'.[165] He achieved his end by speaking in the grand manner, while at the same time pointing out – in Cicero's footsteps – that this mode of speaking, designed to produce action, must not be overdone and was inseparable from the calm style of speaking for purposes of instruction, and the moderate style for purposes of engaging the emotions, both being preparatory to the grand style for urging the action the speaker recommended.[166]

Before giving all this advice Augustine distanced himself from his source: 'I begin by forestalling the expectation of readers who might think that I will provide the rules of rhetoric that I learnt and taught in the secular schools, and I urge them not to expect this from me, not because they are of no use but, if they are of any use, this is to be learnt elsewhere, if perhaps some

---

[163] August. *De Doctrina Christiana* 4.3.4: eloquence should be learned in youth, when it can be done quickly, cf. Cic. *De or.* 3.89; cf. 146.

[164] August. *De Doctrina Christiana* 4.12.27 *dixit enim quidam eloquens, et uerum dixit, ita dicere debere eloquentem, ut doceat, ut delectet, ut flectat. deinde addidit: docere necessitatis est, delectare suauitatis, flectere uictoriae.* Cicero's wording differs somewhat at *Orat.* 69. Copeland 2006: 239–47 discusses the presence of Cicero in *De Doctrina Christiana* along with a Neoplatonist orientation derived from Marius Victorinus' commentary on Cicero's *De inventione* (see above n. 66).

[165] August. *De Doctrina Christiana* 4.24.53.

[166] At *De Doctrina Christiana* 4.20.39–44 Augustine provides examples of the three styles of speaking from Paul's letters. This is followed by further examples from Cyprian and Ambrose. At 4.18.35 Augustine compares topics of Cicero's forensic speeches – money, and even matters of life and death – to ecclesiastical topics, which latter always dealt with matters of ultimate importance: even so, these topics too should be approached by using all three styles. It merits saying that in his extant sermons, Augustine did not follow his own advice, as my colleague Hildegund Müller, whose book on the subject is eagerly awaited, has pointed out to me – I cannot but agree.

good man has time to study this subject, but it should not be expected from me either in this work or elsewhere.'[167]

Yet Augustine lived in a social and cultural world where Cicero's writings were known because they continued being taught in Roman schools. Earlier he had replied impatiently but at some length to enquiries about 'small questions' involving Cicero's dialogues to the Greek Dioscorus who was in Africa for his studies,[168] and before that – unbeknown to himself – he appeared in a dream of his former student Eulogius, who had become rhetor of Carthage and was puzzling over a problem arising from Cicero's *De inventione* that he was to explain to his students.[169] Eulogius later wrote a *Disputatio* about the dream of Scipio which concludes Cicero's *De republica*. Augustine had read those pages too. In the dream, Scipio saw his deceased grandfather the elder Scipio Africanus and his adoptive father Aemilius Paullus in the Milky Way and conversed with them about the eternal reward that the gods bestowed on those who laboured for their homeland. From there, the conversation turned to the music of the spheres and to the smallness of the earth and even of Rome when viewed from the celestial dwelling place of those two eminent Romans. Omitting any comment on, and even mention of, Scipio's dream, Augustine suggested that Cicero had implied a critique of the myth of Er at the end of Plato's *Republic*, a myth that some Christians wanted to understand as referring to the resurrection of the dead. This last point about the resurrection was one that Augustine rejected.[170] Augustine's studious disinterest in the *Dream of Scipio* was obviously not shared by Eulogius who used it as an opportunity to write about the number symbolism he thought was latent in Cicero's text, and about the harmony of the spheres.[171]

A little later, the *Dream* attracted the interest of Macrobius in Rome who not long after AD 430, when he had been praetorian prefect, addressed his *Commentum in somnium Scipionis* to his son Eustathius, 'joy and glory of

---

[167] August. *De Doctrina Christiana* 4.1.2. Augustine did not have happy memories of teaching rhetoric (*Conf.* 5.8.14, and cf. 3.3.6–4.7, his own studies and first encounter with Cicero). Müller 1910 (using mainly Greek sources).

[168] August. *Ep.* 118.2 *Tullianorum dialogorum quaestiunculas* – the entire letter is studded with Ciceronian quotations.

[169] August. *De Cura Pro Mortuis Gerenda* 11.13.

[170] August. *De civ. D.* 22.28. After mentioning Labeo's story of two men who revived after death and thereafter became friends, Augustine pointed out that throughout the topic was about returning to this life, not rising to the next life (this is true of Er and the two friends in Labeo, but not of the elder Scipio and Aemilius Paullus in the *Dream*, even if the *Dream* does not contemplate any resurrection of the body). Ziegler 1958 included the passage about Plato and Cicero (124–5); Powell 2006 omits it. See Heck 1966: 141–2. Cf. below n. 173.

[171] See Weddingen 1957.

my life'.[172] Like Augustine and Eulogius, Macrobius connected the *Dream* with the myth of Er in Plato's *Republic*. Both Plato and Cicero had appealed to the transcendental destiny of just souls so as to lend weight to the idea that 'without love of justice' 'neither the *res publica* nor a gathering of people and not even a tiny household' could stand.[173] But Cicero made his point in a different way. In lieu of Plato's narrative, *fabula*, about Er's return from the other world, ridiculed as it had been by critics, Cicero clothed his message as a *fabula* about visionary experience.[174]

The intellectual and cultural environment inhabited by Macrobius differed greatly from that of Augustine, and from that of the other Christians who had contradicted, commented on and sometimes partially agreed with Cicero. For Macrobius, as earlier for Symmachus, Roman antiquity was something to be revered – the more ancient the better. Macrobius' purpose in the *Dream of Scipio* therefore was not to modify or contradict but to affirm Cicero, who 'by his learning and wisdom', *doctrina et sapientia*, was able to track the path of virtuous souls in the cosmic order, eliciting this knowledge 'from the sanctuaries of philosophy', *de adytis philosophiae*.[175] Macrobius wrote in Rome, during times that were unquestionably Christian, when the Roman religious practice that underlay Cicero's theodicy had become a thing of the past. The *Dream of Scipio* was a *fabula*, an invented narrative, but, so Macrobius specified, it was a *fabula* such as was appropriate to philosophy, distinct and separate from

---

[172] The long debate on the 'date and identity of Macrobius' would appear now to have been settled (Cameron 2011: 231–9); Kaster 2011: xi–xxiv. Accordingly, Macrobius was a Christian. The arguments for this conclusion advanced by Cameron and Kaster raise questions about the religious identity of Augustine's student Favonius Eulogius, taken probably to have been a pagan by Weddingen 1957: 8. For the reasons there given for his paganism at the time of writing the *Disputatio* – i.e. the broadly Neoplatonist ideas there expounded – did not hold up to scrutiny in the case of Macrobius who also expressed such ideas, although more learnedly and elegantly. Dedications of works of learning to sons were something of a tradition in Roman letters; Cicero dedicated *De officiis* to his son Quintus; for Martianus Capella see below at notes 206 and 209.

[173] Macrob. *In Somn.* 1.1.1–2.2; 1.1.4:. The statement is about Plato, but applies equally to Cicero, see Macr. *Somn.*1.1.8–9, where Plato's myth of Er and Cicero's *Dream of Scipio* are juxtaposed.

[174] Macrob. *In Somn.* 1.2.1–16. Macrobius is at pains not to criticize Plato while doing justice to Cicero.

[175] Macrob. *In Somn.* 1.12.18. By death of the soul Macrobius means its descent into the body, and the soul's life is its return to the celestial spheres, see *In Somn.* 1.11.1. At 1.12.3 Macrobius echoes Cic. *Tusc.* 1.74 on the body as the soul's prison (*vincla carceris*). About two kinds of death, see also August. *De civ. D.* 13.2. It is tempting to see Macrobius' description of Platonist teaching about life and afterlife in terms of two kinds of death as a response to Augustine.

the *fabulae* of poets that Augustine and earlier Christians had criticized so severely.[176]

Following upon his definition of different kinds of *fabula*, Macrobius highlighted the political message concerning justice in society and the role of the statesman that he found in the *Dream*, where also his interpretation of Cicero diverged from that of Augustine and earlier Christians. Where Augustine had substituted the shared love of specific goals for Cicero's consent about justice as the bond of society and definition of *res publica*,[177] Macrobius accepted Cicero's view and built on it by describing the virtues as evidenced in the words and emotions that Cicero attributed to the dreaming Scipio. In the process, Macrobius built into his commentary some *aperçus* derived from *De republica* as a whole, while also interpreting the dream and the entire book in a Neoplatonist and more otherworldly sense than Cicero had set down. But political life did remain a central theme. In promising a blessed afterlife to statesmen, Cicero had, according to Macrobius, distinguished between contemplative and active virtues – 'some people are made blessed by the contemplative, others by the active virtues'.[178] Claiming the authority of Plotinus, Macrobius ordered the virtues into four ascending ranks, as pertaining to political life, to the life of purification and that of the already purified soul, and finally the exemplary, paradigmatic virtues of the perfected soul.[179] But he did not intend this to mean that the political virtues whereby a good man ruled first over himself and then over the *res publica* were lowest in rank.[180] The practice of virtue in itself generates blessedness, where the political virtues must be included since Cicero had assigned to those who govern commonwealths a place 'where they for ever enjoy eternity in blessedness'. For, as Cicero had also said, 'of events on earth nothing is more pleasing to that leading god who rules all the world, than councils and gatherings of people brought together by law that we call cities'. Here Macrobius added for clarification: 'there have been groups of

---

[176] Macrob. *In Somn.* 1.2.12; cf. August. *Ep.* 101.2; *De civ. D.* 2.14, on Plato banning poets from his city because of the harm done by their *fabulae*. In his mature and older years, Augustine had no room for a positive view of *fabula*.

[177] See above at notes 147–51.   [178] Macrob. *In Somn.* 1.8.11.

[179] Macrob. *In Somn.* 1.8.5 ascribes the scheme to Plotinus *Enn.* 1.2 (see especially sections 3–7). But see, on Macrobius' use of Porphyry, Courcelle 1948: 20–31 (but dating Macrobius' writing to the later fourth century, for which allowance must be made in consulting these pages).

[180] Macrob. *In Somn.* 1.8.8: having explained that each of the hierarchy of virtues contains all four cardinal virtues, Macrobius concludes: *his uirtutibus* (i.e. the four cardinal virtues and their derivations) *uir bonus primum sui atque inde rei publicae rector efficitur, iuste ac prouide gubernans, humana non deserens* ('through these virtues the good man becomes a ruler first of himself and then of the *res publica*, guiding it justly and with foresight and not abandoning human concerns').

slaves and gladiators making up "federations and gatherings of people", but they were not "brought together by law"'.[181] Whether or not it might be possible to show that Macrobius was responding to Augustine's *City of God*,[182] his affirmation of Cicero's definition of *res publica* is striking.

At the conclusion of the *Somnium* Macrobius returned to the active virtues of the statesman[183] as compared to the contemplative ones of the philosopher, now arriving at a three-fold order of virtues. Men of action like Romulus came first, followed by philosophers like Pythagoras. Next came those who excelled in both spheres, like Lycurgus and Solon, although Macrobius described this group as peculiarly Roman and included in it Numa, the elder and younger Cato 'and many others who drank deeply of philosophy and bestowed a firm foundation on the *res publica*. For of those who were exclusively dedicated to philosophical retirement, of whom Greece produced many, Rome knew nothing.'[184] As Cicero had said more than once, no 'light of Latin letters illumined philosophy'[185] although there had been Roman orators and statesmen in plenty. Where Macrobius went beyond Cicero was in his conclusion that the *Dream* constituted that rare thing, a universal work, comprising the moral life, natural philosophy and the eternal life of the soul.[186]

Macrobius' aim in subsequently writing the *Saturnalia* was similar, for where the *Somnium* exalts Cicero, the *Saturnalia* exalts Virgil, but here also Cicero was present.[187] Macrobius explicitly modelled the *Saturnalia*, a dialogue between Symmachus, Praetextatus, Nicomachus Flavianus, all distinguished Roman pagans of the later fourth century, and their acquaintances and friends, on Cicero's dialogues in which the interlocutors were 'Cotta, Laelius and Scipio',[188] i.e. on *De natura deorum, De amicitia* and *De republica*. The primary themes of the *Saturnalia* were Virgil and Roman religious antiquities of what was, by Macrobius' time of writing, a bygone age, and the interlocutors – as also in those dialogues by Cicero – were all dead.[189] The *Saturnalia* is, *inter alia*, a work of philogical and antiquarian erudition, in which Macrobius drew on earlier sources, among them the *Attic Nights* of Aulus Gellius.

Accordingly, the portrait of Cicero that emerges in the *Saturnalia* is in some respects continuous with the one drawn by this second-century *savant*, and by Fronto, and differs *toto caelo* from the one drawn by the earlier Christian authors and by Augustine. From the outset, just as Aulus

---

[181] Macrob. *In Somn.* 1.8.12, quoting Cic. *Rep.* 6.13.   [182] Cf. above, n. 139.
[183] Macrob. *In Somn.* 2.17.4 referring back to 1.8.   [184] Macrob. *In Somn.* 2.17.8.
[185] Cic. *Tusc.* 1.5.   [186] Macrob. *In Somn.* 2.17.15.
[187] As Virgil was in *Somnium*, but this takes me beyond the theme of this chapter.
[188] Macrob. *Sat.* 1.1.4, for which see now Kaster 2011.   [189] Cameron 2011: 243–7.

Gellius had concluded, Cicero could do no wrong: everything he wrote was worthy of admiration.[190] Periodically, therefore, interlocutors cite his usage as tone-giving,[191] and in understanding Virgil Cicero was adduced for clarification.[192] When the point came to decide whether Virgil or Cicero was more universal, more admirable, the interlocutor assigned to this task found himself hard put to comply and did so only by taking refuge in established opinions about the four modes of speaking, *genera dicendi*.[193] The solemn obligations of theological and religious controversy that occupied so many Christian writers had silenced Cicero's urbanity and his sense of humour, but both came to life again among the interlocutors of the *Saturnalia* when they chronicled what Romans had said, in the words of Cicero, 'wittily, concisely and pointedly'.[194] The dignified Praetextatus who was hosting the interlocutors of the *Saturnalia* did not want to receive a dancer into his house to provide after-dinner entertainment for his guests, but he was happy to allow the conversation to turn to Cicero's jokes, many of which were therefore told.[195] Even some of Cicero's biting but humorous comments, that in their day had offended so many people but had been lovingly collected, now found another hearing.[196]

The *Saturnalia* indicates the extent to which the reception of Cicero depended, generation by generation, not just on those who read and wrote about him, but on copyists of Cicero's writings, and on scholars and teachers in the Roman schools. One of the participants in the dialogue was the grammarian Servius, author of a commentary on Virgil in which he included many citations of Cicero, whom he described as 'the orator' *tout court*.[197] His manner of citing Cicero, however, was that of the grammarian who

---

[190] See above, n. 8, and Macrob. *Sat.* 1.24.4–5, where Symmachus defends Cicero against Evangelus. Kaster 2011 suggests that Symmachus is here referring to his own discussion of Cicero's oratory, at the beginning of Book 3, which is lost.

[191] Macrob. *Sat.* 1.5.5–9; 6.4.8; 6.4.9 on Verg. *Aen.* 1.454 citing as authority Cic. *Att.* 16.6.1 *Paestum et Vibonensem pedibus aequis transmisimus* where Macrobius adds, *quod est transiuimus*, by way of validating Virgil's usage; it is tempting to add to Macrobius, for *pedibus aequis*, *Aen.* 2.724 where the little Ascanius follows his father *non passibus aequis*. *Sat.* 6.7.11 another Virgilian usage justified by reference to Cicero.

[192] Macrob. *Sat.* 4.4.1; 4.4.13–16 on pathos; 6.2.23–4 on Virgilian borrowings from Cicero.

[193] Macrob. *Sat.* 5.1.1–7.   [194] Macrob. *Sat.* 2.1.14, *facete et breuiter et acute*.

[195] Macrob. *Sat.* 2.1.7–16.

[196] Macrob. *Sat.* 7.3.10 also at 2.2.13 and 2.3.6. Cf. 2.1.12 for a book of Cicero's jokes supposedly compiled by Tiro, who, the speaker (Symmachus) suggests, may have authored some of them.

[197] Thilo and Hagen (1878–81): vol. I, on *Aen.* 1.258. The frequency of Servius' citations of Cicero contrasts strikingly with their relative absence in the early third-century commentary on Horace by Pomponius Porphyrio, on whom cf. Sallmann 1997: 259–61.

taught boys their first letters, describing and defining the correct usage of words, as for example in Virgil's line from Evander's speech about the early inhabitants of the site of Rome who received their first instruction in civilization from Saturn: 'he united the stubborn race who were scattered on the mountain tops and gave them laws'. Servius commented: '"stubborn race", for "uninformed". Because "untutored" is what cannot learn at all, and "uninformed" is what has not yet learned . . . This is what Cicero says in the first book of *De inventione*, that human beings who were still barbarous were united by the speech of some great man.'[198] Marius Victorinus, 'rhetor of the city of Rome',[199] whose job it was to teach older boys once they had mastered the rules of grammar and usage, in his commentary on *De inventione* thought about this same passage from a rhetorical and philosophical vantage point, in accord with what he was teaching – and *De inventione* was the same text that Eulogius had difficulties with when preparing his class.[200] Victorinus, while also quoting from Virgil's lines about the savage state of those first inhabitants of the site of Rome,[201] reflected on a broader topic than Servius, on the very origins of eloquence and civilization. Eloquence, he wrote, begins with an exertion of the soul and the active pursuit of the envisioned goal, and this occurred for the first time at the very origin of society, when human beings, preoccupied with meeting their bodily needs, lacked the spiritual energy to ascend to a better state. But nature, Victorinus thought, does not endow all with the same gifts.[202] So it was that 'some great man whose soul had retained its nature so that he understood that all human beings have something divine in them, but that it is hindered and diminished by the failings of the body'[203] was 'impelled to eloquence'[204] to gather those people into a society, a city. In short, Victorinus employed a discursive, argumentative method quite different from that of Servius' grammatical approach. Here as elsewhere, he commented by way of articulating and expanding on the statements of the text, in this case espousing Cicero's ideal that eloquence and philosophy could and should be coextensive, while

---

[198] Verg. *Aen.* 8.321–2: *is genus indocile ac dispersum montibus altis / composuit legesque dedit* . . . Servius on line 321: *IS GENUS INDOCILE pro 'indoctum': nam 'indocile' est quod penitus non potest discere, 'indoctum' quod nondum didicit. hos autem dicit esse conpositos, unde apparet quia 'indocile' dixit pro 'indoctum.' hoc autem est quod dicit Cicero in primo rhetoricorum, feros adhuc homines magni cuiusdam uiri oratione conpositos.* The reference is to Cic. *Inv. rhet.* 1.2.

[199] Thus August. *Conf.* 8.2.3.   [200] See above, n. 169.

[201] As did Grillius, *Commentum in Ciceronis Rhetorica* (Jakobi 2002: 20–1) on *Inv. rhet.* 1.2 *quo tempore magnus uir et sapiens.* Virgil is cited repeatedly to illustrate Cicero's statements, see in particular *Aen.* 1.148–54, on *Inv. rhet.* 1.3; Jakobi 2005: e.g. 76; 77–8; 94–5; 171; 183; 224; 278. The relationship between Cicero and Virgil both as such and in the commentaries on each of them merits attention.

[202] Halm 1863: 160, 21.   [203] Halm 1863: 161, 16.   [204] Halm 1863: 161, 38.

adding his own Platonist understanding of the fall and return of the soul, epitomized by Cicero's 'great and wise man' in *De inventione*.[205]

Among Victorinus' readers was Martianus Capella, who in his old age dedicated a long book of prose interspersed with verse that he titled *De nuptiis Philologiae et Mercurii*, 'Marriage of Philology and Mercury', to his son Martianus.[206] At the pair's wedding feast celebrated in the celestial realms by the Olympian gods, the seven liberal arts each give a speech,[207] where Rhetorica represents, or rather personifies, Cicero, 'my Tullius'.[208] Martianus described *De nuptiis* as a *fabella* or *fabula* that he had heard on a winter night from the personified literary genre Satura,[209] which meant to say, *inter alia*, that the tale was composed of fiction and reality for the instruction and entertainment of the reader. In accord with the sequence of the liberal arts, Rhetorica enters the assembly of the gods after Grammatica and Dialectica. Preceded by a lictor and attired in the 'consular purple' she declaims Cicero's words from the *Second Catilinarian Oration*, 'how blessed we shall be, how fortunate the *res publica*, and how brilliant the renown of my consulship!'[210] But times had changed. Rhetorica, having formerly dominated the law courts, was now reduced 'against my will, to remember the instruction of the young about the threadbare rules of a timeworn discipline'. Yet, given that Cicero himself wrote rhetorical treatises, Rhetorica launched on the topic of explaining her art, where Cicero's *De inventione*, although not mentioned, provided much of the theoretical infrastructure.[211] But here also, Martianus' world was not Cicero's, if only because Cicero

---

[205] Hadot 1971: 81–7. Cic. *Inv. rhet.* 1.2: *quidam magnus uidelicet uir et sapiens.*

[206] Ramelli 2001. On Martianus and Victorinus, see Ramelli 2001: xlviii, citing Hinks 1935 which I have not seen; Hadot 1971: 150–6; 313–21 (regarding Victorinus' lost commentary on Cicero's *Topica*); Grebe 1999: 31. For the allegory of the marriage of Mercury and Philology and its pagan tone, Stahl 1971: 84–98.

[207] Courcelle 1948: 198–205; Simon 1966.

[208] Mart. Cap. 5.436. For the Ciceronian and other sources of Martianus' fifth book, see Johnson with Burge 1971: 115–19.

[209] Mart. Cap. 1.2 addressing his son: *fabellam tibi, quam Satura comminiscens hiemali peruigilio marcescentes mecum lucernas edocuit, ni prolixitas perculerit, explicabo*; 9.997 again addressing his son at the end of the work: *habes anilem, Martiane fabulam, / miscillo lusit quam lucernis flamine / Satura.* On the meaning of Satura in Martianus, see Shanzer 1986: 29–44; Grebe 1999: 37–50 sees Books 3–9 on the liberal arts as 'Fachliteratur'.

[210] Mart. Cap. 5.431 *consularis purpura*, with the words from Cic. *Cat.* 2.10. In 426 she is dressed like this: *subarmalis autem uestis illi peplo quodam circa umeros inuoluto Latiariter tegebatur*, which I am tempted to understand as a toga. The lictor: 5.433–4.

[211] Mart. Cap. 5.436, *inuita compellor scholarium iuuenilium monitus exilia decantatae artis praecepta memorare.* For *Inv. rhet.* in Book 5, see the notes on the text in Ramelli 2001 – although much more can be done. In communicating the rules of Rhetorica's art, Martianus drew on earlier manuals, among them the *Ars rhetorica* of Consultus Fortunatianus; Montefusco 2003: 128.

did not think of eloquence and the teaching and learning of it as being contained in one of the *disciplinae*, the liberal arts, which is what Martianus did think.[212] In the *disciplina* represented by Rhetorica, however, Cicero's speeches provided the primary source of examples, so that not only Cicero's own rhetorical practice,[213] but also the topics and persons about whom he had spoken and written came to life in Martianus' text: the innocent Roscius of Ameria, the notorious Verres, the Catilinarian conspiracy, the defence of Caelius, the speech defending Milo, famous still, even though it had been unsuccessful, the speech for King Deiotarus that had so notably moved Julius Caesar, and the invectives against Antony.[214]

Macrobius, who was praetorian prefect in AD 430, said nothing about the Christian times in which he lived, and neither did Martianus Capella, who wrote around this time.[215] Instead, both wrote about topics that pertained to a past before Christianity became the dominant religion. The long debate as to whether either of them were pagans or not has perhaps obscured the fact that there were different ways of considering the past and its inevitable relevance to the present that were not irreconcilably incompatible. Jerome thought of Cicero when translating the Hebrew Scriptures, and mentioned him in his prefaces. Augustine, without mentioning Cicero, found his rhetorical precepts to be indispensible in *De doctrina Christiana* at a time when all pagan cult had been outlawed – where it may not be irrelevant to note

---

[212] A specific example indicates the complexity of the issue. At *Inv. rhet.* 1.2 Cicero had asked, before launching into his story about the role of his archetypal eloquent and good man in forming the first human society, whether eloquence was an art, a kind of study or the practice of some faculty given by nature; Marius Victorinus, *In rhetoricam Ciceronis* (above n. 66) commenting on the passage redefined the question (Halm 1863: 155, 22 ff.) *antequam ad id unde coepit Cicero, ueniamus, dicendum primum uidetur, quid sit ars, deinde quid intersit inter artem et uirtutem* ('before we can come to the point where Cicero began, it needs to be said what an art is, and then what the difference is between an art and a virtue'); Martianus, with the same issue in mind writes (5.438) *sum ipsa Rhetorica quam alii artem, uirtutem alii dixere, alteri disciplinam; artem uero idcirco, quia doceor, licet Plato huic uocabulo refragetur; uirtutem autem dicunt, qui mihi bene dicendi inesse scientiam compererunt; qui edisci uero dicendi intimam rationem et percipi posse non nesciunt, fidenter me asserunt disciplinam* ('I am Rhetoric, whom some call an art, some a virtue, and some a discipline; an art, insofar as I am taught – we can ignore Plato's opposition to the word; those who call me a virtue do so because they find in me knowledge of speaking well; those who are not unaware that the innermost plan of speaking can be learned and grasped, confidently call me a discipline'). See Hadot 1971: 79–88.

[213] E.g. *translata uerba* 5.512; rhythmic clauses, 5.519–22; on figures, 5.523–37, with examples mainly from Cicero. Martianus' principal source on figures was Romanus Aquila, *De figuris*; Elice 2007: lxxxix–cxv.

[214] E.g. Roscius 5.441; Verres 5.449; 457; 495; 509; Catilina 5.483; 496; Caelius 5.505; Milo 5.446; 453; 455; 461; 469; Deiotarus 5.492; Antony 5.472; 486.

[215] Accepting Cameron's dating (Cameron 1986; Cameron 2011: 206–7; 263).

that the definitive edict to this effect contained an allusion to Horace and another to Virgil.[216] Forgetting is harder than remembering.

Furthermore, cultural, philosophical and religious memories were kept alive and useful by being organized. At some point during the 460s, Sidonius Apollinaris paid a visit to his friend Ferreolus at his villa near Nîmes, which housed a large library. The volumes were organized in two sections, one of works written in *stilus religiosus*, i.e. Christian texts, and the other of works 'enobled by the majesty of Latin eloquence'. But the actual division of the volumes was not quite as clear-cut, since this latter section also contained 'volumes by certain authors who wrote in the same style but about different subjects; for writers of similar erudition were being read, here Augustine and there Varro, here Horace and there Prudentius'. In this section, Sidonius also mentioned translations first of Christian and then of classical texts from Greek into Latin, citing as an example of the latter Cicero's translation of *De corona* by Demosthenes that Jerome too had read.[217] Of course, Christian imitation of pagan models is not the same thing as writing in an autonomous voice about pagan topics as Macrobius and Martianus both did. However, the passage of time produced a softening of boundary lines that is represented by the library of Ferreolus. Some twenty years after Sidonius described this library, Aurelius Memmius Symmachus and his friend Macrobius Plotinus Eudoxius, both of whom were definitely Christians, worked on the improvement of his manuscript of Macrobius' *Somnium Scipionis* in Ravenna,[218] and in 498 Securus Melior Felix, 'rhetor of the city of Rome', assisted by a student, corrected faulty manuscripts of *De nuptiis* 'with the help of Christ', *Christo adiuvante*.[219]

Aurelius Memmius Symmachus was the father-in-law of Boethius, remembered in the *Consolation of Philosophy* as a man, alluding to Cicero's

---

[216] *Codex Theodosianus* 16.10.12 (8 Nov. 392): *in nulla urbe sensu carentibus simulacris vel insontem victimam caedat vel secretiore piaculo larem igne, mero genium* (Horace c. 3.17.14 genium mero), *penates odore veneratus accendat lumina, inponat tura, serta suspendat. Quod si quispiam immolare hostiam sacrificaturus audebit aut spirantia exta consulere* (Aeneid 4.64 *spirantia consulit exta*).

[217] Sid. Apoll. *Epist.* 2.9.4: the number of codices suggested the collection of a scholar, even of the Athenaeum, or a bookseller. Rufinus translated Origen *ad verbum sententiamque* (i.e. both word by word and according to the sense! See above at notes 97 and 98) *ut nec Apuleius Phaedonem sic Platonis neque Tullius Ctesiphontem sic Demosthenis in usum regulamque Romani sermonis exscripserint*. Martianus does not mention Cicero's translations but juxtaposed Cicero and Demosthenes as Cicero had done himself in *Orat*. 104–5, cf. 133 on *De corona*; see also 6; 23–9, defending his own style against the Atticists of his day; Mart. Cap. 5.429–31.

[218] See Zetzel 1981: 217 for the subscription to *Somnium*; Cameron 2011: 420–97 on the production and criticism of pagan and Christian texts; on the subscription to *Somnium*, 235–9.

[219] Cameron 1986.

Pro Cluentio, 'wholly made of wisdom and virtue'.[220] For all his awareness of the *lacunae* in Greek learning that beset his Latin-speaking contemporaries, Boethius was also a reader and admirer of Cicero. Like Cicero,
Boethius aspired to bring Greek philosophy before readers of Latin, albeit
in very different times. Where Cicero had striven during all his active life to
defend the Republic, Boethius, living under the Ostrogothic king Theoderic,
could in about AD 520 write without further ado when discussing syllogisms and maximal propositions in his commentary on Cicero's *Topica*: 'if we want to show that a kingdom is better than a consulship, we
will say: a kingdom when it is good lasts longer than a consulship; now
everything that is good for longer is better than what lasts for a short
time; therefore a kingdom is better than a consulship'.[221] While Cicero
might not have faulted the reasoning, the sentiment in his day would
have made him pause. Even so, Boethius was well informed both about
Cicero's writings and about his life, and knew that the *Topica* was a
late work, written when 'thanks to the troubled times in the *res publica*,
so we conjecture, Cicero withdrew into private life and to the pursuit of
philosophy'.[222]

Boethius' commentary on the *Topica* displaced the earlier one by Marius Victorinus which he criticized periodically for introducing irrelevant
material[223] and for being incomplete and so detailed that it lost sight of the
overall impact of Cicero's work.[224] Not that Boethius himself did not also
have critics, but he thought poorly of their judgement and intelligence.[225]
Boethius did, however, write for his contemporaries, and for practical purposes. Apart from explaining the logical and conceptual content of Cicero's
treatise, he sometimes added historical elucidations, for example in commenting on Cicero's discussion of *gentiles*, members of the same Roman
noble family. For in Boethius' time *gentiles*, so far from being nobility,
were more likely to be pagans, as in the Vulgate, or Goths as opposed to

---

[220] Boeth. *de cons.* 2. pr.4; cf. Cic. *Clu.* 72, *qui esset totus ex fraude et mendacio factus*:
Boethius says the opposite of Symmachus: *uir totus ex sapientia uirtutibusque factus*,
noted by Chadwick 1981: 230.

[221] Boeth. *In Cic. Top.* The quotation is at *Patrologia Latina* 64, 1051D, commenting on
Cic. *Top.* 7–8. Stump 1988; Reinhardt 2003: 29–35; on the impact of Boethius on the
MSS of Cicero's *Topica*, Reinhardt 2003: 77–111. See also Leff 1983: 39.

[222] Boeth. *In Cic. Top.* 1–5, *PL* 64, 1042D.   [223] Boeth. *In Cic. Top.* 28, *PL* 64, 1098AB.

[224] Boeth. *In Cic. Top.*, *PL* 64, 1041B–D. This information was used – along with
information drawn from Martianus Capella and Cassiodorus – to reconstruct
Victorinus' lost work by Hadot 1971: 15–141. See also Chadwick 1981: 117–18, who
finds the criticisms unfair.

[225] To passages cited by Chadwick 1981: 120, add *Patrologia Latina* 64, 1063B–D,
introduction to Book 2 of the commentary, reminiscent of Jerome's attacks on his
adversaries.

Romans.[226] Boethius therefore expanded, adjusted and historicized Cicero's term, explaining that here *gentiles* were distinguished Roman families, like that of the Scipios. Slaves, or those descended from slaves in however remote a past, were not included.[227] Elsewhere, Boethius updated Cicero's legal information by referring to and quoting the post-Ciceronian jurists Gaius, Paul and Ulpian,[228] and engaged with points of law that Cicero had raised. An example is Cicero's discussion of rain water running off roof tops that had also caught the attention of Lactantius because Cicero mentioned it in *De legibus*.[229] He raised it again in the *Topica*, where Boethius – while devoting some attention to this problem – revealed, as he did elsewhere, that his overriding interest was not so much the law as conveying to his contemporaries the towering importance of Aristotle,[230] even if this meant demonstrating that Cicero was sometimes wrong.[231] It was, however, Cicero who provided the precedent for creative disagreement when he wrote in the *Tusculan Disputations* that Greek philosophy had been kept alive by controversy and that he hoped the same would happen at Rome.[232]

Whereas in the commentary on the *Topica* Cicero was ever-present in the words of his own text, when some years later Boethius, now in prison, wrote the *Consolation of Philosophy*, Cicero's presence was of a different nature, more indirect, almost silent, but he was a presence nonetheless. The *Tusculan Disputations* left traces in the *Consolation* because Boethius remembered

---

[226] Pagans: for example, Acts 21.28; Romans 15.27; 1 Corinthians 12.13; Goths rather than Romans, Cassiod. *Var.* 8.11; 8.17; barbarians in general, 2.40; 7.4.

[227] Boeth. *In Cic. Top.* 29, PL 64, 1104 AB.

[228] Boeth. *In Cic. Top.* on Gaius 1095A–C (citing Gaius *Inst.* 1.119; 113; 2.24); Paul 1075D; Ulpian 1071B.

[229] See above, n. 47. The rain-water problem should now be considered in light of Reinhardt's most helpful diagram (2003: 253).

[230] It also occurs in Cic. *Top.* 23–4; 39. On *Top.* 23, at *PL* 64, 1080D Boethius, getting away from the issue in hand, draws attention to his earlier discussion of maximal propositions; more on maximal propositions in 1081B. Commenting on *Top.* 24, where Cicero tacitly concedes that the rain-water problem may not have a legally and practically satisfactory resolution by citing, by way of conclusion, the opinion of the jurist P. Scaevola, Boethius 1082A–D continues with his interest in the types of argument relevant to this problem. Similarly for *Top.* 39, where Cicero returns to the rain-water problem, Boethius in his own right returns to his interest in *genus* and *species PL* 64, 1113A–1114C. His conclusion, 1114BC, is this: *Quod si paululum uidetur obscurius, hic si eos commentarios quos de genere, specie, differentia, proprio atque accidenti composuimus, libris quinque digestos inspexerit, nihil horum poterit incurrere quo caliget* ('If this seems a little obscure to anyone, if he were to consult the commentaries which I have written about genus, species, differentia, property and accident, in five books, nothing of what now darkens his vision will hold him back.')

[231] Chadwick 1981: 119.

[232] Boeth. *In Cic. Top.* 63–4, *PL* 64, 1152AB, quoting Cic. *Tusc.* 2,4–5. This discussion had a significant impact on the manuscript tradition of Cicero's *Topica*: Reinhardt 2003: 77–111.

Cicero's writing about the perturbations and sicknesses of the soul that had also captured the attention of Augustine and others.[233] In the *Tusculan Disputations* philosophy was a physician who treated the *aegritudo* of the soul, and at the end of the final book she achieved a cure, because Cicero had been freed – to some extent at least – from his 'most cruel sorrows', *doloribus*.[234] In the *Consolatio* Boethius followed a similar path: Philosophy was the physician who cured his *aegritudo* and his soul's disturbances.[235] These included 'eagerness for glory and for a reputation of great achievements on behalf of the *res publica*', which Cicero had considered to be most desirable.[236] But it was also Cicero who in the *Dream of Scipio* had spread before the reader a vision of the cosmos: the stars that Scipio saw from the Milky Way 'easily surpassed the size of the earth', and on earth the Roman empire was 'only a tiny section of the habitable parts, which were separated from each other by vast bodies of ocean'.[237] To bring home these points, Macrobius illustrated his commentary with a map, *descriptio*, displaying the parts of the earth, northern and southern, separated by *alveus oceani*, the 'deep of the ocean'.[238] Alluding to Macrobius' *Commentary* and also to Cicero's text of the *Somnium*,[239] Boethius' Philosophy spoke of the great geographical spaces, seas and deserts and the 'infinite spaces of eternity' in which a short human life unfolds, so as to impress on Boethius, just as Cicero's Elder Scipio had impressed on his grandson, that 'fame, even if it

---

[233] Hagendahl 1968: 331–46. *Aegritudo*, soul sickness, and the *perturbationes* afflicting the soul are treated in the middle books of the *Tusculan Disputations*. See e.g. *Tusc.* 3.5 *morbi animi*; for *aegritudo*, *perturbationes* see e.g. 3.7; 12; 74 (cure is by reflection, and 3.80 by will, since *aegritudo* is voluntary); 84 (looking for cure); 4.10 (*perturbatio*); 25 (*gloriae cupiditas*); 36 (soul sickness as intense desire for false goods); 31 (*aegritudo* is voluntary); 57–8; for the four disturbances, *libido*, *laetitia*, *metus*, *aegritudo*, see 4.11 and Verg. *Aen.* 6.733, a classic formulation: *hinc metuunt cupiuntque, dolent gaudentque* with Boeth. *de cons.* 1, metrum 7.25–8; *gaudia pelle, / pelle timorem / spemque fugato / nec dolor adsit.*

[234] Cic. *Tusc.* 3.82; also 1.46; 3.4; 3.84; 4.58.

[235] Boeth. *de cons.* 1, prosa 1.14; 1 prosa 6.9; 2,1 prosa 1.2 with a spin on Cic. *Cat.* 2.6; *de cons.* 1 prosa 6.17 with *Tusc.* 5.70.

[236] Boeth. *de cons.* 2 prosa 7.1–2, with Cic. *De imp. Cn. Pomp.* 7 (the Roman people *semper appetentes gloriae praeter ceteras gentes et auidi laudis fuistis*, as a compliment). For individuals, Cic. *Off.* 2.31–6.

[237] Cic. *Rep.* 6.16; 20.

[238] Macrob. *Somn.* 2.9.7 and 8; also 1.16 on the grandeur of the universe. For different versions of the map, see Neri 2007: 500–7.

[239] Chadwick 1981: 7–8. Boeth. *De cons.* 2, prosa 8 *aetate denique Marci Tullii sicut ipse quodam loco (de re publica 6.2) significat, nondum Caucasum montem Romanae rei publicae fama transcenderat.* For further reminiscences, allusions, quotations, see Gruber 2006. Boethius appears to have read not just the *Somnium*, but the entire *De republica*, or at any rate other parts of it. See Boeth. *de cons.* 2 prosa 7.3 with Cic. *Rep.* 1.26.

endures for a long time, is not simply small, but is as nothing when compared to endless eternity'.[240]

However, this was only the beginning of Boethius' stuggle to free himself of *aegritudo* in the face of the imprisonment that he knew would end in death. Near the end of the *Consolatio*, he raised the age-old question about free will, fate and providence. Philosophy conceded that 'the operation of human reasoning cannot approach the simplicity of divine foreknowledge'.[241] But Boethius still wanted to discuss this 'ancient complaint about providence' that Cicero had written about in *De divinatione*, because he wanted to understand how 'things that are foreknown cannot not happen', and how then there could be such a thing as 'the entire and unconditional freedom of the will' in the presence of divine foreknowledge.[242] For Boethius, Cicero's *De divinatione*, an open-ended book not designed to lead the reader to one or the other conclusion as to whether the gods know the future and communicate it to human beings,[243] had already been filtered by Augustine in the *City of God*. Augustine took Cicero in *De divinatione* and *De fato* to have 'attacked foreknowledge of the future' as being incompatible with free will. As Augustine saw it, a further issue was the subordination of free will to fate, which Cicero would not accept because in such an order of things, 'justice which assigns rewards to the good and punishment to the wicked' would be pointless. As a result – in Augustine's interpretation – Cicero had rejected the existence of divine foreknowledge, of providence and hence even of the existence of God.[244] Augustine therefore asserted, against Cicero, both free will and divine providence.[245] But for Boethius in prison, the *vetus... querela*, 'ancient complaint', looked rather different, because he wanted to know whether it was providence that had led him to prison where he would be executed.[246] Cicero's ancient complaint reappeared in the *Consolatio* because it allowed for a re-examination of the nexus between

---

[240] Boeth. *de cons.* 2 prosa 7.18.   [241] Boeth. *de cons.* 5 prosa 4.2.

[242] Boeth. *de cons.* 5 prosa 4.1 *Vetus... haec est de prouidentia querela Marcoque Tullio, cum diuinationem distribuit, uehementer agitata tibique ipsi res diu prorsus multumque quaesita. De cons.* 5 pr. 4.5 *num enim tu aliunde argumentum futurorum necessitatis trahis, nisi quod ea quae praesciuntur non euenire non possunt. De cons.* 5 pr. 4.9 *manebit ut opinor eadem uoluntatis integra et absoluta libertas.*

[243] See above, n. 143.

[244] The issue is discussed in August. *De civ. D.* 5.9–11. See here *De civ. D.* 5.9 where Augustine recapitulated Cic. *Fat.* 17.40; see Klingner 1921: 100–6. The best guide to the *Consolatio* is Chadwick 1981: 223–53.

[245] August. *De civ. D.* 5.9 quoting Psalms 61.12; *De civ. D.* 5.10 taking up from the preceding chapter Cic. *Fat.* 17.40.

[246] Chadwick 1981: 225–6 writes that the Theta on Philosophy's garment (*Cons.* 1 pr. 1.4) stood for Thanatos, death, the sentence awaiting Boethius. Gruber 2006: 69 thinks this is 'kaum beweisbar' and posits the more amiable alternative interpretation of the letters on Philosophy's garment (sc. for political and theoretical philosophy). But

fate, free will and providence, even though at the very beginning of the discussion Philosophy had already marked the *querela* as unanswerable.

Boethius was executed in AD 524. Cicero, whose destinies we are pursuing, was by this point launched on his journey through the ages. Boethius' *Consolatio* had its own literary and philosophical destiny,[247] in which Cicero had a part. The role of Cicero changed over time, and what he wrote changed, depending on who was reading, and what they were reading. Cicero in his own words was a different matter from Cicero as interpreted by someone else. Boethius read both Cicero himself, and also Augustine's interpretation of Cicero, which led Boethius to see Cicero in a new context. The divine providence that Christians including Boethius thought about was not the same as the divine providence that preoccupied Cicero in *De natura deorum*, *De divinatione* and elsewhere. Even in Boethius' day, many readers will have learnt about Cicero only in the brief notices about him in Jerome's translation of the *Chronicle* of Eusebius and similar works.[248] Others read about him in greater detail in the pagan and Christian writers in whose pages he was present, and yet others read Cicero himself. Beyond all this, Cicero also figured in the organization of knowledge. Augustine organized Christian knowledge in *De doctrina Christiana*, where Cicero, even if nameless, had a part. Macrobius organized knowledge of the Roman past in the *Saturnalia*, and Martianus Capella organized the seven liberal arts, where Cicero was Rhetorica. We thus come to two great organizations of knowledge in which Cicero played a role, the *Institutiones* of Cassiodorus and the *Etymologiae* of Isidore of Seville.

Cassiodorus survived the collapse of the Ostrogothic kingdom on behalf of which he had addressed official correspondence to Boethius and with whom he also claimed family kinship.[249] In his later years Cassiodorus, now retired from the world, wrote the *Institutiones* for the guidance of the monastic community he founded on one of his family's estates. The first book of this work covers divine letters, and the second the seven liberal arts, beginning with grammar.[250] Next came rhetoric and dialectic, for both of

Chadwick's argument, apart from being documented (*pace* Gruber), has the advantage of addressing what for Boethius was a real question with a real look at the prospect that Philosophy had come to help him see and accept (there being no other choice).

[247] Courcelle 1967.   [248] See above, n. 91.

[249] Cassiodorus writing to Boethius on behalf of Theoderic, *Var.* 1.10; 1.45; 2.40. For Cassiodorus' claim of kinship with Boethius, see the *Ordo generis Cassiodorum* also known as the *Anecdoton Holderi*, reproduced with commentary by O'Donnell 1979: 259–66. But no mention of Cassiodorus appears in the writings of Boethius.

[250] Halporn 2004: 64–79; Simon 1966. On Martianus Capella, see Cass. *Inst.* 2.2.17, discussing *ars* and *disciplina* in light of Augustine under whose name Cassiodorus also subsumes Varro and proceeds, *Felix etiam Capella operi suo De septem Disciplinis*

which Cassiodorus derived material from the anonymous *Ad Herennium* that in late antiquity was thought to have been written by Cicero,[251] and especially from Cicero's authentic work *De inventione*.[252] While referring to Cicero with the customary terminology of high praise as the 'singular light of Latin eloquence',[253] Cassiodorus thought about *De inventione* in what had by now become a very long teaching tradition that continued to focus not so much on the rhetorical works of Cicero's maturity, *Brutus*, *Orator* and *De oratore*, but on this one youthful treatise.[254] Among the post-Ciceronian rhetorical works that Cassiodorus consulted was the extensive and ponderous commentary on *De inventione* by Marius Victorinus,[255] of which he left a copy in his library for the benefit of his monks.[256] Victorinus' probable contemporary Consultus Fortunatianus, whom Cassiodorus also read, by contrast wrote his *Ars rhetorica* more invitingly as a dialogue between teacher and student, taking up topics also covered in *De inventione*, quoting from Cicero's speeches and illustrating his points with situations such as might arise in litigation. For example, in answering the

titulum dedit – this is the work otherwise kown as *De nuptiis*. At *Inst.* 2.3.20 Cassiodorus states: *audiuimus etiam Felicem Capellam aliqua de disciplinis scripsisse deflorata, ne talibus litteris fratrum simplicitas linqueretur ignara; quae tamen ad manus nostras minime peruenire potuerunt.* Cassiodorus conflated Martianus Capella's name with that of Securus Melior Felix, *rhetor urbis Romae*, who corrected his faulty manuscript of *De nuptiis* – but perhaps only of Book 1 – see Cameron 2011: 481. If then, Cassiodorus had a copy of Book 1, and not the rest (taking this to be the drift of *minime*), Martianus' treatment of rhetoric (in his Book 5) and dialectic (in his Book 4) in *De nuptiis* was not available to him. In August. *De Ordine* 2.38 the order of the disciplines is grammar, dialectic, rhetoric – where Varro was the source. See also Cassiod. *Inst.* 2.3.2 with quotation from Varro's *Disciplinarum libri*, which, even so, Cassiodorus is most unlikely to have read.

[251] Jer. *Contra Rufinum* 1.16 (*Patrologia Latina* 23, col. 428 AB): *lege Ad Herennium Tullii libros, lege Rhetoricos eius: aut, quia illa sibi dicit inchoata et rudia excidisse de manibus, reuolue tria uolumina De oratore, in quibus introducit eloquentissimos illius temporis oratores, Crassum et Antonium disputantes, et quartum Oratorem, quem iam senex scribit ad Brutum. tunc intelliges aliter componi historiam, aliter orationes, aliter dialogos, aliter epistolas, aliter commentarios.* The *Rhetorici libri* are of course *De inventione*.

[252] For specifics on Cassiodorus' use of *De inventione*, Mynors 1961; see also Halporn 2004 on 2.2.9–12; 15.

[253] Cass. *Inst.* 2.3.10 *Latinae eloquentiae lumen eximium*; cf. *Inst.* 2, preface 92, *ut Poeta dictus intelligitur apud Graecos Homerus, apud Latinos Vergilius, Orator enuntiatus apud Graecos Demosthenes, apud Latinos Cicero declaratur.* Demosthenes and Cicero were juxtaposed elsewhere (note Plutarch's *Comparison* of the two, concluding with a comparison critical of Cicero), e.g. Mart. Cap. 5.429–31.

[254] Cf. above at notes 64–6.

[255] Halm 1863: viii describes Marius Victorinus as *scriptor taedii plenus*. Hadot 1971: 73–102 takes a more generous view.

[256] Cass. *Inst.* 2.3.10; also 2.3.14 where Cassiodorus refers to Victorinus' lost work on syllogisms, on which see Hadot 1971: 157–61.

question as to whether it was always appropriate to use 'grand and splendid words', the student was to answer no, because some situations were more convicingly described in simple terms, as when Cicero made all the greater an impression on his listeners by reciting some among the crimes of Verres concisely and straightforwardly. Similarly, however dignified it might sound to quote the *Twelve Tables* or the Salian hymn, it was unlikely to be useful because the vocabulary was obsolete and would not be understood – a telling indication of linguistic change in late antiquity, that helps to explain the need of that time for repeatedly summarizing and excerpting Cicero's writings.[257] Fortunatianus recurs frequently in the *Institutiones*, his statements intermingled with antecedents from *De inventione* and sometimes from *Ad Herennium*. What appealed to Cassiodorus was Fortunatianus' brevity and *acutissima ratiocinatio*, 'clearsighted reasoning', this being why he made arrangements for a copy of the *Ars rhetorica* – a compact, useful little book unlikely to bore the reader – to be produced for the monastic library.[258] As for *De inventione*, it was to be paired in a more weighty and grand codex with the *Institutes* of Quintilian, the 'outstanding teacher who after the rivers of Cicero's eloquence was able to complement his achievement: for, by undertaking the formation of the virtuous and eloquent man from infancy, he demonstrated that such a person must be instructed in all the noble arts and disciplines of letters'.[259] In short, the writings of Cicero could not be left on their own, but their proper understanding and dissemination required teachers and manuals, among them Cassiodorus' *Institutiones*.

The *Institutiones* are a book of long memories, both Roman and Christian. On the Roman side, for example, the reader was to remember not just Cicero and his exegetes, but formative moments in Roman history and warfare such as Cicero had mentioned in *De inventione* when discussing different types of question with which an orator might have to engage. A simple coherent case was, 'shall we declare war on the Corinthians or not?' A complex one was made up of several questions simultaneously, such as 'should Carthage be destroyed, or should it be returned to the Carthaginians, or should a colony be settled there?' Finally, an orator might have to discuss a case involving comparison, for example 'whether the army should be sent to Macedonia against Philip, to help our allies, or should it be kept in Italy, so as to fight Hannibal with the greatest possible force?'[260] By contrast, in the first part of the *Institutiones* that dealt with Christian literature, the reader found an entirely different kind of history, taken from Scripture and involving

---

[257] Fortunatianus, *Ars rhetorica* 3.5; 3.6.   [258] Cass. *Inst.* 2.3.10.
[259] Cass. *Inst.* 2.3.10. Free translation with help from Halporn 2004.
[260] Cic. *Inv. rhet.* 1.17 quoted in full by Cass. *Inst.* 2.3.7.

different questions that had been expounded among others by Augustine: for example, there was the question as to the meaning of the passage from the First Book of Kings, 'and an evil spirit from the Lord assailed Saul'. Another question from the same book was the meaning of God's words, 'it repenteth me that I have made Saul king', and a third was whether the impure spirit that possessed the witch of Endor was able to make the dead prophet Samuel visible to King Saul so that the two could converse.[261] Here the aim was not to learn public speaking from Cicero, but to learn the discursive contemplation of the eloquence of God, *diuinum eloquium*, in Scripture.[262]

These two worlds, still considered as potentially contrary to each other or simply separate by Augustine when writing *De doctrina Christiana*, were joined for Cassiodorus when commenting on the Psalms. For this commentary, Cassiodorus developed a system of signs to be written in the margins of his text that indicated for the reader the different modes of expression, and the different liberal arts, among them rhetoric, that were relevant to particular statements.[263] When thus commenting on Psalm 118, 'I hated the unrighteous and loved your law', Cassiodorus commented *inter alia*, 'we should know that the argument in this verse is the one described in the *Topica* as "from the opposite", *ex contrario*, when from different topics we conclude our statement with a single resolution'. The argument *ex contrario* does appear in Cicero's *Topica*. Boethius added an extensive commentary on different aspects of this argument, making of the *Topica* a multi-layered text that could be read, like *De inventione* and *Ad Herennium*, in the light both of Cicero's own words and of those of his commentators.[264]

---

[261] Cassiod. *Inst.* 1.2.3.

[262] For *diuinum eloquium*, an expression also used by Augustine, see e.g. Cassiod. *Expositio Psalmorum* (CCSL 97 p. 482), on the conclusion of Psalms 52. The use of colour in this passage might be compared to the panegyric by Cassiodorus on the marriage of Witigis and Mathasuntha, in Mommsen 1894: 481. See also Astell 1999: 63.

[263] A list of these signs is provided in Cassiod. *Expositio Psalmorum* (CCSL 97 p. 2).

[264] Cassiod. *Expositio Psalmorum* on Psalm 118.113 *iniquos odio habui et legem tuam dilexi* (CCSL 98, p. 1108). The reference is to Cic. *Top.* 11. Boethius, *In Topica Ciceronis* 11 (PL 64.1063–4) comments: *ducuntur etiam argumenta ex his rebus quae quodammodo affectae sunt ad id de quo quaeritur. sed hoc genus in plures partes distributum est. nam alia conjugata appellamus, alia ex genere, alia ex forma, alia ex similitudine, alia ex differentia, alia ex contrario, alia ex conjunctis, alia ex antecedentibus, alia ex consequentibus, alia ex repugnantibus, alia ex causis, alia ex effectis, alia ex comparatione maiorum, aut parium aut minorum.* At 1064D, Boethius observes that Cicero divides this *locus inter alia ex contrario.* 1065B *minora majoribus minora sunt, et contraria contrariis contraria, et repugnantia repugnantibus repugnantia sunt.* 1066C after saying that *inimicitia* follows from war, not vice versa, Boethius writes: *repugnantia uero intelliguntur quoties id quod alicui contrariorum*

This multi-layered quality that came to characterize Cicero's texts described a different cultural world from the one where Jerome had experienced his crisis of conscience about being a Ciceronian, or the one where Augustine insisted that he would no longer instruct anyone in the rhetoric that he had learned and taught in the secular schools.[265] In the sixth century classical texts, even if they had earlier constituted a certain patrimony for pagans, no longer did so.[266] What Cassiodorus perceived and quoted in the pages of Cicero was not the same as what Ambrose, Jerome and Augustine had perceived and quoted, even when they read the same texts. Above all, in the fourth and early fifth centuries Cicero was most often read – especially by Christians – for his content, whereas later, interest focused mostly on grammatical points and rhetorical strategies arising from his writings.[267] This is why Cassiodorus was able to instruct his community of monks in both divine and secular letters and to establish a library for them that covered both these fields of knowledge – Cicero's ideas about the state and the statesman, about the gods and fate were not considered or even mentioned.[268]

The same applies to Isidore of Seville who in the early seventh century included the liberal arts in his encyclopaedia, the *Etymologiae*.[269] As in Cassiodorus' *Institutiones*, rhetoric came second after grammar, with dialectic third; moreover, the *Institutiones* provided the bulk of the text for the section on rhetoric and they appear repeatedly in the sections on grammar and dialectic. In rhetoric and dialectic, Cicero is the most frequently quoted author, followed closely by Virgil. Discussing the 'discipline of finding arguments', Isidore took this definition from Cicero's *Topica* or an intermediary,

---

naturaliter iunctum est, reliquo contrario comparatur, ut quoniam amicitiae atque inimicitiae contraria sunt. inimicitias uero consequitur nocendi uoluntas, amicitia et nocendi uoluntas repugnantia sunt, haec quoque ad se contrarietatis similitudine referuntur. The same passage from *Top.* is adduced at Psalm 33.11 (*CCSL* 97, p. 298). Cf. above n. 235 on 'Boethian errors'.

[265] See above, notes 87–8 and 167.

[266] Hence, to ask whether Boethius' *Consolation of Philosophy* is after all a pagan text does not make for a useful enquiry, even if, as Procopius records, during the Ostrogothic siege of Rome, the Sibylline Oracles were consulted, and some Romans tried to open the doors of the Temple of Janus. Procop. *Goth.* 5.24.28–37; 5.25.18–19.

[267] Cassiod. *Inst.* 2.3.13 cites from *Pro Milone* (but perhaps via Quintilian), the *Second Philippic*, and the *First Catilinarian* speech, all of which were known to Jerome and Augustine.

[268] But the distinction of divine and secular texts lived on. Thus, in the late seventh century, the grammarian Vergilius Maro (who knew the name of Cicero and quoted him, but not from direct access to Ciceronian texts) still recommended it, see Holtz 1992: 53–4, quoting Vergilius Maro, *Epistolae* 3, *ut Christianorum libri filosophorum repositi a gentilium scriptis haberentur.*

[269] Fontaine 1983: 211–337 on Isidore's rhetoric; see also, in less technical terms, Fontaine 2000: 167–182.

and then turned to Cassiodorus[270] who produced a wealth of examples from Cicero's speeches and from the *Aeneid*, all of which Isidore copied.[271] But Isidore also added Virgil where he was absent in Cassiodorus, for example in his discussion of figures of speech.[272] Similarly, where Cassiodorus, replicating Fortunatianus, mentioned the three *genera causarum*, Isidore followed suit, but was most interested in the *genus demonstrativum*, which, adapting Cicero's definition in *De inventione*, he described as representing the nature of a thing 'by praising or censuring' it.[273] That said, he illustrated this mode of speaking at length from Virgil, with not a word from or about Cicero.[274]

Things had changed since the time when Macrobius juxtaposed Cicero and Virgil but saw them as distinct. In Roman schools, poetry was taught to younger students primarily by grammarians, and prose to older ones primarily by rhetors. This factor alone helped to maintain grammar and rhetoric as separate disciplines, each dedicated to the study of its own group of texts, although on occasion, grammarians rose socially and professionally by being appointed to the higher position of rhetor.[275] In any case, the boundaries between the two disciplines were porous, and they could not be separated absolutely. The grammarian Servius included a plethora of quotations from Cicero in his commentary on Virgil, and, even in a quite technical sense, the two disciplines of grammar and rhetoric interpenetrated each other. Take figures of speech and thought, *figurae uerborum et sententiarum*, which Cassiodorus discussed as part of grammar while noting their relevance for both grammar and rhetoric.[276] Isidore discussed

---

[270] Cassiodorus and Isidore both place *topica* 'commonplaces' under the heading of dialectic. Rhetoric and dialectic were seen as closely related, see Cassiod. *Expositio Psalmorum*, Psalms 72.17 (*CCSL* 94 p. 666); Cassiod. *Inst.* 2.3.2 (quoting Varro); repeated by Isid. *Etym.* 2.23.1.

[271] Cassiod. *Inst.* 2.3.15 and Isid. *Etym.* 2.2.30.

[272] Isid. *Etym.* 1.36 (under the heading of grammar) *de schematibus ... figurae que fiunt in uerbis uel sententiis per uarias dictionum formas propter eloquii ornamentum.* Here, the examples are from Virgil only. *Etym.* 2.21 (under the heading of rhetoric). Here, the examples are from orators, primarily Cicero, followed by many from Virgil.

[273] Isid. *Etym.* 2.4.5; cf. Cic. *Inv. rhet.* 1.7.

[274] Cassiod. *Inst.* 2.3 derived from Fortunatianus 1.1, providing no examples; Isid. *Etym.* 2.4 with examples from the *Aeneid*. Marius Victorinus, *In Rhetoricam ... Ciceronis* (above n. 66) already used illustrations from Virgil and a few from other poets, but sparingly (for Halm 1863: 217; 218; 224; 228; 239; 249; 302); Grillius, *Commentum* (above n. 67) did it very frequently.

[275] On the career of Ausonius, one of the few to be promoted from grammarian to rhetor, see Booth 1982; further, Kaster 1988: 104–5; 456–8; 461–2; note p. 163, on the views about grammar and rhetoric of the African grammarian Pompeius (Pompeius, *Commentum Artis Donati* in Keil 1855–80: vol. v, 281; 282; 299–304 on figures of thought and speech).

[276] Cassiod. *Inst.* 2.1.2.

figures as part of both grammar and rhetoric.[277] This was not a question of Isidore being confused or disorganized. Rather, even Cicero in the *Topica* had described these figures or ornaments as 'rather undefined'.[278] The grammarian Donatus, whose primary interest was the teaching of Latin literature, resolved the question by assigning figures of speech to the field of grammar and figures of thought to that of rhetoric[279] – a distinction Isidore adopted in name only, because he did not differentiate the two kinds of figure.

Insofar as Cassiodorus and Isidore reflect the state of grammatical and rhetorical instruction in Italy during the later sixth century, and in Spain during the early seventh, the grammarians and rhetors who had been paid by the Roman state to teach their subjects were now a thing of the past. But in thinking about rhetoric and figures of speech and thought, Isidore still bore in mind an orator pleading in court, as Cicero had done: 'An oration is enhanced and dignified by figures of speech and of thought. For since ongoing and continuous delivery produces fatigue and boredom in both the speaker and the listener, an oration should be diversified and varied in form, so as to refresh the speaker by its adornments, and to entertain the judge by changing facial and verbal expressions.'[280] Some centuries earlier, Romanus Aquila would have agreed.[281] But he could not have imagined the context that Isidore devised for Cicero's use of antithesis in the *Second Catilinarian Oration*: 'Antitheta are called *contraposita* in Latin. When balanced, they create beauty of thought, and a most becoming adornment of speech, as in Cicero's *Second Catilinarian Oration*: "on one side fights decency, on the other impudence; chastity on this side, disgrace on the other; here faith, there deceit, here loyalty, there crime"', until finally the *contraposita* culminated in a battle of the virtues and vices: 'here justice, temperance, courage, prudence and all the virtues fight against iniquity, excess, cowardice, rashness and all the vices'. And therefore, what more could be said about *antitheta*? Something could be said: 'in this kind of battle or contest, the book *Ecclesiasticus* employed a similar ornament of speech, saying: "Good is the opposite of evil, and life the opposite of death; so the sinner is the opposite of the godly. Look upon all the works of the Most High, they likewise are in pairs, one the opposite of the other."'[282]

---

[277] Isid. *Etym.* 1.36.1; 2.21.

[278] Cic. *Top.* 34. Further, Quint. *Inst.* 1.8.16; 9.1–2. Quintilian's discussion of genus and species (at 9.1.10–21) is taken up by Boeth. *In Ciceronis Topica* 34, PL 64 col. 1110.

[279] Donat. *Ars Maior* 3.5 in Holtz 1981: 663.

[280] Isid. *Etym.* 2.21.1.   [281] See above, n. 60.

[282] Isid. *Etym.* 2.21.5 quoting Cic. *Cat.* 2.25 and Ecclesiasticus 33.14 (15) where I use the translation of the *New Oxford Annotated Bible*.

Organizing knowledge within the framework of the liberal arts and jux-
taposing these with *divinae lectiones* as Cassiodorus did, and in the larger
framework of the encyclopaedic *Etymologiae* of Isidore, was part and parcel
of communicating this knowledge to future generations.[283] In the preface
to the *Institutiones*, Cassiodorus mentioned the Christian school that with
the support of Pope Agapetus he had hoped to found in Rome. The plan
came to naught when Justinian's armies invaded Italy, 'because the work
of peace has no place in unquiet times'. Years later, returning to his old
idea, but now for the sake of his monastic community, he wrote the *Institutiones* 'to take the place of a teacher'.[284] The monks would be occupied
not in the noisy exercises of the classroom during which so many Romans
had first encountered Cicero,[285] but in quietly reading the scriptural, Christian and secular authors whose writings Cassiodorus arranged to be copied
in codices for the monastic library.[286] Isidore also thought about libraries.
He listed some of the great libraries of the ancient world in the *Etymologiae*, and for a library in his own Seville he wrote verses to identify the
author portraits that adorned the walls. Cicero was not among those mostly
Christian authors, and was nowhere mentioned by name.[287] But the *Theodosian Code*, the base text for the Visigothic *Code of Alaric*, is cited along
with the jurists Paul and Gaius: 'Here is placed the splendid succession
of legal precepts, which govern the Latin lawcourts by truthful speech' –
where Cicero's judicial and political speeches that Isidore quoted in the
section on rhetoric in the *Etymologiae* might have come to the reader's
mind.[288]

---

[283] Fontaine 1988.   [284] Cassiod. *Inst.* Praefatio 1; O'Donnell 1979: 179–85.

[285] Quint. *Inst.* 2.2.12. Cf. *Theodosian Code* 14.9.1 (AD 370) regulating student life in
Rome.

[286] Note Cassiod. *Inst.* 1.15, his instructions for copyists of MSS primarily, in this context,
of Scripture. I thank my colleague Thomas Noble for drawing my attention to
Troncarelli 1998; Radiciotti 1999: 369–70 on writing (as distinct from dictating to a
scribe) as physical as distinct from mental labour and compare Isidore, *Versus in
bibliotheca* (PL 83) xxv, *titulum scriptorii: qui calamo certare nouit cum mortua pelle /
si placet huc ueniat hic sua bella gerat.*

[287] Isid. *Etym.* 6.3. Fontaine 2000: 735–62; 745–6 on Cicero.

[288] Isid. *Versus in bibliotheca*, 15 Teudosius Paulus Gaius. *Conditur hic iuris series
amplissima legum / ueridico Latium quae regit ore forum.* Note Isidore's reluctant
concession to advocates in *Sententiae* (CCSL 111) 3.60.56.1, *de causidicis: negotium
forensium sectatores propter proximi dilectionem saeculare negotium deserere debent,
aut certe, manente proximi caritate, negotium sequantur terrenum. sed quia perrarum
est ut inter iurgantes caritas maneat, postponenda est rei causatio, ut perseueret
dilectio.* See also Isid. *Sententiae* 3.13 *de libris gentilium.* Visigothic literary culture was
primarily Christian and the transmission of Roman texts other than legal ones was very
slender, see Collins 1990: 114–22. When in the early ninth century, the Cordoban

The Cicero whose writings attracted the attention of Cassiodorus and Isidore was a very different person from the Cicero encountered earlier by Augustine and Macrobius, and even, nearly a century later, by Boethius, the early contemporary of Cassiodorus.[289] Minucius Felix, Arnobius, Lactantius and Augustine all read *De natura deorum*, and Augustine also read *De divinatione* and *De fato*.[290] But these dialogues were of much less interest after Christianity could be taken for granted – and again it was Roman institutions that had provided them with their *raison d'être*. Cicero's interest in questions of personal conduct, by contrast, met a different reception. The *Tusculan Disputations* in particular, and also *De officiis*, *De amicitia* and *De senectute* retained a certain relevance that is reflected in more ample manuscript traditions. The same was true of the rhetorical works, especially of *De inventione*, while the speeches, most of all the *Verrine* and *Catilinarian Orations* and *Pro Milone*, filled as they are with the vagaries of human conduct, continued to attract interest, if somewhat selectively – for many of Cicero's speeches have not survived. However, someone in late antiquity complemented the corpus of the speeches that Cicero delivered after his return from exile with a speech titled *Pridie quam in exilium iret*,[291] thereby demonstrating some familiarity with his eventful life, but little appreciation of his eloquence or ability to imitate it successfully.

The history of the text of Cicero's *De republica* – a great success in its day[292] and one of his most important works – is indicative of the profound change in the appreciation of Cicero that occurred in the course of the fifth century. The only extant manuscript of *De republica* is a palimpsest. The original script is a beautiful Italian uncial of the fourth or fifth century, with colophons in rustic capitals. In the seventh century this manuscript was in the library of the monastery of Bobbio and had already lost some of its leaves. There, having been disassembled and the script washed off, the leaves were

---

layman Alvar referred to Cicero, it was at second hand, see his letters 4.19; 5.4; 6.8 and letter to Eulogius, all in Gil 1973: at 174 (citing Jer. *Ep*. 22,29 which he did read), 190, 200, 365 respectively. Contrast another layman, Einhard, below at n. 298.

[289] See Reynolds 1983: 54–142, a survey of the manuscript tradition for all of Cicero's extant works.

[290] But note Cameron 2011: 614: in his critique of polytheism in *De civitate dei*, Augustine used Varro much more than Cicero's *De natura deorum*.

[291] Reynolds 1983: 57–9. The text of *Pridie quam in exilium iret* is included as spurious in Orelli 1826–38; Gamberale 1998 describes the oration as a school *declamatio*. I have not been able to consult Marco 1991.

[292] Cic. *Fam*. 8.1.4, Caelius to Cicero in Cilicia: *tui politici libri omnibus uigent* – referring to *De republica* (and also *De legibus*?). See further Zetzel in this volume (Chapter 11).

combined with leaves from elsewhere, and a new codex was produced, containing Augustine's *Enarrationes in Psalmos*, marked as 'the book of Saint Columbanus in Bobbio'.[293] The fragments of text from this manuscript, when added to further fragments culled from Lactantius and Augustine and to numerous snippets quoted by grammarians and rhetors, make up rather less than one-third of the whole, and the rest is lost. The *Somnium Scipionis* which concludes the sixth book was transmitted autonomously in numerous manuscripts because it was appended to the commentary by Macrobius.[294] Cicero's *De legibus*, the companion volume to *De republica*, lost at least two books in the course of transmission. Like *De republica*, it was of interest to Lactantius and Augustine, and in the *Saturnalia* Macrobius quoted a sentence that he attributed to Book 5; silence thereafter, until the ninth century.[295] This textual history reflects Cicero's authorial intentions. He wrote both books out of love of the *res publica* and concern for its future, a love and concern that even the aged Augustus who in his youth had been complicit in Cicero's death recognized and admired.[296] Cicero's devotion to the *res publica* was still alive for his readers in the fifth century, but not after the fall of the Western empire.[297] While at that point Cicero the statesman and political thinker vanished into oblivion, Cicero the 'celebrated orator' and philosopher lived on, and not only because his edgy advice to writers of Latin in the *Tusculan Disputations* was still meaningful to Einhard when composing the introduction to his biography of Charlemagne: 'To commit one's thoughts to writing without being able to arrange and express them clearly or to attract the reader by some kind of charm amounts to serious abuse of one's leisure hours and also of writing itself.'[298]

---

[293] Lowe 1934 number 34, the *Enarrationes in Psalmos*, 'Liber Scti Columbani de Bobio'; these are the same leaves as number 35, the fragments of *De republica*. A similar story is told by numbers 26a, 26b and 26c, canons of the First Council of Chalcedon; numbers 27–31 are the original components of these same pages, i.e. twenty-seven letters of Fronto; twenty-eight *Scholia Bobiensia in Ciceronem* (cf. above n. 58); twenty-nine fragments of the orations of Symmachus and of Pliny's *Panegyricus*; thirty fragments of the satires of Juvenal and Persius; the only Christian component of this codex is number 31, *Tractatus Arianorum* and *Ascensio Isaiae*, both of dubious orthodoxy: Seider 1979.

[294] See Powell 2006, which does not however supersede Ziegler 1958 for a description of the MS. See also Heck 1966.

[295] Macrob. *Sat.* 6.4.8; Dyck 2004a: 30–4; 40–2.   [296] Plut. *Cic.* 49.5.

[297] For a Greek reader of the early sixth century of Cicero's *De republica*, see Fotiou 1984. In the West, a world without Rome, see Hillgarth 2009: 21–56.

[298] Halphen 1967: preface, quoting Cic. *Tusc.* 1.6.

Further reading

There is no single modern treatment of this topic, though Zieliński 1929 remains a valuable starting-point. Klotz 1911 (on the *Panegyrici Latini*), Hagendahl 1958 (on Jerome), and Eskridge 1912, Testard 1958a and Dodaro 2004 (on Augustine) treat the reception of Cicero in particular authors and genres. Cameron 2011 is major reassessment of the culture of pagan late antiquity.

16

DAVID MARSH

Cicero in the Renaissance

Cicero and Petrarch

Francesco Petrarca (1304–74), who is often called the father of human-ism, devoted most of his life to the study of Latin literature and confessed particular devotion to Cicero from his earliest years:

> From early childhood, when everyone else was poring over Prosper or Aesop, I brooded over Cicero's books, whether through natural instinct or the urgings of my father, a great admirer of that author.[1]

Besides assembling the most complete text of Livy available, he made two notable discoveries of texts by Cicero. In 1333, while travelling in Liège, he found a text of Cicero's oration *Pro Archia*, the defence of a Greek poet that he later cited on the occasion of his poetic coronation in 1341.[2] He also cites the work in his invective *Contra medicum* 27, in order to assert the superiority of poets over physicians. In his list of favourite books, probably written in 1333, Petrarch includes some dozen Ciceronian works.[3]

Then, in 1345, Petrarch visited the cathedral chapter library in Verona, where he found a codex containing Cicero's letters *Ad Atticum*, *Ad Quintum*

---

[1] Petrarch 1992: vol. II, 600. The original Latin of *Seniles* 16.1 is cited in Rüegg 1946: 8–10: '*Siquidem ab ipsa pueritia, quando ceteri omnes, aut Prospero inhiant, aut Esopo, ego libris Ciceronis incubui, seu nature instinctu, seu parentis hortatu, qui auctoris illius venerator ingens fuit.*' Prosper of Aquitaine (379–455) was a follower of Augustine and a historian whose epigrams were used as an elementary Latin text.

[2] See Godi 1970 and Gensini 1980.

[3] For the date, see Ullman 1923: 21–38; and cf. Schmitt 1988: 779: 'Petrarch could include in his list of favourite books – written while he was still young – *Republic* VI, the *Tusculans*, *De natura deorum*, *Paradoxa*, *De inventione*, *De oratore* (not complete) and speeches rare and common, as well as the spurious *Rhetorica ad Herennium*.' For Petrarch's use of Cicero, see Nolhac 1907: vol. I, 213–68; Hinds 2004; Auhagen et al. 2005.

fratrem and *Ad Brutum*, of which he made a copy.[4] Learning how Cicero had thrown himself into the political fray precipitated by Caesar, Petrarch reproved the idealist with having abandoned his philosophical detachment.[5] In a Latin epistle to the Roman orator (*Fam.* 24.3), he cited the words of Brutus, who in a letter reproached him for his friendship with Octavian. Some months later, after Petrarch had recovered from his initial shock, he wrote a second letter (*Fam.* 24.4) praising Cicero's genius – which had made possible his own literary achievements – while censuring his character.[6] A generation later, Petrarch's first letter inspired responses from two men of letters in Padua: the prelate Francesco Zabarella (1360–1417) and the humanist Pierpaolo Vergerio (1370–1444). In 1394, at Padua Vergerio wrote a letter in Cicero's name, in which he insisted that the orator-citizen is obliged to take part in politics.[7] And in a letter of 1396, he wrote that Cicero surpasses all orators and poets in eloquence, although in his 1402 educational treatise *De ingenuis moribus* he only names the orator once in a citation.[8]

Petrarch's Christian view of Cicero is evident in his personal manifesto *De sui ipsius et multorum aliorum ignorantia* 56–84, in which he discusses at length the religious beliefs espoused in Cicero's *De natura deorum*.[9] Although he praises the Roman's sagacity in perceiving the divine order of the universe, Cicero's endorsement of polytheism draws vehement condemnation. Nevertheless, Petrarch admired and imitated one Ciceronian text dear to the Middle Ages – the *Somnium Scipionis* (*Dream of Scipio*) from Book 6 of *De republica*. Cicero's description of a prophetic dream inspired the lengthy dream of Scipio in the first two books of Petrarch's epic *Africa*. And like Dante before him, Petrarch echoed Cicero's heavenly view of the earth and its climatic zones in his *Africa*, *Secretum* and *De remediis utriusque fortune*.[10]

Further discoveries and editions

Beginning in the 1390s, Antonio Loschi (1365–1441) produced a series of Latin commentaries on eleven of Cicero's orations. In 1392, the corpus of Cicero's correspondence was nearly doubled when the Milanese chancellor Pasquino de' Capelli discovered a codex of Cicero's *Familiares* in the

---

[4] The Veronese codex does not survive, but the 1392 Milan copy made for Coluccio Salutati and later emended by Salutati, Niccoli, and Bruni is Mediceus 49.18: Reynolds 1983: 136–7.

[5] Witt 2000: 279–80.   [6] On these letters, see Hinds 2004.

[7] McManamon 1996: 52–9; cf. Schmitt 1988: 420; Witt 2000: 384–6.

[8] Kallendorf 2002: 45: 'as Cicero says, What a happy family books make!' The quotation is from Cic. *Fam.* 9.1. On this passage, cf. Witt 2000: 375–7.

[9] Cf. Petrarca 2003: 274–309; cf. Witt 2000: 258–9.   [10] Marsh 2009: 215–17.

chapter library of Vercelli, and sent a copy to his friend Coluccio Salutati, the chancellor of Florence.[11] Salutati also possessed a codex of the letters *Ad Atticum* (Mediceus 49.18) These more formal letters soon inspired the schoolteacher Gasparino Barzizza (*c.* 1360–1431), who lectured on Cicero at Padua and Milan, to compile a *Liber epistolarum*, which became the first book published in France (Paris: Johann Heylin, 1470). Barzizza, whose pupils in Padua included Leon Battista Alberti and Francesco Filelfo, lectured annually on Cicero's *De oratore*, and his treatise *On Imitation* (1413–17) recommends Cicero as the principal prose model for imitation.[12]

Meanwhile, Poggio Bracciolini, a papal secretary attending the Council of Constance (1414–18) was combing Swiss monasteries for lost classical works. In addition to unearthing texts by Columella, Lucretius, Manilius, Quintilian, Statius and Valerius Flaccus, he found ten of Cicero's orations as well as the commentary of Asconius Pedianus. Shortly thereafter, in 1421 Gherardo Landriani found Cicero's three principal works on rhetoric – *Brutus, Orator* and *De oratore* – in the cathedral library at Lodi.

As the enthusiasm for humanistic studies spread in the early Quattrocento, teachers steered their students towards Cicero. In his treatise *The Study of Literature* (*c.* 1424), Leonardo Bruni (1370–1444) even commends the Roman orator to women with a taste for secular letters.[13] Exemplary new schools, such as those opened by Guarino of Verona in Ferrara and Vittorino da Feltre in Mantua, made Cicero a cornerstone of the Latin curriculum. Educational theory did not lag behind, and fifteenth-century treatises often celebrate the orator as the master of Roman prose. In his *De ordine docendi et studendi* (*Programme of Teaching and Learning*) of 1459, Battista Guarino (the son of the famed educator) recommends Cicero as a supreme model of Latin style, commending his epistles for their elegance, his rhetorical works for their system and his other books for their moral philosophy.[14]

The first books printed in Italy included Cicero's *De oratore*, *De officiis* and *Paradoxa Stoicorum*, all printed at Subiaco in 1465 by Sweynheym and Pannartz, who also printed Donatus and Lactantius in that year. We have some 300 incunabula of Cicero, including 64 editions of *De officiis*, 65 of *De senectute* and *De amicitia*, and 69 of *Paradoxa Stoicorum*.[15] The selection

[11] The MSS survive in the Laurentian Library as Mediceus 49.9 and 49.7: see Reynolds 1983: 138–9; Witt 2000: 320–1.

[12] Mercer 1979; Witt 2000: 462–5.

[13] Kallendorf 2002: 99: 'A woman, on the other hand, who enjoys secular literature will choose Cicero, a man – Good God! – so eloquent! So rich in expression! So polished! So unique in every kind of excellence!'

[14] Kallendorf 2002: 285, 291.   [15] Hankins and Palmer 2008: 42.

indicates that Quattrocento readers were primarily interested in Cicero's discussion of rhetoric and in his popularizing of moral philosophy.[16]

Cicero and the humanities

Cicero's greatest dialogue, *De oratore*, concerned his own profession, that of public speaker and advocate. Besides his exposition of the outlines of classical rhetoric, Cicero's work paints an idealized picture of the Roman nobility and their largely Greek culture. Ever since the development of rhetoric by Greek sophists, dissension arose between theorists who regarded argument as a mere arsenal of persuasive tricks and those who insisted on the orator's true competence in many fields. Siding with the latter, Cicero promotes the notion of what the Renaissance humanists would call the 'universal man', so that the theorist of painting Leon Battista Alberti would insist, in Book 3 of his *De pictura* (1436), on a culture of learning for artists as well as for scholars.

For those seeking a portrait of Cicero the man, the Greek biographer Plutarch was a welcome source of information. His *Vita Ciceronis* was translated twice in the early Quattrocento: by Iacopo Angeli in 1401, and by Leonardo Bruni in 1412, who paired it with the *Vita Demosthenis*.[17] Dissatisfied with Plutarch's treatment, Bruni composed his own biography the following year, which he titled *Cicero Novus sive Ciceronis Vita* (*The New Cicero or Cicero's Life*).[18] In his preface to Niccolò Niccoli, he calls Cicero 'the parent and prince of our literature' (*parens et princeps litterarum nostrarum*), and in discussing Cicero's translations from Greek he notes that the loss of the Roman's versions of Demosthenes and Aeschines moved him to compose his own.[19]

Cicero the rhetorician

During the Middle Ages, the Carolingian Renaissance and the subsequent rise of *ars dictaminis* caused Cicero to be valued above all for his writings on rhetoric. As Zieliński noted, while many other important Ciceronian texts perished, the rhetorical corpus (including the anonymous *Rhetorica ad Herennium*) survived whole.[20] In the legal and notarial culture of late medieval Italy, Cicero gains even more prominence. Dante's teacher Brunetto Latini translated part of the *De inventione* with the title *Rettorica* (1260), and a few years later also made Tuscan versions of the 'Caesarian' orations

[16] Schmitt 1988: 769 n. 17.   [17] Giustiniani 1961: 38.   [18] Bruni 1996: 411–99.
[19] Bruni 1996: 418, 472.   [20] Zieliński 1912: 131.

Pro Ligario, Pro rege Deiotaro and *Pro Marcello*.[21] Cicero's oration *Pro Ligario* enjoyed special popularity, perhaps because of Plutarch's glowing account of its success before Caesar (*Cic.* 39).[22] Latini's translation was followed by the commentaries of Antonio Loschi (1395), George of Trebizond (1438–40) and Giorgio Merula (1478).[23] The Byzantine scholar George of Trebizond (1395–1472) also composed an influential *Rhetoric* (1433–34) that drew heavily on Ciceronian concepts.[24] In his 1459 *Program of Teaching and Learning*, Battista Guarino recommended as the best introduction to rhetoric the treatise *Ad Herennium*, which was thought at the time to be a work of Cicero.[25]

As printing diffused the culture of humanism, Cicero the rhetorician became ever more prominent. A recent bibliography lists over 300 editions and commentaries on Cicero's rhetorical works published between 1460 and 1700.[26] And in the second half of the sixteenth century, Jesuit educators made Cicero the paramount model of oratory. Here are the recommendations for the teacher of humanities as outlined in the Jesuit *Ratio studiorum (Plan of Study)* of 1599:

> For the knowledge of the language, which consists especially in propriety and abundance of expression, the daily lessons should be devoted to teaching Cicero alone of the orators, usually through those books that contain his moral philosophy; Caesar, Sallust, Livy, Curtius, from the historians, and any others like these; from the poets, especially Vergil, setting aside the Eclogues and the fourth book of the *Aeneid*... The brief summary overview of the rules of rhetoric from Cyprian will be given in the second semester, of course. At that time, Cicero's philosophy being set aside, some of the easier speeches, like the *Pro Lege Manilia*, *Pro Archia*, *Pro Marcello* and the others delivered to Caesar can be taken... This will be the schedule: In the first hour in the morning, Marcus Tullius and prosody should be recited from memory.[27]

---

[21] Witt 2000: 183–5; 201–5.

[22] The Jesuit *Ratio studiorum* of 1599 would particularly recommend the 'speeches delivered to Caesar'.

[23] Classen 1993: 76–80. On Loschi, see Viti 2006.

[24] For the influence of George's rhetoric, see Monfasani 1976: 318–37; for his works about Cicero, see Monfasani 1984: 342–477.

[25] Kallendorf 2002: 291: 'No text is more useful or convenient for learning this discipline than the *Rhetorica ad Herennium* of Cicero, where all the parts of rhetoric are set forth, perfectly and succcinctly.'

[26] Green and Murphy 2006: 107–38.

[27] Pavur 2005: 166–7. The original Latin reads as follows: '*Ad cognitionem linguae, quae in proprietate maxime et copia consistit, in quotidianis praelectionibus explicetur; ex oratoribus unus Cicero iis fere libris, qui philosophiam de moribus continent; ex historicis Caesar, Salustius, Livius, Curtius, et si qui sunt similes; ex poetis praecipue Virgilius, exceptis Eclogis et quarto Aeneidos... Praeceptorum rhetoricae brevis summa*

The volume and variety of Cicero's works enhanced his popularity. Thus in a study of editions of the *rhetorica* and school curricula from 1500 to 1700, Joseph S. Freedman notes that anthologies of Cicero's works offered educators a versatile range of rhetorical texts both theoretical and practical.[28] Among the notable anthologies of Ciceronian passages were the *Ciceronianus* of Petrus Ramus (Frankfurt 1530) and the *Ex M. T. Cicerone insignium sententiarum elegans et perutile compendium* of Petrus Lagnerius (Paris 1543).[29]

Cicero the philosopher

Before the era of Scholasticism, a minor text by Cicero played a surprisingly important role in late medieval Italy, for his *Topica* were a principal school text used to teach lawyers logic and argumentation.[30] With the rise of Renaissance humanism, this text was eventually eclipsed by the philosophical works that Cicero had expressly written for a wide readership – his dialogues.[31]

In his *Enquiry Concerning Human Understanding* (1748), David Hume distinguishes between two types of philosophers. The moral philosophers view people as actors in society and seek to teach their fellows the ways to happiness and virtue, whereas the theoreticians consider humankind in its rational aspect and attempt to discover hidden truths for the edification of the learned. The former thinkers, Hume concludes, will always be more popular than the latter, so that 'the fame of Cicero flourishes at present; but that of Aristotle is utterly decayed'. Hume's judgement had been anticipated by many Renaissance humanists, beginning with Petrarch's preference for the Roman's eloquence over the Greek's abstractions.[32]

Adapting the model of the Greek dialogue, Cicero wrote a dozen works expounding Greek philosophy; and to Renaissance humanists from Petrarch onwards Cicero's philosophical works offered more than a survey of

---

ex Cypriano, secundo scilicet semestri, tradetur; quo tempore, omissa philosophia Ciceronis, faciliores aliquae eiusdem orationes, ut pro lege Manilia, pro Archia, pro Marcello, ceteraeque ad Caesarem habitae sumi poterunt... Divisio temporis haec erit: Prima hora matutina memoriter recitetur M. Tullius et ars metrica apud decurionem.'

[28] Freedman 1986.
[29] Green and Murphy 2006: 365 (Ramus), 259 (Lagnerius: some thirty editions between 1543 and 1584).
[30] Witt 2000: 353; Reinhardt 2003. In fact, the popularity of the *Topica* is perhaps not surprising, since it is based on the text by Aristotle, whose works in translation enjoyed a great fortune in the late Middle Ages.
[31] On Cicero's dialogues, see Marsh 1980 and Powell 1995a.
[32] Hankins 2007: 1; Petrarca 2003: 314–17.

Hellenistic doctrines: they provided a model for the secular discussion of virtue and happiness in what might be called a civic forum. In the Italian Quattrocento, Cicero appeared as an icon of civic virtue in pictorial sequences of *Uomini Famosi* or Famous Men.[33] While in his *De divinatione* (*On Divination*) Cicero reviews his achievement in making Greek thought available to a Roman readership, it is his *Tusculan Disputations* that offer the most important statements of his philosophical credo. Thus, as a practical Roman citizen, Cicero concentrates on the ethical branch of philosophy – rather than logic or natural science. In a famous passage of the *Tusculan Disputations* (5.10), he praises Socrates for having brought philosophy back down to earth, preferring ethics to science and metaphysics. To humanists disaffected by the *a priori* dialectic of the Schoolmen, Cicero's word must have sounded a rallying cry.

Cicero's philosophical works offered many elements that attracted Renaissance humanists. As a mediator of Greek thought to a Latin readership, he presents doctrines in balanced debates that inspired humanists to apply his method to ancient schools like the Stoics and Epicureans. With his rhetorical training and its emphasis on arguing both sides of a case – *in utramque partem disserere* – Cicero was drawn to Academic scepticism, and rejected blind allegiance to traditional authorities.[34] In another celebrated passage of the *Tusculan Disputations* (1.10), Cicero censures the dogmatism of the Pythagoreans, who cited their legendary founder, saying *ipse dixit* ('the Master said so') as the definitive authority on any question. From Petrarch onwards, humanists appropriated this critique, and turned it against adversaries who made a similar appeal to an incontrovertible Aristotle, whom they simply called 'the Philosopher'. (In Cicero's day, Peripatetic philosophy was not in vogue, as he notes in his preface to the *Topica*, for much of Aristotle was unknown at Rome until Cicero's own lifetime, when the books that Sulla brought back after the capture of Athens in 86 began to circulate. In fact, the Roman orator cites Aristotle mainly for his writings on rhetoric, including the production of arguments on both sides of a question.[35]) In the event, humanist allusions to Aristotle were often directed against ecclesiastical authorities and canonic dogmas.

---

[33] Jones and Kilpatrick 2007: 377–9.
[34] See A. E. Douglas in Dorey 1965: 135–70, at 143: 'Cicero, by temperament and by training as orator and lawyer, was always ready to see both sides of a question. In his writings he often attacks dogmatism, and is scathing about those who accept the first view they hear or swallow uncritically the dicta of some authority (cf. *Nat. D.* 1.10).'
[35] *De oratore* 3.78: '*sin aliquis exstiterit aliquando, qui Aristotelio more de omnibus rebus in utramque partem possit dicere et in omni causa duas contrarias orationes . . . is sit verus, is perfectus, is solus orator.*' On Cicero's rhetorical interpretation of Aristotle, see Long 1995a.

Rejecting Scholastic argument and rigid dialectic, humanists found in Cicero's rhetorical approach to moral questions a justification for their own eclectic writings. When in the preface to the *Tusculan Disputations* (1.7–8) Cicero professes to treat philosophical topics in a rhetorical manner, he affords justification for much of Renaissance ethical discourse. Thus, Lorenzo Valla, one of the more profoundly original humanists, argued for the superiority of rhetoric to logic in debating moral issues.[36] At the same time, he portrayed Stoicism as a cloak for supercilious piety, thus distancing himself (like Petrarch) from Cicero's predilection for the sect.

As noted above, Cicero's philosophical works were some of the first books printed in Italy, with the moral works – *De officiis*, *De amicitia* and *De senectute* – taking pride of place. As humanists made vernacular translations of Cicero, these same works were usually the first to claim attention, so that between 1481 and 1561 they had been printed in English, French, German, Italian and Spanish, as well as the *Paradoxa Stoicorum* and *Tusculan Disputations*. The philosophical corpus also attracted learned commentators, whose work has not been adequately studied.[37]

Cicero also inspired imitations and adaptations. For example, the Florentine Matteo Palmieri (1406–75) composed an Italian dialogue in three books titled *Della vita civile* (1431–8), which draws heavily on Cicero's *De inventione*, *De officiis* and *Tusculan Disputations*, as well as on Aristotle's *Nicomachean Ethics*.[38]

An interesting chapter in the story of Cicero's fortune involves the role of his *Academica* as a source for the scepticism that characterized the Greek thinkers known as the New Academy (c. 269–87 BC). The *Academica* survives in single books taken from two separate versions of the work, which were known to Petrarch and many Quattrocento humanists, but aroused little interest in sceptical thought. The first figure to use Cicero to outline Academic scepticism was the Sienese humanist Francesco Patrizi (1413–94), who in a letter to his friend Achille Petrucci outlines the history of the Academy, using Diogenes Laertius as well as Cicero.[39] During the sixteenth century, more than a dozen notable scholars – including Victorius, Camerarius, Turnebus and Lambinus – wrote commentaries on the *Academica*; and Daniele Barbaro (1514–70) and Francesco Robortello (1516–67) wrote specific Latin tracts on the subject. This interest culminated in the work of the German scholar Joannes Rosa (1532–71), whose

---

[36] Nauta 2009: 234–5.
[37] Hankins and Palmer 2008: 46–7 list some seventy printed Renaissance commentaries on Cicero's thirteen philosophical works.
[38] Kraye 1997: 149–72.   [39] Schmitt 1972: 49–51; Patrizi's text is printed at 171–7.

lengthy *Commentarius*, printed in 1571, deals with Cicero's *De finibus* and *Academica*.[40]

In Paris, the work gained new prominence as a number of thinkers, led by Petrus Ramus (1515–72), rejecting the dominant school of Aristotelianism with its dogmatic assertiveness, found Academic scepticism useful to their cause. In 1547 and 1550, Audomarus Talaeus (Omer Talon: *c.* 1510–62) wrote commentaries on the two versions of Cicero's dialogue, accompanied by his introductory essay *Academica*. A counter-attack was mounted by Petrus Gallandus (1510–59), who in 1551 composed an oration defending the University of Paris from the 'New Academy of Petrus Ramus' (*Pro schola Parisiensi contra novam academiam Petri Rami oratio*).[41]

After the Reformation, Academic scepticism naturally aroused the suspicion of Catholic thinkers, whose dogmatism rejected what they perceived as atheistic doubt. In 1558, the Italian Giulio Castellani (1528–86) printed a treatise against Cicero's *Academica* (*Adversus Marci Tullii Ciceronis academicas quaestiones disputatio*). In this work, dedicated to the papal legate Cardinal Girolamo Dandino, Castellani divides all philosophers into sceptics and dogmatists, and predictably condemns Ciceronian probabilism in favour of Aristotelian certitude.[42] In 1597, the Cypriot Jason de Nores asserted that Cicero alone combines rhetorical eloquence with methodical treatment, and interpreted the Roman's dialogues as covering the same topics as Aristotle's *Nicomachean Ethics*.[43]

Cicero the model of Latinity

Since antiquity, Cicero had been cited as the paramount model of Latin prose. During the dawn of humanism, he was praised by Petrarch and Salutati, but neither of them strove to imitate Ciceronian prose. As Latinity improved in the course of the Quattrocento, various humanists often cited the influence of Cicero as a major factor in the rebirth of eloquence; but, again, no-one advocated adopting the Roman orator as the sole model. The humanist Biondo Flavio (1392–1463) includes an interesting account of the revival of Latin eloquence in his *Italia Illustrata* (1448–51). In a discussion of Ravenna (6.25–9), he traces the succession of Italian humanists from Petrarch to Giovanni Malpaghini (of Ravenna) to his own Quattrocento

---

[40] Schmitt 1972: 134–57.   [41] Schmitt 1972: 92–102.   [42] Schmitt 1972: 109–33.
[43] Schmitt 1988: 326: 'Nores felt obliged to defend Cicero's moral works by demonstrating that they covered the same territory as the *Nicomachean Ethics*. He therefore argued that *De finibus* corresponded to book I, *De officiis* to books II–VI, the *Tusculan Disputations* to book VII, and *De amicitia* to books VIII and IX. For book X, however, he offered no Ciceronian equivalent.'

contemporaries. In passing, he places great emphasis on the rediscovery and imitation of Cicero's works, specifically the letters and *De oratore*, *Orator* and *Brutus*.[44]

With the diffusion of printed texts, the student of Latin naturally faced a puzzling array of texts to study and imitate; and various humanists began to counsel a restricted diet of Ciceronian works. By the late Quattrocento, battlelines were being drawn up between rigid Ciceronians and the partisans of eclectic imitation. News from the battlefield was quickly reported in print, heightening the conflict. Between 1494 and 1532, the most notable skirmishes took the form of letters exchanged between various Italian humanists: Angelo Poliziano and Paolo Cortesi, Gianfrancesco Pico della Mirandola and Pietro Bembo, and Giovambattista Giraldi Cinzio and Celio Calcagnini.[45]

Meanwhile, the debate spread north of the Alps. The assertion that Cicero alone was the highest model of eloquence provoked the Dutch humanist Erasmus to compose a Latin dialogue, *Ciceronianus* (1528), which impugns the adoption of a single model as an absurdity, echoing Poliziano's remarks on the subject. Many Italians were incensed by Erasmus' irreverent critiques, since behind his stylistic nonconformity they sensed that there lurked some form of religious heterodoxy. In Italy, meanwhile, the scholar Nizolius (Mario Nizzoli 1498–1566) published his *Observationes in Ciceronem* (*Observations on Cicero*) in 1535; a revision of this work was repeatedly printed as *Nizolius, sive Thesaurus Ciceronianus* (*Nizolius, or A Ciceronian Thesaurus*) from 1558 onwards.[46] In 1532, Lilio Gregorio Giraldi commented on the debate, and attempted to resolve it by proposing that beginning students read Cicero alone for a couple of years, and then expand their reading to other prose writers. His compromise was subsequently adopted by Justus Lipsius (1547–1606) in his *Epistolica Institutio* (1591), and soon endorsed by the Jesuit educator Antonio Possevino.[47]

The epistolary debates centre on several questions, especially the contrast between imitation and invention. Pico's letter is titled *libellus de imitatione*, or little book on imitation; and Calcagnini's letter is *super imitatione commentatio*, or treatise on imitation. Those arguing for diverse models observe that nature creates people with different inclinations and talents. Those advancing the cause of Ciceronianism assert that one should imitate the very best model, whom they identify as Cicero. Gradually a sort of compromise emerged as humanists proposed that beginners imitate Cicero closely, but read more widely as they mature.

---

[44] Text and translation in White 2005: 300–9. See the comments of Viti 1999: 81–8 and Witt 2000: 340–2.

[45] DellaNeva 2007: vii–xxxix (introduction).   [46] Green and Murphy 2006: 322–3.

[47] DellaNeva 2007: 190–211.

The Ciceronian debate spread in the first half of the Cinquecento, thus participating in a larger trend in Italian literary culture. For the proliferation of standard editions of canonical authors greatly promoted a literary classicism based on the imitation of recognized models. Such classicism extended to the vernacular, and Pietro Bembo, the editor of Petrarch's *Canzoniere* (1501) proposed a 'classical' standard in Italian based on the adoption of Boccaccio and Petrarch as Italian parallels to Cicero and Virgil. In fact, the Venetian Bembo's *Prose della volgar lingua* (1525), which endorses adherence to Trecento models, is couched in rather artificial Tuscan prose. As for Latin authors, a fixed language – some would say 'dead' language – afforded a more stable target for imitation.

Interestingly, the debate concerning Cicero also addressed the epistolary form, for which the Roman orator furnished a central model. To be sure, readers perused letters by other Romans, such as the epistolary sermons of Seneca and the calculated missives of Pliny the Younger. But Cicero's letters offer an unmatched variety, ranging from the colloquial notes to Atticus and Brutus to the more elevated *Epistulae ad Familiares*.[48] As noted above, Justus Lipsius recommended Cicero as the sole model for beginners in letter-writing. In the eighteenth century, Edward Gibbon would observe that 'Cicero's *Epistles* may in particular afford the models of every form of correspondence.'[49]

Conclusion

Cicero's influence on the Renaissance is central to the movement we call humanism. In three particular areas he furnished a model for the new educator and man of letters. First, his philosophical works were now read with interest, both as an alternative to the Aristotelianism of the universities and as a precedent for the gentlemanly discussion of ethical theories and moral questions. Second, and partly in connection with the new vogue of the *philosophica*, the literary dialogue as a forum of learned discourse enjoyed a remarkable flourishing that reflected the new socialized context of learning, which rejected abstract treatises in favour of intellectual exchange and debate.[50] Third, humanists from Petrarch onwards cultivated the epistle, which in antiquity was conceived of as 'half a dialogue' and for which Cicero's assembled books offered a wide range of stylistic and thematic material to study and imitate. And the adoption of Cicero as a school text in

---

[48] For the use of Cicero's epistles in the classroom, see Grendler 1989: 222–34; Black 2001: 252–5.

[49] Gibbon 1994: 104; cf. the similar endorsement of Battista Guarino above, n. 14.

[50] On the Quattrocento dialogue, see Marsh 1980.

many fields by groups as influential as the Jesuits guaranteed his centrality in humanities curricula for centuries to come.

Further reading

Cicero's central influence in Western letters receives classic treatments in Zieliński 1912 and Dorey 1965. His predominant position in Latin education is examined in complementary studies by Grendler 1989 and Black 2001; while his often dictatorial role as a model of Latin prose, especially in Italy, is illuminated by Sabbadini 1885 and DellaNeva 2007. The fortune of Cicero's philosophical works is examined in Schmitt 1972, Marsh 1980 and Powell 1995a.

17

MATTHEW FOX

Cicero during the Enlightenment

Contexts

The Enlightenment can be characterized as an intellectual movement based upon the pursuit of rational principles: an optimism about the potential of intellectual enquiry and scientific investigation to reveal the secrets of creation, and a corresponding desire to break with restricting, faith-based systems of explanation.[1] The Enlightenment is unusual as a historical category in that the participants recognized themselves as engaged in a coherent project, and the vocabulary of enlightenment, of casting illumination into dark places, of supplanting obscurity with insight, are all consciously employed by writers keen to show that they were committed to breaking with outmoded forms of thought and belief. And the movement was confident of its ability to bring about social progress. The most significant proofs of this confidence, and the reasons why later historians have accepted the self-definition of the Enlightenment thinkers with so little questioning, were two cataclysmic events: the American war of independence (with the consequent establishment of an entirely new social order in the 'New World', founded upon principles characteristic of the Enlightenment) and the French Revolution – an event of a rather more ambiguous character, which (especially after it facilitated the megalomaniacal ambitions of Napoleon I) had much of Europe shuddering in fear of similar social upheaval, and reeling from the sight of noble ideals transformed into slaughter and totalitarianism. Both of these events demonstrate an intersection between political action and intellectual movements: the thinkers of the Enlightenment were, rightly, it turns out, convinced that a more systematic engagement in social debate would ultimately give rise to social change.

[1] The bibliography on the Enlightenment is vast. Two useful introductions are Im Hof 1994 and Outram 2005. More extensive, but still aspiring to a general readership is Israel 2006. Israel 2001 is more specialized, and in both these works Israel pushes the Enlightenment further back in time than is orthodoxy. His work now supplants Gay 1977 (first edition 1966 and 1969) as the standard synoptic study.

Historians, of course, need to be cautious about the way in which historical events are later constructed as part of a pattern: riots in London in 1780 caused considerably more damage to private property than the French Revolution, but, because of the absence of a coherent surrounding narrative of social change, have lacked the impact of more written-about disturbances.[2] The Enlightenment Cicero fits rather aptly into such a context, where issues of hindsight, and the retrospective ordering of events to produce a coherent narrative, require adjustment to the original terms of debate: what is made of Cicero in the Enlightenment today often bears little resemblance to Enlightenment accounts, and to a large extent this is because of changes in thinking about society, education and literature that themselves are the product of those times. A central characteristic of the Enlightenment is the growing systematization of ways of thinking about society: the fields of philosophy, science and economics all begin to aspire to a much greater degree of rigour. The fact that Cicero is not himself a systematic thinker, nor one whose works lend themselves easily to the production of a clear social or political programme, means that he does not appear (as, for example, Lucretius does) as a figure with an easily identifiable significance in this period.[3] And although it can be argued that he did influence a few figures strongly, unless an assumption is made about what Cicero's thought consists of, it is difficult to find a close correspondence between particular theories developed in the Enlightenment and views that can be attributed to Cicero.[4] This is mainly because Cicero's thought does not have any coherent philosophical system, a lack that comes to be seen as a failing on his part only as the Enlightenment nears its end. Enlightenment readers took inspiration from Cicero, but they did not as a rule think of him as the inaugurator of a theoretical vision that could be taken as more than a vague foundation for their own endeavours.[5]

So it is essential to distinguish between those writers and thinkers who tackle Cicero directly (who will provide the material for this chapter), and others (the larger number), for whom he is a more general inspiration. Writings that tackle Cicero head-on display a variety of ways of interpreting him,

---

[2] See Porter 1982: 116.   [3] See Baker 2007; Johnson 2000: 88–102.

[4] Revealing is the index entry for Cicero in Goldie and Wokler 2006: in over 700 pages on the history of thought in the eighteenth century, Cicero's name appears only 6 times. Likewise, in their treatment of Thomas Jefferson's rhetoric, a field where Cicero's influence could reasonably be expected, Golden and Golden 2002 make no reference to Cicero.

[5] Social contract theories are a good example. Although it is possible to see Cicero as the originator of the theory in which the ruler and the ruled make a mutually satisfying deal to act as a regulated society, this theory is in fact first made explicit by St Augustine. He may have been inspired by Cicero, but it would be excessive to regard Cicero as the first proponent of that theory. See Riley 2006: 349.

and they point more clearly than in earlier periods to tensions within Cicero's own writings: in particular the tension between the political figure and the philosopher. That tension had been a significant part of Cicero's reception at least since Petrarch, but it becomes more obvious in Enlightenment responses to Cicero, as thinkers move towards a more clearly articulated discussion of social and political issues that can actually shape opinions or events. In this context, expectations of the relevance of theoretical insights or philosophical endeavour to the world of politics become higher, and Enlightenment readers seem more aware than their predecessors of the difficulty of integrating the veneration of Cicero as a philosopher with admiration of him as a political figure. Readings of Cicero centre firmly upon these issues, and while it is tempting to try to extrapolate from Cicero's general authority to a more specific role as the inaugurator of particular political or social theories, it is a fallacy to imagine that Cicero played a particularly prominent role in the founding values of the American constitution or the French Republic:[6] what the accounts of Cicero from this period reveal is less dramatic, and in a way more predictable. Cicero retains much of his status as a revered thinker and stylist: but the central feature of the Enlightenment reception of Cicero is that the intellectual climate changes significantly, and along with it the use to which Cicero's work can be put.[7]

To understand what happens to Cicero in the Enlightenment it is worth considering the context of literary culture in this period. The Enlightenment brought enormous progress in the production of printed books: printing and paper became cheaper, and the reading public grew.[8] It is in the eighteenth century that usable complete editions of classical authors appear, many of them still usable today; it is also the era of translation. Although, of course, translations had been undertaken continuously since the invention of printing, in the Enlightenment the status of Latin as an international language diminished, and (again in the wake of cheaper book production) a greater value came to be placed upon the establishment of national literatures. So the production of translations of Cicero's complete *corpora* (speeches, letters, philosophical treatises) began, although it was not completed until well into

---

[6] That is not to say that there are no resonances between Cicero's model of the statesman and that employed particularly by the founding fathers: there is an extensive scholarship on the classical roots of their thinking. But it is a highly specialist project to try to demarcate between a specifically Ciceronian influence and a more general classical one. Bederman 2008 provides excellent orientation. See also Connolly 2010.

[7] My case studies are restricted to the British reception of Cicero: a necessary limitation given the wealth of material.

[8] Feather 1988: 93–114 gives an accessible account of the growth of the book trade. Allan 2003 explores the methodological issues regarding readership during the early Enlightenment.

the nineteenth century. The publishing boom had an effect on Cicero, as on most other classical authors, making him more accessible to a wider audience. More significant, however, was the boom in production of learned scholarly works: improving tracts aimed at the wider public, enthusiastic amateurs publishing scientific research, and philosophers and social reformers making a name for themselves by going into print to put their systems of thought before the public. Beyond the ambition of individuals, there is that particular hallmark of Enlightenment literary culture: the encyclopaedia.[9] Often initiated by one key figure (Bayle, Diderot), the encyclopaedia aimed to present knowledge in a systematized, if not necessarily definitive form. And this systematic approach, and the reputation that could be derived from it, had a huge effect upon the reception of classical writings: in essence it substantiated what was known in France as the *Querelle des Anciens et des Modernes* into a concrete distinction between systematic, modern, forms of theory and philosophy, and their more haphazard ancient forerunners. Classical texts, in this worldview, take up a revered, but rather distant position: their function is in part to demonstrate the superiority of the more systematic way of thinking that advances in scientific theory had brought with them. This way of dealing with ancient forerunners is confirmed by Cicero's appearances in the writings of the Enlightenment *savants*: he is occasionally referred to, almost always with respect, and almost always as an authority who can provide useful ammunition for the theories being propounded. So, for example, Molière, in common with many other readers of his time, found Cicero's approach to religion (as expressed in *De natura deorum*, and to a lesser extent *De finibus* and *De divinatione*) an inspiring and useful model for his own brand of anti-clerical rationalism.[10] But crucially, his concern in referring to Cicero is not to shed a particular light upon him, nor to investigate his thought in any detail: but to use him, sporadically, as a way of lending antique authority to his own arguments. The same can be said for Montesquieu, whose views on social order clearly build on Cicero's: Cicero is a springboard, and an eager reader can trace degrees of similarity and difference between isolated remarks in a range of Cicero's work, and the considerably more systematic treatment of related subjects by Montesquieu. Likewise David Hume, who was heavily influenced by Cicero: his *Dialogues Concerning Natural Religion*, a late attempt to systematize his thoughts on religion, effectively bring *De natura deorum* into the world of the eighteenth-century free-thinkers and sceptics. Nevertheless, the influence of Cicero on these authors remains at the level of inspiration, rather than argumentation,

---

[9] Yeo 2001.
[10] MacKendrick 1989: 276–85 is the best survey of Cicero's influence on these thinkers.

because Cicero's philosophy is itself so far from systematic, so little suited to providing the building blocks for particular theories or dogmas.

As a result, the way that Cicero acts as a model depends only to a limited extent upon engaging with or extending his own ideas. Certainly, his views on religion are one area where he can be thought to be particularly influential, and where the influence was recognized explicitly.[11] But beyond that, Cicero's reputation in the Enlightenment rested on the effectiveness of his discourse, whether in oratory, letters or philosophical writings: this appeals to different writers throughout the Enlightenment (and, indeed, later) for its statesman-like authority; its polite, educated quality; its pedagogic value; its republicanism. In none of these areas does Cicero have a monopoly: Pliny is as useful as a model for polite letters; Cato is better as a model for republicanism (only slightly disadvantaged by the failure of his speeches to survive); Plato emerges from obscurity to revolutionize conceptions of what a philosopher is capable of; Seneca's Stoicism is popular, and more rigorous. But it is the respect for Cicero as an orator, and as an all-round literary giant, that sees figures at both ends of the eighteenth century comparing themselves to him in his battle against Verres: better known and more carefully elaborated is Edmund Burke's appropriation of that theme in his impeachment of the corrupt East India Company's official, Warren Hastings, in the late 1780s.[12] In 1710, Jonathan Swift published a translation of a particularly pointed passage from the *Verrines* as an attack on the Earl of Wharton.[13] These comparisons depend for their effect upon Cicero's status as a writer, an orator and a vivid figure from antiquity. The vision of Cicero as a campaigner against provincial corruption responds to a particular way of reading Cicero's *Verrines*. The reading leads to inspiration and imitation, rather than a critical examination or attempt to understand either Cicero's actions or his texts within a context responding to wider historical or literary concerns. And both Swift and Burke derive a potency from the connection with Cicero: their own rhetoric is enhanced by channelling his, by allusion, into the modern context. It is perhaps a mark of their own status as accomplished men of letters that they have the authority and literary reputation necessary to enable the connection to Cicero to be effective. They are sufficiently confident in their own status and rhetorical capacity for the comparison not to back-fire into an expression of their own arrogance. As the title page of a translation of the *Commentariolum petitionis*, published to coincide with an imminent general election in 1714, has

[11] See Gawlick 1963; MacKendrick 1989: 276–85.   [12] See Lock 2006: 75–91.
[13] *Examiner*, Thursday 23 November 1710. See Rogers 1975 and Schmidt 2000: 167–8. See too *The Times*, Friday 9 March 1787: p. 2; col. C, where the two uses of the Verres parallels are juxtaposed.

it, Cicero was 'the greatest scholar, and most consummate statesman then in the world'.[14] It took self-assurance to place oneself on a par with such a figure. But such appropriations of Cicero's status do not rest on a detailed engagement with his writings or history.[15] There are, however, many cases of such engagement, and it is to some of these that I now turn.

Popular perception of Cicero in the early eighteenth century

In looking for a more differentiated view of Cicero in the early Enlightenment, *The Tatler* is a useful source. Not the society and fashion magazine started in the early twentieth century, but the short-lived periodical (1709–11) that inspired it. It is a publication characterized by the energy of its writing, and by the way in which it demonstrates the interconnectedness of the world of politics with the world of letters. Its pages consist of the deliberations of 'Isaac Bickerstaff' (pseudonym of Richard Steele, who subsequently inaugurated *The Spectator*) and letters to the editor on the full range of topical issues, and it appeared three times a week.

> It is impossible to read a page in Plato, Tully, and a thousand other ancient moralists, without being a greater and a better man for it.[16]

This sentiment, of the generally improving quality of Cicero (among other classical authors), is typical of many hundreds of similar comments to be found in eighteenth-century newspapers. Correspondents to (and presumably the readers of) *The Tatler* have a basic acquaintance with the outlines of Cicero's life and career: one writes in quoting from *Pro Archia* (7.16) as an advertisement for the pursuit of the liberal arts (*The Tatler* 140, 2 March 1710);[17] in the same vein, readers are sufficiently familiar with Cicero's work to need no decoding of the trope of praising actors by comparison with Roscius (*The Tatler* 167, 4 May 1710). A more topical theme is the use of Cicero as a model for 'free-thinking', the euphemism for atheistic tendencies in dissenting religious movements, of which *The Tatler* has a low opinion. This is the start of an interest in Cicero as a prototypical atheist that was a major characteristic of his reception by the thinkers of Enlightenment.[18] In issue 135, an article draws a firm contrast between the free-thinkers of antiquity (Socrates and disciples, Cicero, Seneca) and the so-called free-thinkers of today. They are compared to the *minuti philosophi*

[14] Q. Cicero 1714.
[15] For a detailed consideration of the influence of Cicero on Burke, see Browning 1984; Zetzel 2003: 136–7.
[16] *The Tatler* 108, 17 December 1709.   [17] Bond 1987: vol. II, 156.
[18] Cicero's reception by the deists forms the main focus of Gawlick 1963.

of *De senectute* 23.85. The article then refers the reader to *Tusc.* 1.17.40 in which Cicero states that he would rather be in the wrong with Plato than in the right with 'such company'. Here we can see once again the authority of Cicero's thought: in this case applied to reinforce the time-less superiority of antiquity against what is perceived as a misguided mod-ern fad. The accommodation that Cicero achieves between his desire to open philosophical debate and the conventional traditions of Roman reli-gion is something that does not need detailed elaboration to readers of *The Tatler*.

Less predictable than his mention in discussions of religion, in issue 159, 'Isaac Bickerstaff' claims:

> Every one admires the Orator and the Consul; but for my Part, I esteem the Husband and the Father. His private Character, with all the little Weaknesses of Humanity, is as amiable, as the Figure he makes in publick is awful and majestick. But at the same Time that I love to surprise so great an Author in his private Walks, and to survey him in his most familiar lights, I think it would be barbarous to form to our selves an Idea of mean spiritedness from these natural openings of his heart, and disburthening of his thoughts to a wife.[19]

In all these references, the crucial idea is of Cicero as a source of authority. It is authority that derives in part from a veneration of his texts, and in part from a desire to evoke the personality of the man. It is noteworthy here that Bickerstaff touches upon the issue that had dogged Cicero's reputation since Petrarch's discovery of some of his letters in the fourteenth century: the emotional tone of his letters from exile, an issue that was to fuel the debate over the moral worth of Cicero's personality until well into the twentieth century. The standard reaction, the one that Bickerstaff reacts against, is distaste at the degree of despair, and a need to excuse it (here, the excuse is that the letters demonstrate a degree of matrimonial intimacy that is 'natural', and in other respects admirable).

The relationship between Cicero as a man and Cicero as a writer; the role of Cicero as a pioneer of religious scepticism; the reputation of Cicero as a stylistic or literary model. These are the features of the popular perception of Cicero in the early Enlightenment. In the remainder of this chapter I shall explore three case studies: a prospectus for a new edition of Cicero's complete works, and two biographies (one short, one enormous). Through them, it is possible to observe the way these same features were expressed in larger-scale treatments of Cicero.

---

[19] *Tatler* 159, 13 April 1710. Similar praise of Cicero's affection for his family can be found later in the century: *The Times*, Wednesday 20 December 1786: p. 1; col. B.

Case study 1: *Cicero Illustratus*

Cicero Illustratus (1712) by John Toland is a remarkable publication, giving us a detailed understanding not only of Toland's own views of Cicero, but also of characteristics of early Enlightenment thinking into which Cicero could most easily fit. Toland had acquired notoriety with his 1696 publication *Christianity Not Mysterious*, which had been declared heretical, burnt publicly in Dublin, and caused him to leave his homeland for the life of a peripatetic European intellectual. His correspondents included Leibniz and the Prussian Queen Sophie Charlotte; those influenced by him included his compatriot Berkeley.[20] His title is revealing: Toland's aim is to shed light on Cicero. The subtitle lays out further the key preoccupation of the text: to lay down the principles for a properly *critical* approach to Cicero.[21] The book is a prospectus for a new edition of Cicero's complete works that Toland is planning, and is to a large extent determined by the need to show why such an edition is necessary, and how it will differ from its competitors. The prospectus is written in Latin, itself significant: Toland is aiming at an international network of subscribers who would send money towards the edition. The dedicatee is Baron von Hohendorff, aide-de-camp to one of Europe's richest and most powerful figures, Eugene of Saxony, a military genius and avid bibliophile, whose books became the core of Austria's national library. Cicero appears as an inspiration to statesmen and men of action, and the opening chapters of the work, concerned with the dedicatee and his patron, Eugene, elaborate a vision of political and military success predicated upon uniting the world of politics and the world of letters. There is a close connection between this preface and the vision of Cicero that Toland is promoting: Cicero represents the unification of a literary and a political career, and Toland's project is to use an edition to make that vision clearer. First of all, he establishes Cicero as a role model for the literate man of action, then he sets about pointing out why the perception of Cicero by his contemporaries is so different: he blames educational traditions for instilling a hatred of Cicero in the young. They associate him so closely with the punitive regime of the schoolroom that they cannot distinguish between memories of corporal punishment, and memories of reading his works. At the same time, Cicero is someone with such obvious authority that petty local officials confuse their own feeble attempts at rhetorical excellence with the achievements of Cicero, which stand in an entirely different league.

---

[20] On Toland in general, see Israel 2001: 609–14; Champion 2003. I discuss *Cicero Illustratus* more fully in Fox 2007: 275–303.

[21] *Cicero Illustratus: dissertatio philogico-critica: sive consilium de toto edendo Cicerone, alia plane methodo quam hactenus unquam factum.*

I can safely assert nonetheless that this same *Cicero* is practically unknown to many even within the literary world, even if no name finds itself more often on people's lips, and deservedly so. I value genuine teachers of literature more highly; but he has been so carelessly treated by those who make a pretence of teaching literature, by those vulgar wordsmiths, and has been read in such perverse ways, that the majority of them think of him as like themselves.[22]

I've translated Toland's *acceptus* as 'read' here: it is a salutary lesson against assuming that only in the twentieth century were critics sufficiently alert to the changing habits of reading to have a coherent idea of textual reception. Toland, foreshadowing the more clearly articulated theories of 'Reception Studies', is quite aware that *Cicero* (in italics, presumably, so as to distinguish the textual Cicero from the historical Cicero) cannot be defined only in terms of the ancient evidence. He will change according to the preconceptions of different readers, who will be influenced to the greatest extent by their expectations. These expectations, Toland assumes, will be formed by their own preoccupations: the values that correspond to their place in the world, and their profession. From the literature teachers (*grammatici*), Toland moves on to the teachers of rhetoric, lawyers and professional advocates. Like the *grammatici*, they will interpret Cicero in their own image, out of a combination of reverence for him and false self-regard.

This has the effect that he is regarded by the uneducated as verbose, arrogant, mercenary and litigious: the same objectionable slur with which the lowest bawling case-pleaders and litigants abuse the most respectable activities of proper lawyers and advocates. There is no mayor or (in the barbarian tongue) Bürgermeister; no syndic, alderman, or village leader, no public engineer for roads or buildings, who doesn't think himself a Cicero, or that Cicero was thoroughly like him.[23]

To counter the prevailing misconceptions, Toland proposes his new edition, the claims for which are of a methodological character. Toland will present Cicero in a new light, derived from the rationally organized publication of his works, using good-quality paper and clear typefaces, and providing readers with aids to enable them to read more effectively: the standard biographies, and a new one by Toland himself; a limited critical apparatus, giving only the more significant textual variants, and constraining the polemic of the philologists, which in existing editions threatens to obscure the visibility of the text. The notion of criticism is highly significant here. In Toland's view, the role of the critic is to display the texts, and the figure of Cicero himself, in such a manner that readers will be able to form their own opinion of

[22] Toland 1726: 238.   [23] *Ibid.*, 239.

his merits, without interference from the intermediary figure of the critic. The publication of the complete works in a standard edition is the central idea here; Toland's aspiration for a comprehensive account is fully in step with the times, to a large extent simply because of the provision of a legible, accessible text.[24] Toland's view of the critic as the impartial mediator of Cicero, the route to the demolition of ill-founded preconceptions, is likewise characteristic of this phase of the Enlightenment. The clearest forerunner is Bayle's *Dictionnaire Critique* (1695–7), to which Toland contributed the life of Milton. Criticism in that work consists in the provision of all relevant source material, as an aid to banishing prejudice and error: the critic does not aim to impose his own authority by providing a unifying account of the sources, so much as to ensure that the source material is properly displayed. It is true that in the vision of Cicero that Toland presents in the booklet, he is pushing one interpretation: Cicero is a dedicated and successful statesman, and a figure beloved of his countrymen. Toland is, to modern eyes, uncritical in making liberal use of Cicero's own speeches in support of this interpretation, especially *Post reditum in senatu* and *De domo sua*: speeches driven by the need to re-establish his reputation at Rome after his return from exile.

Toland's way of dealing with Cicero combines an unbounded admiration for his subject with a zeal to remain close to the original source material. When describing his own *Dissertatio historico-critica*, he comes quickly to the topic of Cicero's vanity, in a passage that illustrates nicely Toland's manner of interweaving Cicero's texts with his own interpretation.

> You will consult almost no man or book which does not lay a charge against Cicero of dwelling far too often on his own praises. People are quick to mention that he harassed Lucius Lucceius to write a prose history of his consulship (which he himself published in Latin verses and Greek prose) (20). They point out that he asked for the same favour from a certain little Greek (21) to publish the same consulship in Greek verse. They don't even give up hope of carrying off a triumph when they point out that Cicero was blamed (22) by his

---

[24] Several complete editions appeared around this time, mostly following the so-called 'variorum' arrangement, in which excerpts from a large range of earlier commentators would be included with the text: a complete annotated text in four volumes appeared in London in 1680, and a more fully commentated one, in one vast volume, in Basel in 1687: Littleton 1680 and Cicero 1687. Cicero appeared piecemeal within the Dauphin edition, a vast undertaking to publish the bulk of surviving classical literature in a standard format, and with a number of editors, from 1685 onwards. An eleven-volume edition including more commentary was published in Amsterdam in 1724, including some of the materials envisaged for Toland's own edition, such as a defence of Cicero against slanders, and Fabricius' biography: Cicero 1724. An edition in nine volumes edited by Olivet, with commentary, appeared in Paris in 1740: Cicero 1740.

friend Marcus Brutus, because he always had the Nones of December on his lips: the date, of course, on which he overturned the conspiracy of Catiline. I will not linger on the countless examples by which he could defend himself; that immense desire for praise, without which nothing either great or good is ever undertaken, is sufficient justification; *virtue* (he says) (23) *desires no other reward for hard work and dangers, beyond that of praise and glory* . . . [quote from *pro Archia* continues] Although he nobly confesses (24) that he always has this too before his eyes, it is not only the desire to perpetuate his name that drove him on to speak about himself so often. In many other speeches, such as those for *his house, P. Sextio,* & against *L. Piso*, the case concerned his own affairs no less that those whom he was defending or accusing. He was driven by necessity to refute and erase on every occasion the lies and slanders of his enemies.

(20) Epis. fam. l.5. ep. 12.
(21) Pro Archia, c. 11.
(22) Epist. Fam. l.1. ep. 9. ibid. ep. 16. & ep. I. l. ad Att.
(23) Orat. pro Archia Poeta, c. 11 & elsewhere.
(24) Ibid. c. & countless other passages.[25]

Toland seems unaware that it is precisely the kind of self-regard that the elaboration of the theme of glory in the *Pro Archia* encapsulates that had attracted the critics. Nor does it occur to him that what appear in Cicero's own works as the lies and slanders of his opponents might have some kind of justification. It was the historical treatments later on in the century that opened that cleft further, although it is clear from Toland's essay how firmly established the conflict over Cicero's reputation was, in spite of the widespread acknowledgement of his status.

As a dissenting theologian, Toland finds Cicero's religious thinking appealing. But it is surprising how little he makes of it, beyond praising Cicero as the *malleus superstitionis*, the hammer of superstition.[26] More clearly articulated is his interest in the relationship between method and religious scepticism. Cicero's procedure in composing dialogues is frequently overlooked, argues Toland, and arguments that are placed in the mouths of the characters who populate his dialogues are frequently interpreted as belonging to Cicero himself.[27] This misunderstanding has given rise to all kinds of absurdities, in which views that cannot possibly be Cicero's own are attributed to him by careless readers. We should remember that at the time

[25] *Ibid.*, 256–7.
[26] He had made rather more use of *De natura deorum* in the third of his *Letters to Serena*, Toland 1704.
[27] Middleton too was aware how important the appropriate understanding of the dialogue form was to the evaluation of Cicero's religious views: see below, n. 28.

Toland was writing, the dialogues of Plato were barely known (although he would have been familiar with the Ciceronian dialogic tradition, carried on in the Renaissance by figures such as Giordano Bruno and Galileo). Toland's insistence on demarcating between the different (sometimes competing) arguments in a philosophical work and the controlling voice of the author makes this a remarkable moment in Cicero's reception. He calls upon his readers not only to regard Cicero as a pioneer of scepticism, but to approach his texts in an appropriately sceptical manner. But this is an isolated moment in Cicero's reception, one that failed to buck the pervasive trend of reading Cicero as a storehouse of useful philosophical aphorisms, or didactic anecdotes, of the kind that are found in the pages of *The Tatler* and in the isolated references to Cicero in the great thinkers of the period.

Case study 2: *Observations on the Life of Cicero*

While Toland's Cicero is a pioneering religious sceptic, and prototype of the literate man of action, the short historical sketch of Lord Lyttleton (1733) brings us into a different world, where it is the task of the historian (rather than the critic) to bring his judgement to bear directly upon the object of his enquiry, and to be more discriminating in tackling Cicero's writings than Toland aspires to be. Lyttleton established the terms for his evaluation of Cicero right at the start of his short book: there are no figures in Roman history more worthy of attention than those men who were at the helm in Rome at the point where the Republic collapsed into 'an infamous Slavery'. With remarkable concision, he characterizes the change from liberty to servitude as one which expressed the 'general depravity' of the age, and in which the significant historical figures fell into two categories: either they resisted, or they were themselves the agents of the corrupting spirit that resulted in the coming of imperial rule. Lyttleton claims that Cicero is normally regarded as standing alongside figures such as Brutus and Cato, and points out that by his own evaluation 'Rome had not a more unspotted patriot to boast than himself'. The gambit of his work will be to drive a wedge between the aspirations of Cicero's self-presentation and the reality of his political conduct. The unity that motivates Toland to praise Cicero so highly is broken open by the judgement of the historian. The introduction ends by isolating one particular shortcoming: a lack of consistency and steadiness in Cicero's conduct that upsets the glowing reputation that he himself had looked for, and which 'has been given him rather by the partiality of learned men, than from the suffrage of historical justice'.

Lyttleton's account then focuses upon a selection of key episodes in Cicero's career. First, his defence of Sextus Roscius, praised for its boldness in the face of Sulla's power, but rather ambiguously, since Cicero's subsequent trip to Greece is viewed as an attempt to avoid the consequences of having offended Sulla. Lyttleton interprets Cicero's support of the *lex Manilia*, which granted exceptional powers to Pompey, as a demonstration of Cicero's lack of consistent support for the Republican constitution. Pompey's powers were a violation of the principles of that constitution, and Cicero should have done as Hortensius and Catulus did, and opposed them. Cicero's employment of his rhetorical skills in such an unworthy cause is linked directly to the ultimate fall of the Republic, as Lyttleton sees Pompey's powers as an encouragement to the aspirations of Julius Caesar.

After a brief positive evaluation of the events of Cicero's consulship, Lyttleton examines the years between the consulship and Cicero's exile in more detail, criticizing in particular Cicero's hypocritical but dependent attitude to Pompey, and his equally inconsistent relationship with Clodius. Regarding Cicero's conflict with Cato, however, Lyttleton comes down on the side of Cicero's pragmatism over Cato's idealism: 'Hence it was that with admirable intentions for the service of his country, he [Cato] sometimes did a great deal of mischief, for want of distinguishing between what was good in speculation, and what in practice. This was seldom the case with Cicero: when he departed from the interests of the republic, it was for the most part with his eyes open, and without the excuse of error.'[28] With the emergence of the first triumvirate, Lyttleton's scorn is damning: 'Thus he manifestly gave up the care of the commonwealth to a precarious safety and shameful ease', although he is at pains to point out that in the letter where Cicero's position is clearest (*Att.* 2.3) Cicero himself condemns his own behaviour. The account of Cicero's negotiations with Pompey and Caesar, culminating in his ending up on the losing side in the civil war, is energetically written, and circles repeatedly around Cicero's lack of firm principles, his weakness in the face of the power of Pompey and Caesar, as well as his foresight in knowing the likely outcome of events. Lyttleton sums up Cicero's subsequent life as one of servitude and abjection: 'From that time until the death of Caesar, he led a most inglorious and dishonourable life, courting the usurper whom in his heart he hated, with the most abject and servile adulations, entirely forgetting the dignity of his former character, and not even hiding these disgraceful circumstances . . . by a prudent and modest retreat.' Some redemption comes after Caesar's assassination, but Lyttleton makes much of a contrast between Cicero and Brutus, and imagines Cicero as too frail and unprincipled to be included in the conspiracy. Brutus' letters condemning Cicero for his courting of Octavian play a crucial role here

---

[28] Lyttleton 1733: 25–6.

(*Ad Brut.* 1.16 and 1.17), with Cicero emerging even at this point of highest peril as self-seeking and opportunistic. Lyttleton balances this by speculating that Cicero's aim had been to control Octavian, and by concluding (rather in contrast to his condemnation so far), that 'although his behaviour in regard to Caesar was productive of infinite mischiefs, yet he meant well in it to the commonwealth, and that the fault was rather of his judgement than his heart'. The book comes hurriedly to a close, Lyttleton reflecting that the most significant forms of writing, philosophy and oratory, depend for their well-being upon a constitution founded on liberty. Poetry may flourish, he concludes, 'under the smiles of an arbitrary prince; but force and solidity of reasoning, or a sublime and commanding eloquence are inconsistent with slavish restraint, or timorous dependancy [*sic*]'.

The contrast between Toland's evaluation of Cicero's status and Lyttleton's (twenty years later) is striking. In particular, the idea of the received opinion of Cicero that each author holds, in order to give their own work the weight of a polemic, is very different. For Lyttleton, it is essential that Cicero has been overestimated as a great and virtuous historical protagonist. Here we see the beginnings of the republican admiration of Cato that was to give him a less problematic place in the thoughts of American and French revolutionaries than Cicero. Toland, meanwhile, had been rectifying an altogether less favourable vision.

Case study 3: *History of the Life of Marcus Tullius Cicero*

Lyttleton's account is sufficiently brief, and sufficiently little known, to be treated in some detail. The authoritative biography of the period, however, is on an altogether grander scale, and had a much larger influence, being translated, and frequently reprinted over the next century and a half, even if it is seldom read or referred to today. Conyers Middleton's *History* appeared in 1741. It is a huge piece of work, and established Middleton as a figure of considerable significance in the British literary scene.[29] Middleton's life was reprinted continuously for almost two centuries, after the mid nineteenth century in a ubiquitous tome entitled *Cicero's Life and Letters*, in which it was placed alongside Melmoth's translation of the *Ad fam.* and the *Ad Att.* of Heberden.[30]

There are strong links between the approach that Middleton takes to writing Cicero's biography and the critical values elaborated by Toland forty

---

[29] Significance so great that when in 1793 a certain John Adams published a chronicle of significant events in world history, he included among the great events of 1750 the death of Middleton. Adams 1793: 163.

[30] Middleton 1840.

years before. Most striking is the extent to which Middleton relies upon paraphrases and long extracts of Cicero's own writings to provide the body of his text. Like Toland, he is assiduous in citing his sources (extensively in Latin in the footnotes), but has little compunction in taking most of what Cicero says about his own achievements at face value. Middleton's Cicero is a rational, well-meaning individual, who 'chose the middle way between the obstinacy of Cato and the indolence of Atticus'.[31] The combination of a biographical structure, and a heavy reliance on Cicero's own writings, leaves no space for Middleton to develop the kind of critical distance from his subject that is observable in Lyttleton's work. Had Toland produced his projected biography, it would probably have emerged as similar to Middleton's: in spite of the popularity, status and longevity of Middleton's work, it was, methodologically speaking, an anachronism. The continuity with Toland goes beyond method, however: like Toland, Middleton was an energetic promulgator of enlightened religion.[32] In his opening pages, he makes his position clear, being unusually subjective on the subject of the house in which Cicero was born:

> But there cannot be a better proof of the delightfulness of the place, than that it is now possessed by a convent of monks, and called *the Villa of St. Dominic*. Strange revolution! to see Cicero's portico's converted to *Monkish cloisters*! the seat of the most refined reason, wit, and learning, to a nursery of superstition, bigottry, and enthusiasm! What a pleasure must it give to these *Dominican Inquisitors*, to trample on the ruins of a man, whose writings, by spreading the light of reason and liberty thro' the world, have been one great instrument of obstructing their unwearied pains to enslave it.[33]

Such amusing polemic is rare in the book, though: Middleton's account makes hard reading today. There is little evaluation or discussion, and the author's main contribution is to provide a minimal narrative framework (often diligently substantiated by footnoted references to other sources) into which lengthy passages from Cicero's speeches and letters can be set. He follows a model of biography that loosely resembles Suetonius, separating the main achievements and events from an analysis of character, appearance and

---

[31] Middleton 1741: vol. II, 567.
[32] And, like Toland, he courted religious controversy. See Rupp 1987: 275–7. An exchange of letters from 1736 with the deist William Warburton was published posthumously along with a tract directed against Warburton's work. In his letter, Middleton gives a similar, if more precise, account of Cicero's scepticism to the one produced by Toland: [Towne] 1751: 162–72.
[33] Middleton 1741: vol. I, 5–6.

personal life, and a consideration of his philosophical and literary achievements, which appear only after 500 pages of a heavily textual historical chronicle.

Critics were swift to attack Middleton's work. 'He has laid before us a very dry list of facts, which every one that knows any thing at all, has hanging already at his finger's ends', writes 'An Oxford Scholar' in his florid polemic.[34] The remainder of the sentence, however, is revealing: 'and there has left them, as he rightly acknowledges, *to speak for themselves*. He has not dwelt upon such of them as were most important to the character of his hero, or most interesting to the age and nation he was living in; has made no nice observations, or useful reflections upon them for the benefit of those he was writing to.'[35] '[He] has given us, instead of *Cicero*, a *Patch-Work Hero* of his own imagination.'[36] This criticism reveals eloquently the developing sense of methodology, which was to lead to the establishment of firmer principles of historical analysis in the early nineteenth century, that were to prove highly unfavourable to Cicero's reputation.[37] This scholar was reacting precisely to the methodological premises that Toland outlines, but which, by this time, are beginning to look outdated.

Not long afterwards, Colley Cibber, famous as an actor, comic playwright, poet laureate and literary opponent of Pope, brought out his *The Character and Conduct of Cicero Considered*.[38] He situates his undertaking thus: 'Now that we have heard all that the most learned men in the world have said upon the life and times of Cicero – what may we reasonably *think* of it?'[39] Once again, we can see that there is a demand not just for the texts and the facts, but also for opinions. The main outlines of Cibber's version of Cicero are given by an elegant prefatory poem by Laetitia Pilkington, in which it is clear that Cibber will give a more balanced account of Cicero than Middleton, showing the negative side of his character more fully: 'To crown true Glory only with our Praise, and from unworthy brows to tear the bays'.[40] Cibber will also give a more sympathetic comparison of Caesar and Cicero:

---

[34] Oxford Scholar 1741: 13.   [35] Oxford Scholar 1741: 13–14.

[36] Oxford Scholar 1741: 22.

[37] Later in the century, presumably in response to the continuing success of the work, criticisms of supposed plagiarism arose; these seem to be unfounded: Clarke 1983, Dussinger 2004.

[38] Cibber 1747.   [39] Cibber 1747: vi.

[40] Cibber 1747 (the prefatory pages are unnumbered). Pilkington (*c.* 1709–*c.* 1750) was a struggling Irish writer, originally a protegée of Swift, whose most successful work was her autobiographical memoirs. The patronage of Cibber helped her to prominence. Elias 2004.

> Thus while hard Tullius, in the Capitol,
> With unrelenting Eye, sees Caesar fall;
> Tho' 'gainst the patriot you plead Caesar's cause,
> Yet Tullius dying has as just applause.

Like 'Oxford Scholar', Cibber's criticisms have a methodological foundation: readers need to be able to make a swifter judgement of Cicero's character than Middleton's presentation allows. His essay, running to almost 300 Quarto pages, and printed to the same lavish production standard as Middleton's own text, goes through selected passages, giving page numbers, as if to be read alongside it. Much of it is a digressive, anecdotal supplement to Middleton, as when, for example, Cibber enthuses over Middleton's reaction to the nuns of Arpinum, likens Cicero's grandfather to a 'plain old *English* Gentleman', or where he uses the first triumvirate as an opportunity to digress upon the question of ruler and subject, and the longevity of the Roman state.[41] However, from the start, Cibber raises the issue of Cicero's own love of fame, and repeatedly he comes back to Middleton's failure to see through Cicero's own presentation of himself. Once the narrative reaches the conflict between Caesar and Pompey, Cibber's response to Middleton is to reframe the terms of the debate so that they centre not around Cicero (who is sometimes not mentioned for pages at a time), but upon the motivations of Caesar (and to a lesser extent Pompey). Cibber regards Middleton's account as too reliant on, and too uncritical of, Cicero as a source. In this he foreshadows the more systematic critique that characterized the nineteenth-century treatment of Cicero as a historical figure. Cibber, however, is not so much systematic in his criticism, as more cautious about the possibilities of being too heavily influenced by one view or another. In a discussion prompted by Caesar's forced entry into the Temple of Saturn (Rome's public treasury), he writes: 'And tho', I confess, nothing seems more unpardonable or low-minded in an author than a vicious endeavour to sully or depreciate . . . the memorable actions of great men whom history has delivered down to us as objects of praise or emulation, yet to let all pass for gold that has the colour of it, to see only with others eyes, to be borne along by the common stream of opinion, or to take every thing for criminal or virtuous that has been called so, may be running into a contrary error, and be sometimes as great proof of our facility or weakness, as the other of a malevolent sufficiency.'[42] He then quotes Middleton's assessment of these events (that in a civil war, the 'honester side' is more likely to be cautious), and points out that, in this case, it is far from clear which side was in fact the honester.

---

[41] Cibber 1747: 3–4, 112–19.   [42] Cibber 1747: 195, italics and capitals modernized.

The final section of Middleton's history is perhaps the most accessible, but the fate of Caesar being long since sealed, it receives little attention from Cibber. However, in tackling the thorny question of Cicero's vanity and boasting, Middleton suggests (unsurprisingly) that Cicero needs to be judged in the light of circumstance, and with a full picture of all his works.[43] Cibber's final pages are a grumpy response: 'By what obligation are our free thoughts of Cicero never to wander out of the pale of his praise? Or how comes it to be imposed upon us as an article of our historical faith, that his character is immaculate? Or why, at last, is the liberty of supposing a possible flaw in him to incur the contempt or indignation of his more zealous admirers?'[44]

Middleton's *History* reveals an uncritical veneration for the textual Cicero that is to a certain extent typical of its age. The development of a notion of criticism that depends upon the careful encounter with the original text was one of the hallmarks of Enlightenment scholarship. However, the reception which the work received demonstrates the evolution of a different form of reading, one in which the values of the reader, and in particular, the judgement of the reader, are to be given greater priority. This evolution was to take a while before reaching a decisive incarnation, in the famously anti-Ciceronian biographical lexicon of W. Drumann (published 1834–44). But the roots of a version of Cicero less accommodating to his own texts can already be observed in this overtly non-specialist critique.

Conclusion

The work of Lyttleton, and the criticisms to which Middleton was subjected, show Cicero at the centre of a wider debate about the role of the historian and the purpose of perpetuating classical authors. For Toland, the project of Enlightenment was the perfect opportunity to shake the dust from Cicero's image, and liberate him as a pioneering sceptic, methodologically sophisticated, and able to bring together the world of politics with the world of literature. Middleton's biography operates in something of the same direction, but his faith in the ability of Cicero's texts to speak for themselves at such great length lay him open to criticism, and dissipates any sense of edge to Cicero's character or political role: Toland's fear of Cicero being misjudged as a provincial country gentleman was unwittingly realized by Middleton. Conversely, Lyttleton, and the critics of Middleton, look past the texts, and explore notions of character and historical judgement: the comparisons between Cicero and Caesar/Pompey/Cato, which form so

---

[43] Middleton 1741: vol. II, 520–2.   [44] Cibber 1747: 277.

prominent a part of the later evaluation of Cicero, are already visible in these works. At the centre of the Enlightenment reading of Cicero, therefore, lies the dialectic between political and theoretical, precisely the dialectic which was to characterize the major political upheavals to which the Enlightenment gave birth. This struggle was one that was not, on the whole, beneficial to Cicero's reputation. In spite of a general sense of his authority and significance, with the newly rigorous ideas of how theory and practice should relate to each other Cicero's fall from grace had clearly begun.

Further reading

There are few easily accessible treatments of this material: the works of Toland, Lyttleton and Middleton have received very little scholarly attention. Gawlick 1963 discusses Cicero's influence on the deists, while MacKendrick 1989 includes a chapter on the Enlightenment, among a selection of chapters on the reception of Cicero. Fox 2007 discusses Toland's *Cicero illustratus* in more detail. For suggestions for reading on the Enlightenment in general, see n. 1.

18

NICHOLAS P. COLE

Nineteenth-century Ciceros

Throughout the eighteenth century, Cicero's reputation as orator and states-man had remained almost unassailed. A commentator such as David Hume might lament some of Cicero's treatment of those around him, but only as a way of making a broader comment on the morals and customs of ancient societies.[1] Even his failure to take more direct action against Caesar might be alluded to as a positive virtue: 'the zeal of patriots is . . . much less requi-site than the patience and submission of philosophers. The virtue and good intentions of CATO and BRUTUS are highly laudable; but to what purpose did their zeal serve?'[2] Indeed, not only was Cicero a watchword for elo-quence and virtue, but the absence of any modern equal was something to be lamented.[3] Yet over the course of the nineteenth century Cicero's reputa-tion was to come under the severest scrutiny, both in scholarly and in more popular works.

Addressing the students of Harvard in 1810, John Quincy Adams heaped praise on Cicero as an orator – second only to Demosthenes – a rhetorician and, above all, a moralist and model for virtuous behaviour.[4] Closing his remarks, Adams summarized his essay: 'Let us make this the standard of moral and intellectual worth, for all human kind; and in reply to all the severities of satire, and the bitterness of misanthropy, repeat with conscious exultation, "we are of the same species of beings, as Cicero."'[5] As the century progressed, the grounds upon which to judge Cicero shifted. He was recon-sidered principally as a political actor, and the battle over his reputation was fought over the following points: had his actions against the Catilinar-ians been justified? Were his actions in the final years of Rome's Republic noble and virtuous? His literary and philosophical contributions received relatively light discussion, though he was acknowledged always as a great orator. From his public career and his private writings, a judgement would

---

[1] Miller 1987: 128–9. [2] Miller 1987: 30. [3] Miller 1987: 106–7.
[4] Adams 1810: 117–38. [5] Adams 1810: 138.

be made on the nature of his character. On all of the points upon which Cicero's reputation would rest, Conyers Middleton's *The History of the Life of Marcus Tullius Cicero* (1741), which remained a standard work into the nineteenth century, had been clear. Even though Middleton had promised a balanced assessment of Cicero, his work, drawing heavily on Cicero's own writing, presented a glowing assessment of Cicero that condemned almost all other political figures at the end of the Republic. He discussed but dismissed the legal controversy surrounding Cicero's execution without trial of members of Catiline's conspiracy. Indeed, Cicero's actions are praised as an instance of the purest virtue – the deliberate sacrifice of private interest to the public good. Cicero, Middleton suggests, foresaw and ignored the danger to himself that such a course of action would present. 'Here then', he says of the laws that ought to have protected the conspirators, 'was ground enough for Cicero's enemies to act upon, if extreme measures were pursued: he himself was aware of it, and saw, that the public interest called for the severest punishment, his private interest the gentlest; yet he resolved to sacrifice all regards for his own quiet to the consideration of public safety.'[6] Summing up Cicero's contribution to the state after recounting his death, Middleton presented him as a virtuous but practical politician, who had always chosen 'the middle way between the obstinacy of Cato and the indolence of Atticus: he preferred the readiest road to what was right, if it lay open to him; if not, he took the next that seemed likely to bring him to the same end; and in politics, as in morality, when he could not arrive at the true, contented himself with the probable'.[7]

Middleton's account serves as a reference point for evaluating the nineteenth-century criticism. The most famous and damning of Cicero's critics was Theodor Mommsen, whose *Römische Geschichte* (*The History of Rome*) appeared in three volumes in 1854–6, which were quickly translated into English by William Purdie Dickson. The portrait of Cicero could scarcely have been less flattering. In place of Middleton's heroic and virtuous politician, Mommsen presented Cicero as a vacillating coward, whose character-flaws were most evident as the fate of the Catilinarians was being decided. Mommsen noted flatly that Cicero's actions were unconstitutional, but also suggested that he was not himself the originator of the proposal to execute citizens without charge and would 'have gladly rejected the hazardous suggestion'. Cicero was 'indifferent' to the constitutional question, Mommsen suggested, but realized 'how useful it is to an advocate to be called liberal, and he showed little desire to separate himself from the democratic party by shedding this blood'. He was persuaded to pursue a stricter

[6] Middleton 1741: 219.   [7] Middleton 1741: 363.

course, Mommsen alleged, principally by his wife, yet did so 'like all cowards anxiously endeavouring to avoid the appearance of cowardice, and yet trembling before the formidable responsibility'. Mommsen condemned as an act of legally meaningless cowardice Cicero's decision to try the conspirators in the senate, and suggested that Cicero lost control of that debate, being pressed into an action from which he was shrinking. Mommsen's dislike of Cicero is such that he condemns him both for hesitating and yet also for the executions themselves. After an extensive description of the executions and the popular celebration of them, Mommsen remarked, 'Never perhaps has a commonwealth more lamentably declared itself bankrupt, than did Rome through this resolution.' The execution of 'a few political prisoners' not for any grand reason but because 'the security of the prisons was not to be trusted' was an 'act of the most brutal tyranny', and yet one carried out by 'the most unstable and timid of all Roman statesmen'. The whole event seemed to Mommsen to show the 'tragedy' of the fate of the Republic, and he emphasized the irony of the fact that it was Cicero who destroyed 'the palladium of the ancient freedom of the Roman commonwealth, the right of *provocatio*'.[8]

It is difficult to discuss Cicero's nineteenth-century reputation without at least some discussion of similar re-evaluations of Caesar. In common with other nineteenth-century accounts that were critical of Cicero, Mommsen's account criticizes the champion of a bankrupt republic dominated by a corrupt aristocracy so that he can praise Caesar, presented by him as a statesman with the vision to reform the Republic's ills. Caesar had tried to restrain the blow that Cicero allowed to fall against the conspirators and against the constitution, and the fourth volume of Dickson's translation ends with Caesar not only setting to right many points of public policy, but ensuring that Cicero will be punished for his actions. Cicero's banishment is presented as the 'gentlest punishment' in light of the seriousness of his crimes, and as a punishment reflecting the 'cool irony' of Caesar, the master-politician of his generation.[9] These characterizations, however, go far beyond simple assessments of character, and instead reflect the more general criticism in Mommsen's work of the workings of the Republic. Instead, presenting Cicero and the senate as weak and irresolute, unable to take the necessary steps to strengthen the state, he presents Caesar as the author of 'rational and necessary proposals' that are rejected by Rome's aristocracy generally, and by Cato and Cicero in particular, simply out of a spirit of destructive partisanship.[10] His view of Caesar became ever clearer as his

---

[8] Dickson 1894: vol. IV, 482–4. [9] Dickson 1894: vol. IV, 517–18.
[10] Dickson 1894: vol. IV, 510, 516.

work progressed further into the details of Caesar's rule. He praised Caesar as a 'monarch...never seized with the giddiness of the tyrant. He is perhaps the only one among the mighty ones of the earth, who in great matters and little never acted according to inclination or caprice, but always without exception according to his duty as ruler' and who 'made no false step of passion to regret'.[11] His Caesar was indeed a 'democratic' dictator, whose 'monarchy was so little at variance with democracy, that democracy on the contrary only attained its completion and fulfilment by means of that monarchy. For this monarchy... [was] the representation of the nation in the man in whom it puts supreme and unlimited confidence.'[12]

Such a critique seemed to address not only the interpretation of Roman history, but a question that was of greater contemporary resonance: were weak republics legitimately saved by the actions of men such as Louis-Napoleon Bonaparte? Some of his readers thought that Mommsen's answer was in the affirmative, and he clarified his position in his second edition: he approved of Caesar but not of the autocrats of his own day.[13] As his work progressed, he made both the comparison of ancient and modern politics and his rejection of Napoleon III's politics more explicit.[14] His criticism of Cicero he never moderated.

Even if Mommsen rejected too close a connection between ancient and modern dictatorship, the confusion of his readers and the parallels he did draw are nevertheless instructive. Cicero and Caesar's reputations were being evaluated and debated even as Europe's various monarchies and republics were facing uncertain futures. Guided by ancient authors, republicans had long predicted that the biggest threat to popular government was the tyrant who claimed to serve the best interests of the people. In America, popular politicians had attracted unflattering comparison with Caesar since the earliest years of Independence. Accused by his political opponents of trying to undermine the young republic, Alexander Hamilton had written to George Washington warning him about the 'Caesars' of their own day. One of Caesar's most dangerous abilities, he warned, had been his ability to seem like a friend of the republic through his flattery of the people. 'It has been aptly observed', he wrote, making his parallel clear, 'that Cato was the Tory – Caesar the Whig of his day. The former frequently resisted, – the latter always flattered the follies of the people. Yet the former perished with the Republic[;] the latter destroyed it.'[15] In America the charge of Caesarism remained little more than a political slur, but in France

---

[11] Dickson 1894: vol. v, 312.   [12] Dickson 1894: vol. v, 325.

[13] Yavetz 1971: 189–91.   [14] Dickson 1894: vol. v, 312–13.

[15] Hamilton to Washington, 18 August 1792: see Syrett and Cooke 1967: 252.

these fears were made reality, first by Napoleon Bonaparte and then by his nephew. Remarking in an 1865 essay entitled 'Caesarism as it now Exists' on Napoleon III's publication of his history of Julius Caesar, the English commentator Walter Bagehot wrote: 'That the French Emperor should have the spare leisure and unoccupied reflection sufficient to write a biography is astonishing, but...his choice of subject is very natural. Julius Caesar was the first who tried on an imperial scale the characteristic principles of the French Empire...On the big page of universal history, Julius Caesar is the first instance of a democratic despot.'[16]

The debate over a useful definition of 'Caesarism' continued through the nineteenth century and need not detain us further here, except in so far as Caesar's reputation was linked with that of Cicero. Historians and political commentators alike could easily become the partisans of one or other of the men. With some justice, those who reflected on their diverging reputations came to view the positive and negative views of Cicero as dividing along national lines. The French author Gaston Boissier wrote *Cicéron et ses amis: étude sur la Société Romaine du Temps de César* in part to defend Cicero from German criticisms; he noted that English and French authors had generally been more sympathetic, persisting in their 'old habits and their old admirations, and in the midst of so many convulsions criticism at least has remained conservative'. This he attributed to differing attitudes to republican government and differing expectations of politicians. 'Perhaps also the indulgence shown to Cicero in both countries comes from the experience they have of political life. When a man has lived in the practice of affairs and in the midst of the working of parties, he can better understand the sacrifices that the necessities of the moment may demand', he wrote, condemning the German scholars Wilhelm Drumann and Mommsen alike for heaping criticism onto Cicero on the basis of 'theories thought out in solitude and not submitted to the test of experience [become] more severe towards him'.[17]

At its worst this debate over the reputation of Cicero seemed divorced from a detailed analysis of him as a historical figure and instead seemed to be little more than assertion. Even Mommsen's criticisms and analyses of Cicero's motivations rarely result from a critical analysis of particular documents. Boissier went some way towards explaining the character of this criticism when he remarked:

> It is too much the custom now-a-days to seek arms for our present struggles
> in the history of the past. Smart allusions and ingenious parallels are most
> successful. Perhaps Roman antiquity is so much in fashion only because it

---

[16] Bagehot 1968: 111.   [17] Boissier 1897: 22–3.

gives political parties a convenient and less dangerous battle-field where, under ancient costumes, present-day passions may struggle.[18]

At its best, however, this desire to pass judgement upon, or defend, Cicero's actions led to a more detailed and critical examination of his correspondence. To be sure, there was still plenty of room for disagreement over interpretation, but Boissier pleaded for a more sophisticated approach to Cicero's corpus of writing:

> I mistrust those learned men who, without any acquaintance with men or experience of life, pretend to judge Cicero from his correspondence. Most frequently they judge him ill. They search for the expression of his thought in that commonplace politeness which society demands, and which no more binds those who use it than it deceives those who accept it. Those concessions that must be made if we wish to live together they call cowardly compromises. They see manifest contradictions in those different shades a man gives to his opinions, according to the persons he is talking with. They triumph over the imprudence of certain admissions, or the fatuity of certain praises, because they do not perceive the fine irony that tempers them. To appreciate all these shades, to give things their real importance, to be a good judge of the drift of those phrases which are said with half a smile, and do not always mean what they seem to say, requires more acquaintance with life than one usually gets in a German university.[19]

Although setting out to defend Cicero, Boissier's study could not manage to recreate the positive view of him that had been found in Middleton's work. Too many of the modern criticisms had hit home, and Boissier was forced to produce a much more balanced view of Cicero's career as a result. One example is his assessment of Cicero as a political philosopher. Here, the influence of Mommsen is explicit. Cicero, Boissier noted, had not, like Plato, described a merely theoretical model but one close to the Roman constitution as it operated. What Cicero described, 'is in actual existence and working; it is that of his own country'. Yet, he conceded, 'This opinion has been much contested. M. Mommsen thinks it agrees as little with philosophy as with history. Taking it strictly, it is certainly more patriotic than true.'[20] In a passage that reflected on Cicero's ideal constitution, he observed:

> We remember, of course, that Cicero did not bestow this praise on the Roman constitution as it was in his time. His admiration went further back. He recognized that it had been profoundly modified since the time of the Gracchi, but he thought that before it had undergone these alterations it was irreproachable.[21]

---

[18] Boissier 1897: 21. [19] Boissier 1897: 19.
[20] Boissier 1897: 31. [21] Boissier 1897: 32.

Had he been given a choice, Boissier speculated, Cicero would have chosen to have lived in the period following the Punic Wars.

In important respects, it was with this reflection that Boissier set the scene for his consideration of the central events of Cicero's consulship. After some further discussion of his general temperament, Boissier noted, 'We may say then without discrediting Cicero, that he was not altogether fit for public life.'[22] Boissier's Cicero foresaw the danger that the execution of the conspirators would bring, not out of a rigorous sense of duty and virtue, but because when he imagined the future he tended to see the possibility of evil consequences. He nevertheless defended his actions as courageous. Yet Boissier's Cicero did hesitate, and in part because he was simply not temperamentally suited to Rome's politics: 'he had more courage than another who in a moment of excitement would not have seen the danger. One cause of his inferiority and weakness was that he was moderate, moderate by constitution rather than principle, that is to say, with that nervous and irritable impatience which at last employs violence to defend moderation.'[23]

In Boissier's view Cicero's role in defeating Catiline and thwarting his conspiracy was more moderate than Cicero himself believed and Cicero had triumphed as much through luck as through leadership and oratory. Believing that Caesar was behind the conspiracy, Boissier noted that at best Cicero had delayed dictatorship by fifteen years, and had done so through betraying his old allies and at great personal cost.[24]

His analysis of Cicero's consulship was brief, but Boissier offered an extensive account of Cicero's activity during and after Caesar's dictatorship. He criticizes the historians of his own day for offering Caesar too much credit, for painting him as the champion of Rome's people and empire, and for imagining him to have governed with the foresight to imagine benefits that would be the distant consequences of his rule. Cicero, by this sort of analysis, was painted as the champion of the narrow privileges and prerogatives of the Roman elite alone. All of this, Boissier noted, was difficult to sustain from the documentary evidence. Despite offering a much more nuanced analysis than those of previous ages, in the end he declares himself for Cicero: 'Let us call things by their real name', he wrote. 'It was for himself and not for the people that Caesar worked, and Cicero, in opposing him, thought he was defending the republic and not the privileges of the aristocracy.'[25] Whether that republic deserved to be saved he admitted was a question that was much more difficult to answer.[26]

---

[22] Boissier 1897: 34.   [23] Boissier 1897: 35.   [24] Boissier 1897: 49–51.
[25] Boissier 1897: 63.   [26] Boissier 1897: 64.

A more extensive work with many of the same impulses was James Leigh Strachan-Davidson's *Cicero and the Fall of the Roman Republic*, published in 1894. In almost all of his text, Strachan-Davidson avoided direct criticism of other scholarship, though he noted in a short preface that he disagreed with 'almost every page' of Drumann, and offered what was in many ways one of the strongest scholarly defences of Cicero since the eighteenth century. Unlike Boissier, he did not imagine that any nation had a monopoly on praise or condemnation of Cicero: James Anthony Froude's *Caesar: A Sketch* (1879) had proved that Englishmen were as capable as any of damning Cicero and elevating Caesar. The other most famous German condemnation of Cicero seems to have given Strachan-Davidson greater pause: 'In writing Roman history', he remarked in the same preface, 'it is impossible to escape from the genius of Mommsen. Sometimes by suggestion, sometimes by revulsion, his presence is always felt.' Unlike those scholars, he avoided drawing modern parallels except where a concept from English law or a contrast with modern practice might help explain an obscure point.

In keeping with his general view of Cicero, Strachan-Davidson's analysis of the politics of Catiline's conspiracy was presented with a careful account of the extant evidence and yet a detailed defence of Cicero. Caesar and Crassus, he alleges, are already plotting against the state, but betray Catiline whose own ambitions to take control of the state lack their planning and finesse.[27] In the account that follows of Cicero's handling of the crisis, he is considered favourably, always presented as very much in control of events, and Strachan-Davidson does not question his judgement. Quoting from Cicero's speeches, Strachan-Davidson presents an image of the consul fully in command of both the politics and the justice of the situation.[28] He acknowledged, however, that 'no State trial, except perhaps that of Charles I, has ever been the subject of so much controversy' as Cicero's execution of the conspirators. Strachan-Davidson attempted one of the more thorough explanations of the question, examining first the legal problem in Roman law at some length and then the moral and political aspects of the question.[29] On all three grounds he sides with Cicero, concluding that he made 'not a single false step'. Offering a judgement on Cicero's character as a consequence, he concluded that:

> Cicero was a man of mild temper and of constitutional timidity, but of honest heart and sincere purpose. On this occasion, in the presence of great

[27] Strachan-Davidson 1900: 119–20.   [28] Strachan-Davidson 1900: 119–50.
[29] Strachan-Davidson 1900: 151–6.

danger...he rose above himself and exhibited unexpected resources of strength and courage...His own conscience fully approved the deed. Nowhere, even in the periods of darkest depression and suffering, when all the world seems to have turned against him, do we find the least hint of a doubt that he had in very truth been the saviour of his country.[30]

Strachan-Davidson's final analysis of Cicero was complimentary. He had ambition, he said, but not the unlimited ambition of Caesar. He held fast to principle and to patriotic duty, but was more reasonable and practical than Cato, and if he had made mistakes in his predictions or in his decisions it had to be remembered that at many periods of his life he faced only a 'choice of evils'.[31] He was the 'exponent of [the republic's] best thoughts and noblest aspirations, its faithful servant in life and its constant martyr in death'. His character-flaws were obvious, Strachan-Davidson noted, in his private correspondence, but he concluded his account by noting Octavian's judgement on Cicero: 'a great orator and a man who loved his country well'.[32]

Strachan-Davidson's account did not finally settle the question of Cicero's character, nor the legality or wisdom of many of his actions. It did, however, mark the resurgence of a view of Cicero strikingly similar to that advanced by Middleton over a century and a half before. Yet the context in which these observations were made was different, and Cicero in the nineteenth century was never the model for emulation that he had been for Middleton. It was not just that a closer examination of his writings had alerted readers to inconsistencies and flaws in his character. On the one hand, the partisans of dictatorship and critics of democracy had elevated Caesar; on the other, the champions of republican or democratic government no longer looked so firmly to Cicero as a model. Boissier had captured something of this mood when he had written:

> It is curious that, among us, in the seventeenth century, at the height of monarchical government, the learned all pronounced against Caesar without hesitation. Magistrates of the high courts, men cautious and moderate by their offices and character, who approached the king and were not sparing of flattery, took the liberty of being Pompeians and even furious Pompeians in private. 'The First President,' says Guy-Patin, 'is so much on Pompey's side, that one day he expressed his joy that I was so, I having said to him, in his fine garden at Bâville, that if I had been in the senate when Julius Caesar was killed, I would have given him the twenty-fourth stab.' On the contrary, it is in our own days,

[30] Strachan-Davidson 1900: 157.   [31] Strachan-Davidson 1900: 426–7.
[32] Strachan-Davidson 1900: 428–9.

in a democratic epoch, after the French Revolution, and in the name of the revolution and the democracy, that the side of Caesar has been upheld with the greatest success, and that the benefit humanity has reaped from his victory has been set in its clearest light.[33]

Cicero's reputation suffered in part because, while an obvious target of those opposed to republicanism, he was nevertheless also a difficult figure for the champions of popular government to defend wholeheartedly. This problem presented itself all the more sharply in an age when the strength of a polity was increasingly understood in terms of the strength of its institutions rather than the virtue of its citizenry. Even Cicero's most staunch defenders found it hard to make the case that he understood the failings of the Republic or that he had reforms to propose that would have addressed them.

At worst, Cicero's political thought was misunderstood entirely. The most extreme example of misreading, but one which highlights some of Cicero's less flattering descriptions of popular government, occurs in the 1841 translation of Cicero's *On the Republic*, which was dedicated to the Duke of Wellington. Encouraged by the fact that much of the text was a relatively recent rediscovery (1822), the translator, Francis Barham, included an extensive reassessment of Cicero's political theory. He read Cicero's passages on monarchy not as a treatise on ancient political theory, nor (following the similar passage in Polybius) as a description of the Roman state in its ideal form, where discussions of 'monarchy' were used to capture a view of the role and power of the consuls, but as a definitive statement in favour of actual, limited monarchy. Of Cicero's political aims, he wrote:

> Cicero, therefore, desired to restore the monarchical government, and wished to see an emperor or king once more swaying the Roman commonwealth – a fact which will appear manifestly proved in his newly-discovered treatise, De Republica. But while he pleaded for a king, he pleaded not for a king forced on the Romans by ambition or chicanery, but a king universally approved by his political character and conduct, and legitimately elected by the open, free, and unbiassed suffrage of the Senate and the people.[34]

An extensive footnote in Boissier's work defends Cicero against such wild misreadings, and explains that those who read Cicero as favouring monarchy are in error. Monarchy for Cicero was a theoretical or primitive form of government, not an obtainable ideal.[35] Yet even those who did not misread Cicero's theoretical discussions thought that in calling for a guide of the

---

[33] Boissier 1897: 52.   [34] Barham 1841: 15.   [35] Boissier 1865: 40.

state or a director of the commonwealth he was calling for monarchy or dictatorship. Strachan-Davidson, therefore, also writes a brief defence of Cicero, explaining the passages in question as calls for the leadership of ideal citizens, not for a change of constitution.[36]

If Cicero's political thought could be defended, though, it was difficult to hold it up as a model for emulation or for great political insight. Even in his lengthy biography, Strachan-Davidson views Cicero's philosophical and literary output as a 'distraction' from 'drudgery in the law-courts' and 'consolation in his disgust at the political situation'. He allots little more than two pages to a discussion of *De oratore*, *On the Republic* and *On the Laws* together. Cicero seemed to him an uncritical commentator on the Roman political system, preserving 'even the most perverse details of the Roman constitution'. There is little innovative in his work: 'His methods of reasoning are those of the Greek philosophers, his conclusions those of a Roman statesman with all a Roman's limitations.' Summing up his works, Strachan-Davidson wrote that 'Cicero has much to say of the duties of a statesman, but he seems blind to the faults in the machinery of government.' Strachan-Davidson was prepared to accept that Cicero was one of the leading minds of Rome, but thought that the principal problem facing the Roman state in his generation was how to organize a free government on a scale beyond that of a city state, and that this problem had defeated all the minds of antiquity.[37]

To be sure, some bristled at the criticism of the hero, in both scholarly and popular works, but by the end of the century a work such as Anthony Trollope's *Life of Cicero* that still attempted to hold him up as a model of virtue was generally scorned by reviewers.[38] Compared to earlier ages the general mood had shifted to the point that at least some criticism of Cicero was the mark of any serious engagement with ancient history. Even in the works that had most praised him in earlier generations there is an acknowledgement that as a model for modern statesmen, Cicero must be deficient. Discussing Cicero as a model for rhetoric in deliberative assemblies, John Quincy Adams injected a note of warning into his remarks: the modern world was governed by representative bodies rather than by the democratic assemblies of the ancient world. This changed the function as well as the nature of oratory.[39] It is a small comment in a work that otherwise has little but praise for Cicero, but it does highlight a theme that would grow in significance throughout the century. Whether in popular works or in

---

[36] Strachan-Davidson 1900: 293–4.   [37] Strachan-Davidson 1900: 293.
[38] Rosner 1988.   [39] Adams 1810: 266.

scholarly ones, the focus of interest moved from Cicero the moral philosopher to Cicero the practical politician as contemporary debates about the nature of politics themselves de-emphasized the individual virtue of citizens and statesmen and instead focused on the mechanics of politics and political institutions.

Yet what remained a constant throughout the century was the desire to pass judgement on Cicero as a politician and as a moral example. Scholarly and popular authors alike would not content themselves with less, even though the grounds upon which such an assessment was made were narrower than they had been in other ages and hinged upon assessment of his political career above all. Even as his reputation suffered Cicero, the most familiar and (because of the unusually intimate nature of the evidence about his life) most human of ancient historical figures, remained one of the most studied.[40] As Strachan-Davidson put it, 'The time lives again before us in the pages of Cicero, and, thanks to him, he and his contemporaries are not mere lay-figures but actual flesh and blood.'[41] His nineteenth-century readers still hoped to find in his writings an insight into Roman politics 'much more living and true in them than in regular works composed expressly to teach it to us'.[42] The best way of understanding the contested nature of his reputation was as a product of a more sophisticated view of Roman history and a more nuanced view of politics in general. Modern readers of all persuasions thought that they understood Cicero as no previous age had done, even as they projected onto him shadows cast by contemporary debates about the nature of republican government and the desirability of the flexibility and moderation that all agreed were the hallmarks of his career.

Further reading

Readers wishing to explore the themes of this chapter further might like to read more widely the work of nineteenth-century classical scholars. An excellent starting-point remains John Edwin Sandys, *A History of Classical Scholarship*, published in three volumes between 1903 and 1908, the third volume of which concerned the eighteenth and nineteenth centuries. There has been no specific study of Cicero's changing reputation over time, though accounts of the importance of the classics in Enlightenment and modern republican thought invariably mention Cicero. Specific studies of Cicero's place in the curriculum, such as Winterer 2001 also discuss Cicero's nineteenth-century reputation in passing, while studies such as

---

[40] Boissier 1897: 1.   [41] Strachan-Davidson 1900: 3.   [42] Boissier 1897: 1.

Hingley 2000 assert the wider cultural importance of Roman history for the nineteenth century. The conflicting interpretations of Cicero's career outlined in the chapter above continued well into the twentieth century, even if the basic contours of the debate had been well established by the end of the nineteenth.

19

LYNN S. FOTHERINGHAM

Twentieth/twenty-first-century Cicero(s)

Introduction

The British novelist Robert Harris is currently two-thirds of the way through a trilogy about the career of Cicero: *Imperium*, published in 2006, covers the period from his rhetorical training in Greece to his election to the consulship (79–64 BC); *Lustrum* (American title *Conspirata*), published in 2009, takes the story down to the eve of his exile (58 BC). As fictional works in which Cicero is the central character, these novels are unusual, although he is a member of the supporting cast in many novels and a few works for film and television. And yet the life of Cicero is full of drama: he is (or can be) the underdog who achieves high political office; the years after his consulship are filled with easily dramatizable highs and lows, both public and private; his final years can readily be figured as tragedy, of last-stand republicanism or political blindness according to taste.

In this chapter I shall examine Cicero's presence in popular culture – confining myself to works in the English language – in order to discover what sort of presence he *does* have there. Since his appearances on film are so scanty, it is necessary to expand our focus to include written fiction. This necessity may be seen as an advantage, since it opens up a world relatively neglected by scholars of classical receptions, that of the mass-market historical novel. Much work remains to be done here, and this chapter can only make some initial observations and suggestions. I shall also glance at popular history, whether in the form of documentary film or published works.

The films, novels and popular works on Cicero referred to in this chapter will be found in the Further Reading section. Author/date references are to works in the volume bibliography.

Cicero on film

But to start with filmed works, whether destined to be shown in the cinemas or on television. The late Republic is less frequently treated in film than the early empire,[1] and Cicero is on the whole a marginal figure. This is not necessarily a problem for the student of reception. The fact that a historical figure is usually a minor character can itself be an interesting one – it is the starting-point of this chapter. The question of why such a minor figure is included at all can be asked, and the few details included to characterize such a figure can be seen as those which stand out as the most important ones in the popular imagination.

Cicero appears in Shakespeare's *Julius Caesar*, of which there are more than two dozen attested versions listed on the Internet Movie Database (nine by the BBC alone). But Cicero may have been omitted from the early, and short, silent versions (1908, 1911, 1913 . . .), as he is such a minor character; in this respect Shakespeare prefigures most filmic representations of the Republic. In Joseph L. Mankiewicz's *Cleopatra* (1963), Michael Hordern gets only a few minutes' screentime as Cicero. He is simply a representative republican senator, disapproving of Caesar and especially Antony, although he is clearly depicted as having a clever tongue, Cicero's most famous and perhaps most significant characteristic. He is unimportant to the plot: the question of whether he might be included in the conspiracy is not even debated, as it is in Shakespeare, and he does not appear on screen again after Caesar's death, so nothing can be made of his opposition to Antony. Had Mankiewicz been allowed to cut his material into two films instead of one, there might have been more space for Cicero[2] – and if so, the fact that it is Hordern who is cast against Richard Burton's Antony may have been supposed to parallel the relationship between Demosthenes and Alexander, portrayed by the same actors, in Robert Rossen's *Alexander the Great* seven years before. Can a case be made that, even if the film we have is not what the director originally intended, the decision to leave Cicero in the few scenes where he appears was nevertheless consciously made? It might be that he could just not easily be excised from those scenes once filmed, but if we are allowed to imagine that his inclusion, however brief, was a deliberate choice, it is tempting to speculate that it is because of an expectation that the audience would know who he was, and might even look for him in this context. (The parallel with Demosthenes, if it is there, also depends on audience-knowledge.) If such an expectation existed, it might be attributed

---

[1] So Joshel, Malamud and Wyke 2005: 3.
[2] See Solomon 2001: 70–1 on the cutting of *Cleopatra*.

to his presence in the Shakespeare play, or to the importance of Cicero's works in the school Latin curriculum.

But not all film-makers feel that a representation of the last days of the Republic is incomplete without reference to Cicero: although he has a similar minor role in DeMille's *Cleopatra* (1934), he is omitted altogether from two recent television mini-series, *Cleopatra* (1999) and *Julius Caesar* (2002) – the latter supposedly dealing directly with the period of Cicero's hey-day. On the other hand, his appearance in the soft-core pornographic film *The Notorious Cleopatra* (1970) is striking because it is so thoroughly unnecessary. Why is he included, if not because the audience is supposed to know who he is, or perhaps to feel flattered that they are expected to know who he is?[3] Admittedly, since the film is playing games with Shakespeare rather than with the ancient sources, it may be because of Cicero's appearance in *Julius Caesar* that the film-makers ever thought of him. But ironically – and probably accidentally – he is one of the more historically accurate characters in the film, if being represented as clever (making barbed asides, sometimes to the camera), and perhaps as disapproving of Caesar, is enough to count as historical accuracy.

Before I leave the question of how much can be squeezed out of minor appearances, it may be worth commenting on the inclusion of a character named Cicero in Ridley Scott's *Gladiator* (2000): a slave belonging to the protagonist, Maximus. Scott's film is less concerned with evoking ancient sources than with evoking earlier 'epic' films:[4] a cross between *Spartacus* and *The Fall of the Roman Empire* in terms of plot, it refers to *Ben-Hur* and *I, Claudius* – and, with its ultimate (and anachronistic) restoration of the Republic, probably *Star Wars*. Symbolic of this 'intertextuality' is the casting of Derek Jacobi, who played Claudius in the 1970s BBC television series, as an even more anachronistic 'senator Gracchus' than the one played by Charles Laughton in Kubrick's 1960 *Spartacus*: Laughton had been destined to play Claudius in the never-finished 1937 film of Robert Graves' work.[5] Given the fact that Cicero is so minor a figure in earlier films, it is harder to make the case for anything in particular being evoked by this use of the mere name. If, in the 1960s, film-makers might include Cicero because of a dim possibility that people might recognize the character, when Scott returns to ancient-world epic at the end of the century, all that remains of the great

---

[3] Nisbet 2009: 157 might describe this attempt at flattery as 'part of the novice-friendly sales pitch', although his article as a whole argues that there is no real engagement with the 'source' material in such pornographic takes on Shakespeare or the classics.

[4] Winkler 2004.

[5] *The Epic that Never Was*, a 1967 documentary on the abortive film, is available as an 'extra' on the DVD edition of the BBC version of *I, Claudius*.

orator is his name – as if audiences might be expected to recognize that name as Roman without attaching any particular information to it at all.

The 2000s saw no fewer than three television series focused on the establishment of the principate: a mini-series, *Imperium: Augustus* (2003), a slight longer series, *Empire* (2005), and, best known of all, the HBO/BBC co-production *Rome* (two seasons, 2005–7). The first two start not long before the death of Caesar, while the third takes its starting-point further back to before the civil war between Caesar and Pompey. Cicero appears in all three. There is some indication in the first two that the audience of this period is less expected to know who he is. In *Imperium: Augustus* some care is taken, at his first appearance, to indicate explicitly that he is a renowned speaker. In *Empire* he is presented, somewhat astonishingly for the classicist viewer, as Caesar's friend who mourns his death.

In *Rome*, Cicero is given considerably more space than we have seen so far. That this is even possible is because of the much greater length of the work; *Rome* was a weekly serial, which eventually totalled twenty-two episodes of around fifty minutes each.[6] Its nearest rival, *Empire*, trails far behind with six hour-long episodes. So the amount of screen-time allowed to Cicero can be seen, not as a sign of greater interest in the man, but rather as an accidental result of the format of the work. But while he remains a minor character – maybe little more than set-dressing, as in the 1963 *Cleopatra* – the space given to him is symptomatic of some concern for providing a historical background. This is especially true in the first season, where he is less necessary for the main plot. *Rome*, like all the other filmed versions of the ancient world considered so far, turns as much as possible of the historical politics into personal, family drama – ultimately, Caesar's assassination can be said to be brought about by the quarrel between Atia and Servilia (Augoustakis 2008). Even so, the series' creators put some effort into portraying the complexity of late Republican politics: Cicero, Cato and Metellus Scipio feature in the narrative as well as Pompey, Caesar, Antony and Brutus. The serial format makes it possible for an audience with no knowledge of the period to distinguish the characters in a fairly large cast, and to follow a relatively complicated political plot. But politics is an important part of the background in *Rome*, and it is a more detailed, messier politics than is allowed for in the other films: contrast, for example, the extreme simplification of the picture in the 2002 *Julius Caesar*, in which there appear to be only three politicians of any note in post-Sullan Rome: Caesar, Pompey and Cato.

---

[6] Solomon 2008: 25 notes this difference between *Rome* and the 'mini-series' he has been discussing.

The format of *Rome* also aligns it with a completely different kind of predecessor from the ancient-world film or mini-series: the gritty, dystopian worlds of recent HBO serials such as *The Sopranos* (1999–2007) and *The Wire* (2002–8), with their lack of a moral centre. In *Imperium: Augustus* and *Empire*, glib identifications of the senate/nobles as 'corrupt', and Caesar as 'man of the people' construct a black-and-white world in which right, represented by Caesar's heir, will eventually triumph. It is debatable whether any of the characters in *Rome* are treated in a wholly positive light, and it is in this context that any judgement seemingly passed on Cicero must be understood. In the first season his primary attribute is timidity: he is pressurized by Pompey into acting against Caesar, and is manifestly unhappy in the Pompeian camp before defecting to Caesar after Pharsalus. But timidity is not a straightforwardly negative characteristic: the senatorial/Pompeian faction is so driven by fanatical hatred of Caesar, so easily led into false moves, that Cicero's weak resistance to it is to some extent right. In the second season, when the rest of the Pompeians are dead and Brutus and Cassius are in the east, he is the only representative of the senatorial party at Rome: he shows some backbone in standing up to Antony, and he dies bravely. But on the whole, he comes across as faintly ridiculous: the actor, David Bamber, is not particularly attractive, and far too young for the part historically speaking, lacking Cicero's proper gravitas (contrast the white locks/balding pates of Hordern in *Cleopatra*, Gottfried John in *Imperium: Augustus* and Michael Byrne in *Empire*); the character is haunted by memories of the actor's earlier turn as a particularly unbearable Mr Collins in the 1995 BBC *Pride and Prejudice* – well known to viewers on both sides of the Atlantic.

The makers of *Rome* emphasized the physical grittiness of their world as putting a distance between them and earlier films set in the ancient world;[7] the moral darkness of the series can also be seen as performing this function. Another factor contributing to this distance is innovative treatment of events and characters, particularly Brutus (who is difficult to imagine as an effective conspirator – or anything else – on his first appearance) and Cleopatra (Daugherty 2008). To a classicist viewer, there is nothing particularly innovative about the treatment of Cicero; but given his minimal presence in the material from which *Rome* is being distinguished, there does not need to be: a fuller treatment than ever before is innovative enough.

Some other reason than the desire to be different is preferable for the 'innovation' – or 'inaccuracy' – of *Empire*'s alliance of Cicero and Caesar. It

---

[7] See the creators' comments in newspaper articles about the forthcoming series such as Bruni 2004, Walsh 2005.

is just conceivable that the film-makers would defend the notion of Cicero as Caesar's friend on the grounds of their historically attested friendly relations at various times, but to represent him as grieving at his death is simply inaccurate. The best explanation for the inaccuracy is probably the need for simplification combined with the focus on the rise of Octavian, whom Cicero supported against Antony: explaining why he would support the nephew when he rejoiced at the death of the uncle may have seemed too difficult in a work without the leisurely exposition of *Rome* or the explanatory first-person voiceover of *Imperium: Augustus*.

In conducting this survey of filmic versions of Cicero, I have not avoided questions of historicity/authenticity. Much of the scholarship on the ancient world in film has dismissed the question of accuracy as a red herring; Winkler 2004: 16–24 presents the arguments clearly. But as Wyke 1997: 13 acknowledges, the selection of events in the filmic account reveals 'the logic of that account'; so does the changing of elements from the original sources, or 'inaccuracy' as it might be labelled. This is evident in many articles on films set in the ancient world which explicitly subscribe to the view that accuracy is not the be-all-and-end-all of their analysis, but which still find it useful to compare the modern version with the ancient sources, and label individual elements as historical or unhistorical as part of their analysis. Perhaps more important than scholars' views for our understanding of popular culture is the fact that accuracy remains an important part of the way these works are marketed,[8] and of the general public's understanding of what these works are (or should be) doing, as evidenced by consumer dicussions on sites like IMDb and Amazon; one viewer on IMDb specifically criticizes the 2002 *Julius Caesar* for omitting Cicero.[9] An examination of the ways in which the *idea* of accuracy or authenticity operates in the commercial world of historical fiction and popular history would be valuable. I shall find more reason to discuss accuracy in the discussion of print-fiction that follows.

Cicero in print

Turn to the world of publishing, and examples of Cicero as a member of the supporting cast in fictions can be vastly multiplied; the following list is only a sample:

---

[8] See especially the press pack (BBC 2005), and numerous comments by creators in newspaper articles (Bruni 2004, Walsh 2005). Milnor 2008 presents a scholar's take on the creators' desire for authenticity.

[9] Username 'csongor', posting 28.8.08: 'to omit [Crassus and Cicero] is akin to omitting w.t. Sherman and Jefferson Davis from any story about the civil war' (capitalization as in original), www.imdb.com/title/tt0284741/reviews.

Hardy, W. G. *Turn Back the River* (1938)	– focusing on Clodia
Wilder, T. *The Ides of March* (1948)	– death of Caesar (epistolary)
Radin, M. *Epicurus my Master* (1949)	– memoirs of Atticus
Warner, R. *The Young Caesar* (1958)	– memoirs of Caesar
Jaro, B. K. *The Key* (1988)	– memoirs of Caelius
Massie, A. *Antony* (1997)	– memoirs of Antony

In most of these works Cicero has at least more to do than just dress the set, as in *Cleopatra*, although he may not have more of a role than he has in *Rome*.

Interesting comparanda for Harris's Cicero novels, works which develop Cicero as a reasonably important character, include the *Masters of Rome* series by Colleen McCullough (1990–2007) and two series of detective novels set in the same period, Steven Saylor's *Roma Sub Rosa* (1990–present) and John Maddox Roberts's *SPQR* (1990–present). McCullough's series is a comprehensive project to tell the story of the last days of the Republic: seven enormous novels cover the period from 110 to 27 BC, starting with Marius and Sulla and ending with Antony and Cleopatra.[10] Inevitably, such a series has more than one main character, although a case could be made that Julius Caesar is the overall 'hero'. Cicero is among the cast of thousands, naturally more prominent at some points in the story (e.g. 63 BC) than others. Saylor and Roberts both have as central protagonist an invented detective-character: Gordianus the Finder, an apolitical private investigator, in *Roma Sub Rosa*; Decius Caecilius Metellus, a budding politician with an obsession for finding the truth, in *SPQR*. In three of Saylor's novels, the central mystery is derived from a Ciceronian case (*Roman Blood* covers the trial of Roscius Amerinus, *The Venus Throw* that of Caelius and *A Murder on the Appian Way* that of Milo; in addition, *Catilina's Riddle* is centred on Cicero's consulship), and Cicero is a correspondingly prominent figure. Roberts's crimes are invented, although they play cleverly with incidents from the historical record; Cicero is again one of a large cast, his prominence varying depending on the subject matter of the novel.

Three stand-alone novels in which the character of Cicero is reasonably well developed also have elements of the detective story. Despite its title, Kenneth Benton's *Death on the Appian Way* (1974), narrated by Caelius, focuses on the killing of Clodius by Milo in 52 only in the last quarter of the novel, but ends, like many a detective novel, with a revelation of who was ultimately responsible for the crime. Joan O'Hagan invents a murder for *A Roman Death* (1988), which also closes with multiple revelations about the true culprit – Cicero does not quite manage to guess correctly.

[10] Malamud 2005 provides a critical introduction to McCullough's series.

Ron Burns's *Roman Shadows: A Mystery* (1992) has an invented narrator, Gaius Livinius Severus, but focuses on historical events, particularly the relationship between Caesar and Curio. In many of these novels, Cicero is represented positively:

> Marcus Cicero . . . was also a keen and shrewd judge of men even if he did not always act on his judgement. And above everything else he loved . . . Rome well enough to die for it. (Radin, *Epicurus my Master*, ch. 3; Atticus speaking.)[11]

> Underlying his dignity, they felt immediately the tremendous vitality of that challenging, restless intelligence. (O'Hagan, *A Roman Death*, ch. 12; narrator's voice.)

> The lamplight shines on his humorous, intelligent mouth, his thoughtful, experienced, lawyer's eyes . . . I am fascinated as always to watch his mind at work. (Jaro, *The Key*, ch. 1; Caelius speaking.)

> Ah, Cicero, I thought – now there's a statesman . . . I and so many others had sat as pupils at Cicero's feet, enjoying the words of wisdom. (Burns, *Roman Shadows*, ch. 1; invented character speaking.)

At other times he is portrayed more or less negatively:

> To win the consulship, therefore, he was, secretly, prepared to do anything . . . It was with this attitude, betraying itself by a tendency to cringe and to agree a little too eagerly with whatever was said, that he greeted Catulus and Hortensius and Cato. (Hardy, *Turn Back the River*, Part Three, ch. 2; narrator's voice.)

> There was no end to the old man's vanity, which was indeed the cause of his failure as a politician. It made him distrusted, for you can never be certain how the vain main will act since you cannot tell just what will prick his vanity. (Massie, *Antony*, ch. 3; Antony speaking.)

Where Atticus or Antony is speaking, the positive/negative attitude is predictable. Where Caelius is speaking, there is more room for variation; Benton's *Death on the Appian Way* has an interestingly nuanced portrait, with the intelligence acknowledged but also some faults. The broader scope of the long series also allows nuance, and development: 'By this time he had acquired the vanity and self-importance that marred his otherwise admirable character' (Roberts, *The Catiline Conspiracy* [second book in the series], ch. 1). The Cicero of Saylor's *Roma Sub Rosa* series undergoes an interesting development. In the first novel, *Roman Blood* (1990), he is a fairly impressive figure with both nerves and a brain, although the protagonist,

---

[11] I give references to the novels by chapter, as multiple editions for some of them result in varying paginations.

Gordianus, does not entirely approve of the way his intelligence and daring manifest themselves. Four novels later, in *A Murder on the Appian Way* (1996), he is an ineffectual politician and a bit of a jaded hack. Even his faithful servant Tiro seems shocked by his lack of scruples, and one of the climactic moments of the novel is his failure even to produce a decent speech in defence of Milo; admittedly, this farcical scene is taken directly from the ancient accounts of Plutarch and Dio, and appears, despite the manifest unreliability of the sources, in many a biography of Cicero because it is such a good story. Saylor has admitted in interviews that he started off with the idea of making Cicero the detective and protagonist, but as he researched the character he found him more and more difficult to view as either a seeker after truth or a hero.[12] The invented character of Gordianus, who is both, presents Saylor's negative view of Cicero to the reader as first-person narrator of the novels. I shall return below to the question of how Cicero is judged.

It is immediately evident that there is a much greater number of novels than films dealing with the late Republic and featuring Cicero. This is largely a matter of economics: producing a book is relatively cheap compared with producing a film, whether for the big screen or the small. There is still a preference in publishing for the empire over the Republic, a fact that may be because of not only the riches and scandals which the former affords, but also the horrific complexity of late Republican politics, mentioned above in discussing the films. But it could be argued that the novel is better suited to dealing with this complexity than film, given the specific characteristics of the two media. More can be fitted into a book than a film, as is evidenced by most cinematic adaptations of pre-existing novels.[13] And while *Rome* has demonstrated how serial television can allow a more detailed treatment of any particular subject-matter than feature-length cinema, the publishing world also permits serialization; it is difficult to imagine even a long televisual narrative which would fit in as much information as McCullough's *Masters of Rome* sequence. Even *Rome* must simplify: a viewer might easily come away from the series with the idea that there was only ever one consul at a time. Contrast the praise awarded to Robert Harris by some reviewers (such as Kemp 2006) for his ability to make the complexity of the Roman political

---

[12] The most explicit statement of Saylor's disillusionment with the historical Cicero that I have found online is no longer available. But see comments on Cicero in interviews: Cuthbertson 1998; KM 1998; see also the 'Author's Note' at the end of *Roman Blood* for the view of Cicero Saylor had developed by the time he had finished writing this, the first novel in the series.

[13] For a detailed analysis of 'the medium-specific approach' to film adaptations of novels, see Cardwell 2002: 43–51.

system comprehensible. Print therefore allows more detailed exploration of whatever it is the author (and the intended audience) is interested in, whether that be exploration of the characters' emotions, or the accumulation of 'historical' detail: a bigger cast of characters, a bigger selection of attested events, more detailed interaction with the existing sources.[14]

Communicating complexity is potentially a step towards greater historical accuracy, and so the question arises: are the novels, perhaps even by their very nature, more concerned with (some kind of) accuracy than the films? The frequently employed device of the 'Author's Note' at the end of a historical novel may constitute evidence that they are. Here authors can proclaim their research credentials, acknowledge – and recommend – ancient sources and modern historical works, and where necessary explain the narrative or other drives behind the changes they may have made. The fact that this device is used even in such works as Conn Iggulden's *Emperor* series – which makes some startling changes to the historical record, including narrating the Catilinarian conspiracy without any reference to Cicero – implies that the relationship between the novel and the historical record is believed to *matter* in some way. This is confirmed by the hot debate among readers about the merits of the novels on the Amazon website. Buried in the wide variety of opinions are a variety of ideas about authenticity: what it is, how it can be achieved, whether and why it matters. I shall return below to McCullough's Notes, which, like her novels, are more substantial than most.[15]

Films make their own gestures towards historical accuracy, whether in the body of the work itself (e.g. quotations from ancient authors presented as explanatory titles or through sonorous voiceovers), in the credits, in advertising or in accompanying materials, whether press packs and souvenir programmes or DVD 'extras' in the form of commentaries and documentaries. But credits roll quickly, advertising is not always seen by the viewer, and all of this, including the accompanying material with quotes from academics, can be misleading.[16] Even the DVD 'extras', like the film itself, are soon over – yes, in theory you could rewind and take notes, but *do* you? – and not easily checked. A list of sources and explicit analysis in an 'Author's Note' seems more likely to invite the reader to make their own comparison

---

[14] Compare Milnor's comments (2008: 46) comparing her own audience as a teacher to that of *Rome*'s creators.

[15] See Malamud 2005: 219–20 on McCullough's claims to 'authenticity'.

[16] See Haynes 2008: 48–9 on the limitations of claims to accuracy in the commentary; Joshel 2005: 148–9 on the misleading nature of the introductions to the American televising of *I, Claudius*, which nevertheless reinforce the impression of historicity.

with the ancient sources, which may well be found in the same library or bookshop as the novel itself.

Economics may also play a role. As a film costs more to produce, so it needs to reach a wider audience in order to recoup the expenditure involved in its creation; a book does not have to reach as many consumers in order to be profitable. This factor results, as mentioned above, in *more* books than films, but also in a variety of specialist subgenres – romance, military fiction, children's books, mystery novels – catering to only a proportion of the audience that must be reached by a film. One sub-audience which it would be particularly useful to take account of is the amateur history-buffs so well attested in the IMDb and Amazon discussions mentioned above, who expect a particular level of 'authenticity' even from fiction. The purchases of this group may not be restricted to individual subgenres; if they have a relatively greater importance in the world of published fiction, it is because of the fact that, since the audience for a book is smaller than that for a film, the history buffs can in theory constitute a larger proportion of that audience. This is one reason why work on the relative popularity of different publications and on the demographic reached by them would be very interesting.

Cicero in popular non-fiction

Before turning to a more detailed analysis of how Cicero is judged in some of these novels, I should like to expand our focus yet again, to (supposedly) non-fiction works. Here there are works that are more closely comparable to Harris's novels in that they have Cicero as a central character. In television documentary about the end of the Republic, Cicero is no more an essential character than he is in fiction; for example in 'Caesar' (an hour-length episode of the 2006 BBC documentary-series *Ancient Rome: The Rise and Fall of an Empire*), only a small number of the senatorial party can be introduced to the audience: the film-makers choose Cato and Marcellus. A 2005 episode of the long-running BBC series *Timewatch*, 'Murder in Rome' (scripted by Tom Holland), has a much narrower focus. The episode tells the story of Cicero's first big court case, the trial of Sextus Roscius of Ameria in the late eighties. It involves considerable dramatization and indeed fictionalization of the trial and the events surrounding it; an explanatory voiceover and numerous still images of ancient visual evidence, however, identify it as generically as documentary, or 'docudrama'.

Even a programme like this, belonging to the filmic genre with the greatest pretension to historicity, plays fast and loose sometimes. One historically rather implausible aspect of the representation is a clever move in terms of engaging the audience. Cicero is pressurized into defending Roscius at the last minute, and when the trial begins he still knows next to nothing about the case. This turns the trajectory of the episode into that of a murder-mystery. At one point the young orator is shown consulting the proscription lists himself – apparently the first person to do so – at night, by torchlight, searching for 'clues'. The unexpected appearance of a further witness from Ameria also contributes to the detection aspect of the plot. The choice of the murder-mystery format is interesting in the light of the tremendous success of historical murder-mystery *novels* in recent decades. In sharp contrast to Saylor's decision to take the detective role away from Cicero, here our sympathies are further engaged by the fact that Cicero is the detective/protagonist, the seeker after truth. The Roscius episode can be easily played in Cicero's favour, and here he is presented as both a young man, played by a good-looking actor, and an underdog, easily engaging the audience's sympathies. The material from the speech is broken up and redistributed, partly in order to facilitate the gradual revelation of information that is a key part of the murder-mystery plot; Cicero's own handling of the case, in contrast, is remarkable for the early stage at which it reveals the answer to 'who(really)dunnit'.[17] In the docudrama, which squeezes considerable drama out of Cicero's rhetorical abilities, this gradual revelation leads to the splitting up of the trial into repeated encounters between Cicero and the prosecution, rather than single long speeches one after another; this has the result that the trial plays more like a modern trial (and more like a dramatization of such trials) than a late Republican one. This is likely to have been considered beneficial from the point of view of engaging the modern audience, who in any case would have found a continuous delivery of the extant speech visually static and dull.

We find similar fragmentation of sources in Saylor's stories based on Cicero's speeches, which are the novels that engage most closely with individual texts. In *A Murder on the Appian Way*, following the tradition of Cicero's poor performance at Milo's trial allows Saylor to use knowledge gained from the speech in his overall plot – such as the dangerous nature of the countryside immediately outside Rome, where Gordianus himself is kidnapped in ch. 21 – without attributing the knowledge to Cicero's text. By this novel, the fifth in the series, Gordianus/Saylor's negative opinion of Cicero has become quite clear. But practical reasons rather than negative opinion may be the cause of this failure to credit Cicero with the information Saylor has used. Although there is no problem about avoiding static visuals in the novels, the same tendency to break up the speeches appears in other

---

[17] In his speech *Pro Roscio Amerino*, which is 154 sections long, Cicero names Chrysogonus as villain in §6, Magnus and Capito in §17.

novels, including Harris's; this kind of fragmentation of the ancient sources might be an interesting issue to pursue in further work on the interaction between modern popular works and the actual historical record. Saylor's novel, like the *Timewatch* docudrama, must present the information more gradually than the speech in order to allow the process of detection to take place. A third possible factor is that simply replicating the speech is not particularly creative; anyone who wants to read the speech can, after all, go out and buy the Penguin or Oxford Classics translation. With all this in mind, the story about Cicero's failure at Milo's trial is a gift to the novelist, presenting him with the perfect opportunity to scatter elements of the speech through the rest of the novel, without the need to recap them when he gets to the trial-scene itself.

Turning back to print, popular historical works about the late Republic, such as Tom Holland's *Rubicon* (2003), are almost bound to mention Cicero, although their focus tends to remain on the great warlords Marius, Sulla, Pompey and Caesar, who are likewise the main focus of Colleen McCullough's fiction. Where the great orator becomes a dominant figure is in the world of biography. Nineteen biographies of Cicero were published in English in the twentieth century (including two translated from other languages and one published simultaneously in English and German) – even if some of these use Cicero as a lens through which to view his culture, rather than focusing on him alone.[18] The remarkable number of works focusing on Cicero is highlighted by a comparison with biographies of other late Republican politicians such as Sulla, Pompey the Great, Marc Antony and Augustus, none of whom reached double figures over the course of the twentieth century. Cicero's only rival in terms of *number* of modern biographies is his great contemporary, Julius Caesar, with thirteen twentieth-century biographies in English (three translated from other languages).[19] That Caesar should attract attention is no surprise; that he outstrips Antony and Augustus may perhaps be attributed to the wealth of evidence available for his life, thanks in part to his own campaign memoirs but also to the writings of Cicero. This reasoning applies even more to Cicero, the single ancient figure about whom, thanks to the extraordinary survival of so much of his correspondence, we know the most.[20] If only the speeches and philosophical works remained, it is difficult to imagine that Cicero would attract as many

---

[18] E.g. Cowell 1948, Lacey 1978.

[19] There has been a positive explosion in biographies of Caesar since the turn of the twenty-first century, with at least six between 2001 and 2009. I have not included works aimed at children.

[20] This point is a repeated trope in introductions to the biographies, e.g. Petersson 1920: 1, Stockton 1971: vii, Fuhrmann 1992: vii.

modern biographers; although his story is full of human interest, he is too easily relegated as a political failure to be as fascinating as Caesar. I shall return below to the relationship between Cicero and Caesar in the modern imagination.

In calculating these figures I have not attempted to draw a clear demarcation between scholarly and popular works, as the boundary between the two types is not always clear. Authorship does not necessarily settle the matter: scholars may write for more than one audience;[21] conversely, authors who are not classical scholars may still hope for some kind of approval from the scholarly community. Although some biographies will be too scholarly for a general audience, a case could even be made that biography by its very nature is a popular genre, whatever the scholarly credentials of the author. Its clear narrative structure, although it may incorporate scholarly argument, is easily digestible by a wide audience, its drive to include all of a life may lead to the exclusion of thorough discussion of the more disputed points,[22] and its human focus has a wide appeal. What can be observed is that there is a marked difference between the identity of the biographers in the first and second halves of the century. Of the nine works that appeared between 1914 and 1948, only three were produced by classicists working in universities; of the ten biographies between 1966 and 1994 (counting the two volumes by Mitchell as one biography), only one was not – and the author of that one was still an educational professional.[23] The other six authors in the first half of the century were mostly lawyers, politicians and civil servants; one was a doctor and poet. Five of the nine works of this period were by Americans, two by Brits, one by a Hungarian writing in English and one was originally written in French. Two of the biographies produced after 1950 were originally written in German; the remaining eight were produced by education professionals in the UK or Ireland. The next biography of Cicero written by someone from another walk of life was Anthony Everitt's in 2001.[24]

Whereas it was only tentatively suggested above that some of the differences between the sixties film versions and those released at the start of the twenty-first century could be attributed to decline in classical knowledge in the audience, we are on more secure ground with the biographies, since there are so many more of them. The disappearance of biographies of Cicero by anyone other than classical scholars in the second half of the

---

[21] See Stockton 1971: vii–viii, Rawson 1975 (preface to 1983 edition).
[22] Comments along these lines in Stockton 1971: viii, Rawson 1975: xv–xvi, Fuhrmann 1992: vii–viii.
[23] David Taylor was head of OFSTED's Teacher Education and Training team when his short 1973 work was reprinted by Bristol Classical Press in the 1990s.
[24] Everitt was formerly Secretary-General of the Arts Council of Great Britain.

twentieth century may well reflect the decline in Classics as a fundamental element of Anglophone education at this time and indeed earlier: most of the non-classicist biographers of the first half of the century were schooled early in the twentieth or late in the nineteenth centuries. The gradual increase in biographies *by* classical scholars (one between 1851 and 1900, three between 1901 and 1950, ten between 1951 and 2000 – again counting Mitchell's two volumes as one biography) may reflect the ever-increasing importance of numbers of publications to an academic career, but the sheer number produced in the second half of the twentieth century – and especially in the seventies – is remarkable. Some of these works are clearly designed for students (Taylor 1973, Wiedemann 1994), and thus also reflect the changes in classical education during this period – the need for basic works to introduce school pupils and university students, taking courses in Classical Studies/Classical Civilization/Ancient History, to authors and periods which previous generations would have learned about through reading the Latin authors.

The biographies at last provide a range of works focused on Cicero himself that is large enough to make comparisons. In considering the way Cicero is judged in popular culture, I shall, therefore, begin with the biographies.

Judging Cicero (and Caesar)

Scholarly works dealing with (for example) the precise details of Cicero's political activity at a particular time, or the rhetorical style of one of his speeches, can refrain from judging the character of their protagonist – although they do not always do so. Such restraint is rare in the biographies and popular histories. The very intimacy with Cicero which the evidence appears to grant has a tendency to encourage judgement, and popular works inevitably exploit their readers' interest in the human aspects of their subjects; in Cicero's case, even the more scholarly biographies are perhaps more likely to express explicit judgement of the man they have taken as their subject-matter. As for the fictional(ized) works, we should probably be surprised if they did *not* have a point of view.

The familiar arguments are repeated over and over again. Was Cicero a coward? insincere? inconsistent in his policies? a political imbecile? Or was he a staunch and wise republican, a defender of freedom, overwhelmed by events? One might think that biographies and documentaries would be more likely to deal with these questions explicitly and fiction only implicitly, with the reader having to deduce the attitude to Cicero from the way his actions are presented. In fact, the first-person memoir form of historical novel allows explicit judgement, as we have seen, whether immediate or enhanced by hindsight; this is less true of the fictional films, only one of which, *Imperium: Augustus*, has a clear first-person voiceover.[25] On the other hand, the biographies can be remarkably neutral in tone and narrative rather than judgemental in focus. Some do devote a chapter to summary and assessment, notably the works of Sihler (1914) and Taylor (1916), but this appears to be more common in nineteenth-century biographies; it is dropped by successors. Comments on the existence of the debate, however, survive: 'The very things for which he is criticized are evidence of Cicero's finer qualities' (Wilkin 1947: 238); 'Controversy is still rife in many areas, and no portrait of Cicero is likely to achieve unquestioning adherence' (Rawson 1975: 306). Note that Taylor was a Southern American politician and Wilkin an Ohio Supreme Court Judge; awareness of scholarly debate – and the willingness to refer to it – is not confined to classical scholars such as Sihler and Rawson.

Taylor's Chapter 15, 'An Appreciation of Cicero', looks back to the earlier works of Forsyth (1864) and Collins (1871) in its direct references to German scholars Drumann and Mommsen as the principal modern exponents of the anti-Ciceronian point of view; he explicitly identifies 'Caesar worship' as part of Mommsen's motivation (Taylor 1916: 454). The contrast between (modern) attitudes to Caesar and attitudes to Cicero is often evoked by the latter's defenders; Petersson, for example, laments that Cicero is castigated for reading his brother's mail: '[this] sin against morality and good manners, if a sin it was, has sunk far more deeply into the modern consciousness than Caesar's looting of towns and enslaving of whole populations' (1920: 17). Taylor argues, rather optimistically, that 'The effect of the assault of Mommsen upon the political character of Cicero is already a thing of the past...rejected, generally with great emphasis, by high authorities' (1916: 455). But critical assessments of Cicero outnumber positive ones, and few of the twentieth-century writers defend him as ardently as Taylor and his predecessors; the most obvious exception is Habicht 1990.

On the question of cowardice, one of the most interesting approaches is that of Witley:

> He was one of those peculiar characters, who are audacious rather than plucky, but who very often become scared of their own daring. Much as he feared danger, he was unable to check his great hatred, that eventually brought about his ruin. He was afraid of those stronger than himself, and still provoked the

---

[25] The voiceover in the 1963 *Cleopatra* is only occasional, and the voice is certainly not that of one of the characters; that in *Empire* does belong to a character, but not to a major political player, and it is again only occasional. See further Joshel 2005: 139–40 on the impact of character-voiceover in the BBC *I, Claudius*.

anger of his adversaries and enemies with the perseverance of a hunting-hound, only to flee from them again, trembling for his own health and safety.[26]

'A. F. Witley' is a pseudonym of Sándor Forbát/Alex Forbath, a Hungarian doctor and poet, whose other books include a psychological detective novel and an edited volume entitled *Love, Marriage and Jealousy*.[27] In the light of this background, it is not surprising that this biography has a particular theory of Cicero's psychology; his title is *The Tremulous Hero*. But though the extent to which the theory is developed here is unusual, the picture of Cicero as timid and changeable is not. Even his defenders tend to acknowledge his faults, and to point out that many of his contemporaries would come across equally badly if their private correspondence was revealed to the world – an argument that may come across either as perfectly correct or as special pleading, according to the taste of the reader.

It is against this background of competing views of Cicero's merits and faults that the fictionalized accounts must be set. Here, too, we shall find that Cicero's position is identified in contrast to Caesar's. Sometimes Caesar comments on Cicero:

> Cicero has always believed that his conduct during this and the following year [64–63] entitles him to a secure place in history as one of Rome's greatest statesmen. Such a claim is absurd. He has no conception of what is needed by the times, and if he were to outlive me and engage again in active politics he would almost certainly be destroyed. (Warner, *The Young Cicero*, Book Three, ch. 4)

In this first-person novel (by classicist Rex Warner), a supposed memoir written by Caesar shortly before his death, the explicitness of the judgement on Cicero is partly justified by the memoir form; this is cleverly combined with an underscoring of Caesar's own superiority to Cicero in terms of political intellect, which has nothing to do with hindsight: his prediction of the future is spot on. Warner's Caesar, in fact, is near-omniscient, the only man who knows what Rome needs. It is not an uncommon portrait, and it is Mommsen-ian. The contrast between a far-seeing Caesar and a blinkered Cicero can also be communicated outside the memoir form, for example through free indirect discourse as in the following passage:

> Suddenly short of breath, Labienus managed to put his goblet down on the desk without spilling its contents, then stared at Caesar as if he had never seen him before. Why did Caesar see so many ramifications when no one else had? Why hadn't he, Titus Labienus, understood better what Cicero was actually

---

[26] Witley 1939: 140–1.
[27] Forbath's own contribution is 'The question of the mother-in-law'.

doing? Ye gods, *Cicero* hadn't understood! Only Caesar had. (McCullough, *Caesar's Women*, Part Five)

The conversation from which this extract comes is one between Caesar and Labienus on the day of the debate on the Catilinarian conspirators. In terms of the triangular relationship between novelist, material and audience, having Caesar explain the ramifications of the senate's vote to execute the conspirators without trial – ramifications which will eventually include Cicero's being driven into exile, although this is not the thing that concerns the character of Caesar – provides McCullough with a way of giving her readers that explanation. What is startling in a writer usually so concerned to demonstrate her scholarly credentials is the fact that in this conversation Caesar reveals to Labienus his plan to try Rabirius on the charge of treason. The trial of Rabirius is usually placed well *before* the debate about the conspirators.

McCullough explains her reasoning in her 'Author's Note'. One of her arguments is that the lowering of the flag on the Janiculum to bring the trial to an end would have been more effective if 'Catilina was known to be in Etruria with an army ... Many must surely have been expecting ... an assault on Rome.' But she also believes that the trial, with its attack on the (mis)use of the so-called *senatus consultum ultimum*, makes little sense unless it takes place after its (mis)use in executing the Catilinarians. This is tantamount to saying that the bulk of Roman politicians were unaware of the possible negative effects of using the *s.c.u.* to justify the execution of the conspirators; as Labienus thinks in the passage quoted, only Caesar sees the ramifications. It could be argued that this gives Caesar too much credit, and his contemporaries not enough. Ironically, another of McCullough's supporting arguments is that Caesar himself could not have foreseen the possible relevance of the *s.c.u.* earlier in the year. It is not my purpose here to establish the actual motivations for (or timing of) the trial of Rabirius, only to point out the implications, for our understanding of Cicero's intelligence and courage (or lack of either), of moving the trial. If the condemnation of the conspirators came *after* the trial of Rabirius, there is an increased chance that Cicero *knew danger he was facing* in promoting the executions, and *took the risk*. McCullough's alteration of the usual chronology, and the justification which accompanies it, deny this reading. One might compare the attitude of scholars who argue that any sign of awareness of danger to Cicero present in the *Fourth Catilinarian* could not have been part of the originally delivered speech, but must have been added after Clodius had begun his attack on Cicero, in the run-up to the latter's exile.[28] It is hard to

---

[28] McDermott 1972 argues against this, but his view has not been universally accepted.

resist the conclusion that McCullough's decision at least is influenced by a *pre-existing* tendency to judge Cicero as not particularly insightful or brave.

The Cicero created by Robert Harris therefore stands out from the crowd, portraying his virtues and abilities – but without whitewashing him completely. This work takes the form of a first-person memoir, although the narrator is not Cicero himself but Tiro, Cicero's trusted (and attested) slave and secretary. The choice of Tiro as narrator is a clever stroke which enables Harris to create sympathy for Cicero while simultaneously projecting a greater impression of objectivity than might be possible with Cicero as a narrator. In the second novel, *Lustrum*, Harris presents a rather different chronology of the trial of Rabirius from McCullough's: he places it *early*, in January 63: Cicero actually hears about it on the night before his inauguration (ch. 2), and it is over before the landbill of Rullus is finally disposed of. It is this episode that sets the scene for the entire novel:

> 'I realised then,' Cicero confided in me afterwards, 'with the force of a revelation, that the true target of this lynch mob of Caesar's was not Rabirius at all, but me, as consul, and that somehow I had to regain control of the situation before my authority to deal with the likes of Catilina was destroyed entirely.' (ch. 4)

Whether this judgement is supposed to be affected by hindsight depends on how the word 'afterwards' is interpreted, but the direct speech adds vividness, and the impression Cicero at least wants to give is that he reached this judgement at the time. The part likely to be played by Catiline is understood by both himself and Caesar. Harris's Cicero is fully aware of the dangers of executing the conspirators, later in the year:

> 'Dear gods, have I not done enough?' Cicero shouted suddenly. 'I have exposed the conspiracy. I have stopped Catilina from becoming consul. I have driven him from Rome. I have foiled an attempt to burn down half the city and massacre us in our homes. I have delivered the traitors into custody. Am I now supposed to shoulder all the opprobrium for killing them as well? It's time you gentlemen started playing your part.' (ch. 11)

Caesar and Cicero are once more set in opposition. But Harris's Cicero is not infallible, either intellectually or morally – he is not given the role that Warner and others give to Caesar. Immediately after his consulship, Tiro recounts that 'He became, in short – and whoever would have imagined saying this of Cicero – a bore' (ch. 12). It is hard not to imagine that Harris had his tongue in his cheek when he wrote that aside! In the same chapter, Tiro and Atticus agree that his letters to Pompey and his editing of his speeches show lack of judgement, and when Crassus allows him to purchase the house on the Palatine at a bargain price, the stage is set for a complex conspiracy against Cicero's reputation which eventually involves both Caesar and Caelius (culminating in ch. 17). Crassus' motivation for this entrapment is his discovery of a trick played on him by Cicero at the time of the Catilinarian conspiracy, revealed to Tiro in ch. 13: Cicero forged the letters that drove Crassus into informing on the conspirators (an incident recounted in ch. 8). Tiro is shocked but ultimately comments that 'I did not presume to judge Cicero for the morality of his action.' Together with Cicero's own comment to Tiro, this reveals the heart of Harris's approach to Roman politics. Cicero is explaining why he did not involve Tiro in the forgery:

> 'It's a compliment to your honesty. You sometimes have too many scruples for the dirty business of politics, Tiro, and I would have found it hard to carry off such a deception under your disapproving gaze. So I had you fooled then, did I?' He sounded quite proud of himself. (ch. 13)

The description of politics as a 'dirty business' is a key element of Harris's approach,[29] which to some extent protects his Cicero from criticism: it is a realistic approach, doubtless coloured by Harris's own extensive experience as a political journalist, and his connections in the Labour Party.[30] A key element in his representation of politics is the impossibility of maintaining any kind of moral purity once one has entered the business, whatever one's motives for entering. The point was made clear in the first novel, *Imperium*, which presents Cicero, his brother Quintus and his cousin Lucius in a triangular relationship in their attitude to politics: Lucius is the high-minded man of principle, Quintus is the pragmatist who recommends the expedient action, and Cicero's success is in no small part because of his ability to compromise between the two extremes. Something of the cost of this compromise is portrayed in the novels, and the choice of Tiro as narrator allows Harris both to pass judgement and to show sympathy. As a slave, Tiro is completely without volition in the political activity of his master (although he is represented as giving advice – and good advice at that); he can afford the luxury of moral judgement, and despite his claim to eschew such judgement his viewpoint allows Harris to let judgement slip in. He is similar to Saylor's Gordianus in his ability to maintain his own innocence; unlike Gordianus, however, his affection for Cicero allows him (and through him his author) to grant Cicero the benefit of the doubt. It is a pity that in presenting this

---

[29] The reviews of *Imperium* emphasize Harris's affinity with politics, and his claim that politics is not boring: Kemp 2006; Rawnsley 2006.

[30] The dedication of *Lustrum* to Peter Mandelson is noted by reviewers, and invites more suggestions that Harris has modern-day parallels in mind: Sandbrook 2009.

humane and realistic portrait of Cicero, Harris feels it necessary to demonize Caesar as much as Warner and McCullough idolize him. This Caesar is not omniscient, his actions are not ascribed to a vision of what is necessary for Rome; rather he is a talented opportunist, with nobody's interests at heart but his own. When Cicero humbles himself and attempts to take Caesar up on his offer of a legateship to escape the threats of Clodius in the final chapter, Caesar pushes and pushes him until Cicero is driven back to a moral stance and forced to decline the offer. Back at home he tries to explain to Terentia:

> 'Does no one in this city understand? That man won't stop until he is master of the world – he more or less just told me exactly that – and I would either have to go along with him as his junior accomplice or break with him at some later stage, and then I would be absolutely finished.' (ch. 19)

The outburst underlines once more Cicero's intellectual superiority over his contemporaries in his ability to comprehend the danger Caesar represents – the rest simply hate him. By this stage in the narrative Caesar has demonstrated his true colours adequately, but in fact this ability to understand the threat he poses has been used to characterize Cicero's intelligence far earlier in the novels.

Conclusions

It is not, perhaps, surprising to find that judgements of Cicero are tied up with judgements of Caesar. A historical figure must be judged in his historical context, and Caesar looms large in Cicero's historical context. Even the *Timewatch* documentary, which has such a narrow focus on a particular trial, drags in Caesar: in an attempt to persuade the reluctant young advocate to take the utterly hopeless case, Caecilia Metella, Roscius' patron, taunts Cicero with the contrast between himself and Caesar, a younger man who is presented as already more successful than him. Historically it is unlikely that Caesar was even in Rome at this time period, and his status as Marius' nephew and his quiet refusal to comply with all of Sulla's commands cannot have boded well for his career. But this is unimportant. Caesar is mentioned because the audience of the programme can be expected to have heard of, and even to know something about, him. This is not a matter of judgement but merely of contextualization; nevertheless, it is striking that even in a work focused entirely on him, the character of Cicero cannot escape that of his great rival. Caesar himself does not appear; he does not have to. But Cicero is still measured against him.

This chapter has only scraped the surface of modern popular-culture representations of the late Roman Republic. In doing so, it has been able to point at a number of potential avenues for further research: into the effect on popular works of the decline of Classics in education, into the different views of authenticity held by authors/creators and readers/audiences, into the actual market impact of the various novels, into the differences in the ways film and print works can and do transmit information/stories about the ancient world. The enormous number of historical novels might also be studied in more detail with interesting results. On the current very broad canvas it has only been possible to note that there is a wide variety of attitudes to Cicero in the works available. It may be possible, after more research, to track trends in the attitudes to a particular period or character, or to observe the interaction between the scholarly and popularizing worlds by noting when particular scholarly interpretations begin to appear in the published fictions and other works for general consumption. The greater the number of accounts that exist, the higher the probability that they will begin to react to one another as well as to contemporary developments in scholarship and in society as a whole, offering different approaches and interpretations.

Historical fiction both in film and in print-fiction might also be studied in more detail from the point of view of how it is constructed. The effect of employing first-person narrators has been mentioned several times. I have only noted in passing where historical characters are combined with invented plotlines (Cicero's involvement in O'Hagan's *A Roman Death*), and invented characters with historical events (Gordianus' involvement in historically attested trials in Saylor's works). As it happens, all the novels looked at closely in the last section focus on attested characters and attested events; is there a difference in the way that these stories are told when invented characters are added to them? *Rome*, in which top billing is given to the actors playing essentially fictional characters, is a striking case in this connection.[31] I have also proposed fragmentation as a potentially useful theme for structuring investigations into the interactions between modern works and their ancient sources.

But turning from the broad avenues of possible future research back to the question with which I started: why are there not more works of fiction *focusing* on Cicero? The answer may be related to the importance of Julius Caesar, and the historical context more generally, for *judging* Cicero. The

---

[31] Vorenus and Pullo are nominally to be found in an ancient text, Caesar's *Gallic Wars*, but the incidents of their lives narrated in the television series are fictional, as are the characters of their families and friends. For their interaction with historically attested figures, see e.g. Haynes 2008.

high number of biographies was attributed to the vast wealth of information available about Cicero's life, more than is available about any other figure in antiquity. But the texts that inform us in so much detail about Cicero's life also provide us with more information about his period, his context, than we have for any other period of antiquity. As a provider of context, he may seem to belong more to that context, to the background, than to the foreground. And there is also the possibility that the sheer amount of material is daunting for a creator, or that, like simply re-delivering the speech, re-telling Cicero's life seems to lack creativity, to generate biography rather than fiction. If so, the uniqueness of Robert Harris's work is all the more noticeable.

Further reading

Films

'Caesar.' 2006. dir. N. Green. *Ancient Rome: The Rise and Fall of an Empire*. BBC. [television]
Cleopatra. 1934. dir. C. B. DeMille. Paramount. [cinema]
Cleopatra. 1963. dir. J. L. Mankiewicz. Twentieth Century Fox. [cinema]
Cleopatra. 1999. dir. F. Roddam. Hallmark Entertainment. [television]
Empire. 2005. dir. A. Brooks et al. Storyline Entertainment. [television]
Gladiator. 2000. dir. R. Scott. Universal. [cinema]
I, Claudius. 1977. dir. H. Wise. BBC. [television]
Imperium: Augustus. 2003. dir. A. Young. EOS Entertainment. [television]
Julius Caesar. 2002. dir. U. Edel. DeAngelis. [television]
'Murder in Rome.' 2005. dir. D. Stewart. *Timewatch*. BBC. [television]
Rome. 2005–7. dir. B. Heller et al. HBO/BBC. [television]
The Notorious Cleopatra. 1970. dir. P. Perry Jr. Global. [cinema]

Novels

Benton, K. (1974) *Death on the Appian Way*. London.
Burns, R. (1992) *Roman Shadows*. New York.
Hardy, W. G. (1938) *Turn Back the River*. London.
Harris, R. (2006) *Imperium*. London.
   (2009) *Lustrum*. London.
Jaro, B. K. (1988) *The Key*. New York.
McCullough, C. (1996) *Caesar's Women*. London/New York.
Massie, A. (1997) *Antony*. London.
O'Hagan, J. (1988) *A Roman Death*. London.
Radin, M. (1949) *Epicurus my Master*. Chapel Hill.
Roberts, J. M. (1991) *SPQR II. The Catiline Conspiracy*. New York.
Saylor, S. (1990) *Roman Blood*. New York.
   (1996) *A Murder on the Appian Way*. New York.
Warner, R. (1958) *The Young Caesar*. London.
Wilder, T. (1948) *The Ides of March*. London.

Biographies/popular history

Collins, W. L. (1871) *Cicero*. Edinburgh.

Cowell, F. R. (1948) *Cicero and the Roman Republic*. London.

Delayen, G. (trans. F. Symons) (1931) *Cicero* [originally published 1929 as *Sous les masques antiques: M. Tullius Cicéron*. Paris]. London.

Everitt, A. (2001) *Cicero: A Turbulent Life*. London.

Forsyth, W. (1864) *Life of Marcus Tullius Cicero*. London.

Fuhrmann, M. (tr. W. E. Yuill) (1992) *Cicero and the Roman Republic* [originally published 1990 as *Cicero und die römische Republik*. Zurich.] Oxford.

Habicht, C. (1990) *Cicero the Politician* [published simultaneously 1990 as *Cicero der Politiker*. Munich]. London.

Haskell, H. J. (1942) *This Was Cicero: Modern Politics in a Roman Toga*. New York.

Holland, T. (2003) *Rubicon: The Triumph and Tragedy of the Roman Republic*. London.

Lacey, W. K. (1978) *Cicero and the End of the Roman Republic*. London.

Mitchell, T. N. (1979) *Cicero: The Ascending Years*. New Haven.

Mitchell, T. N. (1991) *Cicero: The Senior Statesman*. New Haven.

Petersson, T. (1920) *Cicero: A Biography*. New York.

Rawson, E. (1975) *Cicero: A Portrait*. London. [2nd edition 1983. Bristol/Ithaca.]

Richards, G. C. (1935) *Cicero: A Study*. London.

Shackleton Bailey, D. R. (1971) *Cicero*. London.

Sihler, E. G. (1914) *Cicero of Arpinum: A Political And Literary Biography, Being a Contribution to the History of Ancient Civilization and a Guide to the Study of Cicero's Writings*. New Haven.

Smith, R. E. (1966) *Cicero the Statesman*. London.

Stockton, D. L. (1971) *Cicero: A Political Biography*. London.

Taylor, D. (1973) *Cicero and Rome*. London.

Taylor, H. (1916) *Cicero, a Sketch of his Life and Works, a Commentary on the Roman Constitution and Roman Public Life, supplemented by the Sayings of Cicero arranged as an Anthology*. Chicago.

Wiedemann, T. E. J. (1994) *Cicero and the End of the Roman Republic*. London.

Wilkin, R. N. (1947) *Eternal Lawyer: A Legal Biography of Cicero*. New York.

Witley, A. F. (1939) *The Tremulous Hero: The Age and Life of Cicero, Orator, Advocate, Thinker and Statesman*. London.

CICERO'S WORKS

Title	Date (BC)	Abbreviation	English title
De inventione	91–80	*Inv. Rhet.*	On Invention
Aratea	91–80		Aratea
Pro Quinctio	81	*Quinct.*	On behalf of Quinctius
Pro Roscio Amerino	80	*Rosc. Am.*	On behalf of Sextus Roscius
Pro Caecina	71–68	*Caec.*	On behalf of Caecina
Divinatio in Caecilium	70	*Div. Caec.*	Against Caecina at the preliminary hearing
In Verrem	70	*Verr.*	Verrines
Pro Fonteio	69	*Font.*	On behalf of Fonteius
Pro Roscio comoedo	77–66	*Q Rosc.*	On behalf of Roscius the actor
Pro lege Manilia or *De imperio Cn. Pompei*	66	*Leg. Man.*	On the Manilian Law *or* On the command of Gnaeus Pompeius
Pro Cluentio	66	*Clu.*	On behalf of Cluentius
Pro Cornelio	65		On behalf of Cornelius
De lege agraria	63	*Leg. agr.*	On the agrarian law
Pro Rabirio perduellionis reo	63	*Rab. perd.*	On behalf of Rabirius accused of high treason
De Othone	63		On Otho
In Catilinam	63	*Cat.*	Catilinarians
Pro Murena	63	*Mur.*	On behalf of Murena
Pro Sulla	62	*Sull.*	On behalf of Sulla
Pro Archia	62	*Arch.*	On behalf of Archias
In Clodium et Curionem	61		Against Clodius and Curio
De consulatu suo	60		On his consulship
Pro Flacco	59	*Flac.*	On behalf of Flaccus
Post reditum in senatu	57	*Red. sen.*	Thanks in the Senate after his return
Post reditum ad populum	57	*Red. pop.*	Thanks to the People after his return

Title	Date (BC)	Abbreviation	English title
De domo sua	57	*Dom.*	On his house
Pro Sestio	56	*Sest.*	On behalf of Sestius
In Vatinium	56	*Vat.*	Against Vatinius
Pro Caelio	56	*Cael.*	On behalf of Caelius
De haruspicum responsis	56	*Har. resp.*	On the replies of the soothsayers
De provinciis consularibus	56	*Prov. cons.*	On the consular provinces
Pro Balbo	56	*Balb.*	On behalf of Balbus
In Pisonem	55	*Pis.*	Against Piso
De oratore	55	*De or.*	On the orator
De iure civili in artem redigendo	55		On turning civil law into a discipline
Pro Scauro	54	*Scaur.*	On behalf of Scaurus
Pro Plancio	54	*Planc.*	On behalf of Plancius
Pro Rabirio Postumo	54	*Rab. Post.*	On behalf of Rabirius Postumus
De temporibus suis	54		On his vicissitudes
Pro Milone	52	*Mil.*	On behalf of Milo
De re publica	51	*Rep.*	On the state
De legibus	after 52	*Leg.*	On the laws
Partitiones oratoriae	54–44	*Part. or.*	On oratorical divisions
Brutus	46	*Brut.*	Brutus
Paradoxa stoicorum	46	*Parad.*	Stoic paradoxes
De optimo genere oratorum	46	*Opt. Gen.*	On the best kind of orator
Orator	46	*Orat.*	Orator
Pro Marcello	46	*Marcell.*	For Marcellus
Pro Ligario	46	*Lig.*	On behalf of Ligarius
Marius	before 45		Marius
Consolatio	45		Consolation
Hortensius	45		Hortensius
Academica	45	*Acad.*	Academic books
Lucullus	45	*Luc.*	Lucullus
De finibus	45	*Fin.*	On ends
Tusculanae disputationes	45	*Tusc.*	Tusculans
De natura deorum	45	*Nat. D.*	On the nature of the gods
De rege Deiotaro	45	*Deiot.*	Concerning King Deiotarus
De divinatione	44	*Div.*	On divination
De senectute	44	*Sen.*	On old age

(*cont.*)

Title	Date (BC)	Abbreviation	English title
De fato	44	*Fat.*	On fate
De amicitia	44	*Amic.*	On friendship
De gloria	44		On glory
Topica	44	*Top.*	Topica
De officiis	44	*Off.*	On duties
Philippicae	44–43	*Phil.*	Philippics
Epistulae ad Atticum	68–44	*Att.*	Letters to Atticus
Epistulae ad Familiares	62–43	*Fam.*	Letters to Friends
Epistulae ad Quintum fratrem	59–54	*Q Fr.*	Letters to Quintus
Epistulae ad M. Brutum	43	*Ad Brut.*	Letters to Brutus

BIBLIOGRAPHY

Achard, G. (1987) 'Pourquoi Cicéron a-t-il écrit le De Oratore?' *Latomus* 46: 318–29.
  (1991) *La Communication à Rome*. Paris.
Adams, J. (1793) *Elements of Useful Knowledge, comprehending, among other Interesting Particulars, Short Systems of Astronomy, Mythology, Chronology etc.* London.
Adams, J. N. (1994) *Wackernagel's Law and the Placement of the Copula 'esse' in Classical Latin*. Cambridge.
Adams, J. and Mayer, R. G. (eds.) (1999) *Aspects of the Language of Latin Poetry*. Oxford.
Adams, J. Q. (1810) *Lectures on Rhetoric and Oratory*. Cambridge, Mass.
Adkin, N. (1997) 'Cicero's 'Orator' and Jerome', *Vigiliae Christianae* 51. 1: 25–39.
Ahl, F. (1976) *Lucan: An Introduction*. Ithaca and London.
Aldrete, G. (1999) *Gestures and Acclamations in Ancient Rome*. Baltimore.
Alexander, M. C. (1985) '*Praemia* in the *Quaestiones* of the Late Republic', *CPh* 80: 20–32.
  (2002) *The Case for the Prosecution in the Ciceronian Era*. Ann Arbor.
  (2007) 'Oratory, rhetoric, and politics in the Republic', in *A Companion to Roman Rhetoric*, eds. W. J. Dominik and J. Hall. Oxford and Malden, Mass.: 98–108.
  (2009) 'The *Commentariolum Petitionis* as an attack on election campaigns', *Athenaeum* 97: 31–57 and 369–95.
Alfonsi, L. (1945) *Poetae novi*. Como.
Allan, D. (2003) 'Some methods and problems in the history of reading: Georgian England and the Scottish Enlightenment', *Journal of the Historical Society* 3: 91–124.
Allen Jr, W. (1944) 'Cicero's house and *Libertas*', *TAPhA* 75: 1–9.
  (1954) 'Cicero's conceit', *TAPhA* 85: 121–44.
  (1956) 'O fortunatam natam . . .', *TAPhA* 87: 130–46.
Ando, C. (2000) *Imperial Ideology and Provincial Loyalty in the Roman Empire*. Berkeley.
  (2002) 'Vergil's Italy: ethnography and politics in first century-Rome', in *Clio and the Poets: Augustan Poetry and the Traditions of Ancient Historiography*, eds. D. S. Levene and D. Nelis. Leiden: 123–42.

(2008) *The Matter of the Gods: Religion and the Roman Empire*. Berkeley.

Annas, J. (1993) *The Morality of Happiness*. Oxford.

Annas, J. (ed.) and Woolf, R. (tr.) (2001) *Cicero: On Moral Ends*. Cambridge.

Arena, V. (2007) 'Roman oratorical invective', in *A Companion to Roman Rhetoric*, eds. W. J. Dominik and J. Hall. Oxford and Malden, Mass.: 149–60.

Arweiler, A. (2003) *Cicero Rhetor: Die Partitiones oratoriae und das Konzept des gelehrten Politikers*. Berlin.

Asmis, E. (2004) 'The state as a partnership: Cicero's definition of *res publica* in his work', *History of Political Thought* 25: 369–99.

(2005) 'A new kind of model: Cicero's Roman constitution in *De Republica*', *AJPh* 126: 377–416.

Astell, A. (1999) 'Cassiodorus' Commentary on the Psalms as an Ars Rhetorica', *Rhetorica* 17.1: 37–75

Atkins, E. M. (2000) 'Cicero', in *Cambridge History of Greek and Roman Political Thought*, eds. C. Rowe and M. Schofield. Cambridge: 477–516.

Atkins, E. M. and Dodaro, R. (2001) (eds.) *Political Writings*, by Augustine. Cambridge.

Augoustakis, A. (2008) 'Women's politics in the streets of *Rome*', in *Rome Season One: History Makes Television*, ed. M. S. Cyrino. Oxford: 117–30.

Auhagen, U. et al. (2005) (eds.) *Petrarca und die römische Literatur*. Tübingen.

Austin, M., Harries, J., and Smith, C. (1998) (eds.) *Modus Operandi: Essays presented to Geoffrey Rickman*. London.

Austin, R. G. (1960) *M. Tulli Ciceronis Pro M. Caelio Oratio*. 3rd edn. Oxford.

(1965, reprint of corrected first edn.). *Quintiliani Institutionis Oratoriae Liber XII*. Oxford.

(1977) *P. Vergilii Maronis, Aeneidos liber sextus*. Oxford.

Axelson, B. (1945) *Unpoetische Wörter: Ein Beitrag zur Kenntnis der lateinischen Dichtersprache*. Lund.

Axer, J. (1980) *The Style and the Composition of Cicero's Speech 'Pro Q. Roscio Comoedo': Origin and Function*. Warsaw.

(1989) 'Tribunal – Stage – Arena: Modelling of the Communication Situation in M. Tullius Cicero's Judicial Speeches', *Rhetorica* 7: 299–311.

Badian, E. (1966) 'Early historians', in *Latin Historians*, ed. T. A. Dorey. London: 18–23.

Bagehot, W. (1968) *Collected Works*, ed. N. St. John-Stevas. London.

Baier, T. (1997) *Werk und Wirkung Varros im Spiegel seiner Zeitgenossen*. Stuttgart.

Bailey, D. R. Shackleton (1965–70) (ed.) *Cicero's Letters to Atticus*, 7 vols. Cambridge.

(1971) *Cicero*. London.

(1977) (ed.) *Cicero: Epistulae ad Familiares*, 2 vols. Cambridge.

(1980) (ed.) *Cicero: Epistulae ad Quintum fratrem et M. Brutum*, Cambridge.

(1987a) (ed.) *Cicero: Epistulae ad Q.F. et M. Brutum*, Stuttgart.

(1987b) (ed.) *Cicero: Epistulae ad Atticum*, 2 vols. Stuttgart.

(1988) (ed.) *Cicero: Epistulae ad Familiares*, Stuttgart.

(2002) (ed.) *Cicero: Letters to Quintus and Brutus; Letter Fragments; Letter to Octavian; Invectives; Handbook of Electioneering*, Cambridge, Mass.

Baker, E. (2007) 'Lucretius in the European Enlightenment', in *The Cambridge Companion to Lucretius*, eds. S. Gillespie and P. Hardie. Cambridge: 274–88.

Balot, R. K. (2009) (ed.) *A Companion to Greek and Roman Political Thought*. Malden, Mass.

Bannon, C. (2000) 'Self-help and social status in Cicero's *pro Quinctio*', *Anc. Soc.* 30: 71–94.

Barham, F. (1841) *The Political Works of Marcus Tullius Cicero* vol. 1. London.

Barnes, J. (1989) 'Antiochus of Ascalon', in *Philosophia Togata: Essays on Philosophy and Roman Society*, eds. M. Griffin and J. Barnes. Oxford: 51–96.

Barnes, T. D. (1971) *Tertullian: A Historical and Literary Study*. Oxford.

(1986) 'The significance of Tacitus' *Dialogus de oratoribus*', *HSCP* 90: 225–44

Bartelink, G. J. M. (1980) Hieronymus, *Liber de optimo genere interpretandi (Epistula 57): ein Kommentar*. Leiden.

Barthes, R. (1986) *The Rustle of Language*, trans. R. Howard. Oxford.

(1977) 'The grain of the voice', in *Image, Music, Text*, tr. S. Heath. New York: 179–89.

Bauman, R. (1985) *Lawyers in Roman Transitional Politics: A Study of the Roman Jurists in their Political Setting in the Late Republic and Triumvirate*. Munich.

BBC (2005) *Rome Press Pack*. Available at www.bbc.co.uk/pressoffice/pressreleases/stories/2005/08_august/26/rome.shtml.

Beard, M. (1986) 'Cicero and divination: the formation of a Latin discourse', *JRS* 76: 33–46.

(2002) 'Ciceronian correspondences: making a book out of letters', in *Classics in Progress: Essays on Ancient Greece and Rome*, ed. T. P. Wiseman. Oxford: 103–44.

Beard, M. and Crawford, M. (1999) *Rome in the Late Republic: Problems and Interpretations*, 2nd edn. London.

Beck, H. (2007) 'The early Roman tradition', in J. Marincola (2007), 259–65.

Becker, E. (1938) *Technik und Szenerie des ciceronischen Dialogs*. Osnabrück.

Bederman, D. J. (2008) *The Classical Foundations of the American Constitutions: Prevailing Wisdom*. Cambridge.

Bell, A. (2004) *Spectacular Power in the Greek and Roman City*. Oxford.

Bell, C. (1992) *Ritual Theory, Ritual Practice*. New York.

Bell, S. and Hansen, I. (eds.) (2008) *Role Models in the Roman World: Identity and Assimilation*. Ann Arbor.

Benario, H. (1957) 'Cicero's *Marius* and Caesar', *CPh* 52: 177–81.

Bernard, J.-E. (2007) 'Du discours à l'épistolaire : les échos du Pro Plancio dans la lettre de Cicéron à Lentulus Spinther (*Fam.* I, 9)', *Rhetorica* 25.4: 223–42.

Berry, D. H. (1996a) *Cicero: Pro P. Sulla Oratio. Edited with introduction and commentary*. Cambridge.

(1996b) 'The value of prose rhythm in questions of authenticity: the case of *De Optimo Genere Oratorum* attributed to Cicero', *Papers of the Leeds International Latin Seminar* 9: 47–74.

(2003) '*Equester ordo tuus est*: did Cicero win his cases because of his support for the *equites*?' *CQ* 53: 222–34.

(2004) 'Literature and persuasion in Cicero's *Pro Archia*', in Powell and Paterson (eds.) (2004): 291–311.

(2006) (tr.) *Cicero: Political Speeches*. Oxford.

Bispham, E. (2007) *From Asculum to Actium: The Municipalization of Italy from the Social War to Augustus*. Oxford.

Black, R. (2001) *Humanism and Education and in Medieval and Renaissance Italy: Tradition and Innovation in Latin Schools from the Twelfth to the Fifteenth Century*. Cambridge.

Blom, H. van der (2010) *Cicero's Role Models: The Political Strategy of a Newcomer*. Oxford.

Bloomer, W. M. (2011) *The School of Rome: Latin Studies and the Origins of Liberal Education*. Berkeley.

Boissier, G. (1865) *Cicéron et ses amis: étude sur la Société Romaine du Temps de César*. Paris.

(1897) *Cicero and His Friends: A Study of Roman Society in the Time of Caesar*, tr. A. D. Jones. London.

Bolkestein, A. M. (1998) 'Between brackets: (some properties of) parenthetical clauses in Latin. An investigation of the language of Cicero's letters', in Risselada (1998), 1–17.

Bond, D. F. (1987) (ed.) *The Tatler* vol. II. Oxford.

Booth, A. (1982) 'The academic career of Ausonius', *Phoenix* 36.4: 329–43.

Booth, J. (2007) (ed.) *Cicero on the Attack: Invective and Subversion in the Orations and Beyond*. Swansea.

Bradley, G. J. (2000) *Ancient Umbria: State, Culture and Identity in Central Italy from the Iron Age to the Augustan Era*. Oxford.

Brandt, S. and Laubmann, G. (1890–7) *L. Caeli Firmiani Lactanti Opera Omnia*, 2 vols. CSEL 27. Vienna.

Braund, S. (1997) 'Virgil and the cosmos: religious and philosophical ideas', in *The Cambridge Companion to Virgil*, ed. C. Martindale. Cambridge: 204–21.

Bréguet, E. (1964) 'Les archaïsmes dans le *De re publica* de Cicéron', in Renard and Schilling (eds.) (1964): 122–31.

Brink, C. O. (1989) 'Quintilian's *De causis corruptae eloquentiae* and Tacitus' *Dialogus de Oratoribus*', *CQ* 39: 472–503

Brinton, A. (1983) 'Quintilian, Plato, and the "vir bonus"', *Philosophy & Rhetoric* 16.3: 167–84.

Brittain, C. (2001) *Philo of Larissa: The Last of the Academic Sceptics*. Oxford.

(2006) (tr. and intro) *Cicero: On Academic Scepticism*. Indianapolis.

Broughton, T. R. S. (1936) 'Was Sallust fair to Cicero?', *TAPhA* 67: 34–46.

Brown, D. (1992) *Vir trilinguis. A Study in the Biblical Exegesis of Saint Jerome*. Kampen.

Browning, R. (1984) 'The origin of Burke's ideas revisited', *Eighteenth-Century Studies* 18.1: 57–71

Bruni, F. (2004) 'Rendering unto Caesar's subjects; for a new HBO series, a colorful ancient city springs to life in Rome', *New York Times* 5.4.04.

Bruni, L. (1996) *Opere letterarie e politiche*, ed. P. Viti. Turin.

Brunt, P. A. (1974) 'Marcus Aurelius in his *Meditations*', *JRS* 64: 1–20.

(1982a) 'The legal issue in Cicero's *pro Balbo*', *CQ* 32: 136–47.

(1982b) 'Nobilitas and novitas', *JRS* 72, 1–17.

(1986) 'Cicero's *officium* in the Civil War', *JRS* 76: 12–32.

(1988) *The Fall of the Roman Republic and Related Essays*. Oxford.

Buchheit, V. (1959) 'Catullus Dichtercritik in c.36', *Zeitschrift für klassische Philologie* 87: 309–27.

Bücher, F. (2006) *Verargumentierte Geschichte: Exempla Romana im politischen Diskurs der späten römischen Republik.* Stuttgart.

Buescu, V. (1941) (ed. and tr.) *Cicéron: Les Aratea.* Bucarest, repr. Hildesheim (1966).

Buffon, G.-L. Leclerc (1753) *Discours sur le style.* Paris.

Burger, P. C. (1981) *The Insignia of the Notitia Dignitatum.* New York.

Burnand, C. (2000) 'Roman representations of the orator during the last century of the Republic', DPhil thesis, University of Oxford.

  (2004) 'The advocate as a professional: the role of the *Patronus* in Cicero's *Pro Cluentio*', in *Cicero the Advocate*, eds. J. G. F. Powell and J. Paterson. Oxford: 277–89.

Butler, S. (2002) *The Hand of Cicero.* London.

Calboli, G. (1986) 'Nota di aggiornamento', in Norden (1986): 969–1188.

  (1993) *[Cornifici] Rhetorica ad C. Herennium. Introduzione, testo critico, commento.* Bologna.

Cameron, A. (1986) 'Martianus and his first editor', *CPh* 81.4: 320–8.

  (1995) *Callimachus and his Critics.* Princeton.

  (2011) *The Last Pagans of Rome.* Oxford.

Cape, R. W. (1995) 'The rhetoric of politics in Cicero's *Fourth Catilinarian*', *AJPh* 116: 255–77.

  (2002) 'Cicero's consular speeches', in *Brill's Companion to Cicero: Oratory and Rhetoric*, ed. J. May. Leiden: 113–58.

Cardwell, S. (2002) *Adaptation Revisited: Television and the Classic Novel.* Manchester.

Carney, T. F. (1960) 'Cicero's picture of Marius', *WS* 73: 83–122.

Casson, L. (2001) *Libraries in the Ancient World.* New Haven.

Cébeillac Gervasoni, M. (1998) *Les Magistrats des cités italiennes de la seconde guerre punique à Auguste: le Latium et la Campanie.* Rome.

Cerutti, S. (1996) *Cicero's Accretive Style: Rhetorical Strategies in the 'Exordia' of the Judicial Speeches.* Lanham, NY, and London.

Chadwick, H. (1981) *Boethius. The Consolations of Music, Logic, Theology, and Philosophy.* Oxford.

Chahoud, A. and Dickey, E. (2010) (eds.) *Colloquial and Literary Latin.* Cambridge.

Chamoux, F. (1986) *Marc Antoine, dernier prince de l'Orient grec.* Paris.

Champion, J. (2003) *Republican Learning: John Toland and the Crisis of Christian Culture, 1696–1722.* Manchester.

Charlesworth, M. P. (1933) 'Some fragments of the propaganda of Mark Antony', *Classical Quarterly* 27: 172–7.

Cibber, C. (1747) *The Character and Conduct of Cicero Considered, from the History of his Life, by the Reverend Dr Middleton.* London.

Cicero, M. T. (1687) *M. Tullii Ciceronis opera omnia, cum selectissimis Jani Gruteri & variorum notis.* Basel.

  (1724) *Marci Tullii Ciceronii (sic) opera, quae supersunt, omnia, cum Asconio & scholiaste veteri; ac notis integris P. Victorii et al.* Amsterdam.

  (1740) *M. Tullii Ciceronis opera. Cum delectu commentariorum*, ed. P. J. Thoulier d'Olivet with comm. (9 vols.). Paris.

Cicero, Q. T. (1714) *The Art of Canvassing at Elections*. London.

Cichorius, C. (1922) 'Historische Studien zu Varro', in *Römische Studien*. Leipzig: 189–241.

Claassen, J.-M. (1992) 'Cicero's banishment: *Tempora et Mores*', *Acta Classica* 35: 19–47.

Clackson, J. (2011) (ed.) *A Companion to the Latin Language*. Oxford and Malden, Mass.

Clackson, J. and Horrocks, G. (2010) *The Blackwell History of the Latin Language*. Oxford and Malden, Mass.

Clark, A. C. (1907) *Q. Asconii Pediani orationum Ciceronis quinque enarratio*. Oxford.

Clarke, G. W. (1970) 'Four passages in Minucius Felix', in *Kyriakon. Festschrift Johannes Quasten*, eds. P. Granfield and J. A. Jungmann. Münster: 499–507.

(1974) *The Octavius by Minucius Felix*. New York.

Clarke, M. L. (1983) 'Conyers Middleton's alleged plagiarism', *Notes & Queries* 228: 44–6.

Classen, C. J. (1982) 'Ciceros Kunst der Überredung', in Ludwig (ed.) (1982): 149–84.

(1985) *Recht – Rhetorik – Politik*. Darmstadt.

(1993) 'The rhetorical works of George of Trebizond and their debt to Cicero', *Journal of the Warburg and Courtauld Institutes* 56: 75–84.

Clausen, W. (1986) 'Cicero and the new poetry', *HSCP* 90: 159–70.

Clift, E. H. (1945) *Pseudepigrapha: A Study in Literary Attributions*. Baltimore.

Coleman, R. (1964) 'The Dream of Cicero', *PCPS* 10: 1–14.

Colish, M. (2005) *Ambrose's Patriarchs: Ethics for the Common Man*. Notre Dame.

Collins, R. (1990) 'Literacy and the laity in early medieval Spain', in *The Uses of Literacy in Early Medieval Europe*, ed. R. McKitterick. Cambridge: 109–33.

Collins, W. L. (1871) *Cicero*. Edinburgh.

Connolly, J. (2007a) *The State of Speech: Rhetoric and Political Thought in Ancient Rome*. Princeton.

(2007b) 'Virile tongues: rhetoric and masculinity', in *A Companion to Roman Rhetoric*, eds. W. J. Dominik and J. Hall. Oxford and Malden, Mass.: 83–97.

(2010) 'Classical education and the early American democratic style', in *Classics and National Cultures*, eds. S. Stephens and P. Vasunia. Oxford: 78–99.

Conte, G. B. (1987) *Latin Literature: A History*. Baltimore.

Copeland, R. (1991) *Rhetoric, Translation, and Hermeneutics in the Middle Ages*. Cambridge.

(2006) 'The Ciceronian rhetorical tradition and medieval literary theory', in *The Rhetoric of Cicero in its Medieval and Early Renaissance Commentary Tradition*, eds. V. Cox and J. Ward. Leiden: 239–65.

Corbeill, A. (1996) *Controlling Laughter: Political Humor in the Late Roman Republic*. Princeton.

(2001) 'Education in the Roman Republic: creating traditions', in *Education in Greek and Roman Antiquity*, ed. Y. L. Too. Leiden: 261–87.

(2002) 'Rhetorical education in Cicero's youth', in *Brill's Companion to Cicero: Oratory and Rhetoric*, ed. J. M. May. Leiden: 23–48.

(2004) *Nature Embodied: Gesture in Ancient Rome*. Princeton.

Cornell, T. (2001) 'Cicero on the origins of Rome', in Powell and North (eds.) (2001): 41–56.

Costa, D. (1984) *Lucretius: De rerum natura 5*. Oxford.

Courcelle, P. (1948) *Les lettres grecques en occident de Macrobe a Cassiodore*. Paris.
(1967) *La Consolation de philosophie dans la tradition littéraire*. Paris.

Courtney, E. (1999) *Archaic Latin Prose*. Atlanta.
(2003) *The Fragmentary Latin Poets*, 2nd edn. Oxford.

Cousin, J. (1967) *Études sur Quintilien*. Amsterdam.

Cowell, F. R. (1948) *Cicero and the Roman Republic*. London.

Cox, V. and Ward, J. O. (2006) (eds.) *The Rhetoric of Cicero in its Medieval and Early Renaissance Commentary Tradition*. Leiden and Boston.

Craig, C. P. (1993) *Form as Argument in Cicero's Speeches: A Study of Dilemma*. Atlanta.
(2001) 'Shifting charge and shifty argument in Cicero's speech for Sestius', in *The Orator in Action and Theory in Greece and Rome: Studies in Honor of George A. Kennedy*, ed. C. Wooten. Leiden: 111–22.
(2002) 'A survey of selected recent work on Cicero's Rhetorica and Speeches', in May (ed.) (2002): 503–31.
(2004) 'Audience expectations, invective, and proof', in *Cicero the Advocate*, eds. J. G. F. Powell and J. J. Paterson. Oxford: 187–214.

Craik, E. M. (1990) (ed.) *Owls to Athens: Essays on Classical Subjects presented to Sir Kenneth Dover*. Oxford.

Crawford, J. W. (1984) *M. Tullius Cicero: The Lost and Unpublished Orations*. Göttingen, Vandenhoeck and Ruprecht.
(1994) *M. Tullius Cicero: The Fragmentary Speeches*, 2nd edn. Atlanta, Ga.

Crawford, M. H. (1998) 'How to create a *municipium*', in *Modus operandi: essays in honour of Geoffrey Rickman*, eds. M. Austin et al. London: 37–46.

Crook, J. (1995) *Legal Advocacy in the Roman World*. London.

Crook, J. A., Lintott, A. and Rawson, E. (1994) (eds.) *The Cambridge Ancient History* vol. IX: *The Last Age of the Roman Republic, 146–43 BC*, 2nd edn. Cambridge.

Cugusi, P. (1983) *Evoluzione e forme dell'epistolografia Latina nella tarda repubblica e nei primi due secoli dell'impero*. Rome.

Cuthbertson, S. (1998) 'Toiling in the trenches', *Solander* 4: http://historicalnovelsociety.org/toiling-in-the-trenches/

Dahlmann, H. (1935) 'Marcus Terentius Varro', *RE* suppl. 6: 1172–277.

D'Arms, J. (1970) *Romans on the Bay of Naples*. Harvard.

Daugherty, G. N. (2008) 'Her first Roman: a Cleopatra for *Rome*', in *Rome, Season One. History Makes television*, ed. M. S. Cyrino. Oxford: 141–53.

David, J.-M. (1980) 'Maiorum exempla sequi: l'exemplum historique dans les discours judicaires de Cicéron', *MEFRM* 92.1: 67–86.
(1992) *Le patronat judiciaire au dernier siècle de la République romaine*. Rome.
(2006) 'Rhetoric and public life', in *A Companion to the Roman Republic*, eds. N. S. Rosenstein and R. Morstein-Marx. Oxford and Malden, Mass.: 421–38.

Davidson, I. (2001) (ed.) *Ambrose: De officiis*, with an intro., tr. and comm. 2 vols. Oxford.

DellaNeva, J. (2007) (ed.) *Ciceronian Controversies*. Cambridge, Mass.

Dench, E. (1995) *From Barbarians to New Men: Greek, Roman, and Modern Perceptions of Peoples from the Central Appennines*. Oxford.

(2005) *Romulus' Asylum: Roman Identities from the Age of Alexander to the Age of Hadrian*. Oxford.

(2007) 'Ethnography and history', in Marincola (ed.): 493–503.

Dickson, W. P (1894) *The History of Rome, by Theodor Mommsen: translated with the sanction of the author by the Rev. William P. Dickson*, rev. edn. London, 5 vols.

Digeser, E. D. (1994) 'Lactantius and Constantine's letter to Arles: Dating the *Divine Institutes*', *Journal of Early Christian Studies* 2: 33–52.

(2000) *The Making of a Christian Empire: Lactantius and Rome*. Ithaca.

Diggle, J., Hall, J. B. and Jocelyn, H. D. (1989) (eds.) *Studies in Latin Literature and its Tradition in Honour of C.O.Brink*. Cambridge.

Dodaro, R. (2004) *Christ and the Just Society in the Thought of Augustine*. Cambridge.

Doignon, J. (1993) 'Souvenirs cicéroniens (Hortensius, Consolation) et virgiliens dans l'exposé d'Augustin sur l'état humain d' "ignorance et de difficulté" (Aug. *Lib. arb.* 3,51–54)', *Vigiliae Christianae* 47: 131–9.

Dolganov, A. (2008) 'Constructing author and authority: generic discourse in Cicero's *De Legibus*', *G&R* 55.1: 23–38.

Dominik, W. J. (1997a) (ed.) *Roman Eloquence: Rhetoric in Society and Literature*. London.

(1997b) 'The style is the man: Seneca, Tacitus, and Quintilian's canon', in *Roman Eloquence: Rhetoric in Society and Literature*, ed. W. J. Dominik. London: 50–68.

(2007) 'Tacitus and Pliny on oratory', in Dominik and Hall (eds.) (2007): 323–38.

Dominik, W. J. and Hall, J. (2007) (eds.) *A Companion to Roman Rhetoric*. Malden, Mass. and Oxford.

Dorey, T. A. (1965) (ed.) *Cicero*. London.

Douglas, A. E. (1960) 'Clausulae in the *Rhetorica ad Herennium* as evidence of its date', *CQ* n.s. 10: 65–78.

(1966) *M. Tulli Ciceronis Brutus*. Oxford.

(1973) 'The intellectual background of Cicero's Rhetorica: a study in method', *ANRW* 1.3: 95–138.

Dover, K. J. (1997) *The Evolution of Greek Prose Style*. Oxford.

Drexler, H. (1976) *Die Catilinarische Verschwörung: Ein Quellenheft*. Darmstadt.

Drumann, W. (1834–44) *Geschichte Roms in seiner Übergange zur monarchischen Verfassung*. Köningsberg.

Drummond, A. (1995) *Law, Politics and Power: Sallust and the Execution of the Catilinarian Conspirators*. Stuttgart.

Duff, J. D. (1957) (ed.) *Iunii Iuvenalis saturae XIV*. Cambridge.

Dugan, J. (2005) *Making a New Man: Ciceronian Self-Fashioning in the Rhetorical Works*. Oxford.

(2007) 'Modern critical approaches to Roman rhetoric', in *A Companion to Roman Rhetoric*, ed. W. J. Dominik and J. Hall. Oxford and Malden, Mass.: 9–22.

(2009) 'Rhetoric and the Roman Republic', in *The Cambridge Companion to Ancient Rhetoric*, ed. E. Gunderson. Cambridge: 178–93.

Dussinger, J. A. (2004) 'Middleton, Conyers', *Oxford Dictionary of National Biography* 38: 51–6.

Dyck, A. (1996) *A Commentary on Cicero: 'De Officiis'*. Ann Arbor.

(2001) 'Dressing to kill: attire as a proof and means of characterization in Cicero's Speeches', *Arethusa* 34: 119–30.

(2004a) *A Commentary on Cicero: 'De Legibus'*. Ann Arbor.

(2004b) 'Cicero's *devotio*: the roles of *dux* and scape-goat in his *Post Reditum* rhetoric', *HSCP* 102: 299–314.

(2008a) 'Rivals into partners: Hortensius and Cicero', *Historia* 57: 142–73.

(2008b) *Cicero: Catilinarians*. Cambridge.

(2010) *Cicero: pro Sexto Roscio Amerino*. Cambridge.

Dyer, R. R. (1990) 'Rhetoric and intention in Cicero's *Pro Marcello*', *JRS* 80: 17–30.

Earl, D. C. (1961) *The Political Thought of Sallust*. Amsterdam.

Ebbeler, J. (2007) 'Mixed messages: the play of epistolary codes in two late antique Latin correspondences', in *Ancient Letters: Classical and Late Antique Epistolography*, eds. R. Morello and A. D. Morrison. Oxford: 301–23.

Edwards, C. H. (1993) *The Politics of Immorality in Ancient Rome*. Cambridge.

(1996) *Writing Rome: Textual Approaches to the City*. Cambridge.

(1997) 'Self-scrutiny and self-transformation in Seneca's *Letters*', *Greece and Rome* 44: 23–38.

Elias, A. C., Jr. (2004) 'Pilkington, Laetitia', *Oxford Dictionary of National Biography* 44: 321–3.

Elice, M. (ed.)(2007) *Romani Aquilae De figuris: introduzione, testo critico, traduzione e commento*. Hildesheim.

Eskridge, J. (1912) 'The influence of Cicero upon Augustine in the development of his oratorical theory for the training of the ecclesiastical orator.' University of Chicago dissertation. Menasha.

Evans, R. J. (1994) *Marius: A Political Biography*. Pretoria.

Ewbank, W. W. (1933, repr. 1997) *The Poems of Cicero*. London/Bristol.

Fagan, G. (2011) *The Lure of the Arena: Social Psychology and the Crowd at the Roman Games*. Cambridge.

Fairweather, J. (1981) *Seneca the Elder*. Cambridge.

Fantham, E. (1975) 'The trials of Gabinius in 54 BC', *Historia* 24: 425–43.

(2004) *The Roman World of Cicero's 'De oratore'*. Oxford.

Farney, G. (2007) *Ethnic Identity and Aristocratic Competition in Republican Rome*. Cambridge.

Favez, C. (1937) *La consolation latine chrétienne*. Paris.

Feather, J. (1988) *A History of British Publishing*. London.

Feeney, D. (1986) 'History and revelation in Virgil's underworld', *PCPS* 32: 1–24.

Feichtinger, B. (1991) 'Der Traum des Hieronymus: Ein Psychogramm', *Vigiliae Christianae* 45.1: 54–77

(1997) 'Nec vero sopor ille fuerat aut vana somnia (Hier. ep. 22,30,6). Überlegungen zum geträumten Selbst des Hieronymus', *Revue des Études Augustiniennes* 43: 41–61

Ferrary, J.-L. (1984) 'L'archéologie du *de re publica* (2, 2, 4–37, 63): Cicéron entre Polybe et Platon', *JRS* 74: 87–98.

(1995) 'The statesman and the law in the political philosophy of Cicero', in *Justice and Generosity*, eds. A. Laks and M. Schofield. Cambridge: 48–73.

Flaig, E. (2003) *Ritualisierte Politik: Zeichen, Gesten und Herrschaft in alten Rom*, Göttingen.

Flower, H. (1996) *Ancestor Masks and Aristocratic Power in Roman Culture*. Oxford.

(2004) (ed.) *The Cambridge Companion to the Roman Republic*. Cambridge.

Fontaine, J. (1983) *Isidore de Seville et la culture classique dans l'Espagne wisigothique*, 2nd edn. Paris.

(1988) 'Cassiodore et Isidore: l'évolution de l'encyclopédisme latin du VIe au VIIe siècle', in *Tradition et actualité chez Isidore de Séville*. London.

(2000) *Isidore de Séville: genèse et originalité de la culture hispanique au temps des Wisigoths*. Turnhout.

Fordyce, C. J. (1961) *Catullus*. Oxford.

Forsyth, W. (1864) *Life of Marcus Tullius Cicero*. London.

Fotheringham, L. (2007) 'Having your cake and eating it: how Cicero combines arguments', in Powell (ed.) (2007): 69–90.

Fotiou, A. (1984) 'A reconsideration of Cicero's *princeps civitatis* in the light of new evidence from a sixth century political treatise', in *Classical Texts and their Traditions: Studies in Honour of C. R. Trahman*, eds. D. Bright and E. Ramage. Chico, Calif.: 41–58.

Fox, M. (2007) *Cicero's Philosophy of History*. Oxford.

Fraenkel, E. (1956) 'Eine Form römischer Kriegsbulletins', *Eranos* 54: 189–94.

(1968) *Leseproben aus Reden Ciceros und Catos*. Rome.

Frazel, T. D. (2004) 'The composition and circulation of Cicero's *In Verrem*', *CQ* 54: 128–42.

Frederiksen, M. (1965) 'The Republican municipal laws: errors and drafts', *JRS* 55: 183–95.

Fredouille, J.-C. (1972) *Tertullien et la conversion de la culture antique*. Paris.

Freedman, J. S. (1986) 'Cicero in sixteenth- and seventeenth-century rhetorical instruction', *Rhetorica* 4: 227–54.

Frier, Bruce W. (1997) 'The rule against vouching: *ethos* and the rhetorical position of advocates.' Paper read at the annual meeting of the American Philological Association, Washington, DC.

(1985) *The Rise of the Roman Jurists: Studies in the 'Pro Caecina'*. Princeton.

Frisch, H. (1946) *Cicero's Fight for the Republic: The Historical Background of Cicero's Philippics*. Copenhagen.

Frischer, B. (1996) 'How to do things with words per strong stop: two studies on the *Historia Augusta* and Cicero', in Rosén (ed.) (1996): 585–99.

Fuchs, H. (1964) *Der geistige Widerstand gegen Rom in der antiken Welt*. Berlin.

(1965) *Augustin und der antike Friedensgedanke*. Berlin. (First published 1926.)

Fuhrmann, M. (1990) 'Mündlichkeit und fiktive Mündlichkeit in den von Cicero veröffentlichten Reden', in Vogt-Spira (ed.) (1990): 53–62.

(1992) *Cierco*, trans. W. E. Yuill. Oxford.

Gabba, E. (1973) 'Italia e Roma nella storia di Velleio Paterculo', in *Esercito e società nella tarda Repubblica romana*. Florence: 347–60.

Gaines, R. N. (2007) 'Roman rhetorical handbooks', in *A Companion to Roman Rhetoric*, eds. W. J. Dominik and J. Hall. Oxford and Malden, Mass.: 163–80.

Galletier, E. (1949–55) *Panégyriques latins*. 3 vols. Paris.

Gamberale, L. (1998) 'Dalla retorica al centone nell' *oratio pridie quam in exilium iret*. Aspetti della fortuna di Cicerono fra III e IV secolo', in *Cultura latina pagana fra terzo e quinto secolo dopo Cristo. Atti del Convegno Mantova 9–11 ottobre 1995*. Firenze: 53–75

Gambet, D. G. (1963) 'Cicero's reputation from 43 BC to AD 79', Dissertation. University of Pennsylvania. Philadelphia.

(1970) 'Cicero in the works of Seneca Philosophus', *TAPhA* 101: 171–83.

Gawlick, G. (1963) 'Cicero and the Enlightenment', *Studies on Voltaire and the Eighteenth Century* 25: 657–82.

Gay, P. (1977) *The Enlightenment: An Interpretation*. New York.

Gee, E. (2001) 'Cicero's astronomy', *CQ* 51: 520–36.

(2007) 'Quintus Cicero's astronomy?', *CQ* 57: 565–85.

(2008) 'Astronomy and philosophical orientation in Classical and Renaissance didactic poetry', in *What Nature Does Not Teach: Didactic Literature in the Medieval and Early Modern Periods*, ed. J. Ruys. Turnhout: 473–96.

(2009) 'Borrowed plumage: literary metamorphosis in George Buchanan's *De Sphaera*', in *George Buchanan: Poet and Dramatist*, eds. P. Ford and R. Green. Swansea: 35–58.

Geffcken, K. (1973) *Comedy in the 'Pro Caelio'*. Leiden.

Gelzer, M. (1968) *Caesar: Politician and Statesman*, tr. P. Needham. Cambridge, Mass.

(1969) *Cicero, Ein Biographischer Versuch*. Wiesbaden.

Gensini, S. (1980) '"Poeta et historicus": L'episodio della laurea nella carriera e nella prospettiva culturale di Francesco Petrarca', *La Cultura* 18: 166–94.

Giardina, A. (1997) *L'Italia romana: storie di un'identità incompiuta*. Rome.

Gibbon, E. (1994) *Memoirs of my Life and Writings*, eds. A. O. J. Cockshut and S. Constantine. Bodmin.

Gibson, R. K. (2003) (ed.) *Ovid Ars Amatoria Book 3*. Cambridge.

Gil, Ioannes (1973) (ed.) *Corpus Scriptorum Muzarabicorum*, 2 vols. Madrid.

Gildenhard, I. (2007) *Paideia Romana: Cicero's 'Tusculan Disputations'*. Cambridge.

(2010) *Creative Eloquence: The Construction of Reality in Cicero's Speeches*. Oxford.

Gilliam, J. F. (1953) 'The Pro Caelio in St. Jerome's letters', *Harvard Theological Review* 46.2: 103–7.

Ginsburg, J. (1981) *Tradition and Theme in the Annals of Tacitus*. New York.

(1993) 'In maiores certamina', in *Tacitus and the Tacitean Tradition*, eds. A. J. Woodman and T. Luce. Oxford: 86–103.

Giomini, R. (1995) (ed.) *M. Tulli Ciceronis De optimo genere oratorum*. Rome.

Girardet, K. (1977) 'Ciceros Urteil über die Entstehung des Tribunates als Institution der römischen Verfassung (rep. 2, 57–59)', in *Bonner Festgabe Johannes Straub*, eds. A. Lippold and N. Himmelmann. Bonn: 179–200.

(1983) *Die Ordnung der Welt*. Wiesbaden.

Giustiniani, V. R. (1961) 'Traduzioni latine delle *Vite* di Plutarco nel Quattrocento', *Rinascimento* 2.1: 3–62.

Gleason, M. W. (1995) *Making Men: Sophists and Self-Presentation in Ancient Rome*. Princeton.

Godi, C. (1970) 'La 'Collatio Laureationis' del Petrarca', *Italia medioevale e umanistica* 13: 1–27.

Godwin, J. (1999) *Catullus: The Shorter Poems*. Warminster.

Görler, W. (1988) 'From Athens to Tusculum: gleaning the background of Cicero's *De Oratore*', *Rhetorica* 6: 215–35.

Goldberg, S. (1995) *Epic in Republican Rome*. Oxford.

(1999) 'Appreciating Aper: the defence of modernity in Tacitus' *Dialogus de Oratoribus*', *CQ* 49: 224–37.

(2009) 'The faces of eloquence: the *Dialogus de oratoribus*', in *The Cambridge Companion to Tacitus*, ed. A. J. Woodman. Cambridge: 73–84.

Golden, J. L. and Golden, A. L. (2002) *Thomas Jefferson and the Rhetoric of Virtue*. Lanham, Md.

Goldie, M. and Wokler, R. (2006) (eds.) *The Cambridge History of Eighteenth-Century Political Thought*. Cambridge.

Goodwin, J. (2001) 'Philosophy and rhetoric', *Philosophy and Rhetoric* 34: 38–60.

Goold, G. P. (1989) *Catullus*, 2nd edn. London.

(1992) 'The voice of Virgil: the pageant of Rome in *Aeneid 6*', in *Author and Audience in Latin Literature*, ed. A. J. A. Woodman and J. Powell. Cambridge: 110–23.

Gotoff, H. C. (1979) *Cicero's Elegant Style: An Analysis of the 'Pro Archia'*. Urbana.

(1993) *Cicero's Caesarian Speeches: A Stylistic Commentary*. Chapel Hill and London.

Gowing, A. (2000) 'Memory and silence in Cicero's *Brutus*', *Eranos* 98: 39–64.

(2005) *Empire and Memory: The Representation of the Roman Republic in Imperial Culture*. Cambridge.

(2007) 'The imperial Republic of Velleius Paterculus', in *The Blackwell Companion to Greek and Roman Historiography*, ed. J. Marincola. Malden, Mass.: 411–18.

Graff, J. (1963) *Ciceros Selbstauffassung*. Heidelberg.

Gransden, K. W. (1976) (ed.) *Virgil 'Aeneid' Book VIII*. Cambridge.

Graver, M. (2002) *Cicero on the Emotions: 'Tusculan Disputations' 3 and 4*, tr. with comm. Chicago.

Grebe, S. (1999) *Martianus Capella, 'De nuptiis Philologiae et Mercurii.' Darstellung der sieben freien Künste und ihrer Beziehungen zueinander*. Stuttgart and Leipzig.

Green, L. D. and Murphy, J. J. (2006) *Renaissance Rhetoric Short-Title Catalogue 1460–1700*, 2nd edn. Aldershot.

Green, P. (2005) *The Poems of Catullus*. Berkeley.

Greenidge, A. H. J. (1894; repr. 1977) *Infamia: Its Place in Roman Public and Private Law*. Oxford.

(1901; repr. 1971) *The Legal Procedure of Cicero's Time*. Oxford.

Grendler, P. F. (1989) *Schooling in Renaissance Italy: Literacy and Learning, 1300–1600*. Baltimore and London.

Griffin, M. T. (1988) 'Philosophy for statesmen: Cicero and Seneca', in *Antikes Denken – Moderne Schule*, eds. H. W. Schmidt and P. Wülfing. Gymnasium Beiheft 9. Heidelberg: 133–50.

(1989) 'Philosophy, politics, and politicians at Rome', in *Philosophia Togata: Essays on Philosophy and Roman Society*, eds. J. Barnes and M. Griffin. Oxford: 1–37.

(1995) 'Philosophical badinage in Cicero's letters to his friends', in Powell (ed.) (1995): 325–46.

(1997) 'The composition of the *Academica*: motives and versions', in *Assent and Argument: Studies in Cicero's 'Academic Books'*, eds. B. Inwood and J. Mansfeld. London and New York: 1–34.

Griffin, M. and Atkins, E. (1991) *Cicero: 'On Duties'*. Cambridge.

Grimal, P. (1984) 'Sénèque juge de Cicéron', *MEFRA* 96.2: 655–70.

Gruber, J. (2006) *Kommentar zu Boethius, 'De consolatione philosophiae'*. 2nd edn. Berlin.

Gruen, E. S. (1968) *Roman Politics and the Criminal Courts, 149–78 B.C.* Cambridge, Mass.

(1990) *Studies in Greek Culture and Roman Policy*. Leiden.

Gryson, R., et al. (1994) (eds.) *Biblia sacra: iuxta Vulgatum versionem*, 4th edn. Stuttgart.

Gunderson, E. (2000) *Staging Masculinity: The Rhetoric of Performance in the Roman World*. Ann Arbor.

(2007) 'S.V.B.; E.V.', *Classical Antiquity* 26: 1–48.

(2009) ed. *The Cambridge Companion to Ancient Rhetoric*. Cambridge.

Haarhoff, T. J. (1958) *Schools of Gaul; A Study of Pagan and Christian Education in the Last Century of the Western Empire*. Johannesburg.

Habicht, C. (1990) *Cicero the Politician*. Baltimore.

Habinek, T. N. (1985) *The Colometry of Latin Prose*. Berkeley.

(1989) 'Science and tradition in *Aeneid 6*', *HSCP* 92: 223–55.

(1994) 'Ideology for an Empire in the prefaces to Cicero's dialogues', *Ramus* 23: 55–67.

(1998) *The Politics of Latin Literature: Writing, Identity and Empire in Ancient Rome*. Princeton.

(2005) *Ancient Rhetoric and Oratory*. Malden, Mass.

Hadot, P. (1971) *Marius Victorinus: recherches sur sa vie et ses oeuvres*. Paris.

Hagendahl, H. (1958) *Latin Fathers and the Classics: A Study of the Apologists, Jerome and Other Christian Writers*. Gothenburg.

(1968) *Augustine and the Latin Classics* vol. I: *Testimonia*; vol. II: *Augustine's Attitude*. Stockholm.

Haines, C. R. (1919) (ed.) *The Correspondence of Marcus Cornelius Fronto*, 2 vols. London.

Hall, J. (1994) 'Persuasive design in Cicero's *De oratore*', *Phoenix* 48: 210–25.

(1996) 'Social evasion and aristocratic manners in Cicero's *De Oratore*', *AJPh* 117: 95–120.

(2008) 'The rhetorical design and the success of the *Twelfth Philippic*', in *Cicero's Philippics: History, Rhetoric, Ideology*, eds. T. Stevenson and M. Wilson. Auckland: 282–304.

(2009) *Politeness and Politics in Cicero's Letters*. Oxford.

Halliday, M. A. K. (2004) *An Introduction to Functional Grammar*, 3rd edn., rev. C. Matthiessen. London.

Halm, C. (1863) *Rhetores Latini minores*. Leipzig.

(1867) *Minucius Felix, Octavius*, CSEL vol. II.

Halphen, L. (1967) (ed. and tr.) *Vie de Charlemagne*, by Éginhard. Paris.

Halporn, J. (2004) (tr.) *Institutions of Divine and Secular Learning. On the Soul*, by Cassiodorus, intro. M. Vessey. Liverpool.

Hammer, D. (2009) 'What is politics in the ancient world?', in *A Companion to Greek and Roman Political Thought*, ed. R. K. Balot. Malden, Mass.: 20–36.

Hankins, J. (2007) (ed.) *The Cambridge Companion to Renaissance Philosophy*. Cambridge.

Hankins, J. and Palmer, A. (2008) *The Recovery of Ancient Philosophy in the Renaissance: A Brief Guide*. Florence.

Hardie, P. (1986) *Virgil's 'Aeneid': Cosmos and Imperium*. Oxford.

(2002) *Ovid's Poetics of Illusion*. Cambridge.

Hardy, E. G. (1924) *The Catilinarian Conspiracy in its Context: A Re-Study of the Evidence*. Oxford.

Hariman, R. (1989) 'Political style in Cicero's letters to Atticus', *Rhetorica* 7 (1989): 145–58.

Harries, J. (2002) 'Cicero and the defining of the *ius civile*', in *Philosophy and Power in the Graeco-Roman World*, eds. G. Clark and T. Rajak. Oxford: 51–68.

(2004) 'Cicero and the law', in Powell and Paterson (eds.) (2004): 147–64.

(2006) *Cicero and the Jurists: From Citizens' Law to the Lawful State*. London.

Harrison, S. (1990) 'Cicero's *De temporibus suis*: the evidence reconsidered', *Hermes* 118: 455–63.

(2005) (ed.) *A Companion to Latin Literature*. Malden, Mass. and Oxford.

Haury, A. (1964) 'Cicéron et l'astronomie', *RÉL* 42: 198–212.

Haynes, H. (2008) '*Rome*'s opening titles: triumph, spectacle, and desire', in *Rome Season One. History Makes Television*, ed. M. S. Cyrino. Oxford: 49–60.

Heck, E. (1966) *Die Bezeugung von Cicero's Schrift De re publica*. Hildesheim.

(1978) 'Iustitia civilis, iustitia naturalis: à propos du jugement de Lactance concernant les discours sur la justice dans le *De re publica* de Cicéron', in *Lactance et son temps. Recherches actuelles. Actes du IVe colloque d'études historiques et patristique Chantilly 21–23 septembre 1976*, eds. J. Fontaine and M. Perrin. Paris: 171–84.

Heinze, R. (1960) *Vom Geist des Römertums*, 3rd edn. Darmstadt.

Helm, R. (1956) *Die Chronik des Hieronymus = Hieronymi Chronicon*, 2nd edn. Berlin.

Henderson, J. (2004) *Morals and Villas in Seneca's Letters*. Cambridge.

Hendrickson, G. L. (1926) 'Cicero's correspondence with Brutus and Calvus on oratorical style', *AJPh* 47: 234–58.

(1939) 'Brutus *De Virtute*', *AJPh* 60: 401–15.

Hendrickson, G. L. and Hubbell, H. (1962) (eds.) *Brutus, Orator*, by Cicero, rev. edn. Cambridge, Mass.

Herzog, R. (1993) (ed.) *Restauration et renouveau 284–374 (Nouvelle histoire de la littérature latine, vol. 5)*. Turnhout.

Higgins, C. (2009) '*Lustrum* by Robert Harris', *Guardian*, 17.10.09.

Highet, G. (1972) *The Speeches in Vergil's 'Aeneid'*. Princeton.

Hildebrandt, P. (1894) *De Scholiis Ciceronis Bobiensibus*. Berlin.

Hillgarth, J. (2009) *The Visigoths in History and Legend*. Toronto.

Hinds, S. (2004) 'Petrarch, Cicero, Virgil: virtual community in *Familiares* 24.4', *MD* 52: 157–75.

Hine, H. M. (2005) 'Poetic influence on prose: the case of the Younger Seneca', in Reinhardt, Lapidge and Adams (eds.) (2005): 211–37.

Hingley, R. (2000) *Roman Officers and English Gentlemen*. London.

Hinks, D. (1935) 'Martianus Capella on Rhetoric.' Diss. Trinity College Cambridge.

Hölkeskamp, K.-J. (2000) 'The Roman Republic: government of the people, by the people, for the people?' *SCI* 19: 203–33.

(2010) *Reconstructing the Roman Republic: An Ancient Political Culture and Modern Research*, tr. H. Heitmann-Gordon. Princeton.

Hönscheid, C. (2004) *Fomenta Campaniae. Ein Kommentar zu Senecas 51., 55. und 56. Brief*. Munich.

Holtz, L. (1981) *Donat et la tradition de l'enseignement grammatical. Étude sur l'Ars Donati et sa diffusion (IVe–IXe siècle) et édition critique*. Paris.

(1992) 'Continuité et discontinuité de la tradition grammaticale au VIIe siècle', in *The Seventh Century: Change and Continuity. Proceedings of a Joint French and British Colloquium held at the Warburg Institute 8–9 July 1988*, eds. J. Fontaine and J. Hillgarth. London: 41–57.

Homeyer, H. (1964) *Die Antike Berichte über den Tod Ciceros und Ihre Quellen. Dt. Beiträge zur Alt. Wiss., no. 18*. Baden-Baden. (Reprinted with some minor corrections in *Helikon* 17 [1977]: 56–96.)

Hommel, H. (1968) *Ciceros Gebetshymnus an die Philosophie: Tusculanen V 5*. Heidelberg.

Horsfall, N. (1972) 'Varro and Caesar: three chronological problems', *BICS* 19: 120–8.

(1989) *Cornelius Nepos*. Oxford.

(1999) 'The prehistory of Latin poetry', *Rivista di Filologia e di Istruzione classica* 122: 50–75.

(2000) *Virgil, 'Aeneid' Seven: A Commentary*. Leiden.

(2003) *The Culture of the Roman Plebs*. London.

Hubaux, J. (1960) 'Du *Songe de Scipion* a la vision d'Énée', in *Hommages à Léon Herrmann, Coll. Lat.* 44: 436–45.

Hubbell, H. M. (1949) (tr.) *Cicero: De inventione; De optimo genere oratorium; Topica*. Cambridge, Mass.

Humbert, J. (1925) *Les plaidoyers écrits et les plaidoiries réelles de Cicéron*. Paris.

Hutchinson, G. O. (1995) 'Rhythm, style and meaning in Cicero's prose', *CQ* 45: 485–99.

(1998) *Cicero's Correspondence: A Literary Study*. Oxford.

Im Hof, U. (1994) *The Enlightenment*. Oxford.

Inwood, B. (2005) *Reading Seneca: Stoic Philosophy at Rome*. Oxford.

Inwood, B. and Mansfeld, J. (1997) (eds.) *Assent and Argument: Studies in Cicero's 'Academic Books'*. London and New York.

Israel, J. I. (2001) *Radical Enlightenment*. Oxford.

(2006) *Enlightenment Contested*. Oxford.

Jakobi, R. (2002) (ed.) *Grillius, Commentum in Ciceronis Rhetorica*. Leipzig.

(2005) *Grillius, Überlieferung und Kommentar*. Berlin.

Jefferson, T. (1955) *The Papers of Thomas Jefferson*, eds. J. P. Boyd et al., vol. XII. Princeton.

Jehne, M. (1995) (ed.) *Demokratie in Rom? Der Rolle des Volkes in der Politik der römischen Republik*. Stuttgart.

   (2006) 'Methods, models, and historiography', in *A Companion to the Roman Republic*, eds. N. S. Rosenstein and R. Morstein-Marx. Malden, Mass.: 3–28.

Johnson, R., with Burge, E. (tr.) (1971) *Martianus Capella and the Seven Liberal Arts*. New York.

Johnson, W. R. (1971) *Luxuriance and Economy: Cicero and the Alien Style*. Berkeley.

   (2000) *Lucretius and the Modern World*. London.

Jolivet, R. (ed.) (1948) *Augustine, Dialogues philosophiques. I. Problèmes fontamentaux*. 'Contra academicos'; 'De beata vita'; 'De ordine'. Paris.

Jones, C. P. (1971) *Plutarch and Rome*. Oxford.

Jones, D. M. (1959) 'Cicero as a translator', *BICS* 6: 22–34.

Jones H. and Kilpatrick, R. (2007) 'Cicero, Plutarch, and Vincenzo Foppa: rethinking the Medici Bank fresco (London, The Wallace Collection, Inv. P 538)', *IJCT* 13: 369–83.

Joshel, S. R. (2005) '*I, Claudius*: projection and imperial soap opera', in *Imperial Projections: Ancient Rome in Modern Popular Culture*, eds. S. R. Joshel, M. Malamud and D. T. McGuire, Jr. Baltimore: 119–61.

Joshel, S. R., M. Malamud, and M. Wyke (2005) 'Introduction', in *Imperial Projections: Ancient Rome in Modern Popular Culture*, eds. S. R. Joshel, M. Malamud and D. T. McGuire, Jr. Baltimore: 1–22.

Judge, E. (1974) 'Res publica restituta: a modern illusion?' in *Polis and Imperium: Studies in Honour of Edward Togo Salmon*, ed. J. A. S. Evans. Toronto: 279–311.

Kallendorf, C. and Kallendorf, C. (1987) 'Careful negligence: Cicero's low style and business writing', *Rocky Mountain Review of Language and Literature* 41: 33–49.

Kallendorf, C. W. (2002) (ed. and tr.) *Humanist Educational Treatises*. Cambridge, Mass.

Kamesar, A. (1993) *Jerome, Greek Scholarship, and the Hebrew Bible: A Study of the Qaestiones Hebraicae in Genesim*. Oxford.

Kaser, M. (1993) *Ius Gentium*. Weimar.

Kaster, R. (1988) *Guardians of Language: The Grammarian and Society in Late Antiquity*. Berkeley.

   (1995) *Suetonius: De Grammaticis et Rhetoribus*. Oxford.

   (1998) 'Becoming "CICERO"', in *Style and Tradition: Studies in Honor of Wendell Clausen*, eds. P. Knox and C. Foss. Stuttgart and Leipzig: 248–63.

   (2006) (ed.) *Cicero: Speech on Behalf of Publius Sestius*. Oxford.

   (2009) 'Some passionate performances in late Republican Rome', in *A Companion to Greek and Roman Political Thought*, ed. R. Balot. Chichester and Malden, Mass.: 308–20.

   (2011) *Macrobius, Saturnalia*. Cambridge, Mass.

Keil, H. (1855–80) *Grammatici Latini*, 5 vols. Leipzig.

Kelly, J. N. D. (1975) *Jerome: His Life, Writings and Controversies*. London.

Kemp, P. (2006) 'A long time in politics', *The Sunday Times*, 3.12.06.

Kennedy, G. (1963) *The Art of Persuasion in Greece*. Princeton.

   (1972) *The Art of Rhetoric in the Roman World*. Princeton.

(1994) *A New History of Classical Rhetoric*. Princeton.

(2002) 'Cicero's oratorical and rhetorical legacy', in *Brill's Companion to Cicero*, ed. J. M. May. Leiden: 481–501.

Kidd, D. (1997) *Phaenomena*, by Aratus. Cambridge.

Kinsey, T. (1971) *M. Tulli Ciceronis Pro P. Quinctio Oratio*. Sydney.

Kirchner, R. (2007) '*Elocutio*: Latin prose style', in Dominik and Hall (eds.) (2007): 181–94.

Kittel, H. et al. (2007) (eds.) *Übersetzung – Translation – Traduction: An International Encyclopedia of Translation Studies* vol. ii. Berlin and New York.

Klein, R. (1968) *Tertullian und das römische Reich*. Heidelberg.

Klingner, F. (1921) *De Boethii consolatione philosophiae*. Berlin.

Klotz, A. (1911) 'Studien zu den Panegyrici Latini', *RhM* 66: 513–72.

KM (1998) 'Steven Saylor Interview', http://authortrek.com/steven-saylor.html

Koster, S. (1980) *Die Invektive in der griechischen und römischen Literatur*. Meisenheim am Glan.

Kraus, C. (2005) 'Hair, hegemony, and historiography: Caesar's style and its earliest critics', in *Aspects of the Language of Latin Prose*, eds. T. Reinhardt, M. Lapidge, and J. N. Adams. Oxford: 97–115.

Kraye, J. (1997) (ed.) *Cambridge Translations of Renaissance Philosophical Texts* vol. ii: *Political Philosophy*. Cambridge.

Krebs, C. (2009) 'A seemingly artless conversation: Cicero's *de legibus* 1, 1–5', *CPh* 104.1: 90–107.

Krostenko, B. (2001) *Cicero, Catullus, and the Language of Social Performance*. Chicago.

Kubiak, D. (1981) 'The Orion episode of Cicero's *Aratea*', *CJ* 77: 12–22.

(1990) 'Cicero and the poetry of nature', *Studi Italiani di Filologia Classica* 8: 198–214.

(1994) 'Aratean influence in the *De consulatu suo* of Cicero', *Philologus* 138: 52–66.

Kumaniecki, C. (1962) 'Cicerone e Varrone: storia di una conoscenza', *Athenaeum* 40: 221–43.

Kunkel, W. (1967) *Herkunft und soziale Stellung der Römische Juristen*. Graz.

Kurczyk, S. (2006) *Cicero und die Inszenierung der eigenen Vergangenheit: Autobiographisches Schreiben in der späten Römischen Republik*. Cologne.

Lacey, W. K. (1978) *Cicero and the End of the Roman Republic*. London.

Lamacchia, R. (1964) 'Ciceros *Somnium Scipionis* und das sechste Buch der *Aeneis*', *RhM*. 107: 261–78.

Lambardi, N. (1982) *Il Timaeus ciceroniano: arte e tecnica del 'vertere'*. Florence.

Lancel, S. (2003) 'Entre africanité et romanité', in *Augustinus Afer. Saint Augustin: africanité et universalité. Actes du colloque international Alger-Annaba, 1–7 avril 2001*, eds. P.-Y. Fux, J.-M. Roessli and O. Wermelinger, 1: 53–9.

Landgraf, G. (1914) *Ciceros Rede für Sextus Roscius aus Ameria, herausgegeben und erklärt*. Erlangen.

Langlands, R. (2006) *Sexual Morality in Ancient Rome*. Cambridge.

Lardet, P. (1993) *L'apologie de Jérôme contre Rufin: un commentaire*. Leiden.

Laser, G. (2001) *Commentariolum Petitionis*. Darmstadt.

Laughton, E. (1960) 'Observations on the style of Varro', *CQ* n.s. 10: 1–28.

Laurand, L. (1933) *Cicéron*, 2 vols. Paris.

(1938) *Études sur le style des discours de Cicéron*, 3 vols., 4th edn. Paris.

Laurence, R. (1994) 'Rumour and communication in Roman politics', *G&R* 41.1: 6–74.

Lawless, G. (1987) *Augustine of Hippo and his Monastic Rule*. Oxford.

Leach, F. W. (1999) 'Ciceronian "Bi-Marcus": correspondence with M. Terentius Varro and L. Papirius Paetus in 46 B.C.E.', *TAPhA* 129: 139–79.

(2006) '*An grauius aliquid scribam*. Roman *seniores* write to *iuuenes*', *TAPhA* 136: 247–67.

Le Bonniec, M. H. (1984) 'L'exploitation apologétique par Arnobe du *De natura deorum* de Cicéron', in *Présence de Cicéron: Hommage au R. P. M. Testard*, ed. R. Chevallier. Paris: 89–101.

Lebreton, J. (1901) *Études sur la langue et la grammaire de Cicéron*. Paris.

Leeman, A. (1963) *Orationis Ratio: The Stylistic Theories and Practice of the Roman Orators, Historians, and Philosophers*, 2 vols. Amsterdam.

Leeman, A., et al. (1981–2008) (eds.) *De oratore libri III*, 5 vols. Heidelberg.

Leff, M. (1983) 'The topics of argumentative invention in Latin rhetorical theory from Cicero to Boethius', *Rhetorica* 1.1: 23–44.

(1998) 'Cicero's *Pro Murena* and the strong case for rhetoric', *Rhetoric and Public Affairs* 1: 61–88.

Lenel, O. (1889) *Palingenesia Iuris Civilis*, 2 vols. Leipzig.

Lévy, C. (1998) 'Rhétorique et philosophie: la monstruosité politique chez Cicéron', *RÉL* 76: 139–57.

Lewis, A. M. (1988) 'Rearrangement of motif in Latin translation: the emergence of a Roman *Phaenomena*', in *Studies in Latin Literature and Roman History IV*, ed. C. Deroux. Brussels: 210–33.

Linde, P. (1923) 'Die Stellung des Verbs in der lateinischen Prosa', *Glotta* 12: 153–78.

Linke, B. and Stemmler, M. (2000) (eds.) *Mos Maiorum: Untersuchungen zu den Formen der Identitätsstiftung und Stabilisierung in der römischen Republik*. Stuttgart.

Lintott, A. (1997) 'Cassius Dio and the history of the late Roman Republic', *ANRW* 34.3: 2497–523.

(1999a) *The Constitution of the Roman Republic*. Oxford.

(1999b) *Violence in Republican Rome*, 2nd edn. Oxford.

(2008) *Cicero As Evidence: A Historian's Companion*. Oxford.

Littleton, A. (1680) (ed.) *M. T. Ciceronis opera quae extant omnia . . . Studio atque industria Jani Gulielmi & Jani Gruteri*. London.

Lock, F. P. (2006) *Edmund Burke* vol. II: *1784–1797*. Oxford.

Löfstedt, E. (1928, 1933) *Syntactica: Studien und Beiträge zur historischen Syntax des Lateins*, 2 vols. Lund.

Long, A. A. (1974, 2nd edn 1986) *Hellenistic Philosophy*. London.

(1995a) 'Cicero's Plato and Aristotle', in *Cicero the Philosopher: Twelve Papers*, ed. J. G. F. Powell. Oxford: 37–61.

(1995b) 'Cicero's politics in *De officiis*', in *Justice and Generosity: Studies in Hellenistic Social and Political Philosophy*, eds. A. Laks and M. Schofield. Cambridge: 213–40.

Lowe, E. A. (1934) *Codices Latini Antiquiores: A Paleographical Guide to Latin Manuscripts Prior to the Ninth Century*. Part I: *The Vatican City*. Oxford.

Ludwig, W. (1982) (ed.) *Éloquence et rhétorique chez Cicéron: sept exposés suivis de discussions*. Entretiens sur l'antiquité classique 28. Geneva.

Luisi, A. (1996) '*Pro Archia*: retroscena politica di un processo', in *Processi e politica nel mondo antico*, ed. M. Sordi. Milan: 189–206.

Lyttleton, G. (1733) *Observations on the Life of Cicero*. London.

MacCormack, S. (1981) *Art and Ceremony in Late Antiquity*. Berkeley.

(1998) *The Shadows of Poetry: Vergil in the Mind of Augustine*. Berkeley.

McDermott, W. C. (1972) 'Cicero's publication of his consular orations', *Philologus* 116: 277–84.

McGill, S. (2005) 'Seneca the Elder on plagiarizing Cicero's *Verrines*', *Rhetorica* 23: 337–46.

McGushin, P. (1977) *C. Sallustius Crispus. Bellum Catilinae. A Commentary*. Leiden.

Mack, D. (1937) *Senatsreden und Volksreden bei Cicero*. Würzburg.

MacKendrick, P. (1989) *The Philosophical Works of Cicero*. London.

McLynn, N. (1994) *Ambrose of Milan: Church and Court in a Christian Capital*. Berkeley.

McManamon, J. M. (1996) *Pierpaolo Vergerio the Elder: The Humanist as Orator*. Tempe.

Macmullen, R. (1966) *Enemies of the Roman Order*. Cambridge, Mass.

Machiavelli, N. (1994) *Selected Political Writings*, ed. D. Wootton. Cambridge.

Madvig, J. N. (1876) *M. Tulli Ciceronis De Finibus Bonorum et Malorum*, 3rd edn. Copenhagen.

Malamud, M. (2005) 'Serial Romans', in *Imperial Projections: Ancient Rome in Modern Popular Culture*, eds. S. R. Joshel, M. Malamud and D. T. McGuire, Jr. Baltimore: 209–28.

Malcovati, E. (1943) *Cicerone e la poesia*. Pavia.

(1976) *Oratorum Romanorum fragmenta liberae rei publicae*, 4th edn. Turin.

Mankin, D. (2011) (ed.) *Cicero: De Oratore: Book III*, Cambridge.

Manuwald, G. (2007a) (ed.) *Cicero, Philippics 3–9 vol. I: Introduction, Text and Translation, References and Indexes*. Berlin and New York.

(2007b) (ed.) *Cicero, Philippics 3–9 vol. II: Commentary*. Berlin and New York.

(2011) 'Ciceronian praise as a step towards Pliny's *Panegyricus*', in *Pliny's Praise. The Panegyricus in the Roman World*, ed. P. Roche. Cambridge: 85–103.

Marco, M. de (1991) (ed.) *M. Tulli Ciceronis orationes spuriae. Pars prior. Oratio pridie quam in exilium iret, Quinta Catalinaria, Responsio Cataline*. Milan.

Marincola, J. (2007) (ed.) *A Companion to Greek and Roman Historiography*. Malden, Mass.

Marinone, N. (2004) *Cronologia ciceroniana*, 2nd edn. Rome.

Markus, R. (1970) *Saeculum: History and Society in the Theology of St. Augustine*. Cambridge.

Marrou, H.-I. (1965) *Histoire de l'éducation dans l'antiquité*, 6th edn. Paris.

Marsh, D. (1980) *The Quattrocento Dialogue: Classical Tradition and Humanist Innovation*. Cambridge, Mass.

(2009) 'The burning question: crisis and cosmology in the *Secretum*', in *Petrarch: A Critical Guide to the Complete Works*, eds. V. Kirkham and A. Maggi. Chicago.

Marshall, A. J. (1984) 'Symbols and showmanship in Roman public life: the fasces', *Phoenix* 38: 120–41.

Marshall, B. (1985) 'Catilina and the execution of M. Marius Gratidianus', *CQ* 35: 124–33.

Martin, D. E. (1984) 'The Statilius-subscription and the editions of late antiquity', in *Classical Texts and their Traditions: Studies in Honor of C. R. Trahman*, eds. David F. Bright and Edwin S. Ramage. Chicago: 147–54.

Matijevic, K. (2006) *Marcus Antonius: Consul, Proconsul, Staatsfeind: die Politik der Jahre 44 und 43 v. Chr.* Rahden, Westphalia.

Matthews, J. (1989) *The Roman Empire of Ammianus*. Baltimore.

May, J. M. (1980) 'The image of the ship of state in Cicero's *pro Sestio*', *Maia* n.s. 3: 259–64.

   (1988) *Trials of Character: The Eloquence of Ciceronian Ethos*. Chapel Hill.

   (1996) 'Cicero and the beasts', *Syllecta Classica* 7: 143–53

   (2002) (ed.) *Brill's Companion to Cicero: Oratory and Rhetoric*. Leiden, Boston, and Cologne.

May, J. M. and Wisse, J. (2001) *Cicero: On the Ideal Orator*. Oxford and New York.

Mayer, R. G. (1991) 'Roman historical exempla in Seneca', in *Sénèque et la prose latine*. Entretiens sur l'antiquité classique 36. Geneva: 141–76.

   (2005) 'The impracticability of Latin "Kunstprosa"', in Reinhardt, Lapidge and Adams (eds.) (2005): 195–210.

Mercer, R. G. G. (1979) *The Teaching of Gasparino Barzizza with Special Reference to His Place in Paduan Humanism*. London.

Merrill, W. (1921) *Lucretius and Cicero's Verse*. Berkeley, Calif.

Michel, J.-H. (1975) 'Le droit romain dans le *Pro Murena* et l'oeuvre de Servius Sulpicius Rufus', in *Ciceroniana*, eds. A. Michel and R. Verdière. Leiden: 181–95.

Middleton, C. (1741) *The History of the Life of Marcus Tullius Cicero in Two Volumes*. London.

   (1840) *The Life and Letters of Marcus Tullius Cicero*. London.

Miles, G. (1995) *Livy: Reconstructing Early Rome*. Ithaca.

Millar, F. (1961) 'Some speeches in Cassius Dio', *MH* 18: 11–22.

   (1964) *A Study of Cassius Dio*. Oxford.

   (1973) 'Triumvirate and principate', *JRS* 63: 50–67.

   (1977) *The Emperor in the Roman World*. London.

   (1984) 'The political character of the Classical Roman Republic, 200–151 BC', *JRS* 74: 1–19.

   (1986) 'Politics, persuasion and the people before the Social War (150–90 BC)', *JRS* 76: 1–11.

   (1998) *The Crowd in Rome in the Late Republic*. Ann Arbor.

   (2000) 'The first revolution: Imperator Caesar 36–28 BC', in *La révolution romaine après Ronald Syme: bilans et perspectives: sept exposés suivis de discussions*. Geneva: 1–30.

Miller, E. (1987) (ed.) *David Hume: Essays Moral, Political and Literary*. Indianapolis.

Milnor, K. (2008) 'What I learned as an historical consultant for *Rome*', in *Rome Season One: History makes Television*, ed. M. S. Cyrino. Oxford: 42–8.

Mitchell, T. N. (1979) *Cicero: The Ascending Years*. New Haven.

   (1991) *Cicero: The Senior Statesman*. New Haven.

Moatti, C. (1997) *La raison de Rome: naissance de l'esprit critique à la fin de la République (IIe–Ier siècle avant Jésus-Christ)*. Paris.

Moles, J. (1988) (ed.) *Plutarch: Life of Cicero*. Warminster.

  (1997) 'Plutarch, Brutus and Brutus' Greek and Latin letters', in *Plutarch and His Intellectual World: Essays on Plutarch*, ed. J. Mossman. London and Swansea: 141–68.

  (1998) 'Cry freedom: Tacitus Annals 4, 32–35', *Histos* 2 [no pagination].

Mommsen, T. (1892) *Chronica Minora saec. IV, V, VI, VII* vol. I. Berlin.

  (1894) (ed.) *Cassiodori Senatoris Variae*. Berlin.

  (1898) *Chronica Minora saec. IV, V, VI, VII* vol. III. Berlin.

Monfasani, J. (1976) *George of Trebizond: A Biography and a Study of His Rhetoric and Logic*. Leiden.

  (1984) *Collectanea Trapezuntiana: Texts, Documents, and Bibliographies of George of Trebizond*. Binghamton.

  (1999) 'Cicero', in *Encyclopedia of the Renaissance*, ed. P. F. Grendler, vol. I. New York: 450–2.

Montefusco, L. (2003) 'Ductus and color: the right way to compose a suitable speech', *Rhetorica* 21.2: 113–31.

Morello, R. and Morrison, A. D. (2007) (eds.) *Ancient Letters: Classical and Late Antique Epistolography*. Oxford.

Morgan, M. (1980) 'Catullus and the *Annales Volusi*', *Quaderni urbinati* 4: 60–7.

Morstein-Marx, R. (2004) *Mass Oratory and Political Power in the Late Roman Republic*. Cambridge.

Mouritsen, H. (1998) *Italian Unification: A Study in Ancient and Modern Historiography*. London.

  (2001) *Plebs and Politics in the Late Roman Republic*. Cambridge.

Müller, A. (1910) 'Studentenleben im 4. Jahrh. n. Chr.', *Philologus* 69: 292–317.

Murphy, T. (1998) 'Cicero's first readers: epistolary evidence for the dissemination of his works', *CQ* 48: 492–505.

Mynors, R. A. B. (1961) *Cassiodori Senatoris Institutiones*. Oxford.

  (1964) *XII Panegyrici Latini*. Oxford.

Naber, S. A. (1867) (ed.) *M. Cornelii Frontonis et M. Aurelii Epistulae. L. Veri et T. Antonini Pii et Appiani Epistularum Reliquiae*. Leipzig

Nardo, D. (1970) *Il 'Commentariolum Petitionis': la propaganda elettorale nella 'ars' di Quinto Cicerone*. Padova.

Narducci, E. (1997a) *Cicerone e l'eloquenza romana: retorica e progetto culturale*. Rome and Bari.

  (1997b) 'Perceptions of exile in Cicero: the philosophical interpretation of a real experience', *AJPh* 118: 55–73.

  (2003a) (ed.) *Aspetti della fortuna di Cicerone nella cultura latina : atti del III Symposium Ciceronianum Arpinas : Arpino, 10 maggio 2002*. Florence.

  (2003b) 'Cicerone nella "Pharsalia" di Lucano', in Narducci (ed.) (2003a): 78–91.

  (2005) *Introduzione a Cicerone*, 2nd edn. Rome.

Nauta, L. (2009) *In Defense of Common Sense: Lorenzo Valla's Humanist Critique of Ancient and Medieval Philosophy*. Cambridge, Mass.

Neira Faleiro, C. (2005) *La Notitia Dignitatum. Nueva Edición Crítica y Comentario Histórico*. Madrid.

Nellen, D. (1981) *Viri Litterati. Gebildetes Beamtentum und spätrömisches Reich im Westen zwischen 284 und 395 nach Christus.* Bochum.

Neri, M. (2007) (ed.) *Macrobio. Commento al sogno di Scipione.* Milan.

Nesholm, E. (2010) 'Language and artistry in Cicero's *pro Archia*', *CW* 103.4: 477–90.

Neudling, C. L. (1955) *A Prosopography to Catullus.* Oxford.

Nicolet, C. (1960) 'Consul togatus: remarques sur le vocabulaire politique de Cicéron et de Tite-Live', *RÉL* 38: 236–63.

(1967) 'Arpinum, Aemilius Scaurus et les Tullii Cicerones', *RÉL* 45: 276–304.

(1980) *The World of the Citizen in Republican Rome.* London.

(1991) *Space, Geography, and Politics in the Early Roman Empire.* Ann Arbor.

Nippel, W. (1995) *Public Order in Ancient Rome.* Cambridge.

Nisbet, G. (2009) '"Dickus Maximus": Rome as Pornotopia', in *Classics for All: Reworking Antiquity in Mass Culture*, ed. D. Lowe and K. Shahabudin. Cambridge: 150–71.

Nisbet, R. G. M. (1961) *M. Tulli Ciceronis in L. Calpurnium Pisonem oratio.* Oxford.

(1965) 'The speeches', in Dorey (ed.) (1965): 47–79.

(1990) 'Cola and clausulae in Cicero's speeches', in Craik (ed.) (1990): 349–59.

(1992) 'The orator and the reader: manipulation and response in Cicero's *Fifth Verrine*', in Woodman and Powell (eds.) (1992): 1–17.

Nixon, C. E. V and Rodgers, B. S. (1994) *The Panegyrici Latini. Introduction, Translation and Historical Commentary. With Latin Text of R. A. B. Mynors.* Berkeley.

Nolhac, P. de (1907) *Pétrarque et l'humanisme*, 2 vols., 2nd edn. Paris.

Norden, E. (1898, 1909, 1915, 1923, 1958) *Die Antike Kunstprosa vom VI Jahrhundert v. Chr. bis in die Zeit der Renaissance.* Leipzig (successive editions).

(1916) *P. Vergilius Maro Aeneis Buch VI*, 2nd edn. Leipzig.

(1986) *La prosa d'arte antica dal VI secolo a.C. all' età della Rinascita* (Italian translation of Norden [1958]). Rome.

North, J. (1990) 'Democratic politics in Republican Rome', *P&P* 126: 3–21.

OCD³ = Hornblower, S. and Spawforth, A. J. S. (eds.) (1996) *The Oxford Classical Dictionary*, 3rd edn. Oxford.

O'Daly, G. (1999) *Augustine's City of God: A Reader's Guide.* Oxford.

O'Donnell, J. (1979) *Cassiodorus.* Berkeley.

(1980) 'Augustine's classical readings', *Recherches Augustiniennes* 15: 144–75.

(1992) *Augustine, Confessions* vol. II: *Commentary Books 1–7.* Oxford.

Ogilvie, R. M. (1978) *The Library of Lactantius.* Oxford.

Oksala, P. (1953) *Die griechischen Lehnwörter in den Prosaschriften Ciceros.* Helsinki.

Opelt, I. (1965) *Die lateinischen Schimpfwörter und verwandte sprachliche Erscheinungen.* Heidelberg.

(1966) 'Ciceros Schrift De natura deorum bei den lateinischen Kirchenvätern', *Antike und Abendland. Beträge zum Verständnis der Griechen und Römer und ihres Nachlebens* 12: 141–55.

Orelli, J. (1826–38) *M. Tulli Ciceronis Opera quae supersunt omnia ac deperditorum fragmenta*, 8 vols. Zurich.

Osgood, J. (2006) *Caesar's Legacy: Civil War and the Emergence of the Roman Empire*. Cambridge.

O'Sullivan, T. (2006) 'The mind in motion: walking and metaphorical travel in the Roman villa', *CPh* 101: 133–52.

(2007) 'Walking with Odysseus: the portico frame of the Odyssey landscapes', *AJPh* 128: 497–532.

Outram, D. (2005) *The Enlightenment*, 2nd edn. Cambridge.

Oxford Scholar (1741) *The death of M-l-n in the Life of Cicero. Being a proper criticism on that marvellous performance*. London.

Panhuis, D. G. J. (1982) *The Communicative Perspective in the Sentence: A Study of Latin Word Order*. Studies in Language Companion Series 11. Amsterdam.

Panoussi, V. (2009) 'Roman Cultural Identity in Cicero's *Pro Archia*', in *Antiphilesis: Studies on Classical, Byzantine and Modern Greek Literature and Culture in Honour of John-Theophanes A. Papademetriou*, eds. E. Karama-Iengou and E. Makrygianni. Stuttgart: 516–23.

Passelac, M. (1972) 'Le bronze d'appliqué de Fendeille', *Revue archéologique de Narbonnaise* 5: 185–90.

Patterson, J. R. (1991) 'Settlement, city and elite in Samnium and Lycia', in *City and Country in the Ancient World*, eds. J. Rich and A. Wallace-Hadrill. London: 147–68.

Pavur, C. (2005) (tr.) *The 'Ratio studiorum': The Official Plan for Jesuit Education*. Saint Louis.

Pease, A. S. (1919) 'The attitude of Jerome towards pagan literature', *TAPhA* 50: 150–67.

(1920–3) *M. Tulli Ciceronis 'De divinatione'*, 2 vols. Urbana, Ill.

Pépin, J. (1962) *Théologie cosmique et théologie chrétienne*. Paris.

Perelli, L. (1990) *Il pensiero politico di Cicerone*. Florence.

Perrin, M. (1974) *L'ouvrage du dieu créateur*, by Lactance. *Sources chrétiennes* 213 (introduction and text); 214 (commentary). Paris.

(1988) 'Jérôme, lecteur de Lactance', in *Jérôme entre l'occident et l'orient. XVIe centenaire du départ de saint Jérôme de Rome et de son installation à Bethlèem. Actes du Colloque de Chantilly (septembre 1986)*, ed. Y.-M. Duval. Paris: 99–114.

Peter, H. (1967) *Historicorum Romanorum Reliquiae*, 2 vols. Stuttgart.

Petersson, T. (1920) *Cicero: A Biography*. New York.

Petrarca, F. (2003) *Invectives*, ed. and tr. D. Marsh. Cambridge, Mass.

Petrarch, F. (1992) *Letters of Old Age*, tr. A. S. Bernardo et al. 2 vols. Baltimore and London.

Phillips, E. J. (1976) 'Catiline's conspiracy', *Historia* 25: 441–8.

Pichon, R. (1906) *Les derniers écrivains profanes. Les panégyristes, Ausone, le Querolus, Rutilius Namatianus*. Paris.

Pierini, R. degl'Innocenti (2003) 'Cicerone nella prima età imperiale: luci ed ombre su un martire della repubblica', in Narducci (2003a): 3–54.

Pina Polo, F. (1996) *Contra Arma Verbis: Der Redner vor dem Volk in der späten römischen Republik*. Stuttgart.

(2004) 'Die nützliche Erinnerung: Geschichtsschreibung, Mos Maiorum und die Römische Identität', *Historia* 53: 147–72.

Pinkster, H. (2010) 'Notes on the language of Marcus Caelius Rufus', in Chahoud and Dickey (eds.) (2010): 186–202.

Plasberg, O. (1962) *Cicero in seinen Werken und Briefen*. Darmstadt.

Pocock, J. (1975) *The Machiavellian Moment: Florentine Political Thought and the Atlantic Republican Tradition*.

Pöschl, V. (1936) *Römischer Staat und griechisches Staatsdenken bei Cicero*. Berlin.

Pomeroy, A. J. (1991) *The Appropriate Comment: Death Notices in the Ancient Historians*. Frankfurt am Main.

Poncelet, R. (1957) *Cicéron traducteur de Platon*.

Porter, J. I. (2001) 'Des sons qu'on ne peut entendre: Cicéron, les "kritikoi" et la tradition du sublime dans la critique littéraire', in *Cicéron et Philodème: La polémique en philosophie*, eds. C. Auvray-Assayas and D. Delattre. Paris: 315–41.

Porter, R. (1982) *English Society in the Eighteenth Century*. Harmondsworth.

Porter, S. E. (1997) *Handbook of Classical Rhetoric in the Hellenistic Period 330 B.C.–A.D. 400*. Leiden, New York and Cologne.

Powell, J. G. F. (1988) *Cicero: Cato Maior De Senectute*, edited with an intro. and comm. Cambridge Classical Texts and Commentaries 28. Cambridge.

(1990) (ed. and tr.) *Cicero: 'On Friendship' and 'The Dream of Scipio'*, with intro., tr. and comm. Warminster.

(1994) 'The *rector rei publicae* of Cicero's De Republica', *SCI* 13: 19–29.

(1995a) (ed.) *Cicero the Philosopher. Twelve Papers*. Oxford.

(1995b) 'Cicero's translations from Greek', in Powell (ed.) (1995a): 273–300.

(1999) 'Stylistic registers in Juvenal', in Adams and Mayer (eds.) (1999): 311–34.

(2005a) 'Cicero's adaptation of legal Latin in the De Legibus', in Reinhardt, Lapidge and Adams (eds.) (2005): 117–50.

(2005b) 'Dialogues and treatises', in Harrison (ed.) (2005): 223–40.

(2005c) *Researching Rhetoric: The Ancient Art of Spin*. Inaugural lecture, Royal Holloway, University of London. Egham, Surrey.

(2006) (ed.) *Cicero: De re publica; De legibus; Cato Maior de senectute; Laelius de amicitia*. Oxford.

(2007a) 'Cicero', in Sharples and Sorabji (eds.) (2007) II. 333–45.

(2007b) 'Translation and culture in ancient Rome: Cicero's theory and practice of translation', in Kittel et al. (eds.) (2008): vol. II. 1132–7.

(2007) (ed.) *Logos: Rational Argument in Classical Rhetoric*. BICS supplement 96. London.

(2010) 'Hyperbaton and register in Cicero', in Chahoud and Dickey (eds.) (2010): 163–85.

(2011) 'The Language of Roman Oratory and Rhetoric', in Clackson (ed.) (2011): 384–407.

Powell, J. G. F. and North, J. A. (2001) (eds.) *Cicero's Republic*. BICS supplement 76. London.

Powell, J. G. F. and Paterson, J. J. (eds.) (2004) *Cicero the Advocate*. Oxford.

Prag, J. R. W. (ed.) (2007) *Sicilia nutrix plebis Romanae: Rhetoric, Law and Taxation in Cicero's 'Verrines'*. BICS supplement 97. London.

Preston, R. (2001) 'Roman questions, Greek answers: Plutarch and the construction of identity', in *Being Greek under Rome*, ed. S. Goldhill. Cambridge: 86–122.

Primmer, A. (1968) *Cicero numerosus*. Vienna.

Puelma, M. (1980) 'Cicero als Plato-Übersetzer', *Museum Helveticum* 37: 137–78.

Purcell, N. (1983) 'The apparitores: a study in social mobility', *PBSR* 51: 123–71.

(2000) 'Rome and Italy', *CAH* 11, 2nd edn. Cambridge: 405–43.

Quinn, K. (1970) *Catullus: The Poems*. London.

Quondam, A. (ed.) (1999) *Rinascimento e classicismo: materiali per l'analisi del sistema culturale di Antico regime*. Rome.

Rackham, H. (1942) (ed.) *Cicero: De oratore*, 2 vols. Cambridge, Mass.

Radiciotti, P. (1999), 'A proposito dei manoscritti di Cassiodoro', *Rivista di filologia e di istruzione classica* 127/3: 363–77.

Rambaud, M. (1953) *Cicéron et l'histoire romaine*. Paris.

Ramelli, I. (2001) (ed.) *Marziano Capella: Le nozze di Filologia e Mercurio*. Milan.

Ramsey, J. T. (1980) 'The prosecution of C. Manilius in 66 BC and Cicero's *pro Manilio*', *Phoenix* 34: 323–36.

(2001) 'Did Mark Antony contemplate an alliance with his political enemies in July 44 BCE?', *CPh* 96: 253–68.

(2003) *Cicero Philippics I–II*. Cambridge.

Rawnsley, A. (2006) 'You silver-tongued devil', *Observer*, 10.9.06.

Rawson, E. (1975, 2nd edn 1983) *Cicero: A Portrait*. London.

(1985) *Intellectual Life in the Late Roman Republic*. London.

(1991) *Roman Culture and Society*. Oxford.

(1994) 'The aftermath of the Ides', in *CAH* 9, 2nd edn. Cambridge: 468–90.

Rebenich, S. (2002) *Jerome*. London.

Rees, R. (2002) *Layers of Loyalty in Latin Panegyric ad 289–307*. Oxford.

Reinhardt, T. (2000) 'Rhetoric in the Fourth Academy', *CQ* 50: 531–47.

(2003) *Cicero's 'Topica': Critical Edition, Translation, Introduction, and Commentary*. Oxford.

Reinhardt, T., Lapidge, M., and Adams, J. N. (2005) (eds.) *Aspects of the Language of Latin Prose*. Proceedings of the British Academy 129. Oxford.

Renard, M. and Schilling, R. (1964) (eds.) *Hommages à J. Bayet*. Brussels.

Reynolds, L. (1983) (ed.) *Texts and Transmission: A Survey of the Latin Classics*. Oxford.

Ribbeck, O. (1871) *Tragicorum Romanorum Fragmenta* vol. 1. Hildesheim.

Richardson, L., Jr. (1992) *A New Topographical Dictionary of Ancient Rome*. Baltimore.

Riché, P. (1962) *Éducation et culture dans l'occident barbare. Vie–VIIIe siècles*. Paris.

Richlin, A. (1992) *The Garden of Priapus: Sexuality and Aggression in Roman Humor*, 2nd edn. New York.

(1997) 'Gender and rhetoric: producing manhood in the schools', in *Roman Eloquence: Rhetoric in Society and Literature*, ed. W. J. Dominik. New York: 90–110.

(1999) 'Cicero's head', in *Constructions of the Classical Body*, ed. J. I. Porter. Ann Arbor: 190–211.

(2006) *Marcus Aurelius in Love: The Letters of Marcus and Fronto*. Chicago.

Richter, W. (1968). 'Das Cicerobild der römischen Kaiserzeit', in *Cicero ein Mensch seiner Zeit*, ed. G. Radke. Berlin: 161–97.

Riggsby, A. M. (1991) 'Elision and hiatus in Latin prose', *ClAnt* 10: 328–43.

(1999) *Crime and Community in Ciceronian Rome*. Austin, Tex.

(2007) 'Memoir and autobiography in Republican Rome', in Marincola (2007): 266–74.

Riley, P. (2006) 'Social contract theory and its critics', in Goldie and Wokler (2006): 347–75.

Risselada, R. (1998) (ed.) *Latin in Use: Amsterdam Studies in the Pragmatics of Latin*. Amsterdam.

Robinson, A. (1994) 'Cicero's references to his banishment', *CW* 87: 475–80.

Robinson, O. F. (1995) *The Criminal Law of Ancient Rome*. London.

(2007) *Penal Practice and Penal Policy in Ancient Rome*. London.

Rogers, P. (1975) 'Swift and Cicero: the character of Verres', *Quarterly Journal of Speech* 61: 71–5.

Roller, M. (1997) '*Color*-blindness: Cicero's death, declamation, and the production of history', *CPh* 92.2: 109–30.

Rose, P. (1995) 'Cicero and the rhetoric of imperialism: putting the politics back into political rhetoric', *Rhetorica* 13: 359–99.

Rosén, H. (1996) (ed.) *Aspects of Latin: Papers from the Seventh International Colloquium on Latin Linguistics, Jerusalem, April 1993*. Innsbruck.

(1999) *Latine loqui: Trends and Directions in the Crystallisation of Classical Latin*. Munich.

Rosenstein, N. and Morstein-Marx, R. (eds.) (2006) *A Companion to the Roman Republic*. Oxford.

Rosner, M. (1988) 'The two faces of Cicero: Trollope's *Life* in the nineteenth century', *Rhetoric Society Quarterly* 18: 251–8.

Rowe, G. O. (1997) 'Style', in Porter (ed.) (1997): 121–57.

Ruch, M. (1958) *Le préambule dans les oeuvres philosophiques de Cicéron*. Paris.

Rudd, N. (1998) (ed. and tr.) *Cicero: 'The Republic' and 'The Laws'*, Oxford.

Rüegg, W. (1946) *Cicero und der Humanismus: Formale Untersuchungen über Petrarca und Erasmus*. Zurich.

Rundell, W. M. F. (1979) 'Cicero and Clodius: the question of credibility', *Historia* 28: 301–28.

Rupp, E. G. (1987) *Religion in England, 1688–1791*. Oxford.

Russell, D. A. (1990) *An Anthology of Latin Prose*. Oxford.

Ryan, F. X. (1998) *Rank and Participation in the Republican Senate*. Stuttgart.

Sabbadini, R. (1885) *Storia del Ciceronianismo*. Turin.

Sallmann, K. et al. (1997) *Die Literatur des Umbruchs. Von der römischen zur christlichen Literatur 117–248 n.Chr.* Munich.

Sanchez, P. (2007) 'La clause d'exception sur l'octroi de la citoyenneté romaine dans les traités entre Rome et ses alliés (Cicéron, *pro Balbo* 32)', *Athenaeum* 95: 215–70.

Sandbrook, D. (2009) '*Lustrum* by Robert Harris', *Observer*, 11.10.09.

Sandys, J. E. (1903–8) *A History of Classical Scholarship*, 3 vols. Cambridge.

Scheele, J. (1978) 'Buch und Bibliothek bei Augustinus', *Bibliothek und Wissenschaft* 12: 14–114.

Schmidt, P. L. (2000) *Traditio Latinitatis. Studien zur Rezeption und Überlieferung der lateinischen Literatur*, eds. J. Fugmann, M. Hose and B. Zimmermann. Stuttgart.

Schmitt, C. B. (1972) *Cicero Scepticus: A Study in the Influence of the 'Academica' in the Renaissance*. The Hague.

(1988) (ed.) *The Cambridge History of Renaissance Philosophy*. Cambridge.

Schmitzer, U. (2000) *Velleius Paterculus und das Interesse an der Geschichte im Zeitalter des Tiberius*. Heidelberg.

Schofield, M. (1986) 'Cicero for and against divination', *JRS* 76: 47–65.

(1991) *The Stoic Idea of the City*. Cambridge.

(1995) 'Cicero's definition of *Res Publica*', in *Cicero the Philosopher*, ed. J. Powell. Oxford: 63–83.

(2002) 'Academic therapy: Philo of Larissa and Cicero's project in the *Tusculans*', in *Philosophy and Power in the Greco-Roman World: Essays in Honour of Miriam Griffin*, eds. G. Clark and T. Rajak. Oxford: 91–109.

(2008) 'Ciceronian dialogue', in *The End of Dialogue in Antiquity*, ed. S. Goldhill. Cambridge: 63–84.

Schneider, W. C. (1998) *Vom Handeln der Römer. Kommunikation und Interaktion der politischen Führungsschicht vor Ausbruch des Biirgerkriegs im Briefwechsel mit Cicero*. Zurich and New York.

Sciarrino, E. (2007) 'Roman oratory before Cicero: the Elder Cato and Gaius Gracchus', in Dominik and Hall (eds.) (2007): 54–66.

Scott, K. (1933) 'The political propaganda of 44–30 BC', *Memoirs of the American Academy at Rome* 11: 7–49.

Seager, R. (1973) 'Iusta Catilinae', *Historia* 22: 240–8.

Sedley, D. N. (1998) *Lucretius and the Transformation of Greek Wisdom*. Cambridge.

(2012) (ed.) *The Philosophy of Antiochus*. Cambridge.

Seeck, O. (1962) (ed.) *Notitia Dignitatum. Accedunt Notitia Urbis Constantinipolitanae et Latercula Provinciarum*. Frankfurt.

Seider, R. (1979) 'Beiträge zur Geschichte und Paläographie der antiken Cicerohandschriften', *Bibliothek und Wissenschaft* 13: 101–49.

Setaioli, A. (2003). 'Seneca e Cicerone', in Narducci (ed.): 55–77.

Settle, J. N. (1962) 'The publication of Cicero's orations', PhD diss. Chapel Hill, NC.

Shanzer, D. (1986) *A Philosophical and Literary Commentary on Martianus Capella's 'De Nuptiis Philologiae et Mercurii'. Book I*. Berkeley.

Sharples, R. (1991) (ed.) *Cicero: 'On Fate' & Boethius: 'The Consolation of Philosophy'. IV.5–7, V.* Warminster.

(1997) *Stoics, Epicureans, Sceptics*. London.

Sharples, R. and Sorabji, R. (eds.) (2007) *Greek and Roman Philosophy 100 BC–200 AD*. *BICS* supplement 94, 2 vols. London.

Sherwin-White, A. N. (1982) 'The Lex Repetundarum and the political ideas of Gaius Gracchus', *JRS* 72: 18–31.

Showerman, G. (1904) 'Cicero's appreciation of Greek art', *AJPh* 25: 306–14.

Sider, R. (1971) *Ancient Rhetoric and the Art of Tertullian*. Oxford.

Sihler, E. G. (1914) *Cicero of Arpinum: A Political And Literary Biography, Being a Contribution to the History of Ancient Civilization and a Guide to the Study of Cicero's Writings*. New Haven.

Simmons, M. B. (1995) *Arnobius of Sicca: Religious Conflict and Competition in the Age of Diocletian*. Oxford.

Simon, M. (1966) 'Zur Abhängigkeit spätrömischer Enzyklopädien der artes liberales von Varros *Disciplinarum libri*', *Philologus* 110: 88–101.

Sinclair, P. (1994) 'Political declensions in Latin grammar and oratory 55 BCE– CE 39', *Ramus* 23: 92–109.

Sion-Jenkis, K. (2000) *Von der Republik zum Prinzipat: Ursachen für den Verfassungswechsel in Rom im historischen Denken der Antike*. Stuttgart.

Skinner, M. B. (1981) *Catullus' Passer*. New York.

Skinner, Q. (1978) *Foundations of Modern Political Thought*. Cambridge.

(1996) *Reason and Rhetoric in the Philosophy of Hobbes*. Cambridge.

Skutsch, O. (1985) *The Annals of Q. Ennius*. Oxford.

Solmsen, F. (1990) 'The world of the dead in Book 6 of the *Aeneid*', in *Oxford Readings in Virgil's Aeneid*, ed. S. Harrison. Oxford.

Solomon, J. (2001) *The Ancient World in the Cinema*, rev. edn. New Haven.

(2008) 'Televising antiquity: from *You Are There* to *Rome*', in *Rome Season One: History Makes Television*, ed. M. S. Cyrino. Oxford: 11–28.

Sordi, M. et al. (2008) *Tertulliano. Difesa del Cristianesimo*. Rome.

Soubiran, J. (ed. and trans.) (1972) *Aratea: fragments poétiques*, by Cicero. Paris.

Stahl, W. (1971) *Martianus Capella and the Seven Liberal Arts* vol. I: *The Quadrivium of Martianus Capella. Latin Traditions in the Mathematical Sciences 50 B.C.–A.D. 1250. With a Study of the Allegory and the Verbal Disciplines by Richard Johnson with E .L. Burge*. New York.

Stangl, T. (ed.) (1912) *Ciceronis Orationum scholiastae: Asconius, Scholia Bobiensia, Scholia Pseudasconii Sangallensia, Scholia Cluniacensia et recentiora Ambrosiana ac Vaticana, Scholia Lugdunensia sive Gronoviana et eorum excerpta Lugdunensia. Commentarii*. Vienna.

Steel, C. (2000) 'More, but different', *CR* 50: 76–8.

(2001) *Cicero, Rhetoric and Empire*. Oxford.

(2003) 'Cicero's *Brutus*: the end of oratory and the beginning of history?', *BICS* 46: 195–211.

(2005) *Reading Cicero: Genre and Performance in Late Republican Rome*. London.

(2006) *Roman Oratory*. Greece and Rome: New Surveys in the Classics 36. Cambridge.

(2008) 'Finessing failure: the *Sixth Philippic*', in *Cicero's Philippics: History, Rhetoric, Ideology*, eds. T. Stevenson and M. Wilson. Auckland: 255–65.

(2011) 'Cicero's oratory of praise and blame and the practice of elections in the late Roman Republic', in *Praise and Blame in Roman Republican Rhetoric*, eds. C. Smith and R. Covino. Swansea: 35–47.

Steiner, H. (1989) *Das Verhältnis Tertullians zur antiken Paideia*. Erzabtei St. Ottilien.

Steinmetz, P. (1982) *Untersuchungen zur römischen Literatur des zweiten Jahrhunderts nach Christi Geburt* (Palingenesia XVI). Wiesbaden.

Stem, R. (2006) 'Cicero as orator and philosopher: the value of the *Pro Murena* to Ciceronian political thought', *The Review of Politics* 68: 206–31.

Stevenson, T. (2008) 'Tyrants, kings and fathers in the *Philippics*', in *Cicero's Philippics: History, Rhetoric, Ideology*, eds. T. Stevenson and M. Wilson. Auckland: 93–113.

Stockton, D. (1969) *Thirty-five Letters of Cicero*. Oxford.

  (1971) *Cicero: A Political Biography*. Oxford.

Stone, M. (1999) 'Tribute to a statesman: Cicero and Sallust', *Antichthon* 33: 48–76.

Strachan-Davidson, J. L. (1900) *Cicero and the Fall of the Roman Republic*. London.

Stroh, W. (1975) *Taxis und Taktik: die advokatische Dispositionskunst in Ciceros Gerichtsreden*. Stuttgart.

  (1982) 'Die Nachahmung des Demosthenes in Ciceros *Philippiken*', in Ludwig (ed.) (1982): 1–31.

  (2004) '*De domo sua*: legal problem and structure', in Powell and Paterson (eds.) (2004): 313–70.

Stroup, S. C. (2010) *Catullus, Cicero, and a Society of Patrons*. Cambridge

Stump, E. (1988) *Boethius's 'In Ciceronis Topica'*, tr. with notes and an intro. Ithaca.

Süss, W. (1952) 'Die dramatische Kunst in den philosophischen Dialogen Ciceros', *Hermes* 80: 419–36.

Summers, W. C. (1968) *Select Letters of Seneca*. London.

Sumner, G. (1973) *The Orators in Cicero's 'Brutus': Prosopography and Chronology*. Toronto.

Svavarsson, S. H. (1999) 'On Catullus 49', *CJ* 95: 131–8.

Swain, S. (1990) 'Hellenic culture and the Roman heroes of Plutarch', *JHS* 110: 126–45.

  (1996) *Hellenism and Empire: Language, Classicism and Power in the Greek World, AD 50–250*. Oxford.

  (2002) 'Bilingualism in Cicero? The evidence of code-switching', in Adams, Janse and Swain (eds.) (2002): 128–67.

Syme, R. (1939) *The Roman Revolution*. Oxford.

  (1964) *Sallust*. Berkeley.

  (1968) *Ammianus and the Historia Augusta*. Oxford.

Syrett, H. C. and Cooke, J. E. (1967) (eds.) *The Papers of Alexander Hamilton* vol. XII. New York.

Tan, J. (2008) '*Contiones* in the Age of Cicero', *Classical Antiquity* 27: 163–201.

Tatum, W. J. (1999) *The Patrician Tribune*, Chapel Hill.

  (2013) 'Campaign rhetoric', in *Oratory and Politics in the Roman Republic*, eds. C. Steel and H. van der Blom. Oxford: 133–50.

Taylor, D. (1973) *Cicero and Rome*. London.

Taylor, H. (1916) *Cicero, a Sketch of his Life and Works, a Commentary on the Roman Constitution and Roman Public Life, supplemented by the Sayings of Cicero arranged as an Anthology*. Chicago.

Taylor, J. (1952) 'Political motives in Cicero's defense of Archias', *AJPh* 73: 62–70.

Tempest, K. (2007) 'Saints and sinners: some thoughts on the presentation of character in Attic oratory and Cicero's *Verrines*', in Prag (ed.) (2007): 19–36.

  (2011) *Cicero: Politics and Persuasion in Ancient Rome*. London.

Terrenato, N. (1998) '*Tam firmum municipium*: the Romanization of Volaterrae and its cultural implications', *JRS* 88: 94–114.

Testard, M. (1958a) *Saint Augustin et Cicéron vol. i: Cicéron dans la formation et dans l'oeuvre de saint Augustin*. Paris.

(1958b) *Saint Augustin et Cicéron* vol. ii: *Répertoire des texts*. Paris.

(1986) 'Cicero', in *Augustinus-Lexikon*, ed. C. Mayer, vol. i. Basel: 913–30.

(1988) 'Jérôme et Ambroise. Sur un "aveu" du *De officiis* de l'évêque de Milan', in *Jérôme entre l'occident et l'orient. XVIe centénaire du départ de saint Jérôme de Rome et de son installation à Bethléem. Actes du Colloque de Chantilly (septembre 1986)*, ed. Y.-M. Duval. Paris: 227–54.

(1989) 'Recherches sur quelques méthodes de travail de saint Ambroise dans le *De officiis*', *Recherches augustiniennes* 22: 65–122.

Thilo, G., and Hagen, H. (1878–81) (eds.) *Servii Grammatici qui feruntur in Vergilii carmina commentarii* vols. i–iii. Leipzig.

Thomas, R. (1988) (ed.) *Georgics*, by Virgil, 2 vols. Cambridge.

Thomas, Y. (1991) 'Imago naturae. Note sur l'institutionnalité de la nature à Rome', in *Théologie et droit dans la science politique de l'état moderne. Actes de la table ronde organisée par l'École française à Rome avec le concours du CNRS. Rome 12–14 novembre 1987*. Rome: 201–27.

Thraede, K. (1970) *Grundzüge griechish-römischer Brieftopik*. Zetemata 48. Munich.

Toland, J. (1704) *Letters to Serena*. London.

(1712) *Cicero illustratus*. London.

(1726) *A Collection of Several Pieces of Mr John Toland*. London.

Torelli, M. (1991) 'Il "diribitorium" di Alba Fucens e il "campus" eroico di Herdonia', in *Comunità indigene e problemi della romanizzazione nell'Italia centro-meridionale (IV–III sec. av. C.)*, eds. J. Mertens and R. Lambrechts, Brussels: 39–63.

[Towne, J.] (1751) *The Argument of the Divine Legation Fairly Stated...to which is added an appendix containing letters which passed between the late Dr Middleton and Mr Warburton, on the Characters of Moses and Cicero*. London.

Townend, G. B. (1964) 'The poems', in *Cicero*, ed. T. Dorey. London: 109–34.

Traglia, A. (1950) *La lingua di Cicerone poeta*. Bari.

Traina, A. (1974) *Vortit Barbare: le traduzioni poetiche da Livio Andronico a Cicerone*, 2nd edn. Rome.

Treggiari, S. (1972) *Cicero's Cilician Letters*. London.

(2007) *Terentia, Tullia and Publilia: The Women of Cicero's Family*. Abingdon.

Troncarelli, F. (1998) *Vivarium: i libri, il destino*. Instrumenta Patristica 33. Turnhout.

Tyrrell, W. B. (1973) 'The trial of C. Rabirius in 63 BC', *Latomus* 32: 285–300.

Ullman, B. J. (1923) 'Petrarch's favorite books', *TAPhA* 54: 21–38.

Ungern-Sternberg, J. von (1970) *Untersuchungen zum spätrepublikanischen Notstandsrecht. Senatusconsultum ultimum und hostis-Erklärung*. Munich.

Usher, S. (2008) *Cicero's Speeches: The Critic in Action*. Oxford.

Van den Hout, M. (1988) *M. Cornelii Frontonis Epistulae*. Leipzig.

Vasaly, A. (1993) *Representations: Images of the World in Ciceronian Oratory*. Berkeley.

(2009) 'Cicero, domestic politics, and the first action of the *Verrines*', *Classical Antiquity* 28: 101–37.

Viti, P. (1999) *Forme letterarie umanistiche: studi e ricerche*. Lecce.

(2006) 'Loschi, Antonio', *Dizionario biografico degli italiani* vol. LXVI. Rome: 154–60.

Voessing, K. (2003) 'Saint Augustin et l'école antique: traditions et ruptures', in *Augustinus Afer. Saint Augustin: africanité et universalité. Actes du colloque international Alger-Annaba, 1–7 avril 2001*, eds. P.-Y. Fux, J.-M. Roessli and O. Wermelinger. Fribourg, vol. I, 153–66.

Vogt-Spira, G. (1990) (ed.) *Strukturen der Mündlichkeit in der römischen Literatur*. Tübingen.

Von Albrecht, M. (2003) *Cicero's Style: A Synopsis Followed by Selected Analytic Studies*. Leiden and Boston.

Wallace-Hadrill, A. (1997) '*Mutatio morum*: the idea of a cultural revolution', in *The Roman Cultural Revolution*, eds. T. Habinek and A. Schiesaro. Cambridge: 3–22.

(1998) 'To be Roman, go Greek: thoughts on Hellenization at Rome', in Austin, Harries and Smith (eds.) (1998): 79–91.

(2008) *Rome's Cultural Revolution*. Cambridge.

Walser, G. (1959) 'Der Prozess gegen Q. Ligarius im Jahre 46 v. Chr.', *Historia* 8: 90–6

Walsh, J. (2005) 'New $100m TV epic set to rewrite history', *Independent*, 25.7.05.

Walter, U. (2004) *Memoria und res publica: zur Geschichtskultur der römischen Republik*. Frankfurt.

Ward, J. O. (1995) *Ciceronian Rhetoric in Treatise, Scholion, and Commentary*. Turnhout.

(1999) 'Cicero and Quintilian', in *The Cambridge History of Literary Criticism*, ed. G. P. Norton, vol. III: *The Renaissance*. Cambridge: 77–87.

Waters, K. H. (1970) 'Cicero, Sallust and Catiline', *Historia* 19: 195–215.

Watson, A. (1965) *The Law of Obligations in the Later Roman Republic*. Oxford.

Weber, M. (1978) *Economy and Society*, eds. G. Roth and C. Wittich. Berkeley and Los Angeles.

Weddingen, R.-E. van (1957) *Favonii Eulogii Disputatio de Somnio Scipionis*. Collection Latomus 27. Brussels.

Weil, B. (1962) *2000 Jahre Cicero*. Zurich.

Weische, A. (1972) *Ciceros Nachahmung der attischen Redner*. Heidelberg.

Welch, K. (2002) 'Both sides of the coin: Sextus Pompeius and the so-called *Pompeiani*', in *Sextus Pompeius*, eds. A. Powell and K. Welch. London: 1–30.

Weyssenhoff, C. (1966) *De Ciceronis Epistulis Deperditis*. Wroclaw, Warsaw, Krakow.

White, J. H. (ed. and tr.) (2005) *Biondo Flavio: Italia Illuminated* vol. I. Cambridge, Mass.

White, P. (2010) *Cicero in Letters: Epistolary Relations of the Late Republic*. Oxford.

Whitmarsh, T. (2001) *Greek Literature and the Roman Empire: The Politics of Imitation*. Oxford.

Wieacker, F. (1967) 'The *Causa Curiana* and contemporary jurisprudence', *Irish Jurist* 2: 151–64.

Wiedemann, T. E. J. (1994) *Cicero and the End of the Roman Republic*. London.

Wigodsky, M. (1972) *Vergil and Early Latin Poetry*. Hermes Einzelschriften 24. Wiesbaden.

Wilkin, R. N. (1947) *Eternal Lawyer: A Legal Biography of Cicero*. New York.

Willcock, M. (1995) *Cicero: Letters of January to April 43 BC*. Warminster.

Williams G. (1991) 'Conversing after sunset: a Callimachean echo in Ovid's exile poetry', *CQ* 41: 169–77.

Wilson, M. (2008) 'Your writings or your life: Cicero's *Philippics* and declamation', in *Cicero's Philippics: History, Rhetoric, Ideology*, eds. T. Stevenson and M. Wilson. Auckland: 305–34.

Winkler, M. M. (2004) '*Gladiator* and the traditions of historical cinema', in *Gladiator: Film and History*. Oxford: 16–30.

Winterbottom, M. (1982) 'Cicero and the Silver Age', in *Éloquence et rhétorique chez Cicéron*, ed. W. Ludwig. Entretiens sur l'antiquité classique 28. Geneva: 237–66.

(1989) 'Cicero and the Middle Style', in Diggle, Hall and Jocelyn (eds.) (1989): 125–31.

(2004) 'Perorations', in Powell and Paterson (eds.) (2004): 215–30.

Winterer, C. (2001) *A Culture of Classicism*. Baltimore.

Wirszubski, C. (1950) *Libertas as a political idea at Rome during the late Republic and early principate*. Cambridge.

Wiseman, T. P. (1969) *Catullan Questions*. Leicester.

(1971) *New Men in the Roman Senate, 139 BC–AD 14*. Oxford.

(1992) *Talking to Virgil*. Exeter.

(1994a) *Historiography and Imagination*. Exeter.

(1994b) 'The Senate and the *populares*, 69–60 B.C.', *CAH* 9, 2nd edn: 327–67.

(2009) 'Cicero and Varro', in *Remembering the Roman People*. Oxford: 107–29.

Wisse, J. (2002) 'The intellectual background of the rhetorical works', in May (ed.) (2002): 331–74.

(2007) 'The riddle of the *Pro Milone*: the rhetoric of rational argument', in Powell (ed.) (2007): 35–68.

Wistrand, M. (1979) '*Cicero Imperator*': *Studies in Cicero's Correspondence 51–47 BC*. Gothenburg.

Witley, A. F. (1939) *The Tremulous Hero: The Age and Life of Cicero, Orator, Advocate, Thinker and Statesman*. London.

Witt, R. G. (2000) '*In the Footsteps of the Ancients*': *The Origins of Humanism from Lovato to Bruni*. Leiden.

Wood, N. (1988) *Cicero's Social and Political Thought*. Berkeley and Los Angeles.

Woodman, A. J. (1977) (ed.) *Velleius Paterculus: The Tiberian Narrative (2.94–131)*. Cambridge.

Woodman, A. J. and Powell, J. G. F. (1992) (eds.) *Author and Audience in Latin Literature*. Cambridge.

Wooten, C. (1983) *Cicero's Philippics and their Demosthenic Model*. Chapel Hill and London.

Wright, A. (2001) 'The death of Cicero. Forming a tradition: the contamination of history', *Historia* 50.4: 436–52.

Wright, F. W. (1931) *Cicero and the Theater*. Smith College Classical Studies 11. Northampton.

Wright, M. R. (1963–4) '*Principio caelum (Aeneid 6.724–53)*', *Proceedings of the Virgil Society* 3: 27–34.

Wyke, M. (1997) *Projecting the Past: Ancient Rome, Cinema and History*. London.

Yakobson, A. (2006) 'Popular power in the Roman Republic', in *A Companion to the Roman Republic*, eds. N. S. Rosenstein and R. Morstein-Marx. Malden, Mass.: 383–400.

Yavetz, Z. (1963) 'The future of Catiline's conspiracy', *Historia* 12: 485–99.

(1971) 'Caesar, Caesarism, and the historians', *Journal of Contemporary History* 6.2: 184–201.

Yeo, R. (2001) *Encyclopaedic Visions: Scientific Visions and Enlightenment Culture*. Cambridge.

Zanker, P. (1998) *Pompeii: Public and Private Life*, tr. D. L. Schneider. Cambridge, Mass.

Zelzer, K. (1977) 'Zur Cicero-Imitatio bei Ambrosius, De officiis', *WS* 11: 168–91.

Zetzel, J. (1973) '*Emendavi ad Tironem*: some notes on scholarship in the second century AD', *HSCP* 77: 225–43.

(1981) *Latin Textual Criticism in Antiquity*. New York.

(1995) *Cicero, 'De Re Publica': Selections*. Cambridge.

(1996) 'Natural law and poetic justice: a Carneadean debate in Cicero and Virgil', *CPh* 91: 297–319.

(1998) '*De re publica and De rerum natura*', in *Style and Tradition: Studies in Honor of Wendell Clausen*, eds. P. E. Knox and C. Foss. Stuttgart and Leipzig: 232–49.

(1999) (ed.) *Cicero: 'On the Commonwealth' and 'On the Laws'*. Cambridge.

(2001) 'Citizen and commonwealth in *De re publica* Book 4', in *Cicero's Republic*, eds. J. G. F. Powell and J. A. North. *BICS* supplement 76. London: 83–97.

(2003) 'Plato with pillows: Cicero on the uses of Greek culture', in *Myth, History and Culture in Republican Rome*, eds. D. Braund and C. Gill. Exeter: 119–38.

(2011) '"Arouse the Dead": Mai, Leopardi, and Cicero's *Commonwealth* in Restoration Italy', in *Reception and the Classics*, eds. W. Brockliss, P. Chaudhuri, A. Haimson Lushkov and K. Wasdin. Yale Classical Studies 36. Cambridge, Mass.: 19–44.

Ziegler, K. (1958) (ed.) *Cicero: De re publica*, 4th edn. Leipzig.

Zieliński, T. (1904) 'Das Clauselgesetz in Ciceros Reden', *Philologus* Supplement 9: 591–844.

(1912/1929) *Cicero im Wandel der Jahrhunderte*. Leipzig (4th edn. Leipzig 1929).

Zimmerman, R. (1996) *The Law of Obligations: Roman Foundations of the Civilian Tradition*. Oxford.

Zoll, G. (1962) *Cicero Platonis aemulus: Untersuchung über die Form von Ciceros 'Dialogen', besonders von 'De Oratore'*. Zürich.

Zulueta, F. de (1922) (ed. and tr.) *Digest 41, 1 & 2: Translation and Commentary*. Oxford.

Cambridge Companions to ...

AUTHORS

TOPICS